Why should you adopt and use  mylabschool™?
Where the classroom comes to life!

Because your goal is not only to communicate to your pre-service teachers the important theories of learning and the most useful methods of instruction but also to help them understand the real-life challenges of the teaching profession, we think you will want to use **MyLabSchool**. This state-of-the-art website, available with all Allyn and Bacon Education textbooks, will bring your students closer to the classrooms they will one day inhabit and give them more life-like practice in the methods and strategies they will implement with schoolchildren.

Academic research into teacher training has shown that teaching skills can be improved by watching real teachers manage real classrooms, whether in person or through the use of video (Stigler and Hiebert, 1999). **MyLabSchool** contains hundreds of carefully chosen video clips illustrating how experienced teachers perform their tasks and how typical K–12 students respond. Further, observational questions are included in the program to help teacher candidates focus on the "essential moments" that make for successful teaching.

Researchers have also suggested that working with real-world artifacts, lesson plans, portfolios, and local teaching standards will provide aspiring teachers with the appropriate practice to develop a rich and flexible repertoire of teaching skills (Darling-Hammond and Bransford, eds., 2005). **MyLabSchool's** resources include a variety of grade- and discipline-specific lesson plans and activities provided by master teachers and taken from authentic classrooms. These will

give your students a "starter kit" for the types of activities and lesson plans they will collect as they gain experience in their careers and great examples that they can adapt or learn from as they get closer to entering their own classrooms.

Further, our Lesson Plan/Portfolio Builder allows teacher candidates to easily and quickly create template-driven lesson plans and portfolios and to map them against the teaching standards of any state. These can be emailed to you or to a prospective employer, downloaded to the students' hard-drive or CD, or printed and submitted for grading, or included in a traditional portfolio binder.

Last, in a recent survey, school administrators reported that one of the skills new teachers most need is adequate fluency with classroom technology and computer-based instructional strategies (Levine, 2006). Students who use **MyLabSchool** as they proceed through their teacher training curriculum will become much more comfortable with using technology as an educational tool and better versed in the resources available in the digital realm.

So, do yourself and your students a favor.

MyLabSchool's valuable aggregation of teacher-oriented assets will make your course much more enjoyable, practical, and active. What's more, your students will find using these kinds of materials along with their books and your lectures make the whole world of teaching come alive for them in a meaningful way. We are sure you'll find this program helps your students on their way to becoming effective and successful education professionals.

Darling-Hammond, L., & Bransford, J., Eds. (2005). *Preparing Teachers for a Changing World: What Teachers Should Learn and Be Able To Do.* San Francisco: John Wiley & Sons.

Levine, A. (2006). *Educating School Teachers.* Washington, DC: The Education Schools Project. Accessed at http://www.edschools.org/Educating_Teachers_Exec_Summ.

Stigler, J. W., & Hiebert, J. (1999). *The Teaching Gap: Best Ideas from the World's Teachers for Improving Education in the Classroom.* New York: The Free Press.

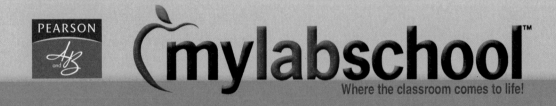

MyLabSchool
SAMPLE INTEGRATION GUIDE
Teaching Students with Special Needs in Inclusive Classrooms

WHAT THESE ACTIVITIES ARE

Professors select MyLabSchool materials for use in their courses all the time. Many are even required by their schools to use technology to teach, and find MyLabSchool to be a lifesaver. But many don't have time to explore MyLabSchool to make those choices before their courses begin. This Sample Integration Guide is a solution to that problem.

What follows is a series of assignable activities found on MyLabSchool, hand-picked to correspond with a course that requires this textbook. In many cases, the activities described here also appear in this text as end-of-chapter MyLabSchool features—in slightly different format and directed at your students—so they can be easily assigned.

If you incorporate MyLabSchool activities other than these into your course, and you'd like to share them with us so that we can pass them along to other professors, please send them to us at mlsactivities@ablongman.com. Be sure to name your school and course, include the instructions you provide to your students, and grant us permission to publish them!

GETTING STARTED

If you have not already created an account, go to www.mylabschool.com and do so, using a pass code from your Allyn & Bacon campus rep.

If your students have not already created their accounts, direct them to www.mylabschool.com to do so, using the access code that came with their texts.

> Instruct your students to email you to verify that they've created their accounts.

CHAPTER 1: INCLUSIVE TEACHING AS RESPONSIVE EDUCATION

VIDEO—"The Inclusive Classroom"

Special education teacher Penny Brandenburg teaches language arts collaboratively with the regular education teacher to a class that includes students with special needs. After the lesson, she meets with her mentor and the classroom teacher to discuss the lesson, including how she allocates her time between students of varying ability levels.

➡ Log onto www.mylabschool.com. Under the **Courses** tab, in **Special Education**, access the "**Inclusion and the Least Restrictive Environment**" videos, and watch "**The Inclusive Classroom.**"

OR

➡ Use the www.mylabschool.com **Assignment Finder** to go directly to these videos. Just enter Assignment ID **SPV2**.

> The simplest assignment is to instruct your students to watch this short video as homework, answer the questions that follow it, and email their responses to you for credit.

If you show the video in class, you may use the following questions as a basis for discussion:

1. This chapter notes that research data about inclusion suggests that student outcomes are positive. Does what you see in the video support these findings? In what ways?

2. How does Penny Brandenburg insure that the general education students in her classroom receive the attention they need, while providing additional help to the students with special needs? Cite specific examples from the video clip.

As a follow up activity instruct students to form small groups and give them the following assignment:

1. Introduce yourself to the other members of your group, sharing why YOU have decided to study inclusive teaching.

2. Using a "T" chart, develop a list of pros and cons your group sees in teaching students within an inclusive environment.

RESOURCE LIBRARY—What Every Teacher Should Know About No Child Left Behind

➡ Log onto www.mylabschool.com. Under the **Resources** tab, navigate to the **WETSKA** publications, and read the booklet entitled **What Every Teacher Should Know About No Child Left Behind**.

OR

➡ Use the www.mylabschool.com **Assignment Finder** to go directly to this publication. Just enter Assignment ID **WETSKA1**.

Instruct students to print and read this booklet for homework. In class, launch discussion of this chapter by having students identify what facts or concepts they learned from the booklet. Assign a student to record all of the points on the board.

Assign a concise, one page explanation of NCLB using the information from the chapter and the WETSKA booklet that would be appropriate to use as a handout for parents explaining this important legislation.

CHAPTER 2: UNDERSTANDING LEARNERS WITH SPECIAL NEEDS: HIGH INCIDENCE DISABILITIES OR CONDITIONS

VIDEO—"ADHD"

Eric is a hyperactive child with social and self-esteem problems. During this clip, his teachers and resource providers discuss his progress.

➡ Log onto www.mylabschool.com. Under the **Courses** tab, in **Special Education**, access the "**Learning Disabilities and Attention Deficit Hyperactivity Disorder**" videos, and watch "**ADHD**."

OR

➡ Use the www.mylabschool.com **Assignment Finder** to go directly to these videos. Just enter Assignment ID **SPV7**.

The simplest assignment is to instruct your students to watch this short video as homework, answer the questions that follow it, and email their responses to you for credit.

If you show the video in class, you may use the following questions as a basis for discussion:

1. Identify some of the behaviors that are causing Eric problems in school. Do you think these behaviors are unique to Eric or students with attention issues?

2. How do teachers typically deal with the types of behaviors exhibited in this video clip?

3. Do you think Eric should be included in a general education classroom? Provide specific evidence for your answer.

RESEARCH NAVIGATOR™—ADHD

➡ Log onto www.mylabschool.com. Under the **Courses** tab, in **Special Education**, navigate to **Research Navigator™**.

OR

➡ Use the www.mylabschool.com **Assignment Finder** to go directly to Research Navigator™. Just enter Assignment ID **SPRN**.

Instruct students to use the search term "ADHD" to locate an article on either EBSCOhost or the *New York Times* On the Web One-Year Archive. Ask students to prepare a 2-5 minute presentation for the class:

1. Present an overview of the article

2. State your opinion on an issue raised within the article

Once all of the students have presented their articles, open the class discussion by asking the students to reflect on how these issues impact classrooms and offer their opinions on the issues presented.

CHAPTER 3: UNDERSTANDING LEARNERS WITH SPECIAL NEEDS: LOW INCIDENCE DISABILITIES OR CONDITIONS

VIDEO—"Physical Disabilities"

Oscar is a high school student with physical disabilities. With the help of an aide and some adaptations, he is able to participate in a regular education classroom.

➡ Log onto www.mylabschool.com. Under the **Courses** tab, in **Special Education**, access the "**Traumatic Brain Injury and Physical Disabilities**" videos, and watch "**Physical Disabilities**."

OR

➡ Use the www.mylabschool.com **Assignment Finder** to go directly to these videos. Just enter Assignment ID **SPV11**.

The simplest assignment is to instruct your students to watch this short video as homework, answer the questions that follow it, and email their responses to you for credit.

If you show the video in class, you may use the following questions as a basis for discussion:

1. Students like Oscar who have paraplegia have many special needs and typically have assigned support staff to aid them. What are some issues that might concern you with situations like Oscar's?

2. How might you address these concerns in your classroom?

VIDEO—"Traumatic Brain Injury"

Matt is a kindergartner who received a traumatic brain injury (TBI) from a car accident. He receives special education, and his teachers discuss his educational plan and how other students interact with him.

➡ Log onto www.mylabschool.com. Under the **Courses** tab, in **Special Education**, access the "**Traumatic Brain Injury and Physical Disabilities**" videos, and watch "**Traumatic Brain Injury**."

OR

➡ Use the www.mylabschool.com **Assignment Finder** to go directly to these videos. Just enter Assignment ID **SPV11**.

The simplest assignment is to instruct your students to watch this short video as homework, answer the questions that follow it, and email their responses to you for credit.

If you show the video in class, you may use the following questions as a basis for discussion:

1. Educational programs for students like Matt, who experienced traumatic brain injury, should focus on retraining impaired cognitive processes while developing new compensatory skills and providing a supportive environment. If Matt's age permitted him to be in your classroom, how might you support his re-entry? Be specific, and support your choices with information from this chapter.

CHAPTER 4: OTHER STUDENTS WITH SPECIAL LEARNING NEEDS

VIDEO—"Challenging Gifted Students"

This clip shows a high school AP teacher using a computer-based social studies simulation. Students use a guidebook with facts and geography to help them make decisions and arguments throughout the simulation.

➥ Log onto www.mylabschool.com. Under the **Courses** tab, in **Special Education**, access the **"Gifted and Talented"** videos, and watch **"Challenging Gifted Students."**

OR

➥ Use the www.mylabschool.com **Assignment Finder** to go directly to these videos. Just enter Assignment ID **SPV12**.

The simplest assignment is to instruct your students to watch this short video as homework, answer the questions that follow it, and email their responses to you for credit.

If you show the video in class, you may use the following questions as a basis for discussion:

1. Are all students in AP classes "gifted"? Would students who are not gifted benefit from the instruction provided in this clip? Explain why or why not.

2. What are some advantages and disadvantages of enrichment or acceleration programs for students identified as gifted and talented? Based on information in the chapter, do you feel such programs are always the best way to support learners who are gifted? Why or why not?

For homework, assign the following activity:

● Using the Lesson & Portfolio Builder, design a lesson plan for your class that includes specific strategies for your students who are gifted and talented. For example, the lesson could contain additional activities or research for your students who are gifted and talented.

VIDEO—"Teaching Bilingual Students"

Teaching in a bilingual classroom poses a unique challenge to a teacher. This clip demonstrates classroom management techniques that one teacher uses in her classroom. A P.E. teacher discusses the need to spend extra time explaining the rules to children with limited English proficiency.

➥ Log onto www.mylabschool.com. Under the **Courses** tab, in **Special Education**, access the **"Cultural and Linguistic Diversity"** videos, and watch **"Teaching Bilingual Students."**

OR

➥ Use the www.mylabschool.com **Assignment Finder** to go directly to these videos. Just enter Assignment ID **SPV6**.

The simplest assignment is to instruct your students to watch this short video as homework, answer the questions that follow it, and email their responses to you for credit.

If you show the video in class, you may use the following questions as a basis for discussion:

1. What are some of the challenges in teaching in a bilingual classroom?

2. What techniques are demonstrated by the teachers in this clip to facilitate instruction? Provide specific examples from the video.

CHAPTER 5: DELIVERY OF SPECIAL SERVICES THROUGH INDIVIDUALIZED PLANS

SIMULATION—"Accessing the General Education Curriculum: Inclusion Considerations for Students with Disabilities"

In this simulation, Ms. Flores and Mr. Ericson from the Wilbur Valley Middle school are reviewing the large-scale assessment data across all grade levels and want to improve the scores of students with disabilities.

➡ Log onto www.mylabschool.com. Under the **Courses** tab, in **Special Education**, access the "**Simulations**" and watch "**Accessing the General Education Curriculum: Inclusion Considerations for Students with Disabilities.**"

OR

➡ Use the www.mylabschool.com **Assignment Finder** to go directly to this simulation. Just enter Assignment ID **SIM02**.

Ask students to watch the simulation and use the following question as a basis for class discussion:

● What does the law say about the instruction and assessment of students with disabilities? Why is it important that students with all ability levels have access to the general education curriculum? What are some ways to help these students access the general education curriculum?

RESEARCH NAVIGATOR™—Individualized Education Programs (IEP)

➡ Log onto www.mylabschool.com. Under the **Courses** tab, in **Special Education**, navigate to **Research Navigator™**.

OR

➡ Use the www.mylabschool.com **Assignment Finder** to go directly to Research Navigator™. Just enter Assignment ID **SPRN**.

Instruct students to use the search term "Individualized Education Programs" to locate an article on either EBSCOhost or the *New York Times* On the Web One-Year Archive. Ask students to prepare a 2-5 minute presentation for the class:

1. Present an overview of the article

2. State your opinion on an issue raised within the article

Once all of the students have presented their articles, open the class discussion by asking the students to reflect on how these issues impact classrooms and offer their opinions on the issues presented.

CHAPTER 6: DIFFERENTIATING INSTRUCTION TO PROMOTE ACCESS TO THE CURRICULUM

CASE STUDY—"A Broken Arm"

This case study focuses on Jim, a high school student who struggles with spelling despite the instructional accommodations made by his resource teacher.

➡ Log onto www.mylabschool.com. Under the **Resources** tab, navigate to the **Case Archive**, and read **"A Broken Arm."**

OR

➡ Use the www.mylabschool.com **Assignment Finder** to go directly to this simulation. Just enter Assignment ID **CS08**.

Instruct your students to print and read the case study for homework. Assign some or all of the following questions.

1. What instructional modifications did Mary make for Jim? Were the modifications effective? Why or why not?

2. When is it appropriate to make instructional modifications?

VIDEO—"Universal Design for Special Needs"

A faculty member from the University of Wisconsin, Milwaukee discusses the development of assistive technology and the principle of universal design. Accommodation is achieved through a series of stages including advocacy, attention and action, and then accessibility. Universal design, when applied to education, means that technologies that make learning accessible to all students should be infused into the general education curriculum.

➡ Log onto www.mylabschool.com. Under the **Courses** tab, in **Educational Technology**, access the **"Assistive Technologies and Universal Design"** videos, and watch **"Universal Design for Special Needs."**

OR

➡ Use the www.mylabschool.com **Assignment Finder** to go directly to these videos. Just enter Assignment ID **ETV13**.

The simplest assignment is to instruct your students to watch this short video as homework, answer the questions that follow it, and email their responses to you for credit.

If you show the video in class, you may use the following questions as a basis for discussion:

1. How does the process of accommodation and creating assistive technology begin?

2. What is the principle of universal design? What are the benefits of this type of accommodation?

3. Explain the metaphor that compares universal design to a volume control 'slider.' How could you adjust your lessons to achieve the goals of universal design?

CHAPTER 7: ASSESSING STUDENTS WITH SPECIAL NEEDS

SIMULATION—"Classroom Assessment"

Ms. Begay is a first year fourth grade teacher. She meets with her mentor teacher Mrs. Hernandez because she is concerned with the progress of three of her students.

➡ Log onto www.mylabschool.com. Under the **Courses** tab, in **Special Education**, access the "**Simulations**" and watch "**Classroom Assessment.**"

OR

➡ Use the www.mylabschool.com **Assignment Finder** to go directly to this case study. Just enter Assignment ID **SIM12**.

Ask students to watch the case study video and use the following questions as a basis for class discussion:

● What kind of information would best help Ms. Begay evaluate her students' learning?

● Why is it important for Ms. Begay to be aware of her students' progress?

● What steps can Ms. Begay take to monitor her students' progress throughout the academic year?

New York Times Education News Feed

The *New York Times* Education News Feed is a collection of education-related stories from the *New York Times*, updated hourly.

➡ Log onto www.mylabschool.com. Under the **Resources** tab, navigate to the New York Times Education News Feed.

OR

➡ Use the www.mylabschool.com **Assignment Finder** to go directly to the *New York Times* News Feed. Just enter Assignment ID **NYTNF**.

Instruct your students to access the News Feed once a day for an entire week. Have them print, read, and highlight the key points of any articles that are related to Assessment in American classrooms. At the end of the week, ask students to compose a journal entry or essay in reaction to the articles found. Students should come to class on the specified day with the articles and the journal entry or essay.

In class, ask students to break off into small groups and discuss their journal entries or essay. They should concentrate on the following factors:

1. Do you detect any trends in the issues presented over the week?

2. How will these issues impact your classroom?

CHAPTER 8: DEVELOPING COLLABORATIVE PARTNERSHIPS

VIDEO—"The Collaborative Process"

In this clip, a classroom teacher works with a special education teacher to provide help for students who need it. They provide a good example of collaboration.

➡ Log onto www.mylabschool.com. Under the **Courses** tab, in **Special Education**, access the "**Professional Collaboration**" videos, and watch "**The Collaborative Process.**"

OR

➡ Use the www.mylabschool.com **Assignment Finder** to go directly to these videos. Just enter Assignment ID **SPV3**.

> The simplest assignment is to instruct your students to watch this short video as homework, answer the questions that follow it, and email their responses to you for credit.

> If you show the video in class, you may use the following questions as a basis for discussion:
>
> 1. In what ways do the students in the video benefit from having the two teachers plan the lesson collaboratively?
>
> 2. As a new teacher, how comfortable do you think you would be with having another teacher in your classroom helping teach a subject? What are some ways you could work with the teacher to make the experience more beneficial to both you and your students?
>
> 3. Why is collaboration important to the process of inclusion?

CASE STUDY—"He's Just a Goofy Guy"

Read this case study that focuses on Jake, an energetic first grader with a learning disability. Betty, Jake's general education teacher, and Sharon, his resource teacher, have differing views on what is best for Jake.

➡ Log onto www.mylabschool.com. Under the **Courses** tab, in **Special Education**, access the "**Case Studies,**" and read "**He's Just a Goofy Guy.**"

OR

➡ Use the www.mylabschool.com **Assignment Finder** to go directly to this case study. Just enter Assignment ID **CS12**.

> Print and distribute this case study in class. Ask students to read the case study and use the following questions as a basis for class discussion:
>
> • Why do you think Betty is resistant to having Jake in her class? Do you think Jake is ready to be placed in a general education classroom full time? Why or why not?
>
> • How can Sharon and Betty work together to best serve Jake's needs?

MyLabSchool Sample Integration Guide

CHAPTER 9: PROMOTING POSITIVE BEHAVIOR AND FACILITATING SOCIAL SKILLS

CASE STUDY—"Back to Square One"

This case focuses on Rachel and Leanne, co-teachers of a combined third, fourth, and fifth grade class. Rachel and Leanne have an equal number of general education students and students with exceptionalities. Thomas, a fourth grade student with learning disabilities and ADHD, exhibits disruptive behavior which proves to be a challenge for Rachel and Leanne.

➥ Log onto www.mylabschool.com. Under the **Resources** tab, navigate to the **Case Archive**, and read **"Back to Square One."**

OR

➥ Use the www.mylabschool.com **Assignment Finder** to go directly to these videos. Just enter Assignment ID **CS09**.

Instruct your students to print and read the case study for homework. Assign either or both of the following questions.

1. How did Rachel and Leanne modify the class behavior plan to address Thomas' disruptive behavior?

2. Considering Thomas' reaction to the reinstatement of the Choices Chart, what other adaptations might the teachers explore to modify his behavior?

VIDEO—"Behavior Disorders"

Nick is a student who struggles with controlling his behavior at home and school. This video shows how behavior intervention helped him to learn to control his behavior disorder.

➥ Log onto www.mylabschool.com. Under the **Courses** tab, in **Special Education**, access the **"Emotional and Behavioral Disorders"** videos, and watch **"Behavior Disorders."**

OR

➥ Use the www.mylabschool.com **Assignment Finder** to go directly to these videos. Just enter Assignment ID **SPV10**.

The simplest assignment is to instruct your students to watch this short video as homework, answer the questions that follow it, and email their responses to you for credit.

If you show the video in class, you may use the following questions as a basis for discussion:

1. What kinds of inappropriate behavior does Nick demonstrate? How have the special educators at Nick's school addressed these behaviors?

2. Nick's teacher notes that he has academic strengths and, while he has behavior problems, he is manageable and responds to feedback and redi-

rection. How might these management strategies be used to reintegrate Nick into a general education classroom?

3. What social skills strategies would you use to help Nick reintegrate into the general education classroom?

CHAPTER 10: TEACHING READING

VIDEO—"Blending Individual Sounds (Phonemic Awareness)"

Students learn to blend individual stretched sounds into words. In this video, the teacher uses direct instruction to teach phonological awareness to struggling readers.

➡ Log onto www.mylabschool.com. Under the **Courses** tab, in **Special Education**, go to the video lab. Access the "**Reading**" videos and watch the "**Blending Individual Sounds (Phonemic Awareness)**" video.

OR

➡ Use the www.mylabschool.com **Assignment Finder** to go directly to these videos. Just enter Assignment ID **SPV13**.

If you show the video in class, you may use the following questions as a basis for discussion:

1. What strategy does the teacher in this video use to teach phonological awareness?

2. Describe the developmental sequence that occurs when children master phonological awareness?

3. Describe three activities (other than the one demonstrated in the video) that could be used to teach phonological awareness?

SIMULATION—"See Jane Read"

This simulation begins with the "Challenge Cycle" showing the following sequence: Challenge, Thoughts, Perspectives & Resources, Assessment and Wrap up. This particular simulation contains a "challenge movie," set in a kindergarten classroom during story time. This is followed by a sequence of self-reflective questions and activities that challenge students to take a close look at how they would ensure that all kindergarten students will learn to read at a grade appropriate level.

➡ Log onto www.mylabschool.com. Under the **Resources** tab, navigate to the **Simulations Archive**, and execute the simulation entitled **"See Jane Read."**

OR

➡ Use the www.mylabschool.com **Assignment Finder** to go directly to this simulation. Just enter Assignment ID **SIM15**.

Instruct your students to access the simulation, watch the "challenge movie" and complete the activities that follow. If you have internet access in the classroom, view the Simulation in class and discuss the questions and activities as a group.

> Homework Assignment:
>
> Instruct students to develop a brief lesson plan centered around a group story-time exercise that will both challenge advanced kindergarten readers and include and facilitate improvement for struggling readers. Require that students develop their lessons using the Portfolio & Lesson Builder tool.

CHAPTER 11: TEACHING WRITING

VIDEO—"Grammar and Punctuation"

This video shows a teacher helping her fifth grade students participate in peer editing. The students edit each others' writing to check punctuation, capitalization, and spelling.

➡ Log onto www.mylabschool.com. Under the **Courses** tab, in **Language Arts**, access "**The Mechanics of Writing**" videos, and watch "**Grammar and Punctuation**."

   OR

➡ Use the www.mylabschool.com **Assignment Finder** to go directly to these videos. Just enter Assignment ID **LAV6**.

> The simplest assignment is to instruct your students to watch this short video as homework, answer the questions that follow it, and email their responses to you for credit.

> If you show the video in class, use the following questions as a basis for class discussion:
>
> 1. What editing strategies from your text are used by the teacher in this video?
>
> 2. Identify two instructional adaptations that may be used to help students who struggle with writing.

SIMULATION—"Providing Instructional Supports"

All of Ms. Price's students struggle with a writing assignment that is based on student participation in the school science fair. This simulation talks about different instructional strategies to help all students succeed in the inclusive classroom.

➡ Log onto www.mylabschool.com. Under the **Courses** tab, in **Special Education**, access the "**Simulations**" and watch "**Providing Instructional Supports**."

   OR

➡ Use the www.mylabschool.com **Assignment Finder** to go directly to this case study. Just enter Assignment ID **SIM23**.

Ask students to watch the case study video and use the following questions as a basis for class discussion:

● What can Ms. Price do to help her class when they struggle with a writing assignment?

● What steps can Ms. Price take to monitor her students' writing progress throughout the academic year?

CHAPTER 12: TEACHING MATHEMATICS

RESEARCH NAVIGATOR™—Mathematics

➥ Log onto www.mylabschool.com. Under the **Courses** tab, in **Special Education**, access **Research Navigator™**.

OR

➥ Use the www.mylabschool.com **Assignment Finder** to go directly to Research Navigator™. Just enter Assignment ID **SPRN**.

Use Research Navigator™ to help your students learn more about teaching mathematics in the inclusive classroom. Ask students to type in the keywords "teaching mathematics". Ask students to review the articles available and select one for an article summary.

VIDEO—"Real-World Math Methods"

This video explores two different math classrooms that make use of real world examples and experiences to teach math concepts.

➥ Log onto www.mylabschool.com. Under the **Courses** tab, in **Math Methods**, access the **"Math Foundations"** videos, and watch **"Real-World Math Methods."**

OR

➥ Use the www.mylabschool.com **Assignment Finder** to go directly to these videos. Just enter Assignment ID **MMV1**.

The simplest assignment is to instruct your students to watch this short video as homework, answer the questions that follow it, and email their responses to you for credit.

If you show the video in class, use the following questions as a basis for class discussion:

1. How will your students benefit from using real world examples to solve math problems?

2. What are some examples of adaptations that can be made for students who struggle with mathematics?

CHAPTER 13: FACILITATING CONTENT AREA INSTRUCTION AND STUDY SKILLS

VIDEO—"Content Area Reading"

In this video, educators discuss the purpose of and strategies for teaching content reading. A third grade teacher demonstrates teaching content area reading in a science curriculum.

➡ Log onto www.mylabschool.com. Under the **Courses** tab, in **Reading Methods**, access the "**Content Area Reading**" videos, and watch "**Content Area Reading**."

OR

➡ Use the www.mylabschool.com **Assignment Finder** to go directly to these videos. Just enter Assignment ID **RMV6**.

The simplest assignment is to instruct your students to watch this short video as homework, answer the questions that follow it, and email their responses to you for credit.

If you show the video in class, use the following questions as a basis for class discussion:

What are some strategies students can use to read in the content areas? What are some examples of adaptations that can be made for students who struggle with reading in the content areas?

VIDEO—"Reading a Textbook"

This video shows Wendy Olsen, an eighth grade math and science teacher, talking with her class about reading textbooks and strategies for reading in the content areas.

➡ Log onto www.mylabschool.com. Under the **Courses** tab, in **Reading Methods**, access the "**Content Area Reading**" videos, and watch "**Reading a textbook**."

OR

➡ Use the www.mylabschool.com **Assignment Finder** to go directly to these videos. Just enter Assignment ID **RMV6**.

The simplest assignment is to instruct your students to watch this short video as homework, answer the questions that follow it, and email their responses to you for credit.

If you show the video in class, use the following questions as a basis for class discussion:

1. Why is it important to help students learn strategies for reading textbooks?

2. What are some examples of adaptations that can be made for students who struggle with reading their textbooks?

From watching actual classroom video footage of teachers and students interacting to building standards-based lessons and web-based portfolios . . . from a robust resource library of the "What Every Teacher Should Know About" series to complete instruction on writing an effective research paper . . . **MyLabSchool** brings together an amazing collection of resources for future teachers. This website gives you a wealth of videos, print and simulated cases, career advice, and much more.

Use **MyLabSchool** with this Allyn and Bacon Education text, and you will have everything you need to succeed in your course. Assignment IDs have also been incorporated into many Allyn and Bacon Education texts to link to the online material in **MyLabSchool** . . . connecting the teachers of tomorrow to the information they need today.

PEARSON **VISIT** www.mylabschool.com **to learn more about this invaluable resource and Take a Tour!**

Here's what you'll find in mylabschool

VideoLab ▶

Access hundreds of video clips of actual classroom situations from a variety of grade levels and school settings. These 3- to 5-minute closed-captioned video clips illustrate real teacher–student interaction, and are organized both topically *and* by discipline. Students can test their knowledge of classroom concepts with integrated observation questions.

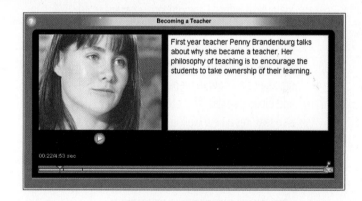

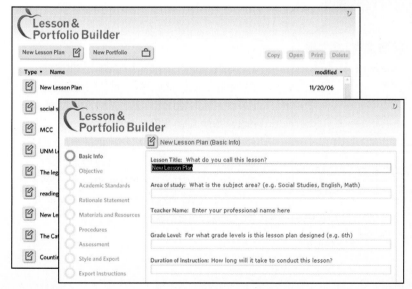

◀ Lesson & Portfolio Builder

This feature enables students to create, maintain, update, and share online portfolios and standards-based lesson plans. The Lesson Planner walks students, step-by-step, through the process of creating a complete lesson plan, including verifiable objectives, assessments, and related state standards. Upon completion, the lesson plan can be printed, saved, e-mailed, or uploaded to a website.

Here's what you'll find in mylabschool

Where the classroom comes to life!

Simulations ▶

This area of MyLabSchool contains interactive tools designed to better prepare future teachers to provide an appropriate education to students with special needs. To achieve this goal, the IRIS (IDEA and Research for Inclusive Settings) Center at Vanderbilt University has created course enhancement materials. These resources include online interactive modules, case study units, information briefs, student activities, an online dictionary, and a searchable directory of disability-related web sites.

◀ Resource Library

MyLabSchool includes a collection of PDF files on crucial and timely topics within education. Each topic is applicable to any education class, and these documents are ideal resources to prepare students for the challenges they will face in the classroom. This resource can be used to reinforce a central topic of the course, or to enhance coverage of a topic you need to explore in more depth.

Research Navigator ▶

This comprehensive research tool gives users access to four exclusive databases of authoritative and reliable source material. It offers a comprehensive, step-by-step walk-through of the research process. In addition, students can view sample research papers and consult guidelines on how to prepare endnotes and bibliographies. The latest release also features a new bibliography-maker program—AutoCite.

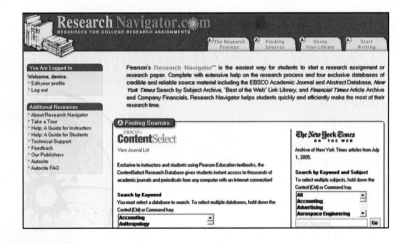

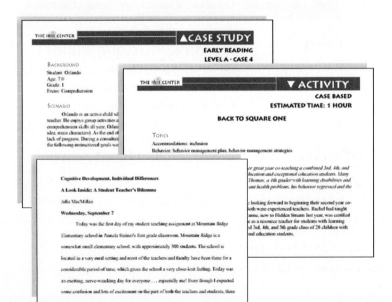

◀ Case Archive

This collection of print and simulated cases can be easily accessed by topic and subject area, and can be integrated into your course. The cases are drawn from Allyn & Bacon's best-selling books, and represent the complete range of disciplines and student ages. It's an ideal way to consider and react to real classroom scenarios. The possibilities for using these high-quality cases within the course are endless.

Teaching Students with Special Needs in Inclusive Classrooms

Diane Pedrotty Bryant
University of Texas at Austin

Deborah Deutsch Smith
Claremont Graduate University

Brian R. Bryant

PEARSON

Boston • New York • San Francisco
Mexico City • Montreal • Toronto • London • Madrid • Munich • Paris
Hong Kong • Singapore • Tokyo • Cape Town • Sydney

Executive Editor and Publisher: Virginia Lanigan
Editorial Assistant: Matthew Buchholz
Senior Marketing Manager: Kris Ellis-Levy
Production Editor: Gregory Erb
Editorial Production Service: Barbara Gracia
Copyeditor: Connie Day
Composition Buyer: Linda Cox
Manufacturing Buyer: Megan Cochran
Electronic Composition: Modern Graphics, Inc.
Interior Design: Denise Hoffman
Photo Researcher: Sarah Evertson
Cover Administrator: Kristina Mose-Libon

For related titles and support materials, visit our online catalog at www.ablongman.com.

Between the time website information is gathered and then published, it is not unusual for some sites to have closed. Also, the transcription of URLs can result in typographical errors. The publisher would appreciate notification where these errors occur so that they may be corrected in subsequent editions.

ISBN 10: 0-205-43092-9
ISBN 13: 978-0-205-43092-5

Library of Congress Cataloging-in-Publication Data was not available at press time.

Photo Credits

Chapter 1: p. 2, © Gabe Palmer/CORBIS; p. 8, © Eric Fowke/PhotoEdit; p. 18, © Michael Newman/PhotoEdit; p. 26, ©Laura Dwight/PhotoEdit; p. 35, ©Michael Greenlar/The Image Works. *Chapter 2*: p. 40, Pearson Learning Photo Studio; p. 46, © Roy Morsch/zefa/CORBIS; p. 51, AP Images/The Indianapolis Star/Adriane Jaeckle; p. 61, © Michael Newman/PhotoEdit; p. 76, © David Young-Wolff/PhotoEdit. *Chapter 3*: p. 82, ©David Young-Wolff/PhotoEdit; p. 91, © Ellen B. Senisi/The Image Works; p. 98, © Robin Sachs/PhotoEdit; p. 102, © Bob Daemmrich/PhotoEdit; p. 111, © Richard T. Nowitz/CORBIS; p. 120, AP Images/Charles Krupa. *Chapter 4*: p. 130, AP Images/Charlie Riedel; p. 139, ©Bob Daemmrich/The Image Works; p. 147, AP Images/MattYork; p. 154, © Michael Newman/PhotoEdit; p. 158, © Robert Harbison. *Chapter 5*: p. 164, © Michael Newman/PhotoEdit; p. 173, © Guy Cali/CORBIS; p. 175, © Michael Newman/PhotoEdit; p. 184, © David Young-Wolff/PhotoEdit; p. 192, © Thinkstock/Alamy. *Chapter 6*: p. 200, © Elizabeth Crews Photography; p. 215, © Ann Cutting/Workbook Stock/Jupiter Images; p. 222, © Bob Daemmrich/The Image Works; p. 229, © Will Hart/PhotoEdit; p. 238, © Ellen B. Senisi. *Chapter 7*: p. 254, © Bob Daemmrich/PhotoEdit; p. 259, © CORBIS; p. 273, © David Young-Wolff/PhotoEdit; p. 287, © Ellen Senisi/The Image Works. *Chapter 8*: p. 300, © Will Hart; p. 310, © Will Hart; p. 314, © Will Hart; p. 321, © Michael

Photo credits continue on page 1, which constitutes an extension of the copyright page.

Printed in the United States of America

10 9 8 7 6 5 4 3 2 1   RRD-OH 11 10 09 08 07

To our special mothers
and special brothers.

And to our children,
who make our lives so very special.

DIANE P. BRYANT is a fellow in the Mollie Villeret Davis Professorship in Learning Disabilities, and a professor in the Learning Disabilities/Behavior Disorders program in the Department of Special Education at The University of Texas at Austin. She is currently the principal investigator of the Response to Intervention Early Mathematics Assessment and Intervention project. She is the project director for an early mathematics project with the Vaughn Gross Center for Reading and Language Arts, also at The University of Texas at Austin. She is the author and co-author of numerous articles, books, tests, and professional development products that focus on learning disabilities, assistive technology, behavior management, reading, and assessment. Her research interests include validating interventions in reading and mathematics for students with early learning difficulties and learning disabilities. She is also the author of *Assistive Technology for People with Disabilities* (Allyn & Bacon, 2003) with Brian Bryant. ●

DEBORAH D. SMITH is a professor of special education at the School of Educational Studies at Claremont Graduate University. She currently is co-principal investigator of the IRIS Center for Training Enhancements, which is funded by the U.S. Department of Education's Office of Special Education Programs (http://iris.peabody.vanderbilt.edu). The national center is charged with developing modules and materials about students with disabilities. These enhancements are designed for use by university faculty in college courses and in professional development activities for education professionals working in inclusive school settings. She also directs IRIS-West, housed at Claremont, where the national outreach component for the IRIS Center is based. Deb is the author of *Introduction to Special Education: Making a Difference*, Sixth Edition (Allyn & Bacon, 2007), and she was the lead researcher for the *Special Education Faculty Shortage Study*. ●

BRIAN R. BRYANT lives and works in Austin, Texas. He has served as director of research for PRO-ED, Inc. for 10 years and has since served as director of the Office for Students with Disabilities at Florida Atlantic University, as project director of the Texas Assistive Technology Partnership (Tech Act project), and as a private consultant. For 15 years, Brian has held an adjunct faculty lecturer appointment in the Department of Special Education at The University of Texas at Austin. For the past 5 years, he has also had an appointment as a research fellow with the Vaughn Gross Center for Reading and Language Arts, also at The University of Texas at Austin. Currently, he is co-principal investigator of the RTI Early Mathematics Assessment and Intervention Model and the program coordinator for the early mathematics project. In addition to his book *Assistive Technology for People with Disabilities* (Allyn & Bacon, 2003) with Diane Bryant, Brian is the author or co-author of dozens of psycho-educational tests, articles, books, chapters in books, professional development materials, and other products dealing with remedial education, learning disabilities, mental retardation, assessment, and assistive technology. His primary research interests are assessment and instruction in learning disabilities (especially reading and mathematics) and mental retardation (especially support provisions), and the exploration of assistive technology applications for children and adults with a variety of disabilities. ●

brief contents

contents

chapter 1

Inclusive Teaching as Responsive Education   2

Understanding Learners with Special Needs: High Incidence Disabilities or Conditions   40

chapter 2

Understanding Learners with Special Needs: Low Incidence Disabilities or Conditions 82

chapter  3

Other Students with Special Learning Needs   130

chapter

Delivery of Special Services Through Individualized Plans   164

chapter

Differentiating Instruction to Promote Access to the Curriculum   200

chapter

- CHAPTER OBJECTIVES   201
- OPENING CHALLENGE: **Planning and Delivering Instruction**   201

How Do We Differentiate Instruction?   204

Universal Design   204

The ADAPT Framework   205

Multicultural and Linguistic Considerations   210

What Instructional Practices Help Students Access and Master the Curriculum?   213

Planning for Instruction   213

Delivering Instruction   222

What Are Some Effective Instructional Grouping Practices?   228

Grouping: Whole Group, Flexible Groups, One-to-One   228

Peer Tutoring   230

Cooperative Learning   230

How Can Instructional Materials Be Adapted?   233

Textbooks   234

Instructional Materials   235

What Are Some Effective Homework Practices?   236

Homework Practices   236

Guidelines for Homework Practices   238

How Can Assistive Technology Help Students Access the Curriculum?   240

Assistive Technology Devices   241

AT Services   248

AT Integration   249

Summary   250

Self-Test Questions   250

Revisit the Opening Challenge   251

Professional Standards and Licensure   252

MyLabSchool Activities   253

chapter

Assessing Students with Special Needs   254

- CHAPTER OBJECTIVES   255
- OPENING CHALLENGE: **Determining What Students Know**   255

Why Do We Assess Students with Special Needs?   257

Purposes of Assessment   257

Legislation Protection Related to Assessment   259

chapter 8

Developing Collaborative Partnerships   300

chapter 9

Promoting Positive Behavior and Facilitating Social Skills   338

Teaching Reading 388

chapter *10*

chapter 11

Teaching Writing   440

chapter 12

Teaching Mathematics   476

Facilitating Content-Area Instruction and Study Skills 534

chapter 13

special features

ADAPT in Action

ADAPT Framework

Considering *Diversity*

Instructional activity

Making a Difference

what WORKS

tech NOTES

WORKING together

preface

To Our Readers

We came together to write this text with one main purpose: to help teachers complete their special education/inclusion course *inspired* to teach students with disabilities in inclusive settings and *equipped* to do so effectively.

With the increased reliance on accountability systems and high stakes testing, the number of students who struggle and who are at risk for school failure has become increasingly apparent to educators. Today, the vast majority of students with disabilities spend more than 80 percent of their school day learning in general education classrooms. Unfortunately, many classroom teachers working in inclusive settings believe they are unprepared to meet the challenges these individual students bring to the learning environment. So we wrote this text to fulfill what we see as our two critical responsibilities to our readers:

- **To increase knowledge of *proven* practices.** A wealth of information exists about instructional practices that are evidence-based and effective for students with special needs who are learning in inclusive settings. We have worked to make this information accessible to you by analyzing the body of research that exists, selecting those practices that have proved to be most effective (and that will be of most help in the teaching situations you will encounter most often), and to present that information in the context of real classrooms. To that end, our text discussion and supporting features focus on *what works.*

- **To improve instructional decision making.** The ADAPT framework that we have integrated throughout this text will help you determine *how, when,* and *with whom* to use the proven academic and behavioral interventions in your repertoire to obtain the best outcomes. The ADAPT framework will help you develop the "habits of mind" needed to respond thoughtfully and flexibly to the challenges you will meet in your classroom long after your coursework is over.

We hope that by the time you have completed your reading of this text, we will have met these responsibilities and you will have confidence in your ability to meet the needs of *all* students in your classroom. We are confident that with the appropriate knowledge and tools, all teachers can make a positive difference in the educational lives of students with special needs.

Organization of This Text

THE FOUNDATIONS OF SPECIAL EDUCATION AND INCLUSIVE EDUCATION
The first four chapters of this text provide an overview of inclusive education and the nature and characteristics of students with disabilities and special learning needs. Chapter 1 examines the meaning of the term *disability,* what is meant by

inclusive education, and the key legislation that has affected the development of inclusive classrooms: the Individuals with Disabilities Education Act of 2004 (IDEA), the No Child Left Behind Act of 2001 (NCLB), and the Assistive Technology Act of 2004 (ATA or the Tech Act). Chapter 2 presents information about the high incidence disabilities—those that teachers are most likely to encounter in classrooms—such as learning disabilities, attention deficit hyperactivity disorder, speech or language impairments, mental retardation or intellectual and developmental disabilities, and emotional or behavioral disorders. Chapter 3 discusses the low incidence disabilities: deafness and hard of hearing, physical disabilities, low vision and blindness, autism spectrum disorders, developmental delay, and other conditions. Chapter 4 offers information about student learners whose needs are not specifically covered by IDEA '04 legislation, including students who are English language learners, students who come from challenging living situations, and students who are gifted and talented.

MEETING THE NEEDS OF STUDENTS WITH SPECIAL NEEDS IN SCHOOLS AND IN CLASSROOMS   In Chapter 5, we discuss individualized education programs (IEPs) and other special services that help teachers meet the needs of their students. Chapter 6 addresses differentiating instruction to promote access to the general education curriculum. This chapter focuses on the steps of the ADAPT framework and the four categories of adaptations, which are then integrated into Chapters 6 through 13. Chapter 7 discusses the evaluation of students' learning and how to modify and adapt assessments for students with special needs. Chapter 8 focuses on the importance of collaborative relationships with professionals, paraprofessionals, and families. Chapter 9 discusses the importance of creating a positive classroom environment by communicating effectively with students, arranging your classroom effectively, teaching social skills, and addressing problem behaviors. In Chapters 10 through 13, we focus on specific content areas: reading, writing, mathematics, and content-area reading and study skills. In these chapters, we present practical, evidence-based strategies for adapting instruction to meet the needs of all students.

Special Features

- An **Opening Challenge** case study begins each chapter. It describes in some detail a specific teaching challenge, which is then revisited throughout the chapter. Students are asked to reflect on their knowledge of the subject matter before reading the chapter and are encouraged to record their responses to **Reflection Questions** in a journal.

• OPENING challenge

Ms. Smith Goes to School

It is the week before the first day of school. Ms. Smith, a first-year teacher, sits in her empty fourth-grade classroom thinking about what it will be like to finally have her own students to teach, her own classroom to organize, and a real paycheck! She remembers years of hard study, taking many late-night classes, traveling across town to observe classroom after classroom, doing week after week of student teaching, staying up late revising lesson plans one more time, and being so excited when she saw the great scores she and her friends received on the state's competency test for teachers. She feels well prepared to assume the responsibility of educating a class of general education students. Ms. Smith has waited so long for this day to arrive; she has wanted to be a teacher since she was in elementary school. She begins to prepare for the school year with great excitement and anticipation.

But as she looks at her class list of 18 students, matching their names with their student files, she is worried. *"The range of their academic skills is so wide; their achievement test scores are all over the map. One of my students has been identified for gifted education, two come to me*

with individualized education programs, and three of my students are English language learners. Plus, I see a couple of the boys are due to continue receiving speech therapy in a group session from the speech/language pathologist twice a week. I haven't heard from any other teachers or resource professionals about special schedules for any of my students. I wish I could go back and take that Inclusion course again!"

• Reflection Questions

In your journal, write down your answers to the following questions. After completing the chapter, check your answers and revise them on the basis of what you have learned.

1. Do you think Ms. Smith is overly concerned about her students' varied needs? Do you think she is just having first-year-teacher jitters? Why or why not?

2. What advice would you give her about planning for her students with disabilities and for those with other special learning needs?

3. How can she learn more about the special education services her students should be receiving this year?

4. In what ways can Ms. Smith be responsive to all of her students' special needs?

Gilbert—High

Gilbert—High
ADAPT in Action • Stakes Testing

Earlier we introduced you to Gilbert, a student in Ms. Grey's class. Gilbert is an honor student who has low vision, and he is scheduled to take his state's high stakes test in English language arts next week. Use the ADAPT framework to determine a way to ensure that the test produces valid results.

A sk, "What am I requiring the student to do?" Ms. Grey thinks about the task that students are to complete. "One section of the test requires that all students read test items and select a response from four or five choices. It is a typical multiple-choice test. Another section asks open-ended questions, and students have to write their answers on from five to eight lines of space in their answer booklet. And one of the writing sections of the test requires the students to write an essay."

D etermine the prerequisite skills of the task. For this task, there are several prerequisite skills that Gilbert will need to have to accomplish the task. Ms. Grey notes, "Gilbert will have to see the print, read the instructions, read the test items and each response choice, tap his language arts knowledge to identify the answer to each question, and mark the answer. Some questions will require Gilbert to write a short answer, and still another segment of the test will require Gilbert to write an essay and edit and proof his work."

A nalyze the student's strengths and struggles. Most of the students have the requisite skills. Gilbert possesses all of the requisite skills, as long as he is able to see the print. But without adaptations, he will not be able to read the questions or provide responses to some items.

P ropose and implement adaptations from among the four categories. Remember that the content of the test has to remain unaltered. Although Gilbert appears to have all of the requisite skills except one, his inability to see standard print will certainly affect his test performance. In this instance, the adaptation is clear-cut. Gilbert will be allowed to use a magnification device (instructional material) because it is listed as appropriate and needed on his IEP.

T est to determine if the adaptations helped the student accomplish the task. Ms. Grey consulted with Gilbert's visual impairment specialist during high stakes tutoring sessions. The specialist worked with Gilbert and Ms. Grey to ensure that a magnification device was appropriate for Gilbert's needs. Throughout the tutoring sessions, including practice test administration, the magnification was effective in allowing Gilbert to read the test items, provide short-answer responses, and write the essay. After the exam, the specialist interviewed Gilbert to discuss the adaptations that were made. Gilbert admitted that the test was difficult, but the difficulty had nothing to do with the input format of the test. He could read the test just fine with the magnification, and he was able to write answers and the essay that were required by the test. The Tech Notes feature provides additional information about assistive technology adaptations available for students with low vision.

- **ADAPT in Action** sections are integrated directly within the text discussion. This illustrative section applies the ADAPT framework, a research-validated problem solving approach, to the student and teacher introduced in the **Opening Challenge** scenarios. In these features, the teacher "thinks out loud" using the ADAPT framework, thus allowing the reader to go through the problem solving steps with him or her.

- **ADAPT Framework** charts summarize the ADAPT model and apply it to practical, oft-encountered teaching and learning topics.

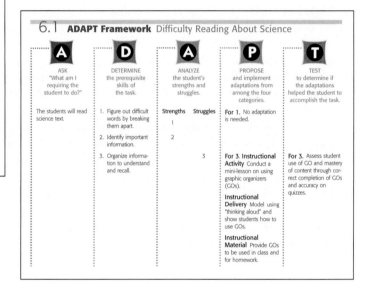

6.1 **ADAPT Framework** Difficulty Reading About Science

A ASK "What am I requiring the student to do?"	**D** DETERMINE the prerequisite skills of the task.	**A** ANALYZE the student's strengths and struggles.	**P** PROPOSE and implement adaptations from among the four categories.	**T** TEST to determine if the adaptations helped the student to accomplish the task.
The students will read science text.	1. Figure out difficult words by breaking them apart. 2. Identify important information. 3. Organize information to understand and recall.	Strengths Struggles 1 2 3	For 1. No adaptation is needed. For 3. Instructional Activity Conduct a mini-lesson on using graphic organizers (GOs). Instructional Delivery Model using "thinking aloud" and show students how to use GOs. Instructional Material Provide GOs to be used in class and for homework.	For 3. Assess student use of GO and mastery of content through correct completion of GOs and accuracy on quizzes.

Making a Difference

Teaching Self-Advocacy Gives Students with Disabilities a Tool for Life

Salle Hill Howes
Colorado Springs, Colorado

Our daughter Hillary was in fifth grade when she was first diagnosed with expressive and receptive aphasia, a language disability that results from damage to the language center of the brain and makes reading, writing, speaking, and processing information especially difficult. Doctors at Denver Children's Hospital told us that, given the significance of her disability, college was an unrealistic aspiration. Fortunately, we live in an enlightened school district in which high school students with learning differences acquire the skills needed for success through a self-advocacy program called LEAD. LEAD (Learning and Educating About Disabilities) is a four-year, accredited course offered to students with learning disabilities and ADHD at Cheyenne Mountain High School in Colorado Springs.

One part of the LEAD curriculum allows students to examine their own test scores and assessments. This knowledge helps them support their requests for the accommodations and modifications they may be entitled to. Students are given information about their specific disabilities and their legal rights under IDEA '04. LEAD students actively participate in their own IEP or 504 plan. They learn to take responsibility for the direction of their own education, not simply to rely on teachers and parents to advocate for them.

Although Hillary entered high school feeling defeated and worthless, the teachers in the LEAD program taught her that a learning disability has nothing to do with intelligence and is nothing to be ashamed of. After a year in LEAD, Hillary began writing letters to each of her teachers, giving them detailed information about her disability and how it affects her in the classroom. This simple act of educating her teachers won her their respect, and a mutual bond was formed. Hillary's teachers not only accepted her need for accommodations but also encouraged her to use them.

Hillary is now a confident and successful student in college, where she continues to advocate for herself and to educate others about her disability. It is my hope that some day all schools will offer a similar program to teach students with learning disabilities the crucial skill of self-advocacy and the importance of self-knowledge. It is equally important that all teachers appreciate and encourage those skills.

More Information on LEAD can be found at www.leadcolorado.org. ●

- **Making a Difference** features are first-person essays, written by classroom teachers, special educators, and parents, that describe their actual experiences and detail their insights into the impact of inclusive settings on the success of students with disabilities and other special learning needs and on their families.

- **Working Together** features offer practical advice on how an idea or concept can be taught using a collaborative approach that involves other school professionals and/or family members.

inclusive education, and the key legislation that has affected the development of inclusive classrooms: the Individuals with Disabilities Education Act of 2004 (IDEA), the No Child Left Behind Act of 2001 (NCLB), and the Assistive Technology Act of 2004 (ATA or the Tech Act). Chapter 2 presents information about the high incidence disabilities—those that teachers are most likely to encounter in classrooms—such as learning disabilities, attention deficit hyperactivity disorder, speech or language impairments, mental retardation or intellectual and developmental disabilities, and emotional or behavioral disorders. Chapter 3 discusses the low incidence disabilities: deafness and hard of hearing, physical disabilities, low vision and blindness, autism spectrum disorders, developmental delay, and other conditions. Chapter 4 offers information about student learners whose needs are not specifically covered by IDEA '04 legislation, including students who are English language learners, students who come from challenging living situations, and students who are gifted and talented.

MEETING THE NEEDS OF STUDENTS WITH SPECIAL NEEDS IN SCHOOLS AND IN CLASSROOMS In Chapter 5, we discuss individualized education programs (IEPs) and other special services that help teachers meet the needs of their students. Chapter 6 addresses differentiating instruction to promote access to the general education curriculum. This chapter focuses on the steps of the ADAPT framework and the four categories of adaptations, which are then integrated into Chapters 6 through 13. Chapter 7 discusses the evaluation of students' learning and how to modify and adapt assessments for students with special needs. Chapter 8 focuses on the importance of collaborative relationships with professionals, paraprofessionals, and families. Chapter 9 discusses the importance of creating a positive classroom environment by communicating effectively with students, arranging your classroom effectively, teaching social skills, and addressing problem behaviors. In Chapters 10 through 13, we focus on specific content areas: reading, writing, mathematics, and content-area reading and study skills. In these chapters, we present practical, evidence-based strategies for adapting instruction to meet the needs of all students.

Special Features

- An **Opening Challenge** case study begins each chapter. It describes in some detail a specific teaching challenge, which is then revisited throughout the chapter. Students are asked to reflect on their knowledge of the subject matter before reading the chapter and are encouraged to record their responses to **Reflection Questions** in a journal.

• OPENING challenge

Ms. Smith Goes to School

It is the week before the first day of school. Ms. Smith, a first-year teacher, sits in her empty fourth-grade classroom thinking about what it will be like to finally have her own students to teach, her own classroom to organize, and a real paycheck! She remembers years of hard study, taking many late-night classes, traveling across town to observe classroom after classroom, doing week after week of student teaching, staying up late revising lesson plans one more time, and being so excited when she saw the great scores she and her friends received on the state's competency test for teachers. She feels well prepared to assume the responsibility of educating a class of general education students. Ms. Smith has waited so long for this day to arrive; she has wanted to be a teacher since she was in elementary school. She begins to prepare for the school year with great excitement and anticipation.

But as she looks at her class list of 18 students, matching their names with their student files, she is worried. *"The range of their academic skills is so wide; their achievement test scores are all over the map. One of my students has been identified for gifted education, two come to me* with individualized education programs, and three of my students are English language learners. Plus, I see a couple of the boys are due to continue receiving speech therapy in a group session from the speech/language pathologist twice a week. I haven't heard from any other teachers or resource professionals about special schedules for any of my students. I wish I could go back and take that Inclusion course again!"

• Reflection Questions

In your journal, write down your answers to the following questions. After completing the chapter, check your answers and revise them on the basis of what you have learned.

1. Do you think Ms. Smith is overly concerned about her students' varied needs? Do you think she is just having first-year-teacher jitters? Why or why not?

2. What advice would you give her about planning for her students with disabilities and for those with other special learning needs?

3. How can she learn more about the special education services her students should be receiving this year?

4. In what ways can Ms. Smith be responsive to all of her students' special needs?

Gilbert—High
ADAPT in Action • Stakes Testing

Earlier we introduced you to Gilbert, a student in Ms. Grey's class. Gilbert is an honor student who has low vision, and he is scheduled to take his state's high stakes test in English language arts next week. Use the ADAPT framework to determine a way to ensure that the test produces valid results.

A sk, "What am I requiring the student to do?" Ms. Grey thinks about the task that students are to complete. "One section of the test requires that all students read test items and select a response from four or five choices. It is a typical multiple-choice test. Another section asks open-ended questions, and students have to write their answers on from five to eight lines of space in their answer booklet. And one of the writing sections of the test requires the students to write an essay."

D etermine the prerequisite skills of the task. For this task, there are several prerequisite skills that Gilbert will need to have to accomplish the task. Ms. Grey notes, "Gilbert will have to see the print, read the instructions, read the test items and each response choice, tap his language arts knowledge to identify the answer to each question, and mark the answer. Some questions will require Gilbert to write a short answer, and still another segment of the test will require Gilbert to write an essay and edit and proof his work."

A nalyze the student's strengths and struggles. Most of the students have the requisite skills. Gilbert possesses all of the requisite skills, as long as he is able to see the print. But without adaptations, he will not be able to read the questions or provide responses to some items.

P ropose and implement adaptations from among the four categories. Remember that the content of the test has to remain unaltered. Although Gilbert appears to have all of the requisite skills except one, his inability to see standard print will certainly affect his test performance. In this instance, the adaptation is clear-cut. Gilbert will be allowed to use a magnification device (instructional material) because it is listed as appropriate and needed on his IEP.

T est to determine if the adaptations helped the student accomplish the task. Ms. Grey consulted with Gilbert's visual impairment specialist during high stakes tutoring sessions. The specialist worked with Gilbert and Ms. Grey to ensure that a magnification device was appropriate for Gilbert's needs. Throughout the tutoring sessions, including practice test administration, the magnification was effective in allowing Gilbert to read the test items, provide short-answer responses, and write the essay. After the exam, the specialist interviewed Gilbert to discuss the adaptations that were made. Gilbert admitted that the test was difficult, but the difficulty had nothing to do with the input format of the test. He could read the test just fine with the magnification, and he was able to write answers and the essay that were required by the test. The Tech Notes feature provides additional information about assistive technology adaptations available for students with low vision.

- **ADAPT in Action** sections are integrated directly within the text discussion. This illustrative section applies the ADAPT framework, a research-validated problem solving approach, to the student and teacher introduced in the **Opening Challenge** scenarios. In these features, the teacher "thinks out loud" using the ADAPT framework, thus allowing the reader to go through the problem solving steps with him or her.

- **ADAPT Framework** charts summarize the ADAPT model and apply it to practical, oft-encountered teaching and learning topics.

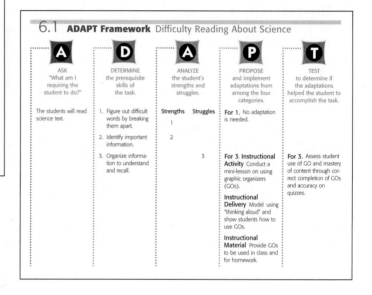

6.1   **ADAPT Framework** Difficulty Reading About Science

A ASK "What am I requiring the student to do?"	**D** DETERMINE the prerequisite skills of the task.	**A** ANALYZE the student's strengths and struggles.	**P** PROPOSE and implement adaptations from among the four categories.	**T** TEST to determine if the adaptations helped the student to accomplish the task.
The students will read science text.	1. Figure out difficult words by breaking them apart. 2. Identify important information. 3. Organize information to understand and recall.	Strengths Struggles 1 2 3	**For 1.** No adaptation is needed. **For 3. Instructional Activity** Conduct a mini-lesson on using graphic organizers (GOs). **Instructional Delivery** Model using "thinking aloud" and show students how to use GOs. **Instructional Material** Provide GOs to be used in class and for homework.	**For 3.** Assess student use of GO and mastery of content through correct completion of GOs and accuracy on quizzes.

Making a Difference

Teaching Self-Advocacy Gives Students with Disabilities a Tool for Life

Salle Hill Howes
Colorado Springs, Colorado

Our daughter Hillary was in fifth grade when she was first diagnosed with expressive and receptive aphasia, a language disability that results from damage to the language center of the brain and makes reading, writing, speaking, and processing information especially difficult. Doctors at Denver Children's Hospital told us that, given the significance of her disability, college was an unrealistic aspiration. Fortunately, we live in an enlightened school district in which high school students with learning differences acquire the skills needed for success through a self-advocacy program called LEAD. LEAD (Learning and Educating About Disabilities) is a four-year, accredited course offered to students with learning disabilities and ADHD at Cheyenne Mountain High School in Colorado Springs.

One part of the LEAD curriculum allows students to examine their own test scores and assessments. This knowledge helps them support their requests for the accommodations and modifications they may be entitled to. Students are given information about their specific disabilities and their legal rights under IDEA '04. LEAD students actively participate in their own IEP or 504 plan. They learn to take responsibility for the direction of their own education, not simply to rely on teachers and parents to advocate for them.

Although Hillary entered high school feeling defeated and worthless, the teachers in the LEAD program taught her that a learning disability has nothing to do with intelligence and is nothing to be ashamed of. After a year in LEAD, Hillary began writing letters to each of her teachers, giving them detailed information about her disability and how it affects her in the classroom. This simple act of educating her teachers won her their respect, and a mutual bond was formed. Hillary's teachers not only accepted her need for accommodations but also encouraged her to use them. Hillary is now a confident and successful student in college, where she continues to advocate for herself and to educate others about her disability. It is my hope that some day all schools will offer a similar program to teach students with learning disabilities the crucial skill of self-advocacy and the importance of self-knowledge. It is equally important that all teachers appreciate and encourage those skills.
More Information on LEAD can be found at www.leadcolorado.org. ●

- **Making a Difference** features are first-person essays, written by classroom teachers, special educators, and parents, that describe their actual experiences and detail their insights into the impact of inclusive settings on the success of students with disabilities and other special learning needs and on their families.

- **Working Together** features offer practical advice on how an idea or concept can be taught using a collaborative approach that involves other school professionals and/or family members.

- **What Works** features present key research-to-practice findings or interesting, classroom-based statistics that are relevant to topics explored within each chapter.

- **Considering Diversity** features examine various issues from a cultural or linguistic perspective; they illustrate how the diversity of our school populations is related to academic instruction and management.

- **Tech Notes** provide readers with information about assistive and instructional technologies that can be employed with students who have learning or behavior problems. Examples from classrooms are used to show practical applications.

- **Instructional Activities,** included in each of the "content-area" chapters (Chapters 10–13), present sample lessons for teaching the skills that students need to succeed in each area. Each activity includes the instructional objective, instructional content, instructional materials, a means to deliver the instruction, and methods to monitor student progress.

- **CEC Content Area Standards and INTASC Principles, and PRAXIS II Core Content Knowledge Areas** are correlated with each chapter in end-of-chapter charts.

- Each chapter closes with a **Summary** section, followed by **Self-Test Questions with Answers** to help readers review material and assess their understanding of key topics. **Revisit the Opening Challenge** questions return readers to the scenarios presented in the **Opening Challenge** and monitor their learning of key concepts in relation to the development of the teacher and student scenarios.

- Each chapter concludes with an activity that draws on the online resource **MyLabSchool,** with corresponding questions for follow-up and further exploration.

what WORKS 6.1

Stages of Learning

Marcus is a fifth-grade student in Mrs. Bell's class who is identified as having a learning disability in mathematics. The individualized education program (IEP) specified annual goals in mathematics, including solving word problems. Mrs. Bell gives a curriculum based assessment to determine which types of word problems Marcus can solve and which types require instruction. Assessment data show zero percent accuracy for solving two-step word problems using whole-number computation. Marcus is in the acquisition stage of learning for this skill. He can solve one-step word problems but does not generalize this knowledge to two-step problems.

Mrs. Bell uses explicit instruction to teach Marcus a strategy for solving two-step word problems. She discusses with Marcus the importance of solving two-step problems, pointing out that problem solving is used in many daily activities (promoting the occurrence of generalization). Marcus continues to build fluency with basic facts because facts are part of the word problem calculations (proficiency stage for facts). It takes Marcus four days to reach mastery (90 percent accuracy) for learning how to solve two-step word problems using the strategy taught by the teacher. Mrs. Bell has Marcus work in a cooperative learning group with his peers to solve one-step (maintenance stage) and two-step word problems (generalization stage). The group works together for a week, at which point the teacher determines through curriculum based assessment that the students can solve two-step problems proficiently. Mrs. Bell then has student groups write their own problems based on situations in the school, at home, or in the community (application stage). The groups share their problems so that different groups solve all the problems. She plans to provide periodic reviews (maintenance stage) of one- and two-step word problems to ensure continued mastery of the skills required for solving them.

Source: Adapted from *Teaching Students with Learning and Behavior Problems,* 3rd ed., by D. P. Rivera and D. D. Smith, 1997, Boston: Allyn and Bacon.

Instructional activity 10.1

Phonics Analogies

INSTRUCTIONAL OBJECTIVE: The students will learn to decode VC and CVC words.

INSTRUCTIONAL CONTENT: Letter–sound correspondence, VC and CVC words

INSTRUCTIONAL MATERIALS: Card with squares, letter tiles, list of VC or CVC words

INSTRUCTIONAL DELIVERY
Grouping: Small group of students who require instruction in phonics analysis

TEACHING PROCEDURE

1. Place the letter tiles in the boxes *m*, *a*, and *n*.
2. Say the first letter sound, /mmm/, while pointing to the letter *m*. The second letter sound, /aaa/, is spoken as the second letter tile is pointed to. The process continues for the final letter sound, /nnn/.
3. Slide your finger below the tiles in a left-to-right sequence as you say the word in elongated fashion (*mmmaaannn*), then quickly (*man*).
4. Say, "If this is *man*, and I change the *m* to a *r* (replaces the *m* tile with a *r* tile), now I have *rrraaannn . . . ran.*"

5. Model the process for other words.

Guided Practice

6. Repeat the process with the students. The process continues with a change of the ending letter tile (e.g., *ran* becomes *rat* then *rag*). Middle letters can also be replaced. The process continues with a variety of VC and CVC words.

Error Correction

7. If students make an error, say, "Stop. I will model the process. Listen, my turn." Model another word. Have students repeat. Then continue with guided practice.

Independent Practice

8. Give each student a couple of words to do alone. Tell the other students to sound out each letter, blending them and then saying the word quickly.

PROGRESS MONITORING: During the lesson, give the student 10 words to decode; check for mastery.

mylabschool

Video—"The Inclusive Classroom"

Special education teacher Penny Brandenburg teaches language arts collaboratively with the general education teacher to a class that includes some students with special needs. In this video clip we see Penny providing assistance to students in the general education classroom. After the lesson, she meets with her mentor and the general education teacher to discuss the lesson.

Log onto www.mylabschool.com. Under the **Courses** tab, in **Special Education,** go to the video lab. Access the "**Inclusion and Least Restrictive Environment**" videos and watch the "**Inclusive Classroom**" video.

OR

Use the www.mylabschool.com **Assignment Finder** to go directly to these videos. Just enter Assignment ID **SPV2.**

1. Describe the roles of the general education teacher and the special education teacher in the video. How can these roles benefit students?
2. How does the special education teacher provide assistance to students with special needs in this classroom?
3. What types of information are discussed in the conference after the lesson? How can conferences such as these support collaborative teaching?
4. The chapter provides a discussion of the "inclusion debate." What guidelines could be used to determine whether the students with special needs in the video clip were appropriately placed in the general education classroom?

Resources for Instructors

INSTRUCTOR'S RESOURCE MANUAL   ISBN: 0-205-59174-4. The Instructor's Resource Manual includes a wealth of interesting ideas and activities designed to help instructors teach the course. Each chapter includes a chapter-at-a-glance grid, chapter overview, lecture outlines, chapter objectives, key terms, discussion topics, activities, websites, and recommended supplementary resources. (Please request this item from your local Allyn & Bacon sales representative; also available for download from the Instructor's Resource Center at www.ablongman.com/irc.)

TEST BANK   ISBN: 0-205-58025-4. The Test Bank includes more than a thousand questions, including multiple choice, short answer, true/false, essay, and Praxis-style cases and questions. Page references to the main text, suggested answers, and skill type, as well as correlations to the CEC Standards and the Praxis Principles have been added to each question to help instructors create and evaluate student tests. (Please request this item from your local Allyn & Bacon sales representative; also available for download from the Instructor's Resource Center at www.ablongman.com/irc.)

COMPUTERIZED TEST BANK   The printed Test Bank is also available electronically through the Allyn & Bacon computerized testing system, TestGen. Instructors can use TestGen to create exams in just minutes by selecting from the existing database of questions, editing questions, and/or writing original questions. (Please request this item from your local Allyn & Bacon sales representative, also available for download from the Instructor's Resource Center at www.ablongman.com/irc.)

POWERPOINT™ PRESENTATION   ISBN: 0-205-58031-9. Ideal for lecture presentations or student handouts, the PowerPoint™ Presentation created for this text provides dozens of ready-to-use graphic and text images. (It is available for download from the Instructor's Resource Center at www.ablongman.com/irc.)

Videotapes for Lecture Presentation

- *Snapshots: Inclusion Video* (22 minutes in length; closed-captioned) profiles three students of differing ages with various levels of disability in inclusive class settings. In each case, parents, classroom teachers, special education teachers, and school administrators talk about the steps they have taken to help the students succeed in inclusive settings.
- *Snapshots II: Learning Disabilities, Mental Retardation, Emotional or Behavioral Disorders;* and *Snapshots II: Hearing Impairment, Visual Impairment, Traumatic Brain Injury* (20–25 minutes in length; closed-captioned) are a two-video set of six segments designed specifically for use in college classrooms. Each segment profiles three individuals and describes their families, teachers, and experiences. These programs are of high interest to students. Instructors who have used the tapes in their courses have found that they help disabuse students of stereotypical viewpoints and put a "human face" on the course material.
- *Professionals in Action Videotape: Teaching Students with Special Needs* (120 minutes in length; closed-captioned) consists of five 15- to 30-minute

modules presenting viewpoints and approaches to teaching students with various disabilities in general education classrooms, in separate education settings, and in various combinations of the two. Each module explores its topic via actual classroom footage and interviews with general and special education teachers, parents, and students themselves.

ALLYN & BACON TRANSPARENCIES FOR SPECIAL EDUCATION, 2008 A set of 100 acetate transparencies related to topics in the text.

COURSE MANAGEMENT **⊜ CourseCompass**™ Powered by Blackboard and hosted nationally, Allyn & Bacon's own course management system, CourseCompass™, helps you manage all aspects of teaching your course. For colleges and universities with WebCT™ and Blackboard™ licenses, special course management packages can be requested in these formats as well, and the Test Bank for this text can be prepared in the appropriate format for importing into your system. Allyn & Bacon is proud to offer premium content for special education in these platforms. (Your sales representative can give you additional information.)

- Allyn & Bacon CourseCompass™ for Special Education, Version 2 (Access code required.)
- Allyn & Bacon Blackboard™ for Special Education, Version 2 (Access code required.)
- Allyn & Bacon WebCT™ for Introduction to Special Education, Version 2 (Access code required.)

Resources for Students

mylabschool *Where the classroom comes to life!* Available as a value-package item with student copies of *Teaching Students with Special Needs in Inclusive Classrooms*, MyLabSchool is a collection of online tools for student success in the course, in licensure exams, and in their teaching careers. Visit www.mylabschool.com to access the following: **video clips** from real classrooms, with opportunities for students to reflect on the videos and offer their own thoughts and suggestions for applying theory to practice; an extensive archive of **text and multimedia cases** that provide valuable perspectives on real classrooms and real teaching challenges; Allyn & Bacon's **Lesson and Portfolio Builder** application, which includes an integrated state standards correlation tool; help with research papers using **Research Navigator**™, which provides access to four exclusive databases of credible and reliable source material, including EBSCO's ContentSelect academic journal database, the *New York Times* On The Web subject archive, the "Best of the Web" Link Library, and the FT.com business archive. MyLabSchool also includes a **Career Center** with resources for Praxis exams and licensure preparation, professional portfolio development, job search, and interview techniques.

COMPANION WEBSITE Created to accompany *Teaching Students with Special Needs in Inclusive Classrooms*, this online site offers **tools and activities** to help students understand and extend the text discussion and study more effectively. It includes, for each text chapter, the chapter objectives, web links, practice tests, and flash cards. Visit www.ablongman .com/bryantsmith1e.

VIDEOWORKSHOP FOR INTRODUCTORY SPECIAL EDUCATION/INCLUSION, VERSION 2.0   An easy way to bring video into your course for maximized learning! This total teaching and learning system includes quality video footage on an easy-to-use CD-ROM, as well as a Student Learning Guide and an Instructor's Teaching Guide—both with questions and activity suggestions. The result? A program that brings textbook concepts to life with ease and that helps students understand, analyze, and apply the objectives of the course. VideoWorkshop is available for students as a value-pack option with this textbook.

Acknowledgments

Thanks to our colleagues who contributed their writing and expertise to Chapter 4, "Other Students with Special Learning Needs": Janette K. Klingner, University of Colorado at Boulder, for her sections on culturally and linguistically diverse students, multicultural education, bilingual education, and culturally and linguistically diverse students and special education; and Margarita Bianco, EdD, University of Colorado at Denver and Health Sciences Center, Denver, Colorado, for her section on students who are gifted and talented.

Thanks to Alison Gould Boardman, University of Colorado at Boulder, for her work on the CEC and INTASC standards correlations and end-of-chapter MyLabSchool activities.

We would like to thank the teachers and parents who contributed the Making a Difference essays that appear in each chapter of the text. Their essays provide a rich understanding of how we can contribute to the success of individuals with special needs in inclusive settings—we *can* "make a difference." Thank you to each of our contributors whose essays appear both within the text and on our Companion Website (www.ablongman.com/bryantsmith1e):

Kathy Bell, special education teacher and consultant, Austin, TX

Kathy Berggren, Cornell University

Nicole Block, Steele Canyon High School, Spring Valley, CA

Carolyn Cohen, Northern Essex Community College

Patricia Davidson, University of Southern Indiana

Michelle Freas, Golden Gate Elementary, Naples, FL

Megan Garnett, Robinson Secondary School, Fairfax, VA

Allison Gillentine, Spring Hill Junior High, Longview, TX

Kimberly Gillow, Dexter Community Schools, Dexter, MI

Salle Hill Howes, Colorado Springs, CO

Vivian M. LaColla, Noxon Road Elementary School, Poughkeepsie, NY

Maria L. Manning, James Madison University

Yvette Netzhammer, Green Park Elementary School, Metairie, LA

Patricia Oliver, behavior analyst, Denver, CO

Quannah Parker-McGowan, Achievement First Charter Schools, New York, NY

Ricki Sabia, Silver Spring, MD

Karin Sandmel, Vanderbilt University

Margaret P. Weiss, learning specialist, Blacksburg, VA

Kelly Wilson, Denver, CO

Our gratitude goes out to the many reviewers, focus group attendees, and advisory council members who have greatly enhanced this project over the years of its writing. Your thoughtfulness and commitment to the project have made this a better book:

Judith Ableser, University of Michigan, Flint

Lynn Bagli, Old Dominion University

Mary Banbury, University of New Orleans

Heather Barker, University of New Hampshire

Dona Bauman, University of Scranton

Kimberly Bright, Shippensburg University

James Burton II, Marshall University

Debbie Case, Southwestern Oklahoma State University

Walter J. Cegel, St. Thomas University

Marlaine K. Chase, University of Southern Indiana

Vivian I. Correa, Clemson University

Kevin Costley, Arkansas Tech University

Christina Curran, Central Washington University

Helen T. Dainty, Tennessee Technological University

Sarah DeHaas, Juniata College

Audrey T. Edwards, Eastern Illinois University

Joseph Feinberg, University of North Carolina at Wilmington

Dan Fennerty, Central Washington University

Marion Fesmire, Florida State University

Connie Flood, State University of New York at New Paltz

Regina Foley, Southern Illinois University, Carbondale

Barb M. Fulk, University of Illinois

Raymond J. Gallagher, California State University, Dominguez Hills

Laurel M. Garrick Duhaney, State University of New York at New Paltz

Gordon S. Gibb, Brigham Young University

Gary Goodman, University of Houston

Paul C. Gorski, Hamline University

Char Gottschalk, State University of New York at New Paltz

Elizabeth L. Hardman, East Carolina University

Genevieve Howe Hay, College of Charleston

Susan Hupp, University of Minnesota

Kimberlye Joyce, University of Richmond

Kim Kelly, Southwestern Oklahoma State University

Timothy Lackaye, Hunter College

Phil Lanasa, Cameron University

Michelle LaRocque, Florida Atlantic University

DeAnn Lechtenberger, Texas Tech University

Robert B. Lee, Fort Valley State University

Gary Louis, Wilmington College

K. Alisa Lowrey, University of South Carolina

David J. Majsterek, Central Washington University

Linda Mechling, University of North Carolina, Wilmington

Heeral Mehta, Columbia University Teacher's College

Susan P. Miller, University of Nevada, Las Vegas

Susan O'Rourke, Carlow University

Theresa Pedersen, Northern Illinois University

John Platt, University of West Florida

Wayne Pyle, Lipscomb University

Melisa Reed, Marshall University

Laura Reissner, Northern Michigan University

Patricia Renick, Wright State University

Joy L. Russell, Eastern Illinois University

Edward J. Sabornie, North Carolina State University

Bruce Saddler, State University of New York at Albany

Mary Schreiner, Alvernia College

Amy Staples, University of Northern Iowa

Qaisar Sultana, Eastern Kentucky University

Donna E. Wadsworth, University of Louisiana at Lafayette

We are deeply grateful for the expertise, support, and commitment of the Allyn and Bacon team to see this project to fruition. Their belief in us and in this project exceeded all reasonable expectations! Many people comprised the team who worked on this book. Although we do not know all of them by name, their expertise with their craft is truly evident; to this team we express our gratitude! We thank Virginia Lanigan—friend, colleague, and editor—for her support, advice, and wisdom as this writing journey unfolded. Virginia inspired us to begin this project and remained steadfast with her encouragement and support throughout challenging times. We could not have finished this work without her continuing encouragement. To Shannon Steed, our developmental editor, we extend our thanks for keeping us on track and enduring the evolution of this book. Shannon's ideas and wisdom are found throughout the book; her partnership was evident as the project evolved in scope and content. We are also very grateful to Erin Liedel who took over when Shannon was on family leave. Erin helped us through the numerous reviewers' comments by providing advice about important changes to ensure the high standards and excellence readers expect. She kept us going by cheering us on when chapters were finished. We would like to thank Greg Erb, our production editor, whose high standards and expectations for guaranteeing quality and meeting timelines ensured that we would indeed finish this text. Greg supported us throughout production and to him we are truly grateful. We greatly appreciate Kris Ellis-Levy's work as marketing manager. Kris offered creative ideas for helping us to make important personal connections with our colleagues. We thoroughly enjoyed working with her! We would also like to thank Barbara Strickland, supplements editor, for expertly coordinating the book's supplemental resources, and to Matthew Buchholz, editorial assistant, for his continued help throughout the process.

Bringing closure to this project could not have occurred without the hard work and attention to detail demonstrated by Barbara Gracia. Her keen eye, efficiency, and professionalism were greatly appreciated to ensure a high quality product for our readers. Barbara was a joy to work with through the endless number of details that required careful scrutiny. We would also like to thank Connie Day, copyeditor, who did an excellent and thorough job in making this book clear to read. It is because of Barbara and Connie that this text is easy to read. Thanks also to Sarah Evertson for her fine work in researching the photos that appear in the book. And, finally, we greatly appreciate the work of Denise Hoffman, who created the beautiful interior design.

You have a textbook that we hope will inspire you as educators to reach out to all students. You will hear the voices of many as you read and learn numerous, practical ways to work with all students across the grades. We wish you the best!

D.P.B.
D.D.S.
B.R.B.

chapter 1

Inclusive Teaching as Responsive Education

After studying this chapter, you will have the knowledge to answer the following questions:

- What is disability?
- What are four perspectives on "disability," and how do they differ from each other?
- How are individuals with disabilities protected by legislation?
- What services are provided by special education?
- What is meant by inclusive education?

● OPENING c h a l l e n g e

Ms. Smith Goes to School

It is the week before the first day of school. Ms. Smith, a first-year teacher, sits in her empty fourth-grade classroom thinking about what it will be like to finally have her own students to teach, her own classroom to organize, and a real paycheck! She remembers years of hard study, taking many late-night classes, traveling across town to observe classroom after classroom, doing week after week of student teaching, staying up late revising lesson plans one more time, and being so excited when she saw the great scores she and her friends received on the state's competency test for teachers. She feels well prepared to assume the responsibility of educating a class of general education students. Ms. Smith has waited so long for this day to arrive; she has wanted to be a teacher since she was in elementary school. She begins to prepare for the school year with great excitement and anticipation.

But as she looks at her class list of 18 students, matching their names with their student files, she is worried. *"The range of their academic skills is so wide; their achievement test scores are all over the map. One of my students has been identified for gifted education, two come to me* *with individualized education programs, and three of my students are English language learners. Plus, I see a couple of the boys are due to continue receiving speech therapy in a group session from the speech/language pathologist twice a week. I haven't heard from any other teachers or resource professionals about special schedules for any of my students. I wish I could go back and take that Inclusion course again!"*

● Reflection Questions

In your journal, write down your answers to the following questions. After completing the chapter, check your answers and revise them on the basis of what you have learned.

1. Do you think Ms. Smith is overly concerned about her students' varied needs? Do you think she is just having first-year-teacher jitters? Why or why not?

2. What advice would you give her about planning for her students with disabilities and for those with other special learning needs?

3. How can she learn more about the special education services her students should be receiving this year?

4. In what ways can Ms. Smith be responsive to all of her students' special needs?

*P*aul is 53 and lives in alternative housing that is responsive to his special needs. There are grab bars in the bathroom, an alarm system in case he needs help, and a contact person to answer questions. He has cerebral palsy, which affects his muscles. He walks with crutches, has good communication skills, and manages his daily living needs. Paul takes special transportation to attend work and physical therapy and to go shopping and visit the bank. Writing and completing tasks that involve using his fingers (such as buttoning his shirt and tying his shoes) are difficult for him because of the cerebral palsy. As a young child, Paul attended a state-funded school for children with physical and cognitive disabilities. The school was isolated from the public schools and was located in a community where Paul did not live. He was transported to school by a special bus. After school, he spent afternoons sitting at home or going for physical therapy at the Children's Hospital. Paul's mother believed that the school system could do better. She believed that Paul was perfectly capable of attending public school with neighborhood children. She also believed that he should be able to graduate from high school like other children. Paul's mother spent years making her case to the local school board, city officials, and state legislators. After years of her determined advocacy for her son's right to a public education, in the mid-1960's Paul started attending public school classes. At that time, specialized instruction and services for students with special needs were not available. In elementary school, he was carried up the stairs to class because there were no elevators and he could not manage stairs with his leg braces. Paul learned basic school skills. He went on to graduate from high school with a special diploma and later graduated from a 2-year vocational training school. He held various part-time jobs and to this day works at a special workshop for individuals with disabilities. In essence, his work environment is a segregated setting. His social world is restricted to telecommunications such as the Internet and cell phone. But even so, Paul is determined to live independently.

We have come a long way since Paul started school in terms of society's perspective on disability, and we have dismantled many of the barriers to individuals' living independent, productive lives. We have laws to protect individuals in most aspects of life, and we have public school systems that must include all students with special needs. We know a great deal about appropriate instruction and services for students with special needs. Yet there is still work to be done to ensure an appropriate education for all students with special needs and to help these students make successful transitions to independent adulthood with employment, social relationships, and living arrangements that all of us strive to achieve.

You might wonder how teaching can be responsive to the needs of students with special learning needs such as Paul's. The simple answer is that education becomes responsive when an array of *individualized* educational interventions, which are monitored for the student's progress, are implemented to improve the outcomes of infants, toddlers, children, and youth with disabilities (U.S. Department of Education, 2006). Education is responsive and, we believe, responsible, when teams of educators work together to address the unique challenges each student brings to school.

You have the opportunity to be part of this work to ensure that all individuals with special needs receive a quality education. However, if you find this opportunity a bit daunting, you are not alone.

Have you had much personal interaction with persons with disabilities so far in your home, school, or community life? If you think not, you probably share that view with many of your colleagues in your program who are preparing to become classroom teachers.

Do you begin this course about teaching students with disabilities with some anxiety about your ability to meet the needs of these students? Again, you are not alone. Although students with disabilities spend more than 80 percent of their school day in general education classrooms, most recently graduated general education teachers report that they do not feel adequately prepared to teach them. And their principals agree with them: New teachers are not doing as well as they should managing behavior or instructing "difficult-to-teach" students (Futernick, 2006; Gaetano, 2006). But rather than being daunted by these reports, we hope you'll recognize in them the great opportunity they present as you prepare to enter the teacher ranks. You can make a tremendous difference in the lives of these students. And the mission of the course (and the text) you are now beginning is to give you the tools to do just that.

Throughout this text, we describe proven practices that will equip you to teach students with special needs in your classes. We focus on *what works* so that you can readily incorporate these practices into your teaching with confidence. We provide the ADAPT framework to help you develop the "habits of mind" to respond thoughtfully and flexibly to the varied challenges you will face in your classroom long after your brief university and in-service coursework is over. The ADAPT framework that we have integrated throughout this text will help you *learn, remember,* and *know when to apply* proven practices in your classroom.

Our goal is that you will develop the confidence you need to teach *all* students in your classes. Our many years working with pre-service and K–12 teachers convince us that teachers *want* to help their struggling students become successful learners but simply feel ill equipped to do so. In this text, we focus on those practices that have been *proved* to work and show you *how, when,* and *with whom* to use each of these practices to the best effect. Nothing builds confidence better than good preparation.

We write this text out of the mission we share with your course instructor: By the conclusion of this course, you will leave *wanting* to teach students with disabilities and other special learning needs in your classroom and *feeling equipped to do so effectively.* You will find (and those of you who have been teaching have already discovered) that *every* student in your classroom comes to you with his or her own areas of strength and struggle, parts of the school day that she or he absolutely enjoys or does not exactly relish, and personality traits that make you laugh, make you cry, or leave you scratching your head.

In this respect, the students in your classroom with identified "disabilities" are no different from the rest of their classmates: They're just kids. But the nature and extent of their particular struggles often require certain specialized teaching approaches to help them succeed. The good news is that we know what those effective approaches are, research has *proved* that they *work,* and they can be done in a *reasonable amount of class time and preclass preparation.* (And, as a bonus, they usually benefit *all* the students in your class, with or without disabilities.) You will learn that even students with the most difficult challenges can overcome, compensate, and achieve remarkable outcomes when your instruction is responsive to their learning needs. Finally, you will come to understand across your teacher education program that as a teacher, you *can* make a real difference in the lives of your students.

What Is the ADAPT Framework and How Do I Use It?

An approach that we have devised called the ADAPT framework is discussed in greater detail in Chapter 6 and used throughout the remaining chapters of this text. It is a framework for instruction and assessment of struggling learners that reflects proven "best practice" in the field. This framework, which we have distilled into the straightforward and (we hope) memorable acronym ADAPT, will help you develop and internalize a mental "drill" for the selection of effective interventions and teaching practices, and it will help you decide what instruction, adaptations, or assistance will most benefit a student with special needs in specific classroom situations. We introduce the ADAPT framework here because it reflects and underscores the mindset we want you to take away from your course: You can use the five steps of the ADAPT framework to help you make informed decisions about adapting your instruction based on individual student's needs and the tasks that all students must complete in school. For now, here's just a quick look at what the ADAPT framework looks like.

1.1 ADAPT Framework—Introducing the Framework

A	**D**	**A**	**P**	**T**
ASK "What am I requiring the student to do?"	DETERMINE the prerequisite skills of the task.	ANALYZE the student's strengths and struggles.	PROPOSE and implement adaptations from among the four categories:	TEST to determine if the adaptations helped the student accomplish the task.
			• Instructional activity	
			• Instructional content	
			• Instructional delivery	
			• Instructional material	

With that in mind, let's begin by first considering disabilities and the special challenges they create.

What Is a Disability?

Some of you might have answered the question "What is a disability?" by expressing the notion that disabilities are absolutes—something an individual simply has or doesn't have. Others might have answered the question by explaining that the concept of disability is complex and that there are many different perspectives on what "disability" is and what "disability" means to each individual, each family, and each culture. You might have included in your answer that the intensity of a disability is the result of different conditions or experiences and that the response (e.g., intensity of instruction, types of services, community supports) to a disability depends on an individual's unique needs. Such answers reflect the idea that individualized accommodations and assistance can reduce the impact of the challenge presented by a disability.

Why did we ask how disability is conceptualized? First, the concept of disability is not as simple as it initially appears. Second, the way people, groups, and cultures think about what it means to have a disability affects how they interact with people with disabilities. In turn, those interactions become events that influence individuals' outcomes (Branson & Miller, 2002; Winzer, 2007). For example, the beliefs of teachers and other professionals who work with students are important to understand because different perspectives result in different responses to a disability; some responses—such as low or unreasonably high expectations—can have long-term negative results (Artiles, 1998, 2003; Harry, 2007). So let's think together about various ways to conceptualize "disability" and also about how attitudes toward disability can influence students' lives.

Different disciplines, cultures, and individuals do not agree about the concept of "disabilities," what disabilities are, or how to explain them (Lynch & Hanson, 2004; Utley & Obiakor 2001). For example, many psychologists, education professionals, and medical professionals describe children and youth in terms of various characteristics, such as intelligence, visual acuity, academic achievement, or behavior. In its manual, *Diagnostic and Statistical Manual of Mental Disorders* (DSM-IV-TR), the American Psychiatric Association (APA) describes many characteristics that help to describe or define a condition or a disability because they set the individual apart from "normal," "typical," or "average" (APA, 2003). With this common approach, human characteristics or traits are discussed by using a continuum; at one end of the continuum very little of the target behavior is observed, and at the other end an unusual amount of the trait is expressed. For example, exhibiting either an excessive amount of a characteristic or not enough of that characteristic marks the individual as different. Here's an example. In the DSM-IV-TR, the APA describes hyperactivity as including the following behaviors:

a. often fidgets with hands or feet or squirms in seat

b. often leaves seat in classroom or in other situations in which remaining seated is expected

c. often runs about or climbs excessively in situations in which it is inappropriate (in adolescents or adults, may be limited to subjective feelings of restlessness)

d. often has difficulty playing or engaging in leisure activities quietly

e. is often "on the go" or often acts as if "driven by a motor"

f. often talks excessively (APA, 2003, p. 92)

Study this definition. Note that all of the behaviors described are expected in children. What leads to the identification of having the condition of hyperactivity is that "too much" of the behaviors listed by the APA are observed in the individual. Now let's look at the reverse situation: An example of when displaying "not enough" or "too few" of the behaviors of concern leads to the

● Some students exhibit problem behaviors and need exemplary teachers. How do federal laws distinguish between students who exhibit problem behaviors and students with attention issues or learning disabilities?

identification of a disability. Here's what the DSM-IV-TR says about depression, a condition that falls under the special education category of emotional or behavioral disorders:

> . . . A persistent and pervasive feeling of dejection, gloominess, cheerlessness, joylessness, and unhappiness. These individuals are overly serious, incapable of enjoyment or relaxation, and lack a sense of humor. They may feel that they do not deserve to have fun or be happy. They also tend to brood and worry, dwelling persistently on their negative and unhappy thoughts. (APA, 2003, p. 788)

Certainly, students with depression require specialized services to help them cope with their condition. These services will undoubtedly involve the classroom teacher who works with the student for a large portion of the school day.

As a teacher, you will hear such descriptions about your students' skills and behaviors. Other perspectives on or orientations toward individuals also guide people's thinking. These perspectives or orientations can provide a framework to understand various actions and reactions to disabilities and special needs. Therefore, let's turn our attention to four different ways of considering or thinking about disabilities:

- Deficit perspective
- Cultural perspective
- Sociological perspective
- Disability as a minority group

The Deficit Perspective on Disabilities

The *deficit perspective* reflects the idea that human behavior and characteristics shared by people are distributed along a continuum. Actually, scores or measurements received by people tend to create a distribution where the majority of people fall in the middle of the distribution and that's why they are called "average." For example, people are of different heights. Some people are short and some tall, but most people's height falls somewhere in the middle; the average of everyone's height is at the center of the distribution. The scores from most human characteristics create such patterns, forming what is called a normal curve, like the one shown in Figure 1.1. Because of the way the distribution tends to fall, with the highest number of scores in the middle and proportionally fewer as the distance from the average score increases, the distribution is also referred to as the bell-shaped curve.

The expectation, according to this idea, is for the academic achievement of all third graders to create such a distribution. The number of students obtaining each score would be plotted on the graph. Few students would obtain low scores on the achievement test, and their scores would be plotted at the left-hand side of the graph. The number of students receiving higher scores increases until the average or mean score is reached. With this scheme, somewhere in the middle of the distribution are typical learners, whose behaviors and characteristics represent the average or majority of students. Then, the progressively fewer students who obtain higher and higher scores on the test complete the right-hand side of the distribution or curve. The number of characteristics that could be counted in this way is infinite, and each individual student probably falls at a different point on each dimension measured. Thus the unusually tall student might have slightly below-average visual acuity and an average score on the distance he or she can kick a ball. Clearly the hypothetical average student, or typical learner, does not actually exist—or exists very rarely—because the possible combinations of human characteristics are endless.

Regardless, in mainstream America, quantifying human performance is the most common method used to describe individuals. Unfortunately, this way of

FIGURE 1.1 **A Hypothetical Distribution of Scores Creating a Normal or Bell-Shaped Curve**

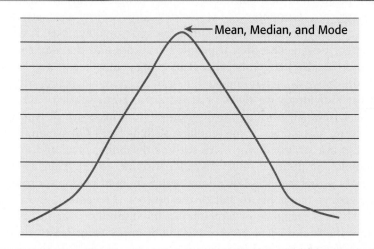

thinking about people puts half of everyone "below average" and forces individuals to be considered in terms of how different they are from the average. For students with disabilities, this approach contributes to the tendency to think about them as deficient or as being somehow less than their classmates without disabilities.

The Cultural Perspective on Disabilities

A second way to think about disabilities and the people who might be affected does not use a quantitative approach; rather, it reflects a *cultural perspective.* Alfredo Artiles of Arizona State University aptly points out that America today includes many different cultures, some of which have values and embrace concepts that differ greatly from mainstream ideas. Nonmajority cultures often hold different views of disabilities, and many do not think about disabilities in terms of deficits or quantitative judgments about individuals (Artiles, 1998, 2003). We believe that this is a very important point for teachers to understand. First, education professionals and the families with whom they work might not share the same understanding of disability. Second, they might not have a common belief about what causes disabilities.

Knowing that not all cultures share the same concept of disability helps us understand why families approach education professionals differently when told that their child has a disability. Because disability does not have a single orientation or fixed definition, it is not thought about uniformly or universally (Harry, 2007; Lynch & Hanson, 2004). Families with whom teachers work are likely to have different understandings about their child from those of school professionals. Also, not all cultures respond the same way to individuals identified as having a disability. In other words, the same individual might be considered "different," or as having a disability, in one culture but not in another (Utley & Obiakor, 2001; Jim Green, 2006 October, personal communication). Or the degree of difference might not be considered uniformly.

The Sociological Perspective on Disabilities

The *sociological perspective* or orientation represents yet another way to think about individuals with disabilities. Instead of focusing on people's strengths or deficits, this perspective views differences across people's skills and traits as being socially constructed (Longmore, 2003; Riddell, 2007). How a society treats individuals, not a condition or set of traits that the individual exhibits, is what makes people different from each other. If people's attitudes and the way society treats groups of individuals change, the impact of being a member of a group changes as well. In other words, according to this perspective, what makes a disability is how we treat individuals we think of as different. Some scholars and advocates hold a radical view, suggesting that disabilities are a necessity of American society, its structure, and values. Some scholars, such as Herb Grossman, believe that when societies are stratified, variables such as disability, race, and ethnicity become economic and political imperatives (Grossman, 1998). They are needed to maintain class structure. Classifications result in restricted opportunities that force some groups of people to fall to the bottom (Erevelles, 1996; Grossman, 1998). Clearly, this rationale or explanation for disabilities is controversial, but let's see how the sociological perspective might apply to at least one disability. Using this perspective, mental retardation exists because society and people treat these individuals poorly. If supporting services were available to help *every* individual when problems occur, then people with mental retardation would not be negatively treated and would be successful. In other words, if individuals with significant differences are treated like everyone else, problems associated with mental retardation will disappear.

Serious issues have been raised regarding sociological perspectives about disabilities. Jim Kauffman and Dan Hallahan, scholars at the University of Virginia, voice many concerns about this orientation and maintain that disabilities are real, not just sociologically constructed. Despite how people are treated, disabilities significantly affect the people involved (Kauffman, 1997; Kauffman & Hallahan, 2005). To them, sociological perspectives arise from a need for "sameness," where everyone is truly alike. They contend that this position is dangerous because it (1) minimizes people's disabilities, (2) suggests that individuals with disabilities do not need special services, and (3) implies that needed services can be discontinued or reduced. All three of these scenarios leave individuals with disabilities vulnerable to diminished outcomes. Whether or not you believe that the sociological perspective can be used to explain disabilities, it does explain why people with disabilities feel they experience bias and discrimination, just like members of other minority groups. Let's turn our attention to these issues now.

Disability as a Minority Group

Paul Longmore—a founder of the disabilities studies movement, director of the Disability Studies Department at San Francisco State, and also a person with disabilities—maintains that like other minority groups, individuals with disabilities receive negative treatment because of discrimination (Longmore, 2002, 2003). The ways in which people are treated by society and by other individuals erect real barriers that influence people's outcomes. Many individuals with disabilities believe that their disabilities (e.g., conditions and impairments) then handicap them (e.g., present challenges and barriers). This belief leads many people to think about people with disabilities as belonging to a minority group, much like race and ethnicity have resulted in African Americans, Hispanics, Native Americans, and Asian/Pacific Islanders[1] being considered part of historically underrepresented groups. Difficult situations occur not because of a condition or disability but, rather, because people with disabilities are denied full participation in society as a consequence of their minority status (Wizner, 2007). In fact, the law that guarantees children with disabilities a right to a public education, the Individuals with Disabilities Education Act (IDEA), is often referred to as a civil rights law. This places IDEA in the same category of laws as the Voting Rights Act of 1965, which put an end to discriminatory practices that denied some Americans their right to vote in state and national elections.

What Are Some Reasons for Disabilities?

We have just discussed four very different perspectives on disabilities; these orientations explain various views about what a disability is and society's reaction to disabilities. Let's return to more traditional views of disabilities and what causes

---

[1]Although regional and personal preferences about specific terms used to identify ethnic and racial groups vary, these terms are the ones used by the federal government. Throughout this text, we use a variety of terms in an attempt to achieve balance.

the conditions that result in disabilities. (Note that we will discuss other special learning needs that schools and society do not consider disabilities, including those prompted by giftedness, social and economic inequities, and cultural and linguistic differences, in Chapter 4.)

Many different systems are used to organize the causes of disabilities. One common way is to divide them into three groups by time of onset—that is, when the event or cause occurred. When this system is used, disabilities are classified in terms of whether they occurred before birth (prenatal or congenital), during the birth process (perinatal), or after birth (postnatal). Prenatal causes often lie in genetics, or heredity. Heredity is responsible for Down syndrome, congenital deafness, and all inherited conditions. Diseases and infections of expectant mothers, such as HIV/AIDS, can devastate an unborn baby, and such events are also considered prenatal. Perinatal causes occur during the birthing process. They include birth injuries due to oxygen deprivation, umbilical cord accidents, obstetrical trauma, and head trauma. They also include low birth weight. One common perinatal cause of disabilities is cerebral palsy (CP). Postnatal causes occur after birth, and here the environment is a major factor. A few examples of postnatal causes are child abuse and neglect, environmental toxins, and accidents.

Another way to consider why disabilities and special needs arise is to classify the reasons in terms of biological causes, environmental causes, and other risk factors. Many of these causes occur across all three periods of onset. Let's briefly consider these reasons for disabilities.

Biological Causes of Disability

Heredity is a biological cause of disabilities, as are diseases and health conditions. Thus, when a virus causes a severe hearing loss, it is considered a biological cause. Seizure disorders such as epilepsy are biological reasons for special health care needs, as are diseases such as juvenile arthritis and polio. In Chapters 2 and 3, where we present information about specific disabilities, we will have more to say about some types of conditions that students bring to school.

Environmental Causes of Disability

In addition to biological reasons, other situations can cause challenges that result in educational difficulties. Some of these are environmentally based. Many of these causes of disabilities are preventable, but many others cannot be avoided. Let's examine a few environmental reasons for disabilities.

Toxins abound in our environment. All kinds of hazardous wastes are hidden in neighborhoods and communities. For example, one toxin that causes mental retardation is lead. Two major sources of lead poisoning can be pinpointed (and, one would think, could be eliminated) in the United States today: exhaust fumes from leaded gasoline and lead-based paint. Leaded gas and lead-based paint are no longer sold in this country. Unfortunately, the lead has remained in dirt children play in and remains on the walls of older apartments and houses where children breathe the lead directly from the air and household dust, eat paint chips, or put their fingers in their mouths after touching walls or window sills. The Children's Defense Fund (CDF) reports that in the United States, some 16 percent of low-income children have lead poisoning, compared to 4 percent of all children in the country (CDF, 2004). Lead is not the only source of environmental toxins that government officials worry about; other concerns include mercury found in fish, pesticides, and industrial pollution from chemical waste (Schettler et al., 2000).

Other environmental issues can trigger problems for children as well. For example, asthma, a health condition that is covered in our discussion of Section 504, is the leading cause of school absenteeism. Problems with asthma can be reduced through the use of simple interventions by teachers and schools. For example, asthma is often triggered by exposure to specific allergens (National Institute of Environmental Health Sciences [NIEHS], 2005). For some students, the chance of an asthma attack is reduced when the classroom is free of chalk dust, plants that generate pollen or mold, cold and dry air, smoke, paint fumes, and chemical smells. For others, the fur of classroom pets can cause an episode. Clearly, exposures to toxins are preventable and the effect of a condition can be reduced.

Who Are Students with Disabilities?

Nationally, some 11 percent of students between the ages of 6 and 17 are identified as having disabilities and are provided special education services (OSEP, 2006). The federal government describes 13 disability-specific categories and one generic grouping that can be used to qualify infants, toddlers, preschoolers, and young students eligible to receive special education services. Within these categories are many conditions. For example, stuttering is included as a speech impairment, attention deficit hyperactivity disorder (ADHD) is included in the category of other health impairments, and Tourette syndrome is included in the emotional disturbances category. Also, in an attempt to avoid either incorrectly labeling young children as having a disability when they do not or identifying them with the "wrong" disability, the federal government provides the option of using a general category (non-disability-specific group) for children under the age of 8 (Müller & Markowitz, 2004; U.S. Department of Education, 2006).

People think about these special education categories, or disabilities requiring specialized educational responses, in different ways. First, the names for these categories differ slightly from state to state and are not necessarily the terms preferred by parent or professional groups. Second, some categories—such as deafness and hearing impairment—often are combined. And they are often ordered and divided by prevalence, or the size of the category: high incidence disabilities (disabilities that occur in greater numbers) and low incidence disabilities (disabilities that occur less often).

Table 1.1 shows an overview of the disabilities and the different ways they are referred to in school settings. The Individuals with Disabilities Education Act (IDEA) of 2004 requires states to use these disability areas to qualify children and youth for special education services. Note that the disability areas are listed by whether the federal government considers them high incidence or low incidence disabilities. Check carefully to see how your state views these determinations about prevalence. Some people make the mistake of thinking that prevalence or incidence relates to severity or significance of the disability. In other words, they assume that high incidence disabilities (those that occur more frequently in the population) are less severe than low incidence disabilities (those that occur less frequently in the population). Remember that all disabilities are serious and that mild to severe cases occur within each disability type.

TABLE 1.1 Special Education's Categories Considered by the Federal Government as Either High or Low Incidence Disabilities

Federal Term	Other Terms	Comments
High Incidence Disabilities		
Specific learning disabilities	Learning disabilities (LD)	Includes reading, language, writing, and mathematics disabilities.
Speech or language impairments	Speech disorders or language disorders; communication disorders	Speech impairments include problems with articulation, fluency problems, and voice problems.
Mental retardation	Cognitive disabilities; intellectual disabilities	Ranges from mild to severe, but often overlaps with low incidence disabilities.
Emotional disturbance	Emotional and behavioral disorders (EBD)	Includes schizophrenia. Does not include children who are socially maladjusted unless it is determined that they have an emotional disturbance.
Low Incidence Disabilities		
Multiple disabilities	Multiple-severe disabilities; developmental disabilities	Does not include all students with more than one disability, varies by states' criteria.
Deafness; hearing impairment	Hard of hearing and deaf	Includes full range of hearing losses; The term Deaf is used to signify those who consider themselves part of the Deaf community.
Orthopedic impairments	Physical impairments (PI); physical disabilities	Category often combined with health impairments because of many overlapping conditions.
Other health impairments	Health impairments; special health care needs	IDEA '04 includes attention deficit hyperactivity disorder (ADHD) in this category, causing overall prevalence to reflect high incidence.
Visual impairments	Visual disabilities; low vision and blind	Includes full range of vision loss.
Autism	Autism spectrum disorders (ASD)	ASD is more inclusive; autism is considered one of five ASD conditions. Actual national prevalence numbers place this group of learners in the low incidence category, although many consider it more frequent.
Deafblindness	Deafblind	This combination causes severe communication and other developmental and educational needs.
Traumatic brain injury (TBI)		TBI must be acquired after birth.
Developmental delay		Allows for noncategorical identification from the ages of 3 to the child's ninth birthday.

What Are the Origins of Special Education?

Although many people believe that U.S. special education began in 1975 with passage of the national law we now call IDEA, special education actually began over 200 years ago. The legend of special education's beginnings is not only famous, it's true! In 1799, farmers in southern France found a young boy in the woods, and they brought that "wild child" to a doctor in Paris. The child was named Victor. Jean-Marc-Gaspard Itard, the doctor who now is recognized as the "father of special education," used many of the principles and procedures of explicit instruction implemented today to teach this boy, who probably had mental retardation.

In the early 1800s, Edouard Seguin, one of Itard's students, came to the United States and began efforts in this country to educate students with disabilities. In fact, these early efforts were taking root across Europe as well. For example, in Italy, Maria Montessori worked first with children with cognitive disabilities and showed that children could learn at young ages through concrete experiences offered in environments rich in manipulative materials. Meanwhile, Thomas Hopkins Gallaudet began to develop deaf education, and Samuel Gridley Howe founded the New England Asylum for the Blind (later, the Perkins Institute). Elizabeth Farrell initiated public school classes for students with disabilities in 1898. Although special education and the idea of educating students with disabilities are not new, they were not uniformly accepted. In the United States, it was another 75 years before education became a right, something all students with disabilities were entitled to receive. You may be surprised to learn, in the next section, that the guarantees in place today were adopted rather recently.

Inconsistent Opportunities

Although positive attitudes about the benefits of educating students with disabilities emerged centuries ago, the delivery of programs remained inconsistent for almost 200 years. In 1948 only 12 percent of all children with disabilities received special education (Ballard, Ramirez, & Weintraub, 1982). As late as 1962, only 16 states had laws that included students with even mild mental retardation under mandatory school attendance requirements (Roos, 1970). In most states, even those children with the mildest levels of disabilities were not allowed to attend school. Children with more severe disabilities were routinely excluded.

In the early 1970s, Congress studied the problem, and here's what it found (20 U.S.C. section 1400 [b]):

- One million of the children with disabilities in the United States were excluded entirely from the public school system.
- More than half of the eight million children with disabilities in the United States were not receiving appropriate educational services.
- The special educational needs of these children were not being fully met because they were not receiving necessary related services.
- Services within the public school system were inadequate and forced families to find services outside the public school system, often at great distance from their residence and at their own expense.
- If given appropriate funding, state and local educational agencies could provide effective special education and related services to meet the needs of children with disabilities.

TABLE 1.2 Landmark Court Cases Leading to the Original Passage of IDEA

Case	Date	Issue	Finding
Brown v. Board of Education	1954	Overturn of "separate but equal doctrine"; integration of public schools	Basis for future rulings that children with disabilities cannot be excluded from school.
Pennsylvania Association for Retarded Children (PARC) v. Commonwealth of Pennsylvania	1972	Public education for students with mental retardation	In the state of Pennsylvania, no child with mental retardation can be denied a public education.
Mills v. Board of Education of the District of Columbia	1972	Special education for all students with disabilities	All students with disabilities have a right to a free public education.

Clearly, Congress, when first considering passage of a national special education law, recognized the importance of special education for children with disabilities. It was also concerned about widespread discrimination. It pointed out that many students with disabilities were excluded from education and that frequently those who did attend school failed to benefit because their disabilities went undetected or ignored. Congress realized that special education, with proper financial assistance and educational support, could make a positive difference in the lives of these children and their families.

Court Cases: A Backdrop for National Legislation

The end of World War II ushered in a time of increased opportunities for all Americans, eventually leading to the civil rights movement of the 1960s and to advocacy for people with disabilities during the 1970s. Before then, the courts had been dealing with issues of discrimination and people's civil rights. Concerns about unfair treatment of children with disabilities and their limited access to education were being brought to the courts and legislatures state by state. Table 1.2 summarizes early landmark court cases that prepared the way for national special education to be consistently offered to all children with disabilities. After years and years of exclusion, segregation, and denial of basic educational opportunities to students with disabilities and their families, consensus was growing that a national civil rights law guaranteeing these students access to the education system was imperative.

What Laws and Court Decisions Protect Students with Disabilities?

The nation's policymakers reacted to injustices revealed in court case after court case by passing laws to protect the civil rights of individuals with disabilities (Florian, 2007). However, until societal attitudes change, advocates must remain vigilant to protect individuals with disabilities from discrimination (Stroul & Friedman, 1986). Federal and state laws are one way to ensure people's rights. Some laws only address children's rights to an education, others focus on individuals' civil rights and access to American society, and still others apply to both schools and society. Table 1.3 lists some of the important laws passed by Congress that affect individuals with disabilities. As you study these laws, you should see how one law set the stage for the next.

TABLE 1.3 Landmark Laws (Legislation) Guaranteeing Rights to Individuals with Disabilities

Date	Number of Law or Section	Name (and Any Abbreviation)	Key Provisions
1973	Section 504	Section 504 of the Rehabilitation Act	• Set the stage for IDEA and ADA • Guaranteed basic civil rights to people with disabilities • Required accommodations in schools and in society
1975	PL 94-142	Education for All Handicapped Children Act (EHA)	• Guaranteed a free appropriate education in the least restrictive environment
1986	PL 99-457	EHA (reauthorized)	• Added infants and toddlers • Provided Individualized Family Service Plan (IFSP)
1990	PL 101-476	Individuals with Disabilities Education Act (IDEA)	• Changed name to IDEA • Added transition plans (ITPs) • Added autism as a special education category • Added traumatic brain injury as a category
1990	PL 101-336	Americans with Disabilities Act (ADA)	• Barred discrimination in employment, transportation, public accommodations, and telecommunications • Implemented the concept of normalization across American life • Required phased-in accessibility in schools
1997	PL 105-17	IDEA '97 (reauthorized)	• Added ADHD to the "other health impairments" category • Added functional behavioral assessments and behavioral intervention plans • Changed ITPs to a component of the Individualized Education Program (IEP)
2001	PL 107-110	Elementary and Secondary Education (No Child Left Behind) Act of 2001 (ESEA)	• Required that all schoolchildren participate in state and district testing • Called for the 100% proficiency of all students in reading and math by 2012
2004	PL 108-364	Assistive Technology Act of 2004 (ATA) (reauthorized)	• Provided support for school-to-work transition projects • Continued a national Web site on assistive technology (AT) • Assisted states in creating and supporting: device loan programs, financial loans to individuals with disabilities to purchase AT devices, equipment demonstrations
2004	PL 108-446	IDEA '04 (reauthorized)	• Required special education teachers to be highly qualified • Mandated that all students with disabilities participate annually in either state and district testing with accommodations or in alternative assessments • Eliminated IEP short-term objectives and benchmarks, except for those who use alternative assessments • Changed identification procedures for learning disabilities • Allowed any student to be placed in an interim alternative educational setting for involvement in weapons, drugs, or violence

Section 504

In 1973 Congress passed Section 504 of the Vocational Rehabilitation Act, which was intended to prevent discrimination against individuals with disabilities in programs that receive federal funds. Section 504 required public buildings to provide accommodations, such as wheelchair ramps, to allow or facilitate access by people with disabilities. Section 504 requires public schools to provide accommodations to students whose disabilities or health conditions require some special attention in order to allow them to participate fully in school activities. This law set the stage for both IDEA and the Americans with Disabilities Act, because it included some protection of the rights of students with disabilities to public education and many provisions for adults with disabilities and their participation in society and the workplace. Let's direct our attention now to the law that specifically targets schoolchildren and their families.

Americans with Disabilities Act (ADA)

Remember that Congress first considered civil rights issues related to people with disabilities when it passed Section 504 of the Rehabilitation Act of 1973. However, after almost 20 years of that act's implementation, Congress became convinced by advocates, many of whom were themselves adults with disabilities, that Section 504 was not sufficient and did not end discrimination for adults with disabilities. It took stronger measures by passing yet another law. On July 26, 1990, President H. W. Bush signed the Americans with Disabilities Act (ADA), which bars discrimination in employment, transportation, public accommodations, and telecommunications. He said, "Let the shameful walls of exclusion fi-

● Federal legislation broadly defines disabilities and impairments that significantly limit one or more major life activities, including walking, seeing, hearing, and learning.

nally come tumbling down." Senator Tom Harkin (D-IA), the chief sponsor of the act, spoke of this law as the "emancipation proclamation" for people with disabilities (West, 1994). ADA guarantees access to all aspects of life—not just those that are supported by federal funding—to people with disabilities and implements the concept of normalization across all aspects of American life. Both Section 504 and ADA are considered civil rights and antidiscrimination laws (de Bettencourt, 2002). ADA supports and extends Section 504 and assures adults with disabilities greater access to employment and participation in everyday activities that adults without disabilities enjoy. ADA requires employers not to discriminate against qualified applicants or employees with disabilities. It requires new public transportation (buses, trains, subways) and new or remodeled public accommodations (hotels, stores, restaurants, banks, theaters) to be accessible to persons with disabilities. ADA has had a substantial impact on the daily lives of people with disabilities, and these changes have become part of American life. For example, it requires telephone companies to provide relay services so that deaf individuals and people with speech impairments can use ordinary telephones. It is thanks to ADA that curb cuts make it easier for everyone to use carts, strollers, and even roller skates when crossing streets. For students who are making the transition from school to adult life, improvements in access and nondiscrimination should help them achieve genuine participation in their communities.

Section 504 and ADA also affect the education system, but there are some important differences between them and IDEA. Section 504 and ADA incorporate a broader definition of disabilities than does IDEA, because they guarantee the right to accommodations even to those who do not need special education services and to those beyond school age. For example, it is under the authority of ADA that college students with special needs are entitled to special testing situations (untimed tests, someone to read the questions to the test taker, braille versions) and that schoolchildren with attention deficit hyperactivity disorder (ADHD) who do not qualify for special education receive special accommodations.

Like IDEA, the ADA law has sparked controversy. On the one hand, some members of the disability community are disappointed because they still cannot find jobs suited to their interests, training, or skills. On the other hand, many small-business owners claim that ADA requires them to make accommodations to their businesses that are expensive and rarely used.

Individuals with Disabilities Education Act (IDEA)

As you just learned, when Congress investigated how students with disabilities and their families were welcomed into the education system, they found widespread patterns of exclusion, denial of services, and discrimination (Knitzer, 1982; Knitzer et al., 1990). Therefore, it decided that a universal, national law guaranteeing the rights of students with disabilities to a free appropriate public education was necessary. The first version of the special education law was passed in 1975 and was called Public Law (PL) 94-142, Education for All Handicapped Children Act (EHA). (The first set of numbers refers to the session of Congress in which the law was passed, the second set to the number of the law. Thus EHA was the 142nd law passed in the 94th session of Congress.) Congress gave the states 2 years to get ready to implement this new special education law, so it was actually initiated in 1977. That law was to be in effect for 10 years, and for it to continue, a reauthorization process was required. After the first 10-year period, the law was to be reauthorized every 3 years.

EHA was reauthorized the first time in 1986. (Congress gives itself a couple of extra years to reauthorize laws so that they do not expire before the congressional committee can complete the job of rewriting the law.) Congress added services to infants, toddlers, and their families in this version of the special education law. In its next reauthorization, Congress (retroactively) changed the name of the law to PL 101-476, the Individuals with Disabilities Education Act (IDEA). Besides changing the name, Congress added two conditions (autism and traumatic brain injury) as special education categories and strengthened transitional services for adolescents with disabilities. In the 1997 reauthorization of IDEA, issues such as access to the general education curriculum, participation in state- and district-wide testing, and discipline assumed prominence. When the law was passed again in 2004, many changes were made in how students with learning disabilities can be identified. This version of the law also encourages states and school districts to help all young students who are struggling to read, in hopes of preventing reading/learning disabilities and also getting help to those who need it as soon as possible (U.S. Department of Education, 2006).

Court Decisions Defining IDEA

It is the role of the courts to clarify laws passed by Congress and implemented by the administration (implementation of IDEA is the responsibility of the U.S. Department of Education). Although Congress thought it was clear in its intentions about the educational guarantees it believed were necessary for children with disabilities and their families, no legal language is perfect. Since 1975, when PL 94-142 (IDEA) became law, a very small percentage of all the children who have been served have been involved in formal disputes. Those disputes concern the identification of students with disabilities, evaluations, educational placements, and the provision of a free appropriate public education. Most disputes are resolved in noncourt proceedings or due process hearings. Some disputes, however, must be settled in courts of law—a few even in the U.S. Supreme Court. Through such litigation, many different questions about special education have been addressed and clarified. Table 1.4 highlights a few important U.S. Supreme Court decisions.

The issues and complaints the courts deal with are significant, and the ramifications of those decisions can be momentous. For example, a student named Garret F. was paralyzed as the result of a motorcycle accident at the age of 4. Thereafter, he required an electric ventilator (or someone manually pumping an air bag) to continue breathing and to stay alive. When Garret was in middle school, his mother requested that the school pick up the expenses of his physical care while he was in school. The district refused the request. Most school district administrators believed that providing "complex health services" to students was not a related service (and hence not the district's responsibility) but, rather, a medical service (excluded under the IDEA regulations). In other words, across the country, districts had interpreted the IDEA law and its regulations to mean that schools were not responsible for the cost of health services. The Supreme Court, however, disagreed and interpreted IDEA differently. The justices decided that if a doctor is not necessary to provide the health service, and the service is necessary to keep a student in an educational program, then it is the school's obligation to provide the "related service." The implications of this decision are enormous (Katsiyannis & Yell, 2000). Not only are the services of additional personnel expensive—potentially between $20,000 and $40,000 per school year—but to these

TABLE 1.4 Landmark U.S. Supreme Court Cases Defining IDEA

Case	Date	Issue	Finding/Importance
Rowley v. Hendrick Hudson School District	1982	FAPE	School districts must provide those services that permit a student with disabilities to benefit from instruction.
Irving Independent School District v. Tatro	1984	Defining related services	Clean intermittent catheterization (CIC) is a related service when necessary to allow a student to stay in school.
Smith v. Robinson	1984	Attorney's fees	Parents are reimbursed legal fees when they win a case resulting from special education litigation.
Burlington School Committee v. Department of Education	1985	Private school placement	In some cases, public schools may be required to pay for private school placements when the district does not provide an appropriate education.
Honig v. Doe	1988	Exclusion from school	Students whose misbehavior is related to their disability cannot be denied education.
Timothy W. v. Rochester New Hampshire School District	1989	FAPE	Regardless of the existence or severity of a student's disability, a public education is the right of every child.
Zobrest v. Catalina Foothills School District	1993	Paid interpreter at parochial high school	Paying for a sign language interpreter does not violate the constitutional separation of church and state.
Carter v. Florence County School District 4	1993	Reimbursement for private school	A court may order reimbursement to parents who withdraw their children from a public school that provides inappropriate education, even though the private placement does not meet all IDEA requirements.
Doe v. Withers	1993	FAPE	Teachers are responsible for the implementation of accommodations specified in individual students' IEPs.
Cedar Rapids School District v. Garret F.	1999	Related services	Health attendants are a related service and a district's expense if the service is necessary to maintain students in educational programs.

costs must be added increased liability for schools, additional considerations for individualized education program (IEP) teams, the administrative costs for increased staff, and the complications of yet another adult in a classroom.

Now let's turn our attention to a law that addresses the education of all students, those with and without disabilities.

No Child Left Behind Act (NCLB)

In the last reauthorization of the Elementary and Secondary Education Act, which is known as the No Child Left Behind Act of 2001 (NCLB), students with disabilities were included in many ways. This law requires that 95 percent of all schoolchildren be full participants in state and district testing. It also includes as a goal that *all* students demonstrate proficiency in reading and mathematics by 2012 (Ziegler, 2002). One major goal of NCLB is to raise academic achievement for all students while closing the achievement gap between poor, inner-city schools and schools in middle-class suburban areas (U.S. Senate, 2004 September 13). Here are a few of the main features of NCLB as they are related to students with disabilities (Browder & Cooper-Duffy, 2003; National Center for Learning Disabilities, 2004):

- Use of scientifically based programs and interventions
- Access to the general education curriculum
- Insistence on highly qualified teachers
- Evaluation of students' performance with appropriate accommodations

Assistive Technology Act of 2004 (ATA)

On October 25, 2004, President George W. Bush signed PL 108-364, the Assistive Technology Act of 2004 (ATA) or Tech Act, into law. This law is of growing importance to people with disabilities, because they are confident that increased accessibility in the future rests, in part, with technology. Like Section 504, the Tech Act applies to both the education system and community access. Assistive technology (AT) is critical to the participation of people with disabilities in the workplace, in the community, and at school; it removes barriers that restrict people's lives. For example, AT allows for people with hearing problems to go to their neighborhood theaters and hear the movie's dialog through assistive listening devices or read it via captions. It allows people with physical disabilities to join friends at a local coffee house by using a variety of mobility options. AT is also spelled out in the law that guides the development of special education for each student with a disability. AT provides text-to-audio translations to those who cannot access printed passages because they cannot see and provides immediate audio-to-text translations to those who cannot hear lectures (Hitchcock & Stahl, 2003). The potential of AT is limited only by our creativity and innovation. However, AT is expensive and far beyond many people's budgets, particularly those who are under- or unemployed. For both students and adults, the Tech Act offers (through the states' loan programs) training activities, demonstrations of new devices, and other direct services. This law allows students to test equipment and other AT devices both at school and at home before actually purchasing them.

Access to information technology is important and unfettering to all of us, and restricted access to it results in barriers with considerable consequences. Here's how the National Council on Disability (NCD) advised the president of the United States about this issue:

> For America's 54 million people with disabilities, however, access to such information and technology developments is a double-edged sword that can release opportunities or sever essential connections. On the one hand, such developments can be revolutionary in their ability to empower people with seeing, hearing, manual, or cognitive impairments through alternative means of input to and interaction with the World Wide Web, information transaction machines, and kiosks. On the other hand, electronic information and technological developments can present serious and sometimes insurmountable obstacles

when, for example, basic principles of accessibility or universal design are not practiced in their deployment. (NCD, 2001 p. 1)

Influential court cases, landmark legislation, and laws related to education and to the greater society have paved the way for special education services as we know them today. We now turn our attention to a discussion about what makes special education "special."

What Is Special Education?

Special education is provided to infants, preschoolers, elementary through high school students with disabilities, and (in some cases) individuals with disabilities up through the age of 21. Special education is specially designed to meet the unique learning needs of each infant, toddler, preschooler, and student with disabilities. This instruction might be delivered in many different types of settings, such as hospitals, separate facilities, and homes, but it is most commonly provided at the student's local school in the general education class with neighborhood friends. Special education reflects a variety of instructional targets: braille for students who are blind, manual communication systems for students who are deaf, social skills training for students with emotional or behavioral disorders, and so on. General education and special education are two educational approaches that are *not* the same. They differ along some very important dimensions. First and foremost, special education and general education are designed for students with different learning, behavioral, social, communication, and basic functional needs (such as daily living skills). Second, some differences are based in law—what is stated in IDEA and its regulations—and result in key components of special education. Third, general education tends to focus on groups of learners, whereas the special education approach focuses on individuals.

One way to gain a better understanding of special education is to study some of its key distinguishing features. Although no single description of special education can be put forth because these services must be designed for each individual to meet his or her unique learning needs, fundamental tenets provide the foundation for the educational services delivered to students with disabilities:

- Free appropriate public education
- Least restrictive environment
- Systematic identification procedures
- Individualized education programs
- Family involvement
- Related services
- Access to the general education curriculum
- Evidence-based practices
- Frequent monitoring of progress

Let's examine each of these features that form the foundation of special education.

Free Appropriate Public Education (FAPE)

Remember that when Congress first passed the IDEA law in 1975, it was concerned that many students with disabilities were being denied a public education or were not receiving all the services they needed to profit from the instruction offered to them. (Review the section on congressional findings earlier in this chapter.) Thus, from the very beginning of IDEA, Congress stipulated that educational services for students with disabilities are to be available to parents at no additional cost to them. These students, despite the complexity of their educational needs, the accommodations or additional services they require, and the cost to a school district, are entitled to a free appropriate public education (FAPE). Note that Congress included the word *appropriate* in its language about the public education to which these students have a right. FAPE must be individually determined, because what is appropriate for one student with a disability might not be appropriate for another.

Least Restrictive Environment (LRE)

The second key feature of special education is that students with disabilities must receive their education in the least restrictive environment (LRE). In other words, special education services are not automatically delivered in any particular place. LRE, and its balance with FAPE, can be confusing. Today, LRE is often misinterpreted as being equal to placement in general education classes. IDEA does *not* mandate that students with disabilities receive all of their education in the general education setting. The U.S. Department of Education, in its 2006 regulations implementing IDEA '04 (the most recent law), explains LRE in this way:

> . . . to the maximum extent appropriate, children with disabilities, including children in public or private institutions or other care facilities, are educated with children who are nondisabled; and that special classes, separate schooling or other removal of children with disabilities from regular educational environment occurs only if the nature or severity of the disability is such that education in regular classes with the use of supplementary aids and services cannot be achieved satisfactorily. (U.S. Department of Education, 2006, pp. 46764–46765)

The federal government goes on, in its explanation of LRE, to discuss an array of placements, in addition to the general education classroom, that are appropriate for some students with disabilities. It does so by describing a continuum of alternative placements that include resource rooms, special classes, special schools, home instruction, and instruction in hospital settings. For some students, exclusive exposure to the general education curriculum is not appropriate. For example, a secondary student with significant cognitive disabilities might need to master functional or life skills essential for independent living as an adult. That student might also need to receive concentrated instruction on skills associated with holding a job successfully. To acquire and become proficient in skills necessary to live in the community and to be employed often requires instruction outside of the general education curriculum, outside of the general education classroom, and beyond the actual school site. This kind of instruction is often best conducted in the community, on actual job sites, and in real situations. In fact, community-based instruction is a well-researched, effective special education approach (Dymond & Orelove, 2001). Thus there is no single or uniform interpretation of LRE. A balance must be achieved between inclusive instruction and a curriculum that is appropriate and is delivered in the most effective setting.

Systematic Identification Procedures

To decide which students qualify for special education—those who actually have disabilities—and what that education should comprise requires systematic identification procedures. Educators must be careful not to identify students without disabilities. Because current methods tend to overidentify culturally and linguistically diverse students as having disabilities and to underidentify them as being gifted and talented, many professionals conclude that the special education identification process is flawed and needs a major overhaul (MacMillan & Siperstein, 2002). New procedures are being developed to identify students with disabilities and to qualify them for special education. We discuss these procedures in greater detail later in the text, but it is important to know that the role of general education teachers in the identification process is evolving and increasing. Teachers have primary responsibility for what is being called the pre-referral process. During this phase, general education teachers are responsible for gathering the documentation necessary to begin the special education referral process (Fuchs & Fuchs, 2001).

The first task is to ensure that difficulties are not being caused by a lack of appropriate academic instruction. The next task is to collect data about the target student's performance, showing that high-quality classroom procedures do not bring about improvements in academic or social behavior for this particular student. Then, for those students who do not make expected gains, further classroom evaluations are conducted (Gresham, 2002). The ensuing classroom assessments include comparisons with classmates who are achieving as expected; careful monitoring of the target student's progress (i.e., progress monitoring through curriculum based measurements); and descriptions of interventions tried, accommodations implemented, types of errors made, and levels of performance achieved (Fuchs, Fuchs, & Compton, 2004; Fuchs, Fuchs, & Powell, 2004; Gregg & Mather, 2002). Students who continue not to profit from instruction in their general education class are referred for formal evaluation and probable provision of special education services.

Individualized Education Programs

We devote an entire chapter to the individualized education programs required by IDEA for all students with a disability who are receiving special education services (see Chapter 5). For now, it is important to know that at the heart of individualized programs are individualized education programs (IEPs) for schoolchildren ages 3 to 21 and individualized family service plans (IFSPs) for infants and toddlers (birth through age 2) with disabilities and their families. In some states, the guarantee of an individualized education is extended to gifted students as well, but because gifted students' special education is not protected by federal law, this is not a requirement. IEPs and IFSPs are the cornerstone that guarantees an appropriate education to each student with a disability. Each of these students is entitled to an individually designed educational program complete with supportive (related) services. The IEP is the communication tool that spells out what each child's individualized education should comprise. Therefore, every teacher working with a special education student should have access to the student's IEP. They should all be very familiar with its contents because this document includes important information about the required accommodations, the special services necessary, and the unique educational needs of the student.

Family Involvement

Expectations for parent and family involvement are greater for students with disabilities than for their peers without disabilities. The importance of family involvement cannot be underestimated, because the strength of families and their involvement in the school can make a real difference in the lives of their children (Garcia, 2001). The roles that parents of students with disabilities play are important. For example, they are expected to participate in the development of their children's IEPs. One idea behind the IEP is for parents to become partners with teachers and schools, so some parents and families expect considerable opportunities for decision making and participation in their child's education. They have the right to due process when they do not agree with schools about the education planned for or being delivered to their children. Also, they are entitled to services not usually offered to parents of typical learners. For example, for infants and toddlers with disabilities (ages birth to 2), parents along with their children receive intensive instruction through special education.

● Parents and family members of students with disabilities have important roles to play. Linking home and school communities is the responsibility of both families and teaching professionals.

Recognizing the challenges that parents often face in raising their children with special needs and in addressing their educational issues at school, advocacy groups and professional organizations have formed over the years to support families and those who work with families. For example, in the area of learning disabilities, the Learning Disabilities Association of America has a long history of advocacy on behalf of individuals with LD and the professionals and families who work with them. The ARC, formerly known as the Association for Retarded Citizens of the United States, is another example of an advocacy group. Its focus includes ensuring that all students are provided appropriate public education services. CHADD (Children and Adults with Attention Deficit/ Hyperactivity Disorder) is another organization made up of hard-working volunteers who provide support and resources to parents and professionals. The Federation of Families for Children's Mental Health is yet another important organization. FFCMH's mission is to provide national-level advocacy for the rights of children with emotional, behavioral, and mental health challenges and their families. It works collaboratively with a national network of family-run organizations on behalf of children and families.

Leaders in these organizations, who often are parents, have greatly influenced successful funding at the state and national levels for appropriate educational services for students with disabilities. Parent advocacy groups are very powerful, as shown by their contribution to successful outcomes in key court cases that have resulted in legislation that now protects students with disabilities in all aspects of the educational system. Thus, family involvement has spurred important safeguards in schools for students with disabilities and their families. Together, families and educators can make an important difference in the lives of students with special needs.

Related Services

Another important difference between special education and general education is the array of services offered to students and their families. These additional services help students with disabilities profit from instruction. In some cases a paraprofessional (sometimes called a paraeducator) supports the special education program and works with a special education student in the general education classroom (Allen & Ashbaker, 2004). In many cases, these professionals' services make inclusion possible because they provide individualized assistance to students with disabilities for extended periods of the school day (Trautman, 2004). Related services are the multidisciplinary or transdisciplinary services that many students with disabilities require if their education is to be truly appropriate. Related services include adaptive PE, assistive technology, audiology, diagnosis and evaluation, interpreters for the deaf, family therapy, occupational therapy (OT), orientation and mobility, paraprofessionals (paraeducators, teacher aides), physical therapy (PT), psychology, recreation and therapeutic-recreation therapy, rehabilitative counseling, school counseling, school nursing, school social work, speech/language pathology, special transportation, vocational education, and work study (U.S. Department of Education, 2006). Related services professionals come together to create flexible teams that go into action to meet the individual needs of students with disabilities. The federal government considers professionals who provide these related services—such as school nurses who perform school health services for students with disabilities and school counselors who provide counseling or guidance to children with disabilities and their families (e.g., parent training or support)—members of the special education team whose costs are in part covered by funding from IDEA '04 (U.S. Department of Education, 2006).

We will discuss related services further in Chapter 5. What is important now is to note that special education is a comprehensive *set of services* designed to support the education of students with disabilities. Related services are typically beyond what general and special education teachers can provide. These services are specified in the student's IEP, so special education consists of many different professions and specialty areas. When some or all of these related services are put into action, the result is multidisciplinary teams of professionals working together to meet the educational needs of each student with a disability. The Working Together feature offers an illustration of the importance of multidisciplinary teams collaborating to address the challenging behaviors of a first-grade student. The clinical psychologist's perspective is presented to illustrate how the idea of collaboration can be approached. Several tips are included to emphasize the importance of sharing information, the different expertise each team member brings to the student's education, effective communication skills, and joint decision making. You will learn more about collaboration and how to work with students who exhibit special needs in Chapter 8.

WORKING together

The Child Study Team

The school's child study team was concerned about the behavior of a 6-year-old, first-grade boy. The team's documentation showed that the boy exhibited erratic, unpredictable behavior, which included throwing chairs in the classroom and having temper tantrums when things did not go his way. The classroom teacher was concerned about how to stop these behaviors, how to teach the student appropriate ways to behave, and how to keep all of her students safe. The team decided to consult a specialist who could advise them on ways to proceed with the student. Although he or she was not a regular member of their child study team, they felt that a specialist's perspective would be helpful. They turned to a psychologist who was part of a practice at the local university's hospital.

Dr. Pedrotty works as a senior clinical psychologist at the University of New Mexico's Carrie Tingley Hospital in Albuquerque, New Mexico. His practice includes providing inpatient and outpatient consultation, psychotherapy, and assessments for his clients and their families. Dr. Pedrotty also consults with child study and behavior intervention teams in the public schools regarding students who demonstrate challenging behaviors that require comprehensive intervention by a multidisciplinary team of professionals.

As Dr. Pedrotty prepared to work with the child study team, he knew that a variety of information was needed to assess the situation from everyone's perspective, including that of the student, parents, teacher, school administration, district's behavioral specialist, school counselor, and school psychologist. Dr. Pedrotty understood the importance of collaborating with the members of the child study team and of including the classroom teacher and parents to ensure that an appropriate plan for addressing the student's needs could be devised and implemented. As part of his preparation, he begins to identify sources of information to assist the team:

- Information about the behaviors should be gathered from the child study team, district behavioral specialist, classroom teacher, and parents. Specific challenging behaviors that can be observed should be recorded, and any events that lead up to or follow the challenging behaviors should be documented. People with whom the student was in contact before, during, and after the challenging behavior should be noted in terms of their interactions.
- Interviews with the professional staff and parents should be conducted to listen to perspectives about the student and the challenging behavior.
- Classroom observations can provide a rich source of information as the student is observed in a natural setting with typical expectations and interactions.
- Psychological assessment can provide additional information to help team members better understand the emotional and social well-being of the student.

The following tips can help make the collaborative process successful.

- All individuals involved in this process are important contributors of information that can be analyzed to help establish an appropriate plan of action for the student. Sharing of information among the child study team (including the classroom teacher, parents, and the district's behavioral specialist) promotes the idea that multiple data sources are valued.
- Reciprocal respect for all individuals in this process reflects the fact that the identity of the "expert" may shift depending on the topic under discussion, such as classroom actions, psychological indicators, or home behavior. For example, only parents can offer a very detailed account of how the child behaves at home.
- Communication skills (including listening, paraphrasing, notetaking, and acknowledging perspectives) are critical to establish a sense of trust and to ensure that people's positions are conveyed and understood accurately.
- Shared decision making helps to establish a plan that is acceptable for most if not all of the individuals who will implement and evaluate the plan to eliminate the inappropriate behavior and replace it with more acceptable behavior.

Most related services specialists are itinerant, working at several schools during the same day and at many different schools across the week. Scheduling these professionals' time can be complicated, but it is important to ensure that no educational opportunity is missed. Educators should remember that related services are part of IDEA's guarantee of an appropriate education. These multidisciplinary teams of experts not only deliver critical services to students with disabilities and their families but are also valuable resources to teachers as they strive to meet the needs of each student. Regardless of the remoteness of a school, the distance a specialist might have to travel, or the shortage of related services specialists, there is no excuse for not making these experts available to teachers or their students with disabilities.

Access to the General Education Curriculum

Another key feature of special education is access to the general education curriculum. In response to some appalling data—only 54 percent of students with disabilities leave school with a standard diploma—parents, policymakers, and advocates insist that these students should participate in the general education curriculum and be part of the accountability measures (e.g., state- and district-wide tests) that monitor all students' progress (OSEP, 2006a). These advocates contend that students who receive their education in inclusive general education classrooms are more likely to have greater exposure to the standard curriculum and a better chance of graduating with a standard high school diploma than those students who receive their education in more restrictive environments, such as self-contained special education classrooms. Therefore, when IDEA was reauthorized in 1997, it required that all students with disabilities have, to the fullest extent possible, access to the general education curriculum and its accountability systems. The 2001 NCLB law strengthened such requirements and expectations by including most students with disabilities in state- and district-wide testing. IEPs must address students' access and participation in the general education curriculum and justify limitations (Wehmeyer et al., 2003). IDEA '04 requires that when a student is removed from the typical general education curriculum, the IEP must specifically explain why the student cannot participate at this particular point in time (U.S. Department of Education, 2006). One interpretation of this requirement is that LRE is being defined as access to a curriculum, rather than access to a place or service. Of course, these concepts often go hand in hand, because the general education classroom is the place where students have the greatest opportunity to access the standard curriculum. It is important to remember, however, that the general education curriculum is not appropriate for all students with disabilities. Some require an alternative curriculum, intensive treatment, or supplemental instruction on topics not available or suitable for instruction in the general education classroom. Here are a few examples of such individualized programs that might require removal from the general education setting and reduced access to its curriculum: orientation and mobility training for students who are blind, learning job skills in community placements, learning how to use public transportation, social skills training, physical therapy, speech therapy for a student who stutters, phonics instruction for a third grader, and so on. Remember that placement issues, LRE, access to the general education curriculum, and alternative curricular options are not mutually exclusive. Each can be in effect for part of the school day, school week, or schoolyear.

Evidence-Based Practices

With passage of NCLB in 2001 and IDEA in 2004, emphasis has been placed on teachers applying evidence-based practices (sometimes referred to as scientifically based practices). These interventions or teaching tactics have been proved effective through systematic and rigorous research. The importance of implementing evidence-based practices cannot be overstated. In fact, according to IDEA '04, there must be documentation that evidence-based practices were implemented with students who are believed to have a learning disability before a referral can be initiated. Furthermore, there must be documentation, through systematic assessment of the student's responses to the evidence-based practices, as part of the learning disabilities identification process. This new process promoted and endorsed in IDEA '04 is known as response to intervention (RTI). More information about RTI appears in the Working Together feature in Chapter 7.

Special education can be defined, in part, by its practices. In some ways, these practices distinguish special education from general education. When a student with disabilities needs intensive intervention on a particular topic or skill, an evidence-based practice should be implemented. Although any teacher (general educator, special educator, or paraprofessional) can successfully implement such interventions, many of these methods differ in various ways (such as focusing on the individual instead of on the group and targeting mastery of skills rather than in-depth understanding) from the methods generally used with typical learners. Special education methods are more intensive and supportive than those used for students without learning problems. What you will notice is that many of these proven interventions share six common features (Deshler, 2003; Torgeson, 1996). That is, effective special education can be thought of as

1. Validated (using practices proved effective through research)
2. Individually determined (matching teaching procedures to individuals)
3. Explicit (directly applying interventions to content and skills)
4. Strategic (helping students apply methods to guide their learning)
5. Sequential (building upon previous mastery)
6. Monitored (evaluating progress frequently and systematically)

It is important to remember that most students with disabilities and most of those with special needs do not require this intensive instruction for all of their education. But when their learning is not on a par with that of their general education classmates, it is time for action. In the Making a Difference feature, both the teacher and the general education students became involved in a successful intervention.

Frequent Monitoring of Progress

Even when teachers carefully select validated practices, there is no guarantee that the individual student will respond positively or sufficiently. For this reason, teachers use progress monitoring—a set of evaluation procedures that assess the effectiveness of instruction on skills while they are being taught. The four key features of this approach are that students' educational progress is measured (1) directly on skills of concern, (2) systematically, (3) consistently, and (4) frequently.

The most effective means of implementing progress monitoring is called curriculum based measurement (CBM). In this approach, the areas of most concern are measured directly to check progress on the curricular tasks, skills, or behaviors to which interventions are being directed (Fuchs, Fuchs, & Powell, 2004).

Making a Difference

Shared Commitment, Flexibility, and Enthusiasm Are Keys to Successful Inclusion

Michelle Freas
Special Education Teacher,
Grades K–5
Golden Gate Elementary
Naples, Florida

I teach students who are deaf and hard of hearing. I work in a public elementary school and have a multigrade, self-contained classroom. We use American Sign Language (ASL) as the primary language of instruction. Throughout the school day, many different school professionals come and go into and out of my classroom—ASL interpreters, the speech/language pathologist, the behavior specialist, and general education teachers—all of whom assist different students at various times. A few of my students are also included in general education classrooms for certain subjects, as determined by their individualized education programs (IEPs).

James, a first-grade student who is Deaf, was included every day for math, science, and calendar or circle time in the general education classroom of Ms. Jackson. At her request, I worked with Ms. Jackson to build her ASL skills, and, though not fully fluent in ASL, she nonetheless became proficient in conversational signing and made particular efforts to sign to our Deaf students at every opportunity. Consequently, she had a very nice rapport with our students. Although Ms. Jackson signed frequently to James during lessons and class discussions, because he had his own ASL interpreter with him during his time in her inclusive classroom, James was always quiet in class and would not use sign language to respond or participate in class discussions. Despite what one would have thought was an ideal "inclusive" situation, he did not seem to be enjoying or benefiting from the experience. So, at Ms. Jackson's suggestion and invitation, I began giving her entire class lessons in sign language three times each week. As time went on, the hearing students' sign vocabulary grew. But even with this increase of signing in the classroom by the hearing students, James still was quiet and off-task much of the time.

One day, James was sitting at his table in Ms. Jackson's classroom during math time. While his ASL interpreter was assisting him, another student who had learned a great deal of sign language (and was eager to use it!) came over to help. She explained the math concept in sign to James, and then she and James signed about math for a little while. With her explanation and assistance, James understood! This outreach from his classmate seemed to help him feel more at ease and open to socialization with his hearing peers. Afterward, James became comfortable answering questions using sign language and participating in class discussions.

In addition to the ways in which it had benefited James, Ms. Jackson told me how much her hearing students had enjoyed learning sign language. As a result, we decided to have my entire class go into her classroom every day for science and social studies and collaborate on various projects and activities. Together we adjusted our lunch times, recess periods, and special classes (music and physical education) to allow this student collaboration to take place. The hearing students became so proficient in their signing skills that they started to interpret for the Deaf students at lunchtime and recess! Our students were also invited to perform a special song for a televised awards event! The learning benefits to the hearing and Deaf students were apparent in their enthusiasm and academic progress; the students who were deaf improved their socialization skills with their hearing peers; and all were generally more accepting of each other. Through the creativity and flexibility of a talented and committed classroom teacher, the professional collaboration of a general and a special educator who shared the same goals for their students, and the energy, enthusiasm, and desire to learn of these young students, we were all able to break down the communication barrier between the hearing and Deaf worlds. ●

Thus, if reading comprehension is being targeted for improvement, then it is this skill that is assessed. Instruction and assessment are linked (Deno, 2003; Fuchs & Fuchs, 2001). These assessments also occur often (perhaps weekly) and provide educators with useful feedback on the basis of which they can quickly modify their instructional approaches (McMasters et al., 2000). Because this approach tailors the special education a student receives (e.g., guiding the selection of practices and monitoring their effectiveness), it is an important element that must not be omitted. You will learn more about monitoring student progress when specific curriculum targets (such as reading) are discussed in Chapter 7.

What Is Inclusive Education?

The answer to this question is not straightforward. Across parents, professionals, policymakers, and the general public, the term *inclusion* has many different meanings. To African American students and their families living in the 1950s and 1960s before *Brown* v. *Board of Education in Topeka, Kansas,* inclusion meant being able to attend an integrated school and not to be separated from other students because of race or skin color. To many families with a child with disabilities living before 1975 and the passage of IDEA, inclusion meant being able to attend a public school, whether that school be a separate school exclusively for students with disabilities or a neighborhood school. In the 1980s, inclusion meant that some students with cognitive disabilities were able to attend school in a separate classroom at their neighborhood school instead of a special center. To adults with disabilities living before 1990 and the passage of ADA, inclusion meant being able to go to a concert or a football game or to have drinks with friends at a local tavern. Or inclusion might have meant living in the community instead of in an institution. And for students who attended school before the ADA law was passed, it might have meant not being able to use the restrooms at school, open the outside door, or even get to the classroom for a required class held on the second floor. Today, however, the term inclusive education usually means that students with disabilities access the standard curriculum in the general education classroom.

Miscommunication can easily occur when the term *inclusion* is used: Whereas one person might use the word to mean that a student attends a neighborhood school and receives most instruction in the general education classroom, to another person it might mean that all of the student's instruction is delivered in the general education classroom. Assumptions that everyone is truly communicating about where a student should be educated are easy to make but often are incorrect. It is wise to be sure everyone is using the same definition before having an in-depth discussion of students' education. To understand the concept of inclusive education better, let's review how it emerged and developed.

Origins of Inclusion

The basic concepts of inclusion and integration of students with disabilities into the public education system have their roots in the original IDEA law passed in 1975. Remember that before 1975, many children with disabilities were denied access to a public education. Thus, to those who were instrumental in developing the original IDEA law, inclusion probably meant that children with disabilities had the right to go to public school and receive a free education.

Neither the type of school nor where the education was delivered was the focus of their advocacy efforts. When education became mandatory for all students with disabilities, the nation saw a rise in the number of separate schools built specifically for students with disabilities. Real growth in the number of special classes—sometimes on the grounds of neighborhood schools, but often in basements and portable buildings—also occurred for this newly included group of students. The first model for inclusive education reflected the idea that students with disabilities should be included in the public education system and mainstreamed, or educated together with peers without disabilities, when possible, (such as in art, music, and physical education).

Was the creation of segregated programs for these students contrary to the concept of inclusion? Most likely, at that time, the answer to this question would have been a resounding "no." Special schools and special classes offered highly specialized programs to students with disabilities and their families. Some special schools offered facilities and services that are feasible to deliver only when students with similar needs are congregated. For example, when all students with severe physical disabilities in one school district attend the same school, the building can include a special therapy pool and the full-time services of many related services professionals (e.g., physical therapists, occupational therapists, and speech/language pathologists). When these students attended their neighborhood schools, they were spread across many different schools and large geographic areas, making the intensity of services available when students are clustered together impossible. Many families believed that the potentially negative aspects of segregation resulting from separate programs were outweighed by the highly specialized services delivered when individuals with similar needs were grouped together. To these families, inclusion meant being provided FAPE and LRE (i.e., where special education is delivered, the placement of students with disabilities was of secondary importance).

As time passed, dissatisfaction with segregated programs, which developed despite the wealth of services available at some special schools and classes, grew. Parents began to question whether separating youngsters from their brothers and sisters and neighborhood friends was the best strategy for the education of students with disabilities. Professionals and policymakers were concerned about the efficacy of special education programs and practices (Finn, Rotherham, & Hokanson, 2001; Gartner & Lipsky, 1987). Policymakers came to believe that separate programs were ethically and morally wrong (Sailor, 1991; Snell & Brown, 2006). In particular, advocates for students with severe disabilities maintained that the benefits of having "typical" role models (illustrating how children without disabilities behave and interact with each other) outweighs intensive services that might be more readily available when groups of youngsters needing a particular program were clustered together (American Association on Mental Retardation [AAMR], 2002; Turnbull, Turnbull, & Wehmeyer, 2007). Across the years, thinking about special education and the students it serves evolved. To many, LRE—that is, access to the general education curriculum—has emerged as the more critical variable to be considered when decisions about special education placement are made.

Of course, participation in the general education curriculum does not automatically result just because students with disabilities are placed in typical classroom settings (Zigmond, 2003). Something special needs to happen. One approach, universal design for learning (UDL), focuses on the curriculum so a broad range of students with very different learning preferences can approach it and learn without an intervention being made especially for them. The second approach focuses on helping students, via assistive technology, to compensate for challenges they bring to the instructional situation. The third and most commonly used approach focuses not on the curriculum but on making adaptations to the instructional situation that match specific students' needs (Fisher, Frey, & Thousand, 2003). In Chapter 6, you will learn about universal design for learning and assistive technology. You will also learn about specific adaptations to help students access the general education curriculum so that they can learn alongside their peers without disabilities.

Inclusive Education Practices

As you have read, inclusive education has many different interpretations. The range of interpretations is the foundation for different inclusive education practices. For example, one interpretation of inclusive education is called full inclusion using pull-in programming, where students receive *all* educational services in the general education classroom. With this practice, speech/language pathologists come to the general education class to work with a student who needs speech therapy, rather than removing the student for individualized work. Another interpretation is called co-teaching, wherein special education teachers come to general education classrooms to work with students needing intervention or share instructional duties across academic content for all students in the class (Friend, 2000; Villa, Thousand, & Nevin, 2004). You will learn more about co-teaching in Chapter 8.

The array of services, or what is often called the special education continuum of services (an older term is *cascade of services*), offers additional practices for serving students with disabilities when they are not receiving some or all of their education in the general education classroom. Pull-out programs include resource rooms, partially self-contained special classes, self-contained special classes, and special education schools (i.e., center schools). For the vast majority of students who receive most of their education in general education classes, the resource room is their option for pull-out special education services. Resource room instruction often consists of small-group instruction focused on areas most in need of intensive intervention. This instruction may occur for 30 to 60 minutes several days a week. However, it is important to know that the number of these classes is shrinking, leaving a reduced number of options available for even short-term, intensive intervention (Moody, Vaughn, Hughes, & Fischer, 2000). For example, in the 2005 school year, 79 percent of all students with disabilities—those with mild to moderate disabilities as well as those with severe disabilities—received at least 60 percent of their education at local public schools in general education classes (OSEP, 2006). The participation rates for students with disabilities in general education classes have increased consistently over the past 15 years, and 4 percent of those students with disabilities attend separate schools or facilities today, down from 20 percent in 1993 (U.S. Department of Education, 1995). Clearly, these data demonstrate a trend toward more "inclusive" education practices.

The Inclusion Debate

At the heart of discussions about inclusive education, particularly full inclusion, is the dynamic tension between FAPE and LRE: the delivery of an appropriate education and participation in the least restrictive environment possible. Let's think about how some of these conversations might unfold. For example, should full-time placement in a general education setting be a goal for every student with a disability, even if some elements of an educational program that an individual needs to achieve to his or her full potential have to be sacrificed? For a high school student with severe disabilities, these parents and educators might have to decide which is more appropriate or more important: access to the standard high school curriculum leading to a diploma (including science and foreign language requirements) or community based instruction where on-the-job training, independent transportation, and home management are taught in real-life settings.

Some scholars argue that full inclusion, where students with disabilities receive all of their education in a general education setting, is not sufficient to support students with more severe needs, whether these needs are academic, emotional, social, or physical. These scholars are concerned that the needs of these students will not be addressed adequately to provide an appropriate education. Other scholars believe that *all* students have a right to fully inclusive educational practices where they can benefit from being integrated into a school setting with their peers. The sense of belonging and active participation in the mainstream are viewed as important dimensions of inclusion. Thus, the role of special education services is to support all students with special needs in general education classes by designing instruction and applying adaptations that accommodate individual learning needs. The "inclusion debate" more often includes perspectives and discussions that range along a continuum where professionals and parents embrace the strengths of different inclusive practices and make decisions based on individual student needs.

Some guidelines can help when challenging decisions are being made. First, special education placement decisions must be individually determined, because services should be tailored to the needs of each student with disabilities. Second, no single answer for all students with disabilities is possible. Third, students with disabilities need an array of services (and placements) available to them for the delivery of individualized education programs that range in intensity and duration (Deshler, 2001; Vaughn, Elbaum, & Boardman, 2001). It is important to recognize that few professionals or parents advocate either for fully inclusive settings or for fully segregated settings. The guiding principle must be based not on placement alone, but on how students can best access the general education curriculum, master academic targets, and develop life skills needed to succeed when they are adults.

● A dilemma for parents and educators of high school students with severe disabilities is which is more appropriate or more important: access to the standard high school curriculum leading to a diploma, or community based instruction where on-the-job training, independent transportation, and home management are taught in real-life settings.

summary

You have now embarked on what we believe is an exciting course of study. You have begun to learn about the challenges that exceptionalities and special needs present to the individuals involved and to their families, teachers, and friends. You have already learned that many of these challenges can be overcome when the educational system is responsive to the individual needs of these students. You also know that responses to such challenges must be rich with evidence-based practices that are supported by teams of professionals working together in collaborative partnerships. For students with disabilities, the education system should be inclusive but also flexible enough to strike an intelligent balance between FAPE and LRE—types of education, services, and placement—for each individual. As you are coming to learn, many provisions, requirements, and legal mandates guide your role as an inclusive educator. Sometimes, these principles can seem overwhelming and confusing, but when all of the hard work pays off, and students soar, the accomplishments are everyone's to share. Across this term, the puzzle of inclusive education will come together as you reach an understanding about how to teach and accommodate every academic and social area where students with disabilities and special needs require intervention.

self-test QUESTIONS

Let's review the learning objectives for this chapter. If you are uncertain and cannot "talk through" the answers provided for any of these questions, reread those sections of the text.

- **What is disability?**

  The concept of disability is not as simple as it appears. The way groups think about what it means to have a disability affects how they interact with people with disabilities. The concept of disability is complex, is not absolute, and is influenced by individuals' and groups' orientations (psychological, medical, sociological).

- **What are the four perspectives on "disability," and how do they differ from each other?**

  Four different perspectives result in different ways of thinking about disabilities. The *deficit perspective* reflects the idea that human behavior and characteristics shared by people are distributed along a continuum. The *cultural perspective* emphasizes that education professionals and the families with whom they work might not share the same understanding of disability. They might not have a common belief about what causes disabilities. In the *sociological perspective,* how a society treats individuals, not a condition or set of traits that are part of the individual's characteristics, is assumed to make people different from each other. Finally, the perspective that focuses on individuals with disabilities as a minority group sees them receiving negative treatment because of discrimination, much like discrimination on the basis of race, ethnicity, and gender. Perceptions about disability also vary across belief systems and cultures, generating different responses to disabilities.

- **How are individuals with disabilities protected by legislation?**

  Section 504 requires public schools to provide accommodations to students whose disabilities or health conditions necessitate some special attention in order to allow them to participate fully in school activities. ADA bars discrimination in employment, transportation, public accommodations, and telecommunications. Public Law (PL) 94-142, the Education for All Handicapped Children Act (EHA), was the first version of a universal, national special education law passed in 1975 that guaranteed the rights of students with disabilities to a free appropriate public education. The most recent reauthorization of this law, the Individuals with Disabilities Education Act of 2004, mandates participation of students with disabilities in state- and district-wide testing, offers more specific guidelines about discipline, and helps explain how students with learning disabilities can be identified. It encourages states and school districts to help all young students who are struggling to read, in hopes of preventing reading/learning disabilities. Finally, it includes the following key components: free appropriate public education, least restrictive environment, systematic identification procedures, individualized education programs, family involvement, related services, access to the general education curriculum, evidence-based practices, and frequent monitoring of progress. The No Child Left Behind Act of 2001 (NCLB) requires that 95 percent of all schoolchildren be full participants in state- and district-wide testing. It also includes as a goal that all students demonstrate proficiency in reading and mathematics by 2012. The Assistive Technology Act of 2004 applies to both the education system and community access, recognizing that AT is critical to the participation of people with disabilities in the workplace, in the community, and at school; it removes barriers that restrict people's lives.

- **What services are provided by special education?**

  The individualized, intensive, explicit, and supportive services offered to students with disabilities balance FAPE and LRE. These services are delivered by multidisciplinary teams of related service providers and incorporate evidence-based practices. They focus on the individual more than on the group and are guaranteed by IDEA, the federal law that gives rights and protections for an array of services, accommodations, and placement options (pull-in programming, co-teaching, pull-out services, and an array of other services) that are evaluated by monitoring students' performance.

- **What is meant by inclusive education?**

  Inclusive education has many different interpretations. It integrates students with disabilities with classmates who do not have disabilities by using neighborhood schools, general education classrooms, and age-appropriate peers to maximize LRE and increase students' access to the general education curriculum. Inclusive education practices include universal design, differentiating (adapting) instruction, and providing assistive technology.

● Revisit the
OPENING challenge

Check your answers to the Reflection Questions from the Opening Challenge, and revise them on the basis of what you have learned.

1. Do you think Ms. Smith is overly concerned about her students' varied needs? Do you think she is just having first-year-teacher jitters? Why or why not?

2. What advice would you give her about planning for her students with disabilities and for those with other special learning needs?

3. How can she learn more about the special education services her students should be receiving this year?

4. In what ways can Ms. Smith be responsive to all of her students' special needs?

Professional Standards and Licensure

CEC Knowledge and Skill Core Standard and Associated Subcategories

CEC Content Standard 1: Foundations
Special educators understand the field as an evolving and changing discipline based on philosophies, evidence-based principles and theories, relevant laws and policies, diverse historical points of view, and human issues that have historically influenced the treatment of individuals with exceptional needs in both school and society.

CEC Content Standard 3
Special educators understand the effects that an exceptional condition can have on an individual's learning in school and

throughout life. They understand the similarities and differences in human development and in characteristics between and among individuals with and without ELN.

CEC Content Standard 7: Instructional Planning

Individualized decision making and instruction is at the center of special education practice. Special educators develop long-range individualized instruction plans anchored in both general and special curricula. Individualized instruction plans emphasize explicit modeling and efficient guided practice to assure acquisition and fluency through maintenance and generalization. Understanding of these factors, as well as the implications of an individual's exceptional condition, guides the special educator's selection, adaptation, and creation of materials, and the use of powerful instructional variables. Instructional plans are modified based on ongoing analysis of the individual's learning progress.

CEC Content Standard 10: Collaboration

Special educators routinely and effectively collaborate with families, other educators, related service providers, and personnel from community agencies in culturally responsive ways. This collaboration assures that the needs of individuals with ELN are addressed throughout schooling.

INTASC Core Principle and Associated Special Education Subcategories

1. Subject Matter

1.03 All teachers understand that students with disabilities may need accommodations, modifications, and/or adaptations to the general curriculum.

1.04 All teachers have knowledge of the major principles and parameters of federal disabilities legislation.

3. Learner Differences

3.03 All teachers understand that a disability can be perceived differently across families, communities, and cultures based on differing values and belief systems.

7. Instructional Planning

7.01 All teachers contribute their expertise as members of a collaborative team to develop, monitor, and periodically revise individualized education plans for students with disabilities.

10. Collaboration, Ethics, and Relationships

10.01 All teachers share instructional responsibility for students with disabilities and work to develop well-functioning collaborative teaching relationships.

Praxis II: Education of Exceptional Students: Core Content Knowledge

I. Understanding Exceptionalities

Basic concepts in special education, including

- Attention deficit/hyperactivity disorder, as well as the incidence and prevalence of various types of disabilities
- The nature of behaviors, including frequency, duration, intensity, and degrees of severity
- The classification of students with disabilities

II. Legal and Societal Issues

Federal laws and legal issues related to special education, including

- Public Law 94-142
- Public Law 105-17
- Section 504
- Americans with Disabilities Act (ADA)
- Important legal issues

The school's connections with the families, prospective and actual employers, and communities of students with disabilities—for example,

- Parent partnerships and roles
- Cultural and community influences on public attitudes toward individuals with disabilities

Historical movements/trends affecting the connections between special education and the larger society—for example,

- Inclusion
- Transition
- Advocacy
- Accountability and meeting educational standards

III. Delivery of Services to Students with Disabilities

Background knowledge, including

- Conceptual approaches underlying service delivery to students with disabilities
- Placement and program issues such as early intervention; least restrictive environment; inclusion; role of individualized education program (IEP) team; due process guidelines; and others

Curriculum and instruction and their implementation across the continuum of education placements, including

- The individualized family service plan (IFSP)/individualized education program (IEP) process
- Career development and transition issues as related to curriculum design and implementation

Video—"The Inclusive Classroom"

Special education teacher Penny Brandenburg teaches language arts collaboratively with the general education teacher to a class that includes some students with special needs. In this video clip we see Penny providing assistance to students in the general education classroom. After the lesson, she meets with her mentor and the general education teacher to discuss the lesson.

> Log onto **www.mylabschool.com.** Under the **Courses** tab, in **Special Education,** go to the **video lab**. Access the "**Inclusion and Least Restrictive Environment**" videos and watch the "**Inclusive Classroom**" video.

 OR

> Use the **www.mylabschool.com Assignment Finder** to go directly to these videos. Just enter Assignment ID **SPV2.**

1. Describe the roles of the general education teacher and the special education teacher in the video. How can these roles benefit students?

2. How does the special education teacher provide assistance to students with special needs in this classroom?

3. What types of information are discussed in the conference after the lesson? How can conferences such as these support collaborative teaching?

4. The chapter provides a discussion of the "inclusion debate." What guidelines could be used to determine whether the students with special needs in the video clip were appropriately placed in the general education classroom?

 To access chapter objectives, practice tests, weblinks, and flashcards, go to the companion website at **www.ablongman.com/bryantsmith1e.**

chapter 2

Understanding Learners with Special Needs
High Incidence Disabilities or Conditions

After studying this chapter, you will have the knowledge to answer the following questions:

- Who are students with special needs?
- Why do students with special needs constitute a group larger than the group of students with disabilities?
- What are the three systems often used to organize disabilities and schoolchildren?
- What is meant by "high incidence disabilities," and which disabilities or conditions are included in this group?

• OPENING challenge

Miss Clarkson's Sorting Them Out

Miss Clarkson is several months into her second year of teaching and is so glad that she was assigned to third grade both years. She loves working at Jackson Elementary School, and she has great kids! The more experienced teachers are always there for her. They answer questions and help her navigate the bureaucracy, figure out how to get paperwork through the system, and think through issues related to her students' programs and how to respond well to their learning challenges. The teachers and administrators all work together as a team. Therefore, when Miss Clarkson received a note from Central Office asking her to come to a meeting because the IEP Team was considering a change of diagnosis for one of her students, she went to some of the senior teachers at her school.

The IEP Team was concerned about a student, Darren, who has received special education services since kindergarten. Miss Clarkson knows Darren's history well and has met with his parents on several occasions. Darren didn't begin talking until he was about 3 years old. As a kindergartener, he was unable to rhyme words, couldn't identify sound–letter relationships as well as his peers, was behind in language development, and seemed to have difficulty keeping up with classmates. Mr. Frank, the kinder-

garten teacher, referred him for speech and language services. Darren qualified for special education and was identified as having language impairments. Now, someone thinks it's important to reclassify Darren as having learning disabilities. Miss Clarkson can't understand why the concern. Darren's receiving special education help, and he is improving! She wonders, *"Why are we going to spend so much time on changing a special education label for Darren? Do all these different special education categories make a difference in how we teach? Will all of the professional time spent on reclassification actually benefit Darren?"*

• Reflection Questions

In your journal, write down your answers to the following questions. After completing the chapter, check your answers and revise them on the basis of what you have learned.

1. Do you think identifying students by specific disability is useful?
2. Why do you think Darren's special education label is being reconsidered at this point in his schooling?
3. Is Darren's situation unusual? Why or why not?
4. Will a change in category influence the way Miss Clarkson teaches Darren?
5. Will it change the services he receives?

ore than 11 percent of all of America's schoolchildren have a disability that affects their educational performance to such a degree that they require special education services (Office of Special Education Programs [OSEP], 2006). It may be surprising to learn that some students with disabilities do not require special education services, and these individuals are not included in the number of special education students. Thus the number of students with disabilities is greater than the federal government or the states report. Also, a substantial number of students do not qualify for special education because they do not have disabilities; regardless, they struggle to keep up with their classmates and need some special accommodations (such as extended time to take tests). When the numbers of these students are added to the number of students with disabilities, it is clear that the percentage of students with special needs far exceeds 11 percent of all students. Teachers who are well prepared, use proven practices and instructional procedures, and provide students with additional assistance or accommodations do make real differences in the educational lives of students with special needs (Futernick, 2006). In this text, we provide you with tools that improve the results of all students. Before you learn about how to teach these students effectively, let's think about which students have special needs.

Who Are Students with Special Needs?

When you think about which students attending public schools today might have special needs, you probably think about students with disabilities, and maybe you include students who are gifted or have special talents. However, these are not the only groups who need a special response to their instruction. Think again. Sadly, many students attending America's schools today are at risk for school failure. In addition, too many others do not achieve to their full potential. The result can be disastrous for the individuals and for society. A great number drop out of school, never complete their education, and find it difficult to obtain gainful employment as adults.

Let's put the number of students who might be considered to have special needs in perspective. First, it might be helpful to know how many students attend America's elementary and secondary schools. According to the National Center for Education Statistics (NCES), some 51 million students attended public schools in 2003 (Hussar & Bailey, 2006). Therefore, when anyone talks about percentages of students falling into one group or another, the number of students can be calculated by multiplying 51 million by that percentage. Considering a reference point when people discuss percentages of individuals is always helpful. For example, if more than 11 percent of the school-age population (ages 6–17) have disabilities and there are over 50 million students in the public education system, then roughly speaking, some 6 million students have been identified as having disabilities. Because students with disabilities do not represent all students who face challenges at school, either with behavior or with academic learning, it is clear that many more students than just those with disabilities have special needs. However, it is difficult to estimate how many students who do not have a disability are also at risk for school failure. One reason for this lack of precision is that school officials do not have to report the number of struggling or at risk students to their state or to the federal government. There is general agreement among teachers, policymakers, parents, and the public that a surprisingly large percentage of America's students face substantial challenges in the education system. In other words, many students have special needs that require a unique response so that they can profit maximally from their educational experiences.

Estimating the number or percentage of students who have special needs is complicated and confusing. But it is important to remember that more students than the almost 12 percent identified as having disabilities belong to this group. Look again at the drawing and description of the "normal curve" that we included in Chapter 1 (see Figure 1.1). Most theorists agree that human traits fall along such distributions, where the mean, or average, appears at the highest point and in the middle of the curve, and other scores or characteristics fall proportionately and systematically away from the center. According to this view of human characteristics, "typical learners" are in the vast majority, and fewer and fewer students find themselves at either end of the distribution. Fewer students have exceptional abilities and talents—being considered gifted, creative, or highly talented—than the number of those students who would be considered about "average." A comparable case exists for students with significant cognitive challenges: There are many fewer of them than there are students with average intellectual abilities.

We believe, however, that the concept of the "normal curve" is not an accurate picture of the distribution or prevalence of students with special learning needs. Accordingly, although it is entirely hypothetical, we drew another graphic (see Figure 2.1) that might help us all better visualize how students might combine along this "special needs" dimension. For this illustration, we thought about all students, and we attempted to include those with all sorts of special needs or considerations. When you think about students with and without disabilities who have special needs, their prevalence could not possibly be represented by a normal, or "bell-shaped," curve. The point we are trying to

FIGURE 2.1 Hypothetical Distribution of Students with Special Needs

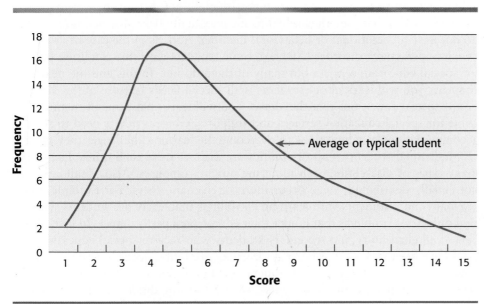

illustrate is that more students than suggested by the normal distribution face challenges at school. These challenges can be caused by many different factors:

- Disabilities
- Having conditions that negatively influence learning
- Receiving unproven instructional strategies
- Being an English language learner

All of these students deserve the additional help they need to be successful. Education professionals are in unique positions to make a meaningful difference in the lives of individuals with all kinds of special needs. However, it is important to know that not all students with special needs qualify for special education services; only those with disabilities do. Let's consider these students now.

Who Are Students with Disabilities?

Only students with disabilities are eligible for special education services, but not all of them actually require special education services to meet their special needs. For example, many students with physical disabilities do not require special education services. They excel as they learn content of the general curriculum alongside their peers who do not experience physical challenges. These students may, or may not, need some assistance or accommodations, such as special floor mats so their wheelchairs can glide easily into the school building or the classroom. These are students who have a disability and have special needs, but they are *not* special education students because their disability does not negatively affect their educational performance. Some physical disabilities do result in the need for special education services—possibly the assistance of a physical therapist and an assistive technologist—to reduce the impact of the disability on learning. Other students may have special needs, and are entitled to some accommodations as well as extra help, but do not have a disability. For example, some students may require some help managing their own behavior so that they do not disrupt the learning environment and so that they themselves profit maximally from instruction, but they do not have an emotional or behavioral disorder. And, as in the case of attention deficit hyperactivity disorder (ADHD), some students with this condition qualify for special education services but many of them do not. In this and the next two chapters, you will learn about students with special needs because of the disabilities or special conditions that they have. You will learn that some of them are eligible for special education services and supports, whereas others need to receive accommodations or adaptations to overcome the learning challenges they face.

Individual students with disabilities are distinct from each other. They have many types of disabilities, each requiring unique responses. Also, disabilities are not equally distributed; some occur more often than others. For example, there are many more students with learning disabilities than there are students with vision or hearing problems that hinder their educational performance. In fact, about half of all elementary and secondary students who receive special education services have been identified as having a learning disability. According to the federal government, about 90 percent of students with disabilities—that is, 90 percent of the almost 12 percent of all students—have a learning disability, or a speech or language impairment, or mild to moderate mental retardation, or an emotional or behavioral disorder. These disabilities are often referred to as high incidence disabilities. The remaining disabilities recognized in IDEA '04—physical and health impairments, low vision and blindness, hard of hearing and deafness, traumatic brain injury, deafblindness, autism spectrum disorders, and multiple-severe disabilities—are sometimes grouped together and called low incidence disabilities because together they represent a very small proportion of students with disabilities (OSEP, 2006). You will learn about these disabilities and the individuals affected in Chapter 3. In Chapter 4 you will learn about other groups of students who do not qualify for special education services and supports, but still require accommodations or extra assistance to fulfill their potential. All of these students have special needs that must be addressed in order for them to succeed at school.

Disabilities create very special needs for the individuals involved, their families, and the education system. You can help students achieve their potential by addressing their special needs, by providing them with many opportunities for learning and for success, and by ensuring that they receive a high-quality educational experience. For now, let's focus on how many of these students there are so that we may better understand who makes up this group of learners with special needs.

As you will learn in this chapter and the next, the federal government, through IDEA '04, defines each disability category and monitors the number and percentage of students included in each special education grouping. Consequently, we know the prevalence of students with disabilities. The federal government, through the U.S. Department of Education's Office of Special Education Programs (OSEP), reports that almost 5.8 million school-age students had disabilities in the 2004–2005 school year, a number that represents about 12 percent of all students (OSEP, 2006). Students with identified or documented disabilities are eligible for additional services and supports through special education. As you learned in Chapter 1, the vast majority of students with disabilities receive nearly all of their education in inclusive general education settings alongside their classmates without disabilities. Although it is not commonplace for students with high incidence disabilities to be grouped together by their identified special education category (e.g., students with learning disabilities in one group and students with mental retardation in another group), the federal government does require that all students older than age 8 be identified and counted in one of the 14 special education categories called out in IDEA '04 (see Chapter 1 for a review).

How Are Disabilities Organized for Special Education?

Three major schemes are used to group, or think about, disabilities. One classification system uses disability types or special education categories (e.g., learning disabilities, mental retardation). Another system groups students by the severity of the disability (e.g., mild, moderate, severe). And the third considers disabilities in terms of how often they occur (e.g., high incidence, low incidence). Let's look at each organizational system in turn.

Special Education Categories

IDEA '04 (the national special education law) and many parent organizations (e.g., Learning Disabilities Association of America, Autism Society of America) encourage the use of disability labels, which translate into special education categories. When it comes to schoolchildren, the government has elected to define disabilities

● While not found in a separate disability category, asthma is the most common chronic illness among children. This student's illness is considered part of the "other health impairments" category.

by using a categorical approach, and states are required each year to use these categories to report the numbers of students with disabilities being served (U.S. Department of Education, 2006). Although many states use terms slightly different from those used by the federal government, the similarities in terms and in definitions used across the nation are obvious (Müller & Markowitcz, 2004). Across the 50 states, the basic definitions of each disability are generally consistent with those found in the IDEA '04 law (Müller & Markowitcz, 2004). Within each of the 14 categories that are defined as disabilities in IDEA '04 and listed in Chapter 1 of this text, many conditions are included. For example, attention deficit hyperactivity disorder (ADHD), asthma, sickle cell anemia, and many other health conditions are part of the "other health impairments" category, not separate categories of their own.

Possibly because it is so difficult to change federal and state laws, the names that these governments use for each disability might not always be what parents and professionals consider modern or up-to-date. In other words, parent and professional organizations sometimes have a different way of conceptualizing and referring to specific disabilities. In this text, we have tried to use terms preferred by individuals who have each specific disability, parents of children with each disability, and the respective professional organizations. Here are a few examples of how terms and thinking about specific disabilities vary. Over recent years, ideas and research about autism have been developing rapidly. Today, this disability is considered a spectrum of at least five similar disorders, with autism being one of the five. Thus, although IDEA '04 still uses the term *autism,* the more current conceptualization of this disability is much broader, as reflected by the name *autism spectrum disorders,* or ASD. IDEA '04 uses the term *specific learning disabilities,* but parents, professionals, and individuals with the condition almost always use the term *learning disabilities.* And although IDEA '04 separates deafness from hearing impairments, it does not separate visual disabilities into two groups (i.e., blindness and low vision).

For schoolchildren, these disability or special education categories developed because of the education that students received. At one time, special education categories related directly to how and where students with specific disabilities were educated and what they were taught. For example, the category of "mental retardation" signaled separate classrooms, separate schools, even separate living and schooling in institutions, and strict adherence to a curriculum of life and self-help skills and training for low-level jobs. Today, educators and policymakers believe that alternative curricula should not be matched to specific disabilities; rather, the general education curriculum should be offered to all students. Different curricular options are then extended to individuals who have demonstrated that they cannot successfully access the standard curriculum offered in general education (McLaughlin & Nolet, 2004). Also, instructional methods are not uniformly effective with all students labeled with a specific disability. Knowing that a student has learning disabilities does not help a teacher figure out which reading method to use. Selection of educational interventions must be matched to the individual learner's performance, not to a special education category (Fuchs, 2004). In other words, reading methods effective with one student with learning disabilities are not effective with all students with learning disabilities. Also, many interventions effective with one student with disabilities are also powerful with classmates without disabilities who find learning a challenging situation. Thus, although special education categories have proved not to offer precision in guiding instructional decision making, they remain the primary way students are identified, are labeled, and qualify for special education services.

Severity of Disability

As we have just noted, many educators believe that special education categories and the resulting labeling of individuals have little or no educational function (Fisher, Frey, & Thousand, 2003; Gargiulo, 2003; Lipsky & Gartner, 1991). These professionals prefer a noncategorical approach wherein students are grouped by the severity of their problems, not by the type of disability they have. How does this system work? Instead of thinking about the specific disability, educators consider how the condition influences an individual's performance. Typically, four groupings are used: mild, moderate, severe, and profound. This system reflects the types of supports the individual needs in life and at school (Luckasson et al., 2002). Individuals with mild disabilities require some accommodations, and those with severe disabilities require intensive supports and assistance for a long time. Several cautions, however, are important when thinking about disabilities by level of severity. First, it is a terrible mistake to assume that one disability is more severe than another. All disabilities are serious, and the effects on the individuals involved and on their families should never be minimized. One disability, such as mental retardation, should not be thought of as inherently more serious than another disability, such as the speech impairment of stuttering. Second, each disability grouping falls along a continuum of severity from mild to severe. It is incorrect, then, to think that all learning disabilities are mild.

Today, both the categorical and noncategorical approaches are used in classrooms. Students are identified and reported to the federal government by disability. However, when it comes to students' education, fewer and fewer separate schools or classes for students with a specific disability are available. For example, "classes for students with mental retardation" or "special schools for students with physical disabilities" were common some 20 years ago, but they are fewer in number every year (OSEP, 2006). Some professionals and advocacy organizations (e.g., TASH, an organization representing individuals with severe and profound disabilities) are advocating for the closure of all segregated programs for students with disabilities (TASH, 2004). Thus, although IDEA '04 requires that students qualify for special education by being identified as having a specific disability, schools typically serve these students according to their needs and educational performance. In both general education classes and special education classes, students with disabilities are classmates but do not always share the same disabilities.

We have just talked about how disabilities can be organized by categories (e.g., physical disabilities, emotional or behavioral disorders) and by severity (e.g., mild, severe). Neither of these systems is related to the number of individuals involved. Another way to organize our thinking about disabilities is to group them by how often they occur. For example, some disabilities (e.g., learning disabilities) occur more frequently than others; more students have mild disabilities than have severe disabilities. Let's consider this type of organizational system.

Prevalence

The third way to think about disabilities and schoolchildren is in terms of prevalence. Figure 2.2 illustrates that disabilities are not equally distributed across special education students. Almost half of all students with disabilities are identified as having learning disabilities, and most other disabilities are very rare. Some believe that the response to more common disabilities, or high incidence disabilities, should be different from the response to less frequent disabilities, or low incidence disabilities. The less frequently occurring disabilities often require specialized services from a multidisciplinary team of professionals (e.g., orientation and mobility specialist, assistive technology specialist, vision teacher who knows braille instruction). To be sure, general education teachers work with many students with high incidence disabilities every school year, but across their entire careers, they may never work with a student with a specific low incidence disability (e.g., blind, deaf). Possibly for these reasons, the U.S. Department of Education often divides disability categories into two groups by prevalence: high incidence disabilities and low incidence disabilities. In this chapter we discuss those disabilities and one condition (ADHD) that occur more frequently, have a greater prevalence, and therefore are considered high incidence conditions. In Chapter 3, we discuss those disabilities that have lower prevalence rates or are often thought of as "low incidence disabilities."

We decided to organize our discussions about students with disabilities and special needs by prevalence. We mentioned earlier that each condition often has

FIGURE 2.2 Prevalence of High and Low Incidence Disabilities

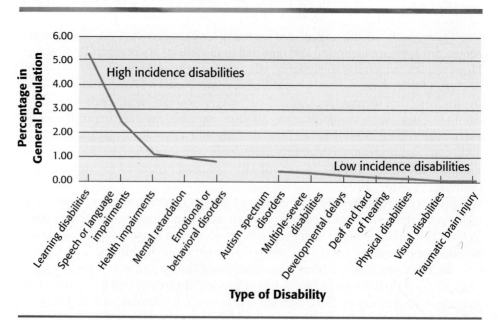

many different definitions. For example, the federal government, through IDEA '04, set forth definitions for each of the 14 disabilities it called out in the special education law. States often use slightly different versions of each disability's definition to identify and qualify students for special education services. And parent groups, advocacy agencies, and professional organizations also use varying definitions. Although not comprehensive, several tables in this chapter provide several commonly adopted definitions for each high incidence condition. Compare these definitions and think about the different perspectives that contributed to each definition's development. By doing so, you will gain a better understanding of the condition and the students involved. Let's start learning about high incidence conditions by thinking about the disability that is the most common among school children: learning disabilities. Clearly, every educator will encounter students with this disability every school day in almost every classroom.

Who Are Students with Learning Disabilities?

Often incorrectly considered a mild condition, learning disabilities (LD) is a serious disability. It is a severe, pervasive, and chronic condition that requires intensive intervention (Bender, 2004; Pierangelo & Guiliani, 2006). Over the years, debate has focused on whether there is a difference between low achievers and students with learning disabilities. Some still question the validity of classifying learning disabilities as an actual disability (Fletcher et al., 2002). However, parents and researchers are confident that learning disabilities is a complex and life-long condition (Goldberg, et al., 2003; Lerner & Kline, 2006).

Definition

Although definitions for learning disabilities differ across the states, the federal government's definition, the one included in IDEA '04, is the basis for them. The IDEA '04 definition, along with the one proposed by the National Institutes of Health (NIH), is found in Table 2.1. Like the NIH definition, many states' definitions reflect a more modern approach that has less of a medical orientation, acknowledge that *learning disabilities* is a general term referring to a heterogeneous group of disorders, allow for other conditions to coexist with learning disabilities (e.g., learning disabilities and visual disabilities), and recognize the problems many of these individuals have with social skills (Müller & Markowitcz, 2004).

Nearly half of all students included in special education are designated as having a learning disability (OSEP, 2006). Look at Figure 2.2 again to see the disproportionate percentage of students included in this special education category. Clearly, parents, policymakers, and education professionals are most concerned about the number of students included in the learning disabilities category. Another concern stems from the way the identification process works. In general terms, the traditional process requires that a student's achievement be 2 years behind what would be expected for that individual. In other words, a third grader reading at the first-grade level is a prime candidate for referral to

TABLE 2.1 **Learning Disabilities**

Source	Definition
IDEA '04[1]	*Specific learning disability* means a disorder in one or more of the basic psychological processes involved in understanding or in using language, spoken or written, that may manifest itself in an imperfect ability to listen, think, speak, read, write, spell, or do mathematical calculations, including such conditions as perceptual disabilities, brain injury, minimal brain dysfunction, dyslexia, and developmental aphasia. Specific learning disability does not include learning problems that are primarily the result of visual, hearing, or motor disabilities; mental retardation; emotional disturbance; or environmental, cultural, or economic disadvantage.
National Institutes of Health (NIH)[2]	Learning disabilities are disorders that affect the ability to understand or use spoken or written language, do mathematical calculations, coordinate movements, or direct attention. Although learning disabilities occur in very young children, the disorders are usually not recognized until the child reaches school age.

Sources: [1]*U.S. Department of Education, 2006, p. 1264*
[2]*National Institutes of Health, National Institute of Neurological Disorders and Stroke, 2006*

special education because of a reading/learning disability. However, this scenario also means that this student has struggled for at least 2 years and has not received specialized attention in a timely fashion. Many maintain that these students struggle without assistance unnecessarily. They can be identified as demonstrating academic difficulties as early as kindergarten, and for many of these students, supplemental evidence-based reading and mathematics intervention prevents years of failure (Bishop & League, 2006; Bryant et al., in press; Vaughn & Fuchs, 2003; Vaughn & Linan-Thompson, 2004). Therefore, IDEA '04 allows for a new way to intervene early and provide systematically more intensive instruction to all students who are struggling with reading and mathematics during the beginning school years. The law also allows for a new way to identify students as having learning disabilities; no longer must there be a significant discrepancy between their ability and their academic performance before those who have learning disabilities get the individualized instruction they need to succeed in school (U.S. Department of Education, 2006). This new system, called response to intervention (RTI), incorporates a multilevel method of intervening before the devastating effects of school failure take their toll (Fuchs & Fuchs, 2006; Kukic, Tilly, & Michelson, 2005). This method is also referred to as early intervening because it is applied as early as possible to every student who is struggling, particularly those having difficulty learning basic reading and mathematics skills. Under the RTI option, those students who do not learn sufficiently with high-quality instruction and do not learn reading and mathematics skills well enough after supplemental evidence-based intervention are identified as having learning disabilities (The IRIS Center, 2006). Once they are eligible for special education services, they receive intensive, individualized intervention.

● Problems associated with academic learning can be overcome with explicit instruction and intensive efforts. What benefits might this student receive from individualized instruction?

Types

To better understand the diversity—the heterogeneity—of these students, let's examine these common profiles or types of learning disabilities:

- Overall underachievement
- Reading disabilities
- Mathematics disabilities

Despite having normal intelligence, students with learning disabilities do not achieve academically on a par with their classmates without disabilities. Some of these students face challenges in almost every academic area. Most experts are certain that cognitive problems, poor motivation, and/or an insufficient instructional response to their learning disabilities can be at the root of some of these students' learning challenges (Fuchs, Fuchs, Mathes et al., 2002; Kavale & Forness, 2000). Some experts think that learning disabilities reflect deficits in the ability to process or remember information (Torgensen, 2002). What appears quite certain is that learning disabilities are resistant to treatment or "resistant to intervention" (Fuchs, 2002; Gresham, 2002). These students do not learn at the same rate or in the same ways as their classmates (Fuchs & Fuchs, 2006; Vaughn, 2005). The instruction or intervention typically used in general education programs is not sufficient and does not help the student improve; more intensive individualized intervention is necessary.

Reading difficulties—very low reading abilities—are the most common reasons for these students' referrals to special education (Fuchs & Fuchs, 2001;

Fuchs, Fuchs, Mathes, et al., 2002). Because reading and writing are intimately related, most students with reading/learning disabilities (sometimes called dyslexia) have problems with written communication as well (Graham & Harris, 2005; Hammill, 2004). Reading and writing, obviously, are important skills; in school, students must be able to read information from a variety of texts (social studies, science, literature) and write in varying formats (essays, reports, creative writing, notes). As the complexity of academic tasks increases, students not proficient in reading and writing cannot keep pace with the academic expectations of school (Jenkins & O'Connor, 2002). As these students progress through school, reading disabilities compound and make it almost impossible to perform well on other academic tasks, contributing to overall underachievement.

Although reading problems are the most common reason for referral, more than 50 percent of students with learning disabilities also have mathematics/learning disabilities (Fuchs & Fuchs, 2003). Some seem to have difficulties with mathematics alone, but for most, this difficulty is part of an overwhelming and pervasive underachievement (Lerner & Kline, 2006). Even so, as you will learn later in this text (in Chapters 10, 11, 12, and 13), many of these problems associated with academic learning can be overcome with explicit instruction and intensive efforts.

Characteristics

Consensus is growing that unexpected underachievement is *the* defining characteristic of learning disabilities (Fuchs, 2002; Vaughn, Elbaum, & Boardman, 2001). These students perform significantly below their peers and below levels that teachers and parents would expect from children of their ability. Although some students have problems in only one academic area, most have pervasive problems that affect the entire range of academic and social domains (Bryant, Bryant, & Hammill, 2000; Gregg & Mather, 2002). Teachers often cite this group's heterogeneity as challenging because it seems that each student requires a unique response (Fletcher et al., 2002). But despite these students' individual differences, some characteristics are commonly seen with learning disabilities; these are listed in Table 2.2.

Compounding these general characteristics are frustrations with the difficulties of learning academic tasks that seem easily understood and mastered by classmates. Students with learning disabilities cannot see the relationship between effort and accomplishment (Hock, 1997; Reid & Lienemann, 2006; Sexton, Harris, & Graham, 1998). When teachers and parents remind students that working hard, studying, and applying effective learning strategies to their schoolwork pays off, youngsters also learn that their efforts can lead to success.

Many of these students are said to be inattentive (Pierangelo & Guliani, 2006). Either they do not focus on the task to be learned, or they pay attention to the wrong features of the task. They are said to be distractible, disorganized, and unable to approach learning strategically (Bender, 2004). Most students with learning disabilities also have problems with generalization; they have difficulty transferring their learning to different skills or situations (Vaughn, Bos, & Shumm, 2006). They might apply a newly learned study skill in history class but not in English class. Generalization can be encouraged by making connections

TABLE 2.2   Characteristics of Learning Disabilities

Academic	Social	Behavioral Style
Unexpected underachievement	Immature	Inattentive
Resistant to treatment	Socially unacceptable	Distractible
Difficult to teach	Misinterprets social and nonverbal cues	Hyperactive
Inability to solve problems	Makes poor decisions	Impulsive
Uneven academic abilities	Victimized	Poorly coordinated
Inactive learning style	Unable to predict social consequences	Disorganized
Poor basic language skills	Unable to follow social conventions (manners)	Unmotivated
Poor basic reading and decoding skills	Rejected	Dependent
Inefficient information processing abilities	Naïve	
Inability to generalize	Shy, withdrawn, insecure	
	Dependent	

clearly between familiar problems and those that are new or novel (Fuchs, Fuchs, Thompson, et al., 2002). When teachers carefully broaden the categories—either the skill or the situation—and point out similar features, students extend their learning more readily. Thus, if a student knows how to solve subtraction problems that require borrowing without zeros in the minuend, for example, teachers should carefully point out the similarities between problems that include zeros (500 − 354 = ?) and those that do not (467 − 189 = ?).

Another long-standing explanation for these students' learning problems is that they have trouble with information processing (Lerner & Kline, 2006). A break occurs somewhere along the processing chain that leads from gaining the information, or input, to understanding the information, to finding an effective means of using new knowledge, or output. A break along the processing chain may be attributed to memory difficulties and how students receive, organize, and store information to aid in recalling it. Many students with learning disabilities benefit from being taught strategies to help them process information and learn academic skills. For example, students can be taught strategies to help them identify, organize, understand, and remember important information in their textbook reading. For learning arithmetic facts, students can be taught strategies for retrieving answers quickly and correctly. Other students with learning disabilities may need to use alternative means or assistive technology to do their schoolwork. For example, a student with severely impaired writing abilities may find that the speech recognition system, a standard feature of personal computers, is helpful when writing term papers. Another student who cannot read well enough to keep up with classmates as they read their sixth-grade social studies textbook might profit from using the digital version of the text and the speech output option.

Finally, it is estimated that about three-fourths of individuals with learning disabilities have problems with social skills, and the results are negative self-concepts, an inability to make friends, ineffective approaches to schoolwork, and poor inter-actions with others (Bryan, Burnstein, & Ergul, 2004; Vaughn, Bos, & Shumm, 2006). For example, many students with learning disabilities are naïve and unable to judge other people's intentions accurately (Donahue, 1997). They cannot under-stand nonverbal behaviors, such as facial expressions, and therefore do not compre-hend other people's emotional messages (Dimitrovsky, Spector, & Levy-Schiff, 2000). This inability puts them at a great disadvantage and results in low accep-tance rates by their peers and teachers. Difficulty with social skills, coupled with low achievement and distracting classroom behavior, influences the social status of children with learning disabilities. Peers consider these classmates as overly depend-ent, less cooperative, and less socially adept (Kuhne & Wiener, 2000). Consequently, these children are less likely to become leaders—or even to be in-cluded in groups. Teachers can play an instrumental role in reducing peer rejection. One approach is pairing these students and classmates without disabilities in areas of mutual interest (Harris & Graham, 1999). For example, teachers might plan ac-tivities for which students with common interests (sports, music, hobbies) are as-signed to work together on an academic task such as a science report.

Prevalence

Learning disabilities is by far the largest special education category (review Figure 2.2), including almost 6 percent of all schoolchildren and nearly half of all stu-dents identified as having a disability (U.S. Department of Education, 2002). Parents, educators, and policymakers are concerned about this special education category for this and other reasons (Bradley, Danielson, & Hallahan, 2002).

1. **Prevalence:** Almost half of all students identified as having a disability are identified as having learning disabilities (OSEP, 2006).
2. **Cost:** Although variation exists across the nation and even district by district, every student with a disability costs more to educate than a classmate with-out disabilities, and usually it is almost three times as expensive (Parrish & Esra, 2006).
3. **Misidentification:** Some experts have called the category of learning disabili-ties a "dumping ground" where any student unsuccessful in the general edu-cation curriculum can be placed (Reschly, 2002).

Not surprisingly, the field of learning disabilities is in a state of transition. Many changes are occurring, and more are on the horizon. For example, the ways in which students with learning disabilities can be identified and become qualified for special education services no longer depend on a significant gap between an individual's achievement and her or his potential. Students no longer must fail for years before receiving specialized and intensive help. One possible benefit of these changes is that the number of students included in this special education category may be far less in future years than it is today. These are exciting times, in particular for those concerned about students who struggle with reading and mathematics, because many have great confidence that these changes will positively affect the lives of students with learning disabilities and their families (Bradley, Danielson, & Hallahan, 2002; Kukic, Tilly, & Michelson, 2005; Vaughn & Fuchs, 2003). One such success story is described in the fol-lowing Making a Difference feature.

Making a Difference

Teaching Self-Advocacy Gives Students with Disabilities a Tool for Life

Salle Hill Howes
Colorado Springs, Colorado

Our daughter Hillary was in fifth grade when she was first diagnosed with expressive and receptive aphasia, a language disability that results from damage to the language center of the brain and makes reading, writing, speaking, and processing information especially difficult. Doctors at Denver Children's Hospital told us that, given the significance of her disability, college was an unrealistic aspiration. Fortunately, we live in an enlightened school district in which high school students with learning differences acquire the skills needed for success through a self-advocacy program called LEAD. LEAD (Learning and Educating About Disabilities) is a four-year, accredited course offered to students with learning disabilities and ADHD at Cheyenne Mountain High School in Colorado Springs.

One part of the LEAD curriculum allows students to examine their own test scores and assessments. This knowledge helps them support their requests for the accommodations and modifications they may be entitled to. Students are given information about their specific disabilities and their legal rights under IDEA '04. LEAD students actively participate in their own IEP or 504 plan. They learn to take responsibility for the direction of their own education, not simply to rely on teachers and parents to advocate for them.

Although Hillary entered high school feeling defeated and worthless, the teachers in the LEAD program taught her that a learning disability has nothing to do with intelligence and is nothing to be ashamed of. After a year in LEAD, Hillary began writing letters to each of her teachers, giving them detailed information about her disability and how it affects her in the classroom. This simple act of educating her teachers won her their respect, and a mutual bond was formed. Hillary's teachers not only accepted her need for accommodations but also encouraged her to use them.

Hillary is now a confident and successful student in college, where she continues to advocate for herself and to educate others about her disability. It is my hope that some day all schools will offer a similar program to teach students with learning disabilities the crucial skill of self-advocacy and the importance of self-knowledge. It is equally important that all teachers appreciate and encourage those skills.

More Information on LEAD can be found at www.leadcolorado.org. ●

Who Are Students with Speech or Language Impairments?

As we have noted, learning disabilities is the largest special education category. However, as with many facts, the situation is not quite so simple. The federal government allows students with disabilities to be reported in only one special education category. Thus, a fourth-grade student with reading/learning disabilities and also a speech problem might well be included in the learning disabilities category but also receive services from a speech/language pathologist (SLP) as a related service. Speech problems and language impairments go hand-in-hand with many disabilities. For example, the co-occurrence of speech or language impairments with learning disabilities is estimated to be 96 percent (Sunderland, 2004). Students with cognitive disabilities typically face challenges in the area of language development (Taylor, Richards, & Brady, 2005). Therefore, many students with disabilities receive services from *both* special education teachers and SLPs. Also, because of the relationship between language problems as a preschooler and later problems with reading and writing, as is shown in Figure 2.3, during the early school years, speech and language impairments is clearly the larger special education category. Consider what might be thought of as primary and secondary disabilities. When both are considered, speech or language impairments are clearly the most common disability among schoolchildren (OSEP, 2006). It is important to recognize that speech and language, in particular, are the foundations for many things we do as human beings. Let's briefly think about how problems in these areas affect learning.

Communication requires the receiver to use eyes, ears, or even tactile (touch) senses (as do those who use braille) to take messages to the brain, where they are understood. Receivers must understand the code the sender uses and must be able to interpret the code so that it has meaning. Communication is unsuccessful if sender or receiver cannot use the signals or symbols adequately. And if either person has a defective mechanism for sending or receiving the information, the communication process is ineffective. It might be helpful to distinguish among three important and related terms: *communication, language,* and *speech.*

- **Communication:** the process of exchanging knowledge, ideas, opinions, and feelings through the use of verbal or nonverbal (e.g., a gesture) language
- **Language:** the rule-based method of communication involving the comprehension and use of the signs and symbols by which ideas are represented
- **Speech:** the vocal production of language

Now let's turn our attention to problems that can interfere with communication by impeding either language or speech.

FIGURE 2.3 Number of Individuals with Speech or Language Impairments and with Learning Disabilities Served Through IDEA '04 by Age

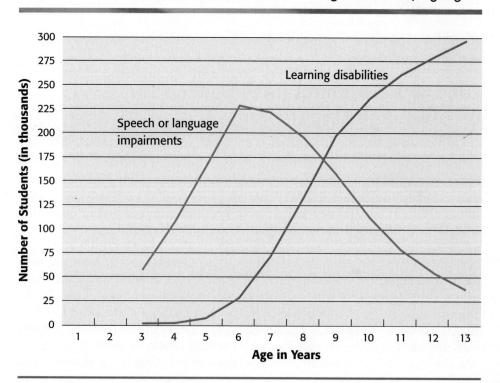

Definition

Although they make up a single special education category, speech impairments and language impairments are really two separate, but related, disabilities. A speech impairment exists when the production of speech sounds is unintelligible, is unpleasant, or interferes with communication (Bernthal & Bankson, 2004; Hall, Oyer, & Haas, 2001). Speech impairments are distracting to the listener and can negatively affect the communication process. A language impairment disrupts communication and interferes with accurate understanding of messages, the intent of communications, and interactions among people. See Table 2.3 for the IDEA '04 definition, as well as the one adopted many years ago by the American Speech–Language–Hearing Association (ASHA), the nation's largest organization representing professionals in the areas of speech, language, and audiology.

Types

Both types of communication disorders—speech impairments and language impairments—can be further subdivided. The three types of speech impairments are

1. **Articulation problems:** The process of producing speech sounds is flawed, and resulting speech sounds are incorrect. (Table 2.4 describes each of the four articulation problems.)
2. **Fluency problems:** Hesitations or repetitions interrupt the flow of speech. (Stuttering is one type of fluency problem.)
3. **Voice problems:** The voice is unusual (in pitch or loudness) given the age and sex of the individual.

It is important that adults understand that some young children (ages 3 to 5) demonstrate misarticulations and dysfluencies (nonfluencies) in the course of normal speech development. These mistakes are not usually indicative of or a problem in need of therapy (Conture, 2001; Ramig & Shames, 2006; Ratner, 2005).

TABLE 2.3 Speech or Language Impairment

Source	Definition
IDEA '04[1]	*Speech or language impairment* means a communication disorder, such as stuttering, impaired articulation, a language impairment, or a voice impairment, that adversely affects a child's educational performance.
American Speech–Language–Hearing Association[2]	A speech and language disorder may be present when a person's speech or language is different from that of others of the same age, sex, or ethnic group; when a person's speech and/or language is hard to understand; when a person is overly concerned about his or her speech; or when a person often avoids communicating with others.

Sources: [1]*U.S. Department of Education, 2006, p. 1265.*

[2]*American Speech–Language–Hearing Association Ad Hoc Committee on Service Delivery in the Schools, 1993, pp. 40–41.*

TABLE 2.4   **Types of Articulation Errors**

Error Type	Definition	Example
Omission	A sound or group of sounds is left out of a word. Small children often leave off the ending of a word (sounds in the final position).	Intended: *I want a banana.* Omission: *I wanna nana.*
Substitution	A common misarticulation among small children; one sound is used for another.	Intended: *I see the rabbit.* Substitution: *I tee the wabbit.*
Distortion	A variation of the intended sound is produced in an unfamiliar manner.	Intended: *Give the pencil to Sally.* Distortion: *Give the pencil to Sally.* (the /p/ is nasalized).
Addition	An extra sound is inserted or added to one already correctly produced.	Intended: *I miss her.* Addition: *I missid her.*

Language impairments are not typically broken down into types, but problems with language are often discussed in terms of the aspect of language where the problem exists.

- **Form:** the rule system used for all language (oral, written, and sign)
- **Content:** the intent and meaning of spoken and written statements
- **Use:** the application of language based on the social content

Rules in each language govern how vowels, consonants, their combinations, and words are used (Small, 2005). The relationship between development of an awareness of sounds in words (phonological awareness) during the preschool years and later ease of learning how to read is now clear (Bishop & League, 2006; Torgesen & Wagner, 1998). To prevent reading failure later during the school years, preschoolers who have problems mastering phonology should be referred to specialists for early intervention.

Characteristics

Although the characteristics of speech or language impairments are important to understand, it is even more critical for teachers to recognize the differences among three language-related situations:

1. Language impairments
2. Language delays
3. Language differences

Being able to distinguish among these types helps general education teachers make correct and prompt referrals and avoid misidentification of students. A typical child at the age of 3 can use some fairly sophisticated language. At the same age, a child with language impairments might speak in only two-word combinations.

It is not just at what rate (how slowly) a child develops language, but also how differently it develops from the way it does in typical peers.

Children with language delays generally acquire language in the same sequence as their peers, but more slowly. Many of these children do not have a disability and catch up with their peers. However, some children acquire language in the correct sequence, do so very slowly, and never complete the acquisition of complex language structures. For example, most children with mental retardation have language delays. Their language development will remain below that of their peers who have normal intelligence and are developing at expected rates (Wetherby, 2002).

What about children who are learning English as a second language? Many teachers have difficulty determining whether a child who is not a native speaker of English is merely language different or has a language impairment (Baca & Cervantes, 2004; Salend, 2005). Truly mastering a second language takes a long time. Many English language learners (ELLs), now beginning to be referred to as English learners (ELs), may appear to be fluent in English because they converse with their classmates on the playground and express their basic needs in the classroom, but even so, they may not yet have developed sufficient fluency in their second language to participate fully in academic instruction. English being a second language does not result in a disability, but some ELLs may be slow in mastering their second language, particularly because of the impact of poverty, and some do have language impairments

Dialects of American English are not impairments either (Payne & Taylor, 2006). Dialects result from historical, social, regional, and cultural influences and are sometimes perceived by educators as inferior or nonstandard. Children from diverse backgrounds who use dialects, whether they are from Appalachia or from a predominantly Black inner-city community, are often misidentified as having language impairments. Teachers need to understand and be sensitive to the differences between dialects and language impairments, but when in doubt, they should seek the advice of specialists. Speech/language pathologists (SLPs) who can distinguish between language differences and language impairments are proficient in the rules of the particular child's dialect and in the use of nondiscriminatory testing procedures. You will learn more about linguistically diverse students in Chapter 4. It is a terrible mistake to assume that students from diverse backgrounds have disabilities because of their cultural or linguistic backgrounds. However, it is also a terrible mistake not to qualify students for services they need, and for which they are eligible due to fear of discrimination.

Prevalence

As we saw in Figure 2.2, official reports show speech or language impairments as the second-largest special education category, behind learning disabilities (OSEP, 2006). In 2005, some 2,780,218 individuals between the ages of 6 and 21 were identified as having a speech or language impairment. For schoolchildren between the ages of 6 and 17, these students represent some 2.3 percent of the entire school-age population. Remember, too, that when *both* primary and secondary disabling conditions are considered, speech or language impairments is clearly the largest special education category (OSEP, 2006).

During the 2005 school year, speech or language impairments was the most common label used for children between the ages of 3 and 5. In fact, over 330,000 preschoolers—more than half of all children in that combined age group—were identified with speech or language disabilities. Only slightly more than 12,000 preschoolers between the ages of 3 and 5, nationally, were identified as having learning disabilities. Look at Figure 2.3 (page 56) again to see how quickly the balance shifts: More and more students by third and fourth grade are included in the learning disabilities category, while the size of the speech or language impairments category declines greatly (OSEP, 2006). Clearly, the prevalence of speech or language impairments is associated with the age of the student and the demands of the curriculum (Bakken & Whedon, 2002). The data shown in Figure 2.3 also confirm what you learned in the previous section about students with learning disabilities. They tend not to be identified early, at the beginning of their school careers, when their struggle to succeed in the curriculum begins. These data contributed to justifications found in IDEA '04 for the application of early intervening procedures and new ways to identify students with learning disabilities.

Who Are Students with Attention Deficit Hyperactivity Disorder (ADHD)?

A growing number of students are being reported to the federal government as having "other health impairments," a disability category that comprises many discrete conditions (e.g., asthma, ADHD, blood disorders). Other health impairments has been traditionally considered a low incidence disability category, but in just the past few years, the number of students included in this category has swelled (OSEP, 2006). In the 2000–2001 school year, health impairments was the fifth-largest special education category, with slightly more than one-half of 1 percent (0.57) of all students reported in this category (U.S. Department of Education, 2002). In 2005, the health impairments category was the third largest, including over 1 percent (1.09) of the general student body (OSEP, 2006). What could have caused one group of students to almost double in size in just a few years? The increase is probably due to the inclusion of attention deficit hyperactivity disorder (ADHD) in the health impairments category when IDEA was reauthorized in 1997.

Although the data make it appear that ADHD is escalating, it is actually impossible to confirm or deny this perception. There are many reasons for this situation; here are three major ones:

1. ADHD is not a separate category called out in IDEA '04, so states do not report these students separately to the federal government.
2. Not all students with ADHD are eligible for special education services because the condition does not adversely influence their academic performance, and those students are not reported to any agency.
3. Few additional students are identified as having a disability because of ADHD. They were served in other categories before the condition was called out within the "other health impairments" category. (Those students who needed intervention, accommodations, and supports were served through other categories, such as learning disabilities.)

It is important to understand that not all students with ADHD qualify for special education services. Students whose ADHD does not seriously affect their educational performance are not eligible. Those students receive accommodations

● It is estimated that over half of all students with ADHD *do not* qualify for special education services because their condition does not seriously affect their educational performance. Those students with ADHD whose educational function is seriously affected by the condition *do* qualify for special education services.

for their unique learning needs through Section 504 of the Rehabilitation Act (see Chapter 1 for a review of this law). In the 1997 reauthorization of the IDEA '04 law, ADHD was called out as a condition within the "other health impairments" category. Until this time, many students with ADHD were identified primarily through one of two special education categories: learning disabilities or emotional or behavioral disorders. Thus, when the federal government made this shift in 1997, it was confident that very few additional students would be included in special education (U.S. Department of Education, 1999). Adding to the confusion surrounding ADHD, it is important to note that many of this condition's symptoms overlap with those of other disabilities. You will understand this condition better when you have learned how it affects the students involved.

Definition

Table 2.5 gives the IDEA '04 and the DSM-IV-TR definitions of ADHD. Perhaps the easiest to understand is the definition that the American Psychiatric Association (APA) developed for its DSM-IV-TR compilation of definitions of psychiatric conditions: ADHD "is a persistent pattern of inattention and/or hyperactivity-impulsivity that is more frequent and severe than is typically observed in individuals at a comparable level of development" (APA, 2003, p. 85). Symptoms of the condition must occur in more than one setting. The DSM-IV-TR also establishes criteria for determining whether a child has ADHD; those criteria are listed in Table 2.6. As you read this table, think about what ADHD is and what it is not.

TABLE 2.5 **Attention Deficit Hyperactivity Disorder (ADHD)**

Source	Definition
IDEA '04[1]	ADHD is listed as one condition within the "Other Health Impairments" category.* *Other health impairments* means having limited strength, vitality, or alertness, including heightened alertness to environmental stimuli that results in limited alertness with respect to the educational environment, that: (i) Is due to chronic or acute health problems such as asthma, attention deficit disorder or attention deficit hyperactivity disorder, diabetes, epilepsy, a heart condition, hemophilia, lead poisoning, leukemia, nephritis, rheumatic fever, sickle cell anemia, and Tourette syndrome; and (ii) Adversely affects a child's educational performance.
DSM-IV-TR[2]	A. Either 1 or 2 　1. Six (or more) of the following symptoms of *inattention* have persisted for at least 6 months to a degree that is maladaptive and inconsistent with developmental level: 　　*Inattention* 　　a. often fails to give close attention to details or makes careless mistakes in schoolwork, work, or other activities 　　b. often has difficulty sustaining attention in tasks or play activities 　　c. often does not seem to listen when spoken to directly 　　d. often does not follow through on instructions and fails to finish schoolwork, chores, or duties in the workplace (not due to oppositional behavior or failure to understand instructions) 　　e. often has difficulty organizing tasks and activities 　　f. often avoids dislikes, or is reluctant to engage in tasks that require sustained mental effort (such as schoolwork or homework) 　　g. often loses things necessary for tasks or activities (e.g., toys, school assignments, pencils, books, or tools) 　　h. is often easily distracted by extraneous stimuli 　　i. is often forgetful in daily activities 　2. Six (or more) of the following symptoms of *hyperactivity-impulsivity* have persisted for at least 6 months to a degree that is maladaptive and inconsistent with developmental level: 　　*Hyperactivity* 　　a. often fidgets with hands or feet or squirms in seat

Types

ADHD is a complicated condition. Students with ADHD tend to fall into three main groups:

1. Those who do not qualify for special education
2. Those who qualify for special education
3. Those who have coexisting disabilities

It is estimated that over half of all students with ADHD do *not* qualify for special education services because their condition does not seriously affect their educational performance (CHADD, 2004). Regardless, most approach learning differently from typical learners. Focusing intently on learning tasks can be difficult, and many students with ADHD tend not to be motivated. They also lack the persistence to make the extra effort to learn when it is difficult for them (Carlson

TABLE 2.5 **Continued**

Source	Definition

    b. often leaves seat in classroom or in other situations in which remaining seated is expected

    c. often runs about or climbs excessively in situations in which it is inappropriate (in adolescents or adults, may be limited to subjective feelings of restlessness)

    d. often has difficulty playing or engaging in leisure activities quietly

    e. is often "on the go" or often acts as if "driven by a motor"

    f. often talks excessively

Impulsivity

    g. often blurts out answers before questions have been completed

    h. often has difficulty awaiting turn

    i. often interrupts or intrudes on others (e.g., butts into conversations or games)

B. Some hyperactive-impulsive or inattentive symptoms that caused impairment were present before age 7 years.

C. Some impairment from the symptoms is present in two or more settings (e.g., at school, work, or home).

D. There must be clear evidence of clinically significant impairment in social, academic or occupational functioning.

E. The symptoms do not occur exclusively during the course of a Pervasive Developmental Disorder, Schizophrenia, or other Psychotic Disorder and are not better accounted for by another mental disorder (e.g., Mood Disorder, Anxiety Disorder, Dissociative Disorder, or a Personality Disorder).

Code based on type:

Attention Deficit Hyperactivity Disorder, Combined Type: if both Criteria A1 and A2 are met for the past 6 months.

Attention Deficit Hyperactivity Disorder, Predominantly Inattentive Type: if Criterion A1 is met but Criterion A2 is not met for the past 6 months.

Attention Deficit Hyperactivity Disorder, Predominantly Hyperactive-Impulsive Type: if Criterion A2 is met but Criterion A1 is not met for the past 6 months.

*Other Health Impairments, besides ADHD, are discussed in Chapter 3 of this text.

Sources: [1]*U.S. Department of Education, 2006, pp. 1263–1264*
[2]*APA, 2003, pp. 92–93*

et al., 2002). Teachers can make a real difference in the educational experience for students with ADHD by

- Providing structure to the classroom routine
- Teaching academic content directly
- Holding high expectations
- Encouraging appropriate academic and social performance

Those students with ADHD whose educational functioning is seriously affected by the condition *do* qualify for special education services. Many of these students experience problems in both academic achievement and social skills. These students' poor academic performance is often due to their distractibility and their inability to focus on assignments for long periods of time. Hyperactivity and poor social skills often lead to rejection by their peers, leaving these individuals lonely and without

TABLE 2.6 Characteristics of Attention Deficit Hyperactivity Disorder (ADHD)

Either inattention or hyperactivity-impulsivity must have persisted for at least 6 months. Either condition must be at a level that is both maladaptive and inconsistent with development and must include six (or more) of the following symptoms:

Inattention

- Often fails to give close attention to details or makes careless mistakes in school-work, work, or other activities
- Often has difficulty sustaining attention in tasks or play activities
- Often does not seem to listen when spoken to directly
- Often does not follow through on instructions and fails to finish schoolwork, chores, or duties in the workplace (not due to oppositional behavior or failure to under-stand instructions)
- Often has difficulty organizing tasks and activities
- Often avoids, dislikes, or is reluctant to engage in tasks that require sustained men-tal effort (such as schoolwork or homework)
- Often loses things necessary for tasks or activities (e.g., toys, school assignments, pencils, books, or tools)
- Is often easily distracted by extraneous stimuli
- Is often forgetful in daily activities

Hyperactivity-Impulsivity

- Often fidgets with hands or feet or squirms in seat
- Often leaves seat in classroom or in other situations in which remaining seated is expected
- Often runs about or climbs excessively in situations in which it is inappropriate (in adolescents or adults, may be limited to subjective feelings of restlessness)
- Often has difficulty playing or engaging in leisure activities quietly
- Is often "on the go" or often acts as if "driven by a motor"
- Often talks excessively
- Often blurts out answers before questions have been completed
- Often has difficulty awaiting turn
- Often interrupts or intrudes on others (e.g., butts into conversations or games)

Also, some hyperactive-impulsive or inattentive symptoms were present before age 7 years.

The symptoms must be present in two or more settings (e.g., at school [or work] and at home).

Clear evidence of clinically significant impairment in social, academic, or occupational functioning must be demonstrated.

The symptoms do not occur exclusively during the course of a pervasive developmen-tal disorder, schizophrenia, or other psychotic disorder and are not better accounted for by another mental disorder (e.g., mood disorder, anxiety disorder, disassociative disorder, or a personality disorder).

Source: Adapted with permission from *Diagnostic and Statistical Manual of Mental Disorders, Fourth Edition, Text Revision,* (Copyright 2003). (pp. 85–90). American Psychiatric Association.

friends (Bryan, 1997; Olmeda, Thomas, & Davis, 2003). They come to judge themselves as social failures and tend to engage in solitary activities (e.g., playing computer games, watching television). This situation can contribute to alienation and withdrawal.

ADHD often coexists with other disabilities, compounding the problems these individuals face (National Institute of Mental Health [NIMH], 2005). Many characteristics of ADHD overlap with other disabilities. For example, compare the characteristics of learning disabilities, found in Table 2.2, with those of ADHD, found in Table 2.6. In some cases the symptoms of ADHD are very similar to those of other disabilities, and in some cases the individuals involved have more than one disability, or have coexisting disabilities. ADHD is likely to be identified in boys with externalizing emotional or behavioral disorders (Reid et al., 2000). For example, a teenager who cannot control his reactions to highly charged situations, or who may even misread social interactions, might engage in hostile and reactive behaviors. When ADHD and antisocial behaviors both occur, the combination can be dangerous (Gresham, Lane, & Lambros, 2000). Violent behaviors tend to happen infrequently, but they also tend to be resistant to treatment. Because events do not occur at a high rate, many of these students have not qualified for special services and therefore did not receive interventions to prevent serious misbehavior. The end result of this situation can be disastrous.

ADHD is now a separate condition included in the "other health impairments" category. However, determining when it is separate, when it coexists with other disabilities, and when its characteristics are merely similar to those found in other disabling conditions can be challenging to professionals. Whether spending the time and effort to make true distinctions is important is open to debate.

Characteristics

The three main characteristics associated with ADHD are

1. Hyperactivity
2. Impulsivity
3. Inattention

The judgment about whether a certain level of a specific activity is too much, or "hyper," is often subjective, and this makes hyperactivity difficult to define. If, for example, the activity is admired, the child might be described as energetic or enthusiastic rather than hyperactive. Nevertheless, the DSM-IV-TR gives some good examples about which there is considerable consensus (APA, 2003, p. 86). Hyperactivity may be manifested by

- Fidgetiness or squirming in one's seat
- Not remaining seated when expected to do so
- Excessive running or climbing in situations where it is inappropriate
- Having difficulty playing or engaging quietly in leisure activities
- Appearing to be often "on the go" or as if "driven by a motor"
- Talking excessively

Students with ADHD, and many with learning disabilities, are said to be impulsive. Impulsivity may explain why these children are unable to focus on the relevant components of problems that need to be solved or on tasks that need to

Making a Difference

Helping a Child with ADHD Through Transitions

Kelly Wilson
Denver, Colorado

"If a child doesn't know how to read, we *teach*.

If a child doesn't know how to swim, we *teach*.

If a child doesn't know how to multiply, we *teach*.

If a child doesn't know how to drive, we *teach*.

If a child doesn't know how to behave,

we . . . . . . teach? . . . punish?

Why can't we finish the last sentence as automatically as we do the others?" Tom Herner (NASDE, president), *Counterpoint* 1998, p. 2

My beautiful son Collin, who is now 13 years old, has historically been quite a challenge. He is now the easiest of my four children—go figure. Collin has struggled with everything from wearing clothes and eating soft food, to any change in routine, such as going from the house to the car or driving on a different street. By the time Collin was preschool age (3 years old), he was diagnosed with attention deficit hyperactivity disorder (ADHD). This label, as I understood at that time, entitled him to special services and extra support in school. Given his extreme hyperactivity and tendency to throw gigantic tantrums (hitting, kicking, spitting, sometimes cursing, and always

screaming and yelling), he was placed in a specialized preschool program for children with disabilities. There were six children in his program and just as many teachers. His intense program included speech and language therapy three times a week, occupational therapy three times a week, and art/play therapy. So much expert attention—a mother's dream. I had no thoughts of inclusion; I understood and agreed that my son needed specialized help that would eventually prepare him for the public arena, and perhaps, someday, a general education setting.

Soon, however, I was getting calls from Collin's school with instructions to come pick him up and take him home because he was having a tantrum. At first they would tell me he was sick; however, by December I was merely told to take him home. The staff was pleasant and helpful and would take one of Collin's arms while I took the other so we could escort—or drag—him to my car. He and I would sit there, in the car, typically for nearly an hour, before he was calm enough to sit for our 5-minute ride home.

be learned. This characteristic may also explain why these students often disrupt the learning environment for an entire class. The third characteristic commonly observed by teachers and researchers is inattention (Mercer, 2004). Children who do not focus on the task to be learned or who pay attention to the wrong features of the task are said to be distractible. The Making a Difference feature describes one family's experience with ADHD.

Many students identified as having ADHD receive medication to control their behavior. Ritalin, Dexedrine, or Concerta does help some children with ADHD focus their attention on assigned tasks and reduce hyperactivity (Forness & Kavale, 2001). Because of its time-release feature, which relieves school personnel of the duties of distributing and monitoring the use of prescription drugs, Concerta probably will replace Ritalin as the drug of choice for schoolchildren in the near future (Newcorn, 2001). Medication, however, does not seem to have a positive effect on academic performance (Gotsch, 2002). Medication is not always necessary and should be considered a last resort, used after behavioral techniques, direct and systematic instruction evaluated on a frequent basis, and highly motivating instructional materials have proved insufficient. In these cases, a combination of behavioral and medical intervention is most powerful in the treatment of ADHD (Jensen, 2000; Pappadopulos & Jensen, 2001).

Halfway through the school year, we moved to another state. In our new school district, I was told Collin would attend the public preschool for half-day sessions four days a week. His services were grouped by a title that simply said "integrated." I was floored. How could Collin be placed in a general education classroom when he could not keep himself under control in a self-contained special education classroom? Collin's new educational team met with me about his program. After discussing our respective concerns, we decided to try the inclusive classroom for one month, during which time we would have open and constant dialog.

On the first day of preschool, Collin reacted exactly as I had expected. He screamed and kicked, clinging fiercely to me when I dropped him off at his new classroom. I was extremely upset on the ride home, letting the tears come once I was out of Collin's sight. Shortly after I arrived at home, the phone rang. It was Judy, Collin's teacher, calling to let me know Collin had settled down and was okay. She told me not to worry and that she would see me in a couple of hours. Again, I was in tears, but this time for a different reason. For the first time, I had received a phone call from school in which the message was "Collin is okay." I was so anxious to get Collin I was a half an hour early. I waited outside the door but did not hear crying; instead, I heard children playing. But then, as I entered the class-

room with the other parents, I heard the familiar sound of Collin crying and screaming. My heart sank. I figured he had probably hit teachers, perhaps pulled hair, maybe even cursed. Judy approached me and I prepared myself for the report; I was just hoping someone would help me get him to my car. Instead, Judy told me Collin had a good first day and fell apart just as they were preparing to leave. What happened next was pivotal for Collin, and for me. Instead of offering an escort, Judy proceeded to explain that Collin was breaking down at these times because he needed extra help through transitions. She asked whether I could wait for a few minutes because she did not want to send him out in a tantrum; rather, she wanted to teach him how to leave the classroom appropriately.

In the next few months, Collin made more progress than he had the whole previous year. It took one teacher to change the trajectory of my child's life. Collin had been headed down the road of exclusion, and I had been his willing and well-intentioned companion. But having witnessed the benefits of an inclusive classroom for Collin through the expertise of Judy and the multidisciplinary team, I now firmly believe that a child cannot learn how to be part of a community without being included in it. Although certain aspects of life continue to challenge Collin, he now has friends, trusted adults, and a community to assist and support him. ●

Prevalence

As we have noted, obtaining precise indications of the number of students who are affected by ADHD is impossible. First, because ADHD is not a separate disability category, the federal government does not require separate reporting (students with ADHD are included in the count of students with "other health impairments"). Second, the government does not require a count of those students with ADHD who do not qualify for special education services but receive accommodations through Section 504. Third, the government does not require the states to report students' secondary conditions or disabilities. When a student's primary disability is learning disabilities and that student's secondary disability is ADHD, the student is reported only in the learning disabilities category.

Regardless of the lack of precision, NIMH estimates that 4 percent of the school-age population in the United States has ADHD (NIMH, 2005). APA places that percentage between 3 and 7 (APA, 2003). Some studies have shown that 70 percent of children with ADHD also have a learning disability (Mayes, Calhoun, & Crowell, 2000; Pierce, 2003). In another study, parents reported that 64 percent of students with emotional or behavioral disorders also had ADHD (Wagner & Blackorby, 2004). Whether a student's ADHD is considered a primary or a secondary condition and whether it negatively influences educational performance or not, ADHD does result in special needs that can be met by perceptive and effective teachers.

Who Are Students with Mental Retardation or Intellectual and Developmental Disabilities?

For more than 50 years this disability, which is characterized by problems with cognition or intellectual functioning, has been called mental retardation. As you will learn in the following sections, this field has been in a state of transition for over 15 years. In 1992 and again in 2002, two new definitions were developed. In 2007, the name of the disability was changed from *mental retardation* to intellectual and developmental disabilities by the field's oldest professional organization, which also changed its own name to reflect the new term. The American Association on Mental Retardation (AAMR) is now the American Association on Intellectual and Developmental Disabilities (AAIDD). In part, these changes in the term and the title of the organization seek to reduce the stigma and bias often associated with this disability (Prabhala, 2007).

For some years to come, these changes may be a bit confusing. The definition supported by AAIDD was developed when this organization was called AAMR. IDEA '04 uses the term *mental retardation,* as do most states' regulations and statues. In this text, when we discuss this disability and its impact on the individuals and families involved, we have tried to balance our use of the terms *mental retardation* and *intellectual and developmental disabilities.*

People often make many incorrect assumptions about mental retardation or intellectual and developmental disabilities. First, they assume that this disability is infrequent and therefore a low incidence condition. Second, they assume that the disability is always severe. Here's what is true: Like all other disabilities or intellectual disabilities, mental retardation occurs along a continuum ranging from mild to very severe conditions. Most important, the foundation for today's special education emanates from mental retardation. Recall the famous story recounted in Chapter 1 about Victor, the young boy found in the forest of southern France by farmers in 1799. That boy became known as the Wild Boy of Aveyron, and the Parisian doctor who cared for Victor, Jean-Marc-Gaspard Itard, is acknowledged as the father of the field of special education.

Definition

In 2002, the American Association on Mental Retardation (AAMR) adopted the current definition of mental retardation, the organization's tenth since 1921. That definition and its five assumptions are found in Table 2.7. How is this modern view of mental retardation different from previous orientations? Before 1992, definitions followed a deficit model, describing the limitations of the individual, such as "significantly subaverage general intellectual functioning." Today, mental retardation is conceptualized in terms of the adaptive behavior each individual possesses and the intensity of supports (intermittent, limited, extensive, or perva-

TABLE 2.7 Mental Retardation

Source	Definition
IDEA '04[1]	*Mental retardation* means significant subaverage general intellectual functioning, existing concurrently with deficits in adaptive behavior and manifested during the developmental period, that adversely affects a child's educational performance.
American Association on Mental Retardation[2]	Mental retardation, now called intellectual and developmental disabilities, is a disability characterized by significant limitations both in intellectual functioning and in adaptive behavior as expressed in conceptual, social, and practical adaptive skills. This disability originates before age 18.

Sources: [1]*U.S. Department of Education, 2006, p. 1263*
[2]*Luckasson et al., 2002, p. 1*

sive) needed for the individual to function in the community as independently as possible (Luckasson et al., 1992, 2002; Polloway, 1997).

One key, defining feature of intellectual and developmental disabilities, or mental retardation, is that the individual has problems with *cognition,* or *intellectual functioning.* The 2002 definition includes a cautious use of IQ scores, and it is important for teachers to be wary as well, because relying on such scores leads to many mistakes and erroneous assumptions about individuals' abilities. These individuals have cognitive abilities "significantly below average," or below levels attained by 97 percent of the general population. When a standardized test is used, the individual must score at least two standard deviations below the mean for that test. Recall the discussion of the normal curve found in Chapter 1. Intelligence is regarded as one of those traits that is distributed among people in a predictable manner and reflected by a statistical distribution representing a bell-shaped curve, also called the normal curve. The majority of a population falls in the middle of the bell, at or around an intelligence quotient (IQ) score of 100, and fewer and fewer people fall at either end of the distribution, having very low or very high intelligence. IQ level is then determined by the distance a score is from the mean, or average, score.

The 2002 definition does use IQ scores as part of the determination of this disability, with a cutoff score of about 70 and below. Further, the definition is helpful because it codes intellectual abilities to express how levels of severity can affect the individual's performance:

- Mild mental retardation: IQ range of 50 to 69
  Outcomes: learning difficulties, able to work, maintain good social relationships, contribute to society
- Moderate mental retardation: IQ range of 35 to 49
  Outcomes: marked developmental delays during childhood, some degree of independence in self-care, adequate communication and academic skills, require varying degrees of support to live and work in the community
- Severe mental retardation: IQ range of 20 to 34
  Outcomes: continuous need of support

- Profound mental retardation: IQ under 20

  Outcomes: severe limitation in self-care, continence, communication, and mobility, continuous need of supports

Adaptive behavior is what everyone uses to function in daily life. "Adaptive behavior is the collection of conceptual, social, and practical skills that have been learned by people in order to function in their everyday lives" (AAMR, 2002, p. 73). People with intellectual and developmental disabilities, as well as many people without disabilities, can have difficulties with such skills that can impair their ability to function independently. Practical skills comprise adaptive behavior: eating, dressing, toileting, mobility, preparing meals, using the telephone, managing money, taking medication, and housekeeping.

Included in this definition is discussion about supports that everyone needs and uses: systems of supports. We ask our friends for advice. We form study teams before a difficult test. We expect help from city services when there is a crime or a fire. We join together for a neighborhood crime watch to help each other be safe. And we share the excitement and joys of accomplishments with family, friends, and colleagues. Supports can be offered at different intensity levels—intermittent, limited, extensive, pervasive—and can be of different types (Chadsey & Beyer, 2001; Kennedy & Horn, 2004).

- **Natural supports:** the individual's own resources, family, friends, and neighbors, as well as coworkers on the job or peers at school
- **Nonpaid supports:** neighborhood and community groups, such as clubs, recreational leagues, and private organizations
- **Generic supports:** public transportation, states' human services systems; and other agencies and services everyone has access to
- **Specialized supports:** disability-specific (e.g., special education, special early intervention services, and vocational rehabilitation) services

Types

One way to consider the types of this disability is to think about causes. Some of these conditions are genetic in origin, others are environmental, and still others are caused by an interaction of biology and the environment. Today, over 500 genetic causes of intellectual and developmental disabilities are known, and because of advances in medical research, more are being identified (The Arc, 2005). Here's an example of a condition identified in 1991 that is now recognized as the most common inherited cause. Fragile-X syndrome affects about 1 in 4,000 males and results from a chromosomal abnormality, a mutation on the X chromosome (Taylor, Richards, & Brady, 2005). The associated cognitive problems can be severe, and it is believed that some 86 percent of fragile-X-affected males have intellectual disabilities and 6 percent have autism.

Another biological example caused by a chromosomal abnormality is Down syndrome. Certain identifiable physical characteristics, such as an extra flap of skin over the innermost corner of the eye, are usually present in cases of Down syndrome. These children's degree of cognitive difficulties varies, depending in part on the speed with which the disability is identified, the adequacy of the supporting medical care, and the timing of the early intervention (National Down Syndrome Society, 2006). Individuals with Down syndrome have a higher prevalence of obesity, despite typically consuming fewer calories (Roizen, 2001). Possibly these individuals' reduced food consumption explains why they are less active than their brothers and sisters and less likely to spend time outdoors. In turn, their opportunities for satisfying friendships, social outlets, and recreation are reduced. Teachers can help by encouraging these individuals to be more active and to play sports with their peers during recess.

In the hereditary condition phenylketonuria (PKU), a person is unable to metabolize phenylalanine, which builds up in the body to toxic levels that damage the brain. If untreated, PKU eventually causes intellectual disabilities. Changes in diet (eliminating certain foods that contain this amino acid, such as milk) can control PKU and reduce the impact of the condition. Because of the devastating effects of PKU, it is critical that the diet of these individuals be strictly controlled. Here, then, is a condition rooted in genetics but brought on by the environment—by ingesting milk. Prompt diagnosis and parental vigilance are crucial to minimizing the associated problems. Teachers can help by monitoring these students' diet and ensuring that snacks and treats provided by classmates' parents do not include milk products that might be harmful. Now let's look at some toxins that do not have a hereditary link.

One well-recognized nonhereditary type of birth defect, considered by Congress as the most common and preventable cause of intellectual and developmental disabilities, is fetal alcohol syndrome (FAS) (U.S. Senate Appropriations Committee, 2004). This condition results from the mother drinking alcohol during pregnancy (The Arc, 2005). The average IQ of people with FAS is 79, very close to the cutoff score for mental retardation. In addition, this group's average adaptive behavior score is 61, indicating a strong need for supports. These data explain why about 58 percent of individuals with FAS have mental retardation and why about 94 percent require supplemental assistance at school. Unfortunately, most of these people are not free of other problems in the areas of attention, verbal learning, and self-control (Centers for Disease Control, 2004). Estimates are that some 5,000 babies with FAS are born each year, and an additional 50,000 show symptoms of the less serious condition fetal alcohol effects (FAE) (Davis & Davis, 2003).

Characteristics

According to AAMR, the three defining characteristics of intellectual and developmental disabilities are

1. Problems with cognition
2. Problems with adaptive behavior
3. Need for supports to sustain independence

Impaired cognitive ability has pervasive effects, whether the disability is mild or severe. It makes simple tasks difficult to learn. Learning new skills, storing and retrieving information (memory), and transferring knowledge to either new situations or slightly different skills are challenges for these individuals. Short- and long-term memory are often impaired, making it hard for these students to remember events or the proper sequence of events, particularly when the events are not clearly identified as important. Even when something is remembered, it may be remembered incorrectly, inefficiently, too slowly, or not in adequate detail. Teachers can help students with memory problems develop memory strategies and learn to compensate by having them create picture notebooks that lay out the sequence of steps in a task that needs to be performed, elements of a job that needs to be done, or a checklist of things to do before leaving the house.

Adaptive behavior comprises the skills one uses to live independently, and through direct instruction and the delivery of supports, adaptive behavior can improve. However, for these gains to happen, it is sometimes necessary for students to receive a separate curriculum that targets life skills. When goals for independent living become the target of instruction, it is not uncommon for the student to have reduced access to the general education curriculum and typically learning classmates.

Making friends has received considerable attention during the last decade, because friends are natural supports and sources of social interactions (AAMR, 2002). Attention has been directed at the development of friendships between people with and people without disabilities. Research findings show that children of elementary school age with and without intellectual disabilities can become real friends who play together, express positive feelings for each other, and respond to each other reciprocally (Freeman & Kasari, 2002). However, as children get older, the odds of real friendships developing between typical students and classmates with disabilities seem to diminish (Hughes & Carter, 2006). During middle school, for example, children without disabilities tend to form friendships with others of similar backgrounds (e.g., age, gender) and interests. Inclusion and friendships between individuals with and without disabilities have benefits beyond those that help the people with disabilities. The attitudes of individuals who attend school alongside students with disabilities are more positive attitudes and reflect a better understanding of the challenges that people with disabilities will face throughout their lives (Hughes & Carter, 2006; Kennedy & Horn, 2004).

Prevalence

According to the federal government, almost 1 percent (that is, not quite 1 out of every 100) of our nation's students between the ages of 6 and 17 are identified and served as having mental retardation as their primary disabling condition through IDEA '04 (OSEP, 2006). During the 2005 school year, some 473,888 children with mental retardation were served across the country. Most students with mental retardation function at high levels and need few supports. In other words, most fall into the mild range.

Who Are Students with Emotional or Behavioral Disorders?

The emotional or behavioral disorders category is the last of the high incidence special education categories. Emotional or behavioral disorders (EBD) are very worrisome, because the connections between this disability and the criminal justice system, violence against self or others, and a life of unhappiness are well recognized (Smith & Lane, 2007; Walker, Ramsey, & Grisham, 2004). There is clear evidence that early intervention makes a real difference in the lives of these individuals. Unfortunately, such services are not delivered often enough to those who exhibit signs of troubling behaviors (Lane, 2004). Let's look more closely at this last high incidence condition.

Definition

Emotional or behavioral disorders are difficult to define. In fact, some think that people are identified as having this disability "whenever an adult authority said so" (Hallahan & Kauffman, 2000, p. 249). In other words, in many cases the application of the definition is subjective. In Table 2.8, IDEA '04 uses the term *emotional disturbance* to describe children whom we refer to as having behavioral or emotional disorders. Remember that this condition is expressed

TABLE 2.8 Emotional or Behavioral Disorders

Source	Definition
IDEA '04[1]	*Emotional disturbance* means a condition exhibiting one or more of the following characteristics over a long period of time and to a marked degree that adversely affects a child's educational performance:
	• An inability to learn that cannot be explained by intellectual, sensory, or health factors.
	• An inability to build or maintain satisfactory interpersonal relationships with peers and teachers.
	• Inappropriate types of behavior or feelings under normal circumstances.
	• A general pervasive mood of unhappiness or depression.
	• A tendency to develop physical symptoms related to fears associated with personal or school problems.
	Emotional disturbance includes schizophrenia. The term does not apply to children who are socially maladjusted, unless it is determined that they have an emotional disturbance.
National Mental Health and Special Education Coalition[2]	The term *emotional or behavioral disorder* means a disability characterized by behavioral or emotional responses in school so different from appropriate age, cultural, or ethnic norms that they adversely affect educational performance. Educational performance includes academic, social, vocational, and personal skills. Such a disability
	• Is more than a temporary, expected response to stressful events in the environment;
	• Is consistently exhibited in two different settings, at least one of which is school-related; and
	• Is unresponsive to direct intervention in general education, or the child's condition is such that general education interventions would be insufficient.
	Emotional or behavioral disorders can coexist with other disabilities. This category may include children or youths with schizophrenic disorders, affective disorders, anxiety disorder, or other sustained disorders of conduct or adjustment when they adversely affect educational performance . . . .

Sources: [1]*U.S. Department of Education, 2006, p. 1262*
[2]*Forness & Knitzer, 1992, p. 13*

over a long period of time, is obvious to many observers, and adversely affects educational performance.

Types

Emotional or behavioral disorders can be divided into three groups:

1. Externalizing
2. Internalizing
3. Low incidence

Students who exhibit externalizing and internalizing behaviors, respectively, are the two main groups of students with emotional or behavioral disorders, but they do not account for all of the conditions that result in placement in this special education category. Externalizing behaviors are characterized by an under-controlled, acting-out style that includes behaviors that could be described as aggressive, arguing, impulsive, coercive, and noncompliant. Externalizing behaviors include aggressive behaviors expressed outwardly, usually toward other persons. These behaviors generally involve some form of hyperactivity, including a high level of irritating behavior that is impulsive and distractible, and persistent aggression. Many of these youngsters engage in bullying and victimize their classmates (Hartung & Scambler, 2006). Table 2.9 provides some examples of externalizing behavior problems. Young children who have serious challenging behaviors that persist are the most likely to be referred for psychiatric services (Maag, 2000). A pattern of early aggressive acts, beginning with annoying and bullying, followed by physical fighting, is a clear pathway, particularly for boys, to violence in late adolescence (Archwamety & Katsiyannis, 2000; Walker & Sprague, 1999). While still in high school, students with emotional or behavioral disorders are 13 times more likely to be arrested than other students with disabilities (Office of Special Education Programs [OSEP], 2001). Some 30 to 50 percent of youth in correctional facilities are individuals with disabilities, and almost half of those have emotional or behavioral disorders (IDEA Practices, 2002).

Internalizing behaviors, the second type of emotional or behavioral disorders, are characterized by an overcontrolled and inhibited style that includes behaviors

TABLE 2.9 Examples of Externalizing Behaviors

• Violates basic rights of others	• Violates societal norms or rules
• Has tantrums	• Steals, causes property loss or damage
• Is hostile or defiant, argues	• Uses lewd or obscene gestures
• Ignores teachers' reprimands	• Is physically aggressive
• Causes or threatens physical harm to people or animals	• Demonstrates obsessive compulsive behavior
• Intimidates, threatens	• Is hyperactive

that could be described as withdrawn, lonely, depressed, and anxious (Kauffman, 2005). Anorexia or bulimia, depression, and anxiety are examples of internalizing behaviors. Anorexia and bulimia are serious eating disorders that usually occur during students' teenage years (Manley, Rickson, & Standeven, 2000). These disorders arise because of individuals' (typically girls') preoccupation with weight and body image, their drive for thinness, and their fear of becoming fat. Often hard to recognize in children, depression includes components such as guilt, self-blame, feelings of rejection, lethargy, low self-esteem, and negative self-image. Children's behavior when they are depressed may appear so different from the depressed behavior of adults that teachers and parents may have difficulty recognizing the depression. Even so, a severely depressed child might try to harm her- or himself. Anxiety disorders may be demonstrated as intense response upon separation from family, friends, or a familiar environment, as excessive shrinking from contact with strangers, or as unfocused, excessive worry and fear.

Additional low incidence conditions are included in the category of emotional or behavioral disorders. Some of these disorders are very rare but are quite serious when they do occur. For example, schizophrenia is an extremely rare disorder in children, although approximately 1 percent of the general population over the age of 18 has been diagnosed as having schizophrenia. When it occurs, it places great demands on service systems. It usually involves bizarre delusions (such as believing one's thoughts are controlled by the police), hallucinations (such as voices telling one what to think), "loosening" of associations (disconnected thoughts), and incoherence. Children with schizophrenia have serious difficulties with schoolwork and often must live in special hospital and educational settings during part of their childhood. It is important to remember that emotional or behavioral disorders include many different specific conditions, including many that are themselves low incidence conditions but still are part of this high incidence category.

Characteristics

Possibly more than any other group of children with disabilities, students with emotional or behavioral disorders present problems with social skills to themselves, their families, their peers, and their teachers (Kauffman, 2005; Wagner & Backorby, 2004). Social skills are the foundation for practically all human activities in all contexts (academic, personal, vocational, and community). We use social skills to interact with others and to perform most daily tasks, but social skills is the major problem area for these individuals. One related characteristic, antisocial behavior, seems to be a prime reason for these students' referrals to special education (OSEP, 2001). Antisocial behavior includes impulsivity and poor interpersonal skills with both peers and adults. These students' behavior patterns can be self-defeating, impairing their interactions with others in many negative ways. Some students with externalizing problems are prone to what Frank Gresham of Louisiana State University and his colleagues call "behavioral earthquakes"—behaviors that occur rarely but are extreme, such as setting fires, being cruel to others, abusing animals, and assaulting adults. Most students with externalizing behavioral disorders exhibit at least some of the following behaviors *in excess:*

- Tantrums
- Aggression
- Noncompliance
- Coercive behaviors
- Poor academic performance

● Emotional or behavioral disorders are difficult to define. Important features of the condition are that it is expressed over a long period of time, is obvious to many observers, and adversely affects educational performance.

On the other hand, students with internalizing patterns tend to exhibit behaviors that reflect

- Depression
- Withdrawal
- Anxiety

Fortunately, intervention can make a difference and improve the outcomes for students with externalizing or internalizing behaviors. For example, instruction in social skills can positively influence the development of social competence (Bullis, Walker, & Sprague, 2001). But such instruction and the use of positive discipline techniques should be initiated no later than first grade (Frey, Hirschstein, & Guzzo, 2000). Effective instruction is embedded within the general education curriculum and includes considerable demonstration and practice. Peers learn to help and provide support for each other, but getting peers to help these classmates can be challenging, because classmates of students with emotional or behavioral disorders tend to reject them (Bullis, Walker, & Sprague 2001).

At the beginning of this chapter, we noted that *all* students identified through IDEA '04 as having a disability have problems with their educational performance. Here, too, even though emotional or behavioral disorders have their roots in social behaviors, the condition negatively affects academic performance. Regardless of intellectual potential, students with emotional or behavioral disorders typically do not perform well academically (Lane & Wehby, 2002; Walker & Blackorby, 2004). Clearly, being in personal turmoil affects one's ability to attend to school tasks and to learning in general. Failure at academic tasks compounds the difficulties these children face not only at school but also in life. Their frustration with the educational system, along with its frustration with them, results in these students having the highest dropout rates of all students (NCES, 2005). The outcomes of students who do not complete high school are not good. There is also evidence that when students are engaged in academic work, their disruptive behaviors decrease (Lane, 2004). Thus, in addition to helping these students with their behavior, it is helpful for teachers to address their academic skills.

Prevalence

The federal government reports that slightly less than 1 percent of all school-children have emotional or behavioral disorders, with some 443,107 students between the ages of 6 and 17 identified with this disability (OSEP, 2006). However, it is likely that these figures substantially underestimate the prevalence of these problems. Why might this be so? First, the definition is unclear and subjective. Second, because the label is so stigmatizing, many educators and school districts are reluctant to identify many children. Some believe that the actual prevalence should be approximately 3 to 6 percent of all students (Kauffman, 2005; Walker et al., 2001). Important factors in prevalence for this group of learners are gender and race.

Clear differences show up in the identification of this disability: Most children (about 74 percent) identified as having emotional or behavioral disorders are male, and this is the highest ratio of boys to girls in all special education categories. The reason for this gender difference is not clear, but it is probably linked to boys' higher propensity to be troublesome and violate school rules, coupled with girls' tendency toward less disruptive, internalizing behaviors that are less likely to result in referral. Whereas Asian American and Hispanic students tend to be underrepresented in this special education category, African Americans are overrepresented: 29 percent of students identified as having emotional or behavioral disorders are Black, even though Blacks represent only about 14 percent of the student population (OSEP, 2006).

• s u m m a r y

The notion that the vast majority of the nation's students are typical learners is inaccurate. The special needs that many students present to their teachers and schools are considerable and varied. Students with disabilities are guaranteed an appropriate and individualized education, tailored to each of their exceptional learning needs, through IDEA. Other students with special needs are entitled to accommodations through Section 504. And many others require a special response to their unique learning challenges so that they can reach their potential and profit maximally from school.

Certainly, special needs arise from disabilities, but they come from a variety of other sources as well. Special learning needs result from conditions that are not disabilities but that still present considerable learning challenges and put students at risk for school failure, dropping out, or underachievement. What you should now understand is that the majority of America's students present an exciting mixture of learning strengths to each classroom situation.

• self-test QUESTIONS

Let's review the learning objectives for this chapter. If you are uncertain and cannot "talk through" the answers provided for any of these questions, reread those sections of the text.

- **Who are students with special needs?**

  Students with special needs are at great risk for school failure and underachievement. They come from many different groups of learners: those with disabilities, those who receive supports and accommodations through Section 504 of the Rehabilitation Act, diverse students, and those with other very special needs (e.g., gifted learners, those who are poor).

- **Why do students with special needs constitute a group larger than the group of students with disabilities?**

  Students with special needs represent the majority of students because they include many different learners. For example, all students with disabilities present unique learning styles and varying abilities. Unique learning styles and abilities result from many different situations beyond disabilities. All special needs demand unique responses so that students' results are optimal.

- **What are the three systems often used to organize disabilities and schoolchildren?**

  One approach, the categorical approach, uses special education labels (e.g., learning disabilities, speech or language impairments). Another focuses on the severity of the disability and is referred to as the noncategorical approach. The third system divides students into two general groups by the disability's prevalence (i.e., high incidence and low incidence).

- **What is meant by "high incidence disabilities," and which disabilities or conditions are included in this group?**

  The largest special education category is *learning disabilities,* which can be severe, complex, pervasive, and life-long. Learning disabilities are characterized as "unexpected underachievement" and as "resistant to treatment."

Problems with reading and writing are the most common.

Speech or language impairments result in problems with communication, language, and/or speech. Speech impairments include articulation problems, fluency problems (stuttering), and voice problems. Language impairments are not the same as language differences, and their prevalence changes by age (the number lessens across the school years).

Attention deficit hyperactivity disorder (ADHD) is a condition included in the IDEA '04 category of "other health impairments." Behaviors associated with ADHD (e.g., distractibility, hyperactivity) are also symptomatic of other disabilities, such as learning disabilities and emotional or behavioral disorders. About half of individuals with this condition are eligible for special education because their educational performance is adversely affected by the condition; most of the other students with ADHD receive supports and accommodations through Section 504.

Mental retardation (the term used in IDEA '04), or *intellectual and developmental disabilities* (the AAIDD term), result in problems with intellectual functioning, adaptive behavior, and independence. Responses to mental retardation include different intensities of supports (i.e., intermittent, limited, extensive, pervasive) and different types of supports (i.e., natural supports, nonpaid supports, generic supports, specialized supports).

Emotional or behavioral disorders can be externalizing (aggressive, argumentative, impulsive, coercive, noncompliant), internalizing (overcontrolled, inhibited, withdrawn, lonely, depressed, anxious), or low incidence (e.g., schizophrenia, Tourette syndrome). Internalizing behaviors (such as anorexia, bulimia, depression, anxiety) are less frequently identified early, and externalizing behavior disorders are highly associated with delinquency. Early intervention is both important and effective.

● Revisit the
OPENING c h a l l e n g e

Check your answers to the Reflection Questions from the Opening Challenge and revise them on the basis of what you have learned.

1. Do you think identifying students by specific disability is useful?

2. Why do you think Darren's special education label is being reconsidered at this point in his schooling?

3. Is Darren's situation unusual? Why or why not?

4. Will a change in category influence the way Miss Clarkson teaches Darren?

5. Will it change the services he receives?

Professional Standards and Licensure

CEC Knowledge and Skill Core Standard and Associated Subcategories

CEC Content Standard 2: Development and Characteristics of Learners

Special educators know and demonstrate respect for their students first as unique human beings. Special educators understand the similarities and differences in human development and the characteristics between and among individuals with and without ELN. Moreover, special educators understand how exceptional conditions can interact with the domains of human development, and they use this knowledge to respond to the varying abilities and behaviors of individuals with ELN.

CEC Content Standard 3

Special educators understand the effects that an exceptional condition can have on an individual's learning in school and throughout life. They understand the similarities and differences in human development and the characteristics between and among individuals with and without ELN.

CEC Content Standard 9

Special educators are guided by the profession's ethical and professional practice standards. They practice in multiple roles and complex situations across wide age and developmental ranges. Special educators are aware of how their own and others' attitudes, behaviors, and ways of communicating can influence their practice.

INTASC Core Principle and Associated Special Education Subcategories

1. Subject Matter

1.03 All teachers understand that students with disabilities may need accommodations, modifications, and/or adaptations to the general curriculum.

2. Student Learning

2.01 All teachers have a sound understanding of physical, social, emotional, and cognitive development. They are familiar with the general characteristics of the most frequently occurring disabilities and have a basic understanding of the ways that disabilities impact learning.

2.03 All teachers recognize that students with disabilities vary in their approaches to learning depending on factors such as the nature of their disability, their level of knowledge and functioning, and life experiences.

3. Learner Differences

3.04 All teachers understand and are sensitive to cultural, ethnic, gender, and linguistic differences that may be confused with or misinterpreted as manifestations of disability.

9. Teacher Reflection

9.04 All teachers reflect on the potential interaction between students' cultural experiences and their disabilities.

Praxis II: Education of
Exceptional Students:
Core Content Knowledge PRAXIS

I. Understanding Exceptionalities

Human development and behavior as related to students
with disabilities, including

- Social and emotional development and
  behavior.
- Language development and behavior.
- Cognition.
- Physical development, including motor and
  sensory.

Characteristics of students with disabilities, including the influence of

- Cognitive factors.
- Affective and social-adaptive factors, including cultural, linguistic, gender, and socioeconomic factors.
- Genetic, medical, motor, sensory, and chronological age
  factors.

Basic concepts in special education, including

- Attention deficit hyperactivity disorder, as well as the inci-
  dence and prevalence of various types of disabilities.
- The causation and prevention of disability.
- The nature of behaviors, including frequency, duration, in-
  tensity, and degrees of severity.
- The classification of students with disabilities.

Video—"Learning Disabilities"

Bridget is a teenager who has been identified as having a learning disability. In this video
clip, she talks about how she deals with other people's perceptions of her disability and
about how their perceptions affect her.

Log onto **www.mylabschool.com**. Under the
Courses tab, in **Special Education**, go to the
video lab. Access the **"Learning Disabilities
and Attention Deficit Hyperactivity
Disorder"** videos and watch the **"Learning
Disabilities"** video.

Use the **www.mylabschool.com Assignment
Finder** to go directly to these videos. Just enter
Assignment ID **SPV7**.

1. In what ways does the description of Bridget's strengths and weaknesses at school fit
   with or diverge from the criteria for learning disabilities that you discovered in Chapter
   2 and/or in your own experience teaching students who struggle with reading?
2. What characteristics did Bridget possess that helped her to succeed in general education classrooms?

Video—"Mental Retardation"

Carlyn is a preschooler with mental retardation. She attends a school where she is included with regular education students. Her parents discuss her progress since birth and her acceptance by peers and family.

Log onto **www.mylabschool.com**. Under the **Courses** tab, in **Special Education**, go to the **video lab**. Access the "**Mental Retardation**" videos and watch the "**Mental Retardation**" video.

 OR

Use the **www.mylabschool.com** **Assignment Finder** to go directly to these videos. Just enter Assignment ID **SPV8**.

1. What skills is Carlyn working on in her preschool classroom?
2. Describe the benefits as well as the struggles of having Carlyn integrated into an inclusive classroom.
3. Do you think the gains her teacher described can be attributed to her placement in an inclusive classroom? Why or why not?

Case Study—"He Just Needs a Little Discipline"

Matt was diagnosed with attention deficit hyperactivity disorder when he was in second grade. By eighth grade he was having frequent outbursts in school. Matt recently confided in one of his teachers that he thought he could focus better if he could go back on Ritalin. The school and Matt's family struggle to find ways to help him succeed at school.

Log onto **www.mylabschool.com**. Under the **Resourses** tab, navigate to the **Case Archive** and read "**He Just Needs a Little Discipline.**"

 OR

Use the **www.mylabschool.com** **Assignment Finder** to go directly to this case study. Just enter Assignment ID **CS11**.

1. Which features of ADHD does Matt exhibit (hyperactivity, impulsivity, inattention)? Provide examples of his behavior to support your answer.
2. If Matt does not go back on medication, list several strategies that you could try to improve his difficult behavior in the classroom.

 To access chapter objectives, practice tests, weblinks, and flashcards, go to the companion website at **www.ablongman.com/bryantsmith1e**.

Understanding Learners with Special Needs
Low Incidence Disabilities or Conditions

chapter **3**

chapter **OBJECTIVES**

After studying this chapter, you will have the knowledge to answer the following questions:

- What is meant by "low incidence disabilities"?
- What are the key features of each low incidence disability?
- Why did IDEA '04 include the special education category "developmental delay"?
- What are some characteristics commonly observed in students with low incidence disabilities?

• OPENING challenge

Ms. Simpkin's New Student

Ms. Simpkin has been teaching general education classes for 10 years. She has successfully included many students with disabilities in her classes and has had great experience working with many special education teachers and related service experts. She has team-taught with special education teachers. Ms. Simpkin has had related service specialists work with students in her classroom so they can better demonstrate effective techniques and also promote generalization.

She has just received a letter from the district office informing her that she is to receive a new student next week. The letter described her new student, Josh, as a student with "low incidence disabilities." She can't remember from her studies in graduate school what that term really means. Her principal has scheduled a meeting with her tomorrow afternoon to discuss this new student. She wants to make sure she plans for Josh's learning and behavioral needs, but she's not sure what considerations she should be thinking about. She decides to review her old textbooks and make a list of questions to ask the principal about Josh. She re-

flects on several questions about her new student, *"What does low incidence mean? What services will Josh need? Am I prepared to work with Josh to address his needs? How can I help my other students accept Josh?"*

• Reflection Questions

In your journal, write down your answers to the following questions. After completing the chapter, check your answers and revise them on the basis of what you have learned.

1. Do you think Ms. Simpkin will need to plan for her new student differently than she has for other students with disabilities? If so, in what ways? If not, why not?

2. What learning characteristics might she have to consider as she makes initial plans for Josh?

3. How might her plans vary after she learns what disabilities Josh has?

4. What topics in her old education textbooks should she review before her meeting with the principal?

5. Provide Ms. Simpkin with five questions or issues she should discuss with her principal.

*I*n Chapter 2 you learned about disabilities that are considered high incidence. Those are the disabilities that are most common, and over 90 percent of all students with disabilities are eligible for special education services through those categories (OSEP, 2006). Low incidence disabilities, by contrast, are just that: They don't occur very frequently. While disabilities affect more than 11 percent of all students between the ages of 6 and 17, low incidence disabilities affect slightly more than 1 percent of all schoolchildren. IDEA '04 calls out nine special education categories that the federal government defines as low incidence disabilities (U.S. Department of Education, 2006). Figure 3.1 illustrates prevalence rates across these special education categories. Note that only "other health impairments," which includes attention deficit hyperactivity disorder (ADHD), affects more than 1 percent of all students.

Who Are Students with Low Incidence Conditions?

Low incidence disabilities share some common features. One such feature is related to prevalence. Not only are these disabilities as a group infrequent in their occurrence, but for three out of the nine low incidence special education categories, their prevalence has remained fairly consistent across the years, increasing much as the general student population does. The exceptions are health impairments, autism or autism spectrum disorders, and developmental delay. We will have more to say about specific reasons for these increases in the following sections of this chapter, but it is important to understand that some changes in prevalence reflect modifications to definitions, allowing more students to be included in the category. You learned of one example of this in Chapter 2 when you studied ADHD, a condition included in the IDEA '04 category of other health impairments.

FIGURE 3.1 **Prevalence of Each Low Incidence Disability**

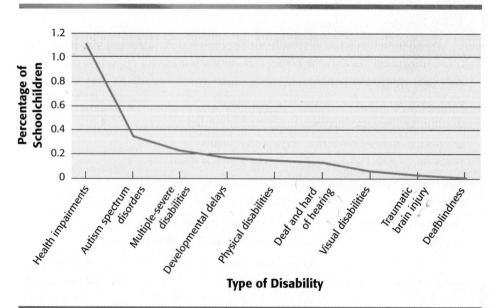

A second common feature of low incidence disabilities involves people's typical, but inaccurate, perceptions about each of these disability categories. Many people assume that if a condition or disability is not common, it must automatically lead to severe problems. In fact, most of these disabilities range in severity from mild to severe (e.g., visual disabilities, hearing problems). Some individuals with low incidence disabilities, like those with some physical problems, do not even qualify for special education because their disability does not negatively affect their educational performance. Of course, some low incidence disabilities do always result in very serious challenges. The conditions classified as multiple-severe disabilities are obvious examples.

No disability should be minimized—they are all serious—but many low incidence disabilities do tend to require an intensive response. When negative assumptions are not permitted and are paired with high expectations and effective interventions, the outcomes can be remarkable. Let's think about a few examples. Possibly the most famous person to have struggled with deafblindness is Helen Keller. Keller was a woman of many accomplishments, but none of her achievements, which included graduating from Radcliffe with honors in 1904, would have occurred without the intensive, pervasive, and sustained supports and interventions she received from her teacher, Anne Sullivan, and her family (Keller, 1988). Today, stories like Helen Keller's are more commonplace. For example, Erik Weihenmayer, a blind climbing enthusiast, scaled Mt. Everest; Marla Ruyan, also blind, qualified for the 2004 Summer Olympics to compete in the 5000-meter run in Greece. Brooke Ellison, paralyzed from the neck down after a car accident, graduated with a bachelor's degree from Harvard with honors and thereafter earned a master's degree in public policy (Ellison, 2002). And Mark Singer, a student with multiple-severe disabilities (his being cerebral palsy and significant hearing problems), graduated from high school and passed his state's competency exams. These folks aren't heroes, they are individuals striving, like most of us, to do the best they possibly can. The clear and single message from these and so many people with low incidence disabilities is that one must never make assumptions about what any individual can accomplish, even if her or his aspirations seem unrealistic.

The third feature commonly associated with these disabilities is that they tend to be more visible or readily observed than high incidence disabilities. What do we mean? Well, nonexperts can usually identify a middle school student who is blind in a relatively short period of time. Classmates know which one of them has a physical disability almost immediately. The same quick recognition of a peer with learning disabilities might not be as common.

The fourth common characteristic related to low incidence disabilities is that you, as a teacher, will probably not teach many students with these conditions during your career. Both the nature of these disabilities and their relatively low prevalence are the reasons. Many children with these disabilities require substantial and intensive special education services and supports outside of the general education classroom. Thus they are few in number and tend to be included in general education classes less frequently than students with high incidence disabilities (OSEP, 2006). Compare the rates of inclusion for those with high and with low incidence disabilities by studying Figure 3.2. You will see that 54 percent of students with learning disabilities (up from 45 percent 3 years prior) received at least 80 percent of their education in general education classes, but only 13 percent of students with multiple-severe disabilities participated in general education classes at that level (OSEP, 2006; U.S. Department of Education, 2002). As you think about these rates of inclusion, remember that nearly all students with ADHD are included in general education classes for much more than 80 percent of the school day. Imagine what these data would look like if the "other health

FIGURE 3.2 Inclusion of Students with High and Low Incidence Disabilities

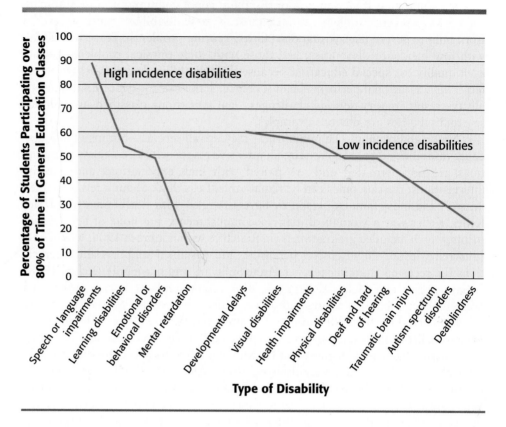

impairments" category did not include ADHD. We believe that the participation rates of students with fragile health are fairly low, possibly as low as 25 percent. Of course, because data about specific conditions contained within a special education category are not reported to the federal government, we can only hypothesize about what the actual facts might be.

Each low incidence disability is unique and presents an array of special needs to those involved. Teachers who understand these conditions make important differences in the lives of these students and their families. Let's think about each of them in the order of their prevalence.

Who Are Students with Health Impairments or Special Health Care Needs?

In Chapter 2, along with discussing other high incidence conditions, we talked about one condition, ADHD, that IDEA '04 includes within the other health impairments category. As we mentioned, a little more than 10 years ago the federal government, during one of its reauthorizations of IDEA (this law is typically reauthorized every 5 years), called out ADHD as one condition in the other health impairments category. Before then, this category was very small, representing some 2 percent of students with disabilities and less than 0.1 percent of all students

(U.S. Department of Education, 1996). We are confident that the disproportionately larger size of this previously "low incidence" category is due to the inclusion of students with ADHD. We have already discussed those students' special needs; in this section, we talk about students with other conditions that are included in the "other health impairments" category. But first, we want to mention several other general issues related to this special education category.

The other health impairments or special health care needs category has an interesting history. It seems to be the birthplace of future special education categories. What do we mean by "birthplace" of categories? In 1990, autism became its own special education category, but before then it was part of the health impairments definition. Today ADHD is called out in the health impairments category, even though it does not seem to share many characteristics with other such conditions. Despite the fact that the APA, in its DSM-IV-TR, considers Tourette syndrome a psychiatric condition, IDEA '04 lists it under "other health impairments" (APA, 2003). So it is important to understand that conditions included in this disability category might not always be predictable.

IDEA '04 separates health problems and physical problems into two different categories; however, these two disabilities often overlap and occur in combination. For example, some individuals with cerebral palsy also have fragile health. Also, like their counterparts with physical disabilities, many students with other health impairments or special health care needs do not need or qualify for special education services, yet they do require accommodations because of their fragile situations. For a listing of illnesses and diseases that often result in special health care needs, see Figure 3.3. And on a final general note, IDEA '04 calls this special education category "other health impairments," but

FIGURE 3.3 An Organizational Scheme for Special Health Care Needs

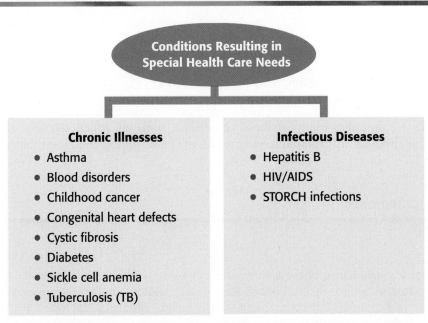

This diagram lists and categorizes the conditions, illnesses, and diseases that can result in special health care needs in children.

we prefer to refer to it as "special health care needs." Many parents and professionals use that term because it better reflects these students' situations.

Definition

The federal government uses the term "other health impairments" to describe, collectively, conditions and diseases that create special health care needs for children. The IDEA '04 definition is given in Table 3.1. Note that many specific health conditions are called out in this federal definition, but also remember that many other conditions—such as blood conditions, cancer, cystic fibrosis, tuberculosis, and STORCH infections (e.g., hepatitis B, herpes, rubella, cytomegalovirus or CMV)—are also included.

For many years the term medically fragile was used to describe all children with special health care needs, but it is now more selectively applied. Medically fragile is a status; it is not assigned to any specific condition but, rather, reflects the individual's health situation. Students can move in and out of fragile status. It is important to understand that because of advances in medical technology, a greater number of medically fragile children survive health crises. In the past, many of these youngsters would not have lived long enough to go to school. Others would have been too sick to attend their neighborhood schools and would have received most of their schooling through hospital-based or home-based instruction with itinerant teachers. Even though many are now stable enough to attend school, they require ongoing medical management. For most, it is necessary for teachers to be familiar with procedures that must be followed if an emergency occurs. The "if, thens" must be carefully outlined and planned in collaboration with doctors and the school's medical professional. Although the contingencies for the "worst case scenarios" must be arranged, in most cases the accommodations required for these children are not terribly dramatic. (However, not having backup power for a child's ventilator could have disastrous results.)

Types

In general, there are two major groups of students with special health care needs:

1. Those with chronic illness
2. Those with infectious diseases

Table 3.2 describes many of these conditions, some of which are very rarely seen in children. All children have episodes of illness during childhood, but most

TABLE 3.1 Health Impairments

Source	Definition
IDEA '04	*Other health impairment* means having limited strength, vitality or alertness, including a heightened alertness to environmental stimuli that results in limited alertness with respect to the educational environment, that is due to chronic or acute health problems such as asthma, attention deficit hyperactivity disorder, diabetes, epilepsy, a heart condition, hemophilia, lead poisoning, leukemia, nephritis, rheumatic fever, and sickle cell anemia; and adversely affects a child's educational performance.

Source: U.S. Department of Education, 2006, p. 1263

TABLE 3.2 Types of Health Conditions

Condition	Description
Chronic Illnesses	
Asthma	*Asthma,* a condition caused by narrowing of the airways accompanied by inflammatory changes in the lining of the airways, may result in severe difficulty in breathing with chronic coughing. Health care needs include appropriate medications, environmental modifications, and monitoring and frequently result in no limitation of activities.
Cystic fibrosis	*Cystic fibrosis* is a genetic birth defect that results in chronic lung infections and digestive difficulties. Health care interventions include aggressive care of lung infections and function and replacement of required enzymes for aiding digestion.
Diabetes	*Diabetes* is the loss of the ability of the pancreas to produce enough insulin, resulting in problems with sugar metabolism. Health care needs include the monitoring of blood sugar levels, appropriate diet and exercise regimens, and knowledgeable response for insulin reactions.
Congenital heart defects	*Congenital heart conditions* can result in high rates of school absences for specialized health care. Most have had surgical intervention and medical monitoring by specialists. Health care needs include taking medications during the school day.
Tuberculosis (TB)	*Tuberculosis,* a disease caused by bacterial infection, rarely causes severe disease in children older than infancy. Most often the bacteria remain sequestered and harmless until late adulthood or when the body's immune system fails. The rates of infection are on the rise in many parts of the United States.
Childhood cancer	*Cancer,* the abnormal growth of cells, can affect any organ. The most common types of cancer in children are leukemia and lymphomas. While going through treatment, children may feel too ill to profit from classroom instruction.
	Leukemia causes an abnormal increase in the white blood cells, which are important in the body's defenses against infection. It often results in anemia and enlargement of the lymph glands, spleen, and liver.
	Lymphomas are malignant and cause enlargement of the lymph nodes.
Blood disorders	*Hemophilia,* a genetic condition typically linked with males, is characterized by poor blood clotting, which can result in massive bleeding from cuts and internal hemorrhaging from bruises.
	Sickle cell anemia, a hereditary disorder, causes a distortion in the red blood cells that restricts their passage through the blood vessels.
Infectious Diseases	
HIV and AIDS	*Human immunodeficiency virus (HIV),* a potentially fatal viral infection that in school-age children results from transmission from a mother infected with the virus to her newborn child or from transfusion with blood or blood products carrying the virus, causes *acquired immunodeficiency syndrome (AIDS).* Health care needs include careful monitoring of general health, specialists to care for potentially overwhelming lung infections, and medications that slow or cure infections. The infection is acquired primarily through the exchange of body fluids in older children, through sexual abuse in younger children, through sexual activity in adolescents, and through intravenous drug use. Health care needs include sources of confidential care, counseling, and health education.
STORCH	*STORCH* is the acronym for a group of congenital infections that have the potential of causing severe, multiple impairments. It stands for syphilis, toxoplasmosis, other, rubella, cytomegalovirus, and herpes.
Hepatitis B	*Hepatitis B,* a viral disease, is infectious and causes inflammation of the liver. It is characterized by jaundice and fever. Cases of this dangerous virus are on the increase.

of these are brief and not very serious. For a small number of children, however, their illnesses are chronic, lasting for years or even a lifetime. Children with chronic illnesses often do not feel well enough to focus their attention on instruction. They also experience many absences, causing them to miss a substantial part of their education.

Asthma is the most common chronic illness of children. This pulmonary disease is the leading cause of school absences among all the chronic diseases (Asthma Foundation of America, 2005; National Institute of Environmental Health Sciences [NIEHS], 2005). A person with asthma usually has labored breathing that is sometimes accompanied by shortness of breath, wheezing, and a cough. Years ago, many people believed that asthma was a psychological disorder. It is not; its origin is physical. Many factors (such as classroom pets, chalk dust, dirt in the environment, dust mites, and pollen) can trigger an asthma attack, as can physical activity or exertion. Many students who have asthma are unable to participate in sports or even in physical education activities. Few of these students actually need special education, but they do need special accommodations so that their illness does not hinder their learning.

One health condition in particular disproportionately affects Blacks, and about 1 in 12 African Americans has the trait (National Institutes of Health, National Heart, Lung and Blood Institute, 2006). Sickle cell anemia is a hereditary, life-threatening blood disorder that causes the red blood cells to become rigid and take on a crescent, or sickle, shape. During what is called a "sickling crisis," this rigidity and the crescent shape of the cells do not allow blood to flow through the vessels, depriving some tissues of oxygen and resulting in extreme pain, swollen joints, high fever, and even strokes. Educators need to know that a correlation seems to exist between the sickling crisis and emotional stress and strenuous exercise (Emory University School of Medicine, 2005). They also need to know that many of these children may be absent from school often. To reduce the stress these students experience when they return to school knowing that they have missed assignments and instruction, teachers should work together and develop strategies with the students and their families to compensate for missed school days. For example, a neighborhood child could serve as a peer tutor who brings assignments home to the student and explains important instructions provided during the school day.

One infectious disease that has received considerable attention over the last 15 years is human immunodeficiency virus (HIV). This potentially fatal viral infection is transmitted primarily through exchange of bodily fluids in unprotected sex or by contaminated hypodermic needles. It is the virus responsible for the deadly acquired immunodeficiency syndrome (AIDS) and can be communicated to a child by an infected mother. Before blood-screening procedures were instituted, the virus was also transmitted in blood transfusions. The effects of the infection in children include central nervous system damage, additional infections, developmental delay, motor problems, psychosocial stresses, and death. HIV/AIDS is an infectious disease, but unlike most others, such as flu and the common cold, it is serious and life-threatening (National Institute of Allergy and Infectious Diseases, 2004). The disease is very uncommon in young children, but unfortunately it is more common in teenagers because of dangerous life choices such as drug use and unprotected sex. For many years, parents and educators were concerned that noninfected children could catch the disease from a classmate. It is now clear that this is highly unlikely. With proper precautions (using latex gloves when treating a child's scrape and following normal sanitary procedures), everyone at school is safe and will not catch this disease.

Characteristics

The health care needs of some children are so consuming that everything else becomes secondary. For them, their health situation requires special accommodations and considerations. The treatment goals for many youngsters are to stay strong, healthy, and active and to lead lives as normal as possible. Accomplishing these goals requires considerable attention to many facets of their lives, including medical management. As with all children, education is also a major component of their childhood, but unlike most of their peers, they face many barriers to efficient learning. Here are a few examples of obstacles that some students experience:

- Fatigue
- Absences
- Inconsistent ability to pay attention
- Muscle weakness
- Loss of physical coordination

Some symptoms are directly related to medications and treatment, and others are a function of the disease, illness, or condition. For example, children who are receiving cancer treatment go through periods of feeling too sick to profit from much of the instructional day, and during this time they may have frequent absences or even some long periods where they do not come to school. Instead they receive a special education option outlined in IDEA '04, home-bound instruction, where an itinerant teacher helps the student maintain progress in the curriculum by coming to the student's home (U.S. Department of Education, 2006). Sometimes, technology helps students stay connected with their classmates. For

● For some students, their health situation requires special accommodations and considerations. The treatment goals for many students are to stay strong, healthy, and active and to lead lives as normal as possible.

example, simple video options now readily available through computers allow a student who cannot come to school to join class discussions about a social studies topic or watch a demonstration science experiment through the Internet. Clearly, opportunities for students with health challenges are much greater today than they were only a few years ago. Possibilities for participating and accessing the general education curriculum from a distance should be available to all students who face such challenges.

Prevalence

Across a 10-year period (1991–1992 to 2000–2001), the special health care needs category increased proportionally more than any other special education category. The number of such students increased almost 400 percent, from 58,749 to 291,850 (U.S. Department of Education, 2002). And between 2002 and 2005 the size of this category doubled (OSEP, 2006). Why might this be so? As we noted in Chapter 2 and earlier in this chapter, the most probable reason is the inclusion of ADHD in the other health impairments federal special education category. ADHD, however, is not the only condition contributing to the increase in this group of students. For example, asthma, the leading cause of school absenteeism and the condition that affects the most schoolchildren, is on the rise (Asthma Foundation of America, 2005). Over 5 million children have asthma, some 8 to 12 percent of all children (NIEHS, 2005). Most of them do not require special education but do need special accommodations and considerations.

Some other health conditions are not increasing because they are better controlled through medication. For example, about 1 percent of the general population has epilepsy, but substantially less than 1 percent of the school population has the condition; for some 70 percent of those affected, medication ends the occurrence of seizures (Epilepsy Foundation of America, 2005a). Although this figure has remained relatively stable, a startling 8 percent of African Americans have inherited sickle cell anemia (National Human Genome Research Institute, 2005). Other conditions are on the decline. Only 92 new cases of pediatric AIDS occurred in the United States in 2002 (National Institute of Allergies and Infectious Diseases, 2004).

Who Are Students with Autism Spectrum Disorders?

Although autism is a relatively rare condition, it has been receiving considerable attention in the media in recent years (e.g., *Time,* May 15, 2006; *Town & Country,* August 2005). The reasons for all this public attention are understandable: The condition is on the rise, the causes remain unknown, and the condition can be very severe.

IDEA '04 still refers to the single disorder of autism, but most parents and professionals have adopted a revised conception of this disability. Rather than autism being a single condition, it is thought that five related conditions make up a spectrum of disorders. The umbrella term autism spectrum disorders (ASD) is a fairly new way of thinking about similar, but different, conditions or syndromes (see Figure 3.4). The previous conceptual framework used the term *autism* as the

FIGURE 3.4 Autism Spectrum Disorders (ASD) Umbrella

name for different conditions or syndromes that share "autistic-like" symptoms and characteristics. However, in today's broader concept, ASD is the larger category and autism is just one disorder within it.

Most experts agree that more children are diagnosed with autism today than received this diagnosis in the past (Burton, 2002). Why might this be so? There is probably no single answer to this question (National Research Council, 2001). One reason is better diagnostic procedures. Another explanation is the use of broader and more inclusive definitions of ASD and autism. Despite all the concern about the increased prevalence of ASD, it is important for educators to keep this disability in perspective. It is a low incidence disability, affecting a small fraction of 1 percent of the school population (some 0.15 percent) (OSEP, 2006). Most general education teachers are likely to have no or little opportunity to meet or work with children who have the disorders or conditions included in this spectrum. Let's take a closer look at ASD and how it affects the individuals involved.

Definition

The federal government has not yet acknowledged in the IDEA law the five types of ASD. It describes only autism in IDEA '04. However, thinking about autism as part of a spectrum is clearly the trend (Simpson et al., 2005). The IDEA '04 definition of autism and the National Research Council's definition of ASD both appear in Table 3.3. Remember, the key idea of ASD is that five related disorders join together to create a spectrum.

TABLE 3.3 Autism Spectrum Disorders

Source	Definition
IDEA '04[1]	*Autism* means a developmental disability significantly affecting verbal and nonverbal communication and social interaction, generally evident before age three, that adversely affects a child's educational performance. Other characteristics often associated with autism are engagement in repetitive activities and stereotyped movements, resistance to environmental change or change in daily routines, and unusual responses to sensory experiences. • Autism does not apply if a child's educational performance is adversely affected primarily because the child has an emotional disturbance • A child who manifests the characteristics of autism after age three could be identified as having autism if the criteria described above are satisfied
National Research Council[2]	ASD varies in severity of symptoms, age of onset, and the presence of various features, such as mental retardation and specific language delay. The manifestations of ASD can differ considerably across children and within an individual child over time. Even though there are strong and consistent commonalities, especially in social deficits, there is no single behavior that is always typical of autism or any of the autism spectrum disorders and no behavior that would automatically exclude an individual child from a diagnosis of ASD.

Sources: [1]*U.S. Department of Education, 2006, pp. 1260–1261*
[2]*National Research Council, 2001, p. 2*

Types

ASD is a broad category that groups together five specific disorders:

1. Autistic disorder, or autism
2. Childhood disintegrative disorder (CDD)
3. Asperger syndrome
4. Rett syndrome
5. Pervasive developmental disorder–not otherwise specified (PDD-NOS)

Because autism is just one of the ASD conditions, the term *autism* should no longer be used as the name for the larger category or spectrum of disorders. Technically, the terms *autism* and *autistic disorder* refer to a specific diagnosis, much as the word *Coke* refers to a specific type of soft drink, rather than generically referring to many brands of cola or to all soft drinks.

The American Psychiatric Association (2003), in its text revision of the fourth edition of the *Diagnostic and Statistical Manual of Mental Disorders* (DSM-IV-TR) provides specific diagnostic criteria for autism (see Table 3.4). Note that according to this description, all children with autism have impairments in communication, impairments in social skills, and restricted and repetitive behavioral patterns or range of interests. The skills of children diagnosed with autism vary greatly. They have different levels of intellectual functioning, exhibit a range of symptoms, and present different degrees of impairment. A unique group of individuals with autism is the group commonly referred to as autistic savants. The

TABLE 3.4 DSM-IV Diagnostic Criteria for Autism

A. A total of six (or more) items from (1), (2), and (3), with at least two from (1) and one each from (2) and (3):

(1) Qualitative impairment in social interaction, as manifested by at least two of the following:

(a) Marked impairment in the use of multiple nonverbal behaviors such as eye-to-eye gaze, facial expression, body postures, and gestures to regulate social interaction

(b) Failure to develop peer relationships appropriate to developmental level

(c) A lack of spontaneous seeking to share enjoyment, interests, or achievements with other people (e.g., by a lack of showing, bringing, or pointing out objects of interest)

(d) Lack of social or emotional reciprocity

(2) Qualitative impairments in communication as manifested by at least one of the following:

(a) Delay in, or total lack of, the development of spoken language (not accompanied by an attempt to compensate through alternate modes of communication such as gesture or mime)

(b) In individuals with adequate speech, marked impairment in the ability to initiate or sustain a conversation with others

(c) Stereotyped and repetitive use of language or idiosyncratic language

(d) Lack of varied, spontaneous make-believe play or social imitative play appropriate to developmental level

(3) Restricted repetitive and stereotyped patterns of behavior, interests, and activities as manifested by at least one of the following:

(a) Encompassing preoccupation with one or more stereotyped and restricted patterns of interest that is abnormal either in intensity or focus

(b) Apparently inflexible adherence to specific, nonfunctional routines or rituals

(c) Stereotyped and repetitive motor mannerisms (e.g., hand or finger flapping or twisting, or complex whole-body movements)

(d) Persistent preoccupation with parts of objects

B. Delays or abnormal functioning in at least one of the following areas, with onset prior to age 3 years: (1) social interaction, (2) language as used in social communication, or (3) symbolic or imaginative play

C. The disturbance is not better accounted for by Rett disorder or childhood disintegrative disorder.

Source: Reprinted with permission from *Diagnostic and Statistical Manual of Mental Disorders, Fourth Edition, Text Revision,* (Copyright 2003). (p. 75). American Psychiatric Association.

number of autistic savants is very small, only about 5 percent of individuals diagnosed with autism, but the public seems fascinated by the almost bizarre inconsistencies in this group's abilities. For example, some such individuals can instantly count the number of wooden matches that have fallen on the floor, remember the dates of important events, or recall the numbers of all of the winning lottery tickets for the past year. Others have outstanding musical talents. Stephan Wiltshire, an English artist with autism, can see a street, landmark, or landscape and replicate it perfectly even many days later. But although these splinter skills are fascinating to the observer, they are rarely functional for the individual.

Another part of the spectrum is childhood disintegrative disorder (CDD). DSM-IV-TR describes CDD as including some of the same behavior patterns as autistic disorder: restricted, repetitive, and stereotyped behavior and interests; impairments in communication; and impairments in social interactions. The most distinguishing aspect of CDD is that these children develop just as their peers without disabilities do until they are 5 or 6 years old, at which time a developmental regression begins. In particular, these children lose already acquired language and social skills. Sadly, their long-term outcomes are far worse than those of many individuals with autism, because their regression continues and fewer new skills develop (APA, 2003).

Dr. Hans Asperger was the first to describe and classify Asperger syndrome as a collection of behavioral characteristics. Asperger syndrome is characterized by problems with social skills and by restricted or unusual behaviors or interests. Although the communication of children with Asperger syndrome may be peculiar, children diagnosed with Asperger syndrome develop speech and language on a par with children without disabilities. Other aspects of communication, however, are problematic. Some children with Asperger syndrome understand language very literally, which can make it difficult for them to form conceptual categories, understand jokes, or interpret nonverbal language (such as gestures). For these individuals, the social use of language can be a particular challenge, as can the ability to comprehend other people's feelings or mental states (Safran, 2001). Unlike children with other ASD conditions, the majority of children with Asperger syndrome have normal intelligence.

The fourth type of ASD is Rett syndrome, sometimes called Rett disorder. The Austrian physician Andreas Rett discovered this genetic condition more than 40 years ago. Atypically among inherited conditions, Rett syndrome is more common in girls. Early development appears normal but then stops. Unlike autism, this disorder is characterized by repeated, stereotypic hand wringing. Symptoms also include communication and social deficits and lack of muscle control. Whereas about half of the individuals with autism have mental retardation, most children with Rett syndrome have mental retardation that is severe.

The last type of ASD is pervasive developmental disorder–not otherwise specified (PDD-NOS). Individuals with PDD-NOS have problems in *all* three areas seen in those with ASD: communication, social skills, and unusual behaviors including restricted range of interests. Those with other ASD conditions or disorders typically have problems in one or two of these areas, but not all three. And in the case of PDD-NOS, the disorder is pervasive and severe.

Characteristics

According to the National Institute of Mental Health (NIMH), all children with ASD demonstrate deficits in

- Social interaction
- Verbal and nonverbal communication
- Repetitive behaviors or restricted interests (Strock, 2004)

Experts with NIMH report that most of these youngsters also have unusual responses to sounds or to the way objects look (Strock, 2004). Like most disabilities, ASD ranges from mild to severe, and as shown in the Making a Difference feature, often a team effort is needed to create a very special educational opportunity. The indicators of ASD used to help in early diagnosis are that individuals

- Do not babble, point, or make meaningful gestures by their first birthday
- Do not speak single words by the age of 16 months
- Do not combine two words by their second birthday

Making a Difference

Working as a Team Helps a Child with Autism Thrive in an Inclusive Classroom

Patricia Oliver
Behavior Analyst
Denver, Colorado

My young friend Mario is a smart, very charming child. He was diagnosed with autism at 18 months of age. I am a board-certified behavior analyst with a solid background in special education. When I met Mario, I was working for an organization that provided free support to families, schools, and professionals dealing with individuals with autism. Mario was one of my clients.

When Mario turned 5, he was ready to go to kindergarten in an elementary school in southeast Florida. The general education kindergarten classroom that Mario was to attend had about 20 students. The teacher was a wonderful elementary education teacher, and she was supported by a special education teacher assigned to a resource room, by a speech/language pathologist, and by an occupational therapist.

When we approached the school about having Mario placed in general education kindergarten, there was a lot of hesitation and doubt from the school's support team. We could understand their concerns, because this was the very first time they were going to attempt full inclusion at this school. We held a series of planning meetings throughout the summer. We designed a plan for Mario's fully inclusive educational experience. By the end of the summer, everyone was ready and anxious (in all senses of that word!) to start working with Mario.

When the school year began, Mario attended that kindergarten class. He participated in daily classroom activities with his peers. To meet Mario's needs, the classroom teacher planned and modified the curriculum weekly. The special education teacher, speech/language pathologist, and occupational therapist came to the classroom to provide Mario with the services speci-

fied in his IEP. He never left his room for special education services. He had a fantastic year and was promoted to first grade with his classmates.

Now, you must be wondering . . . was it really this easy? This sounds like the perfect story! Well, it was *not* easy. The whole school team and the family worked many extra hours to make it happen. I visited the classroom every other week throughout the entire year so that we could brainstorm on those areas where team members were having difficulties. We had to rearrange Mario's hours for speech and occupational therapy many times. Mario did have several total meltdowns in the classroom, and it took a while to teach the rest of the kindergarteners what to do—and what not to do—during these episodes. We had meetings with parents of Mario's classmates. Many of them wondered why Mario was in their child's class. We had to convince the school district (and these parents) that inclusive education could be a great situation for *everyone*. We had to prove this to many, and we did! It was hard work, but it was worth it.

Today, that same school is one of the district's pilot inclusion programs. Mario is now a second grader, and he continues to be fully included. The teachers in the school are now quite eager to include other students with disabilities, and they have done so successfully. Through Mario's example, we learned not only that full inclusion was possible but also that it could be a rewarding experience for everyone involved. It certainly was for Mario. ●

- Do not respond to their names
- Lose language ability
- Have poor eye contact
- Do not play with toys but may be overly attached to one object
- Do not smile or understand facial expressions
- Repeat actions that seem to have little purpose
- Appear to have impaired hearing

From this list, it is apparent why ASD is of such concern to parents, teachers, and other professionals. In addition to these characteristics, children with autism may be sensitive to sensory input, such as loud noises or soft touches (Talay-Ongan & Wood, 2000). They have trouble developing the abilities necessary to understanding other people's perspectives and to predicting others' behavior (Baron-Cohen et al., 2001). Most of these individuals have significant communication problems, and some such children are nonverbal or do not use words to communicate. It is estimated that somewhere between 25 and 60 percent of these individuals remain nonspeaking throughout their lifetime (Owens, Metz, & Haas, 2007). Some children who are verbal merely repeat what they have just heard; this is called echolalia (Strock, 2004). Others generate verbal language but make errors when using personal pronouns. These individuals might confuse *he* for *I* or might not use personal pronouns and instead always use the person's name: "Kathy [referring to herself] wants cookie. Peter wants hot dog and Peter wants pickle."

Children with autism also tend to have problems with social interactions. They often appear to live in their own world and may not seek out the company

● All children with autism have impairments in communication, impairments in social skills, and restricted and repetitive behavioral patterns or range of interests. The skills of children diagnosed with autism vary greatly.

of peers or adults. Many children with autism are said to use people as tools (Powers, 2000). For example, a child may lead an adult by the hand to the refrigerator and push the adult's hand toward the juice the child wants. In this way, the child with autism is using the adult as a means to an end. Children with autism do not generally initiate social situations and do not engage in social turn-taking just for the pleasure of being part of a social interaction.

Most individuals with ASD have repetitive or odd patterns of behavior, stereotyped behaviors, unusual interests, or strange responses to the environment (Autism Society of America, 2006). For example, they may be attracted to specific aspects of a toy, tirelessly spinning the wheel of a toy car or wiggling the string of a pull toy. Many individuals with ASD have rigid or set patterns of behavior. For example, one child might line up his or her toys in a specific way and insist on following the same routine every day. If these patterns of behavior are violated, a tantrum might result to protest the disruption.

Prevalence

Many different prevalence rates for autism and for ASD are cited. For example, DSM-IV-TR reports that the rate of autistic disorder ranges from 2 to 20 per 10,000 individuals (APA, 2003). The Centers for Disease Control (CDC) estimates the rate of occurrence of ASD as 6 individuals in 1,000 (2006). According to the Autism Society of America, as many as 1.5 million Americans, both children and adults, have a condition included in the autism spectrum (Autism Society of America, 2006). And the federal Office of Special Education Programs reported that in 2005, 181,758 of all schoolchildren between the ages of 6 and 17 received special education services because of autism or ASD—up from 74,166 in 2001 (OSEP, 2006; U.S. Department of Education, 2002). This alarming growth is of great concern to parents, policymakers, and professionals, and it is also confusing. Has there truly been a dramatic increase in ASD? Or does the increase reflect a more inclusive definition? The answers to these questions are elusive. Here's what we do know today. In 2003, CDC did find that the rate of autism was greater than it was during the 1980s and early 1990s. The rate of the condition during the late 1990s and early 2000s seems to be stable, however, and is not showing increases at the earlier rate of acceleration (CDC, 2006). Officials at NIMH believe it is clear that more children are being diagnosed with autism today than ever before (National Institute of Mental Health, 2006). But ASD remains a low incidence disability (OSEP, 2006).

Who Are Students with Multiple-Severe Disabilities?

Students with multiple-severe disabilities make up the largest group of low incidence disabilities. Why? Many states assign nearly all children and youths who have more than one disability to this special education category. The combination of disabilities present need not be specified. Thus some students have poor vision and also cognitive disabilities, and others may have a severe hearing loss and substantial mobility issues. Possessing more than one major disability presents unique challenges to the individual and the family. The combined effects of two disabilities create a pattern of problems different from those presented by either of the disabilities alone (Laurent Clerc National Deaf Education Center, 2006). For example, deaf children who also have another disability need teachers who are specialists in more than one area and who also understand the special problems resulting from a unique combination of disabilities.

Teachers need to avoid the temptation of describing these students in terms of deficits, rather than in terms of what they can do through a variety of supports across many of life's dimensions. The emphasis for students with multiple-severe disabilities is on developing skills that promote independence and community presence (McDonnell, Hardman, & McDonnell, 2003; Snell & Brown, 2006). Ironically, in some cases that means teaching individuals how to depend on others to gain the supports they require to achieve maximal independence.

The current outlook for individuals with multiple-severe disabilities is very different from what it was only a few decades in the past. Not long ago, adults with severe disabilities spent their lives in large residential institutions with no access to the community and no chance to participate in mainstream society (Switzky & Greenspan, 2006). Today, these adults have more opportunities than ever before. Many of them live in group homes or in apartments, and they hold jobs in the community. Educational opportunities for these individuals have also increased. Before IDEA was passed in 1975, many of these individuals were excluded from school and had no opportunity to benefit from a special education complete with the related services they needed. For those who did find access to education, it was often in segregated settings. And it was not until the 1960s and 1970s that researchers began to turn their attention to developing and validating instructional procedures and services that are especially effective for these learners (Kochhar-Bryant, Shaw, & Izzo, 2007; Switzky & Greenspan, 2006). In addition to access to the general education curriculum, their education now includes

- Expressions of choice
- Self-determination
- Functional skills
- Social skills training
- Community based instruction
- Supports and planning for the transition to adult life

These individuals' inclusion in school and in the community is relatively recent. Knowledge about best practices and services is still being developed, so the outcomes for the next generations of these students will be even greater!

Definition

Three definitions of multiple-severe disabilities are included in Table 3.5. Each gives a slightly different picture, but all illustrate the complexity of disability and the different conditions that can occur together. The IDEA '04 definition addresses the challenges that are presented when an individual has more than one condition that is severe in nature (U.S. Department of Education, 2006). The one developed by The Association for Persons with Severe Handicaps (the organization goes by its acronym, TASH) provides this description of people with disabilities that are severe and often come in combination with another severe condition

TABLE 3.5 Multiple-Severe Disabilities

Source	Definition
IDEA '04[1]	*Multiple disabilities* means concomitant impairments (such as mental retardation–blindness, mental retardation–orthopedic impairment, etc.), the combination of which causes such severe educational needs that they cannot be accommodated in special education programs solely for one of the impairments. The term does not include deafblindness.
TASH[2]	*Severe disabilities:* Individuals of all ages, races, creeds, national origins, genders, and sexual orientations who require ongoing support in one or more major life activities in order to participate in an integrated community and enjoy a quality of life similar to that available to all individuals. Support may be required for life activities such as mobility, communication, self-care, and learning as necessary for community living, employment, and self-sufficiency.
CDC[3]	*Developmental disabilities* are a diverse group of severe chronic conditions that are due to mental and/or physical impairments. People with developmental disabilities have problems with major life activities such as language, mobility, learning, self-help, and independent living. Developmental disabilities begin anytime during the developmental period up to 22 years of age and usually last throughout a person's lifetime.

Sources: [1]*U.S. Department of Education, 2006, p. 1263*
[2]*TASH, 2000*
[3]*Centers for Disease Control, National Center on Birth Defects and Developmental Disabilities, 2004, p. 1*

(TASH, 2000). The Centers for Disease Control (CDC) elected to describe multiple and severe disabilities by using the term developmental disabilities, describing problems in major life areas, and explaining that these problems typically continue after the school years (CDC, 2004). Combinations of disabilities and conditions lead to unique special needs. For example, an individual with a cognitive disability might need supports to pay bills and manage a budget. If that individual also has a moderate hearing loss, she or he might need an assistant to facilitate communication at the doctor's office but might function at work with only natural supports from coworkers. Let's consider further how different conditions can occur together.

Types

Each individual with multiple-severe disabilities is unique. The possible combinations of conditions are numerous, and the ways in which the symptoms associated with these conditions can manifest themselves make it impossible to group these students by type. So, instead, let's spend a little time thinking about common characteristics these students present to themselves, their families, and their teachers.

Characteristics

Individuals with multiple-severe disabilities display a wide range of skills and abilities, as well as a wide range of problem areas in need of intensive instruction.

According to NICHCY (2004), this group of individuals shares some common characteristics:

- Problems transferring or generalizing learning from one situation to another, one setting to another, and one skill to another
- Limited communication abilities
- Difficulties with memory
- Need for supports for many major life activities (domestic, leisure, community participation, vocational)

Many individuals with multiple-severe disabilities also face other challenges, including medical problems such as seizure disorders, vision or hearing problems, heart disease, and cerebral palsy, along with other health issues. Consequently, they and their families interface with many professionals and disciplines, all with different styles of interaction, terms and jargon, and approaches. Such multiple interactions can complicate an already difficult situation.

One common characteristic of severe disabilities is the response to the challenges to gain independence and participation in the community. Typically, in order for these goals to be accomplished, intensive and pervasive supports from a wide range of individuals and systems must be in place. Technology is one of those supports (Bryant & Bryant, 2003). Technology can also help people with disabilities and their families address and compensate for their disabilities (Reichle, Beukelman, & Light, 2002). The federal government continues to make a considerable investment in technology, because it is clear that technology has improved outcomes for students with disabilities (Office of Special Education Programs [OSEP], 2000). The data on which the government bases these conclusions indicate that technology helps these individuals

- Communicate more effectively
- Increase their levels of independence
- Control their environments
- Have greater mobility
- Gain access to information

● Technology has opened up avenues of communication for many students who are unable to communicate with others through oral speech. What forms of alternative and augmentative communication are available for students with disabilities?

Let's look at one example of how such technology has opened up avenues of communication for many students who are unable to communicate with others through oral speech (Byrant & Bryant, 2003). Augmentative and alternative communication devices (AAC) can be very beneficial to individuals with low incidence disabilities (Noonan & Siegel, 2003). Whether in the form of simple devices, such as communication boards, or complicated speech synthesizers that actually speak for the individual, technology now allows individuals to make their needs known, express their feelings, and interact with others (McCormick & Wegner, 2003). In the most straightforward systems, words and/or pictures are placed on a flat surface or in books. The student communicates by pointing to the appropriate symbols. Symbols are customized to the individual; the words or symbols on the board reflect the individual and salient features of the environments in which he or she operates. Some boards are simple homemade projects; others use quite sophisticated technology. Your job as a teacher is to encourage the use of these techniques and help shape them into a reliable system of communication for the student. When your students have these communication tools, learning and social interaction can take place.

Prevalence

Relatively speaking, few students have multiple-severe disabilities and require intensive educational opportunities to meet their complex needs. Only 0.23 percent of American students are included in the federal special education category of multiple disabilities, representing some 114,364 students ages 6 to 17 (OSEP, 2006). Depending on how states include individuals in one category or another, either fewer or more students can be considered as having this disability. For example, some states do not include in this category students who have learning disabilities and also a hearing problem; other states do. Some states include in the mental retardation category students with a mild visual disability who also have substantial cognitive disabilities; other states report these students to the federal government as having multiple disabilities. Regardless, all students with severe problems are served by special education, and the overall goal for their education usually focuses on achieving independent living in the community.

Who Are Students with Developmental Delay?

Through IDEA, developmental delay was created as an additional disability category in 1991. This action is actually the federal government's first move toward supporting a noncategorical approach to special education. The label developmental delay can be used for preschoolers ages 3 to 5 and for elementary-age students up to the age of 9 (U.S. Department of Education, 2006). Thus, unlike their counterparts without disabilities, these youngsters are entitled to a free appropriate education during the preschool years, and this generic label allows them to receive services without being identified with a specific disability through their early elementary years. The main purpose of this special education category is to reduce the chances of children being misidentified as having one disability when in fact they have another (Simeonsson et al., 2001). For example, a child who is not speaking by the age of 3 is likely to have a problem that could be a significant disability. But which disability? The reason for the communication problem could be mental retardation, ASD, learning disabilities, or a speech or language impairment. Rather than forcing a diagnosis that might be incorrect, IDEA '04 allows preschoolers and children up to the age of 9 to receive special education services without a specific categorical label. The Making a Difference feature shows how the support of family and friends, along with a professional team, can enhance the life of a child with developmental delays.

Definition

Special education services are available to children from birth and for some individuals with disabilities up to the age of 21. Infants and toddlers fall into one

Making a Difference

We're All on the Same Team

Patricia Davidson
University of Southern Indiana

On January 20, 1981, our son Zachary Scott was born, joining our family after just 32 weeks in development. Zach tried to make an appearance at 28 weeks, but the doctors knew best, and the arrival was put on hold for another 4 weeks to give Zach time to develop and grow. As delivery approached, things happened quickly. I began hearing phrases like "fetal heart monitor," "breathing shallow," "distress," and "low APGAR scores." To my husband Tom, a physician, these terms explained the scurrying in the delivery room. To me, they meant a medical problem that I was sure would work itself out and things would be fine. As Zach and I left the hospital a week later, my only concern was getting our son home and into his own crib.

Zach was eventually diagnosed with moderate developmental disabilities. Milestones such as sitting up, crawling, and walking came later to Zach than to typically developing babies. Until the age of 4 years, his vocabulary was limited to one-word utterances. Physical therapists, occupational therapists, and speech therapists have become constant companions for our son. Probably the best "therapist" for Zach, however, was his younger brother. Seth was achieving typical developmental milestones and continually demonstrating them to Zach. With 16 months separating them in age, the boys learned together. Because I had been an elementary school teacher for many years, I was beginning to suspect that we were headed for some challenges, but I never dreamed that the most significant challenges would come from the "systems" we would meet in Zachary's lifetime.

It was in Zach's early school years that my husband and I became aware of how different our sons' lives would be. With Seth, the school years would be a time of learning and growth, socialization, and enjoyment, as they should be. Zach's school years would require our constant prodding and requests to our school, district, and local agencies for each service we felt he should receive. It was at about this time that Tom and I embraced the phrase "No is not an option" when dealing with schools, administrators, physicians, and service agencies. We wanted our son to receive the services he needed so that he could achieve the best possible results. We knew that so much was possible for him when everyone worked together on the same team. We began to approach Zach's needs with not only his well-being in mind; that is, we also adopted the mission of improving a system so this path would be easier for those children and their families who came after Zach. We found that other parents of children with special needs were our biggest resource.

After being out of college for 15 years, I decided to return to school, and I earned a master's degree in special education. Now I possessed that piece of paper that opened doors for me to help plan our son's education. When Zach started school, his special education class-group of young children who can be provided special education and its related services, and preschoolers are in another group. Many of these children are identified as having a disability while they are infants and toddlers. These youngsters typically have obvious physical problems or sensory (e.g., hearing or vision) problems. Some have very serious delays in their motor or cognitive development. By the age of 3, problems that were initially less obvious reveal themselves to parents, medical professionals, and family friends. So as not to mislabel, or incorrectly identify, children with disabilities, IDEA '04 allows states to provide special services without also identifying that child with a specific disability (U.S. Department of Education, 2006). Between the ages of 3 and 9, the unspecific label of developmental delay can be used. The definition for this noncategorical identification outlined in IDEA '04 is found in Table 3.6.

rooms were located in a building that housed used textbooks and equipment. Through the sustained efforts of parents and teachers, the special education classrooms were reassigned to an elementary school's campus, allowing children with special needs to interact on a daily basis with their peers without disabilities.

As Zach approached upper elementary grades, his IEP team, led by Ms. Rosen, director of special services, began to discuss how Zach and general education students could benefit from learning with each other through inclusive education. We began this process by placing Zach in a science class. Zach's fellow students helped him construct, fill, and fly his own hot-air balloon. Zach then chose an art class. His framed paintings decorate our home today. Another class he desperately wanted to attend was "Industrial Woods," a woodworking class. After many before-school and after-school sessions, and with the support of a dedicated industrial arts teacher, Zach learned about the safety issues in a woodworking class. Today, his bedroom contains wooden shelves, a cedar chest, a bookstand, and many other projects he completed in his high school woodworking class. Zach was by no means ready at this point to give up the one-on-one time with his homeroom teacher, Mrs. Sherburne, who worked with him on reading, handwriting, and the math curriculum. By making it a team effort, we were able to make Zachary's school years productive ones.

Our last obstacle arose as we approached our superintendent with the proposal that Zach participate in graduation ceremonies with his high school class of 1999. These were the students he had grown to know and who had been his supporters throughout his school career. We were told that such participation in graduation ceremonies had not been allowed before. The law states that Zach could graduate from high school at the age of 21, but not at 18. If he were to graduate with his classmates, his school services would cease. As we weighed all the options, Zach's fellow classmates made the decision for us. They attended the appropriate school board meeting and explained that Zach was very much a part of the Class of 1999; he was involved in all of their high school class activities, and he was a hit at the senior prom, which he attended with a friend from his Special Olympics team.

His classmates won the battle. Zach walked down the aisle and onto the stage on graduation day. After a standing ovation from his classmates, the teaching staff, and the audience, Zach proudly accepted his unsigned diploma. A huge graduation celebration followed, but more importantly, these events opened the door for others who wished to follow in Zach's footsteps. Zach completed his studies at his high school and transitioned into a work program. Today he works at ARC Industries.

We marvel at the lessons Zachary has taught us. Through these challenging experiences, we have met many wonderful people who have become advocates for a population they might never have had the opportunity to know had it not been for Zach. We are not a unique family. There are thousands of families and teachers across the country who are doing their best to give their special family members and students those opportunities necessary to make their lives rich and meaningful. We are so fortunate to have been a part of this journey. ●

TABLE 3.6 Developmental Delay

Source	Definition
IDEA '04	*Children aged 3 through 9 experiencing developmental delays: A child with a disability* who is experiencing developmental delays, as defined by the State and as measured by appropriate diagnostic instruments and procedures, in one or more of the following areas: physical development, cognitive development, communication development, social or emotional development, or adaptive development; and who, by reason thereof, needs special education and related services.

Source: U.S. Department of Education, 2006, p. 1260

Types

Preschoolers with developmental delays have a wide range of disabilities. Some can be specifically classified during a child's early years, but others cannot. All states use the "developmental delay" option of making children between the ages of 3 and 5 eligible for special education services (Müller & Markowitz, 2004). They use this option for some, but not all, of their young children with suspected disabilities. For example, preschoolers with severe visual disabilities may be identified, whereas children with general delays in language and motor skills may receive services but not be assigned a categorical identification (e.g., mental retardation).

Characteristics

The main characteristic of youngsters with developmental delays is that they have general delays in their development. Professionals use this designation for two main reasons: (1) They are hesitant either to ascribe a potentially incorrect disability label to the child, or (2) they believe that the child may just be developing slowly but may later catch up to peers on critical developmental markers (e.g., talking, motor skills, social skills). Interestingly, even though the federal government has made available the option of noncategorical identification of students up to the age of 9, as the children get older the percentage of students counted in this category decreases dramatically (U.S. Department of Education, 2006).

Prevalence

The special education label of developmental delay is most commonly used with children between the ages of 3 and 5. At the age of 3 years, 72,258 of the 154,196 children identified nationwide were placed in this category—more than in any other of the 14 options available. By the age of 4, two options, speech or language impairments and developmental delay, are used almost exclusively with 213,716 of the 247,697 eligible for special education. As children get older, their problems tend to be more specifically associated with a disability (OSEP, 2006). Thus, at age 6, only 34,982 students are identified as having developmental delays, but 227,386 students are served through the speech or language impairments category, and other disability categories are beginning to grow in size (e.g., autism: 6,704 at age 3 and 18,311 at age 6).

Who Are Students with Physical Disabilities?

Many adults with physical disabilities received a very different education than today's students who face physical challenges. Typically, they were not allowed to join their brothers, sisters, and friends at their neighborhood school. They were bused to special schools equipped with state-of-the-art equipment (e.g., therapy pools) and staffed with related services professionals (e.g., physical therapists, occupational therapists), but these facilities were segregated and only students with disabilities attended. When these individuals grew up, many of them became disability advocates. They have fought hard to enlarge the educational options available to students with disabilities, and specifically, they have sought the closure of separate, center schools for schoolchildren with physical disabilities. The result of their efforts has been that students with physical disabilities attend school alongside typical learners in inclusive school settings. For many of them, their special education consists of therapy from related services professionals. For some, their only teachers are general educators who provide accommodations guided by special education professionals.

Definition

IDEA '04 uses the term orthopedic impairments to refer to conditions that we call physical disabilities and others call physical impairments. The definition used in the law is found in Table 3.7. Individuals with these conditions have problems with the structure or the functioning of their bodies. For such a student to be eligible for special education services, the physical disability must adversely affect the student's educational performance.

TABLE 3.7 Physical Disabilities

Source	Definition
IDEA '04	*Orthopedic impairment* means a severe orthopedic impairment that adversely affects a child's educational performance. The term includes impairments caused by congenital anomaly, impairments caused by disease (e.g., poliomyelitis, bone tuberculosis), and impairments from other causes (e.g., cerebral palsy, amputations, and fractures or burns that cause contractures).

Source: U.S. Department of Education, 2006, p. 1263

Types

The two major groups of physical disabilities are

1. Neuromotor impairments
2. Muscular/skeletal conditions

Many conditions included in each group are listed in Figure 3.5 and described in Table 3.8. When the central nervous system (the brain and the spinal cord) is damaged, the result is a neuromotor impairment because the neurological impairment limits muscular control and movement. Cerebral palsy (CP) and seizure disorders (such as epilepsy) are examples of neuromotor impairments. Individuals with muscular/skeletal conditions usually have difficulty controlling their movements, but the cause is not neurological. Juvenile arthritis and limb deficiencies are examples of muscular/skeletal conditions. Regardless of the type of physical disability, some of these individuals need to use special devices and technology even to do simple tasks—walking, eating, or writing—that most of us take for granted. Let's think about each of these types of physical disabilities in turn.

Two specific neuromotor impairments that teachers should know about because they are more prevalent than other conditions (such as muscular dystrophy, polio, and spina bifida) are seizure disorders (epilepsy) and cerebral palsy (CP). The most common neuromotor impairment encountered at school is epilepsy (Epilepsy Foundation of America, 2005a). This condition is also called a seizure disorder or convulsive disorder. A person with epilepsy often has recurrent seizures resulting from the sudden, excessive, spontaneous, and abnormal discharge of neurons in the brain. The result can be loss of consciousness or changes in the person's motor or sensory functioning. The frequency of seizures may vary

FIGURE 3.5 An Organizational Scheme for Physical Impairments

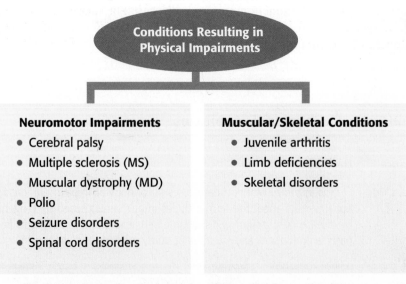

This diagram lists and categorizes the conditions, disorders, and impairments that can result in physical challenges in children.

TABLE 3.8 Types of Physical Conditions

Condition	Description
Neuromotor Impairments	
Seizure disorders	*Epilepsy,* the most common type of neuromotor impairment in children, is a condition of recurrent convulsions or seizures caused by abnormal brain electrical activity. It is treated with medications and frequently is well controlled without any effect on learning or motor skills.
Cerebral palsy (CP)	*Cerebral palsy* is an incurable and nonprogressive condition caused by brain injury that sometimes limits the individual's ability to control muscle groups or motor functioning in specific areas of the body or, infrequently, the entire body. It may be associated with multiple disabilities. Physical therapy offers benefits.
Spinal cord disorders	*Spina bifida,* a neural tube birth defect, is the improper closure of the protective tissue surrounding the spinal cord. It results in limited neurological control for organs and muscles controlled by nerves that originate below the level of the lesion. Increasing numbers of children have suffered traumatic head or spinal cord injuries resulting in permanent disabilities. *Spinal cord injuries,* typically the result of injuries from accidents or abuse, can cause severe motor impairments and even paralysis. Health care needs for both groups include good skin care, management of bladder and bowel care, and physical therapy.
Polio	*Polio,* caused by a viral infection, and almost totally prevented in children immunized in the United States, attacks the spinal cord and can result in paralysis and motor disabilities. Health care needs parallel those for spinal cord disorders.
Muscular dystrophy (MD)	*Muscular dystrophy,* an exceptionally rare, incurable, and progressive disease, weakens and then destroys the affected individual's muscles. Health care needs center on lung function support, prevention of pneumonia, and physical therapy.
Multiple sclerosis (MS)	*Multiple sclerosis,* a chronic disease typically occurring in adults, causes the myelin covering the nerve fibers of the brain and spinal cord to deteriorate, impeding the transmission of electrical signals from the brain to other parts of the body. Health care needs parallel those for MD.
Muscular/Skeletal Conditions	
Juvenile arthritis	*Juvenile arthritis* is a disease caused by an autoimmune process resulting in swelling, immobility, and pain in joints. Health care needs include medication to suppress the process and orthopedic and physical therapy to maintain function in small and large joints.
Limb deficiencies	*Skeletal problems* in which the individual's limb(s) is shortened, absent, or malformed. They may occur from congenital conditions or from injuries. Health care needs focus on adaptive interventions to support or improve functioning of the affected limb(s).
Skeletal disorders	*Dwarfism,* a condition caused by abnormal development of long bones, may result in varying degrees of motor disabilities. Health care needs may include human growth hormone to improve height.
	Osteogenesis imperfecta, sometimes known as brittle bone disease, is a condition in which normal calcification of the bones does not occur, leading to breakage and abnormal healing of bones with accompanying loss of height. Health care interventions include physical therapy and medical care.
	Scoliosis, a curvature of the spine that occurs in children during puberty and may, in severe form, limit mobility of the trunk. Health care needs include monitoring of the amount of curvature of the spine and appropriate interventions to arrest the process.

from a single isolated incident to hundreds in a day. Some children actually anticipate their seizures because they experience a preictal stage, or an aura, and have heightened sensory signals of an impending seizure, such as a peculiar smell, taste, vision, sound, or action. Others might experience a change in their behavior. Knowing about an aura pattern is helpful, because it allows an individual to assume a safe position or warn teachers and classmates before a seizure begins. Cerebral palsy is a result of damage, usually because of insufficient oxygen getting to the brain either before (prenatally), during (perinatally), or immediately after (postnatally) the child's birth (United Cerebral Palsy Association [UCP], 2001). The condition can also be acquired during the first 3 years of life. In these cases, it is usually caused by brain damage resulting from accidents, brain infections, or child abuse. Cerebral palsy is not a disease but, rather, a nonprogressive and noninfectious condition that results in severe motor impairments. Regrettably, once it is acquired, it cannot be cured (at least as of today).

One of the most common muscular/skeletal conditions seen in children, limb deficiencies, can be the result of a missing or nonfunctioning arm or leg. Regardless of whether the impairment occurred before or after birth, the result is a major impediment to normal physical activity and functioning. Emerging technology (particularly robotics) now provides much assistance to those with missing limbs. Artificial limbs now make possible movements that only a few years ago were thought to be impossible. A relatively common muscular/skeletal condition affecting joints and the function of muscles is juvenile arthritis. Although there are many different forms of this disease, it is typically chronic and painful. Juvenile arthritis usually develops in early childhood and can cause many absences from school. These children often need help keeping up with their classmates because they miss so much class instruction. Teachers must understand that their ability to move may be inconsistent (better at different times of the day) and that sitting for extended periods of time can cause them to become stiff and experience considerable pain. These children need to be allowed to move around a lot. Those who have a high rate of absences probably need tutoring and extra help to keep up with their peers (Arthritis Foundation of America, 2002).

Characteristics

One important thing for all educators to understand is that physical disabilities range in severity from mild to severe. And in many cases, they are only one of multiple conditions an individual must face (McDonnell, Hardman, & McDonnell, 2003). However, remember never to make the terrible error of associating a physical disability with a cognitive one. They do not go hand in hand. Also, when responsible educators encounter diseases and conditions they know little about, they seek out all the information they need to provide an appropriate education to the students involved. Let's consider the characteristics of a few physical disabilities.

Some seizures are characterized by short lapses in consciousness, and teachers might not recognize that a student is experiencing anything out of the ordinary (Epilepsy Foundation of America, 2005b). Because some types of seizures are not dramatic, a teacher might wrongly assume that the child is merely daydreaming or not paying attention. With other types of seizures, the individual involved may think that the environment has become distorted and strange and that inexplicable events and feelings have occurred. With these seizures, teachers might incorrectly believe that the child is acting out, clowning around, or exhibiting bizarre behavior patterns. Of course, the most serious type of seizure, the one most of us think of first, is characterized by convulsions and loss of consciousness. The behaviors associated with these seizures may at first be frightening to the teacher and to other students in the class, but knowing what to expect and what to do in the event of a seizure reduces the stress (and the danger to the individual student). The school nurse, the student's parents, or the special education teacher can be a great resource when planning for the special needs of such students.

Individuals with cerebral palsy whose motor functioning is affected show the following characteristics alone or in combination: jerky movements, spasms, involuntary movements, and lack of muscle tone. Many have impaired mobility and poor muscle development. They may also need braces to help support the affected limbs and make them more functional or to prevent more problems and limitations on mobility. Proper positioning of the body also must be considered. Many children need wedges, pillows, and individually designed chairs and work tables so they can be comfortable, breathe easier, avoid more problems, and participate in group activities. Although some degree of intellectual and developmental disabilities is present in about half of these children, others are intellectually gifted. It is a tragic mistake to assume that cerebral palsy and mental retardation always occur together.

The challenges facing students with physical limitations and their teachers are great. All schools must meet the special architectural codes required by the ADA law and must be barrier-free. Regardless, these students' worlds are often filled with physical barriers that must be overcome before they can achieve independence and a "normal" life. Surprisingly, students who use wheelchairs still face physical barriers at some schools. For example, classes scheduled on the second floor although no elevator is available, bathrooms not accessible, and passageways too narrow to pass through are still commonplace (Helman, 2002). These facts may explain why many individuals with a limb deficiency have difficulties adjusting to their situation. Eliminating barriers, even obvious physical ones, can be more difficult than you might think. Often, it is the student's teacher who must advocate for improvements that facilitate these individuals' access both to the curriculum and to the entire school environment (e.g., the bathroom, the lunchroom, the playground, the gymnasium, the music room, the library, and the bus). Remember, too, that barriers are not only physical, and integration may necessitate accommodations beyond the curb cuts, ramps, elevators, and bathroom alterations required by law. Most children will respond warmly and proudly to your subtle reminders that everyone enjoys being included in all aspects of school.

● Some students with disabilities need to use special devices and technology to do basic physical tasks such as walking, playing, eating, or writing.

Prevalence

According to the Annual Report to Congress, some 57,906 students, or 0.14 percent of all schoolchildren between the ages of 6 and 17, have physical disabilities requiring special education or related services (OSEP, 2006). Let's look at the prevalence rates of a few specific conditions. About 1 percent of the general population has epilepsy, but substantially less than 1 percent of the school population has the condition, and 80 percent of all cases are controlled by medication (Epilepsy Foundation of America, 2005b). About 0.03 percent of all children have cerebral palsy, and some of them do not require any special education services (United Cerebral Palsy Association [UCP], 2001). The prevalence of many diseases and conditions that seriously affect children continues to change across time. For example, some, like polio, are almost eradicated in the United States. Other conditions, like cerebral palsy, have remained stable for over 40 years.

Who Are Students Who Are Deaf and Hard of Hearing?

The words deaf and Deaf both refer to individuals with severe and profound hearing losses, but they have very different implications for the individuals involved. Possibly more than any other group of people with disabilities, Deaf individuals unite as a community. To them, their separate language and culture bind them together, much as people who live in different countries feel about each other and about those who do not share the same language, history, literature, and art (Zazove et al., 2004). This group often interprets inclusion differently from those with other disabilities, believing that being separated from others who use the same language system (i.e., manual communication) and included in general education classes is undesirable and restrictive. These individuals are also at the forefront of remarkable technological advances that will change many of their lives. However, it is important to remember that not all people who cannot hear consider themselves Deaf and members of the Deaf community. The best indicator of how people think about themselves in this regard is whether the "D" in *deaf* is capitalized or not.

Perspectives on deafness differ. Some people with average hearing consider deafness a disability, a sad condition that isolates those involved from family and society. To many Deaf people, however, deafness is one aspect binding them together as a minority group rich in culture, history, and language (Davey, 2005). The language of the Deaf community is American Sign Language (ASL), a language that uses signs, has all of the elements of other languages (grammar, syntax, idioms), and is not parallel to English in either structure or word order. ASL is not a mere translation of oral speech or the English language (as is signed English); it is a fully developed language. In fact, many states allow ASL as an option to meet the high school foreign language requirement, and the same is true at many colleges and universities. As the language of the Deaf community, ASL is used in all aspects of their culture. For example, plays are written in ASL and performed by deaf theater groups around the world, and a base of folk literature has developed over the years. This community unites in many ways by coming together socially and to advocate against discrimination and for justice.

Definition

Three definitions of hearing problems that result in disabilities are found in Table 3.9. Deaf students have a hearing loss so severe, with or without help from a hearing aid or an assistive hearing device, that it seriously affects the individual's ability to process spoken or auditory information by hearing. Clearly, these students' educational performance, their interactions with others, and their participation in the community are influenced by their hearing problems.

Students with hearing problems that are less severe—those whose hearing falls into the range considered hard of hearing—are also eligible for special education services. Most states do not specify a specific level of hearing loss that serves as a guideline for which students qualify for special education and which do not. Such states simply indicate that a student's hearing problems (whether permanent or fluctuating) must adversely affect educational performance (Müller & Markowitz, 2004). Experts vary in their definitions of hearing loss and in the point at which they believe it has educational significance. Although 18 states provide a cutoff score, usually including at least a 20-decibel loss in the speech range in the better ear, a precise score on an audiogram cannot guide educators in assessing the significance of a hearing loss because individuals respond differently. Whether a student qualifies in the "deaf" or in the "hard of hearing" group, it is important for teachers to remember that all hearing losses are serious. Of course, at some point the level of severity substantially influences the way in which students need to be taught and how well they understand oral communication.

TABLE 3.9 **Hard of Hearing or Deafness**

Source	Definition
IDEA '04[1]	*Deafness* means a hearing impairment that is so severe that the child is impaired in processing linguistic information through hearing, with or without amplification, that adversely affects a child's educational performance.
IDEA '04[2]	*Hearing impairment* means an impairment in hearing, whether permanent or fluctuating, that adversely affects a child's educational performance but that is not included under the definition of deafness in this section.
Federally Funded Technical Assistance Clearinghouse[3]	A person who is *hard of hearing* perceives some sound and has sufficient hearing to use auditory-based methods of communication, sometimes with visual supplements. Some people who are severely hard of hearing use oral-aural communication, which combines speech, speech-reading, use of personal hearing aids (including the newer cochlear implant technology), and other augmentative devices.

Sources: [1]*U.S. Department of Education, 2006, p. 1261*
[2]*U.S. Department of Education, 2006, p. 1262*
[3]*American Council on Education, HEATH Resource Center, 2005, p. 2*

Types

Different dimensions are used to describe hearing problems. These dimensions are

- Type of loss
- Age of onset
- Degree of loss

The two general types of hearing loss are conductive and sensorineural. Conductive hearing loss is due to blockage or damage to the outer or middle ear that prevents sound waves from traveling (being conducted) to the inner ear. Generally, someone with a conductive hearing loss has a mild to moderate disability. Some conductive hearing losses are temporary; in fact, we have all probably experienced a conductive hearing loss at some point in our lives. For example, you may have experienced a temporary loss of hearing as a consequence of a change in air pressure when flying in an airplane or riding in a car through the mountains. Children often experience head colds and ear infections that result in a temporary loss of conductive hearing. Therefore, it is likely that on any given day, 20 percent of elementary students have a mild conductive hearing loss, and around 80 percent of all children experience such hearing problems at some time between kindergarten and fifth grade (Gordon-Langbein & Metzinger, 2000). With a mild loss, the individual can still hear almost all speech sounds, and can hear most conversations, but has difficulty with distant or faint speech (Owens, Metz, & Haas, 2007). If the hearing loss was caused by a head cold, once the infection clears up, the hearing difficulties also disappear. Other causes of conductive hearing losses can usually be corrected through surgery or other medical techniques. Damage to the inner ear or the auditory nerve results in a sensorineural hearing loss and is more difficult to improve through technology or medicine. Some people refer to this type of hearing loss as "nerve deafness." Individuals affected by a sensorineural loss are able to hear different frequencies at different intensity levels; their hearing losses are not flat or even. Sensorineural losses are less common in young children than the conductive types, but teachers need to understand that hearing aids can have mixed results with sensorineural losses.

The age when the hearing loss occurs, or age of onset, is important. Individuals who become deaf before they learn to speak and understand language are referred to as prelingually deaf. They either are born deaf or lose their hearing as infants. Approximately 95 percent of all deaf children and youth are prelingually deaf, and it is estimated that about half of those born deaf have a genetic reason for their deafness (American Speech–Language–Hearing Association [ASHA], 2005). Their inability to hear language seriously affects their abilities to communicate with others and to learn academic subjects taught later in school. One in ten of those who are prelingually deaf has at least one deaf parent. Children in this group typically learn to communicate during the normal developmental period. However, instead of learning oral communication skills, many learn through a combination of manual communication (sign language) and oral language. One such approach, called the bilingual-bicultural approach, combines English as a second language (ESL) instructional methods and bilingual education so that young deaf children are taught ASL as their native language and learn English as their second language through reading and writing (Evans, 2004; Marschark, 2001). Those whose severe hearing loss occurs after they have learned to speak and understand language are called postlingually deaf. Many are able to retain their abilities to use speech and communicate with others orally.

Although no precise cutoff exists to divide students with hearing problems into two groups, distinctions are made between hard of hearing and deafness. Intensity, or loudness, of sound is measured in decibels (dB). Softer, quieter sounds have lower decibel measurements; louder sounds have higher decibel numbers. Decibel levels ranging from 0 to 120 dB are used to test how well an individual can hear different frequencies; a child with normal hearing should be able to perceive sounds at 0 dB. For examples of what different decibel levels sound like, see Figure 3.6. It is important to recognize that some loud sounds are themselves dangerous and, with continued exposure, can cause hearing loss (Haller & Montgomery, 2004). Common sources of such loud sounds or noise in our environment are also noted on this figure. As a teacher, you can help your students come to understand the importance of being careful with sound. For example, students should know that listening to iPods and MP3 players with their volume turned up too high will eventually result in hearing problems.

The pitch, or frequency, of sounds is measured in a unit called the hertz (Hz). The normal ear hears sounds that range from approximately 20 Hz to 20,000 Hz; speech sounds fall about in the middle of the human hearing range (between 250 Hz and 4000 Hz). An audiogram is used to plot how well an individual hears at various combinations of hertz and decibels and also at various bands of pitch and

FIGURE 3.6 Decibel Levels of Noise in American Environments

Hearing Level in Decibels	Examples of Common Sounds
30	Soft whisper, quiet library
40	Leaves rustling
50	Rainfall, refrigerator
60	Normal conversation, air conditioner
70	City or freeway traffic, sewing machine
80	Hair dryer, alarm clock
90*	Lawn mower, motorcycle
100	Garbage truck, snowmobile
110	Shouting at close range, dance club, race car
120	Jet plane taking off, car stereo turned all the way up
130	Live rock music, jackhammer
140	Firecracker, nearby gunshot blast, jet engine

*Levels 85 decibels and above are considered hazardous.

loudness. Typically, the accommodations and communication styles of these two groups of individuals differ. For example, students who are hard of hearing may need to sit closer to the teacher or have a classmate assist with notetaking, whereas a student who is deaf may well need an interpreter to profit from lectures.

Characteristics

Deaf and hard of hearing students are individuals with different learning styles and abilities, but they share one characteristic: Their ability to hear is limited. Clearly, for whatever reason, students who cannot hear the communications of others have a more difficult time learning through traditional instructional methods. As we have noted, the severity of the hearing loss and the age at which the loss occurred contribute to how well a person will be able to interact with others orally. The characteristics of deaf students are very different from those of students who are hard of hearing. However, teachers cannot make uniform judgments about the types and intensity of accommodations or the services required based on information about an individual student's amount or type of hearing loss. One student with a moderate loss might not profit from typical instructional methods (lectures, oral directions) alone, whereas another student with the same profile might function well without supports.

Another factor is whether the individual has cognitive impairments along with the hearing loss. With some conditions, these disabilities go hand in hand. Estimates are that at least 30 to 40 percent of deaf and hard of hearing children have additional disabilities (Johnson & Winter, 2003). Additional disabilities may include visual disabilities, mental retardation, learning disabilities, behavior disorders, or cerebral palsy. These accompanying disabilities are often by the same disease or accident that caused the hearing loss. Students whose deafness is inherited, however, tend not to have multiple disabilities.

Two areas are of great concern to educators working with deaf students: academic achievement and speech ability. A long-term problem for individuals who are deaf is their academic achievement, particularly in the area of reading (Gallaudet Research Institute, 1994; Johnson, 2001–2002; Moores, 2001). For example, by age 20, half of the students tested read below the mid-fourth-grade level, leaving them unable to read most newspapers, which are written at least at the fifth-grade level. Being able to hear is related to the ability to speak intelligibly. This is clear when we compare two groups of children between the ages of 5 to 10: those with profound hearing loss and those with mild to severe hearing loss. The speech of those with profound loss was not intelligible. Of those with mild to severe loss, 82 percent had intelligible speech (Yoshinaga-Itano & Sedey, 2000).

Technology has changed the lives for many individuals with hearing problems. Improvements in hearing aids and listening devices allow today's students to profit from education alongside their classmates without disabilities, whereas only some 50 years ago, students with mild to moderate hearing problems could not hear teachers' instructions or classmates' discussions. Today, because many hearing problems are corrected either through surgery or by the use of listening devices, some of these students do not even qualify for special education. More improvements are on the horizon. Medical technology holds the promise of both preventing and "curing" deafness at some point in the future. In 2000, children as young as a year old who were deaf were allowed to receive cochlear implants, assistive hearing devices designed to help individuals with sensorineural hearing loss gain useful hearing (National Institute on Deafness and Other Hearing

Disorders, 2006). Although not a cure for deafness, implants hold great promise for many individuals with profound hearing loss.

Prevalence

Think about your own older relatives, because hearing problems are associated with age. Although many people have hearing problems, almost half of them are over age 65. Despite this fact, hearing loss in children is the number-one birth defect in the United States (ASHA, 2002). Approximately 1 in every 1,000 babies is born profoundly deaf, and another 2 to 3 have less severe hearing losses. Remember, estimates are that some 30 to 40 percent of deaf and hard of hearing children have additional disabilities, such as visual disabilities, mental retardation, learning disabilities, behavior disorders, or cerebral palsy (Johnson & Winter, 2003). Typically, children who have multiple disabilities are not counted in the federal deafness or hard of hearing category, so we do not know precisely how many students have hearing problems. For those students whose primary disability is related to their hearing, the federal government reports 0.12 percent of the resident population, or 67,253 students (OSEP, 2006). Remember, these counts do not include those students who do not need special education because hearing aids or assistive devices allow them to hear well enough to participate in typical classroom activities.

Who Are Students with Visual Disabilities?

Today, a large percentage (about 57 percent) of students with visual disabilities spend over 80 percent of their school days in general education classrooms, most likely at their neighborhood school, and receiving support from a resource specialist or itinerant teacher (OSEP, 2006). These students participate in the general education curriculum with their sighted classmates and, if they do not also have multiple disabilities, tend to perform well academically. Most use aids such as glasses or technology that enlarges type to enhance their vision for accessing information and moving independently at school and in the community (Corn & Koenig, 2002).

Definition

When people see normally, two important aspects of their vision are working well: acuity and peripheral vision. Problems can occur in one or both of these aspects of vision, resulting in a disability. Visual acuity is how well a person can see at various distances. Normal visual acuity is measured by how accurately a person can see an object or image 20 feet away. Normal vision is thus said to be 20/20. A person whose vision is measured at 20/40 can see at 20 feet what people who do not need visual correction (glasses or contact lenses) can see at 40 feet away. The width of a person's field of vision, or the ability to perceive objects outside the direct line of vision, is called peripheral vision. This aspect of vision helps people move freely through their environment.

How much impairment results in a disability? Look at Table 3.10 and compare those definitions of visual disability. The definition offered by CDC and the

TABLE 3.10 Visual Disabilities

Source	Definition
IDEA '04[1]	*Visual impairment including blindness* means an impairment in vision that, even with correction, adversely affects a child's educational performance. The term includes both partial sight and blindness.
Professional[2]	*Low vision* . . . a level of vision which, with standard correction, hinders an individual in the planning and/or execution of a task, but which permits enhancement of the functional vision through the use of optical or nonoptical devices, environmental modifications and/or techniques.
United Nations and Centers for Disease Control[3]	*Low vision* . . . visual acuity between 20/70 and 20/400, with the best possible correction, or a visual field of 20 degrees or less.
Federal Government[4]	*Legally blind* . . . central visual acuity of 20/200 or less in the better eye, with best correction, or a diameter of visual field that does not subtend an angle greater than 20 degrees at its widest point.

Sources: [1]*U.S. Department of Education, 2006, p. 1265*
[2]*Corn, 1989, p. 28*
[3]*Centers for Disease Control, 2005, p. 1*
[4]*American Foundation for the Blind, 2005, p. 1*

one used to classify an individual as "legally blind" and therefore eligible for federal benefits both include criteria for visual acuity and peripheral vision. Today, IDEA '04 and most states have adopted eligibility criteria that reflect a functional definition of visual disabilities, a concept initiated by Anne Corn some two decades ago. The basic premise is that a student has a visual disability when, even with correction, educational performance is adversely affected. In other words, the issue is how much residual vision a person has or can use. States and school districts vary in the criteria they use to determine eligibility for special services.

Types

Many professionals talk about visual disabilities in four very different ways:

1. Identifying the reason for the visual loss
2. Considering the severity of the problem
3. Taking into account when the loss occurred
4. Determining whether the criteria for being considered legally blind are met

Numerous conditions can lead to visual loss that results in a disability. The conditions that most of us are familiar with are myopia (nearsightedness), hyperopia (farsightedness), and astigmatism (not being able to focus), but there are many other conditions that damage the eye, compromise its structure, and undermine its functioning. Some of these conditions can be prevented or corrected, and others at the present time cannot.

Typically, persons with visual disabilities are divided into two subgroups:

1. Low vision
2. Blindness

Individuals with low vision use sight to learn, but their visual disabilities interfere with daily functioning. Blindness means that the person uses touch and hearing to learn and does not have functional use of sight. Parents and professionals tend to employ functional definitions for these two subgroups. In other words, children with low vision use their sight for many school activities, including reading. Children who are blind do not have functional use of their vision and may perceive only shadows or some movement. These youngsters must be educated through tactile and other sensory channels and are considered functionally blind.

Blindness can occur at any age, but its impact varies with age. Just as with students who are deaf or hard of hearing, an important issue related to functional use of vision is age of onset (age when the disability occurred):

- Congenitally blind (onset at birth or during infancy)
- Adventitiously blind (onset after the age of 2)

This distinction is important because people who lose their sight after age 2, and hence are adventitiously blind, remember what some objects look like. Those who are congenitally blind were too young when the loss occurred to remember what things look like. The later the disability occurs, the more they remember. Visual memory is an important factor in learning, for it can influence one's development of concepts and other aspects important to learning.

Although it is not related to how well a person can use his or her vision, another way to categorize people with visual problems is in terms of whether they meet the definition of "legally blind." This designation allows individuals to receive special tax benefits and materials from the federal government and private agencies. Because it does not exclude people who have some functional use of sight, many individuals who are legally blind use print to read, and not braille, to gain information.

Characteristics

The way these individuals access information sets them apart as a group and further distinguishes among them (Corn & Koenig, 2002). Contrary to popular belief, the vast majority of people with visual disabilities use vision as their primary method of learning and means of participating in the community. For many of these students, the amount of vision they have left—their residual vision—can be further developed. The vision of some is static, remaining the same from day to day, whereas others find that their ability to see varies with the day, time of day, or setting (CDC, 2004). For some, higher or lower levels of illumination affect how well they can see, but for others, lighting level makes little difference. For some individuals, distance and contrast significantly affect how well they can process information presented through the visual channel. For most, optical aids such as glasses have a positive effect. Literacy is a major concern for these students (National Federation of the Blind [NFB], 2006). Most of them read print, usually via enlarged type. Others read via a tactile system, braille. And many others access printed materials by listening to books-on-tape or a personal reader. Because

● Because of the importance of literacy and the ability to read, IDEA '04 insists that instruction in the use of braille be considered for every student who has a severe visual loss.

of the importance of literacy and the ability to read, IDEA '04 insists that instruction in the use of braille be considered for every student who has a severe visual loss (U.S. Department of Education, 2006).

Although these students participate in inclusive classrooms at a very high rate, they have curricula targets in addition to those of the general education curriculum. These students must also learn skills related to being independent. Here are a few examples of the additional skills they need to learn: accessing transportation, moving freely in one's environment, and life skills. Therefore, orientation and mobility are major curriculum targets for students with severe visual disabilities. Orientation can be described as the mental map people have of their surroundings. Most of us use landmarks and other cues to get from one place to another. Think about how you get from your house to a friend's home or from one class to another on campus. What cues or landmarks do you use? These cues or landmarks make up our mental maps and our orientation to our environments. Remember that these mental landmarks are learned and that students need to know their schools well. As a teacher, you can assist a student with a severe visual loss by helping her or him understand emergency evacuation procedures, recognize exit paths from the school buildings, and learn how to move safely through the school environment both during normal school hours and in times of stress (Cox & Dykes, 2001). You can also make sure the student knows the "landmarks" in the classroom environment so he or she is free to move around independently.

The ability to travel safely and efficiently from one place to another is called mobility. Most adults who are blind use the long cane, also called the Hoover cane, which is named after its developer, Richard Hoover. However, tapping the cane along a sidewalk or pavement of the street does not always help the individual avoid the many obstacles found in modern society. For example, silent traffic signals, escalators, elevators, and public transportation, to say nothing of protruding and overhanging objects that are undetectable with mobility canes, can be very dangerous. These canes do not tell the users where they are or how to get to their next location. Not all people who need help with mobility use long canes; guide dogs or service animals are another option. The number of individuals who use guide dogs is relatively small; there are 1.3 million legally blind children and adults and only about 7,000 (less than 4 percent) use guide dogs to help them move about independently (AFB, 2005). You, as a teacher, can help students who are assisted by a service animal by helping classmates understand that the animal is not a pet and should be left to do the important job that took years of training for it to master.

The new orientation and mobility system for people with severe visual loss may well become "the" mobility system of this century (Bruno, 2006). It combines the global positioning system (GPS) technology used by the navigational devices in cars, long canes, and (in some cases) guide dogs as well.

Prevalence

According to the American Foundation for the Blind (AFB), approximately 1.3 million Americans are legally blind and there are some 10 million with low vision or blindness (AFB, 2005). However, the vast majority of these people are over the age of 65. Worldwide, only 4 percent of all people who are blind are children (Hatton, 2001). Visual disabilities are clearly associated with increasing age. About 4 of every 10,000 schoolchildren (less than 0.05 percent) have visual disabilities and receive special services (OSEP, 2006). Across the nation, only 23,456 children between the ages of 6 and 17 are receiving special education because of low vision or blindness. Remember that this number does not include all students with visual disabilities; for example, it omits those who have multiple-severe disabilities. About half of young children with visual disabilities have more than one disability and are counted in the multiple-severe disabilities category (Dote-Kwan, Chen, & Hughes, 2001).

Who Are Students with Traumatic Brain Injury?

About a million children annually experience a head injury. Of those injuries, some 15,000 to 16,000 have lasting effects and about 500 require hospitalization (Van Kuren, 2001). Prior to the 1960s, most children whose brains were seriously hurt died soon after the trauma. Today's emergency procedures, imaging technology, surgical methods, and pharmaceutical treatments routinely save children's lives after terrible accidents. Unfortunately, the results for some survivors include the need for long-term or short-term special education or special accommodations under Section 504 of the Rehabilitation Act. At some time during your career, you will probably work with at least one child with traumatic brain injury (TBI) (Van Kuren, 2001).

Definition

TBI became a separate special education category when IDEA was reauthorized in 1990. Before then, these students were served and counted in whatever category most closely matched their primary learning needs. For example, because these students often exhibit memory deficits, attention problems, language impairments, and reduced academic performance, many of them are educated alongside their classmates with learning disabilities. Others, because of their head injuries, experience seizures and receive many of the same accommodations as children with epilepsy. The official IDEA '04 definition of TBI is found in Table 3.11.

Types

Like other disabilities, TBI ranges in severity from mild to severe (National Institute of Neurological Disorders and Stroke [NINDS], 2006). Those with more severe head injuries receive home instruction, often for a year, before returning to school part-time. In many cases the effects eventually disappear, but in some cases they are lifelong.

Characteristics

Children with TBI and their families face great emotional turmoil during the time shortly after the injury. Educators must be alert to such additional changes in mood and behavior and seek assistance in helping the individual adjust to changes in ability, performance, and behavior (NICHCY, 2006). Even those with mild cases of TBI must cope with sudden changes in performance and are likely to experience some or all of these symptoms: dizziness, headache, selective attention problems, irritability, anxiety, blurred vision, insomnia, fatigue, motor difficulties, language problems, behavior and emotional problems, cognitive problems, and memory problems (Van Kuren, 2001). What came easily one day is filled with frustration and confusion the next. Many youngsters with TBI tend to have uneven abilities, a fact that is confusing to the individuals and to their teachers. They get tired easily. It is common for these youngsters to have difficulty adjusting to and accepting their newly acquired disability. Because of the frustrations of having trouble doing tasks that used to be easy, many display behavior problems and reduced self-esteem. In these cases, it is also common for the individual to experience depression or withdrawal. Problems caused by TBI can last for a very short time or for years.

Alert teachers can be very helpful in early diagnosis and treatment of TBI (NICHCY, 2006). Many head injuries are the result of activities that children

TABLE 3.11 Traumatic Brain Injury

Source	Definition
IDEA '04	*Traumatic brain injury* means an acquired injury to the brain caused by an external physical force, resulting in total or partial functional disability or psychosocial impairment, or both, that adversely affects a child's educational performance. Traumatic brain injury applies to open or closed head injuries resulting in impairments in one or more areas, such as cognition; language; memory; attention; reasoning; abstract thinking; judgment; problem solving; sensory, perceptual, and motor abilities; psychosocial behavior; physical functions; information processing; and speech. The term does not apply to brain injuries that are congenital or degenerative, or to brain injuries induced by birth trauma.

Source: U.S. Department of Education, 2006, p. 1265

commonly engage in: riding a bicycle, using playground equipment, even tussling in the schoolyard. Often, youngsters do not want to admit that they fell or forgot to wear a protective helmet or were fighting on the playground. But when a student acts differently, becomes unable to pay attention, or seems unusually tired, you should seek help from the school nurse to be certain that he or she has not experienced a head injury.

Prevalence

More than 100,000 children sustain brain injuries each year, and 30,000 of them have permanent disabilities (Lash & DePompie, 2002). Most of these disabilities are mild. According to the federal government, 92,211 students with TBI, aged 6 through 17, were served by special education in the 2005 school year (OSEP, 2006).

Who Are Students with Deafblindness?

A great example of why we should not make assumptions about any person with a disability, even those with the most severe and complex problems, comes from a person with deafblindness. Helen Keller was a woman of many accomplishments, one of which was graduating from Radcliffe with honors. She did this in 1904, when few people *without* disabilities went to college, particularly women, and when people with disabilities never had such opportunities.

Definition

Although every state acknowledges deafblindness, definitions vary by state. Because most of these youngsters have additional disabilities, such as cognitive disabilities and health impairments, many of them are counted in the multiple-severe disabilities category (Miles, 2005). The definition of *deafblindness* is found in Table 3.12.

TABLE 3.12 Deafblindness

Source	Definition
IDEA '04[1]	*Deafblindness* means concomitant hearing and visual impairments, the combination of which causes such severe communication and other developmental and educational needs that they cannot be accommodated in special education programs solely for children with deafness or children with blindness.
National Technical Assistance Center (DB-Link)[2]	Criteria for deafblindness requires that a person needs, at a minimum, to have a visual acuity of 20/70 in the better eye with correction and an auditory deficit of 30 dB in the better ear.

Sources: [1]*U.S. Department of Education, 2006, p. 1261*
[2]Baldwin, 1995, p. 5

Types

When you hear the word *deafblindness,* you probably think of people who have no vision and no hearing abilities and how severely these people's lives must be restricted. Although this is true for some individuals with deafblindness, it is far from true for most of them, because the majority have some residual hearing and/or vision. Almost half of these students have enough residual vision to read enlarged print, see sign language, move about in their environment, and recognize friends and family (Miles, 2005). In fact, according to the National Deafblind Census, more of them have some functional use of their vision than have some hearing abilities (DB-Link, 2006). Some have sufficient hearing to understand certain speech sounds or hear loud noises. Some can even develop speech themselves. Others have such limited vision and hearing that they profit little from either sense. In addition to their visual and hearing losses, the majority of these individuals have other disabilities, such as mental retardation, that further complicate their education. Most individuals with deafblindness need considerable supports for their worlds to be safe and accessible; these students' educational programs need to be carefully thought through and must be uniquely designed to ensure that each of these children meets his or her potential.

Characteristics

The world for children with deafblindness can be exceptionally restricted. For those whose hearing and vision losses are severe or profound, their immediate world may well end at their fingertips (Miles, 2005). The individuals affected by deafblindness, their family members, and their teachers must address problems with feelings of isolation, communication, and mobility.

Possibly the greatest challenge facing individuals with deafblindness is learning to communicate (Miles, 2005). Many adults with this disability have developed outstanding communication skills, but this achievement does not typically happen without considerable effort. Some of these individuals never learn to talk (Stremel, 1998). Others communicate through touch (Chen, Downing, & Rodriguez-Gil, 2000–2001; Miles, 2005). They use various forms of manual communication (e.g., sign language, body language, gestures) to express their needs and "talk" to others. Some use a special kind of sign language called "hand over hand," a system in which two people use the palm of each other's hands to sign through touches.

Prevalence

According to the Deafblind Census, some 7,147 students between the ages of 6 and 21 have deafblindness (DB-Link, 2006). However, for the same year, the federal government reported that only 1,296 students across the entire nation have this condition (OSEP, 2006). Why does such a large discrepancy exist? It is because the federal government insists that states report students' disabilities in only one area, and many deafblind students are reported in other categories because they have so many coexisting problems.

It is unlikely that you as a teacher will meet or work with a student with deafblindness. According to the Deafblind Census, only 591 deafblind students receive their education almost exclusively in the general education classroom (DB-Link, 2006). An additional 511 receive their instruction in both the general education class and a resource room. All of the remaining 6,045 students are educated in separate classes or separate schools. Regardless of the special education category in which a student with deafblindness is included, relatively few students have these problems. And when they do, they need very special instruction and supports.

summary

Although less than 2 percent of all students have low incidence disabilities, these disabilities include hundreds of discrete conditions. The federal government has designated eight disabilities, plus the flexible, noncategorical grouping "developmental delay" for children between the ages of 3 and 9, as being "low incidence." In this chapter, you learned that students with low incidence disabilities exhibit complex and unique learning characteristics that challenge themselves, their families, and their schools. Their conditions and disabilities influence what they are taught and how they are taught to a greater degree than is true for many of their peers with and without disabilities. These students often require unique responses so that they can access the curriculum, participate fully in the school community, and be successful students. The types of supports, accommodations, and instruction must reflect the evidence-based practices you will learn about throughout this academic term. Despite the challenges and barriers many of these students face, they hold great promise of attaining remarkable accomplishments.

self-test QUESTIONS

Let's review the learning objectives for this chapter. If you are uncertain and cannot "talk through" the answers provided for any of these questions, reread those sections of the text.

- **What is meant by "low incidence disabilities"?**

  Low incidence disabilities have a low prevalence, so relatively few individuals and families are involved, but they often require intensive and unique responses to their very special needs. These unique responses include many, and sometimes complex, accommodations, as well as long-term interventions, instruction not typically included in the general education curriculum (e.g., braille), and the inclusion of many different related services professionals (such as assistive technologists, physical therapists, and speech/language pathologists).

- **What are the key features of each low incidence disability?**

  The key features of *multiple-severe disabilities* include the presence of more than one disability; goals that include independence and community presence; provision of supports that are ongoing and intensive; and problems with generalization, communication, memory, and life skills.

  The key features of the five disorders (autism, Asperger syndrome, childhood disintegrative disorder (CDD), Rett syndrome, and pervasive developmental disorder–not otherwise specified) that are included in the *autism spectrum disorders (ASD)* include problems with communication and social skills, unusual behaviors, and cognitive disabilities.

The key features of *physical disabilities* vary with the condition that caused the physical disability. For example, orthopedic impairments, limb deficiencies, and juvenile arthritis result in problems with structure and functioning of the body; cerebral palsy (CP) can have multiple outcomes; and seizure disorders (epilepsy) can result in short episodes that quickly interrupt learning or major events that require major intervention.

The key features of the category *deaf and hard of hearing* vary by type (conductive or sensorineural), age of onset (prelingually or postlingually deaf), and degree of loss (hard of hearing or deafness). All these conditions usually result in problems with communication, academic achievement, and speech ability.

The key features of most *health impairments* or *special health care needs* are fatigue, absences from school, inconsistent ability to pay attention, muscle weakness, and problems with physical coordination. Examples of health impairments include chronic illnesses (asthma, sickle cell anemia) and infectious diseases.

The key feature of *developmental delay* is that disability is noncategorically described (no disability label required). This means of qualifying students for special education services is typically used for preschoolers between ages 3 and 5 but may include children up to the age of 9.

Low vision and blindness is typically categorized in terms of functional use of sight, age of onset (congenitally blind, adventitiously blind), and degree of loss (low vision, legally blind).

Key issues for these individuals are attaining literacy (braille or print), developing orientation and mobility skills, and developing maximal use of residual vision and sight for daily functioning. Those with blindness use touch and hearing as their primary means of accessing information; those with low vision use their sight.

Deafblindness is the occurrence of coexisting hearing and visual impairments; it is important to recognize that neither disability has to be severe or profound in nature. This exceptionally low incidence disability results in problems with isolation, communication, and mobility.

Traumatic brain injury is also called closed head injury. The disability is often temporary, lasting about a year, and most cases are mild. Symptoms are similar to those of learning disabilities. Many of these individuals experience hospital or home instruction for some period of time.

● **Why did IDEA '04 include the disability category "developmental delay"?**

It was included to avoid identifying a young child as having the wrong disability and to provide flexibility and the early delivery of intervention services to preschoolers and those in the early school years.

● **What are some characteristics commonly observed in youngsters with low incidence disabilities?**

These students' special needs are complex and unique, infrequent or uncommon, and typically "visible" or obvious. Although these disabilities are usually identified during the early childhood years, these students' disabilities range from mild to severe. As a group, these students tend to be in general education less than other groups of students with disabilities.

● Revisit the
OPENING challenge

Check your answers to the Reflection Questions from the Opening Challenge and revise them on the basis of what you have learned.

1. Do you think Ms. Simpkin will need to plan for her new student differently than she has for other students with disabilities? If so, in what ways? If not, why not?

2. What learning characteristics might she have to consider as she makes initial plans for Josh?

3. How might her plans vary after she learns what disabilities Josh has?

4. What topics in her old education textbooks should she review before her meeting with the principal?

5. Provide Ms. Simpkin with five questions or issues she should discuss with her principal.

Professional Standards and Licensure

CEC Knowledge and Skill Core Standard and Associated Subcategories

CEC Content Standard 1: Foundations

Special educators understand the field as an evolving and changing discipline based on philosophies, evidence-based principles and theories, relevant laws and policies, diverse historical points of view, and human issues that have historically influenced the treatment of individuals with exceptional needs both in school and society.

CEC Content Standard 2: Development and Characteristics of Learners

Special educators know and demonstrate respect for their students first as unique human beings. Special educators understand the similarities and differences in human development and the characteristics between and among individuals with and without ELN. Moreover, special educators understand how exceptional conditions can interact with the domains of human development, and they use this knowledge to respond to the varying abilities and behaviors of individuals with ELN.

CEC Content Standard 3

Special educators understand the effects that an exceptional condition can have on an individual's learning in school and throughout life. They understand the similarities and differences in human development and the characteristics between and among individuals with and without ELN.

CEC Content Standard 9

Special educators are guided by the profession's ethical and professional practice standards. They practice in multiple roles and complex situations across wide age and developmental ranges. Special educators are aware of how their own and others' attitudes, behaviors, and ways of communicating can influence their practice.

INTASC Core Principle and Associated Special Education Subcategories

1. Subject Matter

1.03 All teachers understand that students with disabilities may need accommodations, modifications, and/or adaptations to the general curriculum.

2. Student Learning

2.01 All teachers have a sound understanding of physical, social, emotional, and cognitive development. They are familiar with the general characteristics of the most frequently occurring disabilities and have a basic understanding of the ways that disabilities impact learning.

2.02 All teachers examine their assumptions about the learning and development of students with disabilities and use this information to create challenging and supportive learning opportunities.

2.03 All teachers recognize that students with disabilities vary in their approaches to learning depending on factors such as the nature of their disability, their level of knowledge and functioning, and life experiences.

3. Leaner Differences

3.04 All teachers understand and are sensitive to cultural, ethnic, gender, and linguistic differences that may be confused with or misinterpreted as manifestations of disability.

9. Teacher Reflection

9.02 All teachers continually challenge their beliefs about how students learn and how to teach them effectively.

Praxis II: Education of Exceptional Students: Core Content Knowledge PRAXIS

I. Understanding Exceptionalities

Human development and behavior as related to students with disabilities, including

- Social and emotional development and behavior.
- Language development and behavior.
- Cognition.
- Physical development, including motor and sensory.

Characteristics of students with disabilities, including the influence of

- Cognitive factors.
- Affective and social-adaptive factors, including cultural, linguistic, gender, and socioeconomic factors.
- Genetic, medical, motor, sensory, and chronological age factors.

Basic concepts in special education, including

- Attention deficit hyperactivity disorder, as well as the incidence and prevalence of various types of disabilities.
- The causation and prevention of disability.
- The nature of behaviors, including frequency, duration, intensity, and degrees of severity.
- The classification of students with disabilities.

Video—"Traumatic Brain Injury"

Matt is a kindergarten student who received a traumatic brain injury (TBI) as a result of a car accident. He receives special education, and his teachers discuss his educational plan and how other students interact with him.

Log onto **www.mylabschool.com**. Under the **Courses** tab, in **Special Education**, go to the **video lab**. Access the "**Traumatic Brain Injury and Physical Disabilities**" videos and watch "**Traumatic Brain Injury**."

 OR

Use the **www.mylabschool.com Assignment Finder** to go directly to these videos. Just enter Assignment ID **SPV11**.

1. Educational programs for students like Matt, who experienced traumatic brain injury, should focus on retraining impaired cognitive processes while developing new compensatory skills and providing a supportive environment. If Matt's age permitted him to be in your classroom, how might you support his re-entry? Be specific, and support your choices with information from this chapter.

Video—"Physical Disabilities"

Oscar is a high school student with physical disabilities. With the help of an aide and some adaptations, he is able to participate in a regular education classroom.

Log onto **www.mylabschool.com**. Under the **Courses** tab, in **Special Education,** go to the **video lab**. Access the "**Traumatic Brain Injury and Physical Disabilities**" videos and watch the "**Physical Disabilities**" video.

 OR

Use the **www.mylabschool.com Assignment Finder** to go directly to these videos. Just enter Assignment ID **SPVII.**

1. What type of assistive technology and other devices did Oscar use? According to the math teacher, was Oscar working toward the same goals as his peers?

2. What was the role of Oscar's aide in the classroom? What are the pros and cons of having an aide work so closely with one student? Provide a rationale for your answer.

3. In what ways was Oscar integrated into the general education math class? List three ways to increase his interaction with peers in this class.

Companion Website

To access chapter objectives, practice tests, weblinks, and flashcards, go to the companion website at **www.ablongman.com/bryantsmith1e.**

chapter 4

Other Students with Special Learning Needs

With contributions by

Janette K. Klingner, *University of Colorado at Boulder*

Margarita Bianco, *University of Colorado at Denver,*
and *Health Sciences Center, Denver, Colorado*

chapter OBJECTIVES

After studying this chapter, you will have the knowledge to answer the following questions:

- How are students with physical and cognitive needs protected under Section 504?
- How can we best meet the needs of students in our culturally and linguistically diverse classrooms?
- Who are students "at risk" and what should we know and do to help them achieve their full potential in school and in life?
- Who are students with gifts and talents, and how can we differentiate our instruction to help them maximize their potential?

● OPENING challenge

Helping Students with Other Special Learning Needs Access the Curriculum

Elementary Grades ● Mrs. Grelak has been teaching in the primary grades at Tyler Elementary School for 20 years. The community surrounding the school and the school's population have changed a great deal since she began teaching. Whereas for years all but a handful of her students were White, and generally middle class, her third-grade class is now culturally and linguistically diverse. This year she has 11 African American students and 19 Latino students, 9 of whom are English language learners at various levels of emerging English proficiency. In addition, she has a new student from Korea who knows very little English. Additionally, most of her students qualify for a free or reduced-price lunch. A resource teacher provides pullout English as a second language (ESL) support for her English language learners for 50 minutes a day. But this seems to be insufficient. Mrs. Grelak feels frustrated and overwhelmed about how best to meet her students' needs. Many of them seem to be struggling to keep up with grade-level material. She is especially concerned about Gabriel and Allen.

Gabriel's family moved to the United States from Mexico about a year and a half ago, and

Secondary Grades ● Mr. Evans loves his job at Campbell Middle School, an urban school with many diverse learners. He is in his third year of teaching sixth grade and believes his greatest strength is differentiating instruction to meet the needs of all his students. This year, however, Mr. Evans is particularly concerned about one of his students and does not know how to help him.

Jerome has been a puzzle for Mr. Evans right from the start of the school year. Jerome seems to be a natural leader in the class, and he sometimes plays the role of class clown (or even class troublemaker). Jerome is very creative and always has wonderful ideas for a new short story or even a screenplay. He also seems to have a natural ability for solving complex problems, but when asked to put his ideas down on paper, Jerome refuses. Although he seems so bright, Jerome is reading well below grade level, has difficulty spelling, and struggles with writing. Mr. Evans reflects on Jerome, *"How can he be so smart yet struggle in so many areas? When I give him extra practice in reading and writing, he attempts the work but either gives up or throws his written work away. What can I do about Jerome?"* ●

Column continues on next page

Gabriel was placed in a first-grade class. He knew very little English when he started school and still is at beginning proficiency level. During his second-grade year he missed almost a month of school, some when he was ill and some when he and his family went to Mexico to visit relatives for Christmas. Now, in third grade, he seems to have made little progress and is reading only at a beginning first-grade level. He has trouble concentrating and appears to lack motivation. Mrs. Grelak is unsure whether to recommend that he be retained; she suspects that he might have a learning disability.

Allen has attended Tyler since kindergarten. Allen was retained after first grade and now is 9 years old. He is well-mannered and good-natured and is popular among his peers. Yet he struggles academically, and he is about 2 years behind in reading as well as math. Allen's mother is concerned about Allen's lack of progress and works with him at home on practice activities that Mrs. Grelak sends home for this purpose. She told Mrs. Grelak that Allen is having much more difficulty than either of his older sisters. Mrs. Grelak has decided to refer him for an evaluation for possible placement in special education. She suspects that he might be developmentally delayed.

Mrs. Grelak thinks, *"I have so many students from diverse backgrounds. I have many students with special learning needs. I'm not sure how to meet all of their needs while trying to teach the curriculum for my grade level. I need to better understand how to help them."* ●

● Reflection Questions

In your journal, write down your answers to the following questions. After completing the chapter, check your answers and revise them on the basis of what you have learned.

1. What should Mrs. Grelak's next steps be with Gabriel?

2. Do you agree that Mrs. Grelak should refer Allen for a special education evaluation? Why or why not?

3. In what ways does his level of English language proficiency seem to be affecting Gabriel?

4. What advice would you give Mr. Evans about instruction for gifted students with learning disabilities?

5. What characteristics does Jerome have that seem consistent with those of a gifted student? What characteristics does Jerome have that seem consistent with those of a student with learning disabilities?

6. How can Mr. Evans challenge Jerome while attending to his other learning needs?

As we learned in Chapter 1, special education services are available for students with identified disabilities according to criteria established in the Individuals with Disabilities Education Act, 2004 (IDEA). These students are entitled to the supports and services they need to benefit from instruction and participate with their peers in the "least restrictive environment." Yet it is almost inevitable that you will have other students with special learning needs in your classroom who may not be eligible for special education services under IDEA but who require special attention in order to fully reach their potential in school. They need academic and other supports to ensure that they can benefit from instruction in the general education classroom. "Inclusive education" is a means to meet the full range of student needs in the classroom by implementing validated practices and providing support systems that help teachers reach *all* their students.

In this chapter, we discuss some of those other special needs that can affect educational outcomes of students in our classrooms. Understanding that the types of needs and life situations that students bring with them are varied and numerous, we do not pretend to approach comprehensiveness in this discussion. Rather, we will discuss some of the more critical and common of these needs and circumstances—health-related, cultural, linguistic, economic, social, and academic—and hope you will recognize that those students, too, require and deserve special attention in your instructional planning and implementation.

Who Are the Students Protected by Section 504, and to What Educational Services Are They Entitled?

Section 504 of the Rehabilitation Act of 1973 is a civil rights law that prohibits discrimination against individuals with disabilities. It requires federal, state, and local governments to provide access to buildings and other public spaces to people with disabilities through such accommodations as alternatives to stairs (ramps and elevators) and barrier-free sidewalks (via curb cuts that allow wheelchairs to roll from sidewalk to street).

Section 504 also requires that publicly funded schools make accommodations and modifications for students with disabilities in order to ensure that they have equal access to an education. Let's review how students qualify for services under Section 504 and the educational accommodations that are available to them.

Qualifying for Services Under Section 504

There are students with special learning needs who are not covered under IDEA. However, they may qualify for services under Section 504 because the definition of disability is broader under Section 504 and extends beyond school age. To be eligible for protections under Section 504, the child must have a physical or mental impairment. This impairment must substantially limit at least one major life activity. Major life activities include walking, seeing, hearing, speaking, breathing, learning, reading, writing, performing math calculations, working, caring for oneself, and performing manual tasks. The key is whether the child has an "impairment" that "substantially limits . . . one or more . . . major life activities" (Wright & Wright, 2007).

If the student has a disability that adversely affects educational *performance,* the student is eligible for special education services under IDEA and would also be automatically protected from discrimination under Section 504. However, the converse is not true: If a student has a disability that does *not* adversely affect educational performance, then the student will *not* be eligible for special education services under IDEA but will usually be entitled to protections under Section 504. For example, a student with AIDS, a student with ADHD, and a student with chronic asthma are all protected from discrimination under Section 504. Each of these students *may* also be eligible for special education services under IDEA (under the category "Other Health Impairments" described in Chapter 3), but those decisions would be based on the specific educational needs of each student (Wrightslaw, 2006). Students with conditions such as drug or alcohol addiction, temporary disabilities resulting from accidents, attention problems, or chronic health issues can qualify as having a disability under Section 504 (Rosenfeld, 2000). Although no funding is attached to this legislation, school districts and general education professionals are expected to implement measures to address any special conditions that they believe would jeopardize a student's ability to learn.

Providing Educational Services Under Section 504

Under Section 504, students who qualify as having a disability are assessed, and a 504 plan is developed and monitored (see Figure 4.1 for an example). The plan includes accommodations and adaptations, the person(s) responsible for implementation, and the procedures for monitoring the effectiveness of the plan. Accommodations and adaptations might include changes to the physical environment (specialized lighting, a quiet study place), adaptations to curriculum and instruction, accommodations in testing, and assistance with organization (Friend, 2008). In addition to instructional programs, the plan can cover other academically related programs such as field trips and summer programs.

How Can We Meet the Needs of All Students in a Culturally and Linguistically Diverse Classroom?

Every one of us has a culture (or cultures), just as we all speak a language (or languages). So what do we mean when we say "culturally and linguistically diverse students"? In the United States, this term has come to mean students with cultural, ethnic, and linguistic backgrounds different from the macro culture and language (i.e., Standard English) of the White majority. Sometimes the term *people* (or *students*) *of color* is used instead of *culturally and linguistically diverse* (CLD) *students.* Any individual belongs not to just one culture, or "macro culture," but to many micro cultures (Gollnick & Chinn, 2006). A macro culture can be thought of as a society that embraces overarching cultural factors. For example, in our society, democracy is one of those factors that is valued as part of our culture. A micro culture is a group whose members share similar language, belief systems, and values (Banks, 2001; Friend, 2008). Thus, students in our classrooms represent a variety

FIGURE 4.1 Section 504 Sample Plan

Sample Components of a 504 Plan for a Student with Diabetes

Student's Name: _____

Birth Date: _____ Grade: _____ Type of Diabetes: _____

Homeroom Teacher: _____ Bus Number: _____ Date: _____

Objectives/Goals of this Plan

The goal of this plan is to provide the special education and/or related aids and services needed to maintain blood glucose within this student's target range of _____ and to respond appropriately to levels outside of this range in accordance with the instructions provided by the student's personal health care team.

1. **Provision of Diabetes Care:** Designated individuals will receive training to be Trained Diabetes Personnel (TDP).

2. **Student Level of Self-Care and Location of Supplies and Equipment:** The student can perform the following diabetes care tasks without help _____ at any time of the day and in any location. The student needs assistance or supervision with the following diabetes health care tasks _____. The student needs a TDP to perform the following diabetes care tasks _____.

3. **Snacks and Meals:** The school nurse, or TDP if the school nurse is not available, will work with the student and his/her parents/guardians to coordinate a meal and snack schedule in accordance with the attached Diabetes Medical Management Plan (DMMP) that will coincide with the schedule of classmates to the closest extent possible. The student shall eat lunch at the same time each day, or earlier if experiencing hypoglycemia. The student shall have enough time to finish lunch. A snack and quick-acting source of glucose must always be immediately available to the student.

4. **Exercise and Physical Activity:** The student shall be permitted to participate fully in physical education classes and team sports except as set out in the student's DMMP.

5. **Water and Bathroom Access:** The student shall be permitted to have immediate access to water and be permitted to use the bathroom without restriction.

6. **Checking Blood Glucose Levels, Insulin, and Medication Administration, and Treating High or Low Blood Glucose Levels:** Blood glucose monitoring will be done at the times designated in the student's DMMP, whenever the student feels her blood glucose level may be high or low, or when symptoms of high or low blood glucose levels are observed. Insulin and/or other diabetes medication will be administered at the times and through the means (e.g., syringe, pen, or pump) designated in the student's DMMP.

7. **Tests and Classroom Work:** If the student is affected by high or low blood glucose levels at the time of regular testing, the student will be permitted to take the test at another time without penalty. If the student needs to take breaks to use the water fountain or bathroom, check blood glucose, or treat hypoglycemia during a test or other activity, the student will be given extra time to finish the test or other activity without penalty.

Emergency Contact:

_____   _____   _____
Parent's/Guardian's Name   Home Phone Number   Emergency Phone Number

Approved and received:

_____   _____
Parent/Guardian   Date

_____   _____
School Representative and Title   Date

Source: Retrieved April 24, 2007, from http://www.diabetes.org/advocacy-and-legalresources/discrimination/school/504plan.jsp

of micro cultures, each with its own identity and perspectives. Our schools must be responsive to and respectful of the richness of diversity as the CLD population continues to increase.

There is growing diversity in the United States, as evidenced by increases in various groups in the population (U.S. Census Bureau, 2000). And this increasing diversity in the general population means more CLD students. Figure 4.2 shows population percentages for racial and ethnic groups in the United States, beginning in 1980 with projected growth to 2050. The U.S. Census Bureau projects that by 2050, the White population will increase by 7 percent and thus constitute an estimated 50.1 percent of the population, compared to the 69.4 percent reported in 2000 (Nieto & Bode, 2008; U.S. Census Bureau, 2000). The African American population is expected to increase from 12.7 percent in 2000 to 14.6 percent in 2050. It is estimated that the Hispanic population will almost double, from 12.6 percent in 2000 to 24.4 in 2050. Finally, the Asian population is expected to increase from 3.8 percent in 2000 to 8 percent in 2050 (Nieto & Bode, 2008; U.S. Census Bureau, 2000). Certainly, the rise in legal immigration and in the numbers of first-generation U.S. residents has contributed significantly to these figures. More than half of these residents are now from Latin America and one-quarter from Asia (Nieto & Bode, 2008).

Changes in the U.S. demographics are also reflected in our schools (Yates & Ortiz, 2004). Over one-third of students in schools are culturally and linguistically diverse, and in most of the major urban school districts, "minority" students represent the majority student population (Yates & Ortiz, 2004). Hispanics are the fastest-growing ethnic group in U.S. schools and have passed African Americans as the largest minority group in the United States (U.S. 2000 Census, 2001). There are now more than 3.5 million children who are English language learners (ELLs) in U.S. schools, which means that these students are learning English as a second or even third language (Nieto & Bode, 2008; U.S. Department of Education, 2003). Seventy-five percent of this linguistically diverse group speaks Spanish, but students speak over a hundred languages in our schools (Yates & Ortiz, 2004).

Think back to the Opening Challenge. How are these changing demographic figures reflected in Mrs. Grelak's classroom? Given the increasing diversity in our

FIGURE 4.2 **Percent of the Resident U.S. Population, by Minority Race/Ethnicity: Selected Years 1980 to 2000 and Projections to 2050**

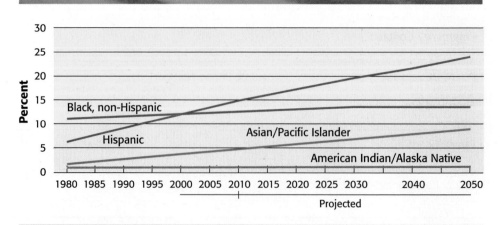

Source: Adapted from *Affirming diversity: The sociopolitical context of multicultural education*, 5th ed., by S. Nieto and P. Bode, 2008, Boston: Allyn and Bacon.

society and schools, educators are challenged to learn more about culture and how it influences our thinking, belief systems, values, and interactions. In other words, culture matters. Let's turn our attention to the definition of culture and to types of programs for CLD students.

Definition of Culture

What is culture? Culture is a way of perceiving the world and of interacting within it. Gollnick and Chinn (2006) note that cultural norms influence our thinking, language, and behavior. Culture is shared; it is the customs and values that bind us together. These customs developed over centuries in response to environmental conditions. And yet culture is not static; rather, it is dynamic, complex, and ever-changing (Gutierrez & Rogoff, 2003). Our cultural identities evolve throughout our lives in response to political, economic, educational, and social experiences.

Cultural identity is learned as part of our ethnic group, but it is also developed as part of our religion, socioeconomic status, geographic region, place of residence (e.g., urban or rural), and gender, to name just a few micro cultures. Participation in some micro cultural groups may take on more importance at different times in one's life. The interaction of these micro cultures within the larger macro culture is also important. Schools and classrooms themselves develop their own patterns of behavior and are said to have a culture.

Culture is involved in all learning (Cole, 1998; Rogoff, 2003). From the time we are quite young, we are socialized to learn in different ways. For example, in her classic study of the children in three different communities, Shirley Brice-Heath (1983) noted that only the middle-class White children started school accustomed to the ways of teaching and learning they encountered in their classrooms. They were not surprised when they were asked questions to which their teachers already knew the answers. They knew how to narrate stories in just the style expected by their teachers. Children from different backgrounds, on the other hand, were not accustomed to being asked questions designed to test their knowledge (e.g., "What shape is this?). Some children had learned in their homes and communities to tell elaborate, complex stories that their teachers did not value because the stories did not "get to the point" quickly enough. In other words, there was a mismatch between home and school cultures, and between ways of teaching and learning. All of the children in the communities that Heath studied started school ready to learn, but their schools were not ready to teach all children. When Heath helped teachers understand these differences, the teachers were able to instruct their students in ways that better capitalized on students' strengths and built on the knowledge and skills they brought to school. The Making a Difference feature in this chapter illustrates how one teacher's determination to communicate in spite of a language barrier both solved a potential problem and taught her how important it can be to learn as much as possible about the experiences of culturally diverse students.

In another classic study, Kathryn Au (1980) observed lessons while school personnel in Hawaii implemented different reading programs that had been found to be effective in other settings. It was not until the discourse of reading lessons became more like the style of day-to-day Hawaiian conversation that reading achievement improved. In other words, there had been a mismatch between the children's home culture and the culture of instruction in their schools. When the match between home and school improved, so did students' learning. Teachers who are culturally responsive strive to match their instruction to their students. They make connections with their students as individuals, while understanding

Making a Difference

Overcoming a Language Barrier to Make a Difference with a Child

Kimberly A. Gillow
*General Education Teacher, Kindergarten
Dexter Community Schools, Dexter, Michigan
Former Speech–Language Pathologist,
Dearborn Public Schools*

My most challenging and rewarding experience as a speech–language pathologist involved a 9-year-old boy named Ali. Ali enrolled in our school in late January. During the initial assessment, I was told that Ali and his family had escaped from a refugee camp in Iraq. Ali spoke Arabic and had a mild cognitive impairment. Not being able to speak Arabic, I was nervous about how I would provide speech and language therapy.

The psychologist, social worker, and bilingual staff worked with him during the first few days, and at the end of the first week, we had a team meeting. At that meeting, Ali's teacher reported that several students were missing their lunches during the week; the children in Ali's class suspected that he was taking the lunches.

I decided to make a social story with pictures to help Ali understand that he should not take food from the other children. The story started with a picture of food and of Ali. Each of the following pages included a picture of food and one of the other students. I asked the bilin- gual staff to write, "I will only eat my own food" in Arabic on the last page. The next day, I read the book to Ali.

At the end of the week, the team met with his parents. They mentioned the book I made for Ali and told our staff that they were "happy to hear that the children were allowed to eat every day in America." That day, I learned that Ali's job at the refugee camp in Iraq had been to find food for his siblings.

I read the book to Ali for months. Eventually, Ali learned that he was safe at our school, the "food finding" stopped, and he grew to feel comfortable and confident as a part of his class. My experiences with Ali taught me that each child comes to school with a unique social, cultural, and family history that affects his school life in many ways—and that my efforts to learn about a student's experiences could help me make informed instructional decisions for him. ●

that there are many sociocultural influences on learning. What can teachers do to help culturally and linguistically diverse students learn and achieve to their potential? What lessons can Mrs. Grelak in our Opening Challenge learn from this research? Multicultural education and bilingual education are two approaches to working with CLD students.

Multicultural Education

Multicultural education has tended to be thought of as something "added on" to the curriculum, focusing on the holidays, traditions, and historical contributions of diverse ethnic groups. But multicultural education is much more than that. It is about making sure that schools are a place where all students feel welcomed, valued, and supported. Nieto and Bode (2008) define multicultural education as

a process of comprehensive school reform and basic education for all students. It challenges and rejects racism and other forms of discrimination in schools and society and accepts and affirms the pluralism (ethnic, racial, linguistic, religious, economic, and gender, among others) that students, their communities, and teachers reflect. Multicultural education permeates the schools' curriculum and instructional strategies, as well as the interactions among teachers, students, and families, and the very way that schools conceptualize the nature of teaching and learning. Because it uses critical pedagogy as its underlying philosophy and focuses on knowledge, reflections, and action as the basis for social change, multicultural education promotes democratic principles of social justice. (p. 44)

Nieto and Bode emphasize that multicultural education should be a central part of comprehensive school reform movements designed to improve schooling for all students and to better prepare them for an increasingly diverse society.

Multicultural education is good for all students. All children benefit from "mirrors and windows"—that is, from seeing themselves reflected in the curriculum as well as from learning about others (Cox & Galdo, 1990). All students benefit from learning that there are multiple perspectives on any issue and learning how to think critically about these issues. Instruction should build on students' experiences as a basis for further learning and should help them make connections with their own lives. Classrooms are a place of acceptance and mutual respect. No one is devalued. For example, during sharing time or storytelling, the teacher recognizes that students bring different ways of talking to school (Heath, 1983). Linking episodes loosely or using a circular narrative structure is just as valid as relating a story in a more linear style. And when a student looks down while the teacher is talking to her, rather than making eye contact, the teacher considers that this might be a cultural norm rather than a sign of disrespect. These also are examples of culturally responsive instruction.

Bilingual Education

Literally, bilingual education means "instruction in two languages." In the United States, a goal of every bilingual education program, regardless of type, is full proficiency in English. Supporters of bilingual education, backed by solid research, advocate instruction in the native language as the best way to support students' development of English (e.g., Greene, 1998; Ramirez, 1992; Thomas & Collier, 2003). Research demonstrates that some instruction in the native language is better than none in promoting students' literacy skills in English—and that more is better than a little (August & Shanahan, 2006; Slavin & Cheung, 2005). Whether proficiency in another language is promoted depends on the type of bilingual program. Some programs strive to help students develop and maintain full proficiency in their native language in addition to English. These are often called maintenance bilingual programs. Others provide instruction in students' home language only temporarily, as a bridge to English, and phase into English-only instruction quickly. These are typically referred to as

● Dual language programs are increasingly popular models that strive to help native English speakers develop proficiency in a second language, while helping students who speak a language other than English develop English proficiency.

transitional bilingual programs. Dual language programs (also called dual immersion programs) are an increasingly popular model; their goal is to help native English speakers develop proficiency in a second language (in the United States this is often Spanish, though not always), while helping students who speak a language other than English develop English proficiency.

Students who are not yet fully proficient in English are typically referred to as *English language learners* to emphasize that they are in the process of acquiring English but are not yet fully proficient. *Limited English proficient* is another term used to mean the same thing and is the label preferred by the government. It is important to consider that English language learners are a very diverse group (Artiles, Rueda, Salazar, & Higareda, 2005). Although Spanish is the home language of the majority of English language learners, other languages (such as Vietnamese, Hmong, Cantonese, Korean, Haitian Creole, Arabic, Russian, Tagalog, and Navajo) are also well represented in U.S. classrooms. Subsets of English language learners are refugees or immigrants, with their own sets of needs (National Center for Education Statistics [NCES], 2005). English language learners also vary in other ways, such as their socioeconomic status; nationality; generation in the United States; status as citizens, legal residents, or undocumented immigrants; and level of education in their home country, as well as the educational attainment of their parents (Suarez-Orozco & Suarez-Orozco, 2001). Some English language learners are already proficient readers in their native language; others are not. Thus, even though English language learners share some needs, such as having their home language and culture valued and respected by their teachers, in other ways their needs vary. Each child is an individual.

Disproportionate Representation of Culturally and Linguistically Diverse Students in Special Education

Culturally and linguistically diverse students are not any more likely than their White peers to have true disabilities. And yet, despite the best intentions of their teachers and other school personnel, they are overrepresented in special education programs relative to what would be expected given their percentages in the overall school-age population (Donovan & Cross, 2002). Notably, culturally and linguistically diverse students are overrepresented only in what are referred to as the high incidence disability categories (learning disabilities, mental retardation, and emotional or behavioral disorders). They are not overrepresented in the low incidence disability categories (such as visual, auditory, or orthopedic impairment) (Donovan & Cross, 2002). These latter disabilities are diagnosed by medical doctors, usually before a child starts school. High incidence disabilities, on the other hand, are usually identified by school personnel after the child has started school. They are referred to as the judgmental categories, because the diagnosis relies so heavily on professional judgment (Gottlieb et al., 1994).

Overrepresentation is most apparent among African American students when nationally aggregated data are the focus (see Table 4.1), yet there are dramatic differences across states (Donovan & Cross, 2002). Donovan and Cross described three ways of calculating students' representation in special education categories: composition indices, risk indices, and risk ratios. The composition index is determined by dividing the number of students in a given racial or ethnic group who are placed in a particular disability category by the total number of students enrolled in that disability category. The risk index is calculated by dividing the num-

TABLE 4.1 Ethnic Representation in Special Education, in Numbers and Percentages (National Aggregates)

	White	Black	Hispanic	Asian/Pacific Islander	American Indian/ Alaska Native	Total
Mental retardation	308,243	205,590	72,695	10,843	6,242	603,613
CI	51.07%	34.06%	12.04%	1.80%	1.03%	
RI	0.74%	1.78%	0.74%	0.43%	0.96%	
RR		2.41	1.00	.58	1.30	
Learning disabilities	1,720,061	538,782	531,299	44,798	42,921	2,877,861
CI	59.77%	18.72%	18.46%	1.56%	1.49%	
RI	4.13%	4.66%	5.42%	1.78%	6.63%	
RR		1.13	1.31	.43	1.61	
Emotional disturbance	285,546	134,265	45,529	5,757	5,991	477,088
CI	59.85%	28.14%	9.54%	1.21%	1.26%	
RI	0.69%	1.16%	0.46%	0.23%	0.93%	
RR		1.68	.67	.34	1.35	
Population	41,677,158	11,564,606	9,804,643	2,517,754	647,581	66,211,742
	62.95%	17.47%	14.81%	3.80%	0.98%	

Note: Mental retardation, learning disabilities, and emotional disturbance are the terms used by Donovan and Cross (2002). CI = composition index; RI = risk index; RR = risk ratio.

Source: U.S. Department of Education, Office of Special Education Programs (2003).

ber of students in a given racial or ethnic group who are placed in a particular disability category by the total enrollment for that racial or ethnic group in the school population. The risk ratio is calculated by dividing the risk index of one racial or ethnic group by the risk index of another racial or ethnic group. The risk ratio provides a comparative index of risk of being placed in a particular disability category and is the indicator of disproportionate representation preferred by the U.S. Department of Education, Office of Special Education Programs (OSEP). Donovan and Cross used White students' risk ratios as the denominators in calculating risk, whereas OSEP is now recommending using a risk ratio in the denominator that includes all racial or ethnic groups, rather than Whites only.

Given that special education provides students with extra resources and specialized services, some researchers and educators wonder why so many people consider overrepresentation a problem. There are numerous reasons for this (Harry & Klingner, 2006). Students in special education may have limited access to the general education curriculum. When students have been placed inappropriately, the services they receive may not meet their needs. Also, disability labels stigmatize students as inferior and abnormal; result in lowered expectations from their teachers, families, and even themselves; potentially separate them from peers; and lead to diminished educational and life outcomes (Patton, 1998). Think back to the Opening Challenge. How does this information on overrepresentation influence your thinking about what Mrs. Grelak should do about Allen?

What can be done to address overrepresentation? Harry and Klingner (2006) and Klingner and colleagues (2005) offer several possible solutions. Change starts with each of us examining our own assumptions about how students learn and why they struggle, and then considering what we each can do to improve learning opportunities for students. Too often, explanations for students' underachievement and inappropriate placement in special education have focused on perceived limitations in students' homes and communities. Culturally and linguistically diverse students can and do excel in some schools, even in low socioeconomic areas (Donovan & Cross, 2002; Taylor et al., 2000). For some students, including students from diverse backgrounds who have disabilities, bilingual and multicultural special education may be an appropriate way to address their special learning needs.

Bilingual and Multicultural Special Education

Regardless of questionable special education referral, assessment, and placement practices, some culturally and linguistically diverse students *do* have disabilities and can benefit from appropriate services in special education programs. The field of bilingual and multicultural special education offers the research base and expertise to guide educators in making well-informed decisions (Baca & Cervantes, 2004; Baca & Valenzuela, 1994). The goals of bilingual and multicultural special education are to reduce inappropriate referrals, improve assessment procedures, and enhance instructional and support services.

The majority of English language learners (ELLs) with disabilities have learning disabilities; reading difficulties are the primary reason (U.S. Department of Education, 2003). Yet compared to ELLs without disabilities, ELLs with disabilities are more likely to receive fewer language support services and more likely to be instructed only in English. Also, ELLs with disabilities tend to receive special education services in segregated rather than inclusive contexts, separated from their peers without disabilities (Zehler et al., 2003).

One area that seems to be particularly problematic is distinguishing between learning disabilities and the process of acquiring English as a second language. There are many similarities, confusing even well-prepared experts. In Table 4.2, we compare and contrast the characteristics associated with learning disabilities, the process of language acquisition, and cultural influences.

Whenever educators are trying to determine why a child is struggling, it is important to consider the learning context and environmental factors that might be influencing learning (Harry & Klingner, 2006). Federal law stipulates that before a child can be considered as having a disability, she must have received an adequate opportunity to learn. Thus, if she has missed too much schooling, she has not received enough instruction. Or if she has attended school but the instruction has not been comprehensible to her or appropriate for her needs, she has not received an adequate opportunity to learn. The following questions can help make this determination:

Instruction

- Is the instruction at the appropriate level for the student—not too difficult or too easy?
- Is the instruction comprehensible—either provided in the student's native language or taught with sufficient supports to be understood?
- Is the instruction meaningful, motivating, and interesting for the student?

Learning/Behavior Problems Often Associated with LD	Expected Behaviors in the Stages of Learning a Second Language (English-L2)	Cultural Behaviors or Values
Preschool Children **Language** Slow speech development Pronunciation problems Difficulty learning new words Difficulty following simple directions Difficulty understanding questions Difficulty expressing needs Difficulty rhyming words **Cognition** Trouble memorizing Difficulty with cause and effect Difficulty with basic concepts **Attention** High distractibility Impulsive behavior Unusually restless Difficulty staying on task Difficulty changing activities **Social** Trouble interacting with others Easily frustrated Withdrawn Poor self-control **Elementary School Children** **Language** Slow learning sound-symbol correspondence Difficulty remembering sight words Difficulty retelling a story in sequence **Attention** Difficulty concentrating Difficulty finishing work on time Difficulty following multiple directions **Social** Difficulty interpreting facial expressions Difficulty understanding social situations Apparent lack of common sense Misinterprets behavior of peers	**The Silent Period Stage** Difficulty following directions Speaks very little English May be silent and not respond when spoken to Difficulty understanding questions Difficulty expressing needs May be withdrawn or show low self-esteem May seem to exhibit poor attention and concentration Pronunciation problems **The Early Production Stage** May be withdrawn Speaks in single words and phrases May seem to have trouble concentrating Phrases may contain notable grammatical errors May be easily frustrated **The Intermediate Stage** Learner is approaching age-appropriate levels in English Still makes errors in speech, reading, and writing May seem more proficient than she actually is May seem slow at processing challenging language May be confused by idioms and slang May understand more than he is able to convey in English May seem to have poor auditory memory	Learner may view time differently (e.g., starting times, deadlines). Anxiety and stress may result from adapting to a new cultural environment. Acting out may reflect lack of experience with formal schooling. Differences in preferred style of learning may reflect cultural norms. External locus of control may be emphasized in some cultures. Time management abilities reflect cultural attitudes toward time. Independent work may be discouraged in favor of group work/collaboration. Coping strategies may vary by culture. Confusion with time and space may be due to lack of familiarity with new cultural expectations. Behaviors involving touch, movement, and proximity to others may vary. Kinesthetic strategies may receive greater emphasis than verbal interactions. Ways of showing respect may vary (e.g., lowered eyes vs. eye contact). Discourse styles may vary (e.g., overlapping talk vs. waiting one's turn). Offering a different opinion may be considered a sign of disrespect. Gender differences may influence the extent to which girls speak. Learners may not be used to learning through question-answer exchanges (e.g., preferring observation).

- Does the instruction explicitly help the student make connections between what he already knows and new learning?
- Are culturally relevant materials and culturally appropriate instructional practices used?
- When the student does not make progress, is he taught in different ways in a more intensive manner?
- Has the instructional model been validated with students who are similar to the student?
- Is the teacher implementing the instructional model with fidelity? If adaptations are made, are they consistent with research?
- Is the student's language acquisition supported?

Assessment
- Is the student's learning of what he has been taught assessed?
- Is the student allowed to demonstrate learning in multiple ways, including in her native language if appropriate?
- Does the assessment process inform instructional decisions?
- How does the student's rate of progress compare with the learning rates of her peers?
- Is the student reaching benchmarks?

Learning Environment
- Is the classroom learning environment a warm, supportive, and collaborative one, where students help each other and all students' contributions are valued?
- Does the teacher build positive, supportive relationships with students?
- Does the teacher work well with students' families and the community?
- Does the teacher help most culturally and linguistically diverse students succeed to high levels?

This last point deserves elaboration. In other words, if most of a student's peers are doing well but he or she is not, that is quite a different scenario than if most students in the class are struggling. If just one or two children are struggling, this reaffirms that they need additional support. If almost everyone is making little progress, the teacher should reexamine his or her instruction. Referring to the Opening Challenge, how can Mrs. Grelak use the information that these questions yield to think about Gabriel's learning problems?

Effective Bilingual Special Education Programs

Culturally and linguistically diverse students with special needs should be taught with validated instructional practices in culturally responsive, supportive learning environments (Ortiz, 2001). This is a theme that resonates throughout the chapters in this book, where you will read about many validated practices to teach instructional content that supports the learning needs of CLD students.

Lopez-Reyna (1996) and Ruiz (1995) observed in bilingual special education classrooms and noted the value of providing an encouraging, helpful learning community. Teachers promoted students' active engagement in authentic learning activities. The most advantageous programs incorporate students' home cultures and include native language instruction as well as a focus on English language development. It is this deliberate and intensive focus on *language* that makes bilingual special education distinct from generic special education (Klingner & Bianco, 2006).

LINGUISTIC SUPPORT   Language development should be an essential goal of instruction, whether in students' native language, in English, or both. Students benefit from explicit instruction in vocabulary, through preteaching and ongoing reinforcement, using visuals and graphic organizers to bring words to life and make them meaningful for students. Instruction should also focus on developing students' higher-order thinking and active problem solving skills. Students should be provided with many and varied opportunities to review and apply what they are learning (Gersten & Baker, 2000).

VALIDATED INSTRUCTIONAL PRACTICES   Several instructional practices show promise when used with English language learners with disabilities. Vaughn and colleagues (2006) effectively provided English language learners with support in reading in their native language. Helpful interventions in English have included focused reading interventions coupled with language development activities, such as the use of repetitive language, modeling, gesturing, visuals, and explicit instruction in English language usage (Linan-Thompson et al., 2003; Vaughn et al., 2005).

Other instructional approaches promote students' reading comprehension and/or content learning. These include graphic organizers (Bos, Allen, & Scanlon, 1989), Collaborative Strategic Reading (Klingner & Vaughn, 2000), Classwide Peer Tutoring (Arreaga-Mayer & Greenwood, 1986), and instructional conversations (Echevarria & McDonough, 1995). All of these approaches except the first include collaboration as an important instructional component, such as through peer tutoring and cooperative learning. You will learn more about these approaches in subsequent chapters.

CURRICULAR MODIFICATIONS   Baca and de Valenzuela (1994) note the importance of providing culturally and linguistically diverse students with curricular modifications. Modifications might include adjusting the method of presentation, developing supplemental materials, tape-recording directions, providing alternative response formats, requiring fewer or shorter responses or assignments, outlining material, or breaking tasks into subtasks (Hoover & Collier, 1989). As much as possible, however, the curriculum should emphasize enrichment rather than remedial activities.

Culturally and linguistically diverse students with and without disabilities benefit from culturally responsive instruction in positive, supportive learning environments. Students thrive when they are valued and cared about, when their strengths are recognized and used in the service of their learning, when their achievement is carefully monitored, and when they are provided with appropriate instruction and effective, timely support when needed. For English language learners, instruction includes a strong oral language component. Thinking back to Gabriel in the Opening Challenge, how can Mrs. Grelak improve instruction to meet Gabriel's needs?

Next, we discuss students who are at risk for school difficulties and deserve special attention to ensure that their learning needs are addressed.

Who Are Students at Risk?

Students are considered *at risk* for school failure or underachievement if their family situations, personal conditions, and life events negatively affect their school lives. Although educators may not be able to influence some of the many factors that place students at risk, educators *can* make a difference in these students' education by carefully identifying academic, behavioral, and social problems that can result from these factors and then implementing and monitoring plans to address these concerns. Here we discuss the types of students who are at risk, possible conditions that contribute to risk, and ways to tackle the problems.

Definition of at Risk

Students who are at risk have experiences, living conditions, or characteristics that contribute to school failure. Informal experiences such as interactions with other children, interactions with adults, and activities contribute to language and cognitive development in the early years of a child's life. Thus, students who have limited life experiences, lower expectations, and fewer academic opportunities because of family situations, family income, and even geography lag behind their peers right from the start when entering school. Living conditions such as poverty, neglect, homelessness, physically and/or verbally abusive situations (including bullying), and drug or alcohol abuse contribute significantly to the risk. Students who are migratory or are refugees or teen parents are in the "high risk" category as well (U.S. Department of Education, 1994; Yates & Ortiz, 2004). Also, students who struggle with depression, exhibit suicidal tendencies, are coping with the death of a loved one, or are experiencing a divorce in their family may have limited capacity to cope with the demands of the educational setting. Careful coordination and collaboration between the family and a team of professionals (such as social workers, school counselors, medical professionals, psychologists, and educators) are needed to tackle the challenges caused by these conditions.

Students at risk benefit from academic and social support services and often respond to the same instructional practices that help students with high incidence conditions learn the general education curriculum.

Many culturally and linguistically diverse students do well in school. However, students who are culturally and linguistically diverse tend to underperform on measures of academic achievement in the United States (Gay, 2000; Yates & Ortiz, 2004). During the 1970s and 1980s, the achievement gaps between African American and White students and between Hispanic and White students narrowed. Yet the achievement gaps then widened in the late 1980s and 1990s and are still large (Lee, 2003). These gaps remain even when analysts statistically control for differences in parental income and housing value. Thus a major educational goal is to close the performance gaps between groups of students.

The achievement gap is often characterized by substandard performance in reading, writing, and computing. Students who lack basic academic skills are limited in economic and employment opportunities when they leave the educational system. Moreover, educational problems contribute to students giving up and dropping out of school. Hispanic students have higher dropout rates than non-Hispanic students (Education Statistics Quarterly, 2000). Unfortunately, the economic picture for students who drop out of high school is bleak because they lack the education and experience employers seek in the more competitive high-salary positions. Many educators suggest that these challenges should be addressed by ensuring that culturally and linguistically diverse students receive an education that is more culturally and linguistically responsive to their needs (e.g., Klingner et al., 2005). In upcoming chapters, you will read about many ways to ensure that education is responsive to the needs of CLD students.

Some Conditions That Contribute to Risk

Many conditions that contribute to risk affect students' performance in schools. In this section, we discuss several of these risk factors to help you better understand them as you work with children in inclusive settings. The conditions contributing to risk that we discuss include poverty, homelessness, migrant family factors, health influences, and the conditions of some schools.

POVERTY   The link among childhood poverty, poor school outcomes, and disabilities is clear and well documented (Lee & Burkam, 2002; U.S. Department of Education, 2002). The most important predictor of student success in school is readiness to learn to read. Unfortunately, many children from high-poverty homes enter school with limited readiness skills. More than any other factor, poverty accounts for poor school performance. Far more poor students than one would expect from their representation in the general population arrive at kindergarten already identified as having a disability (D'Anguilli, Siegel, & Maggi, 2004). Also, diverse students are overrepresented in the poverty category compared to the

● More than any other factor, poverty accounts for poor school performance. However, there are many school services available to students in poverty that can make a real difference, such as free or low-cost meals.

number expected based on their representation in the general population. Thirty-four percent of Black children and 29 percent of Hispanic children are poor, compared to only 9 percent of White children.

HOMELESSNESS   Not all children in poverty are homeless, but the relationship between homelessness and poverty is obvious. Homeless children and those of immigrants and migrant workers often experience disruption and dislocation—circumstances that can adversely affect their physical, mental, and academic abilities (Markowitz, 1999). Children who live in shelters experience daily humiliation at school when peers learn that they have no home (CDF, 2004). These students often change schools every few months, breaking the continuity of their education and leaving gaps in their knowledge that result in reduced academic achievement. Educators must understand that their low academic performance occurs because of many factors, including fragmented education, absenteeism, and high risk for health problems.

Being homeless is difficult for children (Markowitz, 1999; Zima et al., 1998), and, unfortunately, the number of homeless families is on the rise. In 1988, 34 percent of the homeless were children; in 2003, 40 percent of them were children (CDF, 2004). In one study, researchers tested children who were living in an urban shelter and found that 46 percent of them had a disability. The most common disability, affecting some 30 percent of these children, was emotional or behavioral disorders. Because of the lack of social services and shelters, being homeless in rural areas is also challenging. Because of the high percentage of homeless children who also have disabilities, IDEA '04 pays special attention to them and their unique needs.

MIGRANT FAMILIES   Being from a migrant worker's family also places children at risk for poor school performance. Over 80 percent of migrant and seasonal farm workers are U.S. citizens or legal immigrants (Henning-Stout, 1996). These workers earn incomes below the federal poverty level. Most migrant families live in Florida, Texas, or California between November and April and move to find agricultural work the rest of the year. Approximately half a million migrant students live in the United States, and about 75 percent of them are Hispanic.

HEALTH   The Children's Defense Fund (CDF, 2004) gives us some additional and alarming facts to consider when we think about the relationship between the conditions under which children live and the incidence of disabilities in children. Each day in America,

- 390 babies are born to mothers who received late or no prenatal care.
- 860 babies are born at low birth weight.
- 1,186 babies are born to teen mothers.
- 1,707 babies are born without health insurance.
- 2,171 babies are born into poverty.

There is no denying the lifelong impact of poor nutrition, limited or no access to health care (being uninsured), and not receiving immunizations on time during childhood (CDF, 2004). During the school years, the effects can be seen in learning and behavior problems. Across a lifespan, there are adverse effects on employment and life satisfaction.

AT RISK SCHOOLS   School environments can be rated as at risk for a number of reasons. These schools tend to need major renovations, and the classrooms are crowded with too many students. Resources such as technology and instructional materials in these schools are typically limited, which means that students do not have the same learning opportunities and experiences as their peers in better schools. Some of the teachers may be first-year teachers who are not prepared to handle the issues associated with working in an at risk school. Issues include limited resources, low standards and expectations for students, a high dropout rate, and discipline problems. Other teachers may be burned out from grappling with these issues and trying to teach at the same time (Vaughn, Bos, & Schumm, 2007).

Although these issues are complex, they are not insurmountable. For example, No Child Left Behind (2001) requires states to align state assessments with state standards. States must establish annual progress goals for improvement so that all students can achieve proficiency. If goals are not achieved, then schools must implement strategies to improve student performance. Moreover, assessment data must be disaggregated by group to determine how students with disabilities and culturally and linguistically diverse students are performing. Thus, the achievement gap is visible and the schools accountable. School leaders must work strategically to establish appropriate interventions, while keeping abreast of emerging research as they plan instruction at the elementary and secondary levels (U.S. Department of Education, 2003). Finally, well-prepared teachers and high-quality instruction are critical components in how students learn. More attention is now focused on what we as educators are doing to help students learn (Vaughn, Bos, & Schumm, 2007). Research shows that factors such as time engaged in instruction, delivery of effective instructional practices, and monitoring student progress improve students' academic outcomes (U.S. Department of Education, 2003). According to James M. Kauffman,

> If we are going to help students . . . we are going to have to change course. We cannot continue to avoid focusing on instruction! We cannot continue to suppose that consultation and collaboration [and structural changes] will somehow make up for the deficit in instruction. We cannot rely on substitutes for . . . intensive, relentless instruction. (1999, p. 247)

Although Dr. Kauffman was referring to special education instruction, his advice is applicable to instruction for students at risk of school failure and for educators who teach in *all* schools.

Prevention

The best ways to help ensure that students are not at high risk of school failure are through improvements in health care and educational practices.

HEALTH CARE   According to the Children's Defense Fund, the most effective and efficient way to make an enormous difference in the outcomes of children in poverty is to remove the risk variables by

- Improving these children and their families' access to health care
- Guaranteeing universal vaccinations against disease
- Ensuring that these children have safe living environments (CDF, 2004)

Of course, effecting such sweeping social changes is beyond individuals' capabilities, but there are actions that alert educators can take to make a real difference in the lives of children. For example, even without universal health care or guarantees that all workers will be insured, many free services are available to the poor and to people who live in urban centers. Unfortunately, however, available community health care services are often not accessed because families are afraid or unaware of them (Tornatzky, Pachon, & Torres, 2003). Being knowledgeable about resources in your community and then increasing awareness of their availability is one way to help poor parents gain access to medical services that prevent some disabilities from occurring.

EDUCATIONAL PRACTICES   Differentiating instruction to address specific learning needs of students in response to the tasks at hand is one example of an effective educational practice. Differentiating focuses on the tasks that students must perform, their learning needs, and the adaptations that can be made to accommodate individual needs. Thinking back to the ADAPT framework introduced in Chapter 1, you can adapt how you deliver instruction in small groups and with extra instructional support. Specialized materials and adaptations in the content or activity are all ways to make learning more appropriate and individualized.

Another effective educational practice is universal screening to identify students who are performing in the risk category and providing intervention to support the core or regular class instruction. Providing intervention, or additional academic support, to students who are at risk for school failure is imperative if these students are going to have a chance to succeed in the educational system. For example, early identification and intervention to help students with learning and behavior difficulties in kindergarten through grade 3 have received national attention in legislation such as IDEA and No Child Left Behind. The intent of early intervention is to prevent learning problems from escalating and to reduce inappropriate referrals to special education as a result of inadequate or poor instruction.

Screening and intervention are also necessary at the secondary level. Some students with learning problems manage to perform well enough to "get by" in the elementary grades. However, as the curriculum becomes more challenging, academic issues surface and require intervention. For example, students with reading problems may not successfully read and understand subject-area textbooks (history, science), or students with mathematics difficulties may lack the arithmetic and problem solving skills needed for more advanced topics such as algebra. These are the students who are most at risk for dropping out of the educational system because of academic frustration.

Working collaboratively with other professionals and family members is yet another educational practice that is responsive to the special needs of students at risk. Multidisciplinary teams can generate solutions to problems that teachers are encountering in the classroom when trying to work with a range of student needs. Team members can also provide in-class support to implement screening and intervention practices. Finally, connecting to families is critical to learning about their unique situations. The time spent in this endeavor will go a long way in identifying solutions to problems and challenges that families face.

In the next section, we discuss another group of students with special needs. Students with gifts and talents require specialized services to ensure that their abilities are truly nurtured and enriched.

Who Are Students with Gifts and Talents?

Gifted and talented students do not necessarily face the same kind of challenges that most children who receive special education services do. However, because of their unique needs, gifted students confront other obstacles. Many gifted and talented learners are frequently stifled by educational approaches that do not challenge their cognitive abilities or help them achieve to their full potential. For these reasons, many parents, policymakers, and education professionals believe that these students need special services (Gallagher, 2000; Renzulli, 2004).

It is important to remember that IDEA does not offer gifted and talented students protections and rights as it does for students with disabilities. Although many states provide mandated services for gifted students, only eight states have laws or regulations that offer educational protections for gifted students similar to those found in IDEA for students with disabilities (Zirkel, 2005). Education for gifted and talented students is addressed in the Jacob K. Javits Gifted and Talented Students Education Act, initially enacted in 1988 (PL 100-297) and 2001. Let's examine the definition of giftedness, some traits that characterize giftedness, the categories of students who are eligible for this identification, and teaching practices that address their unique needs.

Definition of Giftedness

Why is it important to define giftedness? One reason is that the way a state or school district defines "gifted and talented" influences the identification process that determines who is eligible for special services. Many state departments of education rely on a federal definition of gifted and talented to come up with their own definition. These state definitions are then used as a guide to develop school district policies for identification and eligibility criteria (Davis & Rimm, 2004; Stephens & Karnes, 2000). Table 4.3 provides several commonly used definitions.

TABLE 4.3 Definitions of Gifted and Talented

Source	Definition
U.S. Department of Education (Purcell, 1978, PL 95-561, Title IX, sec. 902)	The term "gifted and talented children" means children and, whenever applicable, youth, who are identified at the preschool, elementary, or secondary level as possessing demonstrated or potential abilities that give evidence of high performance capability in areas such as intellectual, creative, specific academic, or leadership ability or in the performing and visual arts and who by reason thereof require services or activities not ordinarily provided by the school. . . . [G]ifted and talented will encompass a minimum of 3 to 5 percent of the school population.
Jacob K. Javits Gifted and Talented Students Education Act of 1988 (PL 100-297)	Children and youth with outstanding talent [who] perform or show the potential for performing at remarkably high levels of accomplishment when compared with others of their age, experience, or environment. The children and youth exhibit high performance capability, or excel in specific academic fields. They require services or activities not ordinarily provided by schools. Outstanding talents are present in children and youth from all cultural groups, across all economic strata, and in all areas of human endeavor.
Federal government, NCLB (PL 107-110)	Students, children, or youth who give evidence of high achievement capability in areas such as intellectual, creative, or leadership capacity, or in specific academic fields, and who need services or activities not ordinarily provided by the school in order to fully develop those capabilities.

stifled   to keep back
             to have difficulty in breathing

Defining giftedness is a complicated and often controversial task (Davis & Rimm, 2004), and although experts in the field have proposed definitions (e.g., Clark, 1997; Piirto, 1999; Renzulli, 1978; Tannenbaum, 1997), there is no one universally accepted interpretation of what it means to be gifted and/or talented. Some definitions and identification procedures are more restrictive than others and emphasize test performance, including cutoff scores on intelligence and achievement tests. As a result, access to services for the gifted continues to be limited for many students who, despite their high abilities, may not perform well on these measures (Patton, 1997; Reichert, 2003). Other definitions and identification procedures reflect a multidimensional view of gifted abilities with less emphasis on psychometric profiles. Adopting a broader perspective has far-reaching potential for "casting a wider net" to include students who are typically overlooked for consideration as gifted (Granada, 2003).

Types of Gifts and Talents

Howard Gardner's theory of multiple intelligences (1983) provides an excellent example of a broad perspective on intelligence and giftedness. In his book *Frames of Mind* (1983), Gardner proposed that multiple dimensions of intelligence exist. This theory challenged the more traditional notion that giftedness can be defined, assessed, and identified only by standardized tests, which actually measure just a small sample of an individual's aptitude and abilities (Gardner, 1983; 1993; Ramos-Ford & Gardner, 1997). Individuals with outstanding or unusual performance in any one of eight dimensions of intelligence—presented in Table 4.4—could be considered gifted under this scheme (Gardner, 1993).

Characteristics of Giftedness

What characteristics come to mind when you think of a gifted student? You may think of a student who is a natural leader, is an avid reader, has great mathematical aptitude, and excels in just about everything. Although there are some students who can be considered "globally gifted," the majority of gifted students

TABLE 4.4 Gardner's Multiple Intelligences

Linguistic	The ability to think in words and use language in complex ways, whether orally or in writing
Logical-Mathematical	The ability to use numbers effectively—calculate, quantify, and possess a sensitivity to logical patterns and relationships
Spatial	The capacity to visualize or graphically represent visual and spatial ideas—to think three-dimensionally
Bodily-Kinesthetic	The ability to use one's body and hands to express ideas or produce or transform objects
Musical	Sensitivity to rhythm, pitch, melody, and tone
Interpersonal	The ability to understand the moods, feelings, and motivations of others
Intrapersonal	The capacity for self-knowledge—understanding one's own feelings, capabilities, and motivations
Naturalistic	Ability and expertise in the recognition and classification of natural patterns, phenomena, and systems

Source: Adapted from *Multiple Intelligences in the Classroom,* by T. Armstrong, 2000, Alexandria, Virginia: Association for Supervision and Curriculum Development.

excel in some areas and not others. Students who are gifted are a heterogeneous group of students who differ from each other in abilities, interests, motivation, behavior, and needs (Davis & Rimm, 2004). And yet, there are some characteristics that many students who are gifted share (Clark, 2002; Davis & Rimm). Table 4.5 lists some of them.

It is important for educators to be familiar with the characteristics of gifted learners for several reasons. First, understanding how these students learn best can help teachers create an environment conducive to their success. For example, understanding that many students who are gifted learn quickly, have advanced interests, and become bored with drill and practice activities, teachers can differentiate instruction so that once students demonstrate mastery of the content being studied, they can explore topics in greater depth and in more creative ways. Although many of the characteristics listed in Table 4.5 influence students to become highly focused and successful in and out of school, teachers need to understand how some traits, left unattended, can have a negative impact on students.

Sensitivity, perfectionism, and intensity are common among students who are gifted. Sometimes these characteristics can become exaggerated and paralyzing for students, which causes a great deal of stress and contributes to underachievement. For example, dysfunctional perfectionism can lead to an inability to tolerate mistakes, avoidance of demanding tasks for fear of failure, and refusal to turn in assignments that are less than perfect (Schuler, 1999). These students are often extremely sensitive to criticism while striving for unrealistic perfection. By understanding how these traits can manifest themselves in maladaptive ways, teachers can provide a flexible learning environment that challenges intellectual curiosity, while also creating a safe environment for taking risks and accepting mistakes as a natural part of learning.

Prevalence of Giftedness

Because special education for the gifted is not mandated or guaranteed funding by IDEA, states are not required to report these statistics to the federal government. We can only estimate how many gifted and talented students are identified and receive special services.

TABLE 4.5 Common Characteristics of Students Who Are Gifted

• Early and rapid learning	• High levels of curiosity	• Excellent (and adult-like) sense of humor
• Large knowledge base and wide interests	• Interprets nonverbal cues and can draw inferences	• Imaginative and creative
• Superior analytic ability	• Focuses attention on topics of interest	• Self-directed and independent (usually prefers working alone)
• Advanced interests	• Well-organized, goal-directed, and efficient problem solving	• Perfectionist and self-critical
• Inquisitiveness	• Emotional intensity and sensitivity	• Easily bored with routine tasks
• Keen observation	• Strong sense of empathy and social justice	• Sensitive to criticism
• Excellent memory		• Prefers the company of older students and adults
• Energy		
• Abstract and insightful thinking		

● Students with gifts and talents require special attention to help ensure that bias and incorrect perceptions do not keep them from receiving an accelerated or enriched education.

The number of students to serve depends on the concept of giftedness that is being applied and how this concept is defined for identification. In many schools, traditional identification methods based on test scores identify about 2 percent to 5 percent of the school population as gifted (Clark, 2002). But more inclusive approaches—ones that incorporate creativity, leadership, and high achievement in addition to results on tests of intelligence—could increase the percentage receiving at least some special services to somewhere between 10 and 15 percent of all students (Renzulli & Reis, 1997).

There are several subgroups of students who, for many reasons, are underidentified as gifted or talented. These students require special attention to help ensure that bias and different perceptions do not mask their giftedness and keep them from receiving an accelerated or enriched education. Let's turn our attention to three of these groups: culturally and linguistically diverse students, students with disabilities, and females.

Culturally and Linguistically Diverse Gifted Students

Gifted and talented students can be found in every racial, ethnic, socioeconomic, and linguistic group; however, there is concern about the well-documented underrepresentation of culturally and linguistically diverse students among those identified as gifted/talented (Castellano, 2002). As communities become more diverse, the change in the number of students identified as gifted and talented should mirror the demographic changes in the population (Aguirre, 2003), but that is not the case. For example, recent data indicate that African American students are underrepresented in programs for the gifted by as much as 60 percent (Ford, Grantham, & Milner, 2004). Other reports indicate that Hispanic American and Native American students are underrepresented in such programs by 50 to 70 percent (U.S. Department of Education, 1993).

The problem of underrepresentation is compounded for students who have not acquired English language proficiency. Despite the fact that being able to speak two (or more) languages requires keen cognitive ability, bilingualism is frequently treated as a handicap in need of remedial efforts rather than as a strength that requires enrichment. Failure to identify and cultivate giftedness among our diverse student population is unfair to these students and to our society.

Several researchers have investigated characteristics associated with giftedness that may be common among certain culturally and linguistically diverse students. For example, in a study by Frasier and colleagues (1995), characteristics of giftedness in minority, language-minority, and economically disadvantaged populations were explored. Ten core attributes associated with giftedness were identified to provide a basis for establishing procedures to recognize, identify, and plan educational experiences for high-ability diverse students. Additionally, Aguirre (2003) identified characteristics of diverse gifted students in her work with the GOTCHA (Galaxies of Thinking and Creative Heights of Achievement) program, and Robisheaux (2002) created a sample checklist of behaviors to include in initial identification. Many of the characteristics identified by these researchers are presented in Table 4.6.

There are many ways in which teachers can help their culturally and linguistically diverse gifted learners to be successful. It is important for teachers to value students' cultures, languages, and experiences. Often this can be easily achieved by building a connection among home, school, and community (e.g., inviting families to share their history). Teachers should maintain high expectations for all students by providing rich content while incorporating multicultural education and instructional strategies that take advantage of students' strengths, such as problem solving, creativity, and primary-language abilities (Kitano & Espinosa, 1995).

Gifted Students with Disabilities

Gifted students with disabilities—or twice exceptional students—also require special attention. Students with disabilities are frequently overlooked when teachers are considering which of their students are gifted (Bianco, 2005). Teachers have difficulty with the concept of a student both being gifted and having a disability (Baldwin, 1996).

Twice exceptional students exhibit a complex array of abilities, weaknesses, and needs (Davis & Rimm, 2004; Nielsen, 2002; Silverman, 2003). Sometimes students' disabilities mask their giftedness, making it difficult for teachers to recognize their strengths. Unfortunately, many gifted students with disabilities rarely show consistently high achievement, so they remain unidentified as gifted.

Gifted students with learning disabilities have been described as "paradoxical learners" (Tannenbaum & Baldwin, 1983). For example, these students may have advanced mathematical reasoning ability but have great difficulty with simple calculations; they may be extremely knowledgeable about many topics but unable to remember simple facts; they may have excellent problem solving skills but fail to master basic skills. Does this sound like a student you know?

Twice exceptional students can display high levels of creative potential, exceptional analytic abilities, extraordinary spatial abilities, and superior vocabulary. These students can be imaginative and creative with an advanced sense of humor, but despite these documented strengths, they have many characteristic behaviors that affect their learning and hamper their identification as gifted (Nielsen, 2002; Reis & McCoach, 2002; Silverman, 2003).

TABLE 4.6 Characteristics of Culturally and Linguistically Diverse Gifted Students

Frasier et al. (1995)	Aguirre (2003)	Robisheaux (2002)
Highly expressive and effective use of words, numbers, symbols, etc.	Easily shares his or her native culture	Prefers to work independently or with students whose level of English proficiency is higher than his or hers
Transmission and reception of signals or meanings through a system of symbols (codes, gestures, language, and numbers)	Shows strong desire to teach peers words from his or her native language	Is independent and self-sufficient
Produces many ideas; is highly original	Functions at language proficiency levels above those of his or her nongifted English learning peers	Learns English quickly and takes risks in trying to communicate in English
Large storehouse of information on school or nonschool topics	Reads in the native language two grades above his or her grade level	Practices English skills by himself or herself
Exceptional ability to retain and retrieve information	Is able to code-switch	Initiates conversations with native English speakers
Quickly grasps new concepts and makes connections; senses deeper meanings; suddenly discovers the correct solution following incorrect attempts based on primary trial and error	Learns a second or third language at an accelerated pace (formal or informal)	Is curious about new words and phrases
Logical approaches to figuring out solutions	Eagerly translates for peers and adults	Questions word meanings
Highly conscientious, directed, controlled, active, intentional, forward-looking, goal-oriented	Possesses strengths in the creative areas of fluency, elaboration, originality, and/or flexibility	Is able to modify his or her language for less capable English speakers
Ability to synthesize key ideas or problems in complex situations in a humorous way; exceptional sense of timing in words and gestures	Demonstrates leadership abilities in nontraditional settings: playground, home, church, clubs, etc.	Uses English to demonstrate leadership skills; for example, uses English to resolve disagreements and in cooperative learning groups
	Possesses advanced knowledge of idioms and native dialects and the ability to translate and explain meanings in English	Looks for similarities between words in the native language and in English
	Possesses cross-cultural flexibility	Is able to express abstract verbal concepts with a limited English vocabulary
	Has a sense of global community and an awareness of other cultures and languages	Demonstrates social maturity, especially in the home or community
	Balances appropriate behaviors expected of the native culture and the new culture	Has a great deal of curiosity
	Excels in math achievement tests	Does not become frustrated easily
		Becomes easily bored with routine tasks or drill work
		Is curious about American culture
		Has a long attention span
		Is able to use English in a creative way (e.g., to create puns, poems, jokes)

Frustration comes easily and quickly for students with disabilities who are gifted. Imagine how frustrating it must be to have a deep understanding of complex issues and not be able to express adequately or demonstrate this knowledge. Often these students give up on tasks quickly. They are afraid of taking academic risks, have difficulty with fine and gross motor skills, and have low self-esteem, which is frequently masked by inappropriate behaviors (Baum & Owen, 1988). These students often dislike drill and practice activities, have poor organization skills, and have difficulty with spelling (Coben & Vaughn, 1989; Neu, 2003; Silverman, 2003). As a consequence of the frustration caused by a unique combination of skills and deficits, twice exceptional students can be some of the most disruptive students in class. Teachers can make a real difference in the educational experience of twice exceptional students by making sure that their strengths are recognized and nurtured. Thinking back to the Opening Challenge, how can Mr. Evans apply this information to his understanding of Jerome?

Gifted Females

You may be asking yourself why gifted females are being discussed as a separate group requiring special attention. Simply put, girls and young women who are gifted face their own set of challenges both in and out of school. A report from the American Association of University Women (AAUW, 1992) challenges the notion that girls and boys receive equitable treatment in our classrooms and outlines how gender bias shortchanges our young women. This seems particularly true for gifted females. For example, according to the AAUW report, teachers in all grade levels frequently select classroom activities that appeal more to boys' interests and are presented in formats in which boys typically excel. Another interesting finding suggests that boys are consistently given more instructional time, teacher attention, and praise and are called on more often than girls. These interaction patterns appear to be even more pronounced when teachers are dealing with high-achieving students (in the top 10 to 20 percent of the school population) and in science and math classes.

According to Kerr (1994), girls who are gifted struggle with internal barriers that hamper their success and undermine their self-esteem. One example Kerr discusses is the "Fear of Success Syndrome," in which bright girls intentionally hold back effort and enthusiasm in order to please others and avoid competition. The "Impostor Phenomenon," another internal barrier that affects many girls who are gifted, is expressed when young girls and women deny their intellectual abilities despite numerous successes and accomplishments. They are convinced that they perform well only because of good luck or of not being evaluated accurately.

Educators need to develop strategies for recognizing and encouraging gifted girls and for closing the gender gap that exists. One way teachers can help is by paying attention to their own behaviors with students and making sure there is no gender bias in their interactions. Other suggestions include using authentic learning so that science, math, and technology can be applied to solving real-world problems (Fox, Engle, & Sooler, 1999).

Teaching Students Who Are Gifted and Talented

All gifted students should have enhancements to their learning experiences. A differentiated curriculum offers learning experiences above and beyond those provided to typical learners through the general education curriculum (Tomlinson, 2004a & b; Van Tassel-Baska & Stambaugh, 2006). A differentiated curriculum can be achieved in many ways, such as by modifying the standard curriculum's content, the learning environment, or the instruction provided (Gallagher, 2000).

Many different models and instructional techniques are put into practice across the nation (Smith, 2007). Services for students who are gifted and talented are delivered through a variety of placement options: general education classrooms, resource rooms or pullout programs, self-contained classes, and even special schools. Regardless of the method used, these key features define differentiated instruction for gifted learners:

- Problem-based learning
- Abstract thinking
- Reasoning activities
- Creative problem solving
- Content mastery
- Breadth and depth of topics
- Independent study
- Talent development

Acceleration and enrichment are two common educational approaches to teaching students who are gifted and talented. Acceleration is an approach that allows students to move through the curriculum at faster rates than their peers who learn in more typical ways. Enrichment adds topics or skills to the traditional curriculum.

● A differentiated curriculum can be achieved in many different ways—a field trip is one way to enrich the learning environment.

ACCELERATION   Acceleration can take many different forms (Van Tassel-Baska, 2004). One form is grade skipping, which has students advance to a grade ahead of their classmates of the same age. Grade skipping usually happens in the early elementary years, often at or during kindergarten when a child's giftedness is apparent because he or she can already read books, write stories, or solve mathematics problems. Grade skipping is observed with some frequency again toward the end of high school, when students skip their remaining years and attend college through early entrance programs. Another form of acceleration is advanced placement courses, which allow students to take classes that provide more in-depth course content and to earn college credit. Unfortunately, advanced placement is less available to diverse students living in urban areas (Tornatzky, Pachon, & Torres, 2003). Ability grouping, where students of comparable abilities working together in courses or activities in which they excel, is another form of acceleration. Honors sections are one example of ability grouping. Many high schools provide honors sections of academic courses as a form of ability grouping where students must demonstrate superior academic performance for entrance. Research indicates that students who are gifted need at least some ability grouping that focuses on in-depth coverage and accelerated pace of instruction (Rogers, 2002, 2003).

ENRICHMENT   There are several forms of enrichment, which consists of enhancing, rather than accelerating, the typical curriculum. One form is independent study, which means that a student studies topics in more depth or investigates a topic that is not part of the general education curriculum. Independent study focuses on learning to be self-directed and to explore topics in which the individual has an interest. Another form is mentorships, which pair students who have special interests with adults who have expertise in those areas. Mentorships need to be carefully arranged by teachers, but the effects are both immediate and long-term, affecting the students' retention in programs for the gifted and in college and career paths (Grantham, 2004). The mentorship relationship between a gifted student and his or her mentor can reverse persistent patterns of underachievement (Hébert & Olenchak, 2000). Finally, internships are working assignments that allow gifted high school students who have expressed interest in a particular career to gain experience with that profession (Smith, 2007). Thus effective programming, through educational approaches that are responsive to each student's unique needs, is possible and desirable for students who are gifted and talented. Referring to the Opening Challenge, which of these approaches should Mr. Evans consider for Jerome to keep him interested in learning despite his learning difficulties?

summary

Students with other special learning needs encompass a broad range of characteristics and needs. We know that many of these students are protected under Section 504 and that their needs are met through the Section 504 plan, which focuses on their instructional program and on other academically related events such as field trips and summer programs. Thus students with a wide range of needs that are not covered under IDEA may qualify for services under Section 504.

The rapid demographic changes occurring in our nation are reflected in our culturally and linguistically diverse student population. With the numbers of ethnically and racially diverse students expected to grow significantly over the coming years, and with their strong current representation, educators must ensure that the educational system is responsive to the needs of all students. We must strive to understand linguistic and cultural differences so that no students are misdiagnosed as having a disability. Multicultural programs, bilingual programs, and bilingual special education programs are ways in which diverse students' needs are addressed.

Of great concern is the group of students who are at risk for school failure. This group of students is at risk because of experiences, living conditions, and/or specific characteristics that put them in the high-risk category. Educators should understand that students are at risk for many different reasons, such as poverty,

homelessness, neglect, and abuse. They may also be at risk because of their status as a migrant student, refugee, or teen parent. Prevention via improved health care and educational practices can make a difference in the lives of these students who are underachievers and are at high risk for dropping out of school.

Finally, students who are gifted and talented are a unique group of students who have a variety of special learning needs. Teachers should understand the characteristics of these students and must ensure that students from all groups are considered for gifted and talented identification. Specialized programs must be in place for these students to ensure that they receive a rich educational experience to prepare them to maximize their potential.

• s e l f - t e s t QUESTIONS

Let's review the learning objectives for this chapter. If you are uncertain and cannot "talk through" the answers provided for any of these questions, reread those sections of the text.

- **How are students with physical and cognitive needs protected under Section 504?**

  The definition of disability is broader under Section 504 and extends beyond school age. For instance, any condition that greatly limits a major life activity, including the ability to learn in school, is defined as a disability. Students who qualify as having a disability under Section 504 are assessed, and a Section 504 plan is developed and monitored. The plan includes the accommodations and adaptations chosen, the person(s) responsible for implementing the plan, and the procedures for monitoring its implementation.

- **How can we best meet the needs of students in our culturally and linguistically diverse classrooms?**

  Multicultural and bilingual education can address the special learning needs of culturally and linguistically diverse students. Multicultural education should be a part of the school's curriculum, instructional strategies, and interactions. Bilingual education is instruction in two languages. Some programs help students maintain and develop full proficiency in their native language as well as in English. Others provide instruction in students' home language only temporarily, as a bridge to English, and phase quickly into English-only instruction. Dual lan-

guage programs help native English speakers develop proficiency in a second language while helping students who speak a language other than English develop English proficiency. Language support services and instruction in the native language are needed for English language learners with reading disabilities. Bilingual special education students require linguistic support, validated instructional practices, and curricular modifications.

- **Who are students "at risk" and what should we know and do to help them achieve their full potential in school and life?**

  Students who are at risk have experiences, living conditions, or characteristics that contribute to school failure. They are students who represent a variety of situations and conditions, such as poverty, homelessness, abuse, neglect, and poor instruction. Students who are at risk require specialized services to prevent negative outcomes. Health care services must be provided to reduce risk associated with pregnancy, poor nutrition, and lack of regular medical attention. Educational practices such as differentiating instruction, screening and intervention, and collaborative partnerships can be effective in reducing risk and providing necessary support for these students.

  Students who are at risk for school failure exhibit a variety of characteristics, but they consistently have difficulties with achievement compared to their peer group; this condition is known as an achievement gap. Students who are culturally and linguistically diverse tend to underperform on measures of academic achievement in the United States. Students who are at risk are in the high-risk category for dropping out of school.

- **Who are students with gifts and talents, and how can we differentiate our instruction to help them maximize their potential?**

  The majority of students with gifts and talents excel in some areas and not in others. This is a heterogeneous group of students who differ from each other in many ways, including abilities, interests, motivation, behavior, and needs. Even so, they tend to share early and rapid learning, a large knowledge base and wide interests, and superior analytic ability. Gifted and talented students can be found in every racial, ethnic,

socioeconomic, and linguistic group, but culturally and linguistically diverse students are underrepresented among those identified as gifted or talented. Some students are twice exceptional; that is, they have a disability as well as being identified as gifted or talented. For students who are gifted and talented, the key features of differentiated instruction are problem-based learning, abstract thinking, reasoning activities, creative problem solving, content mastery, breadth and depth of topics, independent study, and talent development. Acceleration and enrichment are two common approaches to teaching students who are gifted and talented. Acceleration helps students to move through the curriculum more rapidly than their peers, whereas enrichment adds topics or skills to the traditional curriculum.

• Revisit the
OPENING challenge

Check your answers to the Reflection Questions from the Opening Challenge and revise them on the basis of what you have learned.

1. What should Mrs. Grelak's next steps be with Gabriel?

2. Do you agree that Mrs. Grelak should refer Allen for a special education evaluation? Why or why not?

3. In what ways does his level of English language proficiency seem to be affecting Gabriel?

4. What advice would you give Mr. Evans about instruction for gifted students with learning disabilities?

5. What characteristics does Jerome have that seem consistent with those of a gifted student? What characteristics does Jerome have that seem consistent with those of a student with learning disabilities?

6. How can Mr. Evans challenge Jerome while attending to his other learning needs?

Professional Standards and Licensure

CEC Knowledge and Skill Core Standard and Associated Subcategories

CEC Content Standard 2: Development and Characteristics of Learners

Special educators know and demonstrate respect for their students first as unique human beings. Special educators understand the similarities and differences in human development and the characteristics between and among individuals with and without ELN. Moreover, special educators understand how exceptional conditions can interact with the domains of human development and they use this knowledge

to respond to the varying abilities and behaviors of individuals with ELN.

CEC Content Standard 3

Special educators understand the effects that an exceptional condition can have on an individual's learning in school and throughout life. They understand the similarities and differences in human development and the characteristics between and among individuals with and without ELN.

CEC Content Standard 5: Learning Environments and Social Interactions

Special educators actively create learning environments for individuals with ELN that foster cultural understanding, safety and emotional well-being, positive social interactions, and active engagement. Special educators help their general education colleagues integrate individuals with ELN in regular environments.

CEC Content Standard 6: Language

Special educators understand typical and atypical language development and the ways in which exceptional conditions can interact with an individual's experience with and use of language. Special educators are familiar with augmentative, alternative, and assistive technologies; match their communication methods to individuals' language proficiency and cultural and linguistic differences; provide effective language models; and use communication strategies and resources to facilitate understanding of subject matter for individuals with ELN whose primary language is not English.

CEC Content Standard 10: Collaboration

Special educators routinely and effectively collaborate with families, other educators, related service providers, and personnel from community agencies in culturally responsive ways. This collaboration ensures that the needs of individuals with ELN are addressed throughout schooling.

INTASC Core Principle and Associated Special Education Subcategories

2. Student Learning

2.04 All teachers are knowledgeable about multiple theories of learning and research-based practices that support learning and use this information to inform instruction.

2.03 All teachers recognize that students with disabilities vary in their approaches to learning depending on factors such as the nature of their disability, their level of knowledge and functioning, and life experiences.

3. Learner Differences

3.04 All teachers understand and are sensitive to cultural, ethnic, gender, and linguistic differences that may be confused with or misinterpreted as manifestations of a disability.

6. Communication

6.03 All teachers understand that linguistic background has an impact on language acquisition as well as communication content and style.

6.04 All teachers provide multiple opportunities to foster effective communication among students with disabilities and other members of the classroom as a means of building communication and language skills.

10. Collaboration, Ethics, and Relationships

10.04 All teachers accept families as full partners in planning appropriate instruction and services for students with

disabilities, and provide meaningful opportunities for them to participate as partners in their children's instructional programs and in the life of the school.

Praxis II: Education of Exceptional Students: Core Content Knowledge PRAXIS

I. Understanding Exceptionalities

Human development and behavior as related to students with disabilities, including

- Social and emotional development and behavior.
- Language development and behavior.
- Cognition.
- Physical development, including motor and sensory.

Characteristics of students with disabilities, including the influence of

- Cognitive factors.
- Affective and social-adaptive factors, including cultural, linguistic, gender, and socioeconomic factors.
- Genetic, medical, motor, sensory, and chronological age factors.

Basic concepts in special education, including

- Definitions of all major categories and specific disabilities including attention deficit/hyperactivity disorder, as well as the incidence and prevalence of various types of disabilities.
- The causation and prevention of disability.
- The nature of behaviors, including frequency, duration, intensity, and degrees of severity.
- The classification of students with disabilities.

II. Legal and Societal Issues

Federal laws and legal issues related to special education, including

- Section 504.

The school's connections with the families, prospective and actual employers, and communities of students with disabilities, for example,

- Teacher advocacy for students and families, developing student self-advocacy.
- Parent partnerships and roles.

III. Delivery of Services to Students with Disabilities

Background knowledge, including

- Placement and program issues.

Assessment, including

- Use of assessment for screening, diagnosis, placement, and the making of instructional decisions.

Video—"Challenging Gifted Students"

A high school A.P. teacher uses a computer-based social studies simulation. Students use a guidebook with facts and geography to help them make decisions and arguments throughout the simulation.

Log onto **www.mylabschool.com**. Under the **Courses** tab, in **Special Education,** go to the **video lab**. Access the "**Gifted and Talented**" videos and watch the "**Challenging Gifted Students**" video.

 OR

Use the **www.mylabschool.com Assignment Finder** to go directly to these videos. Just enter Assignment ID **SPV12.**

1. List instances from the video clip where students demonstrate intellectual skills that are commonly seen in gifted students.

2. What differentiates gifted students from other students?

3. Would all students benefit from the instruction in this video clip? If yes, provide a rationale. If no, indicate who might and who might not benefit from this type of instruction.

4. In what ways could the teacher in this classroom support students with gifts and talents who are also culturally and linguistically diverse learners?

Video—"Teaching Bilingual Students"

This video demonstrates several language development techniques for students who are culturally and linguistically diverse learners. The teachers provide a rationale for strategies they use to explain rules to CLD learners.

Log onto **www.mylabschool.com** Under the **Courses** tab, in **Special Education,** go to the **video lab**. Access the "**Cultural and Linguistic Diversity**" videos and watch the "**Teaching Bilingual Students**" video.

 OR

Use the **www.mylabschool.com Assignment Finder** to go directly to these videos. Just enter Assignment ID **SPV6.**

1. The two teachers in the video discuss the importance of taking language into consideration when explaining rules in bilingual classrooms. Describe the strategies discussed in the video and why they are important. What other strategies have you learned about that would be helpful in terms of classroom management and CLD learners?

2. What does this teacher do to emphasize the classroom procedures regarding materials and develop language strategies at the same time? In what ways do strategies such as these support CLD learners?

3. Describe the issues facing CLD learners and the ways they are identified for disability services.

To access chapter objectives, practice tests, weblinks, and flashcards, go to the companion website at **www.ablongman.com/bryantsmith1e**

chapter 5

Delivery of
Special Services
Through
Individualized
Plans

chapter OBJECTIVES

After studying this chapter, you will have the knowledge to answer the following questions:

- Why is a responsive general education important to students who struggle?
- What components of special education must be in place to meet the needs of students with disabilities?
- What steps are followed in the IEP process?
- What tools guarantee students with disabilities an appropriate education?
- What does IDEA '04 require during the IEP process?

• OPENING challenge

Mr. Hernandez Wonders How All These Special Education Services Can Come Together

Mr. Hernandez has been teaching school for several years, but he had not taught a student with complex disabilities in his general education program until now. All of his students with disabilities have had mild to moderate learning challenges, and he has always worked well with the special education teacher to meet those students' needs. It is November, and the school year is well under way. Students have settled down to hard work. They are now assigned to the right groups, and he has a good understanding of each student's strengths and struggles. A new student, Emily, joined his class several weeks ago. She just moved to River City from another state, and her existing individualized education program (IEP) came with her. Because she has complex learning needs, the school's support team decided to implement the IEP process, create their own IEP Team for Emily, and schedule an IEP meeting.

As Mr. Hernandez prepares materials and all the documents for the upcoming IEP meeting, he begins to wonder, *"How many education professionals will be assigned to Emily? Who will be at Emily's IEP meeting? How can I possibly meet all of her needs and still be sure that the rest of the class gets the instruction they need?"*

• Reflection Questions

In your journal, write down your answers to the following questions. After completing this chapter, check your answers and revise them on the basis of what you have learned.

1. Is Mr. Hernandez overly concerned about being able to meet Emily's needs? Why or why not?
2. What advice would you give him about coordinating the supports and services that will be specified in Emily's IEP?
3. What kind of help and assistance should Mr. Hernandez expect from Emily's IEP Team?
4. Is Mr. Hernandez justified in expressing concerns about the educational progress of Emily's classmates? Why or why not?

or an education program to be appropriate for each infant, toddler, and student with a disability, it must be individualized. When education is appropriate, the results can be astounding. It is clear to us that there is no single answer to the educational needs of all students with disabilities: no standard program, no single service delivery option, no single place where education is received, and no single curriculum. For these reasons, the expression first applied to students with disabilities over 20 years ago, "*one size doesn't fit all,*" has become a mantra of special education (Borthwick-Duffy, Palmer, & Lane, 1996). This idea is verified and validated time and time again as the process enacted to develop individualized education programs for each student with a disability is applied.

As a teacher, by implementing an individualized education program you will make a real difference in the long-term results of your students with disabilities. Goals that reflect high, yet realistic, expectations lead to real community presence and participation, independence, and maximal achievement. How are these goals, tailored to each student's abilities and needs, determined and attained? The paths taken by educators, individual students with disabilities, and their families are planned and charted through the individualized special education process. Individualized programs are the heart of the process, guaranteeing every infant, toddler, and student with a disability, as well as their families, the services and supports essential to successful school experiences. Individualized family service plans (IFSPs) for infants and toddlers, individualized education programs (IEPs) for preschoolers and schoolchildren, statements of transitional services for adolescents, and behavior intervention plans are cornerstones that guarantee an appropriate education in the least restrictive environment to each student with a disability. All education professionals must know the key components or essential features of special education, because the responsibility for these individuals' education belongs to all of us.

Let's think first about how general education should be the strong foundation of special education and the educational experiences of students with disabilities. Then we will review the types of services, settings, and personnel that comprise special education. And finally, we'll turn our attention to those plans that put special education's services and supports into action.

How Is Responsive General Education the Foundation for Special Education?

An effective general education program is the foundation for positive special education services because it

- Uses evidence-based instructional procedures
- Supports students who struggle
- Prevents unnecessary referrals
- Welcomes students with disabilities
- Provides instructional adaptations to increase access to the general education curriculum
- Follows through with individualized plans and interventions

These effective principles and practices, when integrated into the general education curriculum and teaching process, can and do make real differences for every student—those with and those without disabilities. We introduced many of these in Chapter 1, and we will discuss them in more detail throughout this text as we talk about specific curriculum areas such as reading, writing, and mathematics. For now, we want to remind you about these major ways of adjusting the delivery of instruction to improve students' access to the general education curriculum.

Evidence-Based Instruction

Evidence-based instruction offered to all students in the general education class is important for many reasons. Education that uses instructional procedures that have been validated through research is responsive to struggling students, prevents school failure, and reduces the number of referrals to special education (McMaster, Fuchs, Fuchs, & Compton, 2005). Because many believe that assignment to special education includes low expectations and locking students into a curriculum that prohibits them from achieving their real potential, prevention of inappropriate referrals is clearly an important role of general education in the lives of many students, particularly those from diverse backgrounds (Obiakor & Ford, 2002). However, when special education services are needed, and when general educators and school leaders (e.g., principals) support those services, the results for students with disabilities can be remarkable (Sataline, 2005).

Differentiating Instruction

In Chapter 1, we introduced the mnemonic ADAPT to remind you about the five steps involved in using that framework to make appropriate instructional adaptations for differentiating instruction. The five steps in ADAPT are as follows: A—Ask, "What am I requiring the student to do?" D—Determine the prerequisite skills of the task. A—Analyze the student's strengths and struggles. P—Propose and implement adaptations from the four categories (instructional activity, instructional content, instructional delivery, and instructional materials). T—Test to determine if adaptations helped the student accomplish the task. Thus different instructional methods might be employed for members of a class who are all learning the same content.

How might instruction be differentiated? Differentiation can be accomplished through the four categories of instructional adaptations. A different instructional activity might be provided to a small group of students to teach a skill when the original activity, using evidence-based practices, was not improving student learning.

Sometimes, teachers need to adapt the instructional content by teaching a portion of the content related to the lesson's objective. Focusing initially on a smaller amount of information may help students be more successful in handling the quantity of information they need to learn. For example, if teachers are teaching the multiplication facts, the "times 5" facts might be taught separately and *then* combined with the "times 6" facts. Controlling the amount of instructional content gives students opportunities to focus their practice and then increase the amount as "chunks" of content are mastered.

Instructional delivery can be adapted by using flexible grouping practices to differentiate instruction (Haager & Klingner, 2005). Flexible grouping practices include same-ability groups and mixed-ability groups. Students with comparable abilities and achievement can be grouped so the pace of instruction can be different from that of other groups (Tomlinson et al., 2003). Or students can be assigned to heterogeneous groups where students complement each other's strengths and can help each other as they solve problems or complete assignments. In this way, flexible grouping practices allow teachers to group students based on the goals of the lesson. Instructional delivery can also be adapted in terms of how teachers present instruction and how students practice their learning.

Finally, instructional materials can be adapted by selecting different types of materials or making adjustments to current materials. For example, worksheets can be changed to include fewer practice items or can be formatted differently to emphasize instructional information or directions. Technology can be used to support instruction, and manipulatives can be used to make math concepts concrete.

Throughout this text, we continue discussions about the ADAPT framework and provide specific examples of its implementation because many students with disabilities require even more changes to their instructional programs to succeed in the general education program. For some instructional topics, students require an individualized change in how instruction is delivered. Differentiated instruction is designed to improve access to the general education curriculum by adapting instruction to each student's learning needs (Haager & Klingner, 2005; Hoover & Patton, 2004). In other words, instruction is adjusted in response to the individual's readiness, interests, strengths, and struggles (Tomlinson et al., 2003). In Chapter 6, you will learn more about differentiating instruction by using the ADAPT framework.

What Components of Special Education Must Be in Place to Meet the Needs of Students with Disabilities?

Although evidence-based instruction and differentiated instruction are important components of general education's foundation for individualized special education services, students with disabilities typically need more intensive interventions and supports to achieve independence and success. It's the multidisciplinary teams and the services they deliver that make special education truly special for students with disabilities and their families. Let's turn our attention to the professionals and services that can be specified for students with disabilities through the individualized education guaranteed by IDEA '04.

Highly Qualified Special Educators

A special educator might be a resource specialist, an itinerant teacher, a special education classroom teacher, a job coach, a home or hospital teacher, or an administrator. The skills needed by special educators are many. They must have in-depth knowledge about differentiating instruction, implementing practices validated through rigorous research, monitoring students' progress, understanding the requirements and expectations of IDEA '04, and ensuring that every student with a disability receives an appropriate education and achieves to the greatest degree possible. Special educators' jobs are complex and require skills that are honed by knowledge and practice. The Making a Difference feature tells about one special

Making a Difference

Data-Based Decision Making: Working by the Book Can Bring Great Results

Maria L. Manning
James Madison University

I have been attending IEP meetings for the past ten years in my roles as a special education teacher, an advocate, and a professor. Successful meetings have certain characteristics that have stood out for me as both the teacher and the parent of a student with a disability. For example, successful meetings usually involve preparation on the part of the teacher, such as sending telephone reminders or e-mails the night before the meeting, greeting the family at the office before the meeting, using nonverbal communication such as nods and eye contact during the meeting, and providing one-on-one question and answer time at the close of the meeting.

However, one particular IEP meeting stands out from all the others, because it used data-based decision making to help shape the future of one student. This IEP meeting was called near the end of the school year to discuss the placement of an upcoming fifth-grade student with Asperger syndrome. Zack had been in general education classrooms all his life. However, the past year had been quite challenging, and the school's support team was considering a change in placement for Zack. The team members were thinking about recommending an assignment at a self-contained behavioral unit for the next year. Zack's mother, however, did not believe the placement would be appropriate, because it would require Zack to move to a new school where the behavioral unit was located. She feared that he would learn more inappropriate behaviors than he already exhibited. The issue created significant tension between the school and the family. Both parties, as often happens, were forgetting that placement decisions should never be subjective.

Zack's multidisciplinary team agreed to call another meeting at the beginning of the upcoming school year.

To provide everyone with important information, a comprehensive functional behavioral assessment (FBA) was conducted and a possible intervention was tried out. The data compiled during the FBA yielded a clear picture of the type and frequency of Zack's challenging behaviors, and an effective intervention became apparent. The data showed that when intervention was consistently applied, the inappropriate behaviors decreased to an acceptable level of 5 percent of the school day.

The IEP team was shocked and pleased with the results! The data certainly presented a different description of Zack and his challenging behaviors—one that didn't match the accounts of his teachers. The data indicated that when supports were implemented effectively, the objectionable behavior became instantly manageable. The team members (an administrator, a special education teacher, a general education teacher, a personal counselor, a diagnostician, a functional behavior specialist, and myself) recommended that an assistant work with Zack one-on-one within the general education classroom (LRE).

I must admit to you now that I am Zack's mother. In spite of my experience as a special educator and a university-level teacher educator, I was just as surprised as the rest of the team. The data were compelling and allowed for a simple solution to a complex issue. With subjectivity removed, everyone involved in the process could bypass the emotions caused by challenging choices and come together as a team working for the best interests of the student—who, in this case, happened to be my son. ●

education teacher who successfully used data-based decision making in determining the placement for one student with a behavioral challenge.

The No Child Left Behind Act of 2001 (NCLB), which is the reauthorization of the federal Elementary and Secondary Education Act, requires all general education teachers to be "highly qualified." NCLB expects teachers to hold a credential, have a degree, or demonstrate competency in every content area in which they teach. When IDEA was reauthorized in 2004, language was included affirming that special education teachers also must be highly qualified. Because of these requirements, co-teaching is gaining in popularity, particularly at the middle and high school levels where it is not possible for individual teachers to meet the requirements of every core subject area that special educators teach. Blending the expertise of general education professionals (e.g., math, science, history, English) and special educators through co-teaching arrangements can make the education that students with disabilities receive truly special (Magiera et al., 2005). This new requirement for highly qualified special education teachers creates many opportunities for middle and secondary teachers to work together, to create wonderful learning opportunities, and to consider the special needs of all students, not just those with disabilities. In Chapter 8, we discuss co-teaching as one way to promote effective collaborative professional partnerships between general and special educators.

Clearly, general educators and special educators are two of the important ingredients of an effective education for students with special needs. But the recipe for success may also include the expertise of professionals who come from different disciplines. It is the IEP process that brings together experts who have unique skills to meet the individual needs of students with disabilities. Let's think about related services and the professionals who provide them.

Related Services and Providers

Many students with disabilities need help beyond that given through the partnership of general and special education. As you learned in Chapter 1, related services are typically beyond what general and special education teachers can provide (Etzel-Wise & Mears, 2004; Neal, Bigby, & Nicolson, 2004). Related services are definitely a unique feature of special education, offering a wide range of services and expertise to students and their families. These experts facilitate the attainment of LRE and FAPE. The three most commonly used related services are speech therapy, physical therapy, and assistive technology. IDEA '04 does not provide a precise list of related services, because its authors did not want to be too prescriptive; these services are to be determined by the exact needs of the individual (Downing, 2004). As Table 5.1 shows, related service professionals may include those who provide assistive technology, audiology, occupational therapy, physical therapy, school health services, speech/language therapy, or other services needed by the student. Unfortunately, particularly for students with high incidence disabilities (such as learning disabilities), IEP Teams (educators who meet to develop the IEP) often fail to fully consider students' needs for related services (Mitch Yell, as quoted in Earles-Vollrath, 2004). It is important for all teachers to understand that students, regardless of their disabilities, are guaranteed needed related services by IDEA '04.

With exceptions for very young children in some states, related services are provided at no cost to the student's family. However, in some cases, costs for related services are paid for by agencies other than schools (such as Medicare or private insurance companies). Some medical services are considered related services. Here's a guideline to whether a medical service is also a related service: If a school nurse can provide the medical services the student needs, they are likely to be related services. If, however, the services need to be performed by a physician, they are not (Bigby, 2004; National Association of School Nurses [NASN], 2004).

Assistive technology is a unique and critical component of many effective programs (Bryant & Bryant, 2003). For these reasons, we highlight such technology in the remaining chapters of this text. For now, remember that assistive technology is both equipment and a related service. Assistive technology is often what

TABLE 5.1 Explanation of Frequently Provided Related Services Specified in IDEA '04

Related Service	Explanation	Provider
Adaptive physical education (therapeutic recreation)	Assesses leisure function, provides therapeutic recreation and leisure education	Recreational therapist
Assistive technology	Assists with the selection, acquisition, or use of any item, piece of equipment, or product system used to enhance functional capabilities (assistive technology device)	Assistive technologist
Audiology services	Identifies and diagnoses hearing loss; determines proper amplification and fitting of hearing aids and other listening devices	Audiologist
Counseling services/ rehabilitative counseling	Provides psychological and guidance services, including career development and parent counseling; develops positive behavior intervention strategies	School counselor, social worker, psychologist, guidance counselor, vocational rehabilitation counselor
Diagnostic and evaluation services	Identifies disabilities	School psychologist, diagnostician, psychometrician
Occupational therapy	Improves, develops, or restores the ability to perform tasks or function independently	Occupational therapist (OT)
Orientation and mobility training	Enables students who are blind or have low vision to move safely and independently at school and in the community	Orientation specialist, mobility specialist
Physical therapy	Works to improve individuals' motor functioning, movement, and fitness	Physical therapist (PT)
School health services	Provides health services designed to enable a student with a disability to participate in FAPE	School nurse
Social work	Mobilizes school and community resources and works in partnership with family members to resolve problems in a child's living situation that affect school adjustment	Social worker
Speech/language therapy	Provides services for the prevention and treatment of communicative disorders	Speech/language pathologist (SLP)
Transportation	Assists with travel to, from, between, and within school buildings, typically using specialized equipment (e.g., special or adapted buses, lifts, ramps)	

Source: Adapted from the U.S. Department of Education Final Regulations for IDEA '04. U.S. Department of Education (2006); pp. 1257–1258, 1284–1294.

allows students with disabilities to access general education, interact with their friends, participate in class discussions, and complete their schoolwork more easily. Like evidence-based practices and differentiated instruction, assistive technology often is an important component of general education's foundation for effective special education services.

As stipulated in IDEA '04, the individualized education program (IEP) Team must consider a student's need for assistive technology and services so that the

tech NOTES

Selection of Assistive Technology Devices and Services

The questions that IEP Team members ask themselves, as they consider what AT services and devices to include in a student's individualized education program, are the following:

1. How can assistive technology (AT) devices and services help the student receive a free appropriate public education?

2. How can AT devices and services help the student receive an education in the least restrictive environment?

3. How can AT devices and services help the student access the general education curriculum and achieve IEP goals successfully?

4. How do the features of the AT device match the strengths and struggles of the student and the tasks of the environment?

5. How will the use of AT devices and services be monitored to ensure successful implementation as well as benefits to the student?

Source: Adapted from A. C. Chambers (1997), *Has Technology Been Considered? A Guide for IEP Teams.* Reston, VA: Council of Administrators of Special Education and the Technology and Media Division of The Council for Exceptional Children.

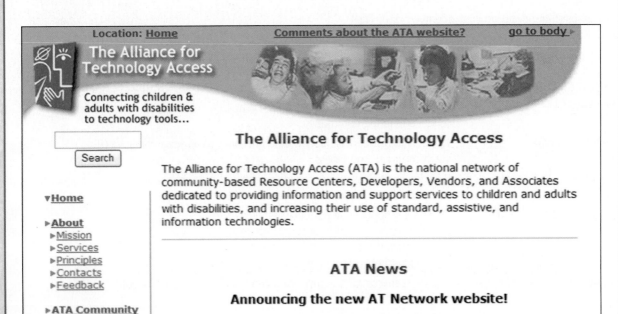

The Alliance for Technology Access, http://ataccess.org, is a network of resources that provides information and support services to children and adults with disabilities including information about assistive services.

student can receive FAPE in the least restrictive environment (LRE) (U.S. Department of Education, 2006). The accompanying Tech Notes feature lists some of the questions that IEP Team members consider when specifying what assistive technology (AT) services and devices are to be included in a student's IEP. When identified in a student's IEP, a device or specific type of equipment becomes part of the student's educational program. However, not every device you can think of is considered assistive technology by IDEA '04. For example, IDEA '04 clarified for school districts and families that costs for the maintenance of surgically implanted medical devices, such as cochlear implants, are not the responsibility of the schools (Kravetz, 2005). The expertise of assistive technologists can be critical to ensure that the latest in technology is available to resolve challenges that some individuals face. In Chapter 6, we present additional information about assistive technology.

You have learned that at the heart of special education are the professionals who join with families to collaborate and provide multidisciplinary services and supports to students with disabilities. These teams are unique because they are individually determined and their membership reflects the individual needs of the student. These multidisciplinary teams of experts not only deliver critical services to students with disabilities and their families but also are valuable resources to teachers as they strive to meet the needs of each

● Many students with disabilities need help beyond that given through the partnership of general and special education. This student requires physical therapy from a related services provider.

student. You as a teacher should always remember that these professionals are available to help you as well as your student. When everyone works together, IEP Teams ensure more than the protection of basic rights guaranteed by IDEA '04: They orchestrate the best education possible! When each individually arranged IEP Team develops partnerships, so that students' programs are coordinated, the results are remarkable, allowing individuals to overcome challenges caused by disabilities.

Now let's think about the process and plans that guide everyone's actions to make these programs a reality.

What Is the IEP Process?

IDEA '04 mandates that an individualized program be delivered to every infant, toddler, and student who is identified as having a disability and is in need of special education. The purposes of these individualized programs are to ensure that each of these individuals

- Receives FAPE
- Is provided an education in the LRE
- Is specific to the student
- Is provided services with the expectation of outstanding results

Students' IEPs are the plans or roadmaps created to guide instruction and the delivery of services that are the foundation for an appropriate education (Kamens, 2004). Although some students with special needs receive accommodations for their special conditions through Section 504 of the Rehabilitation Act, only those with disabilities defined by IDEA '04 are required to have IEPs. Thus some students with a disability that does not require special education services (such as a limb deficiency that does not affect educational performance) do not require an IEP. Conversely, sometimes students without disabilities *do* have an IEP. For example, in some states, students who are gifted or talented are included in special education. Although education of these students is not included in the federal special education law, those states often take their lead from IDEA '04 and develop IEPs for students who are gifted or talented.

IEPs focus on students' strengths and on their individual needs. Parents and school districts' education professionals must agree on these plans for the delivery of special services. IDEA '04 is very specific about the requirements of IEPs and the process to be used in their development and implementation (U.S. Department of Education, 2006). The law spells out the minimum process or steps that are to be used when developing individualized programs offered under the auspices of special education. States often impose further requirements in addition to those that are outlined in IDEA '04 and monitored by the federal government. Because there are many local variations on the rules surrounding IEPs, we present here what the national law requires and do not address specific regulations that various states expect school districts and teachers to follow.

The formation of an individualized program can be organized into seven steps (see Figure 5.1) beginning with pre-referral and ending with evaluation of a student's program. These steps are

1. Pre-referral
2. Referral

FIGURE 5.1 The Seven Steps in the IEP Process

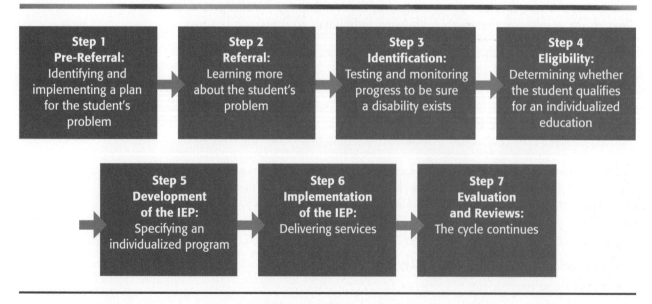

3. Identification
4. Eligibility
5. Development of the IEP
6. Implementation of the IEP
7. Evaluation and Reviews

Now let's look at these seven steps in more detail to get a better understanding of what each means and how they form the IEP process.

Step 1: Pre-referral

The IEP process is initiated through a series of pre-referral procedures and interventions in the general education classroom (NABSE & ILIAD Project, 2002). At this step, the general education teacher and the school's support team ensure that the target student has received high-quality instruction and additional instructional assistance if necessary. During this step, the school's support team must become confident that neither "poor teaching" (the application of practices that are not evidence-based) nor a need to learn the English language explains the student's inadequate performance. The major purposes of this step of the IEP process are to

- Document and explain how and when the student is struggling
- Determine the effectiveness of classroom adaptations and additional assistance
- Monitor the student's progress during the application of high-quality instruction

● Teachers and families may be involved in pre-referral. Pre-referral activities are intended to address individual student's learning or behavior needs in order to prevent unnecessary referrals to special education.

Pre-referral activities include screening students for learning or behavioral difficulties, implementing evidence-based practices, and documenting student responses to these practices. In general, before any formal referral for special education services is made, teachers, school-based education professionals, and family members work together to determine whether the general education teacher alone can resolve a student's educational or behavioral difficulties. The assessments used during this step of the IEP process are intervention-based and conducted in the student's general education class using direct measures of performance (McNamara & Hollinger, 2003). Teachers implement different validated teaching approaches and use assessment measures to document how students respond to this instruction (Barnett et al., 2004). They also systematically differentiate instruction more intensively to address individual learning or behavioral needs.

Pre-referral activities are intended to address individual student's learning or behavioral needs through the use of effective practices to prevent unnecessary referrals to special education, which are costly in time, money, and resources for formal assessments. You as a teacher may receive both assistance and consultation from specialists during this phase of the IEP process. Students whose learning remains challenged—those who continue to struggle—are referred to special education and the next step of the IEP process.

Step 2: Referral

Some students come to school already identified as having a disability and needing special education. Some of these students have already received special education services for many years. Why is this so? For infants, toddlers, and preschoolers, IDEA '04 stresses the importance of an activity called child find, wherein those with disabilities are actively sought (U.S. Department of Education, 2006). In these cases, referrals can come from parents, a social service agency, public health nurses, day care professionals, or a doctor. Young children who are at risk of having disabilities because of improper prenatal care, low birth weight, accident or trauma during infancy, or child abuse are referred for special services. Also, those with visible indications of a disability (such as a missing arm or leg or facial differences resulting from Down syndrome) or other signals of significant developmental delay (such as an 18-month-old child not walking independently or a 3-year-old not talking) are usually identified early and receive early intervention services during infancy or their preschool years. Typically, the referral process begins sooner for children with very severe disabilities, because their disabilities are obvious at birth or during infancy. As children grow older, other signs often trigger referrals. For example, a toddler who does not respond to loud sounds and is not walking by age 2 and a preschooler who tantrums excessively are both candidates for early referrals. Such children and their families usually come to school expecting an individualized education because they have received multidisciplinary services during the preschool years.

Students identified as having disabilities during the elementary or secondary school years present different reasons for referral. For example, students whose academic performance is significantly behind that of their classmates are prime candidates for special education referrals. Also, those students who continually misbehave and disrupt the learning environment often draw the attention of their teachers and are targeted for intervention and (ultimately) referral for special education services.

Step 3: Identification

Assessment is one foundation of the identification process. The purpose of this step in the IEP process is to determine whether a student has a disability, whether special education services are required, and what types of services are needed. Evaluations are conducted by multidisciplinary teams consisting of professionals who have expertise in each area of concern. Each member helps to evaluate the student's unique strengths and struggles. For example, if a student is suspected of having a language impairment, a speech/language pathologist (SLP) is a member of the team. If there may be a hearing problem, an audiologist participates, and so on. For students who are 16 years old or older, evaluation includes assessments related to the need for transition services for moving either from school to work or from secondary to postsecondary education (Madaus & Shaw, 2006).

Information can come from a broad range of sources, including the student's parents and family members. The professional who actually coordinates the identification process varies by state and district. In some states, the assessment team leader is a school psychologist, an educational diagnostician, or a psychometrician. In other states, a teacher from the student's school leads the team's efforts.

At this step, many different types of data are used to inform the team about the student's abilities. Medical history, information about social interactions at school and at home, adaptive behavior in the community, educational performance, and other relevant factors are considered. Evaluations include an array of assessment instruments and procedures. Information should be collected from the student and family. Formal tests—tests of intelligence, of academic achievement, and of acuity (vision and hearing)—are usually part of the information used to make decisions about students and their potential special education status.

Less formal assessments—assistive technology evaluations, school observations of classroom and social behavior, examples of academic assignments, direct measurements of academic performance, curriculum based measurements (CBM) of reading and mathematics skills being taught, and portfolio samples of classroom performance—are also important pieces of evidence used in this step of the IEP process. Together, data from the formal and informal assessments are used to develop a profile of the student. One result of the evaluation step of the IEP process can be a determination that the individual does not have a disability. In these instances the IEP process is discontinued. For those individuals who do have disabilities, this phase of the process results in a baseline of performance data to guide the development of the individualized education program and, later, help judge the program's effectiveness.

Step 4: Eligibility

The information from the assessment step is used to identify students who actually have a disability *and* qualify for special education services. For those students, the IEP Team then determines what components of the full range of special education and related services are needed so that an appropriate education can be planned and ultimately delivered. The education of those students who do not meet the eligibility requirements remains the sole responsibility of general educators; the education of those students with disabilities who are eligible for special education services becomes the shared responsibility of general education teachers and administrators, special education teachers and administrators, and the appropriate related service professionals.

Considering *Diversity*

Don't Confuse Linguistic Diversity with Learning Disability

Culturally and linguistically diverse students are disproportionately represented in special education classes (National Research Council, 2002; Robertson, Kushner, Starks, & Drescher, 1994; Yates & Ortiz, 2004). Inappropriate placements of this sort often occur because educators have limited preparation in providing early interventions to remediate existing underachievement problems. Educators may also have limited preparation in discerning the characteristics of linguistically diverse students from the characteristics of students with language and learning disabilities. However, professionals must provide early intervention to students who are exhibiting achievement difficulties. Documentation of the student's response to this intervention is also required. When these efforts are not successful with individual students, a referral to special education for a comprehensive assessment may be appropriate (Yates & Ortiz, 2004). According to IDEA '04, limited English proficiency cannot be a reason for determining that a student has a disability. Educators may be unfamiliar with questions that can be asked to help determine whether a referral for special education assessment is appropriate. Ortiz (1997) provides guidelines that school-based teams can use as part of the referral process and to eliminate factors besides a disability as the reason for academic underachievement.

- Have the difficulties been noted by a variety of professionals, such as the general education teacher, parents, and the remedial teacher?
- To what extent do the difficulties exist across contexts, such as in classrooms, in "specials or electives" (art, music), and at home?
- What are the student's reading abilities in the native language and in English?
- Are the difficulties evident in the native language as well as in English?
- How is the student progressing compared to other students who had or have a similar level of English language proficiency?
- What concerns have family members expressed about language difficulties?
- Has the student received consistent native language instruction?
- What evidence suggests that difficulties can be explained by factors other than disability, such as cultural differences, school attendance issues, teacher bias or expectations, and teachers not prepared to teach culturally and linguistically diverse students?
- What evidence suggests issues related to assessment, such as measures that are not normed for English language learners, language proficiency of the student that does not match the language in which the assessment was conducted, and results that conflict with documentation about response to intervention?
- What efforts are being made to determine whether the student's language characteristics such as pronunciation, oral language, and comprehension difficulties are a result of learning a second language or a language disability?

At every step along the way, professionals must ensure that culturally and linguistically diverse students who go through the disability identification process (1) have received effective remedial interventions prior to referral and (2) have been thoroughly reviewed to rule out limited English proficiency as the reason for the problem. The Considering Diversity feature includes questions that educators should use during the referral and eligibility process to avoid inappropriate referrals and placements of students with language differences.

Step 5: Development of the IEP

After thorough completion of the pre-referral, referral, identification, and eligibility steps of the IEP process, it is time to develop the actual individualized plan—an IFSP for infants and toddlers, an IEP for preschoolers and schoolchildren, and a transition component of the IEP for those students with disabilities who are 16 years old or older. If behavior is a concern, a behavior intervention plan will be written for the individual student as well. We discuss the development of the IEP in more detail later in this chapter, but for now, it is important for you to know that parents and the education professionals who are all part of the student's IEP Team make important decisions about what services and placements constitute an appropriate education for this individual at this step of the IEP process. The assessment results are used to help make these decisions. It is at this point that the IEP Team begins its work to outline the individualized education needed by the student. Collectively, the team members, who include parents and the student (if appropriate), now use the knowledge they have gained to identify resources needed for that student to access the general education curriculum, determine the appropriate goals for improvement, and then craft a good education program for the student. Of course, goals must include greater success with the general education curriculum or independence and a community presence later in life. It is at this point that the services and supports that become part of the student's appropriate education are specified.

Step 6: Implementation of the IEP

Once the IEP is developed, the student's services and individualized program begin. The IEP has laid out what constitutes an appropriate education for the student, the extent to which the student participates in the general education curriculum, the accommodations the student receives both for instruction and for assessment, and the array of multidisciplinary services from related service providers that support the student's educational program. For students who are participating in a different curriculum or whose goals differ from those of the general education curriculum, the IEP has specified alternate assessment procedures as well.

   Minor adjustments in students' goals or in the benchmarks that indicate attainment of those goals do not signal a need for a new IEP or another IEP meeting. Services continue. However, major changes in goals, services, or placement do require parents to be notified in writing. Some changes, particularly if they involve a more restrictive placement, may necessitate a meeting of the IEP Team and the parent or guardian. Most often, this situation arises when issues surrounding discipline are the reason for the change in placement or services. Later in this chapter, you will learn more about behavior intervention plans, which must be developed as part of students' IEPs when serious behavioral infractions (such as bringing guns or drugs to school, fighting, or being out of control) occur. Also, in Chapter 9, you will learn about effective interventions that should help resolve behavior issues that affect both the individual and his or her classmates when rules are violated.

Step 7: Evaluation and Reviews

IDEA '04 requires accountability for each IEP developed. In most states, students' IEPs are reviewed annually. Under an IDEA '04 pilot program, which is attempting to reduce paperwork and administrative burdens on educators,

15 states conduct these reviews every 3 years. The purpose of the IEP review meetings is to ensure that students are meeting their goals and making educational progress. Because accountability measures determine whether the student is making progress, educators are careful to describe expectations for tasks and skills the student needs to learn in terms that can be evaluated. Whether the IEP process is for an infant or toddler (an IFSP) or for a schoolchild (an IEP and possibly a transition component), the expectation is that frequent assessments of the individual's performance will occur, even if major IEP reviews occur once a year or only every 3 years.

NCLB *and* IDEA '04 require that *all* students participate in annual state- or district-wide testing or in alternate assessments. Because of the importance of these assessments and of each school's collective adequate yearly progress (AYP)—whereby all its students demonstrate their attainment of high levels of achievement—we devote an entire chapter to assessment issues (see Chapter 7). For now, it is important to understand that assessment adaptations are allowed for many students with disabilities while taking these tests. For example, students who use enlarged print or braille to read classroom materials receive these assessment adaptations in the testing situation as well.

For some students, alternate assessments are made available. For example, students who are learning English as their second language and students with disabilities whose IEP goals focus less on accessing the general education curriculum and more on skills related to independence, life skills, and community presence may participate in alternative assessments if these are specified in the students' IEP. Remember, in addition to annual assessments, students with disabilities frequently receive less formal evaluations of their progress. Sometimes these assessments are made weekly or even daily. The purpose of such measurements of progress is to guide instruction and to ensure that scheduled interventions are effective.

Who Are the Members of the IEP Team?

IDEA '04 is very clear about membership in IEP Teams (OSEP, 2006a). The exact language of the regulations is found in Table 5.2, but it is important for you as a teacher to remember that each IEP Team is individually determined according to the specific special needs of the student and his or her disability.

As a teacher attending an IEP meeting for one of your students, you can be most helpful in ensuring that the right people are participating and contributing to the development of a meaningful IEP for your student. Review Table 5.1 (page 171) and consider a student who faces motor challenges resulting from cerebral palsy. Emily is a very bright second grader, but she has difficulty engaging in class discussions because her speech is slow, deliberate, and difficult to understand. She uses a walker and finds it challenging to hold a pencil, but she can use a computer's keyboard. IDEA '04 is specific about the minimum representation of those members who make up IEP Teams for students with disabilities. Who are those essential members? For Emily, IDEA '04 also allows for the inclusion of more multidisciplinary professionals. What additional members would be appropriate for Emily's IEP Team? To answer these two important questions, it might be helpful to know more about the roles of IEP Team members. Some of those roles and responsibilities are highlighted next.

TABLE 5.2 Members of the IEP Team

According to the IDEA '04 regulations, the public agency must ensure that the IEP Team for each child with a disability includes

- The parents of the child
- Not less than one general education teacher of the child (if the child is, or may be, participating in the general education environment)
- Not less than one special education teacher of the child, or, where appropriate, not less than one special education provider of the child
- A representative of the public agency (who has certain specific knowledge and qualifications)
- An individual who can interpret the instructional implications of evaluation results (this person may also be one of the other listed members)
- At the discretion of the parent or the agency, other individuals who have knowledge or special expertise regarding the child, including related service personnel as appropriate
- Whenever appropriate, the child with a disability

The public agency must invite a child with a disability to attend the child's IEP Team meeting if a purpose of the meeting will be consideration of the postsecondary goals for the child and the transition services needed to assist the child in reaching those goals.

Source: The Office of Special Education Programs, Building the Legacy of IDEA 2004, http://idea.ed.gov, Topical Brief: Individualized Education Program (IEP), Team Meetings, and Changes to the IEP, 2006b, pp. 2–3.

Roles of Education Professionals

All education professionals working at every school are crucial to positive experiences for students with disabilities. As we mentioned at the beginning of Chapter 1, it is surprising to us that after some 30 years of including more and more students with disabilities in general education classes, many teachers, principals, and other education professionals still report that they feel ill prepared to accept responsibilities associated with the education of these students (Fisher, Frey, & Thousand, 2003; Futernick, 2006; Hammond & Ingalls, 2003). Those who harbor such attitudes (particularly if they are uneasy with, or even reject, students with disabilities) can negatively influence outcomes for these students (Cook, 2001; Cook et al., 2000). Such negative attitudes are often subtly expressed in the ways in which inadequately prepared educators talk about students with disabilities and the adaptations they need for successful participation in the general education curriculum (Smith, Salend, & Ryan, 2001). We also know that well-prepared educators can and do make a real difference in the lives and the educational achievements of their students (Darling-Hammond, 2005, 2006a, 2006b). We are confident that you, as a teacher thoroughly prepared with knowledge about effective interventions and the ADAPT framework, will positively influence the lives of your students with disabilities.

The school principal is a key person in the collaborative effort at every school (Praisner, 2003; Rodríguez, Gentilucci, & Sims, 2005). Because principals often coordinate management efforts at their site, they can be most helpful in developing and ensuring the delivery of special education services (particularly for large-scale assessments), in monitoring the array of services indicated on every student's IEP, and in ensuring the coordination of services throughout the school and across the district. Effective principals also set the tone for positive attitudes crucial to all students' success. They welcome and facilitate the efforts of the many different professionals who are itinerant, coming to their school to work with individual students such as Emily, whom we described at the beginning of this section. For example, students with challenges similar to Emily's typically receive services from SLPs, physical therapists, experts in assistive technology, and possibly occupational therapists. These members of Emily's multidisciplinary team are not permanent or full-time members of the school staff. Their schedules are complicated and often hard to coordinate because each of them travels from school to school, sometimes long distances, to work with individual students and their teachers who need their services. Also, these professionals often find themselves in crowded schools where they do not have sufficient space or appropriate places to work with individual students or to store their equipment. Principals can lead their school's staff to solve complex coordination issues that itinerant multidisciplinary team members often present, smoothing the way for efficient delivery of related services.

IDEA '04, individual states' regulations, nor school districts' guidelines have established definitive roles for each profession's IEP Team member. Teams must determine each member's role and responsibility when they collaborate as members of IEP Teams and work together to plan for the delivery of an effective and appropriate education for each student with a disability. In part, this lack of uniformity exists because no single or uniform action can reflect what special education services any particular student needs. Also, government officials do not want to dictate how groups of professionals elect to work together. For example, at one school, the principal and IEP Teams might assign duties differently than the principal and team members at another school (Praisner, 2003). At one school, the school counselor coordinates the entire schedule; at another, a special education teacher schedules related services for all students with disabilities, and the principal's assistant develops the other teachers' and students' schedules. In short, the way in which these professionals collaborate is partially determined by how they are organized at each school.

The IEP process, the development of responsive IEP Teams, and the inclusion of students with disabilities require true partnerships among those who share responsibilities for the education of students with disabilities. Fisher and his colleagues help us think about how both general and special education teachers could share responsibilities that typically arise in providing an appropriate education to students with disabilities (Fisher, Frey, & Thousand, 2003). Some of their ideas are presented in Table 5.3.

Roles of Families

IDEA '04 stresses the importance of involving families of students with disabilities in the IEP process and as members of their child's IEP Team (U.S. Department of Education, 2006). The IEP process can help develop partnerships among parents and extended family members, schools, and professionals (Sopko, 2003). This purpose should be actively fostered, for the importance of these partnerships cannot be overestimated (Dabkowski, 2004).

TABLE 5.3 Roles of General and Special Educators in the Education of Students with Disabilities

Role	Special Educators	General Educators
Pre-referral and Referral	Assist with data collection Test effectiveness of educational modifications and accommodations	Conduct pre-referral assessments Use tactics of varying intensity Provide instruction under different conditions
Instruction	Individualize instruction (1:1; 1:3) Apply instruction to small groups Adapt materials and instruction Consult with, and provide assistance to, other educators	Apply instruction to whole class and small groups Ensure maximal access to the general education curriculum by implementing adaptations and accommodations Train and supervise peer tutors
Assessment	Monitor progress frequently Determine appropriate adaptations and accommodations	Develop and maintain portfolios Implement adaptations and accommodations for testing situations
Communication	Foster parent partnerships Communicate with school personnel about needed accommodations	Communicate with parents and families Work in partnership with special education personnel
Leadership	Train and supervise paraprofessionals Advocate for each student with a disability Coordinate students' related services Conduct inservice training sessions about access to the general education curriculum	Work with paraprofessionals Participate in IEP meetings Facilitate the scheduling and delivery of related services Maintain anecdotal records
Record Keeping	Develop the IEP Maintain records of accommodations and IEP progress	Keep records of accommodation use and effectiveness

Source: From "What do special educators need to know and be prepared to do for inclusive school to work?" by D. Fisher, N. Frey, & J. Thousand, *Teacher Education and Special Education, 26* (2003), p. 45. Copyright © 2003 by The Council for Exceptional Children. Partially adapted with permission.

When parent involvement is high, student alienation is lower and student achievement is increased (Brown, Paulsen, & Higgins, 2003; Dworetzky, 2004). Educators need to recognize, however, that many parents believe schools control the special education process. As a result, many families feel disenfranchised or confused about rules, regulations, and the purpose of special education (Cartledge, Kea, & Ida, 2000). Most parents want to participate in their children's education, but sometimes they do not understand the educational system.

Often, families need help to participate effectively in IEP meetings and in the resulting individualized programs (Tornatzky, Pachon, & Torres, 2003). Here are some tips that teachers can give parents to help them better prepare to participate in IEP meetings (Buehler, 2004):

- Make a list of important questions to ask IEP Team members. Examples: What is my child's daily schedule? How is my child doing in school? Does my child have friends? How well does my child behave? What problems is my child having?
- Outline points to make about your child's strengths.

- Bring records regarding your child's needs.
- Ask for clarification.
- Be assertive and proactive, but not aggressive or reactive.
- Listen and compromise.
- Remain involved with the professionals on the IEP Team.
- Know about placement and service options, and explore each with the Team.

For families who do not speak English well enough to understand the complicated language used to talk about special education issues, participation may seem impossible (Hughes, Valle-Riestra, & Arguelles, 2002). In such instances, schools must welcome family members and people from the community who are fluent in the family's native language and also knowledgeable about the special education process and procedural safeguards guaranteed to families through IDEA '04. The law encourages the family's maximal participation, so it requires schools to find interpreters to the fullest extent possible. Remember, it is the obligation of educators to include and inform parents and students about the efforts that will be made on their behalf.

Roles of Students

Review Table 5.2 (page 181) and remember the importance that IDEA '04 places on students participating on their own IEP Teams, particularly when adolescents are about to transition out of high school. The law stresses of student involvement because, because it has found that many students are unfamiliar with

● IDEA law stresses the importance of student involvement in their IEPs because, surprisingly, many students are unfamiliar with the contents and the goals established for them within their IEPs. Involving students in the process has many benefits.

their IEPs and do not know the goals established for them (Lovitt & Cushing, 1994). One result is a lack of "ownership" in the school program especially designed for them. Involving students has many benefits (Test et al., 2004). Particularly if students are active participants, they can learn important skills needed in life. Here are two examples. Self-determination is the ability to identify and achieve goals for oneself. Self-advocacy consists of the skills necessary to stand up and advocate for what one needs to achieve those goals. These two skills are interrelated and can be fostered during the IEP process when students are involved (Wood et al., 2004). Here are some ways in which older students can contribute to their IEP meetings:

- Describe personal strengths, weaknesses, and needs.
- Evaluate personal progress toward accomplishing their goals.
- Bring a list of adaptations and explain how each is helpful.
- Communicate their preferences and interests.
- Articulate their long-term goals and desires for life, work, and postsecondary schooling.

What Tools Guarantee Students with Disabilities an Appropriate Education?

Four tools, or plans for individualized programs, serve to coordinate and document what constitutes the appropriate education for each infant, toddler, and student with disabilities. The tools that guarantee an appropriate education to those with disabilities are

1. The *individualized family service plan (IFSP)*—for infants and toddlers
2. The *individualized education program (IEP)*—for preschoolers through high school students
3. An additional statement of *transitional services*—initiated at age 16 to help those students who require special education services to make successful transitions to independence, community living, and work
4. A *behavior intervention plan*—for those students with disabilities who commit serious behavioral infractions

Let's examine each of these plans in turn.

Individualized Family Service Plans (IFSPs)

Infants or toddlers (birth through age 2) who have disabilities or who are at great risk for disabilities were originally guaranteed the right to early intervention programs through PL 99-457, which was passed in 1986. That right continues today through IDEA '04. (For a review of IDEA legislation, see Chapter 1 and Table 1.3.) Individualized family service plans (IFSPs) are written documents that ensure that special services are delivered to these young children and their families. The IFSP is the management tool that guides professionals as they design and deliver these children's special education programs. Service managers are the professionals who provide oversight and coordination of the services outlined in IFSPs. The key components of these early education management plans are as follows:

- The child's current functioning levels in all relevant areas (physical development, cognitive development, language and speech development, psychosocial development, and self-help skills)
- The family's strengths and needs in regard to the development of their child
- The major outcomes expected, expressed in terms of procedures, evaluation criteria, and a time line
- The services necessary and a schedule for their delivery
- Projected dates for initiation of services
- The name of the service coordinator
- A biannual (every 6 months) review, with the child's family, of progress made and of any need for modifications in the IFSP
- Indication of methods for transitioning the child to services available for children ages 3 to 5

To many service coordinators and early childhood specialists, the IFSP is a working document for an ongoing process in which parents and specialists work together, continually modifying, expanding, and developing a child's educational program. Children and families who participate in early intervention programs often find these years to be an intense period, with many professionals offering advice, training, guidance, and personalized services, as well as care and concern. Also, the transition to preschool at the age of 3 can be particularly difficult and frightening. One reason is that services that were delivered primarily at the family's home now will be delivered at a preschool. Therefore, IFSPs include plans for these youngsters and their families to transition from very intensive and individually delivered interventions to more traditional classrooms (CEC, 1999). IDEA '04 allows states to give families the option of delaying entrance into school-based preschool programs by keeping their child in an early intervention program, but making this decision sometimes results in the family having to pay for some or all of the services (U.S. Department of Education, 2006).

Individualized Education Programs (IEPs)

IEPs are the documents that describe the special education and related services appropriate to the needs of students with disabilities who are 3 to 21 years old. These management tools are the cornerstones of every educational program planned for preschoolers (ages 3 to 5) and students (ages 6 to 21) with disabilities (OSEP, 2006a). IDEA '04 delineated what the IEP *must* contain at the very least, and it is important that every educator know these key components:

- **Current performance:** The student's present levels of academic achievement and information about how the student's disability influences participation and progress in the general education curriculum
- **Goals:** Statement of measurable goals related to participation in the general education curriculum or to meeting other educational needs resulting from the disability

- **Special education and related services:** Specific educational services to be provided, including accommodations, program modifications, or supports that allow participation in the general education curriculum and in extracurricular activities
- **Participation with students without disabilities:** Explanation about the extent to which the student will *not* participate in general education classes and in extracurricular activities alongside peers without disabilities
- **Participation in state- and district-wide testing:** Description of assessment adaptations needed for these assessments, or, if the student will not be participating, a statement listing reasons for nonparticipation and explaining how the student will be alternately assessed
- **Dates and places:** Projected dates for initiation of services, where services will be delivered, and the expected duration of those services
- **Transition service needs:** Beginning at age 16, for those students whose goals are related to community presence and independence, a transition component is included in the IEP to identify postschool goals and to describe transitional assessments and service needs
- **Age of majority:** Beginning at least 1 year before the student reaches the age of majority, students must be informed of those rights that transfer to them
- **Measuring progress:** Statement of how the student's progress toward achieving IEP goals will be measured and how parents will be informed about this progress

To stress the importance of including all of these components in each student's IEP, the federal government provided a template for school districts to use as a model (OSEP, 2006b). This sample form is found in Figure 5.2.

IEPs must be written for each student with a disability, so each IEP will be different from the next. Remember Emily, who was described earlier in this chapter? She needs services from several related service professionals, such as a SLP, a physical therapist (PT), and an assistive technologist. Some students may need help only from a special education teacher or a paraprofessional. Other students may require assistance from many more members of a multidisciplinary team. Academic areas may be reflected, but so may areas not typically part of educational programs for students without disabilities (e.g., fine and gross motor skills and life skills). Services indicated on the IEP *must* be provided, and they cannot be traded for other services, such as more time in the general education classroom. Services not being readily available (including assistive technology devices and services) is no reason for omitting them from an IEP: If the student needs the service, it must be delivered. In other words, if a student needs the services of an assistive technologist and requires some special equipment, those services and devices must be made available. In addition, any changes in placement, related services specified in the IEP, or annual goals necessitate another IEP meeting and mutual approval by the family and the school district.

The contents of a student's IEP must be available to all educators who work with the student (U.S. Department of Education, 2006). IEPs are meant to be a communication tool. Surprisingly, it is not uncommon for teachers to be unaware of the goals, objectives, and services required by their students' IEPs. This situation leads one to ask how an appropriate education can be delivered when the educators who interact with students with disabilities do not understand what the students' education should comprise! The answer is obvious: An appropriate education cannot be delivered under these circumstances.

FIGURE 5.2   Individualized Education Program

The Individualized Education Program (IEP) is a written document that is developed for each eligible child with a disability. The Part B regulations specify the procedures that school districts must follow to develop, review, and revise the IEP for each child. The document below sets out the IEP content that those regulations require.

A statement of the child's present levels of academic achievement and functional performance including:

- How the child's disability affects the child's involvement and progress in the general education curriculum (i.e., the same curriculum as for nondisabled children) **or** *for preschool children,* as appropriate, how the disability affects the child's participation in appropriate activities.

A statement of measurable annual goals, including academic and functional goals designed to:

- Meet the child's needs that result from the child's disability to enable the child to be involved in and make progress in the general education curriculum.
- Meet each of the child's other educational needs that result from the child's disability.

For children with disabilities who take alternate assessments aligned to alternate achievement standards (in addition to the annual goals), a description of benchmarks or short-term objectives.

A description of:

- How the child's progress toward meeting the annual goals will be measured.
- When periodic reports on the progress the child is making toward meeting the annual goals will be provided such as through the use of quarterly or other periodic reports, concurrent with the issuance of report cards.

A statement of the *special education and related services* and *supplementary aids* and *services,* based on peer-reviewed research to the extent practicable, to be provided to the child, or on behalf of the child, and *a statement of the program modifications or supports* for school personnel that will be provided to enable the child:

- To advance appropriately toward attaining the annual goals.
- To be involved in and make progress in the general education curriculum and to participate in extracurricular and other nonacademic activities.
- To be educated and participate with other children with disabilities and nondisabled children in extracurricular and other nonacademic activities.

An explanation of the extent, if any, to which the child will not participate with nondisabled children in the regular classroom and in extracurricular and other nonacademic activities.

A statement of any individual appropriate accommodations that are necessary to measure the academic achievement and functional performance of the child on State and districtwide assessments.

If the IEP Team determines that the child must take an alternate assessment instead of a particular regular State or districtwide assessment of student achievement, a statement of why:

- The child cannot participate in the regular assessment.
- The particular alternate assessment selected is appropriate for the child.

The projected date for the beginning of the services and modifications and the anticipated frequency, location, and duration of *special education and related services* and *supplementary aids and services* and *modifications and supports.*

Service, Aid or Modification	Frequency	Location	Beginning Date	Duration

Transition Services

Beginning not later than the first IEP to be in effect *when the child turns 16, or younger if determined appropriate by the IEP Team,* and updated annually thereafter, the IEP must include:

- Appropriate measurable postsecondary goals based on age-appropriate transition assessments related to training, education, employment, and, where appropriate, independent living skills.
- The transition services (including courses of study) needed to assist the child in reaching those goals.

Transition Services (Including Courses of Study)

Rights That Transfer at Age of Majority

- Beginning not later than one year before the child reaches the age of majority under State law, the IEP must include a statement that the child has been informed of the child's rights under Part B of the IDEA, if any, that will, consistent with 34 CFR §300.520, transfer to the child on reaching the age of majority.

Source: Model Form: Individualized Education Program. U.S. Department of Education, Office of Special Education and Rehabilitative Services, Office of Special Education Programs. 2006b.

Transition Components of IEPs

When IDEA was reauthorized in 1997, plans to help students transition from school to postsecondary experiences became a special education requirement. At that time, such a plan was a separate document—a mini-IEP of its own—for students aged 14 and older and was called an individualized transition plan (ITP). Since the 1997 reauthorization of IDEA, these plans for assessments and services to prepare for postschool life, or statements of transitional services, are a part of the students' IEPs; they are *not* stand-alone documents. IDEA '04 increased to 16 the age for initiation of the transition component of students' IEPs. Transitional planning is very important for high school students with disabilities, because these individual's postschool outcomes have much room for improvement.

Although more students with disabilities graduate from high school with a standard diploma than did some 10 years ago (54 percent), too many still drop out of school (OSEP 2006c). Some 28 percent of students with disabilities recently exited high school with no diploma or certificate of completion (Wagner et al., 2006). Completion rates vary greatly by type of disability. For example, 95 percent of students with visual or hearing disabilities and 85 percent of those with autism and physical disabilities complete high school. However, only 56 percent of those students identified as having emotional or behavioral disorders finish high school. How do these statistics compare to those for students without disabilities? Not well. Almost 90 percent of all students complete high school, and this average takes into account the dismal completion rate of Latino/a students, only 75 percent of whom complete high school (National Center for Education Statistics, 2006).

Of course, high school completion rates influence participation rates in postsecondary opportunities. Students with disabilities participate in postsecondary programs at about half the rate of their peers without disabilities; about 20 percent of students with disabilities attend community colleges or four-year colleges and universities (Wagner et al., 2006). All of these reasons contribute to the fact that individuals with disabilities earn less than their counterparts without disabilities and more often find themselves in jobs that do not provide benefits such as health insurance.

It is also important for teachers who participate in transition planning to understand that as adults, these individuals tend to engage in active leisure activities less than individuals without disabilities. They participate in organized community groups at a rate much lower than would be expected, and they also get in trouble with the law more often than their typical peers (Wagner et al., 2006). Helping students set goals for themselves, gain work experience, and develop skills needed for independent living can be critical to the life satisfaction experienced by adults with disabilities (Neubert, 2003).

The transition component supplements and complements the IEP, and as you can tell, it has the potential of being very important to the long-term results of your students. Whereas the IEP describes the educational goals and objectives that a student should achieve during a school year, the transitional services part of the IEP focuses on the academic and functional achievement of the individual to prepare for adult living (National Center on Secondary Education and Transition [NCSET], 2005). Transition components are designed to facilitate the process of going from high school to any of several postschool options: postsecondary education, vocational education, integrated employment (including supported employment), adult services, or community participation (de Fur, 2003). The last years of school can be critical to the achievement of special education outcomes and to these learners' smooth and successful transition to adulthood.

Behavior Intervention Plans

When any student with a disability commits serious behavioral infractions, IDEA '04 requires that a behavior intervention plan, which is like an IEP but addresses the behavioral infraction, be developed (U.S. Department of Education, 2006). Because inappropriate behavior is so often at the root of special education referrals, of teachers' dissatisfaction with working with students who have disabilities, and of lifelong challenges, we devote an entire chapter to behavior management, development of good social skills, and interventions for serious and persistent behavior issues. Here, we will introduce the plans that IDEA '04 requires for students who have an IEP and also engage in seriously disruptive or violent behavior.

Why did behavioral plans for students who have major behavioral issues become part of students' IEPs? One reason reflects concerns of Congress and the public about violence, discipline, and special education students. Although students without disabilities can be expelled for breaking school rules (for bringing guns to school, for example, or engaging in serious fighting), some students with disabilities cannot. These students can, however, be removed from their current placement and receive their education away from their assigned classroom(s) in what is called an interim alternative educational setting (IAES) for up to 45 school days. Continued progress toward the attainment of IEP goals must be one intention of the IAES placement. Students who cannot be expelled are those whose disruptive behavior was caused by their disability. Under the older versions of IDEA, this protection was called the stay put provision. Through a process called manifestation determination, educators figure out whether the disability caused the infraction. All students with disabilities who are violent or "out of control" must have behavior intervention plans developed for them. These plans focus not only on the control or elimination of future serious behavioral infractions but also on the development of positive social skills.

To develop behavior intervention plans, educators use a process called functional behavioral assessment (FBA), which clarifies the student's preferences for specific academic tasks and determines when the undesirable behavior is likely to occur (Kern et al., 2001). We discuss FBA in some detail in Chapter 9. This assessment process was originally developed for students with severe disabilities. IDEA '04 suggests a broader application of the procedure and emphasizes its use when students with any disability face disciplinary actions. The FBA process leads teachers directly to effective interventions with socially validated outcomes (Barnhill, 2005; Ryan, Halsey, & Matthews, 2003). FBAs help determine the nature of the behavior of concern, the reason or motivation for the behavior, and under what conditions the behavior does and does not occur (Hanley, Iwata, & McCord, 2003).

The goal of the assessment is to determine what activities are associated with problem behaviors and to identify the student's interests and preferences (Shippen, Simpson, & Crites, 2003). Instructional activities are then modified to incorporate the student's "likes" into activities where problems typically occur. Here's how it works: Ethan's behavior during activities that require him to write is highly disruptive. However, he likes to use the computer, so he is allowed to complete written assignments using a word processing program on a computer. The double benefit is that his academic performance is improving and his disruptive behavior has decreased. There is a major caution, however. These assessments often miss behaviors that occur rarely, and this is a real problem because many low-frequency infractions (hitting a teacher, setting a fire, breaking a window) are the most dangerous and serious (Nichols, 2000). Because of the propensity of students with emotional or behavioral disorders to exhibit behavior problems, FBAs are used with most of these students. Therefore, more details about FBA and effective interventions that address problem behaviors are found in Chapter 9. As a teacher, you will need to become proficient in using FBAs and understanding their results.

When and How Are Existing Individualized Plans Evaluated?

Assessments of students' performance have many different purposes. The first purpose of assessments, identifying and qualifying students with disabilities, is an important part of the initial IEP process. Those assessments are conducted before the IEP is developed. The data gathered and judgments made are used to shape the IEP process and help the student's IEP Team determine what services are necessary for an appropriate education. However, once an IEP is developed, there are two primary purposes of evaluating the student's performance:

- Evaluate the student's progress toward IEP goals.
- Evaluate the effectiveness of services or supports.

Monitoring Progress

Students with disabilities are tested and evaluated more than any other group of learners. As we just mentioned, these individuals experience many different kinds of assessments during the IEP process. In addition, students with disabilities participate in assessments

- To determine whether the school is making adequate yearly progress
- To monitor their individual progress toward academic and social targets
- To monitor the school's progress toward adequate yearly progress (AYP)

Like their classmates without disabilities, nearly all students with disabilities participate in state- and district-wide assessments (Ziegler, 2002). For improved school accountability, NCLB and IDEA '04 require all students to participate in annual assessments. Only a very small percentage—some 2 percent—of all students with disabilities can be excused from these tests, and they receive an alternate assessment. The other group excused from tests consists of those students just learning English as their second language (U.S. Department of Education, 2006). Because the overall results from individual schools—their adequate yearly progress—are used to "grade" a school's effectiveness, affect student promotion, and sometimes impact the school's funding, these yearly assessments are often referred to as high stakes testing. The ultimate expectation is that all students will achieve proficiency in reading and math, and if students' test scores indicate that they do not reach those levels, the schools they attend will experience significant disincentives (penalties). All students with disabilities must participate in their school district's accountability system. Those who are participating in the general education curriculum may take tests with accommodations, if such accommodations are called for in the student's IEP (Shriner & Destefano, 2003). Students whose curriculum targets life skills and community presence most often participate in alternate assessments, which evaluate students' progress toward meeting benchmarks for targeted achievement of skills that are not part of the general education curriculum (Thompson et al., 2004; OSEP, 2006b). Very few students with disabilities receive alternate assessments, because IDEA '04 allows states to give this option to only 2 percent of all students with disabilities (U.S. Department of Education, 2006).

Although it is important to monitor the overall achievement of a school and how well its students are mastering the general education curriculum, yearly tests do not provide teachers with enough information about the progress of individual students to guide instruction. Other types of assessments are better suited to monitoring students' progress and adapting instruction accordingly. Careful and consistent progress monitoring is important to avoid wasting instructional time by using a tactic that is ineffective. Teachers need to document these students' improvement in academic achievement, behavior, or attainment of life skills. They use results from these evaluations both to guide their instruction and to communicate with the IEP Team. We provide more details about direct assessment systems in Chapter 7, but to put these procedures in context, we introduce them here.

All students experience assessments of their classroom performance. Weekly spelling tests, math tests, exams after the completion of social studies units, and history papers are all examples of students' classroom work that is graded. Such evaluations of students' work are authentic assessments, because they use the work that students generate in classroom settings as the evaluation measurements (Layton & Lock, 2007). Results on students' class assignments, anecdotal records, writing samples, and observational data on behavior are examples of authentic assessments. In other words, evaluation is made directly from the curriculum and the students' work. Teachers often collect more authentic assessments for students with disabilities than they do for their students without disabilities (Fuchs et al., 2001).

● Authentic assessments use work that students generate in classroom settings as evaluation measurements. Teachers often collect more authentic assessments for students with disabilities than for their students without disabilities.

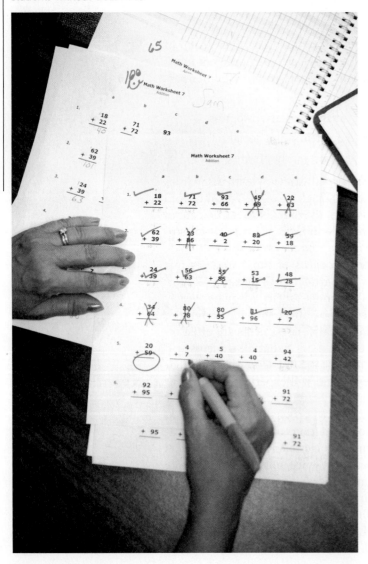

Authentic assessments can be comprehensive and include ongoing, systematic evaluations of students' performance. Portfolio assessment is an example of authentic assessment that includes samples of a student's work, over a period of time, to show her or his growth and development (Layton & Lock, 2007). This evaluation process involves students in both instruction and assessment because they select the exhibits of their work to include (Curran & Harris, 1996; Hébert, 2001). A portfolio may include prizes, certificates of award, pictures, dictated work, photographs, lists of books read, and selections from work done with others. It may also include reports, written by the teacher or by others who work with the child, about challenging situations or patterns of behavior that should be a focus of concern.

Considered both a self-correcting instructional method and an evaluation system, curriculum based measurement (CBM) is a detailed data collection system that frequently measures how well a student is learning specific instructional targets. With CBM, teachers quickly know how well their students are learning and whether the chosen instructional methods are effective (Fuchs et al., 2001; Vaughn & Fuchs, 2003). For example, a teacher instructing a student in math keeps a record of the number or percentage of problems correctly solved across time. Using this system, teachers can track the percentage of words spelled correctly, the number of new arithmetic facts memorized, the number of words correctly read per minute (reading fluency), or the number or percentage of topic sentences included in writing assignments. These records help teachers judge whether the instructional methods selected are both efficient and effective (Fuchs & Fuchs, 2001). CBM is often part of the evaluation system used during the pre-referral stage of the IEP process, particularly for students suspected of having learning disabilities (Bradley, Danielson, & Hallahan, 2002; Fuchs, Fuchs, & Powell, 2004).

Change in Services or Supports

Remember, IDEA '04 guarantees students with disabilities and their families a continuum of services. However, the intention is not for these services to be offered in a fixed sequence. Rather, they are to be a flexible constellation, invoked when supports need to be increased because a student's progress has slowed, or phased down when they are no longer necessary. In other words, the needs of individual students are not fixed but, rather, change across time. A student with a reading disability might, for some period of time, need intensive instruction outside of the general education classroom for some portion of the school day. There, intensive instruction would be delivered to a very small group of learners, all struggling with the task of learning how to read, and all receiving individualized instruction. However, when the reading difficulty is resolved, that student may well move immediately back to the general education setting, where continued progress in reading is monitored every several weeks and then every month or so.

When changes in placement, either more or less restrictive, are considered, the IEP Team, including the family (and, in some cases, the student), must be in communication (U.S. Department of Education, 2006). In some cases, the whole IEP Team, which includes the parents, holds a meeting. In other cases, only selected members of the team who have expertise related to a particular portion of the student's individualized program need to meet. IDEA '04 requires schools to notify parents in writing about changes being made to the student's program. Regardless, for correct decisions to be made about whether a student's services need to be more or less intensive, information must be current and precise. Typically, authentic assessments are used for such decisions.

What Does IDEA '04 Require During the IEP Process?

IDEA '04 includes many requirements about the IEP process and students' IEPs. For example, the law is very specific about these issues:

- IEP Team membership
- Parent participation

- Attendance of IEP Team members at IEP meetings
- When meetings must be held
- Transition components of IEPs
- Blending of IFSP and IEP content in plans for children between the ages of 2 and 3
- Access to IEPs' content
- Transfer of the IEP when a student relocates

As we have noted, states often add steps to the IEP process by expanding components or features of IEPs as they are implemented at the state or district level. Such additional requirements extend beyond what the federal government requires that school districts, schools, and teachers provide to students with disabilities and their families. Federal officials felt that each of the issues above needed to be addressed in IDEA '04, so let's think about each of them in turn.

You have already learned about what IDEA '04 says about who must serve on IEP Teams (review Table 5.2 on page 181). You learned that each IEP Team is a multidisciplinary team of experts who come together to plan an individually designed program to meet the unique needs of each student with a disability. IDEA '04 requires that every team have members from the following groups: the student's parent(s) (or guardian), at least one general education teacher, at least one special educator, a representative of the school district, someone (such as a school psychologist) who can interpret the student's test results, related service providers in each area of need, and the student (when appropriate).

The participation of parents in the IEP process can be a key element in the success of each student's education. However, it can be difficult to schedule and coordinate everyone's time. Parents' work schedules may conflict with the school's schedule. Some parents may not have the transportation to get to and from school at specific times; or they may not be able to arrange baby sitters; or they may feel uncomfortable with the education system. Every effort must be made to assist parents and encourage their participation in the IEP process and IEP Team meetings. As a way to facilitate participation, IDEA '04 now allows for these meetings to be held through different means: conference calls, video conferences, and possibly even e-mails. Many suggest that extended family members also be included, but what is most important is that the schools welcome parents and families of all students with disabilities (Smith, 2007). The Working Together feature provides an example of how IEP Team members come together to ensure that Emily's IEP is serving her needs as her education continues.

IDEA '04 does not require that every member of the IEP Team be present at each and every meeting about the student's educational program (OSEP, 2006a). For example, if an IEP meeting is being held to discuss only the student's speech or language problems, the school psychologist on the team might not have much to contribute. However, that professional may be excused only if both the parent(s) and the school district officially agree in writing.

Unless he or she is part of a pilot program operating in 15 states, every student with a disability must have the IEP reviewed at least annually. However, if major changes are not going to be made, the parents and school district can agree not to hold an official meeting. The IEP Team needs to meet more often than once a year if the student's progress mastering the general education curriculum is less than expected or if unanticipated needs surface. Also, if a major change in the student's services or placement is to occur, a meeting must be called. For example, if the student violates school rules by bringing a gun to campus and a change in placement is to occur, an IEP meeting must be called.

On another note, and addressing a common concern about IEPs, IDEA '04 reaffirms that IEPs are to be open to every education professional who works with the student. However, special education records are confidential, and only those directly involved in administering services described on the IEP have legal access to them. It is important that everyone who works with the child benefit from the collaborative work of the team that developed the IEP. For the same reason, IEPs move with the student. When a family moves to another school, school district, or state, the new education team should benefit from all of the work that went into development of the IEP. Therefore, IDEA '04 stresses the importance of quickly transferring records of students who are relocating.

WORKING together

Reviewing Emily's Progress

Professionals representing related services in addition to the required IEP Team members work together to fine-tune Emily's IEP. The focus of the meeting is to conduct an annual review of Emily's performance in school and to determine what changes to her IEP may be necessary to ensure an appropriate education. The IEP Team consists of Mr. Hernandez, Emily's second-grade teacher, Emily's art teacher, the special education teacher, the principal, Emily's parents, the special education coordinator, and the diagnostician. Also, because of Emily's speech/language and motor needs, the speech/language pathologist, recreational therapist, assistive technologist, occupational therapist, and physical therapist participate on this IEP Team. Different members of the IEP Team have obtained Emily's input about her needs during an interview and observations. All individuals involved in this process should be prepared to discuss Emily's academic, behavioral, social, motor, and language needs from their own perspective. The IEP Team members will bring their summaries about Emily's progress and questions for the team to address. Based on their discussions, Emily's IEP can be adjusted to more appropriately address her needs to ensure successful inclusion in the second-grade class.

Here are some tips that can help ensure the success of this collaborative process:

- Mr. Hernandez should be prepared to discuss how Emily is performing compared to her peers and what techniques he is using to make environmental and instructional adaptations for her. He should also describe how well the computer works as an accommodation to help her do her work and how well Emily is socializing in his class.
- The art teacher should describe how Emily is progressing based on any adaptations that were made to the materials or content.
- The special education teacher should explain how she teams with Mr. Hernandez to support Emily in second grade and how Emily's learning needs are also being addressed during the twice-weekly pull-out sessions with the special education teacher.
- The parents should have an opportunity to express their concerns at home with schoolwork and any other issues that are important for the IEP Team to discuss and resolve.
- The speech/language pathologist can provide an update on therapy sessions to help Emily develop her speech. A discussion about how Emily is doing with her oral language communication in class should also occur.
- The recreational therapist should update the IEP Team on how Emily is performing in adaptive physical education (PE) and provide guidance about how to include Emily in general PE classes.
- The assistive technologist should work with the occupational therapist to reevaluate Emily's use of the computer as an alternative to using a pencil. Discussion about other assistive devices or adaptations to the keyboard may be necessary.
- The physical therapist should evaluate Emily's use of the walker in various school environments and bring this information to the meeting. Issues related to transportation and mobility should be addressed. A discussion with Emily about how the walker helps her mobility can inform discussion in the meeting as well.

Finally, IDEA '04 included language to help students who are transitioning from early childhood programs to school-based programs. This transition period is a very difficult time for many families. For example, for infants and toddlers under the age of 3, service providers often work with both the child and the family at home and in "natural environments," such as community play groups. When children are age 3 or older, education is typically provided at schools. Also, for children under the age of 3, goals and benchmarks of programs planned through IFSPs are not comparable to the education described in IEPs. IFSPs address targets such as school readiness, emerging language, developing motor skills, and preliteracy. IEPs focus more on access to the general education curriculum. To assist in the transition from early childhood programs to school-based programs, the law mandates that the service manager or representative from the early intervention program participate in the young child's initial IEP meeting.

summary

A cornerstone of the federal laws ensuring all infants, toddlers, preschoolers, and students with disabilities a free appropriate education in the least restrictive environment is the individualized education created through the special education process. IDEA '04 guarantees these individuals and their families a tailor-made education program, which is guided by uniquely created planning documents: the individualized family service plan (IFSP) and the individualized education program (IEP). The IEP is further supported, when necessary, by behavior intervention plans and the statement of transitional services. These plans bring together multidisciplinary teams of parents, general educators, special educators, and related service providers for the purpose of helping young children and students with disabilities reach their full potential and achieve community presence and independence as adults.

self-test QUESTIONS

Let's review the learning objectives for this chapter. If you are uncertain and cannot "talk through" the answers provided for any of these questions, reread those sections of the text.

- **Why is a responsive general education important to students who struggle?**

  General education serves as the foundation for effective special education services because high-quality general education uses evidence-based instructional procedures, supports students who struggle, reduces the number of unnecessary referrals, welcomes students with disabilities, provides instructional adaptations and accommodations to increase access to the general education curriculum, and follows through with the individualized plans and interventions.

- **What components of special education must be in place to meet the needs of students with disabilities?**

  Special education is truly special when it builds upon a responsive general education program that incorporates features of universal design for learning, accommodates special needs, differentiates instruction, includes highly qualified special educators, and takes full advantage of the skills and expertise of individually determined multidisciplinary teams of related service providers.

- **What steps are followed in the IEP process?**

  Although states and school districts can add steps and procedures to the IEP process they implement, IDEA '04 requires that these steps, at a minimum, be included in the IEP process: 1. Pre-referral, 2. Referral, 3. Identification, 4. Eligibility, 5. Development of the IEP, 6. Implementation of the IEP, and 7. Evaluation and reviews.

- **What tools guarantee students with disabilities an appropriate education?**

  The plan that guarantees an appropriate education to infants and toddlers (i.e., individuals from birth up to the age of 3) is called the individualized family service plan (IFSP); the plan for preschoolers and schoolchildren is called the individualized education program (IEP). IEPs may have additional components, such as a transition component for students older than age 16 and a behavior intervention plan for students with disabilities who violate schools' conduct codes.

- **What does IDEA '04 require during the IEP process?**

  IDEA '04 mandates that an individualized program be delivered to every infant, toddler, and student who is identified as having a disability and is in need of special education. IDEA '04 is very specific about the requirements of IEPs and the process to be used in their development and implementation. IDEA '04 is also very clear about membership on IEP Teams.

• Revisit the
OPENING challenge

Check your answers to the Reflection Questions from the Opening Challenge and revise them on the basis of what you have learned.

1. Is Mr. Hernandez overly concerned about being able to meet Emily's needs? Why or why not?

2. What advice would you give him about coordinating the supports and services that will be specified in Emily's IEP?

3. What kind of help and assistance should Mr. Hernandez expect from Emily's IEP Team?

4. Is Mr. Hernandez justified in expressing concerns about the educational progress of Emily's classmates? Why or why not?

Professional Standards and Licensure

CEC Knowledge and Skill Core Standard and Associated Subcategories

CEC Content Standard 1: Foundations

Special educators understand the field as an evolving and changing discipline based on philosophies, evidence-based principles and theories, relevant laws and policies, diverse historical points of view, and human issues that have historically influenced the treatment of individuals with exceptional needs both in school and in society.

CEC Content Standard 3

Special educators understand the effects that an exceptional condition can have on an individual's learning in school and throughout life. They understand the similarities and differences in human development and the characteristics between and among individuals with and without ELN.

CEC Content Standard 6: Language

Special educators understand typical and atypical language development and the ways in which exceptional conditions can interact with an individual's experience with and use of language. Special educators are familiar with augmentative, alternative, and assistive technologies; match their communication methods to individuals' language proficiency and cultural and linguistic differences; provide effective language models; and use communication strategies and resources to facilitate understanding of subject matter for individuals with ELN whose primary language is not English.

CEC Content Standard 8: Assessment

Special educators use multiple types of assessment information for a variety of educational decisions and use the results of assessments to help identify exceptional learning needs and to develop and implement individualized instructional programs, as well as to adjust instruction in response to ongoing learning progress. Special educators understand the appropriate use and limitations of various types of assessments. Special educators conduct formal and informal assessments to design learning experiences that support the growth and development of individuals with ELN. Special educators use assessment information to identify supports and adaptations required for individuals with ELN to access the general curriculum and to participate in school-, system-, and statewide assessment programs. Special educators regularly monitor the progress of individuals with ELN.

CEC Content Standard 10: Collaboration

Special educators routinely and effectively collaborate with families, other educators, related service providers, and personnel from community agencies in culturally responsive ways. This collaboration ensures that the needs of individuals with ELN are addressed throughout schooling.

INTASC Core Principle and Associated Special Education Subcategories

1. Foundations

1.04 All teachers have knowledge of the major principles and parameters of federal disabilities legislation.

3. Learner Differences

3.04 All teachers understand and are sensitive to cultural, ethnic, gender, and linguistic differences that may be confused with or misinterpreted as manifestations of disability.

6. Language

6.01 All teachers have knowledge of the general types of communication strategies and assistive technologies that can be incorporated as a regular part of instruction. They understand that students with disabilities may have communication and language needs that impact their ability to access the general education curriculum.

8. Assessment

8.01 All teachers understand the purposes, strengths, and limitations of formal and informal assessment approaches for making eligibility, placement, and instructional decisions for students with disabilities.

10. Collaboration, Ethics, and Relationships

10.01 All teachers share instructional responsibility for students with disabilities and work to develop well-functioning collaborative teaching relationships.

Praxis II: Education of Exceptional Students: Core Content Knowledge PRAXIS

I. Understanding Exceptionalities

Basic concepts in special education, including

- The classification of students with disabilities

II. Legal and Societal Issues

Federal laws and legal issues related to special education, including

- Public Law 94-142
- Public Law 105-17
- Section 504
- Americans with Disabilities Act (ADA)
- Important legal issues

The school's connections with the families, prospective and actual employers, and communities of students with disabilities, for example,

- Parent partnerships and roles
- Cultural and community influences on public attitudes toward individuals with disabilities
- Interagency agreements
- Cooperative nature of the transition-planning process

Historical movements/trends affecting the connections between special education and the larger society, for example

- Inclusion
- Transition
- Advocacy
- Accountability and meeting educational standards

III. Delivery of Services to Students with Disabilities

Background knowledge, including

- Placement and program issues such as early intervention; least restrictive environment; inclusion; role of individualized education program (IEP) Team; due process guidelines; and others

Curriculum and instruction and their implementation across the continuum of education placements, including

- The individualized family service plan (IFSP)/individualized education program (IEP) process

Assessment, including

- Use of assessment for screening, diagnosis, placement, and the making of instructional decisions
- Procedures and test materials, both formal and informal

Professional roles, including

- Specific roles and responsibilities of teachers
- Communicating with parents and guardians and appropriate community collaborators

Video—"Assessment of Special Needs Students"

This video shows that standardized tests may need modifications to accurately measure learning for students with special needs.

> Log onto **www.mylabschool.com**. Under the **Courses** tab, in **Special Education,** go to the **video lab**. Access the "**Inclusion and Least Restrictive Environment**" videos and watch the "**Assessment of Special Needs Students**" video.

 OR

> Use the **www.mylabschool.com Assignment Finder** to go directly to these videos. Just enter Assignment ID **SPV2**.

1. What type of information regarding standardized assessments is contained in the IEP?

2. What alternative forms of assessment or assessment modifications are described in the video for students with disabilities?

Case Study—"Is This Child Mislabled?"

Serge Romanich, a third-grade student and refugee from Serbia, spoke limited English. His education had been sporadic at best, and the new elementary school he was attending had tested him and classified him as having learning disabilities. Now the professionals who work with Serge wonder whether he is appropriately placed in special education.

> Log onto **www.mylabschool.com**. Under the **Resources** tab, navigate to the **Case Archive** and read "**Is This Child Mislabled?**"

 OR

> Use the **www.mylabschool.com Assignment Finder** to go directly to the case study. Just enter Assignment ID **CS13**.

1. Review the IEP steps outlined in the chapter. How could the information provided in the case study be used to qualify Serge for special education services and to develop his IEP?

2. Do you think Serge's skills were adequately assessed? Provide a rationale for your response.

3. What is the role of the general education teacher in developing the IEP?

To access chapter objectives, practice tests, weblinks, and flashcards, go to the companion website at **www.ablongman.com/bryantsmith1e**.

chapter 6

Differentiating Instruction to Promote Access to the Curriculum

After studying this chapter, you will have the knowledge to answer the following questions:

- What is differentiated instruction?
- How can instruction be differentiated?
- What are some effective instructional practices?
- How can grouping practices promote effective instruction?
- What guidelines should be followed for instructional materials and homework?
- What are assistive technology devices and services?

● OPENING challenge

Planning and Delivering Instruction

Elementary Grades ● Mrs. Bell is a fifth-grade teacher who teaches in a suburban public school district outside a major city. She has been teaching fifth grade for 12 years. The community in which she teaches has been growing rapidly in recent years. In response to housing demands and varying socioeconomic levels, developers are building a range of housing options that offer affordable opportunities. The school district's demographics reflect a diverse student population: 26 percent African American, 19 percent Asian, 32 percent Hispanic, 22 percent European American, and 1 percent Native American. In Mrs. Bell's school, 43 percent of the students qualify for free or reduced-cost lunch, and 12 percent are English language learners. Mrs. Bell's class includes two students with reading, writing, and mathematics learning disabilities (LD). These students are performing about 2 years below grade level. Mrs. Bell has two English language learners (ELLs) in her class. These students speak Spanish at home and in school in social situations. They attended bilingual classes in the primary grades. The Language Support Team (LST) in Mrs. Bell's school agreed, on the basis of oral language assessments, that both students were ready to move into English

column continues on next page

Secondary Grades ● Ms. Mendez is a first-year ninth-grade science teacher at a high school in the same school district as Mrs. Bell. The student demographics in her high school are similar to those described for Mrs. Bell's school. Ms. Mendez teaches five class periods a day, with one "prep" period. The ninth-grade science teachers meet weekly to plan units and assess student performance. Because nearly one-third of the student population has low academic performance, the school administration is trying new teacher teaming strategies to address the students' needs. Thus, different support teachers meet with the science team weekly to identify and address student response to academic instruction, behavior concerns, and any other issues that are evident, such as home situations and motivational problems. Ms. Mendez appreciates planning science instruction with her team and the opportunities to problem-solve student issues. Although she feels fairly confident with the science curriculum, she is apprehensive about ensuring that all of her students can access the curriculum and benefit from her instruction. As she prepares for an upcoming team meeting, she reflects on her instructional practices: *"The range*

column continues on next page

instruction classes. Mrs. Bell also has one student with cerebral palsy (CP) who uses a wheelchair for ambulation. Her student with CP has good communication skills but has difficulty with motor tasks such as writing with a pencil. This is Mrs. Bell's first opportunity to work with a student who has CP. She is a little nervous about ensuring that instruction is appropriate for this student. Mrs. Bell reflects about her class: *"I need to be sure that my instruction is appropriate for all of my students. I have a range of abilities and needs this year. In reviewing the fall academic assessment scores, I see that about one-quarter of my class requires extra help with reading, writing, and mathematics. I also have to be sure that I am addressing the needs of my students who are ELLs and students with LD and CP. Differentiating instruction is critical for the success of all of my students."* ●

of reading and writing abilities is challenging, particularly when students read text in class and for homework. I use small groups for class activities, but not all of the students are learning in these groups. I know I should make adaptations to differentiate instruction, but I am not sure where to begin. I will bring up these issues at the next support meeting to find ways to strengthen my instructional practices." ●

● Reflection Questions

In your journal, write down your answers to the following questions. After completing the chapter, check your answers and revise them on the basis of what you have learned.

1. How can Mrs. Bell and Ms. Mendez use the ADAPT framework to differentiate instruction for their students?

2. How can Mrs. Bell and Ms. Mendez differentiate instruction for their multicultural and ELL students?

3. What instructional and grouping practices might help them provide effective, differentiated instruction for their students?

4. How can Mrs. Bell and Ms. Mendez ensure that the instructional materials and homework practices they use are appropriate for all of their students?

5. How can assistive technology help Mrs. Bell's students with disabilities access the general education curriculum?

*I*nclusive schools use a variety of practices to ensure that all students have opportunities to learn and thrive in a supportive, responsive school environment. As you read in Chapter 1, the legal requirements of Section 504 and IDEA were enacted to guarantee the rights of all students to a free appropriate education, including access to the general education curriculum. In Chapter 5, you learned that general education is "the foundation for special education" because educators are responsible for providing evidence-based instruction to struggling students in order to prevent or reduce unnecessary referrals to special education. Moreover, the implementation of individualized education programs (IEPs) in the general education classroom is the cornerstone of an appropriate education for students with disabilities. Thus, by systematically differentiating instruction with evidence-based practices to address individual learning needs, teachers can make the educational setting a responsive environment where all students can succeed and learn. These are broad challenges, but by knowing how to differentiate instruction and how to implement strategies for behavior management and content instruction, educators, in collaboration with special educators and other professionals, can indeed meet the legal requirements that are intended to benefit *all* students.

Having access to the general education curriculum means being able to (1) learn the knowledge and skills that we expect all students to learn; (2) benefit from evidence-based instruction that is designed, delivered, and evaluated for effectiveness; and (3) use materials, facilities, and labs that facilitate learning. For many at risk students and students with disabilities, mastering the critical knowledge and skills in the academic areas is difficult because of problems (such as sensory, memory, communication, motor, behavioral, and cognitive problems) associated with learning. Differentiating instruction, then, is critical to helping them become successful learners.

Differentiating instruction is instruction that is responsive to the diverse needs of all students, with a focus on curriculum, instructional adaptations, services, and instructional intensity. Figure 6.1 depicts a differentiating instruction continuum that illustrates how most of the student population can benefit from less differentiation in order to successfully access and master the general education curriculum. Some students require differentiation, however, and it can take various forms depending on the student's individual needs. For example, differentiating instruction can occur in terms of intensity of instruction. Intensity involves the grouping of students and the amount of time required to provide

FIGURE 6.1 A Differentiating Instruction Continuum

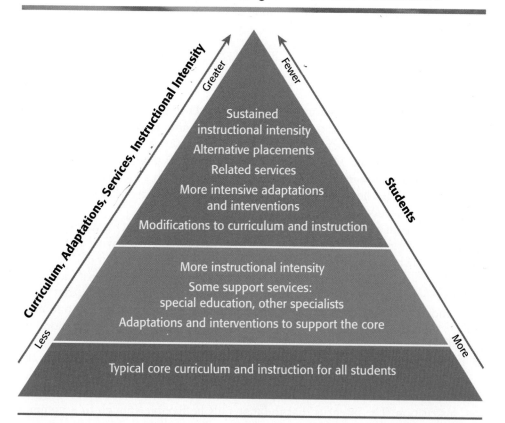

Curriculum, Adaptations, Services, Instructional Intensity

Greater Fewer

Students

Less More

Sustained instructional intensity
Alternative placements
Related services
More intensive adaptations and interventions
Modifications to curriculum and instruction

More instructional intensity
Some support services: special education, other specialists
Adaptations and interventions to support the core

Typical core curriculum and instruction for all students

more individualized instruction. Specialized personnel, including special educators, may be needed to deliver more intensive, adapted instruction. Also, differentiating instruction may occur in different settings, such as the general education classroom, a resource room, or a self-contained classroom, depending on the needs of the student. In some cases, a change in the curriculum emphasizing more life skills may be required.

In Chapter 5, we discussed the ADAPT framework as a tool that you can use to differentiate instruction by making instructional adaptations. Adapting instruction can help students access, learn, and apply the knowledge and skills introduced in the general education curriculum (Bryant & Bryant, 1998; Gelzheiser & Meyers, 1991). In this chapter, we discuss ways to differentiate instruction, including the ADAPT framework. We provide information about multicultural and linguistic considerations when differentiating instruction. We also discuss instructional practices that help students access and master the curriculum, ways to adapt instructional materials, effective homework practices, and assistive technology devices and services.

How Do We Differentiate Instruction?

Differentiating instruction can be accomplished in many ways. We present three ideas for differentiating instruction to meet the needs of all learners. First, universal design focuses on how information is presented and how students can respond accordingly. It ensures that students with special needs can easily access learning. The ADAPT framework, a major feature of this text, is another way in which instruction can be differentiated. Finally, teachers must ensure that instruction is differentiated to address the learning needs of their students from diverse backgrounds.

Universal Design

To set the stage for a discussion about using the ADAPT framework to differentiate instruction, we first offer a broader perspective about accommodating differences. This perspective focuses on the idea of universal design for curricula and instruction. Orkwis and McLane (1998) describe universal design as planning materials and instruction in such a way that all students with a variety of differences in learning, seeing, hearing, moving, and understanding English can access and benefit from instruction.

Let's take an example of universal design based on the ADA law, which requires that the physical environment be made accessible. Removing barriers allows people with disabilities to participate in events and activities of daily life, but removing those barriers also helps people without disabilities. For instance, curb cuts enable people who use wheelchairs to use sidewalks, cross streets, and move independently as they shop or get from a parking lot to a local coffee shop to meet friends. But curb cuts also help parents with strollers and people with shopping carts as they shop and walk through neighborhoods or shopping centers.

Now, let's translate this concept of access to the environment into making the curriculum and instruction more accessible. Applying universal design to curricula and instruction means that adaptations are incorporated into the materials and instruction. The intent is that the materials be flexible enough to accommodate the diverse learning needs evident in most classrooms.

Universally designed curricula and instruction exhibit three special features (Miller, 2002; Orkwis & McLane, 1998). First, there are multiple means of representation; in other words information is presented in various formats to reduce sensory and cognitive barriers. For example, written text can be accompanied by audio for students who are blind, and graphics can be used to enhance the content for students who are deaf or have learning problems. Closed captions on video are another example. The second feature, multiple means of expression, refers to the ability of students to respond in a variety of ways. For example, voice recognition software, scanning devices, and switches help students with physical disabilities access the computer to complete computer-based activities. The third feature, multiple means of engagement, consists of actively involving students in activities and making available more than just a single mode of representation and expression to address their needs and interests. Offering information in various formats *and* making it possible for students to respond either in small groups or as partners. Using the computer is an example of providing different ways to engage students in the learning process.

Digital media offer an excellent example of how universal design features promote access for students with different needs, such as accommodations in learning, seeing, hearing, moving, and/or understanding English (Miller, 2002; Orkwis & McLane, 1998). Current technology and partnerships with textbook publishers now make electronic versions of texts readily available, so print is not the only way to access books. For the student with learning disabilities who has difficulty reading, the computer can be used to immediately translate visual access to the curriculum materials (that is, reading print) into an auditory means of gaining information (listening to the text). Thus, a social studies text can be "heard" instead of "read." By using the same electronic version of the book, the computer can convert print into braille for the student with severe visual disabilities. In this case, the student who is blind uses a tactile means of accessing print can read the social studies text. Universal design allows the broadest spectrum of learners to access the curriculum: students with varying learning needs, those with disabilities, and those with other special needs.

In the Making a Difference feature an elementary science teacher finds that an instructional modification she devised for her special education students benefited everyone, saved her time, and made the lesson *more* inclusive.

The ADAPT Framework

Differentiating instruction can also be accomplished by adapting instruction in the activities used to teach objectives, content that is being taught, procedures that are used to deliver instruction, and materials that support instruction. Bryant and Bryant (1998) proposed an adaptations framework, now known as the ADAPT framework, as a way of identifying appropriate adaptations for students with special needs. Adaptations share three characteristics. They are *individualized,* focusing on the strengths of the individual; they are *relevant* to the objective being taught to all students; and they must be *effective* to ensure that students learn the objectives. If our first attempt at making an adaptation does not help the student benefit from instruction, then we continue to make adaptations until the student meets the objective. By using the ADAPT framework, educators can make decisions about adaptations that are individualized for the student's strengths and needs and are relevant to the task at hand, such as reading and completing homework. Student performance on tasks is a good indicator of the effectiveness of the chosen adaptations.

Making a Difference

Differentiating Instruction Can Benefit *All* of the Students in My Class!

Allison Gillentine
*Spring Hill Junior High,
Eighth-Grade Science
Longview, Texas*

Teaching about the atom and its particles (the proton, neutron, and electron) is part of the eighth-grade Texas Essential Knowledge and Skills curriculum for science. It's a challenging section for most students. I begin this lesson for all of my students by explaining how the periodic table is arranged and how to read an element key. Next, I teach them to find the numbers of protons, electrons, and neutrons in an atom.

My general education students then practice drawing smaller atoms correctly; protons and neutrons are drawn in the nucleus, two electrons are drawn in the first energy level, the remaining electrons go in the second energy level, and so on. However, to reinforce this concept with my special education students, I provide them with small colored-shell candies. Each candy color represents a different particle: protons (orange), electrons (brown), and neutrons (yellow). Each student uses the candies to create atoms on a prepared mat on which I have drawn a nucleus and the appropriate electron energy levels. The special education students do well with this manipulative approach and seem to grasp the abstract concepts of the atom more easily.

Because the manipulative approach worked so well, I expanded my regular education lesson to include the candy exercise. I found that my general education students benefited from "playing" with the atom as much as my special education students did, and they enjoyed helping each other as well. Prior to this experience, I was more likely to do lower-level activities with my special education students only. After this experience, I began to analyze and select my in-class activities and assignments to focus on those that would satisfy *all* of my students, both general education and special education. I found that doing so greatly reduced the need for specific modifications for certain students, and the time I saved by delivering effective full-class instruction was available for me to provide necessary modifications when they were needed and to whoever needed them. ●

The ADAPT framework consists of five steps to guide your decision making about selecting and evaluating adaptations:

1. Ask, "What am I requiring the student to do?"
2. Determine the prerequisite skills of the task.
3. Analyze the student's strengths and struggles.
4. Propose and implement adaptations from among the four instructional categories—content, materials, delivery, and activity.
5. Test to determine if the adaptations helped the student accomplish the task.

We will examine each step to illustrate how to apply the ADAPT framework in your class with students who have special learning needs. Throughout the remaining chapters, you will read about specific ways to use ADAPT in academic, social, and behavioral areas.

ADAPT STEPS The first step is *Ask, "What am I requiring the student to do?"* This step involves the tasks that students are required to perform. For example, in second grade, students are expected to learn basic academic skills, demonstrate the ability to get along with others, and listen to the teacher. In high school, students are required to take notes in class, complete their homework, learn from textbooks, conduct and write about research, and pass end-of-semester exams. These "setting-specific demands" are typical of the core curriculum—content that is taught to all students in the general education setting (Deshler, Ellis, & Lenz, 1996). Students who have difficulty with these requirements are good candidates for teachers to use the ADAPT framework.

The second step is *Determine the prerequisite skills of the task.* It focuses on identifying what students must be able to do to meet teachers' expectations. In this step, teachers "pull apart" the task to identify those specific prerequisite skills. For example, to add two numbers ($9 + 3 = ?$), students must be able to (1) identify and understand the numerical value of the numerals 9 and 3, (2) identify and know the meaning of + and =, (3) use a strategy (such as "Count on 3 from 9") to arrive at the solution, and (4) write the numeral 12 correctly (not 21). All of these steps should be performed rather quickly so that students can keep up with instruction. For older students, taking notes in class may be a required task. The prerequisite skills for notetaking include listening, identifying important information to write down, writing, summarizing the notes, and studying them for a test, which involves its own set of prerequisite skills. Thus, identifying prerequisite skills is an important step in the ADAPT framework, because it forms the basis for addressing the remaining steps.

The third step, *Analyze the student's strengths and struggles,* refers to identifying each prerequisite skill of a task (Step 2) as a strength or struggle for an individual student. This process can be accomplished by using assessment techniques or the teacher's knowledge of the student. For example, in thinking about our addition problem ($9 + 3 = ?$), teachers can use active process assessment (interviewing the student as the problem is solved out loud) to determine how the student solves the problem. By having the student "think aloud," the teacher can figure out whether the steps for arriving at the answer reflect strengths or struggles. For example, if the student reads the numerals and symbols correctly, then these prerequisite skills can be listed as strengths for this task. If the student starts with 1 and counts up to 12 rather than starting with 9 and counting up 3 to get 12, then the teacher suspects that the "Start big and count on" strategy is a struggle. The teacher can also use observation to determine whether numerals are written correctly, which would be a strength. If the numeral 12 were written as 21, then writing the numeral correctly would be a struggle. Referring to our notetaking task, teachers can ask for a copy of a student's notes to analyze them for the prerequisite skills of identifying and recording the important information.

In the fourth step, *Propose and implement adaptations from among the four categories,* the teacher considers the student's strengths and struggles to identify appropriate instructional adaptations. In the ADAPT framework, there are four adaptation categories: (1) instructional activity, (2) instructional content, (3) instructional delivery, and (4) instructional material. Each of these is described below. Returning to our addition problem example ($9 + 3 = ?$), the teacher identifies the need to reteach the "Start big and count on" addition strategy. She decides to work with a small group of students (instructional delivery), all of whom need to be retaught the "Start big and count on" addition strategy. As part of this instruction, the teacher uses easier facts (instructional content), such as $3 + 2$, and then increases to more difficult facts, such as $8 + 2$ and $9 + 3$; reviews the concept of bigger than or greater than (instructional content) to be sure students know which number in a problem is the larger of the two; and uses chips (instructional material) so that students can move a chip to keep track of the "counting on" number (for $8 + 2$, there are 2 chips to move as the student starts big, 8, and counts on 2 to get 10). In our notetaking example, several adaptations come to mind. The teacher can provide a student with carbonless paper (instructional material) to take notes and then can share a copy of these notes with the student who struggles with the task. The student can tape record (instructional material) the lecture and then record key ideas. Or a notetaking strategy (instructional activity) such as Note Shrink, discussed in Chapter 13, can be taught to a small group of students who can benefit from this instruction (instructional delivery).

The fifth step, *Test to determine if the adaptations helped the student accomplish the task,* focuses on the ways in which teachers monitor student progress to determine whether they are benefiting from or responding to instruction. Chapter 7 provides assessment examples of how teachers can determine whether students are being successful with adapted instruction. For example, returning to our addition problem 9 + 3, during curriculum based assessment or one-minute timed assessments, the teacher can check to see whether problems that can be solved with "Start big and count on" are answered correctly. With the notetaking example, a final copy of the notes can be graded, and the exam on which the notes are based can be examined for evidence of the key information in the student's answers.

There are four categories of adaptations from which educators can choose when selecting adaptations that are individualized for the student and relevant to the task (Rivera & Smith, 1997):

- Instructional activity is the actual lesson used to teach and reinforce skills and concepts. Sometimes, a different instructional activity is needed if students do not benefit from the original lesson delivered by the teacher.
- Instructional content consists of the skills and concepts that are the focus of teaching and learning. Instructional content can be thought of as the curriculum that state and local school districts require educators to teach. Content can be located in standards, district documents, and the teachers' guides that accompany textbooks and other materials.
- Instructional delivery is how the activity is taught, including grouping practices, instructional steps, presentation techniques, practice techniques, and student activities. Systematic, *explicit instruction* is included in instructional delivery. Examples of explicit instruction include modeling, when the teacher provides a demonstration of steps to solve the problem; "thinking aloud," when the teacher says out loud the steps he or she is taking while solving a problem; prompts or cues, when the teacher provides assistance (visual, verbal) to increase the likelihood of correct responses; error correction, when the teacher provides immediate feedback to correct error responses; guided practice, when the teacher provides multiple opportunities for students to respond and practice; and pacing, when the teacher provides instruction at an appropriate rate to keep students engaged in learning and to promote understanding.
- Instructional materials are aids such as textbooks, kits, hardware, software, and manipulatives. In any subject area, there are multiple types of instructional materials that teachers can use to address various learning needs. You will read about many examples in later chapters.

Let's take a look at how the ADAPT framework works in the classroom. Recall from the Opening Challenge that Ms. Mendez has students in her class with reading difficulties. She is concerned about their ability to read and understand the science text. She knows adaptations are needed, so she uses ADAPT to make instructional decisions. As you read about how she uses ADAPT, think back to the three characteristics of adaptations and consider whether the adaptation is individualized for the student, relevant for instruction, and effective.

ADAPT in Action • Students with Reading Difficulties

Ms. Mendez's ninth-grade students with reading difficulties are required to read science text in class or for homework. Comprehending text requires many skills, including figuring out difficult words and monitoring one's understanding of the text. Ms. Mendez's students with reading difficulties can figure out difficult words pretty well because they learned skills in earlier grades for breaking words apart to "sound them out." They can identify important information as they read. They struggle, though, with organizing all of this information to help them remember what they read, to see relationships among important ideas, and to comprehend the information from multiple paragraphs within chapters. With so much text to read, they cannot organize the important information to aid their understanding. Ms. Mendez is alarmed by how poorly these students did on a recent quiz she gave on text material. She decides to implement ADAPT to help her choose appropriate adaptations to aid reading comprehension for these students.

Ask, "What am I requiring the student to do?" Ms. Mendez considers the task. "The students need to read the science text in class and at home. Text may be in a book or on a handout for small-group work. Often there are lab assignments that require reading and following instructions that students must comprehend."

Determine the prerequisite skills of the task. "Students need to be able to read the text, identify important information from multiple paragraphs, organize this information to facilitate comprehension, see relationships among important ideas, and pass quizzes that test their understanding."

Analyze the student's strengths and struggles. Ms. Mendez thinks about several of her students who have reading comprehension difficulties. They appear motivated to be successful in her class. They participate in small-group activities and seem to enjoy the lab assignments. Text reading and understanding is her main concern. She works individually with the students to analyze difficulties by asking them to read several paragraphs out loud, identify important information, talk about the relationships among these important ideas, and organize the information in a way that enhances learning and retention. She finds that the students can read many of the words and that they have strategies for figuring out harder words. They can tell her the important ideas but cannot discuss the relationships among these ideas or organize them in a way to promote understanding. For example, they have difficulty comparing and contrasting important ideas related to different types of plants. She gave them a news story about global warming, and they were unable to structure information that focused on cause and effect.

Propose and implement adaptations from among the four categories. Ms. Mendez decides to try graphic organizers (GOs), which are visual aids (instructional material) used to help students organize, understand, see relationships, and remember important information. GOs can be used to structure different types of information, including information about "causes and effects" and "similarities and differences." In a small group of her students with reading difficulties, Ms. Mendez models by "thinking aloud" how to use the graphic organizers as she is reading text (instructional delivery). She gives them a short paragraph, and together they read the material and complete the GO. She sets aside 20 minutes to conduct this mini-lesson (instructional activity), while the other students in her class work in small groups (instructional delivery) on a review exercise.

Test to determine if the adaptations helped the student accomplish the task. Ms. Mendez will review the information included in the graphic organizer as one way to determine the effectiveness of the adaptation. She will also provide a quiz on the material to see how the students understood the content. Can you identify how the adaptation is individualized, relevant, and effective?

If progress is still lacking with her students, Ms. Mendez will try some of the following ideas.

- **Instructional activity:** Develop and teach a lesson on the different types of graphic organizers, including examples of completed GOs. She will also give them blank GOs that students can complete together. If possible, she will obtain the reading teacher's instructional assistance for the lesson.
- **Instructional content:** Reduce the amount of content being studied by selecting one type of GO, "compare and contrast," so as not to overwhelm the students with too many materials.
- **Instructional delivery:** Work one-on-one with the students who are having the most difficulty using the GO.
- **Instructional materials:** Provide written directions on the GO to help students remember the steps for using the material. Have students create GOs on the computer to motivate more interest.

Based on the ADAPT framework in action discussed earlier in the chapter, ADAPT Framework 6.1 summarizes the information Ms. Mendez identified for each of the ADAPT steps. In the remaining chapters, you will encounter many examples of the ADAPT framework in your text, and you will see applications that illustrate quickly and simply how ADAPT can be implemented.

Multicultural and Linguistic Considerations

Ways to differentiate instruction for students from culturally and linguistically diverse backgrounds, including students with identified disabilities, are discussed and illustrated throughout this chapter. For example, the ADAPT framework and instructional practices can be implemented with *all* students. Although it is beyond the scope of this textbook to provide a thorough explanation of effective pedagogy (teaching) for students from diverse cultural and linguistic backgrounds, an overview of such instructional considerations is offered here, and specific ideas related to content areas are provided in Chapters 10 through 13.

Teaching in diverse classrooms should involve practices that are responsive to the cultural characteristics (the beliefs, norms, and customs that differ within and between groups) and linguistic differences of students. Goldstein (2002) describes the attributes of "critical educators" who strive to create an inclusive setting that meets the needs of diverse learners, including those students with special needs. Making connections among students' personal history, experiences, and the community is especially important, as is understanding community expectations and issues, in order to create meaningful connections between school and community. Goldstein also cites the importance of respecting students' ethnic and linguistic backgrounds and being mindful of their prior knowledge and experiences.

6.1 **ADAPT Framework** Difficulty Reading About Science

ASK "What am I requiring the student to do?"	DETERMINE the prerequisite skills of the task.	ANALYZE the student's strengths and struggles.	PROPOSE and implement adaptations from among the four categories.	TEST to determine if the adaptations helped the student to accomplish the task.

		Strengths	Struggles		
The students will read science text.	1. Figure out difficult words by breaking them apart.	1		**For 1.** No adaptation is needed.	
	2. Identify important information.	2			
	3. Organize information to understand and recall.		3	**For 3. Instructional Activity** Conduct a mini-lesson on using graphic organizers (GOs).	**For 3.** Assess student use of GOs and mastery of content through correct completion of GOs and accuracy on quizzes.
				Instructional Delivery Model using "thinking aloud" and show students how to use GOs.	
				Instructional Material Provide GOs to be used in class and for homework.	

How can you translate the characteristics of "critical educators" into differentiating instruction? Cloud (2002) provides ideas for ensuring that the curricula and materials are responsive to the cultural and linguistic diversity of our students. One idea is to learn more about your students' life experiences and background knowledge through discussions, interviews, and parent conferences. Then, when teaching a theme or unit of instruction, you can integrate your students' experiences and their heritages into the content. For example, when studying U.S. leaders, you can include individuals from various ethnic and cultural groups who made significant contributions in a variety of areas (such as the arts, politics, education, and medicine). Thus, your selection of leaders should be inclusive and representative of our country's demographic diversity.

The selection of instructional materials is another consideration when planning instruction. Materials should be selected that represent individuals from diverse backgrounds in situations where they serve as positive role models, free of bias and stereotypes. For example, multicultural literature offers stories with familiar situations, characters, and settings to which students might relate (Cloud, Genesee, & Hamayan, 2000).

Considering *Diversity*

Strategies for Differentiated Instruction for English Language Learners (ELLs)

Scheduling Strategies

- Chunk instruction into shorter segments to allow for time to check work.
- Expand assignments over a longer period.
- Extend wait time for oral responses.
- Plan challenging tasks and subjects earlier in the day or period—or other best time for the student.

Setting Strategies

- Seat ELLs close to speaker, screen, or reader.
- Assign support staff to work with ELLs in addition to the classroom teacher.
- Provide small-group instruction.
- Pair or group ELLs with "buddies" who will assist with modeling and explaining tasks.
- Work one-to-one with students.

Equipment/Materials Strategies

- Introduce and develop new vocabulary visually by using a picture dictionary and other visual aids.
- Use bilingual dictionaries during reading and writing assignments in order to clarify meaning when possible.
- Adapt texts by shortening or simplifying language to make the content more accessible.
- Use technology and multimedia (e.g., software such as Inspiration®, books on tape) and graphic organizers.

Presentation Strategies

- Provide ample repetition of language: repeat, re-state, rephrase, reread.
- Keep language consistent when describing or explaining; synonyms, idioms, and metaphors may be confusing at first; gradually introduce figurative language to expand language development of ELLs.

- Keep explanations and directions brief and concise—focus on key concepts and vocabulary.
- Highlight and explicitly teach key vocabulary needed to accomplish the assigned task.
- Enhance oral presentations with visual (e.g., pictures) and written support, graphic organizers, and modeling.
- Allow students time to check and discuss their understanding of directions and material with peers.
- Present material through multiple modes, using audiovisual and other technology (e.g., books on tape, instructional software, visuals on the overhead projector, presentation software).
- Encourage and allow for nonverbal responses through the use of pictures, manipulatives, and graphic organizers.

Response Strategies

- Encourage and allow for nonverbal responses such as pointing, nodding, drawing pictures, using manipulatives, and completing graphic organizers.
- Adjust expectations for language output (e.g., student speaks in words and phrases, simple present-tense statements).
- Allow shortened responses.
- Require fewer assignments (focus on the quality of a reduced number of instructional objectives).
- Pair ELLs with strong speakers and writers (buddies).
- Encourage "buddies" to take a dictated response during pair work where ELLs explain concepts.
- Allow ELLs to dictate responses into a tape player as evidence of completion of assigned written work.

Source: Adapted from http://www.mcps.k12.md.us/curriculum/science/instr/esolaccom.htmb; *Daily Planning for Today's Classroom* (2nd ed.), by K. M. Price and K. L. Nelson, 2003, Belmont, CA: Wadsworth/Thomson Learning.

When teaching students from linguistically diverse backgrounds, teachers can implement practices recommended by Ortiz and Yates (2001) and Zehler (1994) that are intended to enhance language development and understanding. Teachers should provide opportunities for students to interact with peers and adults. For example, this can be done in cooperative learning groups and through class discussions. Teachers can adjust their level of English vocabulary to the student's level of understanding and can support instructional language by repeating, rephrasing, and extending the student's language. Teachers can use nonverbal cues such as gestures, pictures, objects, and other instructional materials to facilitate understanding. Teachers can also preview new content by teaching key vocabulary, asking questions to stimulate thinking about the new content, and making linkages between students' experiences. Moreover, Gersten and Baker (2000) examined the literature on effective practices for English language learners and found the following procedures to be effective:

- Visuals to teach and reinforce new concepts and vocabulary
- Cooperative learning and peer tutoring methods
- Supportive explanations, in the native language, of more difficult ideas
- Opportunities, both formal and informal, to use English during the day

Finally, the Considering Diversity feature offers ways to differentiate instruction for English language learners.

What Instructional Practices Help Students Access and Master the Curriculum?

In this section, we discuss two important components related to instructional practices. Planning instruction involves considering what you will teach and how you will go about teaching so that all students in your class can benefit from your instruction. Delivering instruction involves specific practices for conveying information and ensuring appropriate student responses.

Planning for Instruction

We discuss three areas that teachers should plan as they prepare to teach lessons. The first subsection discusses different types of knowledge and critical thinking. We provide instructional techniques for teaching this information. The next subsection, on stages of learning, includes information about how students' performance may be affected by their level of acquaintance with the content they will be taught. For example, some students might be unfamiliar with the content, whereas other students might have more knowledge. How we teach students at different stages varies. Finally, we discuss instructional components, which include steps for delivering instruction.

TYPES OF KNOWLEDGE AND CRITICAL THINKING   Different types of knowledge and critical thinking for different content areas are applicable across the grade levels; they include discrimination, factual knowledge, procedural knowledge, and conceptual knowledge, as well as critical thinking (Mastropieri & Scruggs, 2007). Discrimination is the ability to distinguish one item (such as a letter, number, letter sound, math sign, state, or piece of lab equipment) from another. Discrimination occurs during the early stages of learning when students are first learning new information.

Discrimination requires the ability to identify and pay attention to the relevant features of an item. Students with learning difficulties may have problems discriminating among items. Teachers should teach the relevant features of items and then present similar items where discriminations are necessary. For example, students can learn that 12 has a 1 and 2, where the 1 can be color-coded or made larger to emphasize the relevant feature that 1 is first in 12. The same can be done for 21. Once each number can be identified, then the numbers can be presented together for students to name. Students should be given multiple opportunities to practice discriminating among items such as similar letters (b, d, m, w, p, q) and numbers (6, 9, 21, 20, 102, 120); words with similar sounds (pet, pit, pig, big); symbols (+, −, ×, =); and concepts that are similar (e.g., types of plants). For older students, discrimination learning occurs, for instance, when they are required to identify pieces of lab equipment before instruction begins or mathematics tools such as a compass or protractor before a geometry lesson.

Factual knowledge is fundamental to school instruction. Numerous facts across the content areas must be learned so that students can apply information to their learning. Factual knowledge requires the ability to memorize, retain, and recall information. Examples of factual knowledge include math facts, vocabulary definitions, historical events and dates, parts of speech in English or a foreign language, parts of a plant, and parts of the brain and their function. Students with special learning needs may have difficulties learning factual information because of problems with encoding, retaining, and recalling the information. Students with special learning needs benefit from strategies that teach them how to memorize and recall information (Swanson, Clooney, & O'Shaughnessy, (1998). Rehearsing lots of information provides minimal benefit; information must be presented in a meaningful way to aid memory (Deshler, Ellis, & Lenz, 1996). Information is better retained and recalled if it is learned in ways that promote meaningful associations; such learning aids include clustering and organization, elaboration, and mnemonic devices (Deshler et al., 1996; Mastropieri & Scruggs, 2007).

Clustering is categorizing information in a meaningful way. For example, when teaching about states, cluster the states according to the category of geographic region (New England states, West Coast states). Students have a better chance of learning the information when you (or they) reduce the amount of information to learn all at once and organize the information in a meaningful way. Information can also be organized and presented in visual displays such as semantic maps and relationship displays (Bos & Anders, 1990). An example of a visual display is a map that organizes factual information about plants in terms of types, climate, geographic location, and benefits to humanity. Examples of semantic maps and relationship displays are provided in Chapters 10 and 13.

Elaboration means adding more details to facts to aid in memorization, retention, and recall. According to Scruggs and Mastropieri (2000), elaboration helps students remember information. Students can identify what they know about a topic to help them make elaborative sentences. Take the following list of animals: giraffe, elephant, lion, and leopard. Students might create the elaborative sentence "The giraffe and elephant fear the lion and leopard" to help them remember the list of animals.

Mnemonic devices are techniques for aiding memory by forming meaningful associations and linkages across information that appears to be unrelated (Scruggs & Mastropieri, 2000). Mnemonic devices help students learn content-area vocabulary, memorize lists of factual information, and read multisyllabic words (e.g., unconvincing) (Bryant & Bryant, 2003; Ellis, 1992; King-Sears, Mercer, & Sindelar, 1992).

● Mnemonic devices are techniques for aiding memory by forming meaningful associations and linkages across information that appears to be unrelated. How could mnemonic devices help these students memorize the planets in the solar system?

The Keyword Method is one type of mnemonic device. The Keyword Method involves linking information, such as a word, with response information, such as the word's definition. The linkage is made by reconstructing the information pictorially or verbally (Deshler et al., 1996; Pressley, Scruggs, & Mastropieri, 1989). In Chapter 13, we discuss the Keyword Method as a technique to assist students in learning vocabulary meanings.

Acronyms and acrostics are mnemonic devices that aid in recalling lists of information. An acronym is a word that is made from the first letters of the words that convey the information to be learned. For example, the acronym HOMES refers to the Great Lakes (Heron, Ontario, Michigan, Erie, and Superior). Students must learn and remember not only the acronym, HOMES, but also what each letter represents. An acrostic is a sentence wherein the first letters of the words stand for the items to be remembered *and* their order. For example, the first letters in "Every good boy deserves fudge" stand for the notes represented by the lines on a staff for playing music: E, G, B, D, F. Deshler, Ellis, and Lenz (1996) recommend the following steps for the FIRST-letter mnemonic strategy to form a mnemonic for studying lists of information:

STEP 1: Form a word.

STEP 2: Insert a letter(s).

STEP 3: Rearrange the letters.

STEP 4: Shape a sentence.

STEP 5: Try combinations.

As an example of a letter mnemonic, you will read about the HINTS strategy in Chapter 10.

Rules are procedures that must be followed. For example, teachers have rules for student behavior; spelling has rules for various patterns (e.g., for adding suffixes and when a word ends in e [drop the e when adding an ending that begins with a vowel]); and governments impose rules for driving and paying taxes. Rules must be learned through repetition and access to examples of when the rules apply and when they do not. For example, students may find that different teachers have different rules that they must learn. And there may be different rules for different locations in the school, such as the playground, school bus zone, cafeteria, and library.

Procedural knowledge means learning a set of steps that must be followed to complete a task. Examples of procedural knowledge include the steps to solve an arithmetic problem, conduct a lab experiment, develop a historical time line, and use a strategy to read difficult words or to comprehend text. Students with special learning needs may have difficulty with procedural knowledge because it requires memorization of the steps in the correct sequence and the ability to perform the tasks associated with each step. It may also be necessary to teach prerequisite knowledge associated with learning procedures. For example, if students are following a series of steps to multiply a number—say, 32×64—they must know the steps and the prerequisite knowledge of 4×2, 4×3, 6×2, and 6×3. Modeling, practice, and error correction are examples of ways to teach procedural knowledge. Cue cards containing the steps of the procedure can also be useful for students to refer to until they learn the steps.

Conceptual knowledge is the many ideas in content instruction. Concepts are categories of knowledge. Concepts range in level of abstractness from those that are easy to understand and depict concretely or pictorially to those whose meaning is more implicit. For instance, the concept of a table is easy for most students to understand and can be easily represented. The concept of democracy, however, is very abstract and requires multiple examples.

Visual displays can help students understand concepts. For instance, the concept *table* can be described using categories of dimensions, function, and types of construction. Students can create collections of words and pictures that represent a concept. For instance, pictures of different types of tables can be assembled, and descriptive words can be identified to describe the concept (e.g., *claw-legged table*). Price and Nelson (2003) recommend that teachers conduct a concept analysis of content to be taught prior to instruction. The concept analysis should include

- Identification of the critical concepts to be taught as part of a unit or chapter
- Definitions of the concepts
- List of attributes or characteristics of the concepts
- List of noncritical attributes that are not essential for understanding the concept
- List of examples
- List of "nonexamples"
- List of related concepts

Critical thinking involves reasoning to learn new concepts, ideas, or problem solutions (Mastropieri & Scruggs, 2007). Examples of the use of critical thinking include reasoning about how to resolve a social issue, explaining the ending of a novel, determining how to solve a problem, and explaining historical events and their impact on society. Students with learning needs may experience difficulties with critical thinking because they have not been taught how to think critically, they lack the prior knowledge and background that would help them understand issues, and their former instruction may have focused more on factual and procedural knowledge. Therefore, students with special learning needs must be taught to think critically.

Using various types of questions can help students think critically about what they are learning. Students can demonstrate their knowledge about a topic by answering convergent questions. Convergent, lower-order questions usually have one answer and start with *who, what,* or *when.* Answers to these questions are essential to show student understanding about a topic. Divergent, higher-order questions tap critical thinking skills because they require students to make inferences, to analyze or synthesize information, and to evaluate content. These questions may start with *What could happen . . . ? What if . . . ? What do you think caused . . . ? Why do you think . . . ? How were the characters alike and different?* and *How could events be changed to affect the outcome?* Critical thinking must be developed through divergent questioning strategies and coaching. Table 6.1 provides examples of instructional techniques for different types of knowledge and critical thinking.

STAGES OF LEARNING   All learners pass through stages of learning as they learn new skills. As an example, think about a young student learning how to ride a bike. She gets on the bike and starts to pedal, perhaps at first with a parent holding on to the seat to provide support and stability. Shakily, she peddles. As she builds confidence and learns balance, she is able to peddle on her own. She becomes a proficient bike rider, navigating tight areas and making turns with ease. As you read about the stages of learning, think about how this youngster learned how to ride her bike.

Knowing about your students' stage of learning can help you plan instruction and make adaptations to accommodate all of your students' learning needs. Researchers have shown that knowledge of students' stages of learning is important for selecting appropriate instructional interventions. For example, in a classic study, Ayllon and Azrin (1964) and Hopkins (1968) learned that rewards are not *always* effective—there had to be some level of correct responding before reinforcement could be instituted. In another classic study about the stages of learning, Smith and Lovitt (1976) found that students had first to learn how to solve computational arithmetic problems before reinforcement was effective.

In the acquisition stage of learning, the learner may not know how to perform the skill, and the aim is for the individual to learn how to perform it accurately. After a period of instruction, some learners demonstrate that they can perform the task or skill with 90 to 100 percent accuracy; at this point, they have passed through the acquisition stage of learning. Other students, such as students with special learning needs, may require further instruction and adaptations to attain sufficiently high levels of accuracy to demonstrate mastery.

In the proficiency stage of learning, the aim is for the learner to perform the skills, depending on the goal of instruction, fluently (that is, responding is both accurate and quick). The interventions for this stage focus on helping the learner to increase performance fluency. Some examples of skills that should be learned proficiently include answering basic arithmetic facts, saying the letters of the alphabet, writing, and identifying instruments used in a science lab.

There are some very important reasons why proficient levels of performance are necessary goals. For example, if a student can correctly form the letters of the alphabet but does so too slowly, he or she will not be able to complete, in a timely manner, tasks that require writing as a basic skill. Writing a report and taking a spelling test are examples of skills that require proficiency with forming letters.

TABLE 6.1 Instructional Techniques for Knowledge and Concepts

Types of Knowledge and Critical Thinking	Instructional Techniques
Discrimination	Model how to identify the relevant features. For example, point out the lower part of the "b" and say that by adding a similar part to the top you make a "B." Small "b" is in big "B." Present a "d." Point out the lower part of the "d" and say that by adding a similar part to the top you do not make a big "B." So, "d" is not b. Provide practice and error correction on discrimination activities. Prompt students if they require additional help making discriminations. For example, "Can you put a similar part on the top of 'b'?" What letter did you make? What letter is this 'b'?" Initially, teach letters, numbers, and sounds that are dissimilar; then introduce items that are similar and focus on the relevant distinguishing features. For example, a 3 only has one side compared to an 8. Put a line under 6 and 9 to help students distinguish where the circle part of the number appears.
Factual knowledge	Present information in categories rather than in long lists. Have students use visual displays to organize the factual knowledge. Reduce the amount of information to be learned. For instance, focus on multiplication facts ×7, then ×8, and finally ×9 before mixing the facts. Teach strategies to aid in remembering, such as counting strategies for math facts. Starting Big and Counting On and Counting Back are good strategies for specific facts (see Chapter 12). Provide concrete and pictorial examples of content-area factual knowledge. Show videos that depict the factual knowledge. Take field trips that focus on the information to be learned. Provide multiple opportunities for students to engage with content actively and in ways that aid memory associations (such as categorization, visual displays, and mnemonics; see Chapter 13).
Rules	Teach content knowledge and behavior rules. Have students repeat the rules. Provide examples of how the rules "look" in use and what happens when the rules are broken. Provide practice opportunities to help students recall the rules, especially at the beginning of the school year or after a break such as winter or spring break.
Procedural knowledge	Model using "think aloud" to demonstrate how to use a series of steps to solve a problem. Provide repetition and opportunities to practice each step. Chunk instruction so that students learn just a few steps at a time. Coach students through the use of the steps. Allow students to watch a peer use the steps.
Conceptual knowledge	Name and define the concept. Teach the critical and noncritical attributes of the concept. Have students find examples that illustrate the concept. Provide multiple examples of concepts. Provide nonexamples for students to discriminate from examples. Use concrete and pictorial examples. Have students explain in their own words the meaning of the concept. Have students keep a concepts dictionary.
Critical thinking	Ask divergent questions regularly to provide practice for thinking critically. Model how to answer divergent questions using factual and conceptual knowledge. Provide problem situations for student groups to work together to solve.

Source: Adapted from *The Inclusive Classroom: Strategies for Effective Instruction,* 3rd ed., by M. A. Mastropieri and T. E. Scruggs, 2007, Upper Saddle River, NJ: Pearson Education.

Computing basic facts accurately and quickly is another example; here, proficiency is important for more difficult skills such as multiplying multidigit problems. Students need to be able to perform many tasks fluently so that they can perform as well as their peers not only in accuracy but also in completing work in the designated time period. Hasselbring, Goin, and Bransford (1987) noted that the development of automaticity (practicing skills until they require less cognitive processing) is important to success with higher-level skills. Students should be able to perform lower-level cognitive skills automatically so that more emphasis can be placed on those higher-level skills (such as problem solving, comprehending text, and writing reports) that extend knowledge and learning.

In the maintenance stage of learning, the goal is for the mastered skills to remain at the same performance level as during the proficiency stage. Retention of learning is important. For some students with special learning needs, this is a challenging stage of learning because they may forget factual knowledge, rules, or procedures to solve different types of problems. When students do not retain desired levels of performance, teachers must plan for maintenance by periodically reviewing and evaluating what has been taught.

The generalization stage of learning means that the mastered skills should occur across all appropriate situations. For many students, skills learned in the classroom do not automatically occur in other settings, with other people, or with various materials without explicit instruction. An example of a lack of generalization is when a student learns a strategy in English class that helps with the writing process but does not apply the strategy in history class when asked to write a report. Another student may have demonstrated the ability to regroup when subtracting 2-digits minus 1-digit but may not be able to regroup when subtracting 2-digits minus 2-digits. For these students, generalization must be taught (Stokes & Baer, 1977). In fact, some researchers (Deshler et al., 1996) recommend that the concept of generalization be introduced to students during the acquisition stage of learning and specifically programmed following demonstration of skill mastery (when students have passed a quiz, for example). A good way to promote generalization during the acquisition stage of learning is to ask students where they can use a strategy that is going to be taught. For instance, if the students are going to be taught a writing strategy in English, they can identify other classes and situations where the strategy can be used.

Finally, the application stage of learning requires the student to use learning and extend it to new situations. For example, students learn strategies for solving word problems. Then they apply these strategies to real-life situations where they have to use their strategies to solve problems encountered in everyday living (such as determining how much money to take when going to a movie). Students need to be flexible as they apply their learning to new situations. Table 6.2 provides examples of teaching techniques for the stages of learning. What Works 6.1 on page 221 offers an illustration of how students progress through the stages of learning and how teaching techniques vary accordingly.

INSTRUCTIONAL COMPONENTS Research findings have identified specific instructional components that produce positive learning outcomes for students with special learning needs (Engelmann & Carnine, 1991; Gersten, Woodward, & Darch, 1986; Mastropieri & Scruggs, 2002; Swanson, 2001; Swanson, Hoskyn, & Lee, 1999). These components are based on direct instruction and strategy instruction. Direct instruction is teacher directed and focuses on the teaching of skills using explicit, systematic procedures such as modeling, practice opportunities, pacing, error correction, and progress monitoring. Strategy instruction focuses on the process of learning by using *cognitive strategies* (steps for facilitating the learning process) and *metacognitive* (e.g., self-regulatory) cues (Deshler et al., 1996; Swanson, 2001; Wong, 1993). For example, cognitive strategies for comprehending reading material from a textbook include activating background

TABLE 6.2 Examples of Teaching Techniques for the Stages of Learning

Stage of Learning	Instructional Techniques
Acquisition	1. Teach each subskill of a task analysis. 2. Pace the rate of instruction slower than the other stages. 3. Keep materials and types of responses consistent. 4. Use prompts and cues such as color, size, and verbal cues to focus student attention. 5. Use "think aloud" to show the steps. Have students imitate the process. 6. Teach the prerequisite skills for the tasks. 7. Tell what the response should look like. 8. Ask a question or show a fact, and provide wait time for a response. Shorten the wait time. 9. Provide multiple practice opportunities. 10. Focus on error correction; have students practice just the problems that need extra work.
Proficiency	1. Increase the pace of instruction. 2. Provide timed activities as appropriate (writing letters or numbers, naming information, computing facts). 3. Use reinforcement (praise, tokens) to reward increases in fluent responding. 4. Provide goals or benchmarks for students to achieve. 5. Graph weekly fluency scores.
Maintenance	1. Provide weekly, biweekly, and monthly reviews. 2. Provide reinforcement for accuracy. 3. Provide mini-lessons on parts of instruction not retained. 4. Assess cumulative knowledge regularly.
Generalization	1. Provide specific activities across environments, requiring students to generalize their learning. 2. Use role playing and think aloud to teach generalization. 3. Have students work with different people (peers, a paraprofessional) to practice skills. 4. Change the response mode from oral to written. 5. Change the materials, such as showing math facts vertically and horizontally.
Application	1. Provide situations for role playing. 2. Give real-life problems that require the use of skills already taught.

Source: Adapted from *Teaching Students with Learning and Behavior Problems,* 3rd ed., by D. P. Rivera and D. D. Smith, 1997, Boston: Allyn and Bacon.

knowledge, predicting, and paraphrasing; metacognitive strategies include asking oneself, "Can I make connections between my background knowledge and what I am reading?" "Were my predictions accurate?" and "Does my paraphrase contain the most important information and is it in my own words?"

In a major study on the effectiveness of interventions to teach students with learning disabilities (LD), Swanson, Hoskyn, and Lee (1999) found that interventions that used instructional components from direct and strategic instruction

what
WORKS 6.1

Stages of Learning

Marcus is a fifth-grade student in Mrs. Bell's class who is identified as having a learning disability in mathematics. The individualized education program (IEP) specified annual goals in mathematics, including solving word problems. Mrs. Bell gives a curriculum based assessment to determine which types of word problems Marcus can solve and which types require instruction. Assessment data show zero percent accuracy for solving two-step word problems using whole-number computation. Marcus is in the acquisition stage of learning for this skill. He can solve one-step word problems but does not generalize this knowledge to two-step problems.

Mrs. Bell uses explicit instruction to teach Marcus a strategy for solving two-step word problems. She discusses with Marcus the importance of solving two-step problems, pointing out that problem solving is used in many daily activities (promoting the occurrence of generalization). Marcus continues to build fluency with basic facts because facts are part of the word problem calculations (proficiency stage for facts). It takes Marcus four days to reach mastery (90 percent accuracy) for learning how to solve two-step word problems using the strategy taught by the teacher. Mrs. Bell has Marcus work in a cooperative learning group with his peers to solve one-step (maintenance stage) and two-step word problems (generalization stage). The group works together for a week, at which point the teacher determines through curriculum based assessment that the students can solve two-step problems proficiently. Mrs. Bell then has student groups write their own problems based on situations in the school, at home, or in the community (application stage). The groups share their problems so that different groups solve all the problems. She plans to provide periodic reviews (maintenance stage) of one- and two-step word problems to ensure continued mastery of the skills required for solving them.

Source: Adapted from *Teaching Students with Learning and Behavior Problems,* 3rd ed., by D. P. Rivera and D. D. Smith, 1997, Boston: Allyn and Bacon.

were the most effective in helping students with LD be successful learners. They labeled this the combined model and suggested using the following instructional components when planning instruction.

- Sequencing: breaking down the task, providing step-by-step prompts
- Drill–repetition–practice: daily testing of skills, repeated practice
- Segmentation: breaking down skills into parts and then synthesizing the parts into a whole
- Directed questioning and responses: asking process or content questions of students
- Control of task difficulty: sequencing tasks from easy to difficult, teaching prerequisite skills
- Technology: delivering instruction via computer or presentation software
- Teacher-modeled problem solving: demonstrating processes or steps to solve a problem or explaining how to do a task
- Small-group instruction: delivering instruction to a small group
- Strategy cues: reminding students to use strategies, modeling the "think aloud" technique

Delivering Instruction

Here we will review several instructional steps and techniques designed to help all students access and master the curriculum. They include use of an advance organizer, presentation of information, practice, closure, and progress monitoring.

ADVANCE ORGANIZER   An advance organizer consists of activities to prepare students for the lesson's content (Lenz, Alley, & Schumaker, 1987). Advance organizers tell students the purpose of the lesson (objectives), motivate students by sparking their interest, and activate background knowledge by reviewing related information. Such a review helps students "warm up" for the lesson, promotes active responding, and provides teachers with information about students' current levels of understanding before new material is introduced. In planning advance organizers, teachers should consider their students' background knowledge, experience, and ability with prerequisite skills for the new task, the vocabulary to be learned, and the level of abstraction of the new learning (Price & Nelson, 2003). Examples of advance organizers include

- Writing the objective on the board and explaining how the objective will be taught.
- Explaining the importance of learning the objective and asking students to provide examples of how they can use the new information.
- Providing an active technique such as role playing, seeing a clip of a video, or taking a field trip before instruction. In history classes, the teacher can dress up in period clothing as an advance organizer for the historical content.
- Having students map or tell what they know about the content to be studied.
- Providing a review of related information for students to make connections.

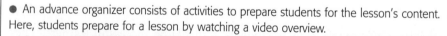

● An advance organizer consists of activities to prepare students for the lesson's content. Here, students prepare for a lesson by watching a video overview.

PRESENTATION OF INFORMATION   In this step, teachers present instructional content related to the instructional objective, such as rules (e.g., spelling, phonics, mathematics), strategies (e.g., reading strategy, paragraph-writing strategy), and concepts (e.g., place value, science vocabulary, health).

When presenting facts, rules, and procedures, teachers should *model,* or demonstrate, the correct responses and model the appropriate thinking processes by using "think aloud." Students can imitate the modeled responses orally, in written form, or motorically (e.g., manipulating objects). If students are in the acquisition stage of learning, modeling is particularly important to help them learn the correct response or set of responses.

Teachers can ask questions to promote discussion and to involve students in the lesson. Teachers should ask different types of questions (what, why, how) and provide sufficient wait time (3 or 4 seconds) between asking a question and calling on a student to answer the question. Asking a question and then calling on a student by name maintains a moderate level of concern, which is student interest in the instruction, and promotes on-task behavior. Calling on a student by name and then asking a question allows other students to "tune out," so the level of concern and on-task time may be diminished.

Examples should be provided to illustrate new information, and nonexamples can help too. For instance, an example of democracy is the right to vote; a nonexample of democracy is being told who will control the government.

Finally, teachers should keep the instruction moving along to keep students engaged in learning and to promote on-task behavior. Ideal pacing is demonstrated when the amount of content does not overwhelm and frustrate students (Algozzine, Ysseldyke, & Elliott, 1997). Keeping up with other students is often a problem for students with special learning needs. For students who are not able to keep up with the pace of instruction, teachers can provide extra practice on chunks or smaller segments of information. For example, math facts can be chunked into segments ($\times 6$ facts, $\times 7$ facts), vocabulary word lists can be segmented, and the number of questions to answer can be reduced.

PRACTICE   Practice can be thought of in several ways. First, there is guided practice, which involves engaging students in practicing what they have learned, usually under the teacher's direction. During guided practice, a variety of techniques can be used to involve students, to help them practice what they have learned, and to check their understanding.

Students with special learning needs benefit from multiple opportunities to practice, or massed practice (i.e., extra practice); active-participation activities can provide these opportunities. Active participation also promotes engaged time and on-task behavior. Engaged time is the amount of time that students are involved in their learning. *On-task behavior* means work on the task that is assigned. Students are making some type of response (oral, written, constructing) or exhibiting behavior (demonstrating eye contact, paying attention) that suggests they are paying attention, listening, and engaged. Figure 6.2 provides examples of active-participation activities for guided practice.

Checking for understanding (CFU) means periodically determining whether students are learning the content. For instance, CFU can be conducted after subject matter is presented or during guided practice. It is necessary to ensure that all students respond. Teachers can use the following techniques to check for student understanding (Price & Nelson, 2003).

- Present information that was taught (factual, rule, procedure) and ask students to show, by signaling thumbs up or thumbs down, whether the information is correct or wrong.

- Use response cards for students to indicate their response to the teacher's statement or question.
- Have the students show their responses using materials such as manipulatives in math.
- Have students write their responses to be turned in for checking.
- Have students write their responses on white boards.

Error correction procedures should be implemented to correct mistakes and to provide feedback. *Error correction procedures* involve stopping the student if an error is made, modeling the correct response for the student, and having the student repeat the correct response. Errors should be corrected to ensure that students do not practice mistakes or learn information incorrectly.

FIGURE 6.2 Examples of Active-Participation Activities

1. Use Jigsaw (Slavin, 1991) as a technique to engage all students in learning and sharing information (see the section on cooperative learning on page 230).
2. Use Think-Pair-Share-Write (students work with a partner to share their response to a question; students turn in their own written responses).
3. Use "Numbered Heads Together" (Kagan, 1990) (students in groups discuss the response to an answer; each student has a number; the teacher calls on one number to provide the answer). This works really well to review the meanings of concepts and terms.
4. Have students brainstorm responses to questions; call on students randomly to provide answers.
5. Require students to take notes.
6. Use peer pairs for practice (see the discussion of small groups in the section on grouping structures).
7. Have students find pictorial representations for content being learned (students can make time lines with significant events pictured or drawn along the timeline).
8. Use response cards. Card 1 can be used when questions require a yes/no or true/false response. Words can be color-coded so that teachers can quickly scan the students to be sure the correct color (word) is displayed. Cards 2 and 3 are pinch cards. The teacher can present a definition and the student "pinches" the answer (puts thumb and forefinger; next to the answer). Students should be told, "Hold your response card at chest level. I will give you a question (or definition). I will say 'think,' and then you show me. Hold up your card with the correct answer or pinch the correct answer."

Card 1 Yes/No or True/False Card	Card 2 Pinch Card	Card 3 Pinch Card
Yes True No False	• Rectangle • Pyramid • Cylinder • Isosceles trapezoid • Parallelogram • Triangle	• Length • Area • Volume • Perimeter

Questioning continues to be an important instructional technique to monitor student comprehension of the instructional objectives. Teachers can use the Response-Dependent Questioning Strategy shown in Table 6.3 to help students arrive at the correct answer to a question.

Independent practice, a type of practice that occurs in the classroom or as homework, implies that students have demonstrated a good understanding of the skill (as determined during progress monitoring) and are ready for activities that do not require direct teacher supervision or guidance. For example, students can practice in small groups or independently at their desks. Students can also be assigned homework (see guidelines later in this chapter) as another opportunity for practice. It is important that the activities undertaken during independent

TABLE 6.3   Response-Dependent Questioning Strategy

STEP 1: OPENING QUESTION

Teacher asks question about subject being presented.

Example: Asks student to make the sound of the digraph, EE.

Response: Student makes correct sound; if incorrect, then proceed to Step 2.

STEP 2: CONSTRUCTED RESPONSE

Teacher seeks correct response by prompting student to focus on specific knowledge or information from which a correct response can be constructed.

Example: Think about the rule we have learned for two vowels together.

Response: Student makes correct sound; if incorrect, then proceed to Step 3.

STEP 3: MULTIPLE CHOICE

Teacher provides choice of two responses; one of the responses is correct.

Example: Is the sound "ee" (makes long e sound) or "e" (makes short e sound)?

Response: Student selects correct sound; if incorrect, then proceed to Step 4.

STEP 4: RESTRICTED ALTERNATIVE

Teacher eliminates the incorrect response from Step 3 but does not provide the answer.

Example: EE (points to letters on chalkboard) does not make the "e" (makes short e sound) sound. What is the correct sound of EE?

Response: Student provides correct response; if incorrect, then proceed to Step 5.

STEP 5: COMPLETE MODEL

Teacher provides correct response.

Example: Teacher points to EE on chalkboard and makes "ee" sound.

Response: Student imitates correct response.

Source: Adapted from *Direct teaching tactics for exceptional children,* by J. J. Stowitschek, C. E. Stowitschek, J. M. Hendrickson, and R. M. Day, 1984, Rockville, MD: Aspen Publications.

practice be related directly to the instructional objective introduced during the presentation of information and that students be capable of high levels of success working independently. Distributive practice, which is practice opportunities presented over time on skills that have been taught, ensures that students continue to get some level of practice (in the maintenance stage of learning, for example) so

what WORKS 6.2

Instructional Steps

Ms. Mendez is teaching a new unit on global warming. She spent several days one week probing her students' knowledge about the concept to determine what they already know from media coverage. She determines her students' stage of learning by assessing overall student performance on key vocabulary and important ideas pertaining to causes and effects and solutions to problems. On the basis of her assessment information, Ms. Mendez decides to use explicit instruction to teach key vocabulary as the beginning of her unit on global warming.

● Advance Organizer

Ms. Mendez tells the students the purpose of instruction. She has them work with a partner to write down their ideas about the meaning of global warming. After several partner pairs share their ideas, which she puts on the chalkboard, she presents five key vocabulary words and explains that to learn more about global warming, they must understand the meanings of these words.

● Presentation of Information

Ms. Mendez reads the list of five words and their definitions, which are presented in two columns and projected for the entire class to see. She covers up one column (the definitions column). She reads one of the words and asks students to state the definition. She reveals the definitions column and covers up the other column (vocabulary words). She has a student read one of the definitions and asks another student to state the word. Next, she uses one word in a sentence and then asks students for examples of the other words in sentences.

● Practice

Ms. Mendez has the students stand. With the list of words and definitions concealed, she says a word and gently tosses a koosh ball to one student, who must define the word. Having defined the word, the student returns the koosh ball to Ms. Mendez, who repeats this process with the remaining words. She provides error correction for any student who is unable to define the word by showing the definition. She also uses this procedure for saying a definition and asking students to supply the word.

Next, she has students work with a partner to match the words and definitions. She gives each pair two envelopes, one with the words and another with the definitions, for them to match. After the timer sounds, each pair turns to a neighboring pair to share their matches.

Finally, Ms. Mendez gives the students a passage about global warming that contains the new words. She asks them to underline the words and to explain how the words are used in the sentences.

● Closure

At the end of the lesson, Ms. Mendez asks students to explain the purpose of the lesson and what they learned. She describes the activities in the unit on global warming that the students will complete over the next few weeks.

● Progress Monitoring

Ms. Mendez gives the students a matching exercise to determine their accuracy in selecting the definitions. She also has them use the new words in sentences.

that their learning of new skills remains intact. Distributive practice on taught skills can be done during independent practice and as part of homework.

CLOSURE   Closure occurs at the end of a lesson when teachers and students wrap up the lesson's activity as it is related to the instructional objective. During closure, which may take only a few minutes, teachers and students review the instructional objective, review the lesson's activity, relate learning to other contexts, and discuss follow-up plans. Closure activities can be brief, but it is an important part of the lesson and needs to be considered when time is allotted to instructional planning.

PROGRESS MONITORING   Progress monitoring is one of the most important instructional steps. Teachers must evaluate students' understanding of the lesson and their ability to perform the skill. Progress monitoring will be discussed in Chapter 7. Examples of ways to monitor progress are provided throughout the remaining chapters.

What Works 6.2 provides an example of how the instructional steps are implemented. In Table 6.4, questions are presented to help teachers reflect on their practices during the steps.

TABLE 6.4 Reflective Questions to Guide Instructional Decision Making

Advance Organizer

Do I have the students' attention?

Is the instructional objective stated specifically?

Do students appear to be interested in the lesson?

Is there sufficient review of background or related content?

Is there vocabulary that needs to be reviewed?

Are students making connections across skills?

Presentation of Information

Are students comprehending the lesson?

Is modeling effective?

Do I need to provide more examples?

Do students understand after error correction?

Guided Practice

Are all students engaged actively in learning?

Do I need to provide more examples?

Are more practice opportunities necessary?

Do I need to give more prompts?

Do students understand after error correction?

Is the grouping practice effective for instruction?

Are there vocabulary words that require further instruction?

Are the instructional materials and textbooks appropriate?

Are the practice opportunities appropriate?

Independent Practice (can also be home work)

Are students ready for independent practice?

Is the grouping practice effective in promoting practice on the instructional objective?

Are students capable of completing activities independently?

Are students achieving high levels of accuracy on independent practice activities?

Am I providing feedback for activities?

Closure

Do I allow enough time for closure?

Do all or most of the students have opportunities to engage in closure activities?

Do I still have students who do not understand the instructional objective?

Are students able to relate the lesson's objective to other learning?

Progress Monitoring

Have students demonstrated mastery of the skill presented in the lesson?

Do I need to reteach or model the skill?

Was my instructional intervention effective?

Is the skill appropriate for students?

Do I need to task-analyze the skill further to meet individual needs of students?

What Are Some Effective Instructional Grouping Practices?

There are a variety of instructional grouping structures, including whole-group instruction; flexible, small groups; and one-to-one teaching. Peer tutoring is another grouping practice to provide additional support to students who can benefit from more opportunities to practice their skills. Finally, teachers have used cooperative learning structures for years to enrich practice in student-centered instruction. Teachers should consider how to use these practices when planning and delivering instruction.

Grouping: Whole Group, Flexible Groups, One-to-One

WHOLE-GROUP INSTRUCTION   In whole-group instruction, the teacher presents a lesson to the entire class. This grouping practice works well where common instructional objectives are identified, the teacher delivers the lesson, and students respond orally or in writing. Whole-group instruction is often chosen to teach content-area subjects, such as science, social studies, and health, and it is common at the secondary level. Examples of activities for whole groups include direct, explicit instruction on new information (vocabulary, rules, concepts), read-alouds, and presentations.

Researchers have shown that whole-group instruction can be effective for students of varying abilities (Gersten, Carnine, & Woodward, 1987). The advantages of whole-group instruction include the ability of students to hear responses from peers, pacing of instruction to maintain academic engaged time, and opportunities for the teacher to work individually with students following delivery of instruction. The disadvantages of this grouping practice include limited error correction, which is problematic for students with special learning needs, a pacing or rate of instruction that may be too fast for some students, and lack of instructional relevance (i.e., instructional objectives not appropriate for certain students). Teachers must be sure that when whole-group instruction is selected as the grouping practice, the objectives are appropriate for most of the students. Time must be allocated for students who require further individualized instruction.

FLEXIBLE, SMALL GROUPS   These groups include same-ability groups and mixed-ability groups. Groupings consist of three to five students. The purpose of small-group instruction varies according to instructional level and the individual needs of students. Flexible grouping practices allow teachers to group students based on the purpose of instruction and the goals of the lesson. Teachers balance same-ability groups with mixed-ability groups in accordance with instructional needs (Elbaum et al., 1999).

All of the students in same-ability groups are performing comparably on a particular skill and require extra or accelerated instruction. For struggling students, extra practice on curricular objectives is often necessary. For students who are high achieving, gifted, or talented, same-ability groups can provide enrichment activities. Same-ability grouping can be used to provide instruction in academic areas, such as reading or mathematics, where students are reading at about the same level or are in need of instruction on the same math objective. Through assessment practices (described in Chapter 7), teachers identify students who are performing at about the same levels academically so that these students can be grouped in same-ability groups for extra instruction and support.

● Students performing at varying levels both academically and socially can learn from one another in mixed-ability groups.

Research supports the efficacy of this grouping practice (Carnine, Silbert, & Kameenui, 1990; Elbaum et al., 1999). Small-group instruction yields better academic outcomes for students with disabilities than whole-group instruction (Erlbaum et al., 1999; Schumm, Moody, & Vaughn, 2000; Vaughn et al., 2001). The major advantage of same-ability group instruction is the ability to provide students with more modeling, prompting, and error correction. Pacing can be tailored to the individual needs of students more easily than in whole-group instruction. The challenge of small-group instruction is to ensure that the rest of the class is engaged actively with meaningful tasks. Having alternative "back-up" tasks ready for those students who require teacher assistance when it is not available, and for those who finish their tasks before small-group instruction concludes, can help ensure that all students are actively involved in learning.

Mixed-ability groups consist of students performing at various levels on skills. This grouping practice can be used, for example, for students to work on projects and to make presentations. Through assessment practices (described in Chapter 7), teachers identify students who are performing at various levels academically and socially so that these students can be grouped in mixed-ability groups.

The advantage of mixed-ability groups is that students can learn from each other. Little evidence exists that mixed-ability groups adversely affect the learning of students who are gifted and talented. Slavin's (1991) review of the evidence confirmed that high-achieving students can benefit from instruction whatever the grouping practice.

ONE-TO-ONE TEACHING   In this grouping practice, teachers provide instruction to individual students on the basis of their specific learning and behavioral needs. For example, a student may need extra assistance (e.g., prompts, feedback, directions) to begin working on or mastering an instructional objective. A student's behavior may warrant individualized instruction away from other students in the classroom. Tutorial assistance might be necessary when preparing for an exam in a content-area class, or individualized assistance might be necessary to correct errors on a homework assignment.

One-to-one instruction has been shown to help students avoid frustration and cope with instructional demands (Bloom, 1984). The advantage of this grouping practice is that individual students receive assistance that promotes their learning. On the other hand, teachers must plan tasks so that other students are engaged as well. Furthermore, one-to-one instruction may not be readily available in general education classrooms because of the number of students and time constraints.

Peer Tutoring

Peer tutoring is an instructional grouping practice wherein pairs of students work on assigned skills, usually for extra practice. There are several models that focus on peer tutoring as a grouping practice to give students extra instructional time with a peer partner. Peer tutoring models include Classwide Peer Tutoring (Utley, Mortweet, & Greenwood, 1997) and Peer-Assisted Learning Strategies (PALS) (Fuchs, Fuchs, & Kazdan, 1999). Research on peer tutoring models has shown that peer tutoring can improve the academic achievement of tutees as well as increase the amount of time students spend on school tasks (King-Sears, 1997). Peer tutoring can be used effectively at the elementary and secondary levels in mathematics (Miller et al., 1996), spelling (Delquadri, Greenwood, Stretton, & Hall, 1983), and reading (Bryant et al., 2000; Fuchs, Fuchs, & Burish, 2000; Simmons et al., 1994). Peer tutoring increases active student involvement and students' opportunities to respond, review, and practice skills and concepts (Delquadri et al., 1986).

In peer tutoring, there is a tutor–tutee relationship, which consists of instruction and feedback to provide efficient instruction to students with disabilities and students who are at risk for academic difficulties (Harper, Maheady, Mallette, & Karnes, 1999). In reading, for example, a higher-performing peer can be paired with a student who is reading at a somewhat lower level and needs additional instructional support. The partners take turns serving as reading coach and reader. The reading coach reads the designated reading passage for a short time period; then the reader reads the same passage for the same time period. Next the partners change roles. The partners provide error correction as needed and praise for good reading. Often this passage reading is followed by comprehension questions. These same procedures can be applied in mathematics, vocabulary development, and spelling.

The advantages of this grouping practice include developing academic skills, promoting self-concept, fostering cooperative relationships, providing extra instructional support, and fostering academic support for students with learning and behavioral problems in general education settings (Mercer & Mercer, 2001). The challenges consist of allocating time to teach tutors their role responsibilities, monitoring tutor–tutee relationships, matching students appropriately, and assessing student progress.

Cooperative Learning

Cooperative learning is a term that refers to mixed-ability small groups that focus on academic and social skills (Rich, 1993). The purposes of cooperative learning are for the students to work collaboratively to achieve common academic and social goals and for them to be accountable to the team for their individual efforts (Johnson, Johnson, & Holubec, 1994).

Extensive research has been conducted in various academic areas (e.g., mathematics, reading, social studies) on cooperative learning with students who have disabilities, students who are typically achieving, and students who come from diverse backgrounds. In most cases, the research has shown that students tend to derive academic and social skills benefits from this instructional arrangement (Slavin, 1991).

Several models of cooperative learning are popular in classrooms. The techniques share similar characteristics: group academic and social goals, arrangement of heterogeneous student groups, task structure, cooperation, and individual and group accountability (Rivera, 1996). Table 6.5 provides information about cooperative learning models.

In preparing for cooperative learning, teachers should consider the following questions:

- What are the academic and social skills objectives?
- What task or activity structure can be used to teach the objectives?
- How can the elements of cooperative learning be promoted?
- How will student groups be formed?
- What environmental factors must be considered?
- What management techniques will be used?
- What is the teacher's role during group activities?
- How will individual and group progress with instructional objectives be monitored?
- What difficulties might students with special needs encounter in cooperative learning groups?

The following are recommendations for ensuring the success of students with special needs in cooperative learning activities (Poplum, 1997).

- Assign a buddy to students who have difficulty reading material in the group.
- Ensure that students can perform the role they have been assigned. Writing or notetaking may be difficult for some students, but using technology such as a laptop computer or tape recorder can circumvent this issue.
- Review behavior and social rules for working in groups.
- Use a reinforcement system (discussed in Chapter 9) to help students stay on task.
- Conduct individual progress monitoring of the skills practiced in cooperative learning groups to be sure students are learning the concepts.

Cooperative learning offers several advantages. First, cooperative learning activities provide opportunities for students to work together toward common goals, thus necessitating some degree of collaborative behavior. Second, group work requires verbal interactions, and this gives students opportunities to develop language skills. Third, cooperative learning focuses on students working collaboratively to solve problems and complete tasks; this means that students, rather than teachers, are responsible for solving problems. Fourth, research has shown that cooperative learning promotes social interactions and peer acceptance (Slavin, 1991).

TABLE 6.5   Selected Models of Cooperative Learning

Teams-Games-Tournaments

Steps

1. Teacher presents material to be studied.
2. Students work in teams to learn material.
3. Students compete in tournament games with peers of similar ability, answering questions about the material practiced in teams.
4. Points are awarded on the basis of performance in tournaments.
5. Team (i.e., original cooperative learning team) scores are obtained from points that members accrue in tournament games.
6. Team standings are announced weekly.

Goals

1. Students learn academic material.
2. Students help team members learn material.

Student Groups

1. Heterogeneous, diverse
2. Four to five students per team

Task Structure

1. Group-paced instruction
2. Teams work together to study material

3. Everyone must learn concepts.

Cooperation

1. Help each other to learn material so members will do well in tournaments.

Accountability/Evaluation

1. Everyone is responsible for his or her own learning.
2. Everyone is responsible for ensuring that other team members learn concepts.
3. Each member's tournament points will be used to compute a group score.

Learning Together

Steps

1. Teacher explains academic task, cooperative goal structure, and criteria for success to group teams.
2. Students are responsible for learning material and making sure group members learn material as well.
3. Students provide encouragement and assistance to team members.
4. Teacher monitors group work and intervenes to provide task assistance or teach collaborative skills.
5. Student work and group functioning are evaluated.

Goals

1. Academic task goal
2. Cooperative/collaborative/social goal

Student Groups

1. Heterogeneous, diverse groups
2. Two to six students per team

Task Structure

1. Group-paced instruction
2. Teams work together to study topic/concept/material/problem— "We all sink or swim together."
3. Everyone must learn concepts and participate.
4. Student roles may be assigned.
5. Only limited materials are provided, thus necessitating interdependence.

Cooperative learning activities require extensive planning and preparation. Teachers must ensure that all students—regardless of their group assignment—participate fully. The bulk of the work should not fall on the shoulders of only a few students. O'Connor and Jenkins (1994) found that in cooperative learning groups where the ethic of "working together" had not been established, students with lower skills were excluded from group participation. Finally, teachers must be sure that students are capable of performing instructional objectives successfully with group members and individually. The Working Together feature provides an illustration of how professionals can collaborate to determine how to differentiate content, instructional approach, grouping, and materials for students who are having difficulties—in this case, during a mathematics lesson.

TABLE 6.5 **Continued**

6. Students are arranged to promote face-to-face interaction.
7. Teams construct one group product.

Cooperation

1. Help each other learn material.
2. Demonstrate collaborative/ social group skills (e.g., providing feedback, elaborating, sharing, staying on task, doing one's share of the work).

Accountability/Evaluation

1. Everyone is responsible for his or her own learning.
2. Everyone is responsible for ensuring that other team members learn concepts.
3. Members may be asked to explain group answers, take a test, or edit another person's work.
4. Student work is evaluated.

Group Processing

1. Group members evaluate their ability to work as a team according to set criteria at the conclusion of their work.
2. Group members determine group skills that should be worked on to promote better collaboration.

Jigsaw

Steps

1. Teaching material is divided into parts and assigned to group members.
2. Students learn how to communicate with and tutor other students.
3. Subgroups with the same material to learn, meet, and then share their material with the original team members.
4. All members of the team must learn all parts of the material.

5. Teachers monitor groups, providing assistance, encouragement, and direction.

Goals

1. Learn a part of the material and then teach this to other team members.

Student Groups

1. Heterogeneous, diverse groups.
2. Four to seven students per team.

Task Structure

1. Cooperative/interdependent.
2. Students learn a section of material pertaining to a topic and then teach that material to group members.

Cooperation

1. All students must work together to learn all of the material on a topic.

Accountability/Evaluation

1. All students are accountable for learning all of the material.

Source: Adapted from *Teaching Students with Learning and Behavior Problems,* 3rd ed., by D. P. Bryant and D. D. Smith, 1997, Boston: Allyn and Bacon.

How Can Instructional Materials Be Adapted?

Textbooks and instructional materials are important components of instruction and must be selected wisely. Textbooks may be assigned to teachers, but those teachers must still analyze them critically to see what difficulties students might encounter when reading the material. Instructional materials are used when concepts are first presented, during guided practice, and as part of independent practice activities. For example, students can use math manipulatives as part of place-value instruction, complete reading comprehension sheets during independent

WORKING together

Collaborating to Differentiate Instruction

Mrs. Bell is teaching her fifth-grade students different ways to represent fractions. She wants her students to compare and order fractions according to fractional parts. She provides a review on different fractions and key vocabulary. She provides a procedure to help students order and compare fractions. Then she has the students work in small, mixed-ability groups to compare and order fractions before they apply this factual knowledge to problem solving. As she circulates among the small groups, she listens to group discussions as they work with the fractions. She notices that several of her students who struggle with mathematics seem confused. She sits with the students and asks questions to check their understanding of the assignment, the vocabulary, and the procedure for comparing and ordering fractions. She decides to model the procedure once more and watches students complete the next example; she also provides error correction as needed. She instructs the students to complete the next few problems as she circulates among the other groups. Mrs. Bell notes in her assessment notebook the difficulties exhibited by students in their groups. She decides to work with the special education teacher and math specialist to implement the ADAPT framework. Together, they will identify ways to differentiate instruction that will benefit her struggling students.

The following information from this process can help Mrs. Bell work more effectively with her students who are having difficulties in math instruction.

- The instructional content may need to be reduced to fewer fractional parts to compare and order.
- The instructional practices should be examined to determine whether struggling students can complete examples after modeling. Additional modeling and "thinking aloud" may be necessary. More checking for understanding may be helpful to determine whether students are benefiting from instruction.
- The grouping practices should be examined to determine how students who exhibit difficulties perform in a whole-group setting and in small, mixed-ability groups. Grouping students with similar performance levels into small, same-ability groups for extra instruction may be needed.
- Additional review of key vocabulary may be necessary.
- Recommendations are needed from the math specialist for instructional materials to represent fractional parts. Students who struggle with mathematics benefit from working with manipulatives that illustrate the concepts.
- The "reflective questions" for the instructional steps (see Table 6.4) should be reviewed to determine whether the design and implementation of the lesson are benefiting students who are having difficulties.
- The progress-monitoring notes in Mrs. Bell's assessment notebook can be analyzed for clues about difficulties observed. Additional ideas for monitoring student progress can be discussed.

seatwork, or use a scale as part of a cooperative learning activity on measurement. These materials must also be chosen carefully to augment instruction.

Textbooks

Basals are textbooks usually adopted by school districts to serve as a primary source for subject-area content. Basals are a good source of instructional content. However, there are issues associated with their use that teachers must consider for their struggling students.

- The reading level of the textbook probably exceeds the reading level of the student with reading difficulties. For students to benefit from reading a textbook, the material should be at the student's instructional reading level (the level at which the reader has 90 to 94 percent word recognition and 90 to 100 percent comprehension).

- The organization or structure of the text content may be hard for students with reading difficulties to follow. The text may lack, or the student may not be familiar with, key words that signal different types of text organization (cause/effect, compare/contrast). Recognizing how text content is organized helps readers comprehend the material.
- Basals usually do not include enough direct, explicit instruction to help struggling students learn content. For example, there may not be sufficient practice opportunities or examples.

In Chapter 10, we provide additional information about textbooks for students with reading difficulties. In Chapter 13, we offer suggestions for selecting and using content-area textbooks with struggling readers, especially at the secondary level.

Instructional Materials

Guidelines for selecting and using instructional materials should address (1) the student and (2) the content and methodology.

Student

- What are the student's present levels of educational performance?
- Can the instructional material be used to meet individualized education program (IEP) goals?
- Does the student seem to be motivated to accomplish tasks and under what conditions?
- Does the student remain focused and persist with tasks? When does the student appear to lose focus and persistence?

Present levels of educational performance can be determined by examining assessment data gathered during the referral, identification, and placement process and from teacher-administered informal assessments. For example, teachers can consult the IEP to identify a student's reading level as they make decisions about the need to adapt instructional materials that require the ability to read. The teacher can also identify a student's reading level by conducting an informal reading inventory, which is discussed in Chapter 7. Finally, it's important to determine a student's interest in content and materials and to identify where in the learning process the student stops trying. Motivation is a key ingredient of successful learning, and their students' level of persistence helps teachers understand their learners' needs more fully.

Instructional Content and Methodology

- Is the content age-appropriate?
- Does the content address state standards and core curriculum?
- Does the instructional material specify a sequence of skills?
- Is information about teaching strategies included?
- Are there sufficient opportunities for practicing new skills?
- Are generalization and maintenance activities included?

Age-appropriateness of instructional materials is a primary concern in the selection process. For example, high-interest/controlled vocabulary materials can be used with older students who have limited reading vocabularies. These materials focus on topics that appeal to older students, such as current events, sports, and entertainment personalities, yet are written with a vocabulary at specific grade levels (such as second grade or third grade) to take into account limited word recognition and reading abilities (Babkie, Goldstein, & Rivera, 1992). Equally important is how the materials are related to the curricular expectations from the school district and state. Teachers are held highly accountable through state assessments to teach the content on which students will be assessed, so materials selected for instruction must reflect this content, which has been specified as appropriate for all students.

Teachers can adopt a sequence for teaching skills and then be sure that the instructional materials match this sequence. For example, if instruction focuses on addition math facts (6 + 9, 7 + 3), then the instructional material should include problems that match this skill. Subtraction math facts should not be included. The next skill in the sequence may include subtraction math facts and materials that focus on these types of problems.

Instructional materials might include review activities (for maintenance), teaching strategies, practice opportunities, and enrichment activities (for generalization purposes). Teachers must examine the materials to determine how the instructional material can best be used in a lesson and what (if any) adaptations are needed.

Very often, teachers need to modify instructional materials to meet an individual learner's needs. Some instructional materials offer suggestions for adaptations, such as extension exercises or alternative methodologies. Other adaptations might include adding more practice options, using only portions of the material, rewording complex directions, and breaking instructional components down into smaller instructional activities. Making instructional adaptations may be necessary to ensure that students with special needs can benefit from instructional materials. Table 6.6 provides examples of ways to adapt instructional materials.

What Are Some Effective Homework Practices?

Cooper (1989) defined homework as "tasks assigned to students by school teachers that are meant to be carried out during nonschool hours" (p. 7). Cooper (1989) identified several positive effects of homework: improved achievement and learning, improved attitude and study skills, more self-discipline, and greater parent involvement. Fatigue, loss of leisure time, parent problems, and cheating were viewed as potential negative effects.

Homework Practices

A variety of national research studies on homework practices in general education classes and on the effects of these practices have yielded interesting findings. For example, in a national survey of homework policies, Roderique, Polloway, Cumblad, Epstein, and Bursuck (1994) found that, on average, elementary students receive homework three nights a week requiring about 40 minutes, middle school students work four nights for about an hour, and high school students have homework requiring about an hour and 40 minutes four nights a week. In recent years, with the emphasis on academic accountability,

TABLE 6.6 **Examples of Adaptations for Instructional Materials**

Task/Instructional Materials	Student Struggles or Challenges	Material Adaptation
Reading directions or instructions/ workbooks, worksheets	Reading or understanding written directions or instructions	Have students underline important words (circle, underline, draw). Rewrite directions or instructions using easier words. Explain the directions or instructions to the student. Say, "Tell me what you need to do first? Next?" Reduce the number of directions or instructions.
Reading books and word lists/textbooks, literature, word lists	Reading words	Put the text on tape for the student to listen to the reading (electronic books). Use high-interest/low-vocabulary materials.
Comprehending text	Comprehending material	Provide graphic organizers (see Chapters 10, 13). Provide questions for students to answer after reading a few paragraphs.
Completing worksheets	Completing items on worksheets	Provide more time. Reduce the number of items. Reformat using borders to separate important information. Use color to highlight important information.
Reading text or worksheets	Seeing the material	Enlarge font size. Use a font that has simple lettering. Provide a magnifier. Use screen magnification software (see the section on assistive technology that begins on page 240). Use color. Contrast the foreground with the background.
Computing mathematical problems using workbooks or worksheets	Identifying symbols (=, +, ×).	Have students circle the symbol and state its meaning. Have students highlight the symbol with color before proceeding. Provide a cue sheet with the symbols and their meaning. Enlarge the font size of symbols to make them more readily visible.

we can surmise that the amount of weekly time spent on homework has probably increased.

Another study showed that teachers typically assign homework for practice and extension opportunities and to allow students time to complete unfinished

● The positive effects of homework include improved achievement and learning, improved attitude and study skills, more self-discipline, and greater parent involvement.

in-class work (Cooper & Nye, 1994; Polloway, Epstein, Bursuck, Jayanthi, & Cumblad, 1994). Research findings have suggested that types of parent involvement in homework practices, teacher discussions of homework assignments, and student consequences for incomplete homework are important factors to consider (Epstein, Polloway, Foley, & Patton, 1993; Polloway et al., 1994). Finally, academic achievement is better when homework is assigned (Cooper & Nye, 1994).

Guidelines for Homework Practices

Research results on homework practices by general and special education teachers suggest several practices to promote the effective use of homework. First, special and general education teachers must work collaboratively to be sure that the homework assignment is appropriate for individual students. Second, teachers must be sure that students understand the assignments and that consequences are in place for compliance and noncompliance. Third, parents can be involved in the process in a structured manner to minimize the problems that homework can create in families. Fourth, homework should be given for skills that students are capable of practicing independently; that is, they have demonstrated acquisition of the skills and now require further practice to attain mastery. Fifth, students with special needs should be taught specific study skills to help them approach homework tasks more efficiently and effectively.

Rivera and Smith (1997) offer the following guidelines for effective homework practices:

- State your policy.
  - Develop a homework policy stating expectations.
  - Share the policy with students, parents, and administrators.
- Teach prerequisite skills.
  - Teach skills necessary for successful homework completion, such as study skills, learning strategies, and problem solving skills.
- Make adaptations.
  - Use the ADAPT framework.
  - Work collaboratively with special education teachers to ensure that homework assignments are adapted to meet individual learners' needs.

- Assign homework.
  - Explain homework assignments; check for understanding.
  - Assign homework as independent practice.
  - Assign reasonable amounts of homework frequently.
- Check homework.
  - Check homework daily.
  - Provide incentives and rewards for completion and accuracy.
  - Involve students in self-monitoring, including correction and evaluation.
  - Establish a routine homework system designating how homework is handled each day (where to turn it in, how to check homework, how to provide feedback to students, when to reward for completion and accuracy, how to provide feedback).
- Make connections to home.
  - Provide specific guidelines for parent assistance.
  - Request parent assistance with rewards and incentives.
  - Ask for parent feedback about homework completion and accuracy.
  - Ask for parent feedback about problems that occur with homework assignments.

Let's see how Mrs. Bell implements some of these homework practices and the ADAPT framework to help Frank be more successful with his writing assignments.

ADAPT in Action ● Frank—Homework in Writing

Frank is a fifth-grade student in Mrs. Bell's class. He gets along well with his peers and works well with them in small-group activities. Frank has an identified learning disability in reading, writing, and mathematics. His educational performance levels show that he is working on a third-grade level in academics. Although he is attentive during whole-group instruction, he learns best in small, same-ability groups for reading, writing, and mathematics. Typically, the teacher works with Frank and two other students during small-group instruction. Homework is an important component of Mrs. Bell's instruction. She recognizes the value of homework as an independent practice time to bolster the skills that students have learned in class. She assigns homework in one subject area four nights per week. Homework in writing requires the students to pick a topic that interests them and write two pages about the topic. She expects students to turn in a clean paper with correct spelling, capitalization, and punctuation and with good sentence and paragraph development. She requires students to write at least four paragraphs about their topic and to include a conclusion. Frank turns in his assignment, but it is short and has errors in spelling, capitalization, and punctuation. The sentences are simple. The paragraphs are not sequenced. Frank's father reports that Frank spends almost three hours working on the assignment. Frank repeatedly rips up his paper, starts over, and seems very frustrated. Frank's father is not sure what to do. Mrs. Bell and Frank's father decide to meet to discuss ways to adapt the homework assignment to ensure success for Frank at home. To prepare for the parent conference, Mrs. Bell considers what went wrong by using the ADAPT framework.

Ask, "What am I requiring the student to do?" Mrs. Bell considers the task. The students need to write a report on a topic of their choice. They need to include several paragraphs and be sure that there are no spelling errors.

Determine the prerequisite skills of the task. Students need to be able to identify a topic and information about the topic. They need to write paragraphs that have a main idea and supporting details. The paragraphs should be logically sequenced. Students need to be able to check their work for spelling, capitalization, and punctuation.

Analyze the student's strengths and struggles. Mrs. Bell thinks about Frank's response to the homework assignment. According to his father, he tried to get it done, and he did indeed turn in his report. However, there were too many requirements for him to complete it successfully. His sentences were simple, declarative statements that were not related to a main idea. The information was disorganized, and content was difficult to follow. His work showed problems with spelling, capitalization, and punctuation.

Propose and implement adaptations from among the four categories. Mrs. Bell decides to try a different instructional activity, brainstorming, as an adaptation. For his homework assignment, she will give Frank several topics from which he can choose one. She will ask him to brainstorm everything he knows about the topic (instructional content) and to write these ideas on his computer at home (instructional material). She knows Frank can type, so that might be easier for him. She will ask Frank to use the spellcheck feature. She will check with Frank's father during their conference to be sure Frank can use the computer at home. The following day, Mrs. Bell will pair Frank with a peer (instructional delivery) in class to go over his ideas. She will then work with him and several other students in a small, same-ability group (instructional delivery) to generate sentences from the brainstormed ideas.

Test to determine if the adaptations helped the student accomplish the task. Mrs. Bell will review the ideas brainstormed by Frank. If progress is still lacking, she will try some of the following ideas.

- **Instructional activity:** Provide main ideas and details about a topic on sentence strips. Talk about how the main ideas and details are related to the topic. Then with the student, organize the main ideas and details into a coherent paragraph.
- **Instructional content:** Provide one topic *and* ideas for Frank to use to create sentences. Teach capitalization and punctuation skills.
- **Instructional materials:** Provide WriteOutloud or CoWriter software program (see this chapter's section on assistive technology, which follows).
- **Instructional delivery:** Work one-to-one with Frank to check his sentences and to teach capitalization and punctuation skills.

How Can Assistive Technology Help Students Access the Curriculum?

Some time ago, International Business Machines (IBM, 1991) provided a training package for assistive technology (AT), in which they noted, "For people without disabilities, technology makes things easier; for people with disabilities, technology makes things possible" (p. 2). Advances in technology have benefited most of society, but it could be argued that for people with disabilities, technology has provided a means to an end, which is independence. That is, AT devices and services serve as a vehicle to help individuals with disabilities do what they want to do when they want to do it, thereby reducing the need to depend on others. The definitions of AT devices and services are provided in the Tech Notes feature.

AT allows students access to the curriculum in inclusive settings and environments at school. By focusing on an individual's functional capability, AT promotes independence for students with disabilities by enabling them to communicate and socialize with their peers; participate across settings such as the playground, classroom, cafeteria, and library; and demonstrate their learning of the curriculum. Functional capability refers to those abilities (such as vision, hearing, communication, mobility, cognition, and motor control) that are used to help individuals compensate for struggles that are disability-related. For example, an individual who has good hearing but is blind might want to read a chapter in a textbook. Listening to the chapter on an electronic book provides access to that material. When selecting AT devices, *we focus on strengths* to select devices that help individuals access their environments.

AT devices can be viewed along a continuum from low-tech to high-tech. Most of us identify as "high-tech" those devices that are usually electronic. Computers with their multiple capabilities, talking calculators, electronic books, screen reader and voice recognition software, and powered wheelchairs are examples of devices that fall at the "high-tech" end of the continuum. Grips for pencils, changes in text font size, a grab bar in the shower, and a magnifier are examples of devices at the "low-tech" end. The point here is that not all AT devices have to have "bells and whistles" to be considered AT. Thus, for a student who has a mathematics learning disability (LD), a calculator may be identified in the IEP as an AT device to help the student compute basic facts when solving word problems. For students who do not have a math LD and who use calculators to check their arithmetic, the calculator is an instructional material.

Teachers should know about devices and services available to help them work with students whose IEP stipulates the use of AT so that they can receive a free appropriate public education (FAPE).

Assistive Technology Devices

An assistive technology device is the unit itself, which can be an item (e.g., a Hoover cane to help a person who is blind with mobility), a piece of equipment (e.g., a motorized wheelchair to help an individual with physical disabilities move about), or a product system (e.g., a computer with speech output software that reads the text on the screen). The intent of the devices is to promote access and independence for individuals with disabilities. An AT device enhances an individual's functioning. A communication board tremendously enhances the life of a student who is unable to communicate orally, by providing the opportunity to "speak." The AT device enables a person with a disability to do something that he or she could not do without the device. Therefore, an assistive technology device is anything that is bought or made that helps a person with a disability accomplish tasks that would otherwise be difficult or impossible (Bryant & Bryant, 2003).

AT devices can be grouped into categories that reflect their purpose and function in promoting access. These categories include positioning and seating, mobility, communication, adaptive toys and games, adaptive environments,

tech NOTES

AT Definitions

Assistive Technology Device: A Definition. The term *assistive technology device* was first defined in the Technology-Related Assistance for Individuals with Disabilities Act of 1988 (P.L. 100-407). In this legislation, which is better known as the Tech Act, it was defined as "any item, piece of equipment, or product system, whether acquired commercially off-the-shelf, modified, or customized, that is used to increase, maintain or improve the functional capabilities of individuals with disabilities."

Assistive Technology Service: A Definition. *Assistive technology service* was defined by the Tech Act as "any service that directly assists an individual with a disability in the selection, acquisition, or use of an assistive technology device." Services include

- A functional evaluation of the person in the individual's customary environment
- Purchasing and/or leasing
- Selecting, designing, and fitting
- Coordinating and using other therapies or interventions
- Training or technical assistance for an individual with disabilities or the family
- Training or technical assistance for a professional

Assistive Technology Devices and Services. How are these two terms related? The answer is quite simple in that the two go together. A device of some sort (such as a wheelchair, a computer, a braille text, or an FM listening system) may be necessary in order for a person with a disability to meet challenges related to impaired mobility, cognitive function, or sensory function. But the services associated with such assistive technology devices must also be carefully considered. How will the device be purchased? Who will assess whether the device and the person are a good match? Who will ensure that the device "fits" with the user's physical, sensory, and cognitive characteristics? Who will train the student to utilize the device properly? How will teachers, other professionals, family members, and others with whom the AT user interacts learn how to provide the user with personal and educational supports, in and out of the classroom? And how will these people and their services be coordinated? These questions must be answered successfully for devices and services to be effective.

For more information about assistive technology devices and services to support students' special learning needs, refer to the following Web sites:
www.closingthegap.com/
www.abledata.com/

♿ **ABLEDATA**
Your source for assistive technology information

Home | MyABLEDATA | Contact | Site Map | Privacy

[ ] Search Advanced Search

Products   Resources   Library   Consumer Forum   About ABLEDATA

Welcome to ABLEDATA

ABLEDATA provides objective information about assistive technology products and rehabilitation equipment available from domestic and international sources. Although ABLEDATA does not sell any products, we can help you locate the companies that do.

Featured Issues

‣ Do you need information on resources for travelers with disabilities?

Highlights
The Building on Family Strengths: 2007 Conference will take place May 31, 2007 to June 2, 2007 in Portland, Oregon, United States. More details.

ABLEDATA is a data source of information on assistive technology. Used with permission.

computer use, and instructional aids (Bryant & Bryant, 2003, *Technology and Media* [TAM], n.d.).

Positioning and seating devices involve the best posture and seating arrangement for a particular function and time period. This might entail moving about from one place to another using a wheelchair, sitting during conversation and instruction, and eating. Physical and occupational therapists are key professionals who work with positioning.

Mobility is the act of movement. When most people think of mobility AT devices, they think of wheelchairs, but mobility devices also include scooter boards, vehicular modifications, and white canes. Rehabilitation engineers, physical therapists, and orientation and mobility specialists are important team members with whom to discuss mobility issues.

Communication devices help people compensate for expressive language (speaking) difficulties by focusing on their capabilities to understand language and to convey their thoughts, ideas, and needs. Augmentative and alternative communication (aug com) devices are included in the communication category. Aug com devices can supplement vocalizations when speech is not understood by a particular communication partner and can provide a way for an individual actually to speak. The speech/language pathologist is a key member of the IEP team when aug com decisions are to be made.

Adaptive toys and games (recreation) give children with disabilities an opportunity to play with toys and games to help them develop cognitive skills and to socialize with their peers. Adaptive toys might include devices with a sound so that children who are blind can discriminate among toys. Games might include large tops on game board markers so that children with motor problems can grasp and hold them. Early childhood specialists work with assistive technologists and occupational therapists to design features that enable all students to interact with toys and games as part of their cognitive and social development.

Adaptive environments (control of the environment) are devices and approaches that enable a person to manipulate the environment to allow for daily living, working, schooling, playing, and so forth. For instance, remote control units can be used to turn lights on and off, respond to the doorbell, open doors, or turn a computer on and off in the home, school, or workplace. In the classroom, something as simple as widening aisles can enhance mobility for a student who uses a motorized wheelchair. Other adaptive environmental devices include curb cuts; braille words for restroom, elevator, and room numbers; grab bars in showers; and automatic door openers. Occupational therapists are important members of a team that makes decisions about ways to adapt the environment.

Computer access devices enable people to use the computer. Examples include keyboard overlays (templates that lie on the keyboard to define the key space for responding), pointers, and screen reader and voice recognition software. For example, by using voice recognition software, a student with physical disabilities whose upper body control is limited but whose speech is a "functional capability" can speak into a microphone and tell the computer what functions to employ. For people who are blind and whose hearing is a "functional capability," alternative output devices for computer use, such as screen reader software, are necessary. Screen reader software reads the text displayed on the computer screen. Educators, occupational therapists, and rehabilitation specialists typically are called upon to assist on issues pertaining to computer access.

Finally, instructional aids provide access to the curriculum, instruction, and instructional materials. This category includes devices that facilitate learning. Instructional aids include technology that offers students access to information (e.g., a screen reader program that allows access to the World Wide Web for research for a student who is blind) or technology that is used for remediation purposes (e.g., math or reading instructional software).

Instructional software can provide students with extra practice on academic and problem solving skills. However, students who can benefit from extra practice using software programs for remedial purposes must continue to receive instruction from the classroom teacher. Instructional software should contain

- Instruction that is geared to the student's performance level
- Easy-to-follow directions
- Modeling
- Examples
- Error correction procedures
- Practice opportunities
- Appropriate reading level
- Documentation of students' progress

Such software should also focus on research-based skills.

Instructional software usually includes words, graphics (e.g., pictures, animation), and features that promote effective learning. It is important for teachers to evaluate these features and to determine the extent to which effective instructional practices are included. Figure 6.3 provides guidelines for evaluating and selecting instructional software.

FIGURE 6.3 Guidelines for Software Evaluation and Selection

A. Basic Information

Name of software _____

Publisher _____   Cost _____

Hardware requirements _____

B. Software Description

Software grade level(s) _____

Software instructional area(s) _____

Reading level of software text (if applicable) _____

Purpose _____

_____ Tutorial   _____ Drill and practice   _____ Simulation   _____ Game

Instructional Objectives ___ yes   ___ no   List objectives if stated _____

_____

How is information presented? (check all that apply)

_____ Speech   _____ Music   _____ Graphics (pictures)   _____ Text (words)   _____ Animation

How do the visuals look? (check all that apply)

_____ Screen is too busy.   _____ Graphics enhance, rather than distract from, purpose.

_____ Print is legible.   _____ Print Size Age-Appropriate

What is the quality of the sound? (check all that apply)

_____ Sound is clear/audible.   _____ Speech is audible.

_____ Sound is distracting.   _____ Rate of speech is appropriate.

Overall impressions/concerns _____

_____

C. Instructional Design

Directions are clear, easy to read, and short.	_____ yes	_____ no
Examples or models are provided.	_____ yes	_____ no
Pacing is appropriate.	_____ yes	_____ no
Practice opportunities are provided.	_____ yes	_____ no
Error correction is provided.	_____ yes	_____ no
Difficulty level can be individualized.	_____ yes	_____ no
Reinforcement (visual and/or auditory) is present.	_____ yes	_____ no
A recordkeeping/evaluation option is available.	_____ yes	_____ no

Overall impressions/concerns _____

_____

D. Software Content

Appropriate to stated objectives	_____ yes	_____ no
Factual and accurate	_____ yes	_____ no
Free of gender, cultural, or racial bias	_____ yes	_____ no
Relates to school's curriculum	_____ yes	_____ no
Relates to student's IEP	_____ yes	_____ no
Sufficient scope and sequence	_____ yes	_____ no

Overall impressions/concerns _____

_____

E. Technical Considerations

User Demands (respond to any that apply)

Academic _____

_____

Physical/motor _____

Computer knowledge _____

Technical vocabulary _____

Problem solving _____

Functions (check all that apply)

_____ Save work in progress   _____ Print in progress   _____ Alter sound

_____ Return to main menu at any point in program   _____ Change pace

Teacher Demands (respond to any that apply)

Amount of instruction to students for using software _____

_____

Installation procedures _____

Level of student monitoring _____

Preparation needed before using software _____

Overall impressions/concerns _____

_____

Source: Adapted from *Teaching Students with Learning and Behavior Problems* (3rd ed.), by D. P. Rivera and D. D. Smith, 1997, Boston: Allyn and Bacon.

Classroom teachers can work with assistive technologists and special education teachers to decide which instructional aids are most suitable to help students with disabilities access the curriculum (Bryant & Bryant, 2003). Table 6.7 provides examples of AT devices that students with disabilities may use, in accordance with their IEPs, in order to access and benefit from instruction and function successfully in various environments.

AT devices will be necessary to help Mrs. Bell's student with cerebral palsy benefit from instruction. The student is performing at grade level academically. However, her fine motor difficulties (holding and grasping objects, turning pages in a textbook, writing, and using math manipulatives) create problems in performing academic tasks. She knows how to use a computer to do her work and is familiar with its word processing and spellcheck features. A laptop computer has been customized to fit on the tray of her motorized wheelchair. The computer keyboard has been equipped with a keyguard, which is an overlap placed on top of the keys to minimize keys being accidentally hit during typing. However, Mrs. Bell notices that the student seems to tire when doing multiple typing assignments and that she has difficulty turning pages in her textbook. She decides to consult the assistive technologist. ADAPT Framework 6.2 shows how Mrs. Bell and the

6.2 ADAPT Framework Writing Answers to Reading Comprehension Questions

A ASK "What am I requiring the student to do?"	**D** DETERMINE the prerequisite skills of the task.	**A** ANALYZE the student's strengths and struggles.		**P** PROPOSE and implement adaptations from among the four categories.	**T** TEST to determine if the adaptations helped the student to accomplish the task.
		Strengths	Struggles		
The students will write answers to reading comprehension questions on a chapter they have read.	1. Is able to read the textbook with understanding.	1		**For 1.** No adaptation is needed.	
	2. Is able to turn the pages in the textbook.		2	**For 2. Instructional Material** Provide an automatic page-turner.	**For 2.** Observe to see if the device is working properly.
	3. Can read, understand, and respond to comprehension questions.	3		**For 3.** No adaptation is needed.	
	4. Can use a pencil to write responses to questions.		4	**For 4. Instructional Material** The student already uses a computer to do written assignments.	**For 4.** Observe to see if the device is working properly.
	5. Can write sentences to answer the questions.		5	**For 5. Instructional Material** Provide CoWriter software.	**For 5.** Observe to see how software works to help the student with sentence production to answer questions.

TABLE 6.7 **Examples of AT Devices**

Use of Device	AT Device
For Students to Access Reading . . .	
To enlarge text	Large-print books, larger font size, hand-held magnifier, closed-circuit television, screen magnifier software, screen magnifier
To enhance text and graphics	Eye glasses, color contrast, pictures, braille text
To convert text to speech	Screen reader software, talking dictionaries, electronic books
For Students to Access Writing . . .	
To increase use of writing tools	Pencil grips, writing paper with colored lines, writing templates
To enhance writing productivity	Electronic/talking spell checker/dictionary, voice recognition software, talking word processor software (WriteOutloud®, CoWriter®), voice dictation input
To use alternative writing tools	Computer, keyboard enhancements (keyguard, repeat rate adjustments ["stickie keys": key remains depressed for longer time]), electronic notetakers (with braille), pointing device to access keyboard, alternative keyboards (Intellitools, on-screen keyboard), switches and scanning devices
For Students to Access Mathematics . . .	
To support calculation	Calculator with print output, "talking calculator," calculator with large keypad, on-screen calculator, graph paper for problems with writing and aligning
To support measurement	Measuring devices with tactile output, measuring devices with speech output, talking thermometers
To support time telling	Talking watches, watches with large faces, watches with tactile output
For Students to Access Study Skills . . .	
To help with time management	Talking watches, calendars as planners with pictures if necessary, speech output devices to remind about dates
To support memory and organization	Hand-held recorders to input important times, dates, and things to do, visual organizers (color-coded folders)
For Students to Be Able to Listen/Communicate . . .	
To listen in class	Hearing aids, assistive technology systems (FM)
To communicate	Communication boards (electronic and nonelectronic), typewriter, speech amplifier, TTY/TTD (teletype devices)
To listen to multimedia	Closed captions on videotapes and TV, computer-generated speech output
To promote safety	Signaling systems (telephone ring signal, door knock signal, smoke alarm with strobe light)
For Students Who Require Mobility Support . . .	
To enhance orientation and mobility	Eye glasses, grab bars, white cane, tactile signage, power or manual wheelchairs, motorized scooter

Source: Adapted from *Teaching Students with Learning and Behavior Problems,* 3rd ed., by D. P. Rivera and D. D. Smith, 1997, Boston: Allyn and Bacon; *The AT Quick Wheel,* by Technology and Media, n.d., Arlington, VA: Council for Exceptional Children; and *Assistive Technology in Special Education: Policy and Practice,* by D. Golden, 1998, Arlington, VA: Council for Exceptional Children.

assistive technologist use the ADAPT framework to ensure that her student with CP uses AT to access the curriculum and instruction. In this case, the students are required to complete a reading comprehension assignment after reading a chapter in their textbook.

AT Services

According to the "Tech Act," there are several AT services that affect classroom teachers and must be provided to ensure that devices are properly identified and used. For example, the selection of appropriate AT devices based on an evaluation of the individual is an important service. Assistive technologists, diagnosticians, audiologists, occupational therapists, speech/language pathologists, and special and general education classroom teachers may participate in an AT evaluation of a student, depending on the needs of the student. Each professional contributes information about how the student is performing in relation to academics, communication, motor development, vision, or hearing. In Chapter 7, you will read about a scale that is used as part of a comprehensive evaluation for assistive technology. This scale, called the *Functional Evaluation of Assistive Technology* (Raskind & Bryant, 2002), enables professionals to rate the performance of a student on listening, speaking, academics, memory, organization, motor tasks, and behavior. Each discipline (such as occupational therapy, speech/language, and audiology) has its own criteria for evaluating student performance.

For example, when AT is being considered during an IEP meeting for a student with an identified reading disability, the AT technologist works with classroom teachers to determine reading strengths and areas of difficulty when completing classroom activities. Classroom teachers may be asked specific questions about reading requirements in the classroom and about the student's performance on these tasks. The AT technologist consults a speech/language pathologist if language difficulties are also noted. Together, professionals can make decisions about devices that can help the student with reading tasks. The evaluation process is ongoing; changes may occur in a student's environment or setting, strengths and struggles, and maturity (Bryant & Bryant, 2003; Raskind & Bryant, 2002).

Training is another example of an AT service (Rieth, Colburn, & Bryant, 2004). Training on AT devices should be provided to the students or users of the devices, their families, and professionals such as classroom teachers, speech/language pathologists, and occupational therapists (Todis, 1996). The use of AT devices in school settings is intended to promote the implementation of IEP goals. Professionals must plan for and implement the integration of the devices into educational settings. Professionals must be trained in how devices work, how to integrate devices into their settings when working with students, how to troubleshoot if a device malfunctions, and how to evaluate students to determine an appropriate match between device and needs. Because of advancements in technology and the changing needs of students, training must be an ongoing priority to ensure that both users and professionals remain informed. Training for educators must be conducted in teacher preparation programs and as a part of ongoing inservice training (Rieth et al., 2004). Additionally, because of the vital role paraprofessionals play in the delivery of services to students with more severe disabilities (see Chapter 8), they too must become competent in the use of AT devices to work effectively with students for whom devices have been assigned (Todis, 1996).

Finally, training must include information for professionals to share directly with families and caregivers of students who use AT devices. Because devices are permitted to go home with students, family members must know how to use the devices properly (Bryant & Bryant, 1998). If electronic devices prove overwhelming, more training may be required for successful implementation (Lemons, 2000).

It is crucial to include families in selecting AT devices and listen to their viewpoints (Bryant et al. 1998). Several key ideas should be included in the AT decision-making process. Team members must consider family viewpoints about disability and how services that are intended to be helpful may be interpreted. Additionally, knowledge about the family's experience and comfort level with technology is very important, especially if they are helping their child use the technology at home. Finally, family members should know what outcomes educators hope to achieve by having the student use a particular AT device. These outcomes should reflect the family's interest and values in promoting their child's independence.

AT Integration

For students with disabilities, the use of AT devices may be the key to promoting learning of the curriculum and access to educational environments. Integration of AT devices into instruction can occur as teachers design, implement, and evaluate instruction.

As teachers design instruction, they can think about the curriculum and objectives that students will be taught and how instruction will be delivered (e.g., grouping, modeling, guided practice). Teachers must also consider the strengths and needs of their students with IEPs and how AT devices can promote their active participation in lessons (Bryant & Bryant, 2003; Rieth et al., 2004). Teachers can think about the environmental requirements for the devices. For example, devices that produce sound or require electricity raise environmental considerations. Students may be able to use headphones with devices such as talking calculators, speech output, and tape recorders. Also, the location of electrical outlets will dictate where devices that require electricity can be set up. Other devices may require batteries, and battery-operated versions are often preferable when mobile environments are part of the setting.

During instruction, teachers should monitor how easy it is to use the device and whether further training is required. The performance (reliability and durability) of devices should also be evaluated (Bowser & Reed, 1995). AT devices that require frequent repair interfere with the student's ability to work. Thus, the use of that device should be reconsidered.

Teachers should monitor their students' ability to keep pace with their peers in completing the tasks (e.g., taking notes in class). For instance, Anderson-Inman and colleagues (1996) found that secondary school students with learning disabilities expressed a need to have fluent keyboarding skills so that they could use specialized software for studying. Practice using the nuances of the device may be necessary so that students can achieve the maximum benefit from the device. Finally, teachers should not overlook the fatigue factor when using the device. Some devices, such as keyboarding with computers, may be tiring and hinder productivity.

Evaluating the effectiveness of integrating assistive technology involves professionals, family members, and students. Teachers should determine whether devices are helping students compensate for specific difficulties (e.g., reading and writing). Evaluation of the devices needs to be ongoing as the student matures and as the tasks change. For example, a pencil grip for a young child may be an appropriate device in the primary grades, whereas using a computer and a word processing program is more appropriate for later grade levels.

summary

Access to the general education curriculum is critical for *all* students. Differentiating instruction to meet the special learning needs of students helps to ensure that students benefit from instruction and learn the curriculum. The ADAPT framework is a tool that can help teachers differentiate instruction that is responsive to the individual needs of students. As teachers plan, deliver, and evaluate instruction, they can identify effective practices from the adaptations categories (instructional activity, instructional content, instructional delivery, and instructional materials) to address specific student learning needs. We know that adaptations should be individualized to the learner, relevant to the curriculum, and effective in order to improve learning outcomes. We know a great deal about what constitutes effective instructional practices for stu-

dents with special needs. These practices focus on planning and delivering instruction, teaching different types of knowledge, and employing techniques that take stage of learning into account. Grouping practices such as whole-group and small-group instruction are a critical component of effective instruction. As part of quality instruction, teachers adapt instructional materials to accommodate learning needs and assign homework by following guidelines for effective practice. Finally, assistive technology devices and services hold great promise in helping students with disabilities be active, independent participants in the educational setting. Differentiating instruction using the ADAPT framework can significantly improve the academic, social, and behavioral outcomes of students with special needs.

self-test QUESTIONS

Let's review the learning objectives for this chapter. If you are uncertain and cannot "talk through" the answers provided for any of these questions, reread those sections of the text.

- **What is differentiated instruction?**

  Differentiated instruction is instruction that is responsive to the diverse needs of all students, with a focus on curriculum, instructional adaptations, services, and instructional intensity. Differentiated instruction can occur in terms of intensity of instruction, such as grouping of students and the amount of time devoted to providing more individualized instruction. Specialized personnel, including special educators, may be needed to deliver more intensive, adapted instruction. Also, differentiated instruction may occur in different settings. In some cases, the curriculum may need to be differentiated if students require a focus on life skills.

- **How can instruction be differentiated?**

  Instruction can be differentiated by including materials that are universally designed, by employing the ADAPT framework, and by considering multicultural and linguistic components

that can be integrated into instruction. The ADAPT mnemonic is as follows:

- **A**sk, "What am I requiring the student to do?"
- **D**etermine the prerequisite skills of the task.
- **A**nalyze the student's strengths and struggles.
- **P**ropose and implement adaptations from among the four categories.
- **T**est to determine if the adaptations helped the student accomplish the task.

The four categories are instructional activity, instructional content, instructional delivery, and instructional materials.

- **What are some effective instructional practices?**

  Effective instructional practices include planning for and delivering instruction. In the course of planning, teachers consider the type of knowledge and critical thinking (discrimination, factual, rules, procedural, or conceptual); the stage of learning of the student (acquisition, proficiency, maintenance, generalization, or application); and the instructional components of direct, explicit instruction and strategy instruction. In delivering instruction, teachers should include the following instructional steps and techniques: an advance organizer, presentation of information, practice, closure, and progress monitoring.

- **How can grouping practices promote effective instruction?**

Grouping practices include whole-group, flexible, small groups; and one-to-one grouping structures. Other effective grouping practices include peer tutoring and cooperative learning. Teachers should consider these practices when planning and delivering instruction. The whole-group format works well where common instructional objectives are identified, the teacher delivers the lesson, and students respond orally or in writing. Flexible, small groups include same-ability groups and mixed-ability groups. Teachers use same-ability groups to provide extra instruction and support to those students who are most in need of additional assistance. Mixed-ability groups can be used for students to work on projects and to make presentations. One-to-one instruction enables teachers to tailor instruction to individual students and their specific learning and behavioral needs. In tutoring via peer partners, pairs of students can work on assigned skills, usually for extra practice. Peer partners can promote active student involvement, opportunities to respond, repetition, review, and practice. Cooperative learning offers a variety of structures to assist students in practicing information in a student-centered format.

- **What guidelines should be followed for instructional materials and homework?**

For instructional materials, consider the student and the instructional content and methodology. Regarding the student, identify the student's present levels of educational performance when selecting materials, and consider whether the material can be used to meet individualized education program (IEP) goals. Regarding content and methodology, decide whether the material is age-appropriate. Determine whether it includes a sequence of skills and teaching strategies. Ensure that there are sufficient opportunities to practice new skills and that generalization and maintenance activities are included.

For homework, guidelines include developing a homework policy to share with students, parents, and administrators. Homework should be explained, assigned in reasonable amounts, and assigned only as independent practice. Teachers may need to teach study skills and learning strategies. Teachers should establish a homework routine, including students correcting and evaluating their work.

- **What are assistive technology devices and services?**

An assistive technology device is anything that is bought or made that helps a person with a disability accomplish tasks that would otherwise be difficult or impossible. AT devices can be viewed along a continuum from low-tech to high-tech. The latter are usually electronic. AT devices can be grouped into categories that reflect their purpose and function in promoting access. These categories include positioning and seating, mobility, communication, adaptive toys and games, adaptive environments, computer use, and instructional aids.

Assistive technology services are those activities that ensure adoption and maintenance of appropriate devices. One such service is evaluating the functional capabilities and struggles of individuals with disabilities to aid in the selection of appropriate devices to promote access and independence. Another service is the training of professionals, paraprofessionals, families, and users. Training should include how devices work, how to integrate devices into settings, how to troubleshoot if a device malfunctions, and how to evaluate students to determine an appropriate match between device and needs.

- ## Revisit the
OPENING challenge

Check your answers to the Reflection Questions and revise them on the basis of what you have learned.

1. How can Mrs. Bell and Ms. Mendez use the ADAPT framework to differentiate instruction for their students?

2. How can Mrs. Bell and Ms. Mendez differentiate instruction for their multicultural and ELL students?

3. What instructional and grouping practices might help them provide effective, differentiated instruction for their students?

4. How can Mrs. Bell and Ms. Mendez ensure that the instructional materials and homework practices they use are appropriate for all of their students?

5. How can assistive technology help Mrs. Bell's students with disabilities access the general education curriculum?

Professional Standards and Licensure

CEC Knowledge and Skill Core Standard and Associated Subcategories

CEC Content Standard 1: Foundations

Special educators understand the field as an evolving and changing discipline based on philosophies, evidence-based principles and theories, relevant laws and policies, diverse historical points of view, and human issues that have historically influenced the treatment of individuals with exceptional needs both in school and society.

CEC Content Standard 4: Instructional Strategies

Special educators select, adapt, and use instructional strategies to promote challenging learning results in general and special curricula and to appropriately modify learning environments for individuals with disabilities. They enhance the learning of critical thinking, problem solving, and performance skills of individuals with disabilities, and increase their self-awareness, self-management, self-control, self-reliance, and self-esteem.

CEC Content Standard 7: Instructional Planning

Individualized decision making and instruction is at the center of special education practice. Special educators develop long-range individualized instructional plans anchored in both general and special curricula. Individualized instructional plans emphasize explicit modeling and efficient guided practice to assure acquisition and fluency through maintenance and generalization. Understanding of these factors, as well as the implications of an individual's exceptional condition, guides the special educator's selection, adaptation, and creation of materials, and the use of powerful instructional variables. Instructional plans are modified based on ongoing analysis of the individual's learning progress.

INTASC Core Principle and Associated Special Education Subcategories

1. Subject Matter

1.03 All teachers understand that students with disabilities may need accommodations, modifications, and/or adaptations to the general curriculum.

4. Instructional Strategies

4.04 All teachers understand that it is particularly important to provide multiple ways for students with disabilities to participate in learning activities. They modify tasks and accommodate individual needs of students with disabilities.

4.06 All teachers adjust their instruction in response to information gathered from the ongoing monitoring of performance and progress of students with disabilities.

4.08 All teachers expect and support the use of assistive and instructional technologies to promote learning and independence of students with disabilities.

7. Instructional Planning

7.02 All teachers plan ways to modify instruction to facilitate positive learning results within the general education curriculum for students with disabilities.

7.04 Design learning environment so that the individual needs of students with disabilities are accommodated.

7.05 All teachers monitor student progress and incorporate knowledge of student performance across settings into the instructional planning process.

Praxis II: Education of Exceptional Students: Core Content Knowledge

II. Legal and Societal Issues

Historical movements/trends affecting the connections between special education and the larger society, for example,

- Inclusion
- Application of technology
- Advocacy
- Accountability and meeting educational standards

III. Delivery of Services to Students with Disabilities

Background knowledge, including

- Conceptual approaches underlying service delivery to students with disabilities
- Integrating best practices from multidisciplinary research and professional literature into the educational setting

Curriculum and instruction and their implementation across the continuum of education placements, including

- Instructional development and implementation
- Teaching strategies and methods
- Instructional format and components

- Technology for teaching and learning in special education settings

Structuring and managing the learning environment, including

- Structuring the learning environment

Case Study—"A Broken Arm?"

Spelling was impossible for Jim despite the accommodations made by his resource teacher.

> Log onto **www.mylabschool.com**. Under the **Resourses** tab, navigate to the **Case Archive** and, read "**A Broken Arm?**"

 OR

> Use the **www.mylabschool.com** **Assignment Finder** to go directly to the case study. Just enter Assignment ID **CS08**.

1. Read the case study and outline the learning issues that are important to the general education teacher and those that are important to the special education teacher.
2. Use the ADAPT strategy to determine how to differentiate instruction in this scenario.
3. In which of the four categories (instructional activity, instructional content, instructional delivery, and/or instructional materials) could adaptations occur?

Video—"Strategies for Teaching Diverse Learners"

In this video, a general education teacher discusses ways that she meets the needs of diverse learners in her classroom.

> Log onto **www.mylabschool.com**. Under the **Courses** tab, in **General Methods,** go to the **video lab**. Access the "**Student Diversity**" videos and watch the "**Strategies for Teaching Diverse Learners**" video.

 OR

> Use the **www.mylabschool.com** **Assignment Finder** to go directly to these videos. Just enter Assignment ID **GMV5**.

1. List the ways in which this teacher meets the needs of the diverse learners in her classroom.
2. Although she doesn't talk about differentiating instruction for individual learners, how are the strategies she uses aligned with those discussed in the chapter?
3. In what other ways could a content-area reading assignment such as the one shown in the video be differentiated for a student with a reading disability?

To access chapter objectives, practice tests, weblinks, and flashcards, go to the companion website at **www.ablongman.com/bryantsmith1e**.

chapter 7

Assessing Students with Special Needs

chapter OBJECTIVES

After studying this chapter, you will have the knowledge to answer the following questions:

- What is assessment, and how does it differ from testing?
- What are the various types of measures that contribute to assessments?
- What is high stakes testing, and how does it affect you and your students?
- What four areas should you consider when adapting assessments for students with disabilities?
- What are interviews, and what is their role in the assessment process?
- How can observations be used to collect information about your students?
- What is portfolio assessment, and what cautions need to be employed in the use of portfolios with students who have disabilities?

● OPENING challenge

Determining What Students Know

Middle School ● Mr. Gomez has been teaching for 4 years. His state has recently revamped its state standards and high stakes tests. Mr. Gomez's students will be taking the test in the spring to determine whether they will move on to grade 7.

Mr. Gomez has a diverse classroom, and the achievement levels range from very low to very high. He is confident that some of his students could take the test now and do quite well. Others in his classroom are so low-achieving that he questions whether he can teach them the skills they need in order to pass the test. He has decided to implement progress monitoring for his entire class. He will collect data on his students' in reading, math, and science, the three areas being assessed in the spring. He will tailor his instruction to their needs and will monitor their achievement throughout the school year.

Two students in particular concern Mr. Gomez. *"Sonya is new to the school and has*

column continues on next page

High School ● Ms. Grey teaches eleventh-grade world history. In addition to teaching her history classes, Ms. Grey tutors students in preparing for her state's exit examination. In the state where she works, students must pass the exit exam to graduate from high school. She has a number of students with whom she works twice a week in preparation for the exam. One of the students in her class, Gilbert, presents a unique challenge. *"Gilbert has low vision, which means that he can read from the text, but the material needs to be adapted for his use. He uses magnification, and that seems to help a great deal."*

Ms. Grey collaborates with the district's visual impairment specialist during tutoring sessions to ensure that Gilbert has access to the study guides and practice tests. *"I have never had a student who is blind or one who is visually impaired, so this is all new to me,"* she states. *"Gilbert has all sorts of tools available to use to help him. He*

column continues on next page

serious reading problems. She is unable to decode words and has very little comprehension of written materials."

"Dondra, my other challenging student, has attention issues. She is very bright and capable but has difficulty paying attention and sitting still." Although Mr. Gomez has worked with students who have attention problems before, "None of my former students compare to Dondra. Her condition is exacerbated by muscle control issues. She has fine motor problems that cause her to struggle when she has to grasp, pick up, or use small objects." ●

is an honor student, so the tools must be effective! It's still the beginning of the school year, so I'm still learning. But so far, so good." ●

● Reflection Questions

In your journal, write down your answers to the following questions. After completing the chapter, check your answers and revise them on the basis of what you have learned.

1. How could Mr. Gomez set up a progress-monitoring procedure?

2. How could he set goals and chart his students' progress?

3. How can Mr. Gomez teach Sonya science and test her abilities when she cannot read?

4. How can Ms. Grey adapt materials for teaching and testing Gilbert?

5. How can she ensure that Gilbert's high stakes testing will yield valid results?

I
n education, assessment is any method by which teachers and other professionals gain information about students. Students may be assessed to measure academic performance, intelligence level, behavior tendencies, or emotional stability. Often, people equate assessment with testing. Tests are one form of assessment, but not the only form of assessment (Taylor, 2003). When working with students who have special needs, teachers use a variety of techniques to gain information about their work and abilities.

Teachers gather assessment information every time they watch children and adolescents do things such as play together or complete an assignment. In assessment terminology, this "watching" is called conducting observation, and it involves not only watching students do something but also thinking about what they are doing, why they are doing it, and what the "doing" means to the students and those around them. Teachers' observations occur over time and are ongoing, which makes them a valuable tool for recording behavioral or academic changes (Venn, 2004). Teachers can also gain information by interviewing the student, the student's teacher(s), or the student's parents or classmates. It is possible to gather information by having the student, parent, or another teacher complete a questionnaire or survey. Assessments help teachers gain valuable information, but only if the results of the various assessments are valid—that is, only if they truly represent the abilities of the students being assessed.

Why Do We Assess Students with Special Needs?

Purposes of Assessment

There are several reasons why we assess students with special needs. Here we discuss a few key purposes.

IDENTIFYING STRENGTHS AND WEAKNESSES   A major purpose of assessment is to gather information about what a student with special needs can do well and what the student struggles with. When teachers gather information across various areas (such as reading, writing, mathematics, classroom behavior, and so forth), they can examine the information to determine a student's strengths (what the student can do) and weaknesses (what the student struggles with). Often, they use assessments that are called diagnostic measures, not because these measures, in and of themselves, diagnose a particular condition, but because they assess a student across a variety of skill areas. Those areas may be within a construct (for instance, they may assess several different reading skills) or more global (they may assess reading, writing, *and* mathematics). More global tests are also called survey batteries, because they assess a lot of different areas and provide an overview of achievement (Venn, 2004).

When teachers compare an individual student's abilities to one another, they are making what is called an intraindividual comparison. These comparisons are important because they enable us to identify what needs to be worked on to help improve any problem areas that might be discovered.

DETERMINING PLACE OF RELATIVE STANDING   In contrast to making intraindividual comparisons, teachers can compare a person's performance to that of others. In this case, the teachers are making interindividual comparisons. Many school districts administer an achievement test in the spring of each year. This test—perhaps the *Iowa Test of Basic Skills,* the *Stanford Achievement Test,* or some similar test—measures students' reading skills, math skills, writing skills, and so forth. After the tests are collected from each classroom, they are usually sent to the test publisher to be scored. Professionals at the publishing company assign normative scores that reflect each student's standing relative to other students across the country (that is, a "national average") and/or to those within the school district (a district average). Sometime a month or two thereafter, the school is sent the test results. Those results, along with a booklet explaining what the results mean, are shared with parents, and the results are placed in each student's cumulative folder, the school's record of each student's academic activity. The results of the test are also used by district superintendents and principals to identify how the schools within the district compare to one another and how a particular district compares to others across the country.

INFORMING INSTRUCTION   One of the first questions that teachers should ask when reviewing assessment results is "What does the assessment tell me about what I should be teaching my student?" This is an example of using assessment data to inform instruction or guide instructional efforts.

For example, when administering a reading test, whether it is a standardized test or an informal reading inventory, teachers observe how students respond to different features of a test. They may conduct a miscue or error analysis to see what words the student misses as he or she reads and to make judgments about the student's word identification skills. If a student continuously leaves off suffixes or inflectional endings, those skills would be targeted for instruction. If the student can correctly respond to literal comprehension questions but misses a sizable proportion of inferential questions, a teacher may decide to focus reading instruction on making inferences.

DOCUMENTING PROGRESS   According to No Child Left Behind legislation, educators must ensure that all students make adequate yearly progress, so it is important for teachers to collect assessment data to determine whether students are making progress toward their end-of-year goals (Smith, 2007). As already noted, the IEP contains annual goals that serve as targets for the teacher and student to reach by the year's end, and assessment data can indicate whether students are making progress toward their annual goals.

Teachers want students to be performing at a certain level by the end of the school year. These end-of-year assessments are sometimes called outcome assessments, because teachers are checking the yearly outcome of their teaching efforts. Teachers can use assessment data to determine, throughout the year, whether their students are performing at a level that will get them where they need to be at the end of the school year. Such use of assessment data is called progress monitoring. All students make some progress throughout a school year, but for some, the progress may be so slow that there is no way for them to reach the annual goals unless changes are made in instruction. By documenting progress on a regular basis via progress monitoring, teachers can use assessment data to make necessary instructional decisions and alterations.

DETERMINING PROGRAM ELIGIBILITY   In some cases, assessment data are used to identify exceptionalities (such as mental retardation, learning disabilities, emotional or behavioral disorders, and giftedness) and to determine that students are eligible to receive special program services. These programs may be special education, Section 504 programs, or dyslexia services, to name but a few. There is no test for exceptionalities per se. Instead, assessment professionals (usually psychologists or educational diagnosticians) administer a battery of tests, make observations, and conduct interviews (in other words, perform a number of assessments) and look at the results with certain criteria in mind. There are established procedures for diagnosing exceptional conditions, and a team of people (a team that includes classroom teachers) talk about the results of the assessments and decide whether the student qualifies as having a particular disability or exceptionality.

The role of the classroom teacher in this process cannot be overemphasized. Teachers are the educational professionals who know the student best, and theirs is an important voice that lends credibility to the assessment findings that shape the decision-making process. For instance, imagine a teacher who has referred a student for having a potential mathematics learning disability. After conducting the assessments, the school psychologist recommends that the student be identified as having a reading learning disability but not a mathematics learning disability. The assessment data did not show a math disability; they showed a reading disability instead. The child's teacher, having observed the student for months, has never noticed a reading problem. In fact, the teacher has always been impressed with the student's abilities as a strategic reader. If the teacher does not speak out during the meeting and provide contrasting evidence, there is a good chance that the student may be misdiagnosed as having a reading learning disability.

GRADING Perhaps the most common form of assessment that teachers encounter involves assessing students for grading purposes— that is, to assign a numeric or letter index based on a student's performance within a specified academic calendar period (usually a semester). To see whether students learned their spelling words, teachers typically administer a spelling test at the end of the week and record the percentage correct in the grade book. An end-of-chapter test might be administered after completion of a science unit. Often these tests will have been prepared by the textbook publisher, but many teachers choose to create their own tests. Whichever approach is used, test grades are assigned and constitute a portion of each student's final grade for the course.

● Perhaps the most common form of assessment teachers encounter involves assessing students for grading purposes.

Legislation Protection Related to Assessment

Over the years, assessment has been used inappropriately to identify people as having disabilities they do not really have or to exclude children from programs for which they would otherwise be eligible. Students from racial or ethnic groups that are not part of the dominant American culture are often at a disadvantage when taking standardized tests. Also, students who have not yet truly mastered English cannot adequately demonstrate their abilities in such testing situations (Thurlow & Lui, 2001). Differences in culture and in language contribute to some students being misidentified as having a disability or being excluded from education programs for students who are gifted (Ochoa, Robles-Pina, Garcia, & Breuning, 1999).

For example, some children who spoke no English or were English language learners (students who are learning English as their second language) were administered intelligence tests in English and diagnosed as having mental retardation because of their low test scores (Smith, 2007). Clearly the results of such tests were not valid, because those results did not reflect the test takers' intelligence. Rather, they reflected the test takers' inability to respond to questions that they did not understand! In many cases, had the questions been asked in the person's native language, correct answers would have been given, and mental retardation would not have been diagnosed in error.

To stress the importance of nonbiased evaluations, IDEA '04 requires that nondiscriminatory testing be established in each state. Assessment authorities have provided numerous procedures that test authors can undertake to reduce bias and therefore create measurement instruments that are nondiscriminatory (Salvia & Ysseldyke, 2001; Sattler, 2001; Taylor, 2003). Before selecting tests for use with students who are culturally and/or linguistically different, teachers, school psychologists, educational diagnosticians, and other assessment professions should consult the tests' technical manuals to see whether procedures were undertaken to reduce test bias. The manuals should provide empirical evidence, in the form of research studies and statistical analyses, supporting the tests' use in nondiscriminatory assessment.

How Do We Assess Students with Special Needs?

Standardized Versus Nonstandardized Procedures

People have debated the merits and abuses of standardized assessments for decades, often without knowing exactly what "standardized" means. Hammill (1987) and Hammill and Bryant (1991) identified four important characteristics of standardized assessments. First, in order for an assessment to be considered standardized, instructions have to be set forth that clearly describe assessment procedures. Little room can be left for the examiner to deviate from the prescribed procedures. Set administration procedures are crucial to all types of standardized measures, be they conventional question-and-answer tests, interviews, direct observations, or analytic teaching techniques.

Second, an assessment procedure can be standardized only if there is an objective system for scoring the measure. If a test involves questions and answers, there must be specific criteria for scoring the correctness of an answer. Most of the time, the scoring procedures are straightforward and well defined. For instance, a math problem that reads "$5 + 3 = X$, solve for X" will have only one correct answer, 8. But consider a reading comprehension question that asks, "Why does Mary feel as she does?" (Accept any reasonable answer.) Here, reliance on the scorer's subjective judgment violates the objective scoring criterion of standardized assessment. An important aspect of objective scoring is to prepare the examiner to see a behavior clearly (either a test response or a student action), to classify it according to a clearly defined system, and to record it correctly.

Finally, a standardized measure must have a specified frame of reference. Interpretations may be norm-referenced, criterion-referenced, or non-referenced.

NORM-REFERENCED INTERPRETATIONS Norm-referenced interpretations interpret a person's performance by comparing it to that of his or her peers (Hammill & Bryant, 1991). We discussed this earlier when we talked about "relative standing." In school, norm-referenced interpretations answer the question "How does my student compare to others of the same age?" This comparison can be made by comparing students to others in their classroom, to others in their school or district, or, most commonly in nationally standardized tests, to others across the country.

When interpreting students' results on a norm-referenced test, it is important to know what the reported test scores mean. Most tests report results using raw scores, standard scores, percentiles, age equivalents, or grade equivalents.

Before we discuss the scores, we need to spend a little time talking about normative samples. A normative sample consists of the people who were given the test to determine an average score with which to compare the scores we are to report. If the test reports national norms, the test has been administered to many students across the country. Best practice dictates that there be at least 100 students in the sample at each age and at least 1,000 people across all ages (Hammill, Brown, & Bryant, 1992). Many tests have normative samples wherein thousands of people were tested at each age. Whatever the numbers, these scores are used to create the "national average" that serves as a comparison score for a particular student.

Thanks to sophisticated computers, test publishers can quickly and accurately provide district norms as well, and the district superintendent may request these. Then, a student is compared not only to a "national average" but also to a more local average. National scores tell teachers how their students compare to those from around the country; they also show principals how their schools compare to those from around the nation and superintendents to see how their students, schools, and districts compare to those from around the country. District norms, sometimes called local norms, allow teachers to compare their students' scores to each other and help a principal and superintendent to see how the schools compare to one another within the district. That is the power of a normative sample.

Test publishers report their normative sample's demographic characteristics (what percentage of the sample is Black, White, Hispanic, and so on), how many are male and how many female, how many in the sample are from urban schools and how many from rural schools, what states the sample was drawn from, and so forth. This important information is called a normative sample's *representativeness*. Teachers should ask, "How representative is this measure's normative sample? Does the sample 'look like' the students in my class?" Fortunately, most major measures used in school systems have representative normative samples (Hammill et al., 1992). Now let's look at the scores that tests yield.

Raw scores are simply the total number of points that a person is awarded. In a test where the student has to spell 30 words and gets 20 out of the 30 correct, a raw score of 20 is recorded. On a rating scale that has a Likert-style rating system (for instance, a behavioral rating scale with behaviors listed, the rater being asked how often a student exhibits that behavior and selecting 1 for never, 2 for sometimes, 3 for frequently, or 4 for always), the raw score would be the total number of points for the ratings. By themselves, raw scores mean little. Think about one test that contains 30 items and another that contains 70 items. Raw scores of 25 on these tests mean different levels of understanding, even though the raw scores are the same. Raw scores are best translated into one or more of the derived scores described below.

Norms for many tests are presented in terms of standard scores, derived scores that have an average score, or mean score, and a set statistical standard deviation. Figure 7.1 depicts the relationship of three standard scores typically reported in tests: z scores, scaled scores, and deviation IQs. Standard scores are valuable because they allow teachers both to make interindividual comparisons (that is, to determine how a student compares to the national or local average) and to assess intraindividual differences (strengths and weaknesses a person exhibits across test scores). We said before that when a student scores 25 raw score points on two different tests that contain different numbers of items, we cannot compare the two raw scores. But we *can* compare standard scores to one another. For example, if a test reports standard scores having a mean of 100 and a standard deviation of 15, we know that a reading score of 125 and a math score of 80 demonstrate a considerable performance advantage in reading over math. Likewise, reading and math scores of 110 and 108, respectively, mean that the student demonstrated similar abilities in both areas.

Percentiles are also provided for most tests. Percentiles, or percentile ranks, as they are often called, are convenient and popular because they are so easy to understand. Percentiles range from 1 to 99, and they represent where the person would rank when compared to 99 of his or her peers. If a student achieves a percentile of 59 on a math test, it means that that only 40 people scored as well as or better than he or she did on the test. Figure 7.1 depicts the relationship among percentile ranks, various standard scores, and the normal curve. The normal curve, which is sometimes called a bell curve because of its appearance, is a theoretical construct of the typical distribution of human traits such as intelligence and achievement.

Percentiles should not be confused with percentages correct for a test. A percentile rank of 59 does not mean that a student got 59 percent of the items correct on a particular test. This is a common misconception. A percentile indicates a person's standing relative to his or her peers based on test performance, not the percentage of items he or she got right on a test.

FIGURE 7.1 Relationship Among Various Types of Derived Scores

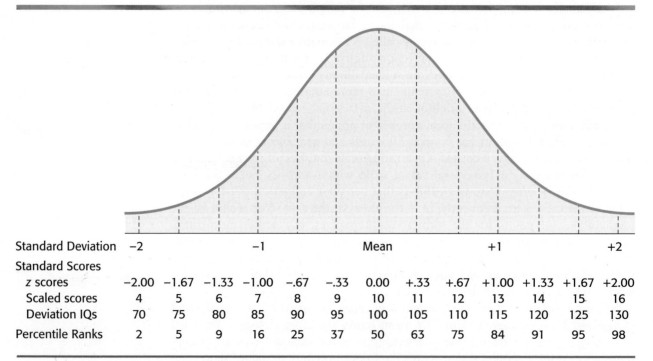

Standard Deviation	−2				−1			Mean			+1			+2
Standard Scores														
z scores	−2.00	−1.67	−1.33	−1.00	−.67	−.33	0.00	+.33	+.67	+1.00	+1.33	+1.67	+2.00
Scaled scores	4	5	6	7	8	9	10	11	12	13	14	15	16
Deviation IQs	70	75	80	85	90	95	100	105	110	115	120	125	130
Percentile Ranks	2	5	9	16	25	37	50	63	75	84	91	95	98

Source: R. Taylor (2003). *Assessment of Exceptional Students.* (6th ed.). Boston: Allyn and Bacon. Reprinted with permission.

Age equivalents are provided for many test scores. These values indicate the age level that corresponds to the student's raw score on each of the tests taken. Basically, an age equivalent indicates the age of the students in the normative sample who got the same raw score as the student on a particular test. For instance, for a fifth-grade student who was administered an intelligence test, an age equivalent of 3 years, 4 months simply means that the students of that age in the normative sample scored the same raw score as the older student. Be cautious: This result does *not* mean that the older student has the same intelligence (or mental age, as it is sometimes inappropriately called) as a 3-year-old.

Grade equivalents also may be assigned to test scores, especially achievement tests. Similar to age equivalents, these values indicate the grade level that corresponds to a raw score made by a student on each of the tests or subtests administered.

Grade equivalents are reported frequently in achievement testing, but they are often misinterpreted. When a reading test reports a grade equivalent of 3-2 (third year, second month of school), it does not necessarily mean that the student reads like a third grader. It means simply that the student achieved the same raw score as children in the third grade, second month of the school year when they took the test.

Informal reading inventories (IRIs) are unique tests that report their test scores in terms of grade equivalents (McLoughlin & Lewis, 2005). Informal reading inventories typically consist of a graded word list that students are given to read (a list of first-grade words, a list of second-grade words, and so forth). The highest level of word list read at 90 percent or 95 percent provides a grade equivalent index. For instance, if an eleventh grader reads a graded word list and can read successfully only words on the sixth-grade list (reads the seventh- and eight-grade lists at less than 90 percent accuracy), he or she would have a grade equivalent *based on that inventory* of the sixth grade. That does not mean he reads like a sixth grader; it simply means that he couldn't read words at a higher level *on that list*. The inventory may stop there, or it may have the student then read graded passages, usually passages from the kindergarten level up to the grade 12 level. When the student can no longer read 90 percent to 95 percent of the words correctly, the examiner stops and assigns a grade equivalent "reader level" for the student.

CRITERION-REFERENCED INTERPRETATIONS   Unlike norm-referenced interpretations that compare performance against that of peers, criterion-referenced interpretations compare performance to mastery of the content being tested (Hammill & Bryant, 1991). The most common reason for evaluating students is to determine whether they have learned what has been specifically taught. For example, imagine that a teacher has given a daily lesson on adding two-digit numerals to three-digit numerals and then follows up by giving a quiz. If the students get most of the subsequent items correct, the assumption is that the students have mastered the subject matter. If a student answers only half of the items correctly, then there is little doubt that the student has not mastered the content and that reteaching is needed.

Most assessment experts agree that mastery can be determined only when the student has had a sufficient number of opportunities to demonstrate competence (Bryant & Rivera, 1997). That is, giving a single item to a student and using the student's response for demonstrating mastery is not sufficient. Missing the item is no guarantee that the student would not answer the next 99 items correctly if given the opportunity. Likewise, answering the item correctly is no guarantee that the student wouldn't miss the next 99 opportunities. As a rule of thumb, only when a student can correctly answer 80 percent to 90 percent (or better) of the items can it be assumed that mastery has been achieved. Thus, it would be unwise to base mastery on fewer than five items; a student with at least five items can slip up on one item and yet still demonstrate mastery by answering four of the five items correctly. Assessing for mastery should include the opportunity to make a careless mistake without making a misleading interpretation inevitable.

Let's look at one way in which teachers can make their own criterion-referenced test for mathematics. Examine the scope-and-sequence chart example from a basal math textbook and identify skills to be assessed (see Figure 7.2). For our purposes, we'll keep our example brief and select only six skills.

Next, write five items for each skill (see Figure 7.3). Write ten items for each skill if 90 percent is to be set as the mastery level. Remember, children should be given an opportunity to miss one item and still demonstrate mastery. Because we have set our mastery for these skills at 80 percent, we can write five items per skill.

Finally, administer and score the test, and check for mastery. For each row of items, did the student get at least four correct? If so, it can be assumed that the student has mastered the skill. If not, then assume that the student has not mastered the skill, and continue teaching the skill. Teachers should review each skill periodically to ensure that students have maintained their mastery. Students need ongoing practice to maintain their skill sets.

NON-REFERENCED INTERPRETATIONS   Some measures lend themselves neither to norm-referenced interpretations nor to criterion-referenced interpretations. In 1987, Don Hammill introduced the term non-referenced interpretations to describe these types of assessment interpretations.

Some measures are intended to identify strategies a student is using during problem solving. When given a problem, individuals rarely arrive at a solution haphazardly. There is almost always a reasonable explanation of how a solution was derived. One of the most challenging yet interesting purposes for assessing math performance, for example, is to target the strategies that a student employs during computation or problem solving. It is intriguing to find out why a student generates a correct or incorrect response.

Rivera and Bryant (1992) suggested that no mathematics assessment, for instance, is complete without assessing strategies using what they termed process assessment. Simply put, the goal of process assessment in mathematics is to de-

FIGURE 7.2 Sample Scope-and-Sequence Chart

This scope-and-sequence chart for addition is representative of what can be found in elementary mathematics teacher's edition textbooks. We provide it as an example of content criterion reference measures.

Addition of two 1-digit numbers to 10, horizontal alignment

Addition of two 1-digit numbers to 10, vertical alignment

Addition of two 2-digit numbers (no renaming)

Addition of two 3-digit numbers (no renaming)

Addition of two 2-digit numbers, zero in addend (no renaming)

Addition of two 3-digit numbers, zero in addend (no renaming)

FIGURE 7.3 Sample Items Based on the Math Scope-and-Sequence Chart in Figure 7.2

2 + 3 =	5 + 1 =	4 + 4 =	2 + 8 =	0 + 9 =
3 + 6	0 + 4	2 + 5	8 + 1	2 + 3
13 + 25	43 + 52	28 + 50	57 + 21	64 + 33
183 + 215	637 + 121	843 + 126	241 + 530	389 + 410
25 + 50	61 + 20	48 + 30	27 + 60	85 + 10
243 + 305	727 + 102	631 + 250	814 + 105	174 + 620

termine the manner in which students derive a particular answer when solving a problem. More often than not, students solve math problems conventionally by utilizing standard school methods (i.e., algorithms). At times, however, students arrive at correct answers through what Ginsberg (1987) termed invented procedures. That is, students are unable to grasp the taught algorithm, so they design alternative means to derive the answer.

By way of illustration, consider the problem $43 - 27 = X$. The correct difference, 16, can be derived by (a) understanding the conceptual nature of place value and applying proper regrouping techniques, (b) failing to grasp the nature of place value conceptually, yet knowing how to apply regrouping techniques, or (c) knowing nothing about either place value or regrouping, but solving the problem using an invented procedure (for instance, by *counting on* from 27 to 43 and writing down the number of counts made along the way).

Process assessments allow one to identify the strategies by which students arrive at their answers. Rivera and Bryant (1992) noted two procedures that can be employed in a process assessment—passive assessment and active assessment. A passive process assessment is conducted by looking at a completed worksheet and analyzing a student's answer to a given problem. For example, consider the problem $43 - 27 = X$ presented earlier. A student's answer of 24 could well be the result of a regrouping miscue: The student probably thought something like "Three minus seven . . . can't do it because you have to subtract the smaller number from the larger one, so seven minus three is four. Four minus two is two . . . 24." Although this answer commonly results from overgeneralizing the basic rule that numbers of lesser values must be subtracted from numbers of greater value, one cannot be certain that this was indeed the strategy employed during problem solving. Perhaps instead the student counted on from 27 but forgot how many counts it took to get to 43. Memory failure is a common source of error in counting on to higher numbers. The obvious disadvantage with passive process assessment, therefore, is the uncertainty that exists when examining errors for defective strategy employment.

The second procedure, active process assessment, generally employs some form of flexible interviewing, whereby the student discusses aloud what she or he thought during computation. For instance, a student may be asked to "think out loud" while doing a math problem. By listening to the student's explanation, one can identify the strategies employed. The teacher generally asks follow-up questions to probe further the strategies being utilized by the student. To illustrate, consider a student who calculates 43 − 27 and states, "Three minus seven can't be done, so I borrow one from here (tens place) and put three, then I put one next to three (ones place), and 13 minus 7 is 6, three take away two is one . . . 16." A follow-up question might be "Okay. Tell me why you crossed out the four and put three above it." Based on the student's response, the teacher can gain insight into the student's knowledge of place-value concepts.

Up to this point, we have discussed the three key ingredients of standardized assessment: set administration procedures, objective scoring criteria, and a specified frame of reference. But proof of standardization entails examining the measures' reliability and validity. In order for a measure to be adequately standardized, there must be evidence of its reliability; in other words, it must yield consistent results (Anastasi & Urbina, 1997). Results achieved on a measure one day should match results achieved if the assessment is conducted again a short time later. And measures must also yield valid results; in other words, scores must reflect performance on the construct that the test claims to be assessing (Linn & Gronlund, 2000). A spelling test that consists of addition and subtraction items is not a spelling test, obviously, and the test's scores would never be considered a valid performance estimate of spelling abilities. But spelling test authors must go further than simply creating a measure that *looks* like it is assessing spelling. Spelling test authors must demonstrate that the items come from a legitimate source and meet basic statistical criteria (have content validity), produce results similar to established spelling tests (have criterion-related validity), and produce results that are associated with the construct being measured (have construct validity). Test authors can demonstrate their test's construct validity by showing that the measures produce results that relate to other written language skills; showing that students get higher test scores as they get older and become better spellers; demonstrating that the test differentiates known poor spellers from known good spellers; and so forth (Hammill et al., 1992).

We conclude this section on standardized versus nonstandardized assessments by pointing out that standardization is a matter of degree (Hammill & Bryant, 1991). There are few, if any, truly nonstandardized assessment procedures. All procedures include some instructions on how to give the test, conduct an observation, and so forth. They also, to some extent, guide the examiner in how to record student responses or behaviors. And the results have to be interpreted somehow. Thus it is not a question of whether an assessment is standardized or nonstandardized but, rather, of *how* standardized it is. Is it highly standardized or less standardized? Standardization should be considered along a continuum, and assessment instruments should be selected on the basis of evidence of their standardization, reliability, and validity. We now continue our discussion of how we assess students with special needs by looking at various measures that are used in assessment.

Screening Procedures

Sometimes teachers wish to identify quickly and efficiently who is struggling in a particular area (e.g., math, reading) and who is not. Usually, teachers can identify their students who are having problems just by working with them, but administering a screening measure helps validate those impressions. Although the most efficient screeners are group administered because good group tests provide valid scores in a short time, individual tests can be given. The screening process often leads to more diagnostic, comprehensive testing (Spinelli, 2002).

SCREENING USING VARIOUS PROCEDURES   Various types of screening instruments are available, some of them highly standardized and others less so. Torgesen and Bryant's (2005) *Test of Phonological Awareness* (TOPA-2+) is an example of a highly standardized instrument that can be used to screen students for phonological awareness and phonics skills. The test is group administered to kindergarten, first-grade, or second-grade children, and students who score below a set benchmark (a predetermined standard for success) are in need of more comprehensive testing.

But not all screening needs to be highly standardized. Several researchers have found that teachers know their students well enough to be able to complete rating scales about their abilities and provide valid and reliable information that can be used for screening purposes (Bryant, Bryant, Hammill, & Sorrells, 2004). Teachers who have had a month or two to observe and work with their students can be asked simply to rate each student's performance along a 5-point continuum from Poor, to Below Average, to Average, to Above Average, to Superior. Or they can be asked to complete a more detailed rating scale that spans academic and behavioral areas (see Figure 7.4). This scale was specifically created by Raskind and Bryant (2002) to be used as part of a comprehensive evaluation for assistive technology use, but it can also be used to gather information from teachers for screening purposes. When used properly, this scale and all other screening procedures can identify students who are in need of further testing.

SETTING BENCHMARKS   We described benchmarks earlier as predetermined standards for success. Although there is no preset benchmark that is established for all measures, Lynn Fuchs (2003) indicates that benchmarks are often established by the local school district and that many select the 25th or 16th percentile (Torgesen et al., 2001, Vellutino et al., 1996). Students whose screening results are below the set benchmark are typically administered more comprehensive, diagnostic assessments.

Diagnostic Assessments

Diagnostic measures can be compared to survey tests, because they survey, or assess, numerous different areas. Diagnostic measures provide more in-depth assessment than screening measures and take longer to administer. For that reason, screening measures are used to limit the number of students who need to be administered the longer, more time-consuming diagnostic measures. In our example

FIGURE 7.4 Sample Rating Scale Used for Screening Purposes

FEAT Functional Evaluation for Assistive Technology Checklist of Strengths and Limitations	**Name:** _____ **Rater:** _____ **Date:** _____

Directions: During technology evaluations, specific limitations that may require compensatory intervention must be identified. It is also critical to identify specific strengths that the technology can tap into during compensation. Place a check in the appropriate column (Weak, Average, Strong) that in your opinion best depicts the abilities of the person being rated, when compared to age-mates, in the areas being evaluated.

Listening	Weak	Average	Strong
Differentiates between relevant and irrelevant information	_____	_____	_____
Hears and understands the spoken word	_____	_____	_____
Understands basic directions	_____	_____	_____
Pays attention to speaker for an appropriate timespan	_____	_____	_____
Comprehends rapid speech	_____	_____	_____
Distinguishes differences among sounds/words	_____	_____	_____
Responds appropriately to requests/instructions	_____	_____	_____
Other (specify)	_____	_____	_____

Overall Listening Skills

Speaking	Weak	Average	Strong
Pronounces words clearly and consistently	_____	_____	_____
Speaks with appropriate vocabulary	_____	_____	_____
Speaks with appropriate grammar	_____	_____	_____
Speaks well in everyday situations	_____	_____	_____
Discusses content that is appropriate to situation	_____	_____	_____
Can adjust language based on communication partner	_____	_____	_____
Speaks well, with appropriate tone, pitch, loudness	_____	_____	_____
Other (specify)	_____	_____	_____

Overall Speaking Skills

Reading	Weak	Average	Strong
Has requisite visual abilities	_____	_____	_____
Reads words accurately	_____	_____	_____
Understands meaning of individual words	_____	_____	_____
Reads with speed/fluency	_____	_____	_____
Is able to maintain place on page	_____	_____	_____
Understands different sentence structures (e.g., simple, complex)	_____	_____	_____
Understands the meaning of connected text (i.e., phrases, sentences, paragraphs)	_____	_____	_____
Other (specify)	_____	_____	_____

Overall Reading Skills

Writing	Weak	Average	Strong
Applies capitalization/punctuation rules	_____	_____	_____
Spells correctly	_____	_____	_____
Writes neatly with little difficulty	_____	_____	_____
Uses appropriate grammar	_____	_____	_____
Uses appropriate vocabulary	_____	_____	_____
Edits/proofs well	_____	_____	_____
Writes well conceptually	_____	_____	_____
Applies sense of audience effectively	_____	_____	_____
Other (specify)	_____	_____	_____

Overall Writing Skills

Mathematics	Weak	Average	Strong
Understands basic number concepts	_____	_____	_____
Calculates basic arithmetic problems	_____	_____	_____
Knows basic math vocabulary	_____	_____	_____
Calculates quickly	_____	_____	_____
Applies math concepts to life situations	_____	_____	_____
Has a sense of reasonable versus unreasonable answer (i.e., can estimate)	_____	_____	_____
Other (specify)	_____	_____	_____

Overall Mathematics Skills

Memory	Weak	Average	Strong
Has long-term recall of previously learned information (words/objects/designs/pictures)	_____	_____	_____
Has short-term recall of recently presented information (words/objects/designs/pictures)	_____	_____	_____
Follows simple directions in sequence	_____	_____	_____
Follows complex directions in sequence	_____	_____	_____
Other (specify)	_____	_____	_____

Overall Memory Skills

Organization	Weak	Average	Strong
Understands cause/effect relationships	_____	_____	_____
Manages personal and work time	_____	_____	_____
Manages personal and work space	_____	_____	_____
Makes plans to accomplish tasks	_____	_____	_____
Organizes ideas into a cohesive whole	_____	_____	_____
Can understand abstract concepts	_____	_____	_____
Other (specify)	_____	_____	_____

(continues)

FIGURE 7.4   Continued

Overall Organization Skills

Physical/Motor	Weak	Average	Strong
Exhibits physical strength/endurance	_____	_____	_____
Has good posture	_____	_____	_____
Controls objects (grasps/manipulates)	_____	_____	_____
Moves about freely	_____	_____	_____
Has good positioning/orientation	_____	_____	_____
Other (specify)	_____	_____	_____

Overall Physical/Motor Skills

Behavior	Weak	Average	Strong
Stays on task	_____	_____	_____
Can work with peers	_____	_____	_____
Takes care of personal/school property	_____	_____	_____
Cooperates with people of authority	_____	_____	_____
Other (specify)	_____	_____	_____

Overall Behavior Skills

Summary/Remarks

_____

_____

_____

_____

Source: From *Functional Evaluation for Assistive Technology,* by M. Raskind and B. R. Bryant, 2002. Austin, TX: Psycho-Educational Services. Reprinted with permission.

of the TOPA-2+, students who did not meet benchmarks might then be administered the *Comprehensive Test of Phonological Processes* (CTOPP) (Wager, Torgesen, & Rashotte, 1999) to identify strengths and weaknesses across phonological awareness abilities. Alternatively, they might be given the *Test of Word Reading Efficiency* (TOWRE) (Torgesen, Wager, & Rashotte, 1999) to assess in-depth phonics skills.

Two types of diagnostic measures are typically used in schools. The first is a global achievement measure that examines a variety of areas. The *Woodcock-Johnson Revised Test of Achievement* (WJ-R) (Woodcock & Mather, 1989, 1990) is one such diagnostic measure. It contains over a dozen subtests that examine reading, writing, mathematics, and other areas of achievement. By administering all WJ-R subtests, examiners obtain a comprehensive overview of a student's skills across subject matter.

The *Gray Diagnostic Reading Test,* 2nd Edition (GDRT-2) (Bryant, Wiederholt, & Bryant, 2004) is a second type of diagnostic measure. This test examines only reading, but it does so by examining many subcomponents of reading, such as comprehension and vocabulary. Comparing and contrasting scores within the measure provides for an intraindividual analysis of reading strengths and weaknesses. Many such tests provide detailed analyses of strengths and weakness across mathematics, writing, and other academic skills.

Diagnostic measures also exist for assessing behavior, attention, anxiety, adaptive behavior skills, and other areas related to school success. With these scales, "diagnostic measure" takes on a subtly different meaning. Not only are the measures broad-based in their content, but they may actually be used to diagnose a condition. One of the most popular scales used for assessing attention problems is the *Conners Teacher Rating Scale—Revised* (Conners, 1997). Because ADHD must be observed across several settings, this rating scale is completed by parents and teachers, who report on the child's behaviors at home and in the classroom. Such a procedure allows for an ecological assessment, because it looks at behavior across settings and locations and collects data from multiple sources—in this case, the parents and one or more teachers. With the Conners scale, the teacher reads a list of student behaviors and rates the extent to which each behavior is present for a particular child. The more behaviors the student exhibits that correspond to those who have ADHD, the greater the likelihood that the student has ADHD.

The *Learning Disabilities Diagnostic Inventory* (LDDI) (Hammill & Bryant, 1998) serves a similar purpose for LD identification. The rater reads a list of behaviors that the student exhibits. The more he or she "looks like" a student with LD, the greater the likelihood that the student *has* LD. The measure's results, when combined with other assessment information, may lead to a diagnosis of LD.

Before we continue, we should make one additional comment about diagnostic measures. We noted earlier that diagnostic tests are not so named because they "diagnose" conditions. Although usually true, this statement requires clarification. The results of diagnostic tests may lead to a diagnosis of a disability by special education team members. The team is typically composed of the student's parents, psychologists, diagnosticians, teachers, a representative from special education, and the principal and other professionals. Team members examine the data provided by diagnostic tests, observations, work samples, and so on and come to a decision about a person's eligibility for special education services. Although test scores are key contributors to the process, it is important to remember the oft-cited dictum, "Tests don't diagnose, people diagnose" (Hammill & Bryant, 1998).

Observations

Teacher observations provide valuable data that should be combined with the data accumulated using other assessments to make educational decisions (Kubiszyn & Borich, 2003). There is an old saying by one of professional baseball's greats, Yogi Berra, a man known for making statements that are somewhat off-base. He once said, "You can observe a whole lot just by watching." On the surface, this statement seems redundant; watching and observing are seemingly the same. But this is not necessarily true. Rather, people watch so that they can observe. Watching is seeing. Observing is seeing *and* learning *and* making decisions about what you are seeing.

There are numerous ways that teachers can observe students and make performance judgments (see the chapter on behavior). Here, we provide an example that yields objective data on students as they work.

It is important to observe students during seatwork to identify whether inadequate performance is due to inability or a lack of effort. Try using a record-keeping device similar to the one offered by Deno and Merkin (1977). With this device, incidents of off-task behavior are noted for the student *and* for peers in alternating 30-second intervals. Figure 7.5 illustrates the technique.

FIGURE 7.5 Example of a Behavior Observation Record Used During Observations

Target Student _____											
Behavior	1	2	3	4	5	6	7	8	9	10	Total
Talking aloud without permission											
Acting out											
Touching/hitting											
Leaving seat											
Making noise											
Other											

Peers

Behavior	1	2	3	4	5	6	7	8	9	10	Total
Talking aloud without permission											
Acting out											
Touching/hitting											
Leaving seat											
Making noise											
Other											

Comparison

Behavior	Target Student	Peers	Ratio
Talking aloud without permission			
Acting out			
Touching/hitting			
Leaving seat			
Making noise			
Other			

Source: Adapted from *Data-based Program Modification,* by S., Deno, and P. Merkin, 1977, Reston, VA: Council for Exceptional Children.

The approach is quite simple. Determine beforehand which students in the class will serve as the peer observants (for instance, two students in a row). Then observe the target student for 30 seconds. If the student is on-task (that is, involved in seatwork) for the entire 30 seconds, a plus (+) is recorded in the box. If off-task behaviors (these must be defined) are observed at any time in the 30-second interval, a minus (−) is recorded. Then observe the first peer student for 30 seconds, recording on-task or off-task behavior in the same way. The target student is observed again, then the second peer student, and so forth until the twenty 30-second intervals have passed (ten for each student). Peer performance is important because it serves as a basis for comparison. One would not expect the target student to be on-task when everyone else in the class was not. To arrive at an assessment of on-task performance, simply divide the target student's total number of pluses by the number of pluses for the peers. The resulting quotient provides an index of on-task behavior. Such data are helpful when one is trying to identify why a student performs poorly on seatwork; the student's off-task behaviors cannot help but affect performance and should be considered in conjunction with other performance measures.

Interviews

Teachers can obtain a great deal of important information about the children they teach from their students' parents or guardians. When developing a diagnostic profile of a student, evaluators ask parents or guardians questions about their child's birth, developmental milestones, illnesses, social skills, and interests. This case history can provide basic information that helps the teacher or educational

● Teachers can obtain a great deal of important information about the development of a child from their students' family members.

diagnostician better understand the child's overall development. However, because recall of developmental history may be sketchy or not totally accurate, one should not rely too heavily on this information. Rather, one should interpret it, along with information obtained from other teachers and from the students themselves, within the total context of assessment data.

Teachers and students can also be interviewed. Overton (2000) suggests that teachers are in a unique position to consider five important characteristics of their students:

1. How is the student prepared for class each day?
2. Describe how the student begins assignments during class.
3. How does the student perform during distractions?
4. How often does the student complete homework assignments?
5. How often does the student respond during class discussions? (p. 331)

Think-aloud interviews can be used with students and are a type of process assessment aimed at identifying, insofar as possible, the cognitive strategies students use to solve mathematics problems, comprehend reading material, explore a social studies scenario, conduct a science experiment, and so forth (McLoughlin & Lewis, 2005). In the think-aloud interview, one asks a student to think out loud as he or she performs a task. Interview interjections might include (a) "What are you thinking?" (b) "How will you solve this task or problem?" (c) "What is another way to solve the problem?" (d) "What do you think the answer might be and why do you think that?" and (e) "How would you explain this problem to another student?"

Several factors must be present for the think-aloud interview to be used appropriately. First, the "interviewer" must be a good observer of student performance. Second, the person must be knowledgeable about the scope and sequence of the curriculum being used. Third, the interviewer must be familiar with cognitive strategies that the student may be employing (McLoughlin & Lewis, 2005). For example, if a student is asked to explain (think out loud) how to add a group of four blocks to a group of five blocks, and the student puts the two groups together and then starts counting from one to arrive at the answer, this student must be assessed (interviewed) further to determine the extent of her or his knowledge of numbers and groups and of her or his ability with the "count on" addition strategy. The interview questions might include "What is an easier way to count all the blocks besides starting with one?" and (given five blocks) "What different arrangements can you make with the blocks to show five?"

Through the think-aloud interview, it is possible to gain an understanding of how a student approaches the problem or task and of what strategies are being used. This information may lead to the development of new instructional objectives or to a change in the intervention. The interview information, along with other data, can help teachers better understand the processes their students use to solve problems or tasks and the effectiveness of these processes.

Although "thinking out loud" can be effective, many children with learning problems have difficulty expressing their thoughts aloud and require a different interviewing method. Zigmond, Vallecorsa, and Silverman (1983, p. 219) provide an example of a second type of interview, wherein the teacher (T) and student (S) engage in dialog about the problems on a worksheet.

T: Tell me what you did in problem 3, step by step [638 + 294, to which the student answered "8132"].

S: I added 8 and 4, put down the 2 and carried the 1. 1 and 3 is 4 and 9 is 13. 6 and 2 is 8.

T: Why did you carry the 1 when you added 8 and 4 (points to ones column) and not when you added 4 and 9 (points to tens column)?

S: I think you only do that here (points to ones column).

T: OK, now tell me what you did in problem 6 [74 − 38 = 44].

S: 8 take away 4 is 4. 7 take away 3 is 4.

T: Now go to number 10 [In the number 56,493, what number is in the thousands place—student responded 56; tens place—9; hundreds place—493; ones place—3: ten thousands place—56493]. How do you know which is in the ones place?

S: It's the first place.

T: What do you mean?

S: It's always over here (points to the number on the right).

T: How do you know which is the tens place?

S: It's next to the ones.

T: What about the hundreds place?

S: I don't know. I forget.

T: Can you write the number one hundred?

S: (writes) 100

T: Can you write the number one hundred thirty-six?

S: (writes) 10036

T: Can you write forty-two?

S: (writes) 42

T: Sixty-seven?

S: (writes) 67

Both interviewing methods serve the same purpose. Teachers may choose one to use consistently or may alternate the methods for the sake of variety. The key is to use some form of interview to identify efficient and inefficient strategies that are being employed.

Rating Scales and Checklists

Rating scales and checklists are valuable sources of information that can be used as part of the assessment process (Reynolds, Livingston, & Willson, 2006). Typically, rating scales and checklists provide a listing of skills or abilities, and the rater provides responses indicating how well a person performs each skill. Sometimes the responses are dichotomous—that is, the skills are either present or absent. Dichotomously scored rating scales are really checklists. Other scales offer a range of responses and use a Likert-type response format, named after Rensis Likert who first used the procedure (Kubiszyn & Borich, 2003). Figures 7.6 and 7.7 provide examples of these types of scoring options.

Figure 7.6 demonstrates the use of a checklist to examine phonological awareness (PA) skills; Figure 7.7 is a rating scale to examine writing skills. Here the user divides skills into two categories: composition and transcription (Smith, 1982). Composition skills are those associated with the cognitive complexities of the writing task. Transcription, on the other hand, entails more editorial or clerical skills.

FIGURE 7.6 Sample Dichotomously Scored Rating Scale (Checklist) for Phonological Awareness (PA)

Phonological Awareness Rating Scale

Based on your knowledge of _____, rate the student's skill level using the following criteria:

0 = The skill is never demonstrated or is emerging.   1 = The skill is approaching mastery or has been mastered.

PA Skill: The ability to	0	1	PA Skill: The ability to	0	1
Match the ending sounds of words, starting with the vowel sound (rhyming)	____	____	Segment the initial consonant or consonant cluster from the vowel and sounds spoken after it (onset-rime blending)	____	____
Produce groups of words that begin with the same initial sound (alliteration)	____	____	Blend phonemes into words (phoneme blending)	____	____
Segment sentences into spoken words (sentence segmentation)	____	____	Segment words into individual phonemes (phoneme segmentation)	____	____
Blend syllables to say words (syllable blending)	____	____	Manipulate phonemes in spoken words (phoneme manipulation)	____	____
Segment words into syllables (syllable segmentation)	____	____			
Blend the initial consonant or consonant cluster with the vowel and sounds spoken after it (onset-rime blending)	____	____	Total	____	____

Comparing ratings allows one to examine the strengths and weaknesses across components within writing abilities.

A different type of writing rating scale is depicted in Figure 7.8. Here, a student's writing skills can be evaluated along a continuum. We have labeled this a holistic evaluation scale, but that really is somewhat of a misnomer. Even though a single, overall rating is assigned, the scale is somewhat *analytical* (broken down, as opposed to a unified whole) because it considers specific elements of writing.

Work Samples

Work sample analysis is a procedure that helps teachers assess academic skills by looking at their permanent products (McLoughlin & Lewis, 2005). Teachers can examine student work to identify types and frequencies of errors. This information can help teachers establish instructional objectives or select a new intervention.

The most common type of work sample analysis is error analysis, which is fairly easy to conduct. The teacher (a) examines work sample products, (b) documents error types, (c) asks students to explain how they arrived at an erroneous solution, and (d) makes instructional recommendations. For instance, in mathematics, the teacher could (a) examine story problems completed by students, (b) record the percentage correct, (c) examine each problem to determine the types of

FIGURE 7.7　Sample Likert-type Rating Scale

Written Language Rating Scale

Based on your knowledge of _____, rate the student's skill level using the following criteria:

1 = The skill is never demonstrated.

2 = The skill is emerging.

3 = The skill is sometimes demonstrated but erratic.

4 = The skill is approaching mastery, but not there yet.

5 = The skill has been mastered.

Composition Skills: The ability to	1	2	3	4	5
Generate ideas	____	____	____	____	____
Select words	____	____	____	____	____
Place words in proper syntactic order	____	____	____	____	____
Subtotals	____	____	____	____	____
Total _____					

Transcription Skills: The ability to	1	2	3	4	5
Spell words correctly	____	____	____	____	____
Use proper punctuation	____	____	____	____	____
Capitalize correctly	____	____	____	____	____
Write legibly	____	____	____	____	____
Subtotals	____	____	____	____	____
Total _____					

errors made (for instance, erroneous computation, incorrect diagram to depict information, incorrect use of "key word" technique), (d) ask students to explain how they solved the problems, and (e) identify additional instructional objectives, based on the error types and student explanations, to rectify the problems. In oral reading, the teacher could record error types (such as substitutions, omissions, additions) and the number of errors. If the number of incorrect responses is significant, a remedial plan can be instituted.

The error analysis procedure can yield good information for designing the instructional program. It is important to ask students to explain their answers. Through careful analysis of work samples, coupled with student explanations, teachers can pinpoint faulty conceptual or procedural knowledge that can then be remediated.

School Records

Teachers glean information about their children from a variety of sources, such as the measures we described above. But they can also find information in students' cumulative folders (or cumulative records or files, as they are also called), which contain academic and behavioral history data (Spinelli, 2002).

FIGURE 7.8 Holistic Rating Scale for Writing Samples

Examinee/Writer: _____   Passage Title/Topic: _____

Circle the appropriate rating below:

Score of 6: Superior

- Addresses the topic fully and explores ideas thoughtfully
- Shows substantial depth, fullness, and complexity of thought
- Demonstrates clear, focused, unified, and coherent organization
- Is fully developed and detailed
- Evidences superior use of vocabulary, syntactic variety, and transition; may have a few minor flaws
- Devoid of spelling, capitalization, and spelling errors
- Written neatly (if handwritten)

Score of 5: Strong

- Addresses the topic clearly and explores ideas
- Shows some depth and complexity of thought
- Is effectively organized
- Is well developed with supporting details
- Evidences control of vocabulary, syntactic variety, and transition; may have some flaws
- Almost no spelling, capitalization, or spelling errors
- Written with adequate legibility (if handwritten)

Score of 4: Competent

- Adequately addresses the topic and explores ideas
- Shows clarity of thought, but may lack complexity
- Is organized

- Is adequately developed, with some detail
- Demonstrates competency in vocabulary and syntax; may have some flaws
- Some spelling, capitalization, and spelling errors
- Written legibly (if handwritten)

Score of 3: Weak

- Some distortion of ideas
- Shows simplistic thought and lacks complexity
- Has problems with organization
- Provides few supportive details; may be underdeveloped
- Demonstrates considerable flaws in vocabulary and syntax
- Many spelling, capitalization, and spelling errors
- Sections of the passage have poor legibility (if handwritten)

Score of 2: Very Weak

- Demonstrates serious inadequacies in one or more of the areas listed . . . [for a score of] 3 above

Score of 1: Incompetent

- Fails in the attempt to discuss the topic
- Is off topic
- Is so incompletely developed as to suggest incompetence
- Is wholly incompetent with regard to spelling, capitalization, and punctuation
- Is nearly or completely illegible

Source: From *Teaching and Assessing Writing* (2nd ed.), by E. M. White, 1994, San Francisco: Jossey-Bass.

School records can be a valuable source of information about student academic and social progress. Records of attendance, achievement test scores, curricular materials used during instruction, anecdotal notes, and student work can be examined to provide a composite overview of the student's progression through the grades. The information can be used to document particular problems that might have been evident in earlier grades, attendance patterns, techniques that were implemented previously, classroom and behavioral interactions, and teacher concerns. Again, although this is important information, some pieces (such as anecdotal notes) may need to be interpreted cautiously because of reliability concerns. That is, people may be inconsistent in their interpretation of information found in the records.

Portfolio Assessments

Portfolio assessment is used as a means of monitoring student learning and evaluating the effectiveness of instructional programs and decision making. Portfolios contain student-selected work samples and may contain student notes about how the samples were created and edited or improved.

Portfolio assessment can be used to examine student progress as it is related to curricular objectives and instructional methods, to focus more on process rather than just on product, to measure student academic achievement and classroom learning more directly, and to assist in evaluating the effectiveness of instruction.

Reynolds and colleagues (2006) note that portfolios are typically scored using evaluation rubrics. These scoring rubrics should

- Specify the evaluation criteria to be considered when evaluating the students' work products.
- Provide explicit standards that describe different levels of performance on each criterion.
- Indicate whether the criteria will be evaluated in a holistic or an analytical manner. (p. 263)

For students with learning and behavior problems, portfolio information should be related to curricular goals included in the IEP. Obviously, such information typically would include academic and social skills, but information can also be provided on behavior and adaptive functioning, academic and literacy growth, strategic learning and self-regulation, and language and cultural aspects that can be linked to the IEP (Swicegood, 1994).

Students with learning and behavior problems typically lack specific academic skills and effective cognitive strategies that promote efficient learning. Therefore, portfolio assessment should include examples of completed products (for instance, math problems or writing samples), with analyses that document the types of strategies employed during problem solving or drafting/editing. Writing samples can be accompanied by notes taken during writing conferences.

Frequent measures of student progress can help teachers monitor learning and implement decision-making criteria. For example, it is possible to measure fluency in oral reading twice a week to determine the effect of the instructional intervention: Collect rate data and analyze student growth, implement decision rules regarding rate of student progress, and store graphs in the portfolio until the next timing. The important point about the time line used for collecting and assessing portfolio items is frequency. For students with learning and behavior difficulties, monitor progress regularly to determine whether instructional techniques are indeed promoting student academic growth. See the Making a Difference feature to learn how a special education teacher's effective use of alternative assessments was a real turning point in one student's education.

Making a Difference

The Benefits of Student Self-Determination in the Assessment Process

Quannah Parker-McGowan
Director of Special Education
Achievement First Charter Schools
New York, NY

Victoria had a severe processing disorder and had been in a self-contained special education classroom since the second grade. By the time she came to our school for sixth grade, where she would be fully included in the general education classroom, she had developed an angry and defiant attitude as a way of compensating for her feeling of inadequacy in school. My challenge as her special education teacher was (1) to adapt assessments so that they did not rely heavily on visual input, and (2) to administer these assessments to Victoria in a way that was not intimidating for her.

Over a period of months, we settled into a system that met her learning needs and made her feel successful. In mathematics, Victoria had severe difficulty in distinguishing between different symbols such as "x" and "+." To help her see the difference, I would highlight "x" in pink highlighter and "+" in blue. In reading, I would read passages aloud after she read them independently, and then she would read them again to herself.

I collaborated with the general education teacher to help institute the use of portfolios for all the students in the class as a method of ongoing assessment. Victoria and I met regularly to pick out samples of work that showed gains toward attainment of her IEP goals. Allowing Victoria to participate in the portfolio process not only allowed her to see the concrete academic gains she was making but also made her a contributing member of her own instructional "team."

Finally, I worked with general education teachers to switch from standard paper-and-pencil tests to project-based assessments for subjects such as history and science. At the end of a unit, the entire class would take part in a week-long independent project that demonstrated mastery of a skill or topic. This type of assessment was not threatening to Victoria because it was hands-on, yet it still required her to demonstrate her knowledge.

Finding ways to authentically gauge Victoria's learning in a way that increased her confidence rather than her anxiety was difficult but possible, and it transformed her as a student. Victoria came to me in the sixth grade as an angry student and left as an eighth grader more confident in her abilities. ●

Performance Assessments

Salvia and Ysseldyke (2001) described performance assessments as those in which students are required to perform specific skills, such as writing a story. This is contrasted with giving separate tests for capitalization, punctuation, and spelling, for example, and using the total score as a means to estimate writing performance.

Teachers often conduct performance assessments in writing throughout a semester. We have already provided an approach for evaluating writing samples in Figure 7.7. Of course, writing is not the only area in which a performance evaluation is conducted. In science and chemistry classes, students may be required to do laboratory work as part of a test. Or perhaps part of a biology test involves fieldwork, where students are required to go outside to photograph examples of specific kinds of plant or animal life. Obviously, the authenticity of such a test is greater than that of a multiple-choice test that has students respond to paragraphs they read or questions they have to answer.

Behavioral Assessments

All students go through periods in their lives that affect their behavior and personality. Events at home or with their peers can cause children to act out or to become depressed or anxious. Typically, these periods do not last long, and the students bounce back. For some students, however, behavior problems occur for a long time and are systematic. For these students, assessments can help identify emotional problems that are symptomatic of disabilities.

There are several assessments that are designed to identify behavior problems in children and adolescents. One such measure is the *Behavior Rating Profile—Second Edition* (BRP-2) (Brown & Hammill, 1990), which assesses children for behavior disorders. We mention this scale because it provides for an ecological assessment. That is, it contains ratings scales that are completed by the students' parent(s), the students' teacher, and the students themselves to provide data from three different perspectives. For the BRP-2, behaviors are listed that correspond to what researchers have determined to be indicative of emotional problems. The BRP-2 Teacher Rating Scale takes about 20 minutes to complete and includes 30 phrases that the teacher reads and rates as Very Much Like the Student, Like the Student, Not Much Like the Student, or Not at All Like the Student. Representative items include:

- Tattles on classmates
- Is an academic underachiever
- Doesn't follow class rules

The Parent Rating Scale takes about 30 minutes to complete and is similar to the teacher scale (of course, "the Student" is replaced with "My Child" in the ratings). Sample items include:

- Is verbally aggressive to parents
- Is shy, clings to parents
- Won't share belongings willingly

The Student Rating Scale actually provides three scores, one dealing with the home, one dealing with school, and one dealing with the student's peers. Home items include:

- My parents "bug" me a lot
- I have lots of nightmares and bad dreams
- I often break rules set by my parents

School items include:

- I sometimes stammer or stutter when the teacher calls on me
- My teachers give me work I cannot do
- The things I learn in school are not as important or helpful as the things I learn outside of school

Finally, peer items include:

- Some of my friends think it is fun to cheat, skip school, etc.
- Other kids don't seem to like me very much
- I seem to get into a lot of fights

www. sd 88. org

the scales, the responses to any one of these items may not be indica-
rious behavior problem. But students whose ratings are consistently
may well have serious behavioral or emotional conditions. The ad-
using ecological assessments, whether gathered in one scale or across
sures, is that they allow teachers and others to determine whether the
ccur in just one setting or are pervasive across multiple settings and
provide several examples of less standardized assessment procedures
9 on behavior concerns. All of the techniques contribute to identifying
haviors and ameliorating them.

ss-Monitoring Assessments

onitoring involves collecting data periodically and using the data to
uctional decisions. Curriculum based assessment (CBA) has gained in
as a technique for monitoring student performance while considering
goals and instructional techniques. Accordingly, CBAs are typically the
assessments of choice for monitoring student progress over time. Professionals use
assessment measures that determine how students are performing not only in relation to the peer group, but also in relation to the curriculum and instruction that
are presented daily. Recently, progress monitoring has also become a critical feature of learning disability identification procedures that employ the response to in-

WORKING together

RTI Implementation

With the passage of IDEA '04, school districts can now
use the response to intervention (RTI) procedure to
help in the learning disability identification process. This
procedure may use a multitiered approach to identify
early those students who may be at risk for having
learning disabilities and to intervene in kindergarten,
grade 1, or grade 2 to help reduce the likelihood that
students will be misidentified as having LD.

General education teachers work closely with special
educators to help set up a multitiered system wherein
young children are given curriculum based assessments (CBAs) in the fall of the school year. Those students who fall below preset benchmarks, usually set at
the 25th or 16th percentile, are targeted for small-
group supplemental instruction in the second tier.
Students receiving the supplemental instruction continue to receive regular class instruction in the core curriculum but also are provided additional, small-group
instruction using validated practices designed to help
them increase their skill levels to those of their peers.

Special educators can help general education teachers
identify reliable CBAs that yield valid results and can
also help teachers identify research-
based supplemental instructional procedures.

Every 2 weeks or so, CBAs are readministered
and provide an index of growth for each student receiving supplemental instruction. If the students are
making progress, no changes are made to the supplemental program. However, instruction for students
who are not making sufficient progress is modified to
better meet student needs. After 8 to 12 weeks of
supplemental instruction, midyear testing is used to
determine whether the students can exit the second
tier of intervention or need to continue such instruction for an additional 8 to 12 weeks. After spring
testing, students who do not make sufficient progress
may be identified as having LD if they meet additional, federally prescribed criteria.

Clearly, assessment plays a critical role in the RTI
process. Additional testing using highly standardized
tests may also be administered in the determination of
a learning disability, but CBA is at the heart of the assessment process.

tervention (RTI) procedure. See the Working Together feature for information about how general education teachers collaborate with special educators to establish a multitiered service delivery system for RTI implementation.

To assist educators in designing, implementing, and evaluating instruction to meet the needs of an increasingly diverse student population, assessment procedures must be versatile yet valid. With CBA, the content of the curriculum and the content found in the assessment are the same. The teacher uses material from the students' curricula to determine where students should be placed, what their instructional objectives should be, and how they are progressing. In this section, we describe (a) the purposes of CBA, (b) how to design curriculum based assessments, (c) data collection and analysis procedures, and (d) procedures for pairing instruction and evaluation. (The reader is referred to the literature on curriculum based measurement and precision teaching; both are excellent examples of CBA that use graphing, decision-making rules, and intervention recommendations to guide the instructional process.) As you read each section, think about a student you may know or have observed who has a disability. What considerations should occur at each step to help reduce the need for later adaptations based on the test's and the student's characteristics?

PURPOSES   Curriculum based assessment has several purposes:

- To measure directly the curriculum that is being taught
- To establish a link between students' IEPs and classroom instruction
- To provide a means for monitoring student progress and evaluating the effectiveness of the intervention being used to teach the instructional objective
- To obtain data during the pre-referral stage about students' progress in the general education setting without special education services
- To provide a more "culture-fair" means of assessing the progress of youngsters from culturally and linguistically diverse backgrounds
- To determine initial placement in a task analysis of skills

Thus, CBA offers an alternative to standardized testing as a means for teachers to place, monitor, and evaluate instructional programs and student progress.

DESIGNING CURRICULUM BASED ASSESSMENTS   There are two types of curriculum based assessments: CBA to identify the initial instructional objective placement, and CBA to measure students' progress with the identified instructional objective. Here, we borrow from Rivera and Smith (1994) to discuss procedures for designing CBA based on IEP goals. These CBAs are applicable for oral reading, mathematics, and language arts. To assess progress in social studies and science, teachers may want to use textbook chapter tests, teacher-made tests, and oral discussions and questioning. For assessment of written expression, teachers could use the procedures described below or analyze written work for the presence of story elements, mechanics (that is, spelling, handwriting, grammar, punctuation, and capitalization), or writing components (ideas, sequence, development, main ideas, and supporting details). For story problem solving and reading comprehension, teachers could use the procedures described below or the "think-aloud" procedures described previously in this chapter.

PLACEMENT   Before identifying instructional placement within the designated curriculum, teachers should refer to the IEP and identify the goals that are designated for instruction. By examining the goals, teachers can begin to develop an idea of the content and skill areas that require instruction. The next step is to design the placement CBA. Taylor (2003) listed five steps to follow when constructing curriculum based assessment for instructional placement purposes (some school districts have CBAs already designed, and some instructional materials may contain CBAs).

STEP 1: Identify the goal to be assessed.

Examine the student's goals on the IEP. An example of a goal might be "The student will compute whole numbers."

STEP 2: Identify the instructional objectives (task analysis).

Task analyze Step 1 into smaller steps that can become instructional objectives. Instructional objectives for the goal identified in Step 1 might include: two-digit + one-digit numbers with no regrouping, two-digit + two-digit with no regrouping, three-digit + two-digit with no regrouping, three-digit + three-digit with no regrouping, two-digit + one-digit with regrouping, two-digit + two-digit with regrouping, three-digit + two-digit with regrouping, and three-digit + three digit with regrouping to the tens and hundreds place. Each of these steps could be treated as an instructional objective, depending on the student's ability level.

STEP 3: Develop test items for each instructional objective.

Develop sufficient items (four or five) for each objective to ensure that the student has enough opportunities to respond in the time frame allowed in the testing situation. Develop several versions of the CBA for testing across several days.

STEP 4: Determine standards of performance (mastery levels).

Identify a performance standard for each objective. The criterion can be stated in percentage correct (80 percent or 90 percent accuracy) or rate (100 words per minute correct); data collection procedures are discussed below. To determine an appropriate performance standard or criterion, (a) have students in the general education classroom perform the skill, and take the average of those scores as the criterion, or (b) use a "percentage-correct" criterion or fluency criterion based on the type of skill being assessed (acceptable percentage-correct criteria usually range from 80 to 100, depending on the skill; fluency depends on the skill), or (c) use the school district's performance standards.

STEP 5: Administer and interpret the CBA instrument.

Have students take the CBA several times; one administration is not sufficient to give an accurate picture of students' instructional abilities. Analyze test item results for each instructional objective; the scores can be averaged to arrive at the student's instructional levels of performance. Instructional objectives with results that fall below the criterion level are targeted for instruction. Students should know the time limits in which they will work and the standards that apply (for instance, work quickly, skip problems you don't know, reduce fractions, show your work, finish all of the pages).

DATA COLLECTION AND ANALYSIS PROCEDURES   A major component of curriculum based assessment is the collection and evaluation of data for determining placement and progress in an instructional sequence. A data collection system that accurately measures the targeted skill is selected, and teachers implement specific data analysis procedures to determine whether their intervention is indeed making a difference with the students.

Teachers can incorporate charting into their progress monitoring using CBA data. An example of this is found in Figure 7.9. Here, a student has been given

FIGURE 7.9   Sample Chart Depicting Correct Calculations Per Minute (CCPM)

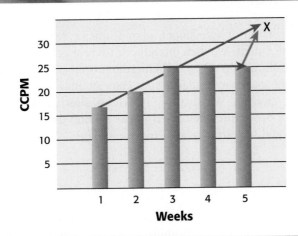

forty addition and subtraction facts to calculate in 1 minute. The number of items answered correctly in that time span (calculations correct per minute, CCPM) is graphed on a sheet of paper. The students can do this themselves in order to see their own progress. In our sample, the student's scores were graphed weekly. Through week 3, the student was making progress toward his end-of-semester objective (marked with an X). But then, for three consecutive weeks, the student's scores plateaued (remained steady). We have drawn an arrow to show how much progress is needed in the short time remaining before the end of the semester. The arrow demonstrates that changes must be made in the program in order to ensure sufficient progress toward the student's goal.

How Do We Adapt and Modify Assessments for Students with Special Needs?

Assessment adaptations involve any change in administration, scoring, and interpretation procedures that are made specifically because of a test taker's ability. Assessment adaptations are made in order to level the playing field. The "playing field" comparison is often heard in discussions of assessment adaptations (Dolan & Hall, 2001), because such adaptations are designed to ensure that each test taker has the same chance as any other student to succeed, whether the assessment is a high stakes test or Friday's spelling quiz.

McLoughlin and Lewis (2005) noted that test adaptations can take a variety of forms. The *Assessment Accommodation Checklist* (Elliott, Kratochwill, & Gilbertson, 1998) provides more than 70 adaptations within eight domains:

- Motivation
- Assistance prior to administration of the test
- Scheduling
- Setting
- Assessment directions

- Assistance during assessment
- Use of equipment or adaptive technology
- Changes in format

We begin our discussion of assessment adaptations by exploring universal design as it applies to assessment. We then introduce different adaptations categories. We will conclude our discussion of assessment adaptations by examining two specific applications where assessment adaptations may or may not be warranted: high stakes testing and grading. We also briefly discuss alternative assessments. Many of the adaptations procedures described in the section can be generalized to any number of additional scenarios related to assessments.

Universal Design

The term universal design refers to barrier-free systems that meet the needs of everyone, including people with disabilities (Smith, 2007). Initially used in conjunction with accessible housing for people with and without disabilities, universal design has expanded to teaching and testing. The premise is that curricula and assessments should be made accessible to all students.

Universal design has always been about equity and fairness—establishing a mindset that whenever something is being constructed, whether it is a house or a lesson or a test, that "something" should be constructed in such a way that all people can use it. But fairness can best be achieved by considering access when that "something" is being built, not afterwards. As Heubert and Hauser (1999) put it, "fairness, like validity, cannot be properly addressed as an afterthought once the test has been developed, administered, and used. It must be confronted throughout the interconnected phases of the testing process, from test design and development to administration, scoring, interpretation, and use" (p. 81). For classroom applications, teachers can create classroom assessments for universal access and choose commercially prepared tests that are likewise universally accessible.

With regard to universal design, Thompson, Johnstone, and Thurlow (2002) provide some suggestions for making tests more accessible to all students:

- **Inclusive assessment population.** When developing items, think about all students who will participate in the assessment. Ideally, examinees would be afforded equal opportunity to prepare for a test.
- **Precisely defined test content.** Define what is to be tested so that irrelevant cognitive, sensory, emotional, and physical barriers can be removed.
- **Accessible, nonbiased items.** Build accessibility into items from the beginning, and use bias review teams to ensure that quality is retained in all items.
- **Amenable to accommodations.** Test design must facilitate the use of need accommodations (for instance, all items can be communicated in braille).
- **Simple, clear, and intuitive instructions and procedures.** Make sure that students are easily able to follow the directions for taking a test.
- **Maximum readability and comprehensibility.** For example, use plain language strategies and other approaches that reduce ambiguity and increase understandability.
- **Maximum legibility.** Characteristics that ensure easy decipherability are applied to text, tables, figures and illustrations, and response formats.

● To make assessments accessible to all students, teachers should give simple, clear, and intuitive instructions and ensure that students are easily able to follow the directions.

Adaptation Categories

Adaptations tend to cluster around four basic areas: input adaptations, output adaptations, time and/or schedule adaptations, and location adaptations. We add a fifth area, academic qualifications, that deals more with curriculum issues than with testing adaptations.

INPUT ADAPTATIONS   Input adaptations involve how students access test stimuli and questions. Hammill et al. (1992) identified three testing input formats: listening (the test taker listens to instructions and/or test questions), reading print (words and numbers), and looking at stimuli, such as spatial tests that have the student look at a one-dimensional, unfolded drawing and ask what the object would look like if folded into a three-dimensional object. The input of test items should suit the needs of all students, including those who have a disability. For example, a student with a reading learning disability is unlikely to do well on a science test if he or she has to read the question. In this instance, recognizing student needs allows teachers to adapt the test input to allow the student to demonstrate acquisition of science knowledge.

One of the key considerations for input adaptations deals with the content that is being assessed by the test. Think about Sonya, a student we met earlier in Mr. Gomez's class. In 2 weeks, she is going to take two tests, back-to-back, that involve reading paragraphs and responding to multiple-choice questions. Both input formats involve reading print. The first test is a measure of reading comprehension, and the second test assesses knowledge of science concepts. Because Sonya has a learning disability in reading, she struggles with both test formats, so she decides to speak with Mr. Gomez about possible input adaptations.

Probably, Sonya will not be allowed to use an adapted input format for the reading comprehension test, but she is likely to receive adaptations for the science test. Why? The content of the reading test is *reading*. Adaptations that remove reading from the task defeat the purpose of the test; in other words, changing the input format changes the content being measured. This is one litmus test of any assessment adaptation. If the content being measured by the assessment is altered, the adaptation proposal is likely to be unsound.

Science, on the other hand, would not be altered in terms of content by removing reading as the input format. This is a science test that uses reading as an efficient way to test large numbers of students' understanding of science, because the assumption is that all (or at least most) test takers can read the paragraphs and questions. But reading ability itself is not being tested. Thus, because the content of the assessment is not being changed, the proposed adaptation is legitimate.

OUTPUT ADAPTATIONS Output adaptations involve how a test taker records responses to test questions. Hammill et al. (1992) identified several output formats: speaking, minor (providing a one- or two-word response); speaking, major (responding with sentences); manipulating objects (such as blocks or coins); marking an answer sheet (the familiar "fill in the bubble," for example); pointing; drawing; and writing print. If a test's output format interferes with its ability to provide valid scores for a student who has a disability, output adaptations can be made.

Consider Dondra, who has a neurological impairment that affects her fine motor skills. As a result of this disability, Dondra has trouble grasping a pencil, and when she finally controls it, she has difficulty using the pencil to write or make identifiable marks. Dondra is studying to take a social studies exam in 3 days. This exam requires students to read multiple-choice questions and respond by filling in bubbles of a Scantron sheet. Thus, the test's output format will make it nearly impossible for Dondra, because of her disability, to mark the answer sheet (completely filling in a bubble without going outside the bubble). Clearly, the test's content has nothing to do with filling in bubbles on an answer sheet. The test is measuring social studies skills. Therefore, it is likely that Mr. Gomez will alter the test's output format for Dondra to allow her to better respond to the test questions.

TIME AND/OR SCHEDULE ADAPTATIONS When appropriate, teachers may extend testing time and may also change the way the time is organized. Extended time is a common test adaptation. The idea is that people with reading disabilities, even if they are able to read the text, read at a much slower rate than their peers without disabilities. Thus, the slow readers will not have the same opportunity to complete the test as their peers without disabilities.

Most tests have time limits. As a rule of thumb, students are expected to complete about 75 percent of the test in the prescribed time allocation, and/or 80 percent of the students are expected to have an opportunity to respond to all items. Students with disabilities may not be able to complete the test in the allotted time, so time adaptations may be made. In addition, a test may be organized to provide 25 minutes for one test to be taken, give students a 5-minute break, and then call for a second test to be administered after the break. Some students, by the nature of their disability, may be fatigued and require a longer break between test administrations. Depending on the circumstances, the students may be allowed to wait longer before completing the rest of the test. Such an adjustment is a schedule adaptation.

LOCATION ADAPTATIONS   Location adaptations may change the setting in which a test is administered or the conditions of the test setting. Some students have disabilities that affect their ability to perform when distractions occur around them. For these students, a conventional testing setting, such as the classroom, may be inappropriate, and an isolated setting may be an appropriate location adaptation. In addition, some students with behavior issues may need to be tested in a situation that minimizes the effects of their behavior.

ACADEMIC QUALIFICATIONS   Although they are not really adaptations in the true sense of the word, academic qualifications are used to identify whether a person should take the test in the first place. Most students with disabilities, by law, participate in the general education curriculum, so they will take the same tests as their nondisabled peers. However, some students with severe disabilities have IEPs that focus on special academic areas such as life skills. In this instance, alternate assessments would be deemed more appropriate than a test that measures mastery of content that the students haven't been taught.

Adaptations for High Stakes Testing

The term high stakes testing implies that something important is at hand. It is generally applied to the testing that is mandated by state education agencies and local education agencies across the country to measure student achievement. High stakes testing has critical implications for students, parents, and schools:

> The use of large-scale achievement tests as instruments of educational policy is growing. In particular, states and local school districts are using such tests to make high-stakes decisions with important consequences for individual students. Three such high-stakes decisions involve tracking (assigning students to school, programs, or classes based on their achievement levels), whether a student will be promoted to the next grade, and whether a student will receive a high school diploma. These policies enjoy widespread public support and are increasingly seen as a means of raising academic standards, holding educators and students accountable for meeting those standards, and boosting public confidence in the schools. (Heubert & Hauser, 1999, p. 1)

Two of the three major uses of high stakes testing are most important for your students who have disabilities: promotion and graduation. The other use, tracking (or placement), usually is addressed though the students' IEPs. Promotion and graduation are based on students' knowledge of the curricular content, as demonstrated by their performance on the high stakes tests. For students with disabilities, test adaptations may be made to ensure that valid results are obtained on the high stakes measures.

CURRICULAR CONTENT   Usually, a team of experts meets and creates, for each subject area, a list of skills that they want taught to their state's students. Essentially, they are telling teachers across the state what it is important for all students in their classrooms to learn in kindergarten, grade 1, and so on through high school. Through this process, state departments of education tell their teachers and population, "This is important for all children in _____ (insert any state here). We care enough about our children's education that we have created a set of skills that all children should have before they go on to the next grade." Supposedly, when students have learned everything they should know in the third grade, they are ready to learn the material in the fourth grade, and so on until graduation.

ASSESSMENT ISSUES   Once the curriculum skills are set, a team of experts creates a test to measure those skills, and these state exams form the basis for most states' high stakes testing. Think about the logic behind the testing. It begins with "These are the skills that all students in the state of _____ need in order to graduate from high school." Then it moves to "If students need to know this information by the end of high school, what skills do they need at the end of the ninth grade? We'll create a test of those skills, which students will take at the end of ninth grade. If they fail the test, they have to repeat the ninth grade until they are ready for the tenth grade." Most states do not test at every grade level; they pick key grades for testing, usually 2 or 3 years apart. For most students in states with this policy, high stakes testing can begin as early as the third grade.

High stakes testing has a dramatic effect on teachers and students. First, teachers have to teach the skills that the state has specified. Fortunately, most publishers of basal textbooks understand this, so they work to ensure a correspondence between these enumerated skills and the skills that are taught in textbooks. If there are gaps, teachers are responsible for filling in those gaps to teach the skills that are mandated by the state but are not included in the textbooks.

Students are dramatically affected because if they fail the high stakes test (usually they have several opportunities to pass the test), they cannot be promoted and/or cannot graduate. It is easy to understand why high stakes testing was so named. The stakes are *very* high.

As we have already noted, not all students have to participate in high stakes testing. If a student has a disability, the student's IEP may state that he or she is exempt from such testing. However, states are increasingly devising alternative tests for students with disabilities. This approach stems from the belief that all students should be accountable for learning.

ADAPTATIONS ISSUES   If a student with a disability is going to take a high stakes test, test adaptation may be made to compensate for the student's disability. The decision whether test adaptations are warranted for any student is not made haphazardly. Usually, states and districts have set policies for making such a decision. Let's look at a six-step procedure that Bryant, Patton, and Vaughn (2000) created for making this decision. (*Note:* Throughout this section, we deal with disability-related adaptations for high stakes testing. For adaptations related to English language learners, see the Considering Diversity feature.)

STEP 1: As a committee, discuss whether the student should participate in state and district assessment.

This step involves three components:

1. IEP committees should examine a student's IEP goals and the content of the educational program or the state's curriculum.
2. IEP committees should examine the purpose of the state- and district-wide assessments and the content of the assessments.
3. IEP committees should determine the extent of the match between the student's educational program and the content of the assessment.

If these steps are taken, and if there is no match between the student's educational program and the content of the assessment, the student may be exempted from the testing. If there is a match, the next step in the process is to determine whether adaptations are warranted.

STEP 2: As a committee, discuss the student's need for test adaptations.

- IEP committees should examine the input and output formats of the state- and district-wide assessments.
- IEP committees should examine the IEP and student work samples to determine whether the formats of the assessment will yield valid results.

If the committee determines that the formats match the student's abilities, then there is probably no need for adaptations. If, however, the formats preclude achieving valid results because they tap into the student's limitations (for example, Sonya's inability to read precludes using reading as an input format that yields valid results), adaptations may be needed. Bryant, Seay, and Bryant (1999) have called this "tapping into the student's limitations" functional dissonance. There is dissonance, or conflict, between what Sonya can do and what she is being asked to do. When such a conflict exists, adaptations should be made.

STEP 3: As a committee, identify test adaptations that respond to the student's needs identified in Step 2.

In a previous section, we described several areas where adaptations typically take place. To review, are there input concerns that preclude obtaining valid results in a typical setting? Does the output format need to be altered to ensure that the student can complete the task? Or, if he or she reads slowly because of the disability, is more time needed to complete the task? Or, if the student is easily distracted, is a different testing location needed? All of these issues require attention in this step of the adaptations process.

STEP 4: As a committee, ensure that the committee's decision is documented.

On the IEP, it is important to document the committee's decision about whether a student should participate in testing and whether adaptations are needed if the student does participate. If the IEP committee decides that the student should not participate, then the committee should recommend an appropriate alternative assessment.

STEP 5: As a committee, collect data and develop procedures for monitoring the effectiveness of adaptations.

What type of data should teachers collect? Usually, there are four sources of data. First, collect student scores on two versions of the same test, with and without adaptations. Remember that it is entirely possible that the student will fail the test because he or she does not know the answers to the test items. Adaptations don't guarantee success; they are designed to guarantee only that the results are valid. If the student doesn't know the content and, with adaptations, demonstrates that lack of knowledge, then the results are valid.

Interview the student after testing to gauge his or her reactions. Did the adaptations work? What other issues may have arisen during testing that you need to know about?

Teachers also must be interviewed. This interview can be conducted at any time to learn about the student's academic characteristics, but it is important to know whether test adaptations have been used successfully in class. Ideally, each teacher will be a member of the committee and will provide input during each stage of the process.

Finally, interview the student's parents. What are their perceptions of the testing process and how it involves their son or daughter? Parents will be dramatically affected by the results of the high stakes assessment, so they need to have input throughout the process, and their reactions to the committee's findings and the testing process should be documented. Ideally, they too have been members of the committee, but that is seldom the case.

Considering *Diversity*

Adaptations for High Stakes Testing of English Language Learners

The National Assessment of Educational Progress (NAEP) periodically publishes the Nation's Report Card, which reviews educational testing information from America's schoolchildren. NAEP provides assessment adaptations guidelines to be followed during the administration of its supported assessments.

Frequently Provided Accommodations/ Adaptations for English Language Learners	Permitted by NAEP?
Native language version of test	No
Bilingual version of test (Spanish/English)	No (except for mathematics and science)
Bilingual word lists or glossaries (Spanish/English)	No (except for science)
Bilingual dictionary without definitions	Yes* (except for reading)
Directions translated aloud into native language or presented by audiotape	No
Student's oral or written responses translated into written English	No
Passages, other stimulus materials, or test questions read aloud in English or presented by audiotape	Yes (except for reading)
Directions read aloud in English or presented by audiotape†	Yes
Passages, other stimulus material, or test questions translated aloud into native language or presented by audiotape‡	No
Small group	Yes
One-to-one (tested individually)	Yes
Extended time	Yes
Preferential seating	Yes

*Not provided by NAEP, but school, district, or state may provide after fulfilling NAEP security requirements.

†Standard NAEP practice. Not considered an accommodation.

‡For Spanish/English bilingual mathematics and science, this would be standard NAEP practice. Not allowed otherwise.

Source: Adapted from http://nces.ed.gov/nationsreportcard/about/inclusion.asp

ADAPT in Action ● Gilbert—High Stakes Testing

Earlier we introduced you to Gilbert, a student in Ms. Grey's class. Gilbert is an honor student who has low vision, and he is scheduled to take his state's high stakes test in English language arts next week. Use the ADAPT framework to determine a way to ensure that the test produces valid results.

Ask,"What am I requiring the student to do?" Ms. Grey thinks about the task that students are to complete. "One section of the test requires that all students read test items and select a response from four or five choices. It is a typical multiple-choice test. Another section asks open-ended questions, and students have to write their answers on from five to eight lines of space in their answer booklet. And one of the writing sections of the test requires the students to write an essay."

Determine the prerequisite skills of the task. For this task, there are several prerequisite skills that Gilbert will need to have to accomplish the task. Ms. Grey notes, "Gilbert will have to see the print, read the instructions, read the test items and each response choice, tap his language arts knowledge to identify the answer to each question, and mark the answer. Some questions will require Gilbert to write a short answer, and still another segment of the test will require Gilbert to write an essay and edit and proof his work."

Analyze the student's strengths and struggles. Most of the students have the requisite skills. Gilbert possesses all of the requisite skills, as long as he is able to see the print. But without adaptations, he will not be able to read the questions or provide responses to some items.

Propose and implement adaptations from among the four categories. Remember that the content of the test has to remain unaltered. Although Gilbert appears to have all of the requisite skills except one, his inability to see standard print will certainly affect his test performance. In this instance, the adaptation is clear-cut. Gilbert will be allowed to use a magnification device (instructional material) because it is listed as appropriate and needed on his IEP.

Test to determine if the adaptations helped the student accomplish the task. Ms. Grey consulted with Gilbert's visual impairment specialist during high stakes tutoring sessions. The specialist worked with Gilbert and Ms. Grey to ensure that a magnification device was appropriate for Gilbert's needs. Throughout the tutoring sessions, including practice test administration, the magnification was effective in allowing Gilbert to read the test items, provide short-answer responses, and write the essay. After the exam, the specialist interviewed Gilbert to discuss the adaptations that were made. Gilbert admitted that the test was difficult, but the difficulty had nothing to do with the input format of the test. He could read the test just fine with the magnification, and he was able to write answers and the essay that were required by the test. The Tech Notes feature provides additional information about assistive technology adaptations available for students with low vision.

tech NOTES

Assistive Technology Accommodations for Students with Low Vision

Students who have low vision generally can read print as effectively with handheld magnifiers, when trained in their use, as with large print. Researchers have noted that students who use magnifiers attain an increase in reading speed and comprehension with regular print (Corn et al., 2002). Portable optical devices or assistive technology devices can be applied in most environments, including the classroom and libraries or study areas. Students who rely on nonportable devices, such as closed-circuit television (CCTV), to access print are obviously restricted when such devices are not available.

Students with low vision need to develop multiple options for accessing print in the environment. This would include the use of a number of nonoptical devices, prescription optical devices, and/or assistive technology, and the ability to use readers. Of course, students must be taught to use each option and match the most appropriate option to the task to achieve optimum efficiency.

A nonoptical device that may be helpful to some print readers is the use of theater gels (colored acetate) placed on the print. The student's functional vision evalu-

A closed-circuit TV system is one example of an assistive technology that can help students with visual disabilities.

ation should recommend the color that works best for a particular student. In all cases, general education teachers who have students with low vision in their classroom should work collaboratively with vision specialists so that they can best meet the students' needs on a daily basis. Inservice workshops on assistive technology devices for students who are blind or have low vision can be of great benefit to general education teachers as well.

Adaptations for Grading

Often, you will have to make adaptations in order for a test to yield valid results for your students who have special needs. For example, a student who uses a wheelchair and an augmentative communication device cannot be expected to take a spelling test using the conventional dictate–write testing procedure. Certainly, asking the student to write the spelling word will not result in a valid indication of spelling abilities. Thus, assessment adaptations must be considered.

ADAPT in Action ● Sonya—Adapting Test Input

Earlier we introduced you to Sonya, a student in Mr. Gomez's class. Sonya is new to the school and has serious reading problems. She is unable to decode words and has very little comprehension of written materials. Mr. Gomez has just completed a science unit and is about to administer a paper-and-pencil, multiple-choice test to his students. Think about Sonya and the problems such a test might present. Use the ADAPT framework to find a way to test Sonya's knowledge of the science unit that produces valid results.

Ask, "What am I requiring the student to do?" Mr. Gomez thinks about the task he had the students complete. "I am requiring that all students read test items and select a response from four choices. It is a typical multiple-choice test."

Determine the prerequisite skills of the task. For this task, there are several prerequisite skills (or requisite abilities, as they are also called) that Sonya will need to accomplish the task. Mr. Gomes notes, "Sonya will have to listen to my instructions, read the test items and each response choice, tap her science knowledge to identify the answer to each question, and circle the answer: A, B, C, or D."

Analyze the student's strengths and struggles. Sonya is able to listen to the teacher's instructions, tap her science knowledge to find the answer to each question, and circle her answer. But she will struggle with reading the test items and each response choice.

Propose and implement adaptations from among the four categories. Remember that the content of the test has to remain unaltered. Although Sonya appears to have all of the prerequisite skills except one, the one area with which she will struggle will probably mean that her test score will not be a valid indication of her science knowledge. There are several possible adaptations that could be made. First, Mr. Gomez could choose to administer the test orally to Sonya, who could say aloud the letter of her response. However, this could occur only away from the rest of the class. Mr. Gomez decides to put the questions on tape and instruct Sonya to follow along on the test sheet as each question and response choice is read aloud to her (instructional delivery) via the tape player (instructional material). She will circle her response to each question on the test, just like all of the other students.

Test to determine if the adaptations helped the student accomplish the task. Mr. Gomez has decided to administer the test twice, using alternative input formats. First, Sonya will take the test in typical fashion, by reading the test items and response choices. She will then retake the test after school using the tape player. If she does better on the listening format than on the reading format, Mr. Gomez will have evidence that the adaptation was successful and that Sonya was able to successfully complete the task.

After the tests were taken, Mr. Gomez scored the tests and found that Sonya did much better on the exam when she listened to the tape player than when she read the questions on her own. He decided that for all remaining tests, he will have one of his Advanced Placement students in another class record the items on tape for Sonya so that the results of the test can provide a valid indication of her content knowledge. Mr. Gomez considered several adaptations that he might try with Sonya after considering the ADAPT framework.

- **Instructional content:** Reduce the number of test items. He could sample the material and select the items that best differentiate between successful and unsuccessful students. These items could constitute Sonya's test.
- **Instructional materials:** As noted, Sonya could use a tape recorder to listen to the test questions and response choices.
- **Instructional delivery:** Mr. Gomez could read the items to Sonya, and she could either circle her answers on the scoring sheet or say her answers aloud.

Alternative Assessments

Students with disabilities are required to be a part of the national accountability system that involves high stakes testing. Such a requirement is designed to ensure that *all* students receive high-quality instruction and profit from their education. We have shown how students with disabilities may receive assessment adaptations to ensure that high stakes tests yield valid results—that is, that they provide a true indication of student abilities.

Although states differ in the options they make available to students with disabilities in high stakes testing, three different testing options are typically available.

1. Partial participation in testing: Students take parts of the test but do not have to take the entire test.
2. Out-of-level testing: Students may take a test from a lower grade level.
3. Alternative assessment: Students take a different assessment designed for a unique group of learners or an individually designed assessment.

Alternative assessments most broadly apply to students with severe disabilities and warrant attention here. It is important to realize that states and districts are still working out what alternative assessment means and how such results are to be included in a school's overall performance report (Turner et al., 2000). In Kentucky, students with severe disabilities (some 0.6 percent of all students) are assessed through alternative portfolios. As we have already seen, many students experience portfolio assessments, wherein their schoolwork becomes part of the documentation of their progress at school. Alternative portfolios are much like traditional ones, but their contents are somewhat different. Instead of including a term paper or notes from a writing conference, an alternative portfolio might include information about a student's performance across six areas:

1. Performance on IEP goals and objectives and student participation in developing a portfolio
2. Use of natural supports
3. Where the student performs the target behavior(s) or skills(s)
4. Number of settings in which the skill is used
5. Social interaction
6. Generalization of skills and knowledge

How well a student performs in these six areas can then be judged, and this evaluation is included in the school's overall assessment data. Such systems of accountability ensure that all students, even those with the most severe disabilities, are included in discussions about school improvement and accountability (Frase-Blunt, 2000).

summary

This chapter focuses on gathering data on students for a variety of purposes using a variety of methods and measures. We call this gathering of information assessment. Teachers have at their disposal many techniques and tools for gathering information about students, including those with special needs who are in their classroom. They can use tests, conduct interviews, and conduct observations using a variety of measures that differ in their level of standardization. Some measures and techniques are highly standardized, and some are less so, but teachers and other education professionals can gather information using procedures that are reliable and yield valid results. A combination of technically adequate measures that provide for norm-referenced, criterion-referenced, and non-referenced interpretations can be used to gather information about how well students are progressing toward their annual goals, about a student's intraindividual strengths and weaknesses, about how students compare to their peers along selected skill areas, and so on.

Increasingly, curriculum based assessments are being used in schools to gauge and monitor students' academic progress. Teachers can purchase commercial tests, but they can also create and use their own CBAs. These measures are administered frequently to ensure that students are making adequate yearly progress.

Periodically, students may be administered high stakes tests that determine whether they will pass on to the next grade and, ultimately, whether they will graduate from high school.

For students with disabilities, it is important that adaptations be made to ensure that the measures are yielding valid results. We examine two opportunities to consider how assessment adaptations could be made using the ADAPT framework: one dealing with high stakes testing and the other for grading purposes. We conclude the chapter by briefly addressing alternative assessments that can be conducted for students with severe disabilities as part of the current IDEA and No Child Left Behind accountability policies.

● self-test **QUESTIONS**

Let's review the learning objectives for this chapter. If you are uncertain and cannot "talk through" the answers provided for any of these questions, reread those sections of the text.

● **What is assessment, and how does it differ from testing?**

Assessment in education is a method by which you can gain information about students. Testing is one form of assessment, but it is not the only way you can get information. You gather assessment information by making observations, conducting interviews, and creating assessment portfolios.

● **What are the various types of measures that contribute to assessments?**

Norm-referenced tests compare a person's performance to that of his or her peers. Criterion-referenced tests measure abilities against a mastery standard. And non-referenced tests examine the strategies that a person uses when problem solving. Curriculum based measures provide information that is curriculum-specific, and performance based assessments allow for authentic information gathering that cannot be obtained using conventional assessments.

● **What is high stakes testing, and how does it affect you and your students?**

High stakes testing is testing that is mandated by state educational agencies and local education agencies across the country to measure student achievement. High stakes testing has critical implications for students, because failure on the tests can prevent students from moving on to the next grade or even from graduating from high school.

● **What four areas should you consider when adapting assessments for students with disabilities?**

Input adaptations are related to how students access test stimuli and questions (listening, reading print, and looking at stimuli). Output adaptations are related to how a test taker records responses to test questions: speaking, minor; speaking, major; manipulating objects; marking an answer sheet; pointing; drawing; or writing print. Time and/or schedule adaptations provide extended testing time and may also change the way the time is organized. Finally, location adaptations may change the setting in which a test is administered or the conditions of the test setting.

● **What are interviews, and what is their role in the assessment process?**

Interviews are conversations with parents and teachers that can provide important information about students from those who know them best. Student interviews can be used in process assessments to gain insight into the strategies they use during problem solving.

- **How can observations be used to collect information about your students?**

  Watching children and adolescents do such things as schoolwork or playing is called observing, and it involves not only watching people do something but also thinking about what they are doing, why they are doing it, and what the "doing" means to the students and those around them.

- **What is portfolio assessment, and what cautions need to be employed in the use of portfolios with students who have disabilities?**

  Portfolios, collections of student work that exhibit the student's efforts, progress, and

achievements in a variety of areas, are used to examine student progress as it is related to curricular objectives and instructional methods. Portfolio assessment can also be used to focus on both process *and* products, to measure more directly student achievement and learning, and to help evaluate the effectiveness of day-to-day instruction. Alternative portfolios can be used for students with severe disabilities who are exempt from high stakes testing. The portfolios ensure that accountability standards remain in place for all students.

● Revisit the
OPENING challenge

Check your answers to the Reflection Questions in the Opening Challenge and revise them on the basis of what you have learned.

1. How could Mr. Gomez set up a progress-monitoring procedure?

2. How could he set goals and chart his students' progress?

3. How can Mr. Gomez teach Sonya science and test her abilities when she cannot read?

4. How can Ms. Grey adapt materials for teaching and testing Gilbert?

5. How can she ensure that Gilbert's high stakes testing will yield valid results?

Professional Standards and Licensure

CEC Knowledge and Skill Core Standard and Associated Subcategories

CEC Content Standard 8: Assessment

Special educators use multiple types of assessment information for a variety of educational decisions and use the results of assessments to help identify exceptional learning needs and to develop and implement individualized instructional programs, as well as to adjust instruction in response to ongoing learning progress. Special educators understand the appropriate use and limitations of various types of assessments. Special educators conduct formal and informal assessments to design learning experiences that support the growth and development of individuals with ELN. Special educators use assessment information to identify supports and adaptations required for individuals with ELN to access the

general curriculum and to participate in school, system, and statewide assessment programs. Special educators regularly monitor the progress of individuals with ELN.

INTASC Core Principle and Associated Special Education Subcategories

8. Assessment

8.01 All teachers understand the purposes, strengths, and limitations of formal and informal assessment approaches for making eligibility, placement, and instructional decisions for students with disabilities.

8.02 All teachers use a variety of assessment procedures to document students' learning, behavior, and growth within multiple environments.

8.03 All teachers collaborate with others to incorporate accommodations and alternate assessments into the ongoing assessment process of students with disabilities when appropriate.

8.04 All teachers engage all students, including students with disabilities, in assessing and understanding their own learning and behavior.

8.05 All teachers understand that students with disabilities are expected to participate in district and statewide assessments and that accommodations or alternate assessments may be required when appropriate.

Praxis II: Education of Exceptional Students: Core Content Knowledge   PRAXIS

III. Delivery of Services to Students with Disabilities
Assessment, including
- Use of assessment for screening, diagnosis, placement, and the making of instruction decisions.
- Procedures and test materials, both formal and informal, typically used for pre-referral, screening, referral, classification, placement, and ongoing program monitoring.
- How to select, construct, conduct, and modify informal assessments.

Where the classroom comes to life!

Video—"Forms of Assessment"

This video shows an eighth-grade teacher who uses a rubric to assess a project-based learning assignment. Experts discuss various forms of assessment and the interdependence of assessment and instruction.

Log onto **www.mylabschool.com**. Under the **Courses** tab, in **Foundations/Intro to Teaching**, go to the **video lab**. Access the **"Assessment"** videos and watch the **"Forms of Assessment"** video.

 OR

Use the **www.mylabschool.com Assignment Finder** to go directly to these videos. Just enter Assignment ID **FDV7**.

1. Explain why a rubric is an appropriate assessment tool for the science project shown in the video.
2. In what ways does instruction guide the types of assessment that are used, and in what ways are assessments used to help teachers design instruction?
3. List four assessment procedures described in the video or in the chapter, and explain the circumstances in which each would be used.
4. In the video, one of the expert states, "You can't really tell where the instruction stops and the assessment begins." Explain the meaning of this statement.

Companion Website

To access chapter objectives, practice tests, weblinks, and flashcards, go to the companion website at **www.ablongman.com/bryantsmith1e**.

chapter *8*

Developing Collaborative Partnerships

chapter OBJECTIVES

After studying this chapter, you will have the knowledge to answer the following questions:

- What are the characteristics of collaboration?
- What foundation skills are critical for effective collaboration?
- What are applications of professional collaboration?
- How can teachers and paraprofessionals develop collaborative partnerships?
- What practices promote collaborative partnerships with families?

● OPENING challenge

Promoting Collaborative Partnerships to Meet the Needs of All Students

Ms. Warren's inclusive classroom is made up of students with an array of strengths and special needs that are addressed collaboratively with assistance from professionals, her paraprofessional, and connections to the families of her students. Ms. Warren is committed to providing all of her students with an appropriate education that is responsive to their needs. In her classroom, she is working with several students who are struggling with reading and mathematics. These students require interventions that support typical classroom instruction. She also has several students with emotional disturbance who need structured routines and management procedures so that they are ready to learn. Ms. Warren has several students who are English language learners (ELLs) and need extra instructional support in vocabulary development. One of her students receives services from the speech/language pathologist to correct articulation problems. Ms. Warren thinks about the related services providers and other individuals who are involved in the school community to help all students. *"How can I work collaboratively with so many people who are involved with*

my students? I want to build strong partnerships with my colleagues and my students' families." Ms. Warren finds herself in a situation that is very common. Developing and nurturing collaborative partnerships with many individuals, both families and service providers in inclusive classrooms, requires certain skills and practice. Collaborative partnerships can be developed to enhance the learning of all students and to build connections between students' home and school environments.

● Reflection Questions

In your journal, write down your answers to the following questions. After completing the chapter, check your answers and revise them on the basis of what you have learned.

1. What professional collaborative practices can Ms. Warren use to help her students who have special learning, behavior, and language needs succeed in the general education classroom?

2. How can Ms. Warren collaborate effectively with her paraprofessional?

3. How can Ms. Warren effectively structure parent–teacher conferences and develop home–school communication effectively?

We know that many students with special needs receive most, if not all, of their education in the general education classroom. Therefore, it is important to establish collaborative partnerships among professionals, paraprofessionals, and families to ensure that all students are receiving appropriate educational services in inclusive settings. (We use the term *families* to denote various family structures, such as extended families, children with guardians, single-parent families, and "blended" families.) Collaboration is an interactive process whereby individuals with diverse expertise choose to work together to provide quality services to all students in inclusive classrooms and their families (West & Idol, 1990). Collaboration occurs when two or more individuals work together voluntarily to accomplish a common goal (Cook & Friend, 1993; Halvorsen & Neary, 2001). It can be informal, as, for example, when two teachers meet to develop a plan together to help a student with special needs, or it can be formalized through a team approach involving related service providers. Collaboration also occurs when teachers work with paraprofessionals who are important members of the educational team. Finally, educators must utilize effective practices to collaborate with families, for they are the ones who know the most about the students we serve.

In this chapter, we provide information about the characteristics of collaboration and the foundation skills that are critical for establishing effective, collaborative partnerships. We also discuss models of professional collaboration and ways to develop collaborative partnerships with paraprofessionals and families. We include multicultural considerations when establishing collaborative partnerships and demonstrate how the ADAPT framework can be used during collaborative activities.

What Are the Characteristics of Collaboration?

Collaboration is a key ingredient of the efforts of inclusive schools to meet the needs of all students in different settings and activities. For example, collaboration can occur when teachers are conducting pre-referral interventions to prevent inappropriate referrals to special education; when service providers are delivering related services; when a bilingual instructor and a special education teacher are developing a lesson plan together; when secondary school teachers are co-teaching a science lesson; when the speech/language pathologist and general education teacher are team-teaching an instructional unit; or when general and special educators are consulting about a student with behavior problems. According to Halvorsen and Neary (2001), the collaborative process aims to successfully include all students in general education activities, to identify adaptations of content and materials, and to develop and implement specialized instruction as appropriate. The following characteristics of collaboration can ensure that the process will be successful.

Shared Problem Solving

Shared problem solving involves the identification, implementation, and evaluation of a plan to solve a mutually agreed-upon problem. In shared problem solving, participants problem-solve and make decisions together. Shared problem solving can be complex, because different perspectives on how to address and resolve issues often arise and must be included in the process of problem solving (Friend & Cook, 2000). Problem solving can be accomplished best when participants in the collaborative process (1) assess the current situation using specific criteria (such as behavior, time, situational factors, achievement information, nonverbal signals, or verbal comments); (2) identify together the specific behavior that is of concern (such as homework completion, reading comprehension, lateness to collaboration meetings, or following through on collaboration plans; (3) specify objectives for solving the problem; (4) develop a plan of action, including tasks, persons responsible, and time lines; and (5) evaluate the plan periodically (Heron & Harris, 1993).

Shared Responsibility

Each member of the collaborative team is equally responsible for ensuring that tasks are accomplished during the process. This usually entails team members dividing up the work in ways that promote parity among team members (Friend & Cook, 2000). For instance, one person might be responsible for observing a student who is misbehaving in class, and another team member might contact the family to talk about how the student is performing in school. In the classroom during co-teaching, teachers assume shared responsibility for teaching and promoting positive behavior. Teachers also share the function of grading assignments and planning instruction.

Voluntary Involvement

Collaboration is a process that individuals should volunteer to engage in, rather than being assigned by school- or district-level administration. Collaboration is most successful when participants choose to get involved in identifying issues and solutions of mutual concern. Collaboration will not occur merely because someone is assigned to a team. In addition to characteristics of collaboration, we know that there are important prerequisite skills to ensure effective collaborative partnerships.

What Are Critical Prerequisite Skills for Effective Collaboration?

Establishing collaborative partnerships with professionals, paraprofessionals, and families is a necessary component of effective schools. Partnerships involve working with people, and to do this well, teachers must be prepared in those critical prerequisite skills that foster collaboration. In this section, we discuss communication skills, conflict resolution skills, and multicultural and linguistic diversity considerations that can develop a foundation upon which effective collaborative relationships can be built.

Communication Skills

Heron and Harris (1993) conceptualized the communication process as consisting of a message that is encoded and transmitted, and a received message that is decoded and comprehended. For this process to occur successfully, the speaker and listener must possess an array of skills. Successful communication requires effective listening skills, the ability to decode (or figure out) a message, and verbal, encoding skills to convey one's thoughts. Additionally, communication partners have to be aware of and interpret nonverbal signals in messages they send and receive.

Listening is an important skill to develop for decoding and improving communication. Listening involves more than just politely hearing what someone else is saying before you speak (Vaughn, Bos & Schumm, 2007); it involves maintaining appropriate eye contact, acknowledging the speaker's message with verbal feedback, and maintaining appropriate nonverbal signals. Deterrents to effective listening include being preoccupied and not listening, talking more than listening, second-guessing what the speaker will say and responding inappropriately, making judgments, being distrustful, using language not appropriate to the situation (too technical, for instance, or unmindful of cultural and ethnic values and perceptions), fatigue, and strong emotions (Mostert, 1998).

One of the most effective types of listening is called active listening (Gordon, 1980). Learning this method of listening involves becoming aware of ways to listen and respond to communication partners more effectively. The purpose of active listening is to engage the listener in the message being sent, to demonstrate to the speaker that the listener is interested in the message, to enable the speaker to convey specific concerns, and to provide feedback to the speaker to ensure that the message was correctly received and perceived. Active listening can be used effectively in many types of interactions and, particularly, during conversations that may be emotionally charged. There are six types of active listening:

1. *Acknowledging* tells the speaker you are listening and may include appropriate nonverbal signals and verbal comments.
2. *Paraphrasing* provides feedback to the speaker about the received, perceived message. The listener repeats to the speaker, in his or her own words, the message that was conveyed.
3. *Reflecting* involves telling the speaker the feelings he or she is verbalizing.
4. *Clarifying* asks for more specific information to help the listener better understand the message.
5. *Elaboration* involves asking the speaker to provide more information about an idea or about the whole message to broaden the content conveyed to the listener.
6. *Summarizing* requires the listener to reiterate the main ideas of the conversation and the actions that will be taken, if any. Summarizing gives closure to a conversation and provides feedback for all members about the key points discussed.

Besides having good listening skills, communication partners must be able to convey their message in such a way that it is correctly understood. Messages can be transmitted orally or in writing. Messages conveyed verbally can be analyzed in terms of how the message is being received, the nonverbal language emitted by the listener, and the feedback from the listener that signals accurate interpretation. Through careful self-analysis and feedback from speakers, listeners can improve their skills so that more effective communication occurs. Idol (2001) recommended the following procedures for facilitating effective verbal communication:

- Before speaking, organize your thoughts to be sure that they are relevant to the conversation and can be stated succinctly.
- Demonstrate good listening behaviors (see above) to show that you are indeed interested in the speaker's message.
- Use feedback to show that you are listening and understanding the speaker's message.
- Avoid being judgmental and evaluative.
- Be aware of extraneous factors (such as a receiver who doesn't feel well or who has a personal crisis, a parent who may be very angry at another professional yet unconsciously projects the anger onto you, a paraprofessional who feels that the tasks she or he is assigned are demeaning). These factors may interfere with the communication process.
- Avoid technical jargon that educators may use as convenient shorthand among themselves. Be specific without using acronyms that the speaker may not be familiar with.

Written communication is another way in which information can be conveyed. Because people are so busy today, written communication is a frequently used method of communication; that is, professionals communicate with others via newsletters, the Internet, and notes. Although written communication reduces the need for face-to-face interactions, participants must be sure that written messages are conveyed appropriately to ensure accurate interpretation. For example, written messages containing spelling or syntactical errors make it clear that the writer has not proofread his or her work or that the writer lacks some basic skills. The use of jargon in written communication should be limited. Long, detailed messages probably lose their effectiveness simply because of their complexity and the recipient's lack of time to read them thoroughly. Finally, written communication should include a signature, date, and request for a response (West, Idol, & Cannon, 1993).

Nonverbal communication is another aspect of communication that requires careful analysis to ensure that the speaker sends appropriate signals and that the listener understands the intended message. According to Heron and Harris (1993), nonverbal communication includes facial expressions, body posturing and movement, use of space, and touch. Nonverbal messages are a powerful form of communication because they tend to be quite genuine, and they may be more easily conveyed than verbal messages that are emotionally laden.

There are several types of nonverbal communication that should be considered when sending or receiving messages. For example, facial expressions can be very informative about feelings, trust, disdain, or interest. Elevated eyebrows, lack of or regular eye contact, smiles, and frowns convey specific messages to speakers. Facing the speaker, crossing one's arms, and sitting in a relaxed position are all examples of body posturing and movements that need to be recognized as part of the way speakers and listeners interact. A distance between speakers and listeners of 2 to 4 feet is an acceptable use of space when participants know each other and can interact comfortably. Touch is a form of communication that needs to be monitored carefully. Some people prefer that speakers or listeners not touch their arms or hug them, for instance.

How we communicate with each other can enhance or impede successful collaborative partnerships. When working in diverse settings, individuals should take into consideration cultural and linguistic factors that are part of the communication process. For example, an interpreter should be available if family members do not speak or understand English. Body posture such as nodding one's head, smiling, and leaning forward convey openness, interest, and attentive listening. Teachers should learn about the values, perceptions, and culture of communicative partners. This information can go a long way in enhancing communication and establishing trust on which to build a collaborative partnership. Conflict resolution skills are another important prerequisite for collaboration. We now turn our attention to this critical area.

Conflict Resolution Skills

In most collaborative partnership endeavors, a plan is developed for the benefit of a student. Very often professionals, paraprofessionals, and families are faced with complex problems that require careful consideration and action to help children; often these interactions may be plagued with issues that lead to conflict. This conflict must be resolved so that the partners can move forward with their plans.

Conflict is defined as the disagreement of interests or ideas (Heron & Harris, 1993). In a collaborative relationship, conflict may stem from differences in opinions about strategies, facts, or values. Conflict may arise from any of the following situations:

- People perceive that they are forced into situations (e.g., working together, having students with disabilities in their classrooms full-time, implementing a strategy for which no training occurred).
- Roles (e.g., special education teacher as consultant) are not clearly defined.
- Philosophies (e.g., humanistic, disciplinarian) clash.
- Levels of expertise and professional development do not match the demands of the situation (e.g., first-year teacher asked to chair a committee).
- Interpersonal styles (e.g., introvert, extrovert, direct, indirect) vary significantly.
- People are resistant to change (e.g., issues of "territory," power, and interest in trying new research-based ideas). (Heron & Harris, 1993)

For example, two professionals may be working on a plan that they had jointly developed for a student; however, one member falls short in completing his or her agreed-on tasks. In this situation, conflict could easily arise, because the plan for the student is not fully implemented. This issue would need to be addressed in a constructive manner that would facilitate progress toward implementing the plan. Thus, participants who enter into collaborative partnerships of any type must possess conflict resolution skills so that plans can be developed and any conflict can be resolved in a productive manner.

Conflict is inevitable even in the best of circumstances; therefore, developing conflict resolution skills is beneficial. Here are several guidelines for conflict resolution:

- Do not expect the conflict to go away; it may diminish, but if problems and feelings are not discussed, they will emerge again at another time.
- Confront conflict when it occurs by stating your feelings using an "I-message" (refer to Chapter 9 for more information about I-messages). For example, "I'm feeling uncomfortable with this situation," "I'm sensing that

maybe we're not on the same wavelength," or "What are your thoughts about how to proceed?" In essence, this is a reality check—an effort to determine whether your perceptions are accurate. If not, then promptly discussing the situation as you perceive it could prevent further misperceptions and possible problems.

- Avoid being judgmental or accusatory: "You're not listening," "You're late again," "That idea didn't work the last time and won't work this time."
- Use self-disclosure if appropriate. "I'm feeling really unsure about how to handle this problem and could use some assistance."
- Maintain open, ongoing communication even if the communication is just notes to other members. A major source of conflict is lack of communication between partners and the perception (or observation) that one person is moving ahead without talking the plan through with others.
- Use active listening: send I-messages, paraphrase, summarize, and clarify. These techniques can go a long way in developing a better understanding of how members feel and how they perceive situations.
- Discuss conflict at a time when members are not pressed to return to their classroom and are not in the midst of a situation that might interfere with the process of conflict resolution. Timing is an important consideration.
- Use problem solving steps to reach consensus and identify a plan of action. This helps members to focus on a procedure that promotes communication, discussion, and resolution.
- Recognize that sometimes conflict may not be resolved and that partnerships may be terminated for the time being. Many reasons (including lack of interest, power, insecurity, bad timing, mistrust, and inability to establish congruent objectives) account for the inability of members to resolve conflict. Focus on letting go and finding an alternative, productive way to handle the situation if further action is required.

Multicultural and Linguistic Diversity Considerations

The cultural, ethnic, racial, and linguistic composition of American society is changing dramatically, and this is reflected in our school-age population. Some students may qualify for a range of services, including bilingual programs, ESL (English as a second language) programs, and special education programs. Thus, it behooves educators to obtain preparation in working with diverse populations so that individual student needs, including special needs, can be met successfully and appropriately (Baca, 2002).

We have already discussed several considerations for collaborating effectively with individuals from diverse cultural, ethnic, and linguistic heritages. For example, we discussed the issue of recognizing diverse values and perceptions and the importance of communicating with people in their primary language. We also mentioned the issue of being aware of different communication styles of collaborative partnerships.

Researchers (Garcia, 2002; Harris, 1991; Ortiz & Yates, 2001) have identified consultation competencies for educators who work with culturally and linguistically diverse students who have special needs. These competencies include (1) reflecting on one's own perspective—that is, one's beliefs and values related to students with special needs who are from diverse backgrounds and the professionals who work with them; (2) fully understanding the roles, values, perceptions, and beliefs of collaborative partners; (3) interpersonal, communicative, and problem solving skills needed to promote successful collaboration; and (4) appropriate assessment and instructional strategies (such as language and cultural considerations for assessment, specific strategies, and adapting curricula). For example, Garcia (2002) recommends that educators must examine their own cultural self-awareness and the influences of these cultural values on their behavior toward others. Understanding roles in the collaborative process is another critically important competency, because conflict can arise when there are misunderstandings about roles and responsibilities. Regarding assessment strategies, Figueroa (2002) recommends that, when assessing English language learners, personnel should observe the student's behavior and performance across multiple contexts, observe over a period of time rather than drawing conclusions on the basis of one or two observations, and draw on the expertise of informed professionals in arriving at diagnostic decisions.

Finally, Nancy Cloud (2002) talks about culturally and linguistically responsive instruction that focuses on cultural characteristics, which are beliefs, norms, and customs that vary within and between groups; language differences; and identified disability needs. Teachers can integrate culturally and linguistically responsive instruction in the areas of curriculum and materials, classroom discourse (discussions), instructional techniques, management, and parent involvement.

In any discussion of diversity, it is important to keep in mind that the notion of "culture" permeates all of society and all interactions. We all belong to some cultural group that is distinguishable in terms of customs, traditions, beliefs, foods, dress, and so forth. Additionally, cultural groups may be distinguished by a specific ethnicity, religious affiliation, or racial background. Culture emerges in group interactions, clubs, social gatherings, and so forth. Heron and Harris (1993) have pointed out that there is a culture specific to co-teaching, collaborative consultation, and family units. Thus educators must be aware of their own cultural values, how they have been socialized professionally, and the cultural values of their collaborative partners (Garcia, 2002).

How Can Professionals Work Together Collaboratively?

Many professionals, such as general and special education teachers, school psychologists, counselors, social workers, administrators, and speech/language, physical, or occupational therapists, are part of the school community that is responsible for working together to provide a quality education for all students. Because of the individual needs of students with special needs, a variety of professionals work together to plan and implement individualized education programs (IEPs). In Chapter 5, you read about related services and the professionals who provide them. For example, speech/language pathologists provide services for the prevention and treatment of communication disorders. In this section, we talk about the need for collaborative professional partnerships and models of collaboration that promote inclusive practices.

The Need for Collaborative Partnerships with Professionals

As you know from Chapter 1, the Individuals with Disabilities Education Act (IDEA) of 2004 requires that students with disabilities be educated to the greatest extent possible in the general education setting. Moreover, general education teachers are required to be part of the IEP Team and are responsible for implementing the adaptations identified on the IEP to help students access and master the curriculum. Thus, there is a need for collaborative models among professionals to provide the support needed when educating all students in inclusive classrooms.

Making a Difference

Communication and Collaboration Among Team Members Ensures Successful Inclusion

Nicole Block
Special Education Inclusion Support Teacher and Department Head
Steele Canyon High School
Spring Valley, California

I collaborate with twelve general education teachers to develop and deliver differentiated curricula for students with disabilities enrolled in tenth-grade world literature and world history, twelfth-grade multicultural literature, and twelfth-grade creative writing. I am also responsible for the design and implementation of the training, given in the peer tutor elective course where students learn instructional skills to support students with disabilities in their general education classes.

When I accepted a position as an inclusion support teacher at a high school in California in 2002, I felt fully prepared to collaborate with a team of English and history teachers across two grade levels. But what I thought was going to be a co-teaching assignment turned out instead to consist of my serving as a consultant teacher working *outside* of the classroom. I felt like my feet were on roller skates! I never spent very much time in any one classroom before I was off to work with another group of students. My approach to this challenging schedule was to maximize my instruction time with students during the school day and then spend my evenings reviewing content standards to develop modified curricula. My colleagues and I collaborated weekly to develop common curricula and assessments. I considered these collaboration sessions "sacred time" well spent communicating about differentiation and students' needs.

In my second year on the job, I continued to collaborate with tenth-grade classes and added twelfth-grade English. Immediately, I noticed a positive difference in my effectiveness with students. I had increased knowledge of the curriculum, had developed an understanding of how to connect with and motivate students, and had established strong and productive working relationships with my colleagues. Once the classroom teachers understood how to utilize my skills, and I learned how best to apply my knowledge in a supportive role to meet their curricular goals, our team dynamic shifted. The general education teachers learned effective behavioral and instructional practices from me, and I gained valuable content area knowledge from them. Students recognized that our united team spoke with one voice in the classroom and responded accordingly.

Although I entered my first year fully expecting my school colleagues and me to have near-instant rapport and collaborative practices, in reality developing our "team" relationship and curriculum took us approximately 2 years. Now our emphasis is on analyzing data and revising our methodologies accordingly. It is the constant communication among our school team that allows us to react to both our successes and our challenges in ways that inform and improve our work with the students. Our instructional approach continues to be child-centered, supportive of the individual's needs, and, most important, inclusive of students and teachers in a way that maintains high standards for all. ●

See the Making a Difference feature on page 309 for an example of the importance of collaboration in inclusive instruction. Collaborative models are prevalent in classrooms across the nation where educators are working together to ensure that *all* students can access the general education curriculum. For example, the "class within a class" model developed by Dr. Floyd Hudson promotes more academic interventions for students with learning problems in the context of the general education setting. This model permits students with various learning problems, including those students who qualify for special education services, to benefit from the expertise of special education intervention. Collaboration–consultation and co-teaching are other models that are described in the next section. We will also discuss collaboration considerations for English language learners.

Models of Collaborative Partnerships with Professionals

There are several models of collaborative partnerships with professionals to help students with special needs function more successfully in the general education classroom.

COLLABORATION–CONSULTATION The collaboration–consultation model focuses on the partnership between the general education and special education teachers, tapping the expertise of both to provide appropriate services to students (Idol, Nevin, & Paolucci-Whitcomb, 1994). In this model, collaboration involves planning, implementing, and evaluating student programs wherein teachers work together to meet the needs of all students (Foley & Mundschenk, 1997). Intervention plans are developed that are typically implemented by general education teachers with ongoing support from the special education teacher. The expertise of both professionals, then, is applied in creating and evaluating plans. The

● Collaborative consultation is an interactive process that enables groups of people with diverse expertise to generate creative solutions to mutually defined problems.

intervention plans could be part of pre-referral activities to prevent academic problems or could be developed to address the academic, behavioral, or social skills of students in inclusive classrooms.

Idol and colleagues (1994) identify six stages of the collaboration–consultation process.

STAGE 1: Gaining Entry and Establishing Team Goals

This stage consists of establishing rapport between or among participants and identifying specifically each member's goals, agenda, and outcomes for the collaborative process. In this stage, it is important to ensure that each participant is clear about what he or she would like to see occur during the collaborative process and to determine what each member is capable of contributing to the partnership in terms of time, expertise, and commitment.

STAGE 2: Problem

Identification In this stage, participants engage in assessment practices (see Chapter 7 for information about assessment techniques) to determine the student's current level of academic performance, behavioral considerations, and affective/emotional status. Assessment data may be obtained from previously administered measures and behavioral rating scales, teacher observation, and current informal assessment measures. On the basis of available data, the participants develop a profile of the student's strengths and weaknesses and identify specific problems that may account for academic and/or behavior problems.

STAGE 3: Intervention Recommendations

Specific interventions are recommended for the problem(s) identified in Stage 2. An important aspect of this stage is identifying interventions that teachers can implement easily *and* that accommodate the special needs of the student. Other students for whom the intervention(s) may be appropriate and effective could be identified during this stage as well.

STAGE 4: Implementation of Recommendations

During this stage, the intervention is implemented for the targeted problem. The special education teacher may be asked to model the intervention or provide feedback to the classroom teacher about the implementation process. The general education teacher may model an intervention for the special education teacher to learn, or both teachers may work together to implement a behavior management plan. There is room for flexibility in how interventions are implemented and how participants in the collaborative process work together to facilitate the plan's success.

STAGE 5: Evaluation

Monitoring student progress to determine the effectiveness of the intervention(s) is extremely important. Classroom teachers can administer evaluation measures that help participants in the collaborative process determine whether the intervention is effective.

STAGE 6: Follow-up

Essential to an effective collaborative partnership for promoting student success are regularly scheduled meetings of participants to determine whether the intervention was effective and to identify additional potential problem areas that could be addressed during the collaborative process. During Stage 1, participants should designate a time schedule that is mutually convenient for discussing student progress. Then, participants will need to adhere to the schedule or find alternative meeting times to ensure that communication is maintained.

Figure 8.1 shows an example of a form that can be used to document collaborative decisions. The following case study shows how collaboration–consultation might work where professionals work together to identify solutions for students who are having academic, social, and emotional difficulties.

FIGURE 8.1 Collaborative Decisions

Collaboration Plan

Date _____   Student_____   Grade_____

General Education Teacher _____

Team Member(s) _____

I. Academic, behavioral, and social/emotional issues for collaborative decision making
(Provide specific, observable, measurable information.)

Academic _____

Behavioral _____

Social/emotional _____

II. Recommended interventions/Person(s) responsible
(Provide techniques to address the issues; identify who will implement the techniques.)

Academic _____

Person(s) responsible _____

Behavioral _____

Person(s) responsible _____

Social/emotional _____

Person(s) responsible _____

III. Evaluation
(Provide techniques that will be used to evaluate student progress, timelines, and person responsible.)

Academic _____

Person(s) responsible _____

Behavioral _____

Person(s) responsible _____

Social/emotional _____

Person(s) responsible _____

IV. Follow-up
(Specify follow-up dates to review the student's response to the interventions and to examine the data.)

Follow-up dates: 1._____   2._____   3._____

4._____   5._____   6._____

AN EXAMPLE OF THE COLLABORATION–CONSULTATION PROCESS   Ms. Warren is concerned about how Felipe is progressing in developing oral reading fluency compared to the other students in her class. She has tried working individually with Felipe to practice reading, but she doesn't have enough time during the school day to meet his needs. Ms. Warren has collected and graphed data on Felipe's oral reading weekly for six weeks, and it is clear that he is not benefiting from instruction. She decides to initiate the collaboration–consultation process with the special education teacher to identify the next steps to take.

In Stage 1, they agree to develop a plan for Ms. Warren to implement in the general education classroom to improve Felipe's oral reading performance. Ms. Warren states that she needs an intervention that won't take too much more of her time because she is already working with Felipe and a few other students in a small group to improve their reading.

In Stage 2, Ms. Warren shares Felipe's reading data; they all agree that Felipe is not responding sufficiently to small-group reading instruction and that he needs an additional intervention to improve his reading fluency. The graphed data show improved reading in terms of the number of words read correctly each week, but the improvement is too slow for him to catch up to his classmates by the end of the school year.

In Stage 3, the special education teacher and Ms. Warren discuss the possibility of taped assisted reading as an intervention for Felipe. This intervention involves taping reading passages and having Felipe practice the reading passages several times each day before he works in a small group with the teacher. Ms. Warren agrees to have her paraprofessional tape-record the passages, and she will continue to collect weekly data on Felipe's reading performance.

In Stage 4, the special education teacher models for Ms. Warren and Felipe how to implement the tape-assisted reading. Ms. Warren continues the implementation process each day for four weeks. She has her paraprofessional oversee the process.

Stage 5 involves data collection, which in this case means recording the number of words read correctly during a one-minute timing each week. Ms. Warren collects the data to share at the follow-up meeting.

Finally, in Stage 6, Ms. Warren, her paraprofessional, and the special education teacher meet, four weeks after the intervention began, to review the data. At this time, they decide that Felipe's reading performance is much stronger with the tape-assisted intervention. They agree to continue the intervention and meet again in another four weeks. They also decide that if the data do not continue to show adequate improvement, they will reconvene sooner.

CO-TEACHING   Marilyn Friend, one of the leading authorities on educational collaboration, defined co-teaching as "a service delivery model in which two educators, one typically a general education teacher and one a special education teacher or another specialist, combine their expertise to jointly teach a heterogeneous group of students, some of whom have disabilities or other special needs, in a single classroom for part or all of the school day" (Friend, 2006, p. 140). Both professionals take part in planning, teaching, and evaluating student performance. Co-teaching is based on specific underlying assumptions about teaching and professionals' expertise. One assumption is that the co-teaching team can bring to the classroom combined knowledge and expertise, which will greatly enhance instruction. Another assumption is that team members can meet individual students' needs more effectively than one teacher (Walther-Thomas, Korinek, McLaughlin, & Williams, 2000).

● In a co-teaching classroom, both teachers take part in planning, teaching, and evaluating student performance.

Co-teaching involves collaborative instructional planning, implementation, and evaluation among team members. For example, in a co-teaching situation that consists of a speech/language pathologist and a special education teacher, the language expertise of the speech/language pathologist can be combined with the special education teacher's expertise in instructional content to produce a lesson rich in language *and* content development. Alternatively, the special education and general education teachers can work collaboratively to plan, co-teach, and evaluate a lesson presented in the general education classroom. There are many variations of co-teaching partnerships, including teaming for one instructional period, teaming for the entire day, and a special education and general education team assigned to one class all year long (Cook & Friend, 1993).

Co-teachers may consist of general education teachers, special education teachers, counselors, bilingual/ELL teachers, and speech/language pathologists. The IEP Team determines the co-teaching members; the instructional content to be taught; and the student's academic, behavioral, and social needs to be addressed by the co-teaching members. Vaughn, Schumm, and Arguelles (1997) identified four models of co-teaching that are described in What Works 8.1.

Walther-Thomas, Korinek, McLaughlin, and Williams (2000) similarly identified four variations of co-teaching. The *interactive teaching* variation consists of partners presenting concepts, reviewing, demonstrating, and monitoring. This provides more opportunities to monitor student performance and to address instructional and behavioral issues. The *station teaching* variation involves students working in small groups at teacher-directed or independent workstations to learn new information or practice what was previously taught. This variation of co-teaching promotes student-centered learning and collaboration among peers. In the *parallel teaching* variation, students work in mixed-ability groups under the direction of one of the teachers. This variation effectively reduces the pupil–teacher ratio to permit more instruction that is focused on the group's needs. Finally, the *alternative teaching* variation involves a big group and a small

what WORKS 8.1

Instructional Models for Co-Teaching

- ### Model A: One Group—One Lead Teacher, One Teacher "Teaching on Purpose"

Student Grouping: Whole class

Teachers' Roles: One teacher takes the lead in instruction; one teacher provides instruction.

"Teaching on purpose" is giving mini lessons to students during or as a follow-up to whole-group instruction.

1- to 2-Minute Purpose: Work with student after instruction to follow up on lesson ideas and check for understanding.

5-Minute Purpose: Reteach and review concepts and vocabulary.

10- to 12-Minute Purpose: Provide a short lesson on a part of the lesson.

- ### Model B: Two Mixed-Ability Groups—Two Teachers Teach Same Content

Student Grouping: Two mixed-ability groups

Teachers' Roles: Each teacher instructs one group.

Use as a follow-up to Model A. Divide the class into two groups with each teacher instructing one group. The purpose of this model is to monitor students' responses and knowledge.

- ### Model C: Two Same-Ability Groups— Teachers Teach Different Content

Student Grouping: Two large, same-ability groups

Teachers' Roles: Each teacher instructs one group.

Students are divided into two groups on the basis of their skill level in the topic area. One teacher re-

teaches information in a different way, while the other teacher provides additional information or enrichment activities.

- ### Model D: Multiple Groups—Teachers Monitor/Teach

Student Grouping: Mixed-ability or same-ability

Teachers' Roles: Each teacher monitors and/or teaches.

Model D can be used in cooperative learning groups, instructional groups, and work centers.

Grouping Suggestions

- Several groups may be mixed-ability while one or two are same-ability. Teachers work with individual groups.
- Small groups work on academic activities while other groups work on practice activities to improve specific skills.

- ### Model E: Whole Class—Two Teachers Teach Together

Student Grouping: Whole class

Teachers' Roles: Teachers work together to teach a whole-class lesson.

In Model E, teachers work cooperatively to teach a lesson. One teacher may lead the class lesson while the other teacher provides elaborations and questions for clarification. The general education teacher typically focuses on the curriculum material, and the special education teacher focuses on strategies.

Source: Adapted from "The ABCDEs of Co-Teaching," by S. Vaughn, J. S. Schumm, and M. E. Arguelles, 1997, *Teaching Exceptional Children, 30*(2), pp. 4–10.

group taught by different teachers. The big group may receive enrichment work while the small group obtains additional intervention support. An example of how some of these variations might work is presented in ADAPT Framework 8.1. Refer to Ms. Warren's opening challenge to see how she used co-teaching variations to provide additional support in her classroom.

8.1   **ADAPT Framework**   Workstations and Special Education Teachers' Assistance

A ASK "What am I requiring the student to do?"	**D** DETERMINE the prerequisite skills of the task.	**A** ANALYZE the student's strengths and struggles.		**P** PROPOSE and implement adaptations from among the four categories.	**T** TEST to determine if the adaptations helped the student to accomplish the task.
		Strengths	Struggles		
Students must possess reading and math skills to work independently and successfully in workstations.	1. Attends to and attempts to perform activities.	1		**For 1.** No adaptation is needed to increase attention.	
	2. Reads word problems in workstation to complete the tasks independently.		2	**For 2. Instructional Delivery** During *workstations teaching,* pair the student with a stronger reader to help read the word problems without teacher help.	**For 2.** Observe during *workstations teaching* to ensure that the student is receiving reading support.
	3. Knows the steps for solving word problems.	3		**For 3.** Use alternative teaching by having the special education teacher provide small-group instruction on word problem solving strategies. Ms. Warren will work with the big group to provide additional problem solving activities.	**For 3.** Provide word problems for the student to solve independently. Assess accuracy.
	4. Works well with other students in small groups.	4		**For 4.** No adaptation is needed.	

There are certain procedures that teachers should implement in a co-teaching or teaming arrangement (Salend, Gordon, & Lopez-Vona, 2002). First, they must mutually define roles in the teaming relationship that pertain to instruction, behavior management, and evaluation. By identifying role responsibilities, teachers can prevent ambiguities and miscommunication. Second, team members need to spend time discussing instructional philosophies to determine whether a mutual, collaborative relationship can be established. This is important to the development of team rapport. Third, teachers must explain what they hope to gain from a team effort instructionally and for students. Such disclosure can promote effective communication right from the start of a teaming relationship. Fourth, team members should convey to students the teachers' roles and explain how instruction and discipline will be handled in the classroom. Both teachers should

WORKING together

Co-Teaching

Mr. Sanchez and Mrs. Voress will use co-teaching as a way to provide more support for students with special needs in Mr. Sanchez's class. Teaming can help them address the academic needs of students with learning disabilities and of other students who have similar academic difficulties as well. They decide to proceed by working through the following steps.

1. Establish a co-teaching partnership.
   - Identify goals and expectations of the partnership.
   - Share beliefs and values about teaching, discipline, and expectations of students for learning.
   - Identify how the partnership will be communicated to parents and the principal.
   - Designate a workspace within the classroom for each teacher.
   - Identify roles and responsibilities. Possible questions to consider:
     - How will discipline be handled?
     - Whose materials will we use to teach lessons?
     - How will we manage progress monitoring and grading?
     - How will we coordinate team instruction?
2. Identify students' needs.
   - Identify each student's strengths and weaknesses.

- Discuss IEPs for students with disabilities.
- Consider adaptations needed for each student to benefit from instruction.
3. Develop an instructional plan.
   - Find time to plan. Try to have at least 45 minutes a week to co-plan. Time for planning is the most frequently cited issue in co-teaching. Work with your principal to establish time.
   - Identify a classroom and behavior management system together.
   - Identify student groupings. Group students on the basis of the specific goals and purpose of a lesson and/or the needs of the students. Balance homogeneous grouping with other grouping formats to implement flexible grouping (Elbaum, Vaughn, Hughes, & Moody, 1999).
   - Select a co-teaching model to suit the instructional purpose and students' needs (see What Works 8.1).
   - Develop a plan.
4. Monitor student performance together.
   - Become familiar with standards and accountability for all students.
   - Measure student progress regularly.
   - Develop a record-keeping system.
   - Make instructional-based decisions.
   - Discuss and assign grades together.
   - Conduct teacher–parent conferences together whenever possible.

maintain a similar level of authority when working with the students. Finally, team members need to meet regularly to work through problems, evaluate student progress, communicate with families, and plan further instruction. The Working Together feature provides examples for building and implementing the co-teaching partnership.

Research on collaborative models suggests that teachers note many positive effects of working together. For example, in a three-year study of effective co-teaching teams, Walther-Thomas (1997) found that general education and special education teachers reported increases in

1. Academic and social gains for students with disabilities
2. Opportunities for professional growth
3. Professional satisfaction
4. Personal support

Other studies have shown that special education teachers have felt subordinate to the general education teacher and that time for planning was an issue (Salend et al., 1997; Trent, 1998). Careful planning, communication about roles and philosophies, and regular meetings are important.

Weiss and Lloyd (2002) studied co-teaching at the secondary level. These researchers questioned whether it is possible for students with disabilities to receive the specialized education that they need in co-taught secondary classrooms. Weiss and Lloyd also noted that building principals are responsible for ensur-

Considering *Diversity*

Intervention Strategies and Collaborative Partnerships for English Language Learners

Issue	Strategy
Student experiences difficulty, implement clinical teaching cycle	• Clinical teaching cycle Teach skill or content Re-teach using different strategies if student experiences difficulty Conduct informal assessments to identify difficulties Adapt instruction based on assessment results Monitor student response to instruction regularly
Problem persists, request assistance from Teacher Assistance Team	• Teacher assistance team process The teacher requests assistance from the team. The team leader reviews the request and obtains additional information if necessary. The leader arranges a classroom observation. A team meeting is held. The team designs an intervention plan. The teacher implements the plan with assistance as appropriate. A follow-up team meeting is held to determine student progress. If the problem continues, the process is repeated.
Problem still persists, refer student to alternative general education programs and services	• Alternative programs and services One-to-one tutoring Cross-age tutoring Remedial programs Student and family support groups Family counseling

Source: From "Prevention of school failure and early intervention for English language learners," by A. Ortiz, 2002. In A. J. Artiles and A. A. Ortiz (Eds.), *English language learners with special education needs,* Washington, DC: Center for Applied Linguistics and Delta System Co.

ing that enough resources, time, and training are provided for co-teaching to be successful.

Finally, Murawski and Swanson (2001) conducted a review of literature on co-teaching research in 2001. Based on the existing research, these authors concluded that co-teaching demonstrated strong effects in language arts, moderate effects in math, and negligible effects for social outcomes. They also noted that more research is needed to determine the effects of co-teaching on achievement outcomes of students with disabilities.

Collaboration Considerations for English Language Learners

Ortiz (2002) and Yates and Ortiz (2004) stress the need for early intervention for students who are English language learners (ELLs) and are experiencing learning problems in the general education classroom. As soon as learning problems are identified, teachers should implement strategies to address special learning needs. Classroom teachers can collaborate with bilingual specialists who can provide assistance on effective instructional practices for English language learners. Ortiz (2002) and Yates and Ortiz (2004) recommend four strategies that build on the concept of pre-referral interventions: the clinical teaching cycle, peer or expert consultation, the teacher assistance team process, and alternative programs and services for early intervention for struggling students.

The clinical teaching cycle consists of sequenced instruction, re-teaching if necessary, and informal assessment procedures, including assessment of academic and conversational language proficiency (Ortiz, 2002). Peer or expert consultation can involve teachers observing their peers and providing interventions to English language learners who need supplemental instruction. Support can also be provided in consultation with an ESL (English as a second language) teacher. The ESL teacher can furnish information on how to integrate ESL strategies into academic instruction.

The teacher assistance team process (Chalfant & Van Dusen Pysh, 1989) can be utilized as another option to assist teachers in providing appropriate instruction for English language learners. In this model, Ortiz (2002) describes a collaborative, team approach that discusses the problem, identifies possible interventions, and assists the teacher as needed in implementing strategies. Finally, Ortiz (2002) provides ideas for alternative programs and services that teachers can implement in collaboration with colleagues and families. The Considering Diversity feature offers information about each of these strategies.

Next, we will talk about developing collaborative partnerships with paraprofessionals. These individuals are critical players in addressing the needs of students with special needs, especially students with more severe disabilities.

How Can Professionals Collaborate with Paraprofessionals?

Paraprofessionals, or paraeducators, are individuals who are hired as teacher assistants to work with teachers in a supportive role under the supervision of licensed professionals (IDEA, 2004). Their titles vary across schools and districts;

paraprofessionals may be called paraeducators, nonteaching assistants, classroom assistants, teaching assistants, or special support assistants, among other titles. Whatever their title, they are members of the instructional team in classrooms and other educational settings, and they often deliver direct services to students and their families (Werts, Harris, Tillery, & Roark, 2004).

Paraeducators are increasingly being relied on to provide special education services to students with more severe disabilities. In addition to performing clerical tasks and providing student supervision, daily needs care, mobility support, and behavior support (Downing, Ryndak, & Clark, 2000; Minondo, Meyer, & Xin, 2001), paraeducators are increasingly being required to teach instructional lessons (Pickett & Gerlach, 2003).

Why are paraeducators being given increasing responsibilities, particularly with students who have severe needs? Giangreco, Edelman, Broer, and Doyle (2001) cite Kozleski, Mainzer, and Deshler (2000) and Pickett (1999) as stating that there is a decreasing number of qualified special educators and there is concern that excessive paperwork, expanded caseloads, inadequate administrative support, and other factors that cause poor working conditions force school administrators to hire more paraeducators to fill the void. One result of such a change in hiring practices is that teachers may be less involved in teaching students who present severe challenges. Giangreco and his colleagues provide a citation that illustrates the problem when they quote Brown, Farrington, Ziegler, Knight, and Ross (1999) as suggesting that students with the most complex challenges to learning "are in dire need of continuous exposure to the most ingenious, creative, powerful, competent, interpersonally effective, and informed professionals" (p. 252).

What is known about paraprofessionals? Studies have shown that most paraprofessionals are women who typically live in the area served by the school in which they work (Balshaw & Farrell, 2002; French, 2004). In many cases, paraprofessionals can bridge linguistic and cultural connections between the school and the community (Chopra et al., 2004). Thus paraprofessionals can make connections between their schools and the families and community affiliated with their schools. In a study by French and Chopra (1999), parents indicated that they viewed paraprofessionals as important links between home and school. In a study on demographics of paraprofessionals, Blalock (1990) found that of 136 individuals working in a large school district in a southwestern state, 92 percent were female, 54 percent were Hispanic, 34 percent and 38 percent were between the ages of 30–39 and 40–49, respectively, and 78 percent had a high school diploma or had obtained a GED. No Child Left Behind (2002) indicates that paraprofessionals must now have a high school diploma or its equivalent. Additionally, paraprofessionals who provide instructional support must have

- Completed two years of study at an institution of higher education,
- Obtained an associates (or higher) degree, or
- Demonstrated, through a formal state or local assessment, knowledge of, and ability to assist in, reading, writing, and mathematics instruction

These criteria aside, researchers have noted that paraeducators' qualifications and educational backgrounds vary widely (Balshaw & Farrell, 2002). Very few paraeducators come to their jobs with any training or experience in general education or special education (Riggs & Mueller, 2001).

Paraprofessionals are important members of the school team. Their role has become one of serving a more diverse student population and supporting the inclusion of students with more significant disabilities in the general education classroom (Bernal & Aragon, 2004; French, 2004). Paraprofessionals account for more than half of the nonteaching staff that provides services to students with special needs (White, 2004). Yet Giangreco and Doyle (2007) note that "at present, there is no international consensus about the extent to which teacher assistants [paraeducators] should be utilized, circumstances that warrant their involvement, there duties they should appropriately perform, or what constitutes adequate training and supervision" (p. 437). The concern of adequate training and supervision is the focus of the remainder of this section, because only through collaborative partnerships can such training and supervision be adequately addressed.

The Need for Collaborative Partnerships with Paraprofessionals

At one time paraprofessionals spent most of their time performing clerical duties; monitoring the halls, playground, and cafeteria; and supervising students who were being disciplined for behavior problems. However, the role of the paraprofessional has evolved with increased awareness of the valuable contributions they can make in diverse and inclusive educational settings. Increased training opportunities have led to many paraprofessionals developing important skills that can benefit educational teams.

● Paraprofessionals account for more than half of the nonteaching staff that provide services to students with special needs.

According to Blalock (1991), since the 1960s paraprofessionals have been in great demand to assist in the delivery of services to students with disabilities. Today, that demand continues as more students with disabilities receive their instruction in general education settings. These students may require services beyond those that general educators can reasonably provide. In addition to working in special education and general education classes, paraprofessionals are needed to assist with the implementation of instruction that is based in the community. Community-based instruction may involve paraprofessionals riding public transportation with students to their job sites, assisting students with disabilities on job site tasks, and participating with students and teachers in community activities designed to promote recreational and social skills.

Thus, as options expand for providing services and effective instruction to students with special needs, the need for collaborative relationships with paraprofessionals to work with students with special needs remains an important part of the collaborative process in inclusive schools. Several areas must be considered for developing collaborative partnerships with paraprofessionals, including the establishment of roles and responsibilities and the provision of supervision and training. The next two sections address these areas.

Roles and Responsibilities of Paraprofessionals in Collaborative Partnerships

According to IDEA (2004), teachers are responsible for ensuring the delivery of services specified in the IEP. However, paraprofessionals have an important role to play in supporting the delivery of these services. Communication about roles and responsibilities helps everyone understand the expectations when providing services to students and their families.

Clear job descriptions, specifying roles and responsibilities, can enhance communication between teachers and paraprofessionals and foster appropriate expectations. Paraprofessionals and teachers should know about one another's job descriptions so that each is familiar with the requirements of the positions. Typically, job descriptions include a definition of the job, general responsibilities, and specific hiring requirements (e.g., amount of education, contractual duty day, and length of school year). Because of the guidelines provided, reviewing job descriptions is a good place to begin a discussion about roles and responsibilities. The job description usually provides information that school district administrative personnel feel is important for particular roles; thus, teachers and paraprofessionals must abide by the established job guidelines.

Once job descriptions have been reviewed, teachers and paraprofessionals can work together to delineate specific roles and responsibilities. It is important to specify roles in order to clarify classroom responsibilities and to establish the authority of the teacher as supervisor and evaluator in the paraprofessional–teacher relationship. Specific roles can be identified, and responsibilities pertaining to each role can be discussed. For example, roles might include instruction, administration, behavior management, assessment, and communication with families and other professionals. Together, teachers and paraprofessionals can develop a responsibilities list for each role and can identify areas for training, philosophical discussion, and further explanation (Blalock, 1991). Teachers have the responsibility for the development, implementation, and evaluation of their students' individualized education programs (IEPs) and for the safety and well-being of the students. However, paraprofessionals can greatly assist in a collaborative way to support these responsibilities. The following include examples of possible responsibilities for paraprofessionals:

Assessment

- Conducting curriculum based assessments
- Scoring curriculum based assessments

Behavior Management

- Implementing behavior management programs designed with the classroom teacher
- Awarding points to students for appropriate behavior
- Monitoring of behavior in small or whole groups

Instruction

- Providing instructional adaptations for lessons taught by teachers
- Monitoring student work in learning centers
- Providing small-group instruction to students who require more assistance

Communication

- Serving as a link between special education and general education teachers
- Meeting regularly with the classroom teacher to discuss specific student needs, instructional programs, successes, and concerns
- Facilitating communication with parents for whom English is not their primary language

Clerical Support

- Conducting tasks to maintain classroom organization and management
- Developing instructional materials

Student Support

- Working with students in community job-related settings
- Escorting students during hallway, recess, and lunch activities

Professionalism

- Attending professional meetings with their teachers or with other paraprofessionals

The years of experience with employment and community connection of the paraprofessional can influence the dynamics between the teacher and the paraprofessional. Often the paraprofessional is older than the teacher, has been at the school longer, and may have strong community connections with families, businesses, and children. These dynamics must be respected; however, the dynamics should not be allowed to undermine the role of the teacher as supervisor of the paraprofessional and as the person contractually responsible for the education of the students.

Through effective communication techniques, teachers can tap the valuable knowledge that paraprofessionals possess through their connections with the school and community. Alternatively, teachers should be sensitive to the needs of younger paraprofessionals who may lack experience and educational expertise.

Thus, it is important for teachers to invest time in establishing rapport and team-building behaviors so that a truly collaborative partnership can be nurtured. The following are examples of possible barriers to the development of collaborative partnerships with paraeducators and solutions for removing the barriers.

Barriers	Solutions
Time	Try to set aside 30 minutes several days a week, before or after school, to discuss students' progress.
Roles and responsibilities	Discuss roles and responsibilities clearly so that each person knows his or her duties.
Years of experience	Tap the expertise of paraprofessionals who have been working at the school longer than the teacher; help build the self-confidence of new paraprofessionals.

Experienced paraprofessionals contribute important information to any dialog regarding ongoing respectful relations between themselves and teachers. For example, Riggs (2005) presented a list of what paraprofessionals identified as being important for beginning teachers to know about working with them.

- Know their name, background, and interests.
- Know about district policies for paraprofessionals.
- View the paraprofessional as a member of the professional team.
- Define roles and responsibilities.
- Supervise the paraprofessional.
- Communicate with the paraprofessional.
- Acknowledge the paraprofessional's experiences and knowledge.
- Be respectful of paraprofessionals.
- Assume "ownership" of all students.

Supervision and Training of Paraprofessionals

Teachers are typically responsible for supervising and evaluating paraprofessionals with whom they work. In some cases, principals may share in the supervisory and evaluative process, but usually teachers assume the greater part of this responsibility.

Ongoing communication is vital to any supervisory situation. Paraprofessionals, like any employee, should be given opportunities to work with their supervisors in determining how they will be supervised and evaluated. Teachers and paraprofessionals must review job descriptions, roles, and responsibilities as a starting point in the supervisory process. Specific tasks and expectations must be communicated effectively to reduce role ambiguity and misinterpretations. At a minimum, weekly meetings are recommended to review the paraprofessionals' tasks and job performance. Paraprofessionals should be given feedback about their performance, both positive and negative, on a regular basis.

Teachers should examine their supervisory style to ensure their adoption of practices that foster collegial relationships. An authoritarian style will not promote a spirit of collaboration, but a sharing, direct approach, where the teacher and paraprofessional have an equal opportunity to reflect on situations, can facilitate a collaborative partnership. Paraprofessionals also should have an opportunity to discuss practices by their supervisors that either impede or foster communication and the fulfillment of role responsibilities. Teachers can ask the following questions to promote communication and build a collaborative partnership:

- How do you think we are doing working together as a team?
- What can we do to make our team stronger, to help students more, or to work better with each other?
- What would you like to discuss with me about how our teaming is working?
- What is important to you to make our teaming work well?
- How would you describe our team to others?
- What advice would you offer to another teacher–paraprofessional team just beginning together?

Teacher training in effective supervisory practices and evaluation criteria makes it easier to serve in the role of supervisor and evaluator. If training is not available, teachers should seek assistance from their building principal and special education coordinators to identify ways to become an effective supervisor and to conduct employee evaluations. Often, school districts have career ladders for paraprofessionals where promotion depends on positive evaluations. Therefore, it is in everyone's best interest for teachers to learn about (1) evaluation criteria, (2) ways to conduct an evaluation (e.g., providing feedback, stating strengths and weaknesses, problem solving, conflict resolution), and (3) techniques to foster professional development in areas where improvement is needed.

Vasa, Steckelberg, and Hoffman (1986) recommended that the paraprofessional evaluation process include a self-evaluation, a parent evaluation, an observation checklist by the teacher, and the school district's classified personnel evaluation. The data from these evaluations across different sources and experiences should yield a descriptive profile of the paraprofessional from which specific strengths and weaknesses can be identified and a follow-up plan developed to foster growth.

Training for paraprofessionals is a critical element of effective supervisory practices. It is not enough to tell someone about weaknesses without offering options for improvement. School district human resources offices could team with teachers to determine specific areas in which paraprofessionals might benefit from inservice training. Many paraprofessionals may be working for the first time with children who have disabilities; thus, they may not possess the skills necessary to meet individual students' needs (e.g., educational, health, medical, and/or language). Paraprofessionals may be individuals who have effective interpersonal skills and a caring attitude but may need to acquire skills specific to the populations with whom they are working. Therefore, school district administrators should consider training options for these critical team members.

A variety of training options are possible. First, local community colleges can provide classes geared to developing skills that paraprofessionals will need to work in the public schools. School district and community college personnel could easily develop a curriculum to serve this training need. Second, teachers can provide informal training in their classrooms as they work with children. Through modeling, prompting, and "think-aloud" situations, teachers can instruct paraprofessionals in the skills they will need to work effectively with students. Periodic meetings between teachers and paraprofessionals can ensure that proper feedback is provided to correct problems and reinforce successes. Third, school district and university personnel can collaborate to offer a menu of inservice training opportunities for paraprofessionals (Blalock, 1991). We now turn our attention to collaborative partnerships with families. This is an important component of providing appropriate services to all students in inclusive schools.

How Can Professionals Collaborate with Families?

Families are an integral part of the school community; they know their children better than anyone and can provide critical information that can help teachers understand the students' individual needs. For years, families have been influential in the development of special education services; this influence continues as educational reform efforts (e.g., NCLB, IDEA) at the elementary and secondary level contribute to the modification and/or creation of service delivery options for students with special needs. In this section, we talk about the importance of developing collaborative partnerships with families and about situations in which this collaboration can be facilitated. The following are possible barriers and solutions for working with families.

Barriers	Solutions
Time	Be sure to meet with parents at times that are mutually agreeable. This may necessitate early-morning or late-afternoon meetings to accommodate busy work schedules.
Language	Have an interpreter present during meetings for parents who do not speak English. Be sure that written communication is in the parents' primary language.
Professional jargon	Avoid technical terms and acronyms that may be unfamiliar to parents.

The Need for Collaborative Partnerships with Families

Collaboration with families is indispensable. Families have been a significant contributor to the establishment of special education as a field. They have formed organizations, raised revenue, initiated litigation, pushed for legislation, formed advocacy groups, and demanded a free, appropriate public education in the least restrictive environment for all students with disabilities. They have clout, and they know their children.

Collaboration with families should be a major goal of all schools. However, for this goal to be achieved, educators must better understand families and their dynamics. As Pugach and Johnson so aptly noted, our "students are all members of families first and students second" (1995, p. 225). We must recognize the powerful effect that families have on the students with whom we work and must nurture collaborative relationships with families and family members. Like all students, students with special needs cannot be viewed in isolation; they are members of the total school community, of the community at large, and of their families (Smith,

tech NOTES

Collaboration to Support Technology Solutions

Within moments of Ernest's birth in 1989, we were told that he had Down syndrome. He began "school" two months later at an early childhood and infant program. Ernest began saying words at 12 months by using a sign language program (called "Makaton"). He took his first steps at the age of $2\frac{1}{2}$ with the encouragement of his friends at preschool. Over the years, Ernest's disabilities have introduced us to many wonderful professionals. My husband and I have worked hard to foster a team spirit, which has resulted in a deeply committed staff and mutual trust. The vision that our family shares of Ernest's future has been well received and enlarged beyond our expectations by professionals, teachers, and students in Ernest's classes. At one time, Ernest's occupational therapist saw our request for a classroom computer as an abandonment of learning handwriting, but

that was never our intention. Ernest has continued to work on his handwriting, although keyboarding will probably be his future means of writing. That same therapist became one of Ernest's best advocates. Ernest has been fortunate because our school is technology-rich. Ernest's special education consultant has been very good at acquiring software with discretionary funding. Ernest uses computers at school and at home. We would like to see Ernest continue learning in the regular classroom for at least part of the day, with one-to-one teaching of specific skills. Our ultimate expectation for his education is for Ernest to thrive in the real world as an adult. We are firm believers that the only way to learn life skills is for Ernest to experience life, even though it might be messy, more time-consuming, and less safe.

Source: Adapted from *Assistive Technology for People with Disabilities,* by D. P. Bryant and B. R. Bryant, 2003. Austin, TX: Psycho-Educational Services. Reproduced with permission.

Ernest's family used Makaton to help in his language development. Learn more about this tool for students at www.makaton.org.

2007). Therefore, we must come to know our students' families and understand their dynamics; only then can we be begin the process of developing effective collaborative partnerships. In the Tech Notes feature, one parent shares her story about her child and how technology is an integral part of his life. The story aptly illustrates the importance of listening to parents and understanding the dynamics in their lives with their children.

Collaborative Partnerships with Families

Using the critical prerequisite skills for effective collaboration discussed earlier in this chapter, successful partnerships with families can be nurtured to build a strong, positive relationship between families and the schools. In a variety of ways, educators can develop collaborative partnerships with families. We discuss the family systems approach as a technique for focusing on school–home relationships within a framework that is responsive to families' needs. We offer tips for working with families from diverse backgrounds. And, ideas are provided to facilitate successful parent–teacher conferences and home–school communication.

FAMILY SYSTEMS APPROACH   Collaborative efforts with students' families can be developed through a family systems approach where families' needs and support are defined according to resources, interactions, functions, and the life cycle (Turnbull et al., 2005). Families may have specific issues, such as reactions to a family member with a disability, economic needs, and future planning. Collaborative efforts can be greatly enhanced between home and school if teachers are aware of (1) the family unit (e.g., one- or two-parent family, extended family); (2) resources needed by families to function; (3) family interactions that may affect the children's mental health and school success; (4) the economic, vocational, and educational needs of families; and (5) the adult and child development cycles that influence how individuals cope with and respond to their environments.

As part of the family systems approach, educators must come to understand that families of children with disabilities will probably need different types of support systems that change as the children mature. For example, children with learning problems may manage during the preschool years, but when they enter school, issues related to learning may surface for families. Teachers should be prepared to

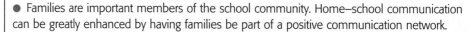

● Families are important members of the school community. Home–school communication can be greatly enhanced by having families be part of a positive communication network.

explain instructional programs and services. Some families may wonder what the future holds for their child's postsecondary education.

For families of children with behavior problems, school may be just another arena in which difficulties surface and negative encounters with "authorities" occur, resulting from misconduct. These families may not view the schools as partners in their child's education if encounters focus on what the child is doing wrong rather than on how we can help the child. For families of children with severe disabilities, an array of services involving various professionals may be offered across the grade levels. However, as these children become older, parents will want to know how their child's specific needs will continue to be addressed after high school. Aging parents will want to be assured that their child with severe disabilities will be served.

A coordinated effort among professionals is necessary to ensure that communication with families is seamless across services and that the families' evolving issues and concerns are addressed. By viewing collaborative partnerships through a family systems approach, educators can tailor their interactions with families to each family's unique configuration and needs. For example, families may have difficulty finding transportation or child care services so that they can attend school meetings. They may be dealing with health or social issues that preclude their involvement in school activities. Thus, school personnel should determine the needs of their school community and provide necessary accommodations that promote family involvement in school activities.

DIVERSITY CONSIDERATIONS   Deborah Smith (2001) examined the literature on increasing family participation, particularly that of diverse families, and generated a helpful list of suggestions for family and community involvement.

- Develop an atmosphere of trust and respect.
- Be sure families and communities feel welcome.
- Select and involve community leaders to serve as representatives of both school and home.
- Identify families' preferred means of communication and use it effectively.
- Communicate on a regular, ongoing basis (not just when there is a problem).
- Use interpreters who are knowledgeable about schools and their programs for effective communication and participation.
- Incorporate materials that reflect the diversity of the community.
- Seek meaningful ways (e.g., actively sharing culture, art, music, and re-creational activities) to involve families and communities (as they feel comfortable).
- Treat families with individual respect, and avoid stereotyping on any basis (race, ethnicity, language, or socioeconomic class).
- Hold meetings with families at times and places that are manageable for them. (p. 100)

Values and perceptions are additional areas of the family systems approach that must be addressed by professionals and paraprofessionals as they work with students and family members. A person's value system and ways of perceiving information are important factors that can impede or promote effective home–school communication and collaboration. Values and perceptions are learned from significant adults, home environments, peers, cultural and ethnic groups, and religious and social affiliations. Unfortunately, it is all too easy to fall into the trap of "assigning" negative or positive opinions to another person's value system and perceptions on the basis of misconceptions, stereotypes, miscommunication, and one's own value and perceptual systems.

Students who represent a rich cultural and linguistic heritage attend today's schools, and like all students they come from a spectrum of socioeconomic environments ranging from homelessness to considerable affluence. The challenge for educators is to become more sensitive to all types of diversity, to become better educated about differences in values and perceptions, and to focus on ways to promote collaborative relationships that tap the diverse ways of viewing home–school partnerships.

Teachers are challenged to build effective communication bridges that convey information about school activities and to take the initiative in speaking with families to demonstrate an interest in establishing collaboration. Collaborative partnerships can be developed with parents and other family members through parent conferences and home–school communication.

what
WORKS 8.2

Stages and Steps of Parent–Teacher Conferences

● Pre-Conference Stage

1. Notify families of the time, day, and purpose of the conference. Notification should be written in the primary language spoken at home. Provide options for conference times and days that are mutually convenient for parents as well as for teachers (and other professionals, such as counselors, who might be attending the conference). In many families, both parents now work, and in single-parent homes, the parent is usually employed full-time. Flexibility in conference times and days is important to increase the likelihood of parental participation (Smith & Rivera, 1993).

2. Review assessment data that describe how the child is progressing academically, socially, and behaviorally. Prepare a summary of important data and information that will help families understand their child's progress. Samples of work can be gathered as evidence of progress or of the need for remediation. Share with families the plans for promoting academic success and addressing instructional problems.

3. Develop an agenda for the meeting, including the starting and stopping times, questions that will be asked, a statement of purpose for the meeting, and time to develop a plan if necessary. Ask family members what topics they would like to discuss as part of the agenda.

4. Arrange the environment to foster a collaborative spirit, including chairs that are designed for adults (a problem at the primary level), the removal of barriers (such as tables with large spaces between families and teachers or teacher desks), and the elimination of distractions (such as intercom interruptions).

5. Identify key professionals and paraprofessionals who can contribute important information to the conference. This is especially important if the child works with a speech/language pathologist or counselor. The challenge is to ensure that there are not too many professionals present, which might be intimidating to families. In some cases, an initial parent–teacher conference might be a good approach, followed by a second meeting with other professionals, as needed. The key is to create an initial meeting in which rapport and trust can be built.

6. Make arrangements for an interpreter if English is not the primary language or if sign language is needed. In some school communities, a home–school liaison delivers the conference information so that families can communicate with school personnel right from the start.

PARENT–TEACHER CONFERENCE The parent–teacher conference is a regular forum for families and teachers to develop collaborative, communicative partnerships (Pugach & Johnson, 1995). Parent–teacher conferences can be used as a time to establish rapport with family members, to convey information about class activities, to identify individual students' strengths and weaknesses for educational planning, and to discover values and perceptions that can be nurtured to promote collaboration and communication. According to Turnbull and colleagues (2005), there are four purposes for the parent–teacher conference:

1. To jointly share information about the child educational progress
2. To work together in finding solutions to problems
3. To establish rapport and joint responsibility for the child's educational program
4. To exchange information that might contribute to a better understanding of the child's progress and individual needs

● Conference Stage

1. Provide a warm welcome; greet family members at the door and guide them to the conference meeting table. A warm greeting and comfortable environment pave the way for a positive start.

2. Present the agenda, and be sure that parents' questions and concerns are readily noted for discussion. Specify the time limits, which is important to help keep the conversation on track.

3. Begin with an explanation and display of the child's strengths. Showing work samples and describing positive situations can begin the establishment of rapport and trust.

4. Apprise family members of their child's progress and of the instructional plan for the child. Talk to families about ways to support instruction at home and tips for developing effective study and homework habits.

5. Provide opportunities for family members to discuss their concerns throughout the conference. Don't just leave the last few minutes for them to "ask questions."

6. Watch for nonverbal and verbal communication cues that might be signaling discomfort, anger, joy, and so forth. In situations where feelings begin to escalate, acknowledge points, and use the communication techniques discussed in this chapter.

7. Jot down important points during the conference; however, check with families about this practice to be sure it does not hinder communication. Writing on carbonless paper provides copies of the notes for each participant and thus eliminates the "secrecy" aura of notetaking. Writing is especially critical if a plan of action must be developed where families and teachers agree on responsibilities for solving a problem.

8. End on a positive note, summarizing issues, successes, and plans for improvement. This can foster trust and boost the likelihood of other successful conferences occurring.

● Post-Conference Stage

1. Review any notes that were taken during the conference to see whether specific activities must be planned for the following school day. If an agreement is made that certain activities (such as moving the child's desk or talking to the child privately more often) will occur, then teachers should be sure that this action is taken the following school day.

2. Discuss with other professionals, as needed, concerns about the child and follow-up plans to address those concerns. This may require the scheduling of an additional conference or the establishment of stronger home–school communication efforts.

Source: Adapted from *Teaching Students with Learning and Behavior Problems*, 3rd ed., by D. P. Rivera and D. D. Smith, 1997, Boston: Allyn and Bacon.

There are three stages of an effective parent–teacher conference: pre-conference, conference, and post-conference. Specific actions can occur during each stage to foster collaboration and communication (Pugach & Johnson, 1995). Descriptions of the steps involved in each stage are presented in What Works 8.2 (page 330). Parent–teacher conferences are a critical component of building collaborative relationships, and time must be invested in this endeavor to ensure success.

HOME–SCHOOL COMMUNICATION Families are important members of the school community; therefore, establishing rapport and effective communication procedures at the beginning of the school year are key factors in promoting collaborative partnerships. Home–school communication can be greatly enhanced by having families be part of a positive communication network (Smith & Rivera, 1993).

Oftentimes, an initial contact with families focuses on a concern or problem (e.g., a disciplinary concern, lack of homework, truancy) that requires parental notification and action. Smith and Rivera (1993) suggested that teachers make attempts, at the beginning of the school year and throughout the year, to focus on the positive—good news about class activities, student progress, and behavior go a long way in building communication bridges that foster collaboration. Then, if a contact must be made regarding concerns, teachers have a positive foundation on which they can discuss current issues.

Smith and Rivera (1993) and Turnbull et al. (2005) offered several suggestions for promoting communication. For example, teachers can send home weekly or monthly newsletters describing events, giving special student recognition, mentioning important dates, and so forth. Keep in mind that some students in all grades, and secondary school students in general, may not want to be singled out; recognizing *groups* of students might be one way to address this issue. Students can participate in the design, layout, and production of the newsletter as a language arts activity, especially with the many desktop publishing software programs now available for students of all ages.

Notes recognizing a child's accomplishments can be sent home periodically. This can be done quietly with the student to minimize public display (this is especially important at the secondary level). Experience has shown that many secondary school students do like special recognition; the key point is how the teacher handles it. Elementary school students usually can deal with public recognition.

Teachers can make telephone calls periodically to inform families of their child's progress. Calling families to say, "I just wanted to tell you the good news . . ." can help tremendously in building communication and trust.

Weekly samples of work can be collected by students and taken home to their families. This informs family members of how their children are progressing with the skills that were designated as areas to focus on for the semester or school year. Samples can include good work and work that needs improvement (with an "improved" paper included as well). This shows that students are progressing with their academic goals.

Establishing parent groups is an excellent way to form a home–school communication network; such groups can be conducted with the school's counselor. Teachers who have been teaching for several years may be ready to begin a parent group that focuses on topics of concern for many families (e.g., finishing homework, establishing study skills, building self-esteem, ways to promote reading at home). Involving a counselor will ensure that another qualified professional addresses issues beyond the teacher's area of expertise. Also, when child care is provided, more family members can take advantage of parent group training and bonding.

Some teachers involve families in the classroom. There are many ways in which teachers can solicit parent involvement. For instance, families can come to class on a regular basis just to read with students during reading time. They can share a special skill or information from a trip. Families can work as individual tutors (be sure to provide some initial training and be specific about tasks they should do). Holidays are a good time, in particular, to involve families who can bring cultural and ethnic traditions and customs to share. Families can help teachers make bulletin board displays and learning materials—have a designated night to explain these needs and see the wonderful items you get!

Weekly report cards that require a signature are another way to keep families informed, to signal areas of growth and concern, and to share a note about a special achievement. These regular report cards also give children an opportunity to discuss their progress with their families.

Developing communication bridges takes time and effort, and teachers must be aware of cultural and linguistic factors to consider when working with families. Frequent positive and informative communication, which is written in the parents' primary language, is important. In the long run, the benefits usually are great and promote the type of home–school communication that contributes to the children's progress.

summary

Collaborative partnerships are an important component of effective inclusive practices. The collaboration process involves individuals who choose to work together to address educational issues in schools. Collaboration consists of shared problem solving, shared responsibility, and voluntary participation in the process. Collaborative members need to be skilled in communication skills that foster trust, respect, caring, and openness. Effective conflict resolution skills and an awareness of diversity issues, particularly in the context of communication styles, are critical to effective collaboration.

Developing collaborative partnerships with professionals, paraprofessionals, and families is an important component of school communities. A variety of models and procedures can be used to ensure that educators and families collaborate effectively to benefit all students.

self-test QUESTIONS

Let's review the learning objectives for this chapter. If you are uncertain and cannot "talk through" the answers provided for any of these questions, reread those sections of the text.

• **What are the characteristics of collaboration?**

Successful collaboration includes shared problem solving, shared responsibility, and voluntary involvement. These characteristics imply that

the individuals choose to share expertise, decision making, and involvement to promote effective inclusive practices for all students.

• **What foundation skills are critical for effective collaboration?**

Communication and conflict resolution skills are important for promoting effective collaborative partnerships. Professionals must also be aware of the cultural, linguistic, and socioeconomic backgrounds of their students and must accommodate differences in values and perceptions.

- **What are applications of professional collaboration?**

  Effective practices include collaboration–consultation, co-teaching, and strategies for English language learners, such as the clinical teaching cycle, peer or expert consultation, the Teacher Assistance Team process, and alternative programs and services.

- **How can teachers and paraprofessionals develop collaborative partnerships?**

  The establishment of roles, supervision and training, and teaming are some approaches that

promote effective partnerships between professionals and paraprofessionals. Paraprofessionals should be given opportunities to express their issues and concerns.

- **What practices promote collaborative partnerships with families?**

  Professionals should use a family systems approach when working with families. This approach takes into consideration the range of needs that families have regarding their child's education and well-being. Professionals can also use parent–teacher conferences and home–school communication as opportunities to develop partnerships. Professionals should be mindful of cultural considerations as they work with families.

● Revisit the
OPENING challenge

Check your answers to the Reflection Questions in the Opening Challenge and revise them on the basis of what you have learned.

1. What professional collaborative practices can Ms. Warren use to help her students who have special learning, behavior, and language needs succeed in the general education classroom?

2. How can Ms. Warren collaborate effectively with her paraprofessional?

3. How can Ms. Warren effectively structure parent–teacher conferences and develop home–school communication effectively?

Professional Standards and Licensure

CEC Knowledge and Skill Core Standard and Associated Subcategories

CEC Content Standard 1: Foundations

Special educators understand the field as an evolving and changing discipline based on philosophies, evidence-based principles and theories, relevant laws and policies, diverse historical points of view, and human issues that have historically influenced the treatment of individuals with exceptional needs both in school and society.

CEC Content Standard 3: Individual Learning Differences

Special educators understand the effects that an exceptional condition can have on an individual's learning in school and

throughout life. They understand the similarities and differences in human development and the characteristics between and among individuals with and without ELN.

CEC Content Standard 5: Learning Environments and Social Interactions

Special educators actively create learning environments for individuals with ELN that foster cultural understanding, safety and emotional well-being, positive social interactions, and active engagement. Special educators help their general education colleagues integrate individuals with ELN in regular environments.

CEC Content Standard 7: Instructional Planning

Individualized decision-making and instruction is at the center of special education practice. Special educators develop long-range individualized instructional plans anchored in both general and special curricula. Individualized instructional plans emphasize explicit modeling and efficient guided practice to assure acquisition and fluency through maintenance and generalization. Understanding of these factors, as well as the implications of an individual's exceptional condition, guides the special educator's selection, adaptation, and creation of materials, and the use of powerful instructional variables. Instructional plans are modified based on ongoing analysis of the individual's learning progress.

CEC Content Standard 9: Professional and Ethical Practice

Special educators are guided by the profession's ethical and professional practice standards. They practice in multiple roles and complex situations across wide age and developmental ranges. Special educators are aware of how their own and others' attitudes, behaviors, and ways of communicating can influence their practice.

CEC Content Standard 10: Collaboration

Special educators routinely and effectively collaborate with families, other educators, related service providers, and personnel from community agencies in culturally responsive ways. This collaboration assures that the needs of individuals with ELN are addressed throughout schooling.

INTASC Core Principle and Associated Special Education Subcategories

7. Instructional Planning

7.02 All teachers plan ways to modify instruction, as needed, to facilitate positive learning results within the general curriculum for students with disabilities.

7.03 All teachers collaborate to plan instruction related to expanded curriculum in general education classrooms for students with disabilities.

3. Learner Differences

3.02 All teachers recognize that a specific disability does not dictate how an individual student will learn.

5. Learning Environment

5.03 All teachers take deliberate action to promote positive social relationships among students with disabilities and their age-appropriate peers in the learning community.

7. Instructional Planning

7.02 All teachers plan ways to modify instruction to facilitate positive learning results within the general education curriculum for students with disabilities.

9. Teacher Reflection

All teachers continually challenge their beliefs about how students with disabilities learn and how to teach them effectively.

10. Collaboration, Ethics, and Relationships

10.01 All teachers share instructional responsibility for students with disabilities and work to develop well-functioning collaborative teaching relationships.

10.04 All teachers accept families as full partners in planning appropriate instruction and services for students with disabilities, and provide meaningful opportunities for them to participate as partners in their children's instructional programs.

Praxis II: Education of Exceptional Students: Core Content Knowledge

II. Legal and Societal Issues

Federal laws and legal issues related to special education, including

- Public Law 105-17

The school's connections with the families, prospective and actual employers, and communities of students with disabilities, for example

- Parent partnerships and roles
- Cultural and community influences on public attitudes toward individuals with disabilities

Historical movements/trends affecting the connections between special education and the larger society, for example

- Inclusion
- Advocacy
- Accountability and meeting educational standards

III. Delivery of Services to Students with Disabilities

Background knowledge, including

- Conceptual approaches underlying service delivery to students with disabilities
- Placement and program issues such as early intervention; least restrictive environment; inclusion; role of individualized education program (IEP) team; due process guidelines; and others

Curriculum and instruction and their implementation across the continuum of education placements, including

- The individualized family service plan (IFSP)/individualized education program (IEP) process
- Instructional development and implementation
- Instructional format and components

Structuring and managing the learning environment, including

- Structuring the learning environment

Professional roles, including

- Specific roles and responsibilities of teachers
- Communicating with parents, guardians, and appropriate community collaborators

Video—"Classroom Aides"

In this video, a paraprofessional talks about working one-to-one with a student with special needs who is included in a general education classroom.

Log onto **www.mylabschool.com**. Under the **Courses** tab, in **Special Education,** go to the **video lab**. Access the "**Professional Collaboration**" videos and watch the "**Classroom Aides**" video.

 OR

Use the **www.mylabschool.com Assignment Finder** to go directly to these videos. Just enter Assignment ID **SPV3**.

1. What is the role of the paraprofessional in this classroom? Do you think a paraprofessional is needed to assist this student? Explain.

2. How are the experiences discussed by the paraprofessional in this video related to what you have learned in the chapter about working with paraprofessionals?

Video—"The Collaborative Process"

In this video, a classroom teacher works collaboratively with another teaching professional. Their combined teaching efforts provide additional help for students. They offer a good example of collaboration.

Log onto **www.mylabschool.com**. Under the **Courses** tab, in **Special Education**, go to the **video lab**. Access the "**Professional Collaboration**" videos and watch the video "**The Collaborative Process**."

 OR

Use the **www.mylabschool.com Assignment Finder** to go directly to these videos. Just enter Assignment ID **SPV3**.

1. Describe the features of effective collaboration expressed in the video.
2. In what ways do the students in this video benefit from having these two teachers plan the lesson together?

To access chapter objectives, practice tests, weblinks, and flashcards, go to the companion website at **www.ablongman.com/bryantsmith1e**.

Promoting Positive Behavior and Facilitating Social Skills

chapter OBJECTIVES

After studying this chapter, you will have the knowledge to answer the following questions:

- What practices can be used to foster student relationships and communication?
- How can classroom arrangements promote positive behavior and social interactions?
- Why do students misbehave, and what are the components of positive behavioral supports?
- What interventions can teachers use to prevent and address behavior problems?
- How can teachers assess behavior and social skills?
- What curricular and instructional interventions can teachers use to teach social skills?

● OPENING challenge

Ms. Martinez Is Puzzled About Behavior and Social Problems

It is October of Ms. Martinez's second year of teaching fifth grade, and she is planning lessons for the upcoming week. She connects her lessons to her school district's curriculum. She makes sure that there are activities that keep her students engaged. Depending on the lesson, she pairs students with disabilities with students who have stronger skills. However, things are not going very well for her students with disabilities. Ms. Martinez is puzzled about three students who seem to challenge her day in and day out. She has read their school folders, but she feels that she doesn't know them well.

One student, Sam, is identified as having attention deficit hyperactivity disorder (ADHD). She studied this condition in her teacher-preparation program, and even worked with one student with ADHD during student teaching, but having a student with ADHD in her class all day long is wearing her out. Ms. Martinez begins to question her ability to work effectively with Sam: *"How can I get him to pay attention? How can I help him get organized? He forgets what to do and can't re-*

member to return homework. Why does he have so few friends? Am I really prepared to help this child learn?"

Her second student, Eric, is identified as having a mild emotional or behavioral disorder. He was retained in first grade. Ms. Martinez worries about Eric: *"I don't really understand his disability. Why is he so defiant? He seems to do things on purpose just to be disruptive and get everyone's attention. What can I do with him so that he will stop interfering with my teaching? Why does he bully the other children? Shouldn't he be in a special education classroom?"*

Finally, Ms. Martinez turns her thoughts to Luisa, who has a learning disability in reading and writing: *"She seems so lost during group instruction and spends way too much time fiddling with things in her desk, sharpening her pencils, and being off task. Why can't she work with the other students? What's wrong?"*

"How can I help these students behave? What can I do about their social skills? How do I know whether my teaching practices are working?"

339

Reflection Questions

In your journal, write down your answers to the following questions. After completing the chapter, check your answers and revise them on the basis of what you have learned.

1. What advice would you offer Ms. Martinez about getting to know her students better?

2. How can she foster student relationships and communication?

3. How can Ms. Martinez help her students with their behavior?

4. How can she facilitate the students' social skills?

5. How can she determine whether student behavior and social skills are improving?

6. How can Ms. Martinez use the ADAPT framework to promote positive behavior and facilitate social skills?

The classroom is a social environment in which academic instruction must thrive. For teaching to be successful, teachers must create, nurture, and manage a classroom environment that supports student learning and interactions, minimizes situations that contribute to the occurrence of problem behaviors, and addresses those unacceptable behaviors that interfere with teaching and learning. For example, consider Sam, Eric, and Luisa in the Opening Challenge. Practices are readily available that teachers can employ to help students with their behavior and social problems. Some of these practices are presented in this chapter. Research has confirmed that teacher attention to nurturing and managing the classroom, student behavior, and social aspects of learning contribute significantly to promoting an environment that is conducive to teaching and learning (Marquis et al., 2000; Polsgrove & Ochoa, 2004; Rosenberg, Wilson, Maheady, & Sindelar, 1997; Wolfgang, 1995).

This chapter presents practices that teachers can use to improve student relationships and communication. You will learn about ways to promote appropriate behavior and to facilitate the social skills of *all* students. You will also learn about interventions that may be necessary for a small number of students so that these students can succeed in inclusive settings. Assessment techniques will help you to identify behaviors and social skills that require intervention and to determine if these interventions are effective. Finally, you will learn about positive behavioral supports, a process supported by IDEA (2004), and also about ways to promote safer schools. The ADAPT framework will be implemented throughout the chapter so that you can learn how to use the framework to promote positive behavior and to facilitate social skills in your classroom.

What Practices Can I Use to Foster Positive Relationships with My Students?

There are a number of practices you can adopt to cultivate good relationships with—and among—the students you teach.

340

Get to Know Your Students

Students' attitudes, beliefs, experiences, and backgrounds influence their perceptions of school and learning and how they approach their relationship with their teachers. Teachers who get to know their students quickly can structure their teaching according to students' interests, background experiences, and attitudes. By doing so, teachers show they care about their students and make connections between their students and teaching. Getting to know students by taking time to talk with them (before school, between classes, during a conference, and in small groups) is one of the most powerful techniques for fostering positive relationships and creating an effective learning community.

How can teachers learn more about their students with disabilities? A good place to begin is by examining students' individualized education programs (IEPs) (for a complete discussion on IEPs, see Chapter 5) to determine their academic and social goals. IEPs can provide helpful information about those areas in which the students need support. Such areas might actually be prerequisite skills for those behavior and social skills tasks that teachers expect from their students. For example, students are expected to follow classroom directions. If the student's IEP states that assistance is needed to help the student follow directions, then the teacher may need to adapt the delivery of directions for that student by shortening the length of directions and including cues and reminders. With practice, these simple adaptations can be implemented very naturally and without much effort. Oftentimes, simple adaptations benefit many students in the classroom, including those who have IEPs.

Teachers can also get to know their students through a variety of activities. For example, students can complete an interest inventory, which consists of a series of questions geared for a particular age group. It can help teachers find out more about their students' background, interests, and perspectives. Questions that help teachers get to know students better include the following:

- "How many brothers and sisters do you have?"
- "What is your favorite movie and why?"
- "What was the name of the last book you read that you enjoyed?"
- "What is your favorite sport?"
- "What do you like to do after school?"
- "What do you like to do on the weekends?"
- "What is your favorite television show?"
- "Who is your hero and why?"
- "How do you know if someone is your friend?"
- "How can we help people who are mean to other people?"
- "If you could change one thing about school, what would it be and why?"
- "What do you like most about school?"
- "How do you spend time with your family?"
- "If you could change one thing in your life, what would that be?"

Answers to these sample questions, obtained orally or in writing, can provide teachers with information about their students. Information from the interest inventory can be used to initiate discussions, to help decide which books to select for the reading center or for class literature groups, or to identify a topic for group work and research. Interest inventory answers also can provide important information about students' cultural backgrounds and experiences (Rivera & Smith, 1997).

Use Motivational Practices

Implementing practices to motivate students is another way that you can foster positive student relationships. When designing or implementing instruction, it is important to focus on what motivates students to perform well, whether academically, behaviorally, or socially. For example, at times students may be bored or frustrated with the academic materials presented to them. Those who have been identified as gifted and talented may not be challenged sufficiently in inclusive settings with the core curriculum. Enrichment activities provided in instructional materials or in basal textbooks (i.e., those used to teach subject-area content) can be good sources of extra stimulation needed by those students who are gifted and talented. In contrast, students with learning and behavior difficulties have experienced varying degrees of success and failure with academic and social interactions during their school years. These successes and failures influence their motivational levels for classroom activities and assignments.

Later in this chapter, information about functional behavioral assessment (FBA) is presented. This process can help teachers determine possible reasons why students are not motivated to do their best in class. Identifying specific reasons through FBA can influence how teachers approach teaching. For example, if some students are reluctant to work on a research project, giving them more instruction in the steps for doing research or in getting online to locate research materials may increase their motivation to complete a research project.

Older students, in particular, may present challenging behavior that is often driven by a lack of motivation for tackling tasks that continue to frustrate them. For example, older students with reading difficulties have spent years struggling with textbook reading. As the demands of the classroom shift from "learning to read" to "reading to learn," older students may exhibit problem behavior that is a manifestation of their frustration. Given that older students may legally drop out of school, teachers of older students with academic and behavioral problems are challenged to implement effective techniques for motivating them.

In an important research study, Center, Deitz, and Kaufman (1982) examined the relationship between students' abilities and the academic tasks presented to them. They found a strong relationship between academic difficulty and inappropriate behavior; that is, as the task became too difficult or too easy for students, problem behavior occurred. This relationship is dramatic and clear. For students who misbehave because the instructional material is either too difficult or too easy, simply adjusting the materials and instructional groups can reduce or eliminate most of the disruption that these students create and can thus have a positive effect on the learning community.

When working with students of all ages, it is important to distinguish between students with a skill deficit (i.e., the student has not mastered specific skills) and those with a performance deficit (i.e., the skill or behavior is not consistently exhibited even though it is in the student's repertoire). For students who exhibit a skill deficit, teachers should spend time teaching them new skills. Oftentimes, learning new skills is motivating for some students who may have spent years struggling. Empowering students with new knowledge and the recognition that they *can* do it can go a long way toward providing motivation and creating a positive learning community. In contrast, students who exhibit performance deficits require different procedures. These are students who have learned the skill but lack the motivation to perform under certain circumstances or with certain people. For these students, some of the motivational techniques in Table 9.1 may be helpful for fostering a positive learning community.

Some students see little reason for tackling the academic activities of the day. They may not see the relevance of the tasks or be interested in the way in which activities are presented. To increase motivation, activities must be presented in a meaningful way. What are some examples of meaningful activities? Meaningful activities relate learning to students' interests and encourage students to become actively involved in learning. Student-centered learning is a type of learning that engages students actively in the learning process through the use of hands-on tasks, discussions, and decision making. It is widely supported as an effective means for teaching and learning (Huitt, 2001). Creating exciting learning experiences, such as class plays, group assignments, mock TV news productions of historical events, and field trips, encourages student involvement. Actively engaging students in the learning process and helping them make connections to real-life situations increases their motivation for participating in and completing activities (Rivera & Smith, 1997).

TABLE 9.1   Practices for Motivating Students

Category	Practices
Preconditions	Know the student's abilities.
	Manage the environment to encourage risk taking.
	Select and monitor task difficulty.
High expectations	Ensure high rates of success.
	Help students set realistic goals in a short time period.
	Through modeling and feedback, show students that the amount and quality of effort contribute to success.
Extrinsic motivators	Provide rewards for achieving goals; tailor the reward to the age and interest level of the student.
	Implement purposeful competition that taps the abilities of students.
	Use contracts.
Intrinsic motivators	Tailor tasks to match student interests.
	Provide opportunities for students to choose tasks or to set the schedule for completion of tasks.
	Use student-centered, activity-based learning to complement teacher-directed instruction.

Source: Adapted from *Preventing School Failure. Tactics for Teaching Adolescents* (2nd ed.), by T. Lovitt, 2000, Austin, TX: PRO-ED.

Be Responsive to Cultural Differences

Demographic changes within our society mean that today's classrooms include students from diverse linguistic, ethnic, racial, and socioeconomic backgrounds (U.S. Census Bureau, 1999). This rich heritage of diversity, coupled with a wide range of familial experiences, serves as a strong foundation for classroom instruction and has created a new context for teaching (Hernandez, 2001). Teachers should be informed about the social and behavioral norms of various cultural, ethnic, and racial groups. Teachers should determine how these norms may be manifested in classroom settings and how they may interact with the "norms" found in classrooms and in a pluralistic society (Vaughan, 2004). Fostering positive student relationships requires educators to be sensitive to the diverse norms brought to classrooms so that they can understand the behavior of different groups and be responsive to these cultural variations (Sleeter, 1995; Vaughan, 2004). For example, in some cultures (e.g., Native American, Hawaiian) the spirit of cooperation is contrary to the focus on competitiveness that is found in White culture and in many of today's classrooms (Smith, 2007).

It is important for teachers to understand behavioral patterns that are socially acceptable in certain cultures so that they can avoid the risk of misidentifying students as possibly having behavioral disorders. For example, students who exhibit behavioral interactions that are counter to "mainstream" behavior could be mistakenly identified as having emotional or behavioral disabilities. The potential long-term and negative effects on school achievement when students are misidentified as having disabilities are both obvious and well documented (Obiakor, 1999). The misdiagnosis of a disability and inappropriate placement in special education can be disastrous for a student. The results can be reduced expectations from parents and teachers, low self-esteem, and feelings of inferior achievement.

For example, in Chapter 4 you read about the disproportionate representation of African American and Hispanic students in special education. Some parents, educators, and policymakers believe that one reason for these students' disproportionate representation may rest in a conflict between teachers' perceptions and students' cultural identity (Neal, McCray, Webb-Johnson, & Bridgest, 2003). Take a few moments to read the example in the Considering Diversity feature on the potential conflict between a teacher's perceptions and a student's cultural identity.

Research by Nancy Cloud, a specialist in the delivery of curricula and instruction for students with diverse cultural backgrounds and ability levels, offers information about being responsive to cultural differences. Cloud (2002) and her colleagues (2000) found that differences across cultures in people's interactional behaviors—in the ways people interact with one another—influence how people behave. It takes time for students from different groups to understand the behaviors that may be expected in a formal classroom setting where Anglo-American norms may be in effect. These differences include the following:

- **Amount of adult guidance**—preferences about the level of adult guidance in accomplishing tasks
- **Comfort with an individual versus a group response**—participation as a group member rather than individually representing ideas
- **Eye contact**—whether direct eye contact or avoidance of it signals respect for authority figures
- **Comfort with guessing**—willingness to guess versus preference to refrain from answering unless sure of responses

Considering *Diversity*

Mixed Messages?

One expression of cultural identity among African American male adolescents is a walking style that many educators consider "nonstandard." The *stroll*, as it is sometimes called, is characterized as a "deliberately swaggered or bent posture, with the head held slightly tilted to the side, one foot dragging, and an exaggerated knee bend (dip)." This raises interesting questions about making assumptions on the basis of behaviors related to cultural identity. For instance:

How can a student's walk contribute to a teacher's perceptions about individual student achievement, aggression, or need for special education?

How might a teacher's perceptions about students' behavior influence referrals to special education?

Some answers to these questions come from research. Based on students' styles of walking, teachers made the following decisions about middle school boys:

Boys, regardless of race or ethnicity, who stroll are more likely to be judged by teachers as having lower achievement than those who use standard walking styles.

Those who stroll are viewed as being more aggressive and deviant.

Without information about academic achievement, these boys are also thought of as being in need of special education.

In other words, teachers are likely to mistake cultural differences, such as walking style, with cognitive and behavioral disabilities, placing those students at risk for underachievement, inappropriate referrals to special education, and misidentification as students with disabilities.

Source: From The effects of African American movement styles on teachers' perceptions and reactions, by L. V. I. Neal et al., 2003, *The Journal of Special Education, 37,* 49–51.

How can teachers better understand the cultural values and norms in today's diverse classrooms? How can they plan and implement practices that are responsive to cultural and ethnic norms? Teachers can learn more about their students through observation, questionnaires, and student–teacher conferences (Cloud, 2002). They can ask students how they like to work (alone or in a group), how large a group they prefer, how they seek adult feedback, how they feel about being praised publicly and privately, how they respond to rewards, and how they are disciplined. Student input will help teachers create student-centered activities. Teachers can learn how students from diverse backgrounds perceive the rules and expectations imposed by the teaching staff and the school. Additionally, it is important for teachers to understand how families perceive school environments and the discipline of their children. Teachers can strive to integrate these values and norms into a more cohesive learning community.

Conduct Student Meetings

William Glasser (1992) presented the *classroom meeting* as a way for teachers and students to confront problems and issues constructively as a group. Through group participation and ownership of issues, a positive climate can be created and positive relationships with students can be fostered. Glasser describes three types of meetings:

- The open-ended meeting is for students to discuss how they would deal with possible problems and take a "What would you do if . . ." approach to problem solving. This gives teachers a chance to discuss hypothetical problems to help students think about possible resolutions before problems come up.
- The educational/diagnostic meeting determines what students know and what they do not know about a topic to be studied. "What is . . . ?" and "Why is that a problem?" are examples of questions for learning about students' knowledge of a topic.
- The problem-solving meeting focuses on a problem exhibited in class that may be related to the handling of materials, class procedures, or a specific student. Students are asked to explain the problems they see, their effects, and possible solutions. The meeting concludes with an agreed-upon plan (Wolfgang, 1995).

Making a Difference

One-to-One Time Helps Behavior Management

Megan Garnett
*General Education Teacher,
Grades 10 and 12
Robinson Secondary School
Fairfax, Virginia*

In my over eight years of teaching high school history, I have learned that most classroom management issues stem from frustration related to learning problems and/or disrespect of the teachers, the school, or the subject matter. External factors also play a role, as achievement is negatively impacted when students struggle with issues at home or with their peers. Knowing this, I make a concerted effort each year to impress upon my students that I care about them and will do whatever it takes to ensure their success. I show this by engaging students on a personal level before, during, or after class time, or in a one-to-one conference.

I like to spend time with the kids who get to class a little early or stop by my desk after school, or I may chat briefly with individuals or groups during class activities as I move around the classroom. For some students, however, it can be more challenging, and my commitment may not be conveyed to them until I have had a serious one-to-one conversation about my concerns regarding their academic progress or their poor classroom behavior. The one-to-one conference has been one of my most effective strategies for handling classroom management issues. I make a point to do this after class or before class, because I don't want to draw negative attention to a par-

ticular student. I usually ask them why they think I have pulled them aside, and typically, they know why. I clarify or agree with their assessment of the situation; I highlight what I see as their positive qualities; and then I ask them how we can fix whatever problem we have identified. I will often come right out and say, "Whatever it takes, that's what I'll do to help you." I believe in collaborating with my students in order to develop a plan to improve academic performance or discontinue inappropriate behavior. Occasionally, I draw up a written contract on which we can both agree. I will not involve parents at first because I want my students to self-advocate and feel a responsibility for their success. These are strategies that have been effective for all of my students, but they have been particularly successful with students with diagnosed learning and/or behavior problems who have struggled in school for some time.

Students who enter my classroom with IEPs are typically classified as having a learning disability. Their level of difficulty varies, but reading comprehension and/or writing

For older students, Lovitt (2000) recommends a peer-forum technique that was implemented by Lewandowski (1989) as a means for students to discuss issues and resolve problems. The peer forum is a panel of students who have had trouble in school and who have agreed to talk with their peer group about how they handled these difficulties. Panel members discuss problems they encountered in school and offer positive advice about how they handled their problems. Additionally, panel members discuss strategies for being successful in school, such as study techniques, counseling, and how to access additional resources. By engaging older students who have dealt with their problems in conversations with peers who may be experiencing similar problems, students demonstrate problem solving, enhancing the opportunity for a more positive community approach to learning and problem resolution. In the Making a Difference feature, you will read about one teacher's effort to work one-to-one with a student who needed extra support. Next, we discuss techniques for promoting effective communication.

are common challenges in history classes. Recently, I had a student, Bonnie, who had difficulties with both reading and writing. Frequently tardy and rarely on task, she often distracted her peers. My notes of encouragement and suggestions to stay after school for help went unheeded. I felt at this point that I needed to contact her parents, and I learned from them that she had trouble focusing and keeping organized, thus making her late for school. Her lack of focus and organization also impacted her ability to complete assignments and/or turn them in on time. I shared some of my frustrations with her parents after I was forced to assign detention for Bonnie after she was tardy several days in a row. Her parents were supportive. So was Bonnie's Basic Skills teacher, who had worked with Bonnie on study skills and time management skills, who had helped her with projects and smaller homework assignments, and who elaborated on her difficulties and gave me some perspective on her past experiences in history. It was clear that part of Bonnie's issue was that she had not been particularly successful in her history classes in the past.

I needed Bonnie to see that I would not let her fail, so I told her I knew she was frustrated, but I could help. I explained that her behavior was hurting her academically and was disrespectful to her peers and me. Purposefully, I timed the detention for the day before a history test so we could complete the study guide together, in a one-to-one conference. I modeled strategies like utilizing images, highlighting, color-coding, and note-taking using one's own words. I further helped her by creating a study guide and scaffolding complex writing assignments by breaking down her large assignments into smaller parts. Scaffolding is critical to making long-term projects manageable, and it gives me an opportunity to provide students with feedback at various checkpoints.

The next day, Bonnie showed up *on time*—hesitant, but ready to tackle the test. After school I excitedly shared the "B" grade she'd earned, and we discussed her success and difficulties. Motivated, she continued to improve both academically and behaviorally. Bonnie was also motivated to come to my study sessions, and I invited her to stay after the study session if she needed additional help. I have worked with other students one-to-one to model study strategies using my study guides; these students really just need a little time, guidance, and focus. It may take a little more time on my part, but the payoff is well worth it. There is nothing more exciting than watching a student grow in confidence and experience success after repeated difficulties. My experiences have taught me that positive, sincere, one-to-one conferences and encouragement enhance student–teacher relationships, leading to fewer classroom management problems. ●

How Can I Communicate Effectively with Students?

In addition to using techniques that promote a positive learning community, managing *teacher* behavior can facilitate the accomplishment of expected behavioral and social skills tasks by all students.

Communicate Clear and Consistent Messages

Communication is a critical component of any classroom learning community. Poorly articulated behavioral and social expectations and inconsistent ways of handling the results of mixed messages detract from a positive tone in any classroom. Behavioral and social expectations, and the consequences for following (or not following) them, should be communicated to students. Consequences, both positive and negative, must be consistent if students are to take teachers' messages seriously. For example, if tardiness is an unacceptable behavior, then it should be addressed each time it occurs. Ignoring the problem sometimes and addressing it at other times sends mixed messages to students about expected behavior and social skills. Table 9.2 presents examples of behavior tasks and the corresponding prerequisite skills that most teachers expect from their students. These expected tasks should be communicated clearly to students.

Sometimes, despite clearly communicated expectations for behavioral and social tasks, students continue to struggle. Thomas Gordon's (1988) work is helpful in understanding how to handle some of these problem situations. Gordon's approach is based on the work of Carl R. Rogers, who conducted research on emotional and self-concept development. Rogers believed that people respond to an emotionally supportive approach that includes openness and understanding. According to Gordon, if a problem behavior infringes on either the teacher's or the other students' rights or if it is a safety issue, then the teacher owns the problem (Wolfgang, 1995). Teachers can respond to such problems by using I-messages. Teachers can use I-messages to communicate feelings to students about the effects of their behavior (Larrivee, 1992). With an I-message, the teacher tells students his or her feelings without blaming the students. Let's compare a good I-message and a poor one, both offered to address the same problem.

> **Problem:** Several students interrupt the teacher when she is explaining assignments.
>
> **Good I-message:** "When students interrupt (*problem behavior*) me when I am speaking, I have to repeat what I just said (*effect of the behavior*), and that frustrates me (*feelings*)."

This example tells the students the problem, its effect, and the feelings of the person sending the I-message.

> **Poor I-message:** "I want you to stop interrupting me. If you do that again, you'll have to stay after school."

This example orders the student to stop a behavior and uses a threat to curb it. The teacher is in a position of power. According to Gordon, practices such as ordering, threatening, and warning are roadblocks to effective communication.

TABLE 9.2 Examples of Behavior Tasks and Prerequisite Skills That Facilitate Teaching and Learning

Behavior Tasks	Prerequisite Skills
Works independently	Knows how to do the work
	Remains on task without assistance
	Knows where to find answers if assistance is needed
	Refrains from talking during independent work
Is punctual	Knows how to tell time
	Can estimate time needed to get to class on time
Is prepared	Knows what supplies and materials are needed
	Remembers to bring supplies and materials
	Is organized
Follows directions	Can verbalize the directions
	Can follow multistep directions
	Complies with the directions
Raises hand	Knows when to raise hand
	Does not call out
Follows the rules	Remembers the rules
	Understands the rules
	Understands the consequences

Gordon acknowledges the need for teachers to use strong directives such as ordering, but only if danger is present. Gordon stresses that overusing commands can result in conflict between the teacher and students. Thus, clearly communicated behavioral and social skills tasks, delivery of consequences, and the use of I-messages all contribute to effective communication.

Explain the Rules and Consequences

Rules are a necessary part of society; this is true for the classroom as well. Rules provide parameters, structure, and predictability. Rules set the limits! Without rules, students are left to their own devices to determine the teacher's expectations and guidelines for appropriate behavior and social skills. Sometimes, teachers assume that students know how they are supposed to act in class. The codes of school conduct often are implied and not communicated carefully. Unfortunately, in some school situations students learn about the rules only when they break them and are punished for their infractions. How can teachers communicate rules so that students can meet the behavioral and social expectations of the classroom? Teachers can use a class meeting to involve students in establishing classroom rules by asking them, "What rules do we need so that I can teach and you can

● When students exhibit minor problem behavior, teachers can intervene by giving instruction on how to behave appropriately.

learn in a safe classroom?" Here are a few tips for selecting rules (Canter & Canter, 2001):

- Four to six rules are enough; having too many rules makes it difficult to monitor compliance.
- State rules in a positive manner, focusing on the positive, such as "Follow directions."
- Select observable rules that apply throughout the day. "Be respectful" is difficult to observe, is too vague, and may require the teacher to take instructional time to ask "Is that respectful?" A more specific rule, such as "Raise your hand to speak in group discussion," will be more effective.
- Involve students in setting the rules. This is especially important for older students so that they feel they have a voice in the decision-making process.

Once rules are selected, they should be shared with the principal and students' families. The rules should also be posted. Rules should come with both positive recognition and consequences. When students follow the rules, praise, special notices, privileges, and other types of positive recognition provide helpful reinforcement (Canter & Canter, 2001; Wolfgang, 1995).

When rules are broken, consequences must follow. Here are some things to consider when deciding on consequences:

- The consequence should match the infraction; that is, the consequence must make sense for the misbehavior or broken rule. For example, the consequence for being late to class once should be different from that for being late four days in a row.

- The consequence should be something that the teacher can manage. If the consequence is "stay after school," the teacher may have to give up planning time at the end of the day.
- Consequences should be applied consistently and as soon as possible after the infraction. If consequences are applied inconsistently, students get mixed messages about following the rules.
- Consequences need to be communicated clearly to students. They should know what will happen when rules are broken and when they are followed.

Is it necessary to teach rules? Yes! Rules must be explained, reinforced, and reviewed regularly (Jones, 2004). Teachers should work closely with special education colleagues regarding enforcement of rules and logical consequences for students with disabilities. For instance, a student with mild emotional or behavioral disabilities may have an IEP with certain guidelines for rules. Likewise, students who lack the ability to shift among different settings and teachers may need extra guidance in remembering the rules as situations and teachers change during the day.

Explain the Daily Schedule

Most people like to be informed about the schedule of events so that they know what to expect during the course of the day, week, or even vacation period. By communicating a schedule to students, teachers can prepare them for what to expect each day; they will know what is going to happen and be prepared for it. A classroom schedule establishes routines and communicates to all students the activities of each day.

The teacher can develop a classroom schedule and post it for students to review throughout the week. Several routines can be part of one week. For example, one routine can be used on two days and a different routine on three days. The teacher can help students by reviewing the schedule for the day or for the class period.

For students who struggle with certain academic subjects or tasks, problems might occur during specific times of the day associated with those subjects or tasks. For instance, if reading is a demanding activity for a student, it is not surprising that the student might get out of his or her seat, start talking to a friend, or take extra time to go to the reading table for instruction. Think back to Luisa in the Opening Challenge. Luisa has a learning disability in reading and writing. Her teacher identified problems with her remaining on task and getting her work done.

What can a teacher do about this academic problem, besides adjusting the work? The Premack Principle is a highly effective technique for motivating students to accomplish tasks (Premack, 1959). With this method, activities that are more demanding or challenging (such as reading and writing for Luisa), and thus less preferred, are conducted earlier in the day or class period. Less demanding and more preferred activities are scheduled for later in the day or class period so that students have something to work towards. In some cases, earned or free time (i.e., designated time during the school day that is provided for students who have completed their work) can be scheduled later in the day. Some parents use the Premack Principle to get their children to eat: "When you finish your dinner you can have dessert!" Astute teachers have used the Premack Principle for years to help students accomplish classroom tasks.

Provide Good Directions

What does it mean to provide good directions? If students understand what they are supposed to do, remember the directions, and follow them, then the teacher probably has provided good directions. Here are some tips for providing good directions and communicating them effectively:

- Be concise; too many words may confuse students or be difficult to remember. Two or three single-step actions are sufficient.
- State directions right before the activity.
- Check student understanding of the directions. For example, consider the following directions: "In pairs, I want you to first (*use a visual signal showing one-finger*) read the paragraph together; second (*showing two fingers*), underline words you don't know; and third (*showing three fingers*), write two sentences about the paragraph." The teacher does a quick check for understanding by asking students what they are supposed to do.

Let's return to Eric and the Opening Challenge. Recall that Ms. Martinez views Eric as a student who causes class disruptions.

ADAPT in Action • Eric—Following Directions

Ms. Martinez notes that Eric tends to act out in class by talking to his neighbors when he is supposed to be working or listening for directions. Ms. Martinez notes that Eric seems to misbehave when she gives directions for different tasks. Sometimes, he refuses to get to work. She is not sure why he does this. Ms. Martinez decides to use the ADAPT framework to figure out how to address Eric's behavior.

Ask, "What am I requiring the student to do?" Ms. Martinez thinks about Eric's behavior, "I need Eric to follow directions when I give them to the class. With a few exceptions, most of the students handle this well."

Determine the prerequisite skills of the task. Ms. Martinez identifies the skills that are needed to follow direction: "Understanding what I am asking and remembering the directions are important. Being willing to follow the directions is also important. Which of these skills seem problematic for Eric?"

Analyze the student's strengths and struggles. Ms. Martinez gives the class directions for independent reading work. She notes that rather than getting to work, Eric starts bothering his neighbors. She thinks about how she tends to scold Eric for not getting to work and then repeats the directions to him. She wonders if Eric is just trying to get her attention, or maybe he doesn't understand what to do. She talks privately with him to do a little diagnostic work on his ability to follow directions. When asked, Eric had difficulty remembering the three directions she gave the class, but he was able to explain how to do the work in the reading workbook. She concludes that remembering a series of directions may be interfering with his ability to get to work and contributing to his off-task behavior of bothering his neighbors. Because she needs students to work independently while she conducts small-group reading instruction, she decides to make adaptations to help Eric.

P ropose and implement adaptations from among the four categories. Typically, Ms. Martinez gives directions and checks the class's understanding by asking a few students to repeat the directions. This practice seems to work well, because the students start working. Ms. Martinez thinks that Eric may not be able to remember a series of directions. She decides to provide a buddy (*instructional delivery*) for Eric who can check that Eric can follow the directions and get to work. She decides also to periodically give Eric a sticker (*instructional material*) for following directions and getting to work. Although she does not usually give out stickers for following directions, Ms. Martinez is willing to try this adaptation. Ms. Martinez thinks a couple of other students may also benefit from these adaptations.

T est to determine if the adaptations helped the student accomplish the task. Ms. Martinez decides that when she sees Eric following directions by getting to work more consistently, she will gradually reduce the frequency of the stickers and provide verbal praise for getting to work.

Describe Transition Procedures

Why is transition time so important? Transition is the time when students are changing activities or classes. Often it is a less structured time, so transition can be a challenging time for students who need structure as part of their routine. Students may struggle with shifting from one activity to another either in the classroom or across settings in the school. When students complete small-group work, the expectation is that they can return to their desks without problems. Unfortunately, this is not always the case.

Difficulties with transition times occur for a variety of reasons. Sometimes, teachers do not pay enough attention to student movement in the classroom during transitions. At other times, the teacher has not clearly communicated expectations for student behavior during transitions. Also, the procedures that teachers use to make transitions may not be the most effective ways for students to change activities. For example, asking all students to line up for lunch or all students to move into group work at the same time may invite problems (Evertson, Emmer, & Worsham, 2003).

How can teachers communicate effectively during transition times? Smith and Rivera (1995) offer the following transition practices:

- Signal to students that it is time to finish their work because soon they will be moving to the next activity. Providing a verbal reminder, "Finish up what you are doing because the bell will ring in 10 minutes," signals how much time students have to complete their work and get ready for the next activity or class.
- Gain student attention prior to the transition to provide directions for the transition. Teachers can use their proximity (e.g., standing at the front of the classroom), a visual signal (e.g., flickering the lights), or a verbal signal (e.g., counting backwards from five to one) to gain students' attention. Then, directions for the transition to another activity in the classroom or to another location, such as the next class or the cafeteria, can be provided. One teacher shared her strategy for gaining student attention. She said, "All eyes on me." Her students were taught to reply in unison, "All eyes on you." It works!

- Communicate the transition plan and behavioral expectations. For instance, younger students could be told that they need to meet in their spelling groups at the carpet area and that they should walk to the mat quietly. Older students could be told that they should return to their seats and gather their belongings to get ready for the bell to change classes.

- Praise students who follow the transition plan and meet behavioral expectations. Provide specific praise; thank students for following the directions given; and demonstrate the appropriate behavior if convenient. For example, announcing "The Red group went to the mat quietly with their spelling materials; thank you for following the directions" or "The group working on computers did a nice job of logging off and returning to their desks quietly" tells students specifically what they did appropriately that related to following transition directions.

Use Specific Praise Judiciously

Specific praise is complimenting or verbally rewarding students for their accomplishments. Providing specific praise is a very simple way to communicate behavior and social expectations. Praise can serve as a reward for proper behavior and social interactions and as a reminder about expectations for students. Specific praise is a form of attention and feedback that has been studied for many years, and it has been shown to be very powerful in bringing about positive behavior in classrooms (Emmer, Evertson, & Worsham, 2003; White, 1975). Although easy to implement, specific praise is underutilized in many classroom settings. In a classic study, White (1975) found that elementary-level teachers provided higher rates of specific praise than middle school teachers, who more often reprimanded than praised students. Thus, one of the easiest interventions for managing behavior remains untapped in many classrooms. Think back for a moment to Sam in the Opening Challenge; recall his problems with being prepared and organized. Ms. Martinez gives him a box to hold his supplies (*instructional material*) and provides specific praise (*instructional delivery*) when she "catches" him putting his supplies neatly in the box and storing it in his desk. She can also do a periodic "desk check" to see how organized his supplies are and to give him specific praise for managing his space.

What guidelines are important to consider when using specific praise to promote positive behavior?

- Make the praise specific. For example, a teacher who wants students to raise their hands to speak during group discussions can acknowledge a student who demonstrates this task by saying, "Thank you, Eric, for raising your hand to speak instead of shouting out." This praise is specific to the task of raising a hand, which the teacher expects students to demonstrate during class discussions. This praise also gives Eric positive attention.

- Consider the age of the student or students being praised. For instance, teachers cannot praise tenth-grade students in the same way they do first graders. Older students may not respond favorably to a teacher who praises them publicly, but a private word can mean a great deal.

- Use praise judiciously. This means that teachers should focus on the behavior or social skill that they want students to demonstrate. Excessive praise loses its reinforcing value.

What Are Effective Classroom Arrangement Practices?

Your classroom is the stage on which the educational experience unfolds. It pays to plan the setting thoughtfully.

Physical Arrangements

The physical arrangement of the classroom is an important component of effective classroom management. What are some considerations for designing the environment? Arranging activity-based centers in less distracting parts of the room can minimize problems. For example, in elementary classrooms the reading, writing, and listening centers could be placed next to one another, assuming that students are using headphones in the listening center. The art center, however, should be placed away from students' seats and quieter centers. At the secondary level, instructional supplies and materials for students could be stored away from students' desks. Computers can be arranged in another section of the room.

Traffic Patterns

Traffic patterns, the paths students take to move about the classroom, are another issue to consider. How can traffic patterns make a difference? The arrangement of furniture and the location of instructional materials (e.g., pencil sharpener, computers, books, lab instruments) may influence how students move about the classroom as they go from large-group to small-group instruction and from independent seatwork to the pencil sharpener. The following tips can help to manage classroom traffic patterns:

- Separate instructional areas.
- Provide adequate movement space.
- Provide access to the most-frequented areas (Emmer, Evertson, & Worsham, 2003; Evertson, Emmer, & Worsham, 2003).

Emmer and colleagues (2003) recommend that teachers simulate student movement about the classroom to determine possible problem areas. For instance, a student who uses a wheelchair will require more navigational space in the classroom; the room arrangement will require wider spaces to accommodate the student's movement about the room.

Seating Arrangements

How students' desks are arranged is yet another consideration (Lovitt, 2000; Smith & Rivera, 1993). The types of activities and desired interactions should influence desk arrangements and seating patterns, such as rows and groupings. In addition, specific student behavioral needs will influence how the desks are arranged and where certain students' desks are located in proximity to the teacher and other students. For instance, students who are distracted easily or who like to socialize will require preferential seating (i.e., closer to the teacher or with students who can ignore "talkers"). A student who is easily distracted should sit in an area that is less traveled by peers, rather than in an area (such as by the pencil sharpener) that is frequented during the day.

With-It-Ness

Teachers must be able to see all of the students all of the time to be aware of interactions; this is referred to as with-it-ness (Kounin, 1970). Why is with-it-ness so important? A lack of teacher awareness of classroom activities and student behavior can contribute to misbehavior and social problems. Nooks and crannies may offer students "private space," but they limit teachers' abilities to be aware of classroom activities. In addition, teachers who position themselves in the classroom where visibility is limited are inviting problems that they cannot see or stop. Thus, teachers must have "eyes in the back of their heads" and let students know such is the case (Jones, 2004). Designing the classroom's physical environment to maximize visibility of all students makes it possible to prevent behavioral and social problems or to address them as situations warrant (Smith & Rivera, 1993).

Classroom Observation

Taking time to observe the environment, including traffic patterns, seating arrangements, and student interactions, will provide information about changes that may be needed. Through observation, teachers can reduce behavioral problems and increase student involvement with those students who tend to be quiet or uninvolved with their peers. Asking students, particularly older ones, about environmental factors such as temperature, noise, furniture, and arrangements can also inform decision making about creating an environment that is conducive to learning, managing behavior, and facilitating social interactions (Lovitt, 2000).

   This section presented practices that teachers can use to help *all* students understand and accomplish behavior and social skills tasks in the classroom. We know there is also a group of students who exhibit difficulty managing their behavior. For these students, it is helpful to understand the "goals" of misbehavior and to be familiar with interventions that can address problem behavior.

What Are the Goals of Misbehavior?

For many years, researchers have studied student behavior to better understand why problem behaviors occur and to identify ways to promote positive behavior. Differing viewpoints about the causes of inappropriate behavior have influenced the development of approaches and systems for managing it. For example, inspired by Alfred Adler's work on the relationship of behavior to social acceptance, Rudolph Dreikurs (1968) and Dreikurs and Cassel (1972) believe that people's behavior, including misbehavior, is goal driven—specifically, that it is performed to achieve social acceptance. If students are not successful in achieving social acceptance, misbehavior occurs that can be annoying, hostile, destructive, or helpless. But students who believe that inappropriate behavior will garner an adult's positive attention are mistaken. The attention they get is negative. These students are desperately seeking positive acceptance but do not know how to achieve it.

They need to learn appropriate prosocial behaviors—behaviors that are positive and that build relationships—to achieve the acceptance they are seeking.

Teachers can help students recognize their misguided goals and can offer alternatives for social acceptance (Wolfgang, 1995). When teachers understand the goals of misbehavior, an appropriate intervention plan can be implemented to support positive behavior and to decrease or eliminate inappropriate behavior. Table 9.3 provides information about the goals of misbehavior and offers examples of techniques for handling mistaken goals.

What Interventions Are Available for Less Serious Behavior Problems?

Sometimes, specific interventions must be implemented to promote positive behavior in the classroom.

Planned Ignoring

Planned ignoring, sometimes referred to as the *ignore strategy,* is the planned, systematic withdrawal of attention by the individual from whom the attention is sought. This individual could be the teacher but could also be a classmate.

TABLE 9.3 Goals of and Techniques for Handling Misbehavior

Goal	Description of Misbehavior	Techniques
Attention getting	The student engages in behavior that demands excessive praise or criticism.	Ignore the behavior. Give an I-message. Lower your voice. Change the activity. Praise appropriately behaving students.
Power and control	The student tries to manage situations, get his or her own way, or forces himself or herself on others.	Leave the scene. Have the student repeat the desired behavior. Remove the student from the group. Change the topic.
Revenge	The student engages in hurtful and malicious behavior.	Implement a timeout. Take away a privilege.
Inadequacy	The student does not cooperate or participate and avoids or escapes situations.	Adapt instruction. Break tasks down into smaller steps. Provide more praise. Showcase successes. Teach positive encouraging talk, such as "I can do it."

Source: Adapted from *Solving Discipline Problems* (3rd ed.), by C. H. Wolfgang, 1995, Boston: Allyn and Bacon.

Planned ignoring is an appropriate intervention if the behavior is a minor infraction that poses no threat of harm to others (Evertson, Emmer, & Worsham, 2003). Behaviors such as threatening others or fighting will probably not be influenced quickly enough by ignoring and should be dealt with quickly and directly. The landmark research that clearly demonstrated the power of adult attention on nursery school children's behavior was conducted more than 40 years ago (Allen et al., 1964). Results showed the correlation between behavior and the application and withdrawal of teacher attention.

What guidelines apply to planned ignoring? First, the person who is doing the ignoring must be the individual whose attention is being sought. Thus, it is important to know whose attention a student is seeking. How can a teacher determine whose attention the student is seeking? Adult attention is extremely important to younger children, which is why teachers see immediate, and often dramatic, changes when they praise or ignore younger students. However, as students get older, the attention of the peer group increases in importance, and the teacher's influence lessens. This is why ignoring older students when they are off task probably will not be effective. Second, planned ignoring must be implemented consistently, even if the behavior of concern increases. It is common for inappropriate behavior to escalate when planned ignoring is first introduced. Notably, some students will purposefully exhibit inappropriate behavior to gain the teacher's attention. However, planned ignoring can quickly become an effective intervention when teachers implement it consistently, even during the brief escalation period. As noted by Bacon (1990), "when the behavior fails to gain the desired attention, the behavior will eventually stop" (p. 608). However, teachers should become aware of students who engage in attention-seeking behavior and provide them with positive attention for appropriate behavior as much as possible.

Redirect Inappropriate Behavior

Redirection is the process of informing a student that an error was made and asking the student to describe the appropriate behavior. The student is provided an opportunity to demonstrate the appropriate behavior with reinforcement. Redirection is an effective way to help a student stop a problem behavior and receive further instruction on appropriate behavior in a relatively short amount of time. Much like specific praise and planned ignoring, redirection is a helpful intervention if the behavior is relatively minor and stems from the need to remind students about appropriate behavior.

When students exhibit minor problem behaviors, the teacher can intervene by giving instructions on how to behave appropriately. Students should be told the desired behavior and provided with positive support for demonstrating the appropriate behavior. With a focus on the positive, a reprimand—a negative response to problem behavior—is avoided. A reprimand does not provide the student with the opportunity to practice the correct behavior and receive reinforcement. For example, if a student calls out rather than raises his hand during discussion, the teacher can talk privately with the student, stating that calling out is inappropriate and asking the student to explain what he should have done during discussion (raise his hand to contribute). Then, in further class discussion, contingent on handraising, specific praise could be provided for the appropriate behavior. Redirection is a positive intervention and helps students become aware of and practice the desired behavior (Colvin, Kame'enui, & Sugai, 1993). In thinking back to Eric from the Opening Challenge, who calls out and may be seeking Ms. Martinez's attention, she can redirect his calling out by privately having him explain to her what he can do besides calling out and by praising him with positive attention each time he raises his hand.

Contingent Observation

Sometimes problem behavior occurs during small-group work or an activity when peers may be reinforcing the student's misbehavior. Peer reinforcement may result in increased levels of the problem behavior. Contingent observation is a form of timeout whereby a disruptive student is removed from an activity but is still allowed to observe the proceedings (Gast & Nelson, 1977). Contingent observation can be implemented in such situations if it appears that the peer group is contributing to the problem behavior. The advantage of this intervention is that the student can observe others participating appropriately in the group work, which can reduce the loss of instruction. It is important to ensure that the contingent observation period is long enough to make a difference, but not so long that interest is lost in rejoining the group.

● Classroom rules should be posted. Rules should come with both positive recognition and consequences. When students follow the rules, praise, special notices, privileges, and other types of positive rewards may be earned.

Criterion-Specific Rewards

With criterion-specific rewards, students earn privileges only as they reach desirable levels of the target behavior. This intervention is used widely in schools. Rewards are given to students who achieve designated levels of improvement (the criterion level) for a specific academic, behavioral, or social skill. Rewards may include the following:

- Tangible items, such as food, trinkets or prizes
- Token reinforcers, such as happy faces, stickers, or points toward a "payoff"
- Social reinforcers, such as praise, positive notes, or positive calls to parents
- Activity reinforcers, such as a one-night no-homework pass, 10 minutes of extra recess time, or earned time to select a desired activity in the classroom (listening to a tape) (Axelrod & Hall, 1999; Morgan & Jensen, 1988)

It should be noted that a reward for one student might not have the same appeal for another; therefore, it is necessary to find out from students what rewards are most desirable to them. Also, something that is rewarding in September may not be appealing to students in November. Rewards will probably lose some of their value to students over time, so they must be changed to achieve results. Table 9.4 provides a list of suggested rewards for elementary- and secondary-level students (Smith & Rivera, 1993, 1995).

TABLE 9.4 Suggested Rewards for Elementary and Secondary Students

Elementary Level	Secondary Level
Activity Reinforcers	**Activity Reinforcers**
Leader for classroom chores	No-homework pass
Running errands to the office	Working on games or puzzles
No-homework pass	Listening to music
Working on games or puzzles	Field trips
Extra recess	Decorating the bulletin board
Working as a tutor	Working on the computer
Field trips	Helping the teacher with clerical tasks
Decorating the bulletin board	Helping in the front office
Working on the computer	
Extra library time	**Tangible Reinforcers**
Working at the listening center	Food treats
	Prizes
Tangible Reinforcers	Pencils, markers
Food treats	
Prizes	**Token Reinforcers**
	Stickers
Token Reinforcers	Stars
Stickers	
Stars	**Social Reinforcers**
Chips	Note home to parents
	Earned time to visit with friends
Social Reinforcers	
Note home to parents	
Sitting next to a friend	
Having lunch with the teacher	
Visiting with the counselor	

Source: From Discipline in special education and general education settings, by D. D. Smith and D. Rivera, 1995, *Focus on Exceptional Children, 27*(5), 1–14.

Think back to the Opening Challenge; Ms. Martinez is reflecting about Sam. Recall that he has been identified as having ADHD. He has difficulties staying organized and being prepared to work. See how Ms. Martinez uses a certificate as a reward when Sam achieves the desired goal of an organized desk, which in turn helps him be prepared for class.

ADAPT in Action • Sam—Preparing for Class

Ms. Martinez thinks about Sam as he participates in class. He really tries to get his work done and seems to understand instruction, as indicated by his responses on written work. However, Sam lags behind his classmates in getting to work and finishing on time. Ms. Martinez observes that he spends too much time managing his materials and getting organized. Ms. Martinez decides to implement the ADAPT framework to identify a positive reinforcement system to help Sam be prepared for class.

Ask, "What am I requiring the student to do?" Ms. Martinez notes, "I expect all of my students to be prepared for class so that we can focus on the lessons at hand."

Determine the prerequisite skills of the task. Ms. Martinez realizes that being prepared means that her students have supplies and materials readily available in their desks and that they are organized for learning.

Analyze the student's strengths and struggles. Ms. Martinez reflects on Sam's preparation for class: "He lost his pencil four times last week and left his homework at home twice. Sam said he knew he was supposed to have a pencil and bring back his homework. When I asked him where he put his pencil, he couldn't seem to remember. He said he forgot his homework but that he did it! His desk is a mess; it's a wonder he can find anything. I have to stop my small-group work to help him get organized so that he can do his work. What can I do to help him be more prepared?"

Propose and implement adaptations from among the four categories. Ms. Martinez thinks that Sam may have difficulty organizing his space enough to keep track of his pencils and that he may have problems organizing himself at home to remember to return his homework. She decides to implement a behavior management system with Sam. First, she and Sam clean out his desk and develop an organization system (*instructional delivery adaptation*). She views the organization system as an instructional delivery adaptation because being prepared is really a prerequisite for instruction. She told Sam that once a week she would do a "desk check" with him to see if the books and supplies are organized. If so, he will earn a "Being Prepared" certificate (*instructional material adaptation*) to take home. Ms. Martinez also sent home a chart (*instructional material adaptation*) for Sam to look at before leaving the house to go to school. The chart simply asks, "Do you have your homework?" Sam's mom said that she would tape the chart to the door as a reminder.

Test to determine if the adaptations helped the student accomplish the task. As the days progress, Ms. Martinez notes that Sam remembers to bring his homework to school. She praises him for being so good at remembering to do this. The "desk checks" are also beginning to work. At first, she finds herself quietly reminding him about his desk organization, but by the second week he is developing the habit of organizing his books and storing supplies, including his pencil, in the box in his desk. He confided that things were going better for him because he could find his pencil when he needed it. Thus, with a little extra effort, Ms. Martinez helped Sam to develop better organization skills and the ability to remember his homework, which seems to improve his preparation for class.

Contracting

Contracting involves setting up a written agreement between two parties that designates a targeted behavior that needs improvement. This technique is sometimes necessary for students whose problem behaviors do not seem to respond to other interventions. Alberto and Troutman (2005) suggested that contracts can be an effective intervention for teachers to implement because the conditions for reinforcement are written down, which can help busy teachers remember how behavior for certain students will be managed.

The following are simple guidelines for implementing contracts:

1. The desired behavior and a reward that is meaningful to the student must be identified.
2. The conditions for earning the reward must be stipulated as part of the contract, including the desired behavior and the time frame.
3. The contract should contain an *If . . . then* statement and include the behavior, condition, criterion, and reinforcer (Alberto & Troutman, 2005).
4. The teacher and the student should sign the contract. A sample contract is shown in Figure 9.1.

Interdependent Group Contingencies

Students and teachers respond well to group contingency interventions because they are typically arranged as classroom games (Babyak, Luze, & Kamps, 2000). They take a little more time on the teacher's part to manage, but they can be effective for dealing with problem behaviors that are resistant to other interventions, such as planned ignoring and redirection. With interdependent group contingencies, students earn reinforcement when they achieve a goal that has been established for the group. Group contingencies focus on using the peer group as a resource to encourage positive changes in behavior. Interdependent group contingencies are effective for all age groups, particularly when the peer group's attention and reactions are the reasons why the undesirable behavior occurs. Interdependent group contingencies have been used for years because they are very effective in reducing rates of inappropriate behavior and increasing the occurrence of desired behaviors (Barrish, Saunders, & Wolf, 1969).

Here are a few guidelines to keep in mind when using interdependent group contingencies. First, be certain that the student involved is capable of performing the desired behavior and stopping the inappropriate behavior. If not, undue pressure could be placed on an individual who causes the group to lose its opportunity for the reward. Second, plan for the possibility that several students might actually enjoy subverting the program for the group. If this occurs, special arrangements must be made for the subversive students.

FIGURE 9.1 **Sample Behavior Improvement Contract**

IF John Evans [the student] is in his seat and prepared to work [the desired behaviors] when the bell rings [the condition] every class period for a week [the criterion], THEN he will earn a "no-homework pass" for one assignment for the following week [the reinforcer, or reward].

_____   _____
(Student/date)   (Teacher/date)

Let's return to Ms. Martinez. She decides to implement the "Good Behavior Game," which was developed by Barrish, Saunders, and Wolf in 1969. Ms. Martinez is concerned that many of her students don't work well independently while she is conducting small-group work. In particular, Luisa struggles with this expected task. Ms. Martinez decides to focus on improving the behavior of working independently. She divides the class into teams. When the timer sounds, the team whose members are on task during independent work is given a point. At the end of each day, the team with the most points earns 10 minutes to work on an activity of their choice (something the class values as important). The members of the other team who haven't earned enough points have to continue with their independent work. Eventually, Ms. Martinez sets a criterion of five points as the goal for earning the reward. Although the Good Behavior game increases on-task behavior during independent work time, Ms. Martinez observes after two days that Luisa's inability to work independently prevents her teammates from earning a point. Recall that Luisa has a learning disability in reading and writing. In ADAPT Framework 9.1, you will read about how Ms. Martinez applied the ADAPT framework to identify possible adaptations for Luisa related to the tasks that she expected in class.

9.1 ADAPT Framework for Luisa

A ASK "What am I requiring the student to do?"	**D** DETERMINE the prerequisite skills of the task.	**A** ANALYZE the student's strengths and struggles.		**P** PROPOSE and implement adaptations from among the four categories.	**T** TEST to determine if the adaptations helped the student to accomplish the task.
		Strengths	Struggles		
The students will complete an independent reading assignment quietly at their desks during small-group instructional teaching.	1. Knows how to do the reading assignment.		1	**Instructional Content** 1. Determine that content is at student's independent reading level; if not, then provide easier reading material.	1. Have student read to determine if material is appropriate.
	2. Remains on task without assistance.		2	2. Observe on-task behavior to see if appropriate reading level of material reduces off-task behavior.	2. Observe on-task behavior.
	3. Knows where to find answers if assistance is needed.	3		3. No adaptation is needed.	3. On a behavior chart, tally the number of talking behaviors during independent work. Determine if praise reduces talking behavior.
	4. Refrains from talking during independent work.		4	**Instructional Delivery** 4. Provide specific praise for working quietly.	

Self-Regulation

Self-regulation occurs when individuals monitor their own behavior. Using self-regulatory techniques, individuals attempt to avoid situations that lead to inappropriate behavior or stop problem behavior if it has already started. Self-regulation is a type of self-management (i.e., the implementation of specific interventions by the targeted student to manage his or her own behavior). Studies have shown that self-management techniques are effective for both elementary and secondary students (Hughes & Boyle, 1991). Self-management techniques are appealing because they actively involve the individual in the learning process and promote independence and decision making (Lovitt, 2000). Examples of self-regulation techniques include "counting to ten," using self-talk to work through a problem, and walking away from a potentially problematic situation. Obviously, these techniques require the teacher to help the student know how to recognize a problem situation and when to use the appropriate technique.

Let's examine some guidelines for implementing the self-regulation intervention. Modeling and role playing are good ways to help students learn self-regulation techniques. It will be necessary to determine which techniques are more appropriate for younger or older students. The students' use of self-regulatory techniques will increase as they receive reinforcement and see the effects of the techniques. Figure 9.2 is an example of a "Countoon." Students can use the Countoon to self-regulate by recording occurrences of a desired behavior, such as "raising hand during class discussions," and the problem behavior, such as "calls out." The technique of self-recording to monitor one's own behavior can lead to increases in the desired behavior and to decreases in the problem one.

● Self-management techniques are appealing because they actively involve the individual in the learning process. These techniques require the teacher to help the student know how to recognize a problem situation and when to use the appropriate technique.

FIGURE 9.2 Countoon

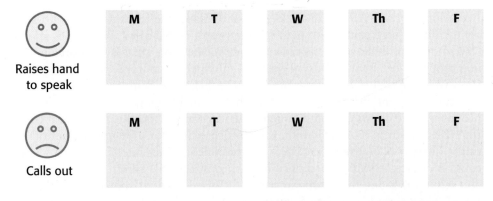

Directions: Put a tally in the box of the behavior that represents you during each day's class discussion time.

Raises hand to speak

| M | T | W | Th | F |

Calls out

| M | T | W | Th | F |

What Interventions Are Available for More Serious Behavior Problems?

Sometimes, students may exhibit problem behaviors that require more intensive interventions. We provide examples of interventions that you can use to reduce or eliminate these problem behaviors.

Restitution

Restitution is an effective intervention when students damage or destroy their surroundings or others' belongings. For example, behaviors such as writing on desks or in books; defacing a surface, such as a wall or restroom stall; wadding up wet paper towels and throwing them on the ceiling; or destroying someone's personal belongings can be corrected using restitution practices. Cleaning desks, erasing marks in books, painting a wall, and scrubbing the restroom stalls are examples of how restitution could be implemented for related misbehavior. When implementing restitution, consider the following guidelines proposed by Burke (1992):

- The student should have been observed engaging in the problem behavior; this ensures that the student who is receiving the restitution intervention actually committed the problem behavior.
- The match between the problem behavior and the amount and kind of restitution should be logical.
- The student should be expected to perform the restitution even if adult prompts are necessary.
- The intervention should not be something the student particularly likes, nor should it be done at a time of the day when the student would otherwise be engaged in an activity (such as reading) that she or he may want to avoid. For example, graffiti on bathroom walls unfortunately is common in student

restrooms, especially at the secondary level. Students who are caught writing graffiti have to pay restitution. Staying after school to remove the graffiti is a logical consequence for this inappropriate behavior.

Timeout and Seclusion Timeout

According to Lane (1976), in the early 1800s Itard, the teacher of a "wild student," Victor, used timeout to manage inappropriate behavior. Timeout is an intervention that removes the student from a situation that is reinforcing the inappropriate behavior. Seclusion timeout, in which the pupil is placed in an isolated room, is used for severe, out-of-control behavior. With seclusion timeout, the student is removed from a situation that is encouraging and maintaining the problem behavior and placed in a neutral environment. Usually, the neutral environment is a small room where the student is isolated for a designated period of time (Alberto & Troutman, 2005). Seclusion timeout has gained in popularity because it offers the student a chance to calm down, think about what happened, and rejoin the group in a short time period. White, Nielsen, and Johnson (1972) found that a period from 1 to 5 minutes is effective for producing the desired results. As with restitution, guidelines for using seclusion timeout are helpful to consider. Here are some guidelines for using seclusion timeout:

- The student should have been given an opportunity to correct the problem behavior prior to the use of seclusion time out.
- The school staff should monitor the student's behavior to ensure that it is severe enough to warrant an intervention that will remove the student from instruction.
- An evaluation of the student's academic work or social demands should be conducted to determine if the work is too difficult or the social situations are problematic. Adjustments to either academic work or social situations could adjust the problem behavior. If, through misbehavior, the student can avoid a difficult assignment or social situation, misbehavior will most likely worsen rather than decrease.
- An appropriate space must be identified that is available when the problem behavior occurs. The space should be examined to ensure proper ventilation, safety, and size (at least 6 feet by 6 feet).
- The space must offer the opportunity to supervise the student.
- Campus administration and parents should be aware that seclusion timeout will be implemented for severe problem behavior that is resistant to other positive behavioral interventions.
- The use of seclusion timeout should be documented, including the events leading up to the incident, the actual behavior, the amount of time in seclusion timeout, and positive interventions that were tried (Smith & Rivera, 1995).

In-School Supervision

In-school supervision is recommended only for severe behavior problems, and only after other positive interventions have been tried but failed over a period of time. Because students miss class, this intervention is usually reserved for major disruptive acts, such as fighting (Emmer et al., 2003). School privileges are suspended, and students must spend their time completing schoolwork in a quiet environment (Bacon, 1990). Students should not consider in-school supervision a better place to be than in class. The advantage of this intervention for teachers is that they do not have to miss their lunch breaks or planning periods to supervise disorderly students; rather, someone is assigned to supervise the in-school suspension room. The advantage for students is that they are required to complete schoolwork and are in school rather than out on the streets. The in-school supervision procedure serves as a deterrent to future disruptive behavior.

How Can I Identify and Assess Problem Behaviors?

How can positive and problem behaviors be described when they occur? What behaviors are acceptable? How can the occurrence of problem behaviors be assessed? Teachers must be able to describe behaviors that are desirable as well as those that are intrusive to teaching so that they can design and assess intervention plans.

Behavior Identification

Teachers must be able to describe problem behavior. An identified behavior should be observable, measurable, consistent over time, and of great concern (e.g., interfering with teaching or learning). For example, "calling out" can be observed, and it can be counted for a designated period. "Calling out" is a behavior that, although not serious, interferes with class discussions and can be labeled as rude and relatively disruptive. Returning to the Opening Challenge, "How many times Eric 'calls out' during a 15-minute discussion after viewing the film" tells us that "calling out" is the behavior that is being observed for 15 minutes. Ms. Martinez can measure it consistently over time by using a tally system to record how many times Eric calls out. Information on the identified behavior can help Ms. Martinez to describe the problem behavior (calling out during a discussion), determine how often it occurs (measuring the behavior for a time period), and know if the behavior (calling out) is decreasing and if a desirable behavior (hand raising) is increasing when an intervention plan is implemented.

Identified behavior can be stated in the form of behavioral objectives that include a condition, a behavior, and a criterion for improvement. The following examples include these three components and relate to our three students from the Opening Challenge.

- In the reading group (*condition*), Luisa will stay in her seat (*behavior*) for 20 minutes (*criterion*).
- During the daily 10-minute whole-class morning discussion (*condition*), Eric will raise his hand (*behavior*) each time (*criterion*) he wishes to participate.
- For writing activities (*condition*), Sam will have his pencil (*behavior*) each day (*criterion*) to complete the writing assignments.

Observational Techniques

For students who engage in minor infractions, simply recording observations of positive and problematic behavior anecdotally in a notebook or on lesson plans may suffice to keep track of how they are progressing with behavior intervention programs or to identify possible issues. However, in many cases systematic observational systems can provide information helpful in the design, implementation, and evaluation of behavior programs.

Observational systems can determine how frequently or how long a problem behavior occurs. Table 9.5 provides observational systems that can be used to gather data about the identified behavior and to assess the effectiveness of the intervention plan. Think about behaviors you have seen in classrooms and select the observational system you would use to measure that behavior. Keep in mind that

TABLE 9.5 Systems for Observing and Assessing Behavior

System	Description and Example Behaviors
Event recording	Number of occurrences of the identified behavior is recorded using a count or tally (e.g., 1111 = 4).
	Session time period (and hence opportunities to respond) is held constant.
	Example behaviors: hand raising, talk-outs, tardiness, pencil sharpening, tattling.
Interval recording	Number of intervals in which the identified behavior occurs or does not occur is counted.
	Session time period is divided into small intervals (e.g., 10-minute group time is divided into 10-second intervals).
	Occurrence of the identified behavior *during any portion* of the interval is noted by a plus (+); nonoccurrence is noted by a minus (–).
	Each interval has only one notation; percentage of occurrence of the identified behavior for the session time period is calculated by dividing the number of intervals in which the behavior occurred by the total number of intervals and multiplying by 100. It can be challenging to record occurrences of behavior and teach at the same time, but this method provides a more accurate picture of the occurrences of a behavior than time sampling.
	Example behaviors: out of seat, talking with neighbors.
Momentary time sampling	Number of intervals in which the identified behavior occurs is counted.
	Session time period is divided into larger intervals (e.g., 1-hour group time is divided into 10-minute intervals).
	Occurrence of the identified behavior *at the end* of the interval is noted by a plus (+); nonoccurrence is noted by a minus (–).
	Each interval has only one notation; percentage of occurrences of the identified behavior for the session time period is calculated by dividing the number of intervals in which the behavior occurred by the total number of intervals and multiplying by 100. In momentary time sampling, it is easier to record occurrences of behavior and teach, but it provides a less accurate picture of the occurrences of behavior than interval recording.
	Example behaviors: out of seat, talking with neighbors, not working on an assignment.
Duration recording	How long a high-rate or continuous behavior occurs.
	Session time period can be a short period of time, a day or week; at the onset of the identified behavior, a stopwatch is started to record the cumulative time.
	Example behaviors: out of seat, temper tantrums, staying with one's group.

the system should be sensitive to the behavior. For example, if a student continuously and rapidly taps a pencil on the desk, it would be hard to use event recording to capture each occurrence of this distracting behavior. Rather, interval recording would be a more appropriate system to use to get a sense of the occurrence of the behavior.

Oftentimes, it is helpful to display data. Figure 9.3 shows one way to depict data collected on an identified behavior. Data displays provide an easy way to see what is happening. In this example, the teacher was concerned about Patricia's talking with her neighbors when she was supposed to be writing independently in her journal for 10 minutes each day. The teacher chose the interval recording system to collect data. Prior to implementing a behavior management plan, the teacher collected the first four data points. As shown in the figure, Patricia's percentage of talking was quite high. However, a dramatic decrease in talking (the remaining four data points) is noted with the introduction of a behavioral intervention. What intervention from those discussed in this chapter would you use to reduce the inappropriate talking behavior?

Events that occur either before or after the behavior may contribute to its occurrence. Descriptive observation of these events can reveal important clues about how to manage the behavior. The Antecedent Behavior Consequence (ABC) log is a good tool for recording observations. "A" stands for events that occur before the behavior of concern, "B" is the behavior of concern, and "C" stands for the events that happen after the behavior occurs. The ABC log can be used for gathering data about what is going on with the student and the environment. These data can help the teacher make informed decisions about why problem behavior is occurring. An example is provided in Figure 9.4. Review the data and try to determine what is triggering or maintaining the behaviors. Based on your idea, what would you do next? For example, Luisa's reading abilities can be assessed with the possibility of providing more intensive reading intervention to help her learn to read better.

The ABC log technique can be easily adapted for use with older students in a format that offers them the opportunity to self-evaluate and self-manage their

FIGURE 9.3   Displaying Data Collected with Interval Recording

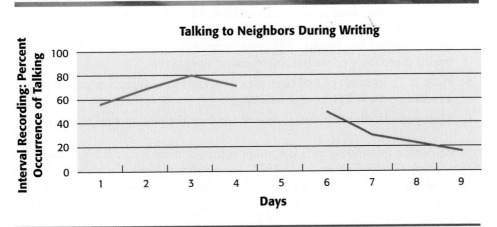

FIGURE 9.4 ABC Log

Date/Time	Antecedent Events or Situations	Behaviors	Consequences
12/01 10:30	**1. Teacher (T):** "Luisa, Sarah, and Ben come for reading."	**2. Luisa:** "I need to sharpen my pencil." Luisa sharpens her pencil. She stops and talks to Ricardo. Luisa pokes Stephanie with her pencil. Stephanie hits Luisa. **4.** Luisa wanders around the room.	**3. T:** "Okay, stop that." The teacher goes over to the students and separates them. Stephanie cries. **5.** The teacher sends Stephanie to the nurse and has a private conference with Luisa, who loses recess for the day.

The team hypothesized that Luisa's pencil sharpening and poking served the purpose of avoiding the reading task because of her difficulties with reading. The incident itself attracted the attention of the whole class. And although she lost recess for the day, she had the teacher's undivided attention, negative as it was, during the conference.

Source: Adapted from *Preventing School Failure. Tactics for Teaching Adolescents,* by T. Lovitt, 2000, 2nd ed., Austin, TX: PRO-ED.

own behavior. Lovitt (2000) provides several steps to teach older students how to use the ABC log for self-management purposes:

1. Explain what each letter (A, B, and C) means. Provide examples of antecedents, behaviors, and consequences from real-life experiences. Ask students for their own examples. Get them to think about what triggers their actions, both positive and negative, so that they can see the connection between antecedents and consequences.
2. Discuss with students how to discriminate between antecedents that trigger positive behavior and those that trigger negative behavior.
3. Discuss with students what happens to them after positive and negative behaviors occur.
4. Develop a plan with students for dealing with the antecedents that trigger negative behaviors. For example, if the trigger is "name calling," walking away could be the positive behavior rather than getting into a fight, which would cause the student to receive disciplinary action.
5. Have students select one of their own behaviors to change. Students can keep a record of the behavior in a journal.
6. Meet periodically with the student to see how the plan is working.

Reviewing existing records is another source of data. Records can include office referrals (Taylor-Greene et al., 1997), attendance records, counselor information, and cumulative school folders. Also, interviews of family members and support personnel can yield important clues about the events that trigger or maintain problem behavior.

What Are the Components of Positive Behavioral Supports?

Positive behavioral support (PBS), or positive behavioral interventions and support (PBIS) (Gagnon & Leone, 2002), is defined by the Office of Special Education Programs (2000, p. III-8) as an "application of a behaviorally based systems approach to enhancing the capacity of schools, families, and communities to design effective environments that improve the fit or link between research-validated practices and the environments in which teaching and learning occur." PBS is a proactive process that uses behavioral interventions. PBS focuses on preventing problem behavior by identifying and altering situations that could contribute to problem behavior and by teaching and evaluating more appropriate behavior (Carr et al., 1999). PBS procedures were originally implemented with students who had severe behavioral and cognitive disabilities to reduce aggressive and self-injurious behavior. These procedures have been validated as effective to help students learn more appropriate behavior and ways to respond (Marquis et al., 2000).

The implementation of PBS procedures in inclusive settings has gained in popularity because of the success of PBS with students who have severe disabilities and because of the requirements of IDEA (2004) legislation. That is, IEP Teams, which include general education teachers as part of the teams, are required to explore strategies and support systems to address the behavior problems of students with disabilities if the behavior impedes the student's learning or that of others. Also, within 10 days of disciplinary actions taken by school personnel, IEP Teams must develop a functional behavioral assessment plan and behavior intervention plan or review and revise, if needed, a current behavior intervention plan for those students whose behavior is of concern (IDEA, 2004). According to Kennedy and colleagues (2001), PBS should be implemented not only with students who are receiving special education services, but also with those students whose behavior places them in the risk category for special education identification. This requirement suggests that general education and special education teachers, along with various campus-based and school district support services, are responsible for collaboratively identifying, implementing, and evaluating positive behavioral supports for students.

PBS procedures include the following:

- Conduct a systematic functional behavior assessment (FBA) to identify inappropriate behaviors and environmental conditions that support those inappropriate behaviors.
- Develop a behavior intervention plan to teach new skills that will take the place of inappropriate behaviors while increasing desirable "prosocial" behaviors.
- Evaluate the effectiveness of the plan (Horner, 1999).

Functional Behavior Assessment

Simply put, functional behavior assessment (FBA) is a process for identifying the events that trigger and maintain problem behavior (Demchak & Bossert, 1996; Repp & Horner, 1999). Individuals engage in behavior because it gets them something they want (e.g., teacher attention) or helps them avoid something they do not want (e.g., timeout). Thus, the behavior has a function, goal, or purpose. Conditions in the environment also can cause behaviors to occur. FBA is used to determine what the individual is doing and under what conditions.

The goals of the FBA are as follows:

- Describe the problem behavior and the conditions that trigger and reinforce its occurrence.
- Generate hypotheses or educated guesses of why the behavior is occurring.
- Identify goals for decreasing the problem behavior.
- Develop an intervention plan.

The ABC log, student and parent interviews, and review of school records and documents are examples of ways to collect data as part of the FBA and to write the behavior intervention plan.

Behavior Intervention Plan

Teachers who can explain the function or purpose of problem behavior can respond more effectively to students by planning appropriate interventions (McCart & Turnbull, 2003). A behavior intervention plan provides teachers with a road map for changing inappropriate behavior and teaching new, appropriate skills. The behavior intervention plan is developed on the basis of findings from the FBA.

The behavior intervention plan includes the following components:

- Change the environmental events that trigger the inappropriate behaviors.
- Teach the student new skills to use instead of the inappropriate behaviors.
- Implement a reward system that reinforces appropriate behavior to improve the student's behavior. This component may include establishing positive relationships and engaging in appropriate activities.
- Evaluate the plan's effectiveness (Carr et al., 1999; Fad, Patton, & Polloway, 2000; Horner & Carr, 1997).

Drawing from research on identifying behavior, planning effective instruction, and monitoring instruction, the behavior intervention plan described in What Works 9.1 shows how research can be applied to practice.

Classroom teachers can expect other school personnel, such as the special education teacher, the school psychologist, and counselor, to work together to conduct the FBA and to write, implement, and evaluate the behavior intervention plan. An example of how professionals collaborate to conduct the FBA and to write the behavior intervention plan is shown in the Working Together feature on page 374. Take a moment to read this example.

We will now discuss social skills and how teachers can facilitate the development of these skills in their classroom through the ADAPT framework. Good social skills are extremely important for peer group acceptance. The social skills of some students with disabilities and at-risk students may not be adequate to promote peer acceptance. Thus, it is essential to devote attention to ways teachers can facilitate social skills in inclusive settings.

what WORKS 9.1

Behavior Intervention Plan
Student: Mark Friar   **School:** Fairview Middle School   **Grade:** 6 (Language Arts & Reading)
General Education Teacher: Mrs. Franklin   **Special Education Teacher:** Mr. Garcia

● **Results from FBA**

Antecedent Events (A): Request by the teacher to work in a small group; small group involves students with average reading abilities; small-group tasks involve reading aloud.

Problem Behaviors (B): Student refuses to move to and work with small group.

Consequences (C): Teacher attention (redirection, reprimands); instructional time lost because of lack of compliance for working in small groups.

Hypotheses: Because of low reading skills and the setting demands of the small group, the student may have feelings of inadequacy and thus is engaging in behavior to avoid the reading tasks. He may seek acceptance through attention-getting behavior and isolating himself from the group.

● **Intervention Goal**

To increase compliance for working in small groups on literacy tasks

Intervention	Person Responsible	Assessment
Have the student practice the reading passages that will be used in small groups.	Special education teacher during resource time	Observation: student is reading aloud in-group.
Provide the passages on tape for the student to practice at home.	Special education teacher	Observation: student is reading aloud in-group.
Change group membership to be more heterogeneous.	General education teacher	Observation: student works with group members.
Give the student a strategy for letting the teacher know when the reading material is too difficult and thus will cause embarrassment.	School counselor	Conference between counselor and teacher to assess when the student is using the strategy.
Provide specific praise (in note format) for using the strategy.	General education teacher	Observation: student uses the strategy.

What Is Social Competence?

Social competence means that a person uses social skills well enough to obtain positive reactions and to reduce the likelihood of negative reactions from others (Rivera & Smith, 1997). Being socially competent means that an individual has the ability to perceive when and how to use social skills depending on the situation and social context. The result contributes to acceptance by others. Unfortunately, research studies suggest that many individuals with special needs tend to have difficulty with an array of social behaviors, including, for example, choosing appropriate social behaviors for different situations, predicting behavioral consequences, reading social cues, and adapting their behavior in social situations (Bender & Wall, 1994;

WORKING together

Functional Behavior Assessment and a Behavior Intervention Plan

The process of conducting a functional behavior assessment (FBA) and developing a behavior intervention plan is a team effort that can involve the special education teacher, general education teacher, counselor, speech/language pathologist, and other professionals, as appropriate. Consider the following example to learn about possible roles for each professional and the student.

Mrs. Evans, the eighth-grade social studies teacher, was concerned about the behavior of one of her students with a diagnosed emotional or behavioral disability. She has tried several interventions to address the misbehavior, to no avail. She called together the school support team to work with her on the next step. The team decided that the needs of the student warranted an FBA.

Mrs. Evans indicated that she could use the ABC log to collect data on the situational events prior to and following the behavior of concern. She agreed to do this for a week. The special education teacher agreed to collect quantitative data using an observational system so that the frequency could be identified. The counselor thought that interviewing the student's mother would help shed light on events at home that could help the team understand the student's behavior. Finally, the counselor agreed to review school records and interview the student.

After the FBA was finished, the data analyzed, and the hypotheses generated, the team wrote the behavior intervention plan together. Collectively, they identified the interventions that could reasonably be implemented to teach the student more appropriate behavior and to reduce the misbehavior. They agreed to give the plan two weeks and then reevaluate.

The following tips can help make the collaborative process more successful:

- Each person must state what is reasonable to implement and what is not. Making promises to implement interventions that are just not possible will stall the process.
- The interventions need to be clearly stated and communicated to all involved so that everyone understands what needs to be done.
- Roles need to be clearly articulated so that people understand what is expected of them.
- Evaluation to determine the effectiveness of the intervention(s) should occur frequently and should be data based.

Gresham, Sugai, & Horner, 2001; Haager & Vaughn, 1995). Think about the three students—Sam, Eric, and Luisa—from the Opening Challenge. Review their social skills issues. Table 9.6 provides examples of social skills tasks and prerequisite skills. How do Sam, Eric, and Luisa's social skills problems compare to this list of social skills tasks that teachers expect in the classroom?

Curriculum

Social skills curricula have been developed for elementary, middle, and high school students. Social skills can be categorized into a variety of domains, such as communication skills, problem solving skills, getting along with others, and coping skills. Figure 9.5 includes sample social skills curricula for elementary- and secondary-level students. Take a moment to review this information. Using Figure 9.5, on page 376, which social skills activities would you recommend for Sam, Eric, and Luisa? If you said "getting-along skills" for Sam, "negotiation" and "coping skills" for Eric, and "conversation" for Luisa, then you're on track for matching interventions to struggles with prerequisite skills for social skills tasks.

TABLE 9.6 Examples of Social Skills Tasks and Prerequisite Skills That Facilitate Teaching and Learning

Social Skills Tasks	Prerequisite Skills	
Gets along with others	• Is able to compromise • Accepts others' points of view • Knows how to share	• Is polite • Is helpful
Converses appropriately	• Initiates conversation • Listens to others • Takes turns in conversation	• Uses an appropriate tone • Can maintain a conversation • Can end a conversation appropriately
Makes and keeps friends	• Makes an effort to talk with others • Has good hygiene	• Cooperates • Is loyal
Gives feedback	• Offers feedback in a positive manner • Can use I-messages to give feedback	• Is able to express own needs • Can say "no" to peer pressure
Solves problems	• Can identify the problem • Can generate solutions	• Can initiate solutions • Can evaluate the effects of solutions
Exhibits self-control	• Recognizes situations that are provoking • Initiates action to remain calm • Can evaluate the effects of actions	• Can self-monitor behavior • Is able to resolve conflict • Accepts consequences

Social Interactions

Research about the social acceptance and interactions of students with disabilities in inclusive settings has yielded conflicting results. For example, in studying the social acceptance of students with cognitive disabilities in general education classes, Freeman and Alkin (2000) found a lower rating for these students than for typically achieving students. Students with learning disabilities have been shown to have lower peer acceptance rates than other students in general education settings and are disproportionately represented in negative social status classifications (Bryan & Bryan, 1978; LaGreca & Stone, 1990; Vaughn & Lancelotta, 1990). Asher and Gazelle (1999) found that students with language impairments have more problems with peer interactions. Language plays an important role in the development of social relationships and interactions—students must be able to use language to send and receive messages and to resolve conflicts. For students with severe communication disorders, technology can be liberating. Take a moment to read the Tech Notes feature on page 377 for an example of how augmentative communication can be used to increase social interactions for many of these students.

Finally, and contradictory to other studies about students with disabilities and social acceptance and interactions, Rosenblum (1998) found older students with visual impairments to be more socially adjusted in inclusive settings. With increased emphasis on including students with disabilities in general education classes, just placing students in these environments will not, in and of itself, increase acceptance and interactions. For students with disabilities, the teacher can begin by examining the IEP to determine the social skills that need to be taught

FIGURE 9.5 **Sample Social Skills Curricula and Programs**

The ACCEPTS Program: A Curriculum for Children's Effective Peer and Teacher Skills

By H. M. Walker, S. McConnell, D. Holmes, B. Todis, J. Walker, and N. Golden

ACCEPTS is a curriculum for teaching classroom and peer-to-peer social skills to children with or without disabilities in grades K through 6. Different instructional groupings can be used. Included is a 45-minute videotape that shows students demonstrating the social skills that ACCEPTS teaches. The curriculum includes the following social skills:

- **Classroom skills:** Listening to the teacher, doing your best work, and following classroom rules
- **Basic interaction skills:** Eye contact, using the right voice, listening, answering, taking turns
- **Getting-along skills:** Using polite words, sharing, following rules, assisting others
- **Making-friends skills:** Grooming, smiling, complimenting, and friendship making
- **Coping skills:** When someone says no, when you express anger, when someone teases you, when someone tries to hurt you, when someone asks you to do something you can't do, and when things don't go right

ASSET: A Social Skills Program for Adolescents

By J. S. Hazel, J. B. Schumaker, J. A. Sherman, and J. Sheldon

ASSET consists of eight teaching videotapes that contain four vignettes, which focus on specific social skills areas. The curriculum includes the following social skills:

- **Giving positive feedback:** Thanking or complimenting others
- **Giving negative feedback:** Expressing criticism or disappointment in a calm, nonthreatening manner
- **Accepting negative feedback:** Listening calmly to criticism, asking permission to tell your side of the story
- **Resisting peer pressure:** Saying no, giving a personal reason, suggesting alternative activities
- **Problem solving:** Identifying problems, considering consequences, determining possible solutions
- **Negotiation:** Resolving conflicts with others, suggesting solutions, asking for alternatives, learning to compromise
- **Following instructions:** Listening carefully, acknowledging, clarifying, following through
- **Conversation:** Interacting with others, introducing yourself, initiating and maintaining a conversation

The ACCESS Program: Adolescent Curriculum for Communication and Effective Social Skills

By H. M. Walker, B. Todis, D. Holmes, and G. Horton

ACCESS is a curriculum for teaching social skills to students at the middle- and high-school levels. The program teaches peer-to-peer skills, skills for relating to adults, and self-management skills. The curriculum includes the following social skills:

- **Relating to peers:** Listening, greeting others, having conversations, offering assistance, complimenting, making and keeping friends, interacting with the opposite sex, negotiating, being left out, handling group pressures, expressing anger, and coping with aggression
- **Relating to adults:** Getting an adult's attention, disagreeing with adults, responding to requests, doing quality work, working independently, developing good work habits, following classroom rules, and developing good study habits
- **Relating to yourself:** Taking pride in your appearance, being organized, using self-control, doing what you agree to do, accepting the consequences of your actions, coping with being upset or depressed, feeling good about yourself

---

and reinforced. To succeed in inclusive settings, students must be able to compete academically *and* socially. Thus, students need to be taught appropriate social skills to improve their social competence and to facilitate the use of these skills during the school day. In the area of social skills, let's return to Ms. Martinez as she reflects on Sam's difficulty with social interactions that interfere with his ability to make friends and work in groups.

tech NOTES

The Communication Board

Melissa is a 14-year-old student who is a ninth grader in the local high school. She was born with a severe form of spastic cerebral palsy that makes it difficult for her to produce intelligible speech. For mobility she uses a motorized wheelchair, which can be operated with a joystick. She is able to keep up with the work in general education classes with appropriate adaptations and modifications. To communicate, Melissa uses an electronic communication device as a means to express her needs, to interact with teachers and friends, and to function in her classes.

Because of Melissa's cognitive and receptive language strengths, the communication device contains features that provide a range of communicative interactions. A scanning system is used that searches by row and column an array of communicative choices. When the choice is highlighted, Melissa activates a switch that emits the oral response. Switch-activation capabilities are appropriate for Melissa because of her motoric challenges.

The use of the communication device is a good start for enhancing social interactions because it gives the user a tool for expressive language. However, com-

Using a communication board can enhance social interaction for students with disabilities.

munication partners should exhibit patience by giving the user a chance to manipulate the device (motor control) and by allowing time for the rate of communication utterances (electronic emission) to occur. Students are likely to be intrigued by this tool, and if appropriate, the operator may enjoy "being the expert" and showing them how it works.

ADAPT in Action • Sam—Working with Others

Ms. Martinez is concerned about Sam's difficulties with social interactions in small groups. Sam tries to participate during group time, but he does not act as if he understands how to get along with the other students. He is capable of doing the work, but the social interactions cause problems for him. Ms. Martinez decides to use the ADAPT framework to help Sam.

Ask, "What am I requiring the student to do?" Notice the task, "gets along with others," that Ms. Martinez expects. This is an important social skill that is necessary for students to work well together. Ms. Martinez gives a group assignment and reminds students to follow the group rule of getting along with others in the group.

Determine the prerequisite skills of the task. Ms. Martinez realizes that for students to get along, they need to be able to compromise, be respectful of other points of view, share, be polite, and be helpful.

Analyze the student's strengths and struggles. In thinking about Sam, Ms. Martinez notes: "He seems to try to get along with the other students but shows difficulties. Just the other day, he was working in a group but didn't want to share the materials. I heard the other students explain their need to use the materials, but his response was rude. I'm afraid the other students won't want to work with him in small groups. He was able to tell me what he said that was rude, but I don't think he understands the other students' perspectives. He seems to have problems compromising. I need students to be able to get along with each other in their small-group work. How can I help him with this task?"

Propose and implement adaptations from among the four categories. Ms. Martinez thinks about how to help Sam get along with others: "Maybe a reminder about getting along is not sufficient for Sam. I'll get the groups working and then give Sam private directions about what getting along looks and sounds like (*instructional delivery*). I'll provide specific praise (*instructional delivery*) when I hear or see him getting along with his peers."

Test to determine if the adaptations helped the student accomplish the task. Ms. Martinez decides to keep an observational chart of Sam's group work. She decides to use the ABC log to determine whether certain events trigger problems and to see the effects of her extra instructions and praise.

What Interventions Can Be Used to Teach Social Skills?

Each of the following procedures can be effective in teaching social skills. With a little practice, students' can improve their social skills in the classroom and with peers.

Role Playing

Role playing is an activity where students practice the desired behaviors under the guidance of their teacher or counselor. Role playing includes a combination of effective teaching practices to teach skills and provides an opportunity for students to practice with guidance. You can construct contrived situations in which students role-play particular behaviors. How can role playing be used to teach social skills?

- The teacher can model the appropriate social interaction skills. By "thinking aloud," students learn the steps and thinking process used to initiate the social interaction skills successfully.
- The teacher can provide examples of the appropriate use of the target skills and examples of failure to exhibit them. This step helps students see how the interaction *should* look and how it *should not* look.
- Students should practice the desired social interaction behaviors in contrived situations while the teacher prompts the desired behaviors.

Coaching

Coaching focuses on encouraging appropriate behaviors through modeling and feedback. Coaching has been used to teach many different social skills (Lane, Gresham, & O'Shaughnessy, 2002). It involves the teacher providing guidance and feedback on appropriate social behaviors in natural settings. Costa and Garmston (2002) described coaching as an interactive process that facilitates self-directed learning.

How does coaching work? Coaching involves the use of direct verbal instructions, followed by the opportunity for students to rehearse or practice the target skill in a nonthreatening situation. Use the following steps in a coaching situation:

1. Present the rules or standards for the target behavior.
2. Model the desired behavior.
3. Have students rehearse the skill.
4. Ask the students which behaviors in their opinion went well and which went not so well.
5. Ask students how they could do things differently next time.
6. Provide feedback on the rehearsed performance.
7. Make suggestions for future performances.

● Teaching problem-solving and decision-making skills is an important part of the social skills curriculum at all grade levels. What social skills are needed to help these students complete their group assignment?

Problem Solving and Decision Making

Most students understand what is deemed acceptable behavior at school and in society. However, students can benefit from interventions that teach them how to solve problems and make good decisions. Students who struggle with social skills benefit from interventions that teach them how to choose socially acceptable behaviors in specific situations. Tanis Bryan and her colleagues have studied social skills challenges of students with learning disabilities for a number of years. Some of their findings relate to problem solving and decision making. For example, students had difficulty identifying the problem when a specific situation was described. They could not identify options for handling a situation or predict the consequences for the solutions they suggested. In fact, many youngsters with special needs tended to select antisocial behaviors, particularly when pressured by their peers (Bryan & Bryan, 1978).

Therefore, teaching problem-solving and decision-making skills is an important part of any social skills curriculum at all grade levels. Martin and Marshall (1995) and Wehmeyer (1995) identified skills for inclusion in a problem-solving and decision-making program. Teaching procedures for these skills are presented in Table 9.7. As with any social skill, thinking aloud, modeling, role playing, and coaching are good interventions to teach the steps.

TABLE 9.7 Decision-Making and Problem-Solving Steps

What Is the Step?	What Is Involved?	What Intervention Can I Use?
STEP 1: Gathering information	Identify information needed to make a decision and solve the problem.	Hold a class meeting. Conduct a brainstorming session. Have students collect data. Use the ABC log process. Involve the school counselor.
STEP 2: Problem identification	State the precise nature of the problem in observable, measurable terms.	Have students identify the problem; use the criteria—observable and measurable—to evaluate the wording. Take a vote to obtain consensus about the problem.
STEP 3: Solution generation	Describe specific solutions to the problem.	Brainstorm solutions with students. To help students generate solutions, have them answer the following questions: • What happens when the problem does not occur? • What does our classroom look like when this problem does not occur? • Who needs to help solve this problem? • What would happen if . . . ?
STEP 4: Decision-making criteria	Establish criteria for selecting the best solution.	Use data from the ABC log to help guide solution generation. Have students describe the resources needed for each possible solution. Rule out those solutions that require unrealistic resources (e.g., too much time, too many people, money). Rank-order possible solutions with 1 = best idea.
STEP 5: Action plan	Develop a specific plan using the solution, including who does what, by when.	Write the action plan using either a class meeting or a designated team of students. Post the action plan.
STEP 6: Evaluation	Meet to determine whether the action plan is working and whether the problem has been solved.	Conduct a class meeting to assess the action plan. Revise if necessary. Set another time line for reevaluating.

How Can I Assess Social Skills?

Assessing social skills provides information about students' social behavior and how interventions are working. Several techniques can be used to assess social skills. For example, the ABC log described elsewhere in this chapter can be used to determine what social skills are problematic and what events and individuals may be triggering or increasing the occurrence of the inappropriate social behavior. Rating scales found in many social skills curricula can be used to determine which students are exhibiting poorer skills than their peers. Also, sociometric surveys and sociograms can be used to identify peer relationships in the classroom.

Sociometric Survey

Sociometrics, or peer-nominating techniques, help teachers learn about peer relationships. Through the use of a sociometric survey—a set of questions answered by students regarding their perspectives on their peers—teachers can learn which students may be popular, which may be rejected, and which may be isolated within the classroom or peer group. The sociometric survey can be conducted by asking students to respond to several of the following questions:

- Who would you most like to eat lunch with?
- Who are your top three choices to sit next to?
- Who do you not want to sit next to?
- Who would you invite to your birthday party?
- Who do you get together with during the weekend?
- Who would you not want to be in your working group?

Some of these questions relate to relationships within the classroom and others relate to after-school activities. By asking these types of questions and having students record their responses confidentially, teachers can learn a great deal about students who are popular and students who are disliked. Teachers also can learn which students may be isolated. This information can help teachers plan social skills training and instructional groupings to foster better peer relationships in the classroom.

Sociogram

Drawing a sociogram—a graphic depiction of peer relationships—of the information gleaned from the sociometric survey can help a teacher see quickly what relationship patterns are evident in the classroom. A sociogram is shown in Figure 9.6 to graphically display students' answers to the first question from the sociometric survey. See if you can figure out the relationships in this classroom.

FIGURE 9.6 Sociogram

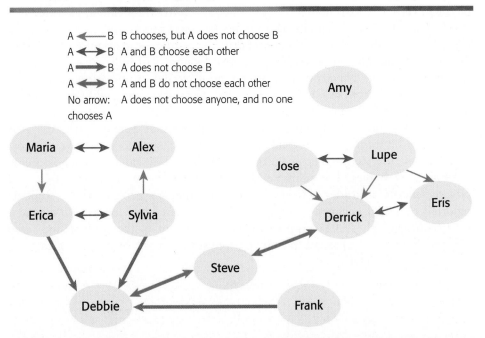

How Can We Promote Safer Schools?

Recent events in some high schools across the country are vivid reminders of the importance of making connections with our youth and identifying potential problems before they become serious.

Guidelines for Safer Schools

Educators are looking at ways to address violence and aggressive acts to help make schools safer. According to Smith (2004), adhering to the following guidelines makes for safer schools (McLane, 1997; Walker & Gresham, 1997; Walker & Sprague, 2000).

- Consistent rules, expectations, and consequences across the entire school
- Positive school climate
- Schoolwide strategies for conflict resolution and dealing with student alienation
- High level of supervision in all school settings
- Cultural sensitivity
- Strong feelings by students of identification, involvement, and bonding with their school
- High levels of parent and community involvement
- Well-utilized space and lack of overcrowding

Bullying

Bullying has received national attention as educators strive to address this critical issue in schools. Bullying is deliberate behavior performed with the intent of harming the victim (Craig & Pepler, 1996; Nansel et al., 2001). Bullying can be physical, verbal, or psychological (Nansel et al., 2001). It occurs at all grade levels. The person doing the bullying attempts to assert power and control over the person being bullied. Bystanders are reported to be present in about 85 percent of the incidents of bullying (www.bullying.org). Examples of bullying include physical attacks on the playground or after school, verbal intimidation, and exclusion from social networks. Gang attacks, dating attacks, and child abuse involve bullying (Pepler & Craig, 1997).

Boys are noted as asserting more physical types of bullying, whereas girls tend to exhibit more psychological types of bullying, such as excluding and gossiping about the victim (Pepler et al., 1997). Both boys and girls report being victimized by bullies. For example, a study of 15,686 students in public and private schools in grades 6 through 10 found that 13 percent of the students reported they had engaged in bullying ranging from a moderate to a frequent level (Nansel et al., 2001). Approximately 11 percent of the students indicated that they had been subjected to bullying (physical, verbal, or psychological) frequently or moderately.

In examining student traits, Nansel and colleagues (2001) indicated that individuals who engage in bullying and victims of bullying share several characteristics. Both exhibit problems with social and psychological adjustment, as shown in demonstrated difficulties with friendships and reported feelings of isolation.

What can teachers do about this critical problem? Remember that in the Opening Challenge, Ms. Martinez identified bullying as an issue for Eric. But students who engage in bullying may or may not have an identified disability. Strategies for all students can be implemented to address the bullying problem:

- Make bullying prevention and intervention part of the curriculum. Students should understand that there are bullies, victims, and bystanders who reinforce the bullying behavior. Provide information about the types of bullying—physical, verbal, and psychological—including examples. Students may want to describe examples of bullying as well.

- Involve school administrators, teachers, families, and the community. School procedures for preventing and responding to bullying should be developed and shared with students and families.

- Work with the school counselor to identify effective strategies to handle and report acts of bullying. Have the school counselor conduct age-appropriate discussions with students about power, aggression, and control. Ask the school counselor to meet privately with students to conduct individual or small-group discussions about feelings related to self-concept, social relationships, and other situations in school or at home that may be problematic.

- Sociograms can reveal students who are viewed less favorably by many classmates (note Amy and Debbie on the sociogram in Figure 9.6). Although sociogram results should be interpreted cautiously, evidence should be gathered to support possible problems with social relationships. For example, the teacher can observe students' behavior toward one another in class and note students who are frequently withdrawn from the group.

summary

This chapter presents techniques for promoting positive behavior and facilitating social skills. Both of these areas can greatly influence a teacher's success in promoting an atmosphere for learning. Identifying specific behavioral and social tasks will help teachers to plan effective adaptations and interventions that can provide students with skills to use not only in the classroom but also schoolwide and in the community.

By utilizing assessment practices, teachers will realize quickly how successful their adaptations and intervention programs are in promoting an environment that is conducive to learning. Implementing practices discussed in this chapter will help students with disabilities become more involved in the classroom and be better accepted by their peers.

self-test **QUESTIONS**

Let's review the learning objectives for this chapter. If you are uncertain and cannot "talk through" the answers provided for any of these questions, reread those sections of the text.

- **What practices can be used to foster student relationships and communication?**

  For student relationships

  Get to know your students.

  Use motivational practices.

  Be responsive to cultural differences.

  Conduct student meetings.

  For communication

  Explain the rules and consequences.

  Provide good directions.

  Describe transition procedures.

  Use specific praise judiciously.

- **What classroom arrangements promote positive behavior and social interactions?**

  Arrangements include physical arrangements, traffic patterns, seating arrangements, and classroom observations.

- **Why do students misbehave and what are the components of positive behavioral supports?**

  Goals of misbehavior

  Attention getting, power and control, revenge, inadequacy

  Positive behavioral supports

  Functional behavioral assessment, behavior intervention plan

- **What interventions can teachers use to prevent or address behavior problems?**

  Less serious behavior

  Planned ignoring

  Redirect inappropriate behavior

  Contingent observation

  Criterion-specific rewards

  Contracting

  Interdependent group contingencies

  Self-regulation

  More serious behavior

  Restitution

  Timeout or seclusion timeout

  In-school supervision

- **How can teachers assess behavior and social skills?**

  Behavior: Behavior identification and observational techniques

  Social skills: Sociometric survey and sociogram

- **What instructional interventions can teachers use to teach social skills?**

  Instructional interventions

  Coaching, modeling, role playing, problem solving

Revisit the OPENING challenge

Check your answers to the Reflection Questions from the Opening Challenge and revise them on the basis of what you have learned.

1. What advice would you offer Ms. Martinez about getting to know her students better?

2. How can she foster student relationships and communication?

3. How can Ms. Martinez help her students with their behavior?

4. How can she facilitate the students' social skills?

5. How can she determine whether student behavior and social skills are improving?

6. How can Ms. Martinez use the ADAPT framework to promote positive behavior and facilitate social skills?

Professional Standards and Licensure

CEC Knowledge and Skill Core Standard and Associated Subcategories

CEC Content Standard 4: Instructional Strategies

Special educators select, adapt, and use instructional strategies to promote challenging learning results in general and special curricula and to appropriately modify learning environments for individuals with disabilities. They enhance the learning of critical thinking, problem solving, and performance skills of individuals with disabilities, and increase their self-awareness, self-management, self-control, self-reliance, and self-esteem.

CEC Content Standard 5: Learning Environments and Social Interactions

Special educators actively create learning environments for students with disabilities that foster cultural understanding, safety and emotional well-being, positive social interactions, and active engagement Special educators shape environments to encourage the independence, self-motivation, self-direction, personal empowerment, and self-advocacy of individuals with disabilities. Special educators use direct motivational and instructional interventions with individuals with disabilities to teach them to respond effectively to current expectations.

CEC Content Standard 8: Assessment

Special educators conduct formal and informal assessments of behavior, learning, achievement, and environments to design learning experiences that support the growth and development of individuals with disabilities.

CEC Content Standard 9: Professional and Ethical Practice

Special educators view themselves as lifelong learners and regularly reflect on and adjust their practice. Special educators are aware of how their own and others' attitudes, behaviors, and ways of communicating can influence their practice. Special educators understand that culture and language can interact with exceptionalities, and are sensitive to the many aspects of diversity of individuals with ELN and their families.

INTASC Core Principles and Associated Special Education Subcategories

4. Instructional Strategies

4.07 All teachers use strategies that promote the independence, self-control, and self-advocacy of students with disabilities.

5. Learning Environment

5.02 All teachers help students with disabilities develop positive strategies for coping with frustrations in the learning situation that may be associated with their disability.

5.03 All teachers take deliberate action to promote positive social relationships among students with disabilities.

9. Teacher Reflection

9.04 All teachers reflect on the potential interaction between a student's cultural experiences and their disability. Teachers regularly question the extent to which they may be interpreting student responses.

Praxis II: Education of Exceptional Students: Core Content Knowledge

I. Understanding Exceptionalities

Human development and behavior as related to students with disabilities, including

- Social and emotional development and behavior.

III. Delivery of Services to Students

Curriculum and instruction and their implementation across the continuum of educational placements, including

- Instructional development for implementation.
- Teaching strategies and methods.
- Instructional format and components.

Assessment, including

- How to select, construct, conduct, and modify informal assessments.

Structuring and managing the learning environment, including

- Classroom management techniques.
- Ethical considerations inherent in behavior management. Professional roles, including
- Influence of teacher attitudes, values, and behaviors on the learning of exceptional students.

Communicating with parents, guardians, and appropriate community collaborators.

Video—"Behavior Disorder"

Nick struggles with controlling his behavior at home and school. This video shows how a school-based intervention helped him to learn to control his own behavior.

Log onto **www.mylabschool.com**. Under the **Courses** tab, in **Special Education**, go to the **video lab**. Access the **"Emotional and Behavioral Disorders"** videos and watch the **"Behavior Disorder"** video.

 OR

Use the **www.mylabschool.com** **Assignment Finder** to go directly to these videos. Just enter Assignment ID **SPV10**.

1. Describe the problem behaviors that Nick exhibited.

2. What differentiates Nick as someone with an emotional or behavioral disorder from other students with behavior problems who do not qualify for special education services?

3. What types of interventions do the special education teachers describe that seemed to be effective in supporting Nick at school?

Case Study—"Encouraging Appropriate Behavior"

This case study unit outlines positive behavior management techniques that can be employed with individual students who have behavioral concerns that are not effectively addressed by comprehensive classroom rules. It features scenarios of students at varying grade levels, ranging from elementary to high school.

Log onto **www.mylabschool.com**. Under the **Resources** tab, navigate to the **Case Archive** and read "**Encouraging Appropriate Behavior**."

 OR

Use the **www.mylabschool.com Assignment Finder** to go directly to the case study. Just enter Assignment ID **CS02**.

To answer the following questions, read one of the case studies provided in this case study unit.

1. Read the STAR (STrategies And Resources) sheets associated with the case study. Briefly summarize each strategy.

2. Now select one strategy that you might implement in your own classroom. What are the possible benefits of this strategy? What cautions should you keep in mind when using it?

3. Identify and describe additional strategies or resources described in the chapter that might assist you in meeting this student's needs.

To access chapter objectives, practice tests, weblinks, and flashcards, go to the companion website at **www.ablongman.com/bryantsmith1e**.

chapter *10*

Teaching Reading

chapter OBJECTIVES

After studying this chapter, you will have the knowledge to answer the following questions:

- Who are students with reading difficulties?
- What are the five components of reading?
- How can teachers provide effective reading instruction for the components of reading?
- How can teachers make instructional adaptations for the components of reading?

● OPENING challenge

Ensuring Appropriate Reading Instruction

Elementary Grades ● Mrs. Evans is in her sixth year of teaching at the elementary level in a suburban school district. The district's demographics reflect a rich heritage of diversity. The district also supports a large percentage of students who qualify for free or reduced-cost meals. Mrs. Evans taught first grade for 3 years and is now in her third year of teaching second grade. She is reviewing results from the reading assessment that is intended to screen students for reading problems so that she can provide extra reading support. The district's policy requires teachers in kindergarten through second grade to assess all of their students in the fall, winter, and spring to identify those who are at risk for reading difficulties and to monitor their progress as they engage in reading instruction throughout the year. She learns that of her 22 students, 6 scored at the "somewhat at risk for reading difficulties" level and 2 scored at the "high risk for reading difficulties" level. In examining the results, she reflects: *"These students have problems with word identification—they lack ways to identify words in a list or in their reading passage. Decoding results show that some of the students lack basic skills to figure out unknown words. Some*

column continues on next page

Secondary Grades ● Mr. Williams is in his third year of teaching sixth-grade reading in a large, urban middle school. In his school district, all students are required to take a reading course in sixth grade to develop and refine their reading skills. He has, on average, 35 students per class, with 5 classes daily. Last summer, he took a reading course that focused on strategies for students who have difficulty reading content-area textbooks. He took the course because in the previous school year he observed that many of his students lacked basic reading skills or had problems understanding the text. These problems made it difficult for them to read the novels in his class. He observed that they were often unable to figure out words in the novels, let alone understand the text. Mr. Williams learned from the other sixth-grade teachers that many of his struggling students cannot read their content-area texts well enough to understand the material. Mr. Williams worries that if he doesn't provide support for students who are having reading problems, these students will never be able to read novels successfully. He asked Mrs. Levy, the reading specialist, to help him conduct reading assessments of his class. He reflects on the assessment results: *"I have 20*

column continues on next page

students have difficulty with identifying individual phonemes and can't seem to blend or segment sounds to form words. I am concerned that this problem may affect their decoding and spelling skills. All of these students exhibit difficulty with oral reading. Their reading is choppy because they don't know the words by sight. Problems with reading fluency affect their ability to understand the text. I will have to provide them with extra reading support in addition to my regular reading and writing instruction for the entire class." ●

students across all of my classes who are reading two to three grades below grade level. Some of them have problems with word identification, which causes them difficulties with decoding multisyllabic words found in the novels. They won't read out loud in class during literature circles, and I suspect that it's because they have problems with the words in the books and that they are embarrassed. Mrs. Levy indicated that their oral reading fluency is quite low for their grade level. Other students scored well on word identification and moderately well on fluency but exhibit serious problems with comprehension and vocabulary skills. Maybe if I help them use the strategies I learned this summer, they can improve their reading abilities." ●

Mrs. Evans and Mr. Williams have something in common: they both have groups of students in their classrooms who have so much trouble reading that intervention and instructional adaptations are necessary. Both of these teachers can provide their students with additional support to ensure their success.

● Reflection Questions

In your journal, write down your answers to the following questions. After completing the chapter, check your answers and revise them on the basis of what you have learned.

1. What specific difficulties might students in Mrs. Evans's and Mr. Williams's classes exhibit in phonological awareness, word identification, reading fluency, reading vocabulary, and reading comprehension?

2. How can Mrs. Evans and Mr. Williams use practices for effective reading to structure their reading activities?

3. How can these teachers provide adapted lessons to students who require additional instruction, while meeting the needs of the rest of the class?

4. How can teachers monitor their students' progress or response to intervention?

The ability to read is a fundamental skill that is needed to succeed in school and life. Ensuring that students learn how to read is a major responsibility for all educators. We know the ramifications when students do not learn how to read: (1) students are at higher risk for academic failure and school dropout than students who develop proficient skills in the first years of formal schooling and (2) students are at increased risk for referral and placement in special education. We also know that reading failure is largely preventable given the proper instruction and support. Although a group of students may be identified as having reading disabilities, these students, more often than not, can learn to read. We have the ability to identify struggling readers in the early grades, and we know what constitutes effective reading instruction. We also know that, unfortunately, some students who have reading difficulties or disabilities continue through the grades without the proper reading instruction and adaptations to facilitate their reading abilities in the general education setting. Thus, providing appropriate reading instruction and adaptations throughout the grades is an essential feature of education.

Reading instruction has been the focus of national attention. Supported by mounting evidence of the benefits of early reading instruction to prevent reading difficulties in many students and by concern about scores on national assessments of reading performance, especially for culturally and linguistically diverse students, efforts to address reading problems have been initiated at the national level. For example, the National Research Council established the Committee on the Prevention of Reading Difficulties in Young Children. Their work resulted in the report *Preventing Reading Difficulties in Young Children* (Snow, Burns, & Griffin, 1998). In 2000, the National Reading Panel, which was commissioned by Congress to evaluate the evidence for early reading instruction, published *Teaching Children to Read: An Evidence-Based Assessment of the Scientific Research Literature on Reading and Its Implications.* Combined, these reports documented the benefits of a balanced approach to reading instruction, including instruction in phonological awareness, phonics, reading fluency, reading comprehension, and vocabulary.

Phonological awareness focuses on a variety of listening skills, including rhyming, blending, and segmenting. Phonics is the teaching of letter–sound patterns so that students can figure out unknown words they encounter in text. Reading fluency is the ability to read text accurately, quickly, and with expression. Reading comprehension is the ability to understand what is read, which is influenced by the reader's vocabulary (knowledge of the meaning of words). Figure 10.1 depicts these five components and illustrates their relationship as part of good reading instruction. According to the National Reading Panel (2000), reading instruction must occur in each of these components. Good readers use skills from each of these five components in combination and effortlessly as they read a variety of texts, such as novels, magazines, newspapers, and textbooks.

Jean Chall, in her classic 1996 text *Stages of Reading Development,* described five stages of reading acquisition. Chall's (1996) work is based on the assumption that students "learn to read" during the primary grades and then, in

FIGURE 10.1 Reading Components

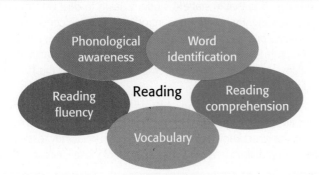

later grades, "read to learn." Reading progress across the grade levels may be broadly described as evolving through the following categories:

- Prereading (preschool)
- Reading acquisition (grades K–2)
- Rapid development (grades 3–5)
- Application (grades 6+)

Students generally develop prereading skills in preschool and then engage in reading acquisition from kindergarten through second grade. They next progress through the rapid-development stage in the third through fifth grades, and they may not arrive at the application stage until they are in their late teens. Unfortunately, some students never progress past the rapid development stage and will probably experience difficulty in most subject areas their entire academic life. Chall's developmental stages are summarized in Figure 10.2.

FIGURE 10.2 **Chall's Stages of Reading**

STAGE 0. *Prereading:* Birth to age 6. During this stage, children who grow up in literate surroundings are exposed to letters, words, and books. As a result, the children develop many of the requisite abilities, commonly called *readiness skills,* associated with early reading success. Such skills include the top-to-bottom and left-to-right orientation skills associated with books, control over syntax and words, and auditory and visual discrimination.

STAGE 1. *Initial Reading, or Decoding:* Grades 1 and 2, ages 6 to 7. During this stage, children learn the arbitrary sets of letters and associate these with the corresponding parts of spoken words. Insight is gained about the nature of English spelling and the alphabetic principle.

STAGE 2. *Confirmation, Fluency, Ungluing from Print:* Grades 2 and 3, ages 7 to 8. With the decoding skills, the syntax, and the vocabulary developed during earlier stages, students can take advantage of these skills and concentrate on the meaning of a story or book. Of importance during this stage is the reader's ability to use context to gain fluency and speed. In addition, some of the more complex phonic elements are mastered.

STAGE 3. *Reading for Learning the New: A First Step:* Middle school, ages 9 through 13. Once the students have "learned to read," they are now ready to "read to learn." Reading at this stage is employed to gain factual information, learn new concepts, and, as a result, learn how to accomplish new tasks. There is a growing importance of word meaning and prior knowledge of the students, but they still use decoding skills learned earlier to derive meaning.

STAGE 4. *Multiple Viewpoints:* High school, ages 14 through 18. The difference between this stage and stage 3 is that in stage 4 students learn to deal with more than one point of view in reading. By having been introduced to basic concepts in stage 3, students in stage 4 are prepared to be exposed to different interpretations and theories of, for instance, Columbus's "discovery" of America. The views of Native Americans, Spanish historians, and others provide alternative renditions of the historical accounts that can be discussed and debated.

STAGE 5. *Construction and Reconstruction—A World View:* College, age 18 and above. At this stage, students are able to use selectively the printed materials that are of interest to them. Readers learn to construct knowledge for themselves in what they read—that is, to balance their comprehension of the ideas read, their analysis of those ideas, and their own views.

Source: Adapted from *Stages of Reading Development,* by J. S. Chall, 2nd ed., New York: McGraw-Hill.

National attention now is focusing on older students who continue to demonstrate problems learning to read sufficiently to be able to read content-area textbooks found in the upper grades and secondary schools. Older students who continue to struggle with the demands of reading may exhibit motivational issues, behavioral concerns, and self-concept problems that may result in their dropping out of school. For many students, problems learning to read are preventable. With evidence-based instruction in the early grades and a focus on reading comprehension and vocabulary instruction in the upper grades, most students can learn to read.

This chapter presents information on students with reading difficulties. The five components of reading instruction and practices for teaching these components to struggling readers are presented. Instructional lessons and adaptations based on the ADAPT framework are provided to help you teach students who need extra support and instruction.

Who Are Students with Reading Difficulties?

It is estimated that one in three students has difficulty learning to read. Of those students who exhibit problems learning to read by the end of

● Reading skills are fundamental for success in school. How can you provide appropriate reading instruction and adaptations for all of your students?

first grade, about 85 percent will continue to struggle through the fourth grade and beyond (U.S. Department of Education, 2002). Results from the National Assessment of Educational Progress (2000) indicate that approximately 40 percent of all fourth graders read below grade level. The percentages of reading below grade level for students from diverse backgrounds and students who are living in poverty are even higher.

Research has identified specific reading difficulties demonstrated by students who are struggling readers (Adams, 1990; Scarborough, 1998). These problems are present to varying degrees for each student. In some cases, students may have trouble discriminating sounds in rhyming activities or identifying sounds in words. Further deficits may be noted in the ability to connect sounds to letters and letter combinations. Some students may show adequate abilities with phonological awareness skills but may struggle learning sound–symbol relationships and have limited sight vocabularies (Al-Otaiba & Fuchs, 2002). Reading fluency may be slow and choppy; problems with fluency hamper students' ability to comprehend text. Students who find reading to be laborious and difficult often don't read independently for pleasure. Yet extensive reading is one of the best ways to increase reading vocabulary. Thus, vocabulary development may be affected because of limited reading exposure.

Older students may also exhibit reading difficulties that remain unchecked from the elementary years. These students may have limited strategies (techniques) for figuring out multisyllabic words. Strategies for breaking words apart, sounding out the parts, and blending the parts together to read the word may be lacking. Also, secondary teachers often note that students with reading difficulties have problems comprehending text and are hampered by a limited vocabulary (Bryant et al., 2001). In classes where the textbook is the major source of information for students, comprehension and vocabulary problems can greatly affect the student's ability to succeed at the secondary level. Table 10.1 lists characteristics that differentiate good and poor adolescent readers. Given the heavy demands of textbook reading at the secondary level, it is important to be aware of the difficulties struggling readers encounter when reading content-area textbooks.

Factors Contributing to Reading Difficulties

Why do some students learn to read effortlessly whereas others struggle? Teachers and researchers have wrestled with this question for over a century, with various reasons for reading failure cited at one time or another. Some have identified low intellect as a factor, but many students with low intelligence quotients (IQs) learn to read better than students with higher IQs. It has been suggested that vision problems cause reading problems, but some students who have very poor vision, and some who are legally blind, read better than students who see with no difficulty. Many have argued that deficits in phonological awareness cause reading failure, but research has shown that many students with phonological awareness problems learn how to read just fine. Some blame socioeconomic factors, but many students from poor families read better than students from more wealthy families. Others suggest that students' reading failure results from their parents' inability to read, but many adults who are illiterate have children who learn to read easily and proficiently.

TABLE 10.1 Summary of Research Findings Differentiating Good and Poor Adolescent Readers

Good Readers	Poor Readers
Are aware of variables that interact in reading.	Are less aware of variables that interact in reading.
Are able to identify main ideas from a passage and determine their relative importance.	Have difficulty identifying a passage's main ideas and determining their relative importance.
Use headings, subheadings, and other text features to aid in comprehension.	Struggle with making connections among headings, subheadings, text features, and text meaning.
Attempt to correct comprehension breakdowns by rereading material.	Tend to move through the text even if they do not understand what they have read.
Employ a variety of reading strategies and adapt their reading to the material.	Have few alternative reading strategies in their repertoire.
Bring considerable experience and background knowledge to the reading process.	Have limited experience and prior knowledge to help them understand new material.

The most preventable reason for poor reading is poor teaching; some teachers simply are not good reading teachers (Hammill & Bartel, 2004). Teachers hold the power to open doors for students to pick up a book and experience things that are otherwise impossible to experience. Readers can help solve mysteries, travel to worlds (and solar systems) unknown, share the joys and sorrows of teenage development, be there when the winning points are scored in an athletic contest, feel the fear of a young solider at war, and do just about anything or go anywhere through access to books.

There is no single cause for reading failure. Instead, reading problems result from many factors and are usually intrinsic to the individual; that is, they are specific to a particular person (Wiederholt & Bryant, 1987).

Dyslexia

A developmental reading disability, or dyslexia, is thought to affect 15 percent of school-aged students (Orton Dyslexia Society, 1993). Dyslexia is a lifelong condition that affects people from all backgrounds. Dyslexia tends to run in families (Honig, Diamond, & Gutlohn, 2000). Dyslexia is a language-based reading disability that affects the following areas to varying degrees, depending on the severity of the disability (Honig et al., 2000; Caswell-Tuley, 1998):

- Learning to speak
- Decoding unknown words
- Word recognition
- Learning letter–sound associations
- Memorizing facts
- Comprehension
- Spelling
- Writing
- Discriminating sounds
- Learning a foreign language

Bryant and colleagues (2004) identified research-based behaviors associated with dyslexia. These behaviors are shown in Figure 10.3. Appropriate instruction and the implementation of instructional adaptations can help most struggling readers learn to read. Teachers must focus on teaching the skills of the five components of reading shown in Figure 10.1 (see page 391) and help students apply these skills to various types of text.

What Is Phonological Awareness and How Do I Teach It?

Phonological awareness (PA) is defined as "one's sensitivity to, or explicit awareness of, the phonological structure of words in one's language" (Torgesen & Mathes, 2000). PA is considered to be an important skill in early reading because it prepares students for being able to manipulate letter sounds to form words.

FIGURE 10.3 Behaviors Associated with Dyslexia

Evidence-based research has shown that the following behaviors are associated with dyslexia:

Sound–letter association errors when reading aloud

Poor memory for letters and words

Slow oral reading

Slow silent reading

Substitution of words of similar meaning while reading aloud (e.g., substitutes *thermos* for *flask*)

Substitution of phonetically similar words while reading aloud (e.g., substitutes *chair* for *cheer* or *then* for *when*).

Oral reading with flat, disjointed, or nonmelodic (dysrhythmic) intonation

Does not remember letter sequences in printed syllables

Interchanges short words, especially articles (e.g., substitutes *a* for *the*) when reading orally

Omits inflectional endings (such as, *-s, -ed, -ing*) when reading aloud

Cannot break a word into syllables

Cannot combine syllables into words

Reverses sounds (e.g., *pan* as *pna*) when reading aloud

Reads as though each word is encountered for the first time

Cannot call pseudowords (e.g., *nim, klep*).

Calls words correctly but does not know their meaning

Adds words when reading aloud

Cannot retell what has been read

Cannot comprehend a passage without reading it more than once

Although technically a skill that involves listening and speaking (Hammill & Bryant, 1998), PA has long been studied in relation to reading, usually as auditory discrimination, which is the ability to identify speech and other sounds, such as environmental sounds. When auditory discrimination involves discrimination of speech sounds, it is the same as phonological awareness. Lundberg (1991), among others, asserted that a "causal link in fact exists from phonological awareness to reading acquisition" (p. 50). Morais (1991) acknowledged that a statistical relationship exists between the two constructs but stopped short of calling the relationship causal (i.e., did not assert that phonological awareness problems *cause* reading problems).

One type of PA, phonemic awareness, is the ability to segment, blend, and manipulate individual phonemes, which are the smallest units of sound that influence the meaning in words. Phonemic awareness is considered to be the most important type of PA because it is related to the alphabetic principle (recognizing that letters of the alphabet represent sounds in language), phonics instruction, spelling, and learning to read.

Types of Phonological Awareness

Phonological awareness typically involves a developmental sequence including the awareness of words, rhymes, and syllables at the preschool and kindergarten levels and individual phonemes during the kindergarten and first-grade years (Honig et al., 2000). Table 10.2 identifies the different types of PA. Although earlier-developing skills, such as rhyming, sentence segmenting, and syllable blending and segmenting, are part of typical development, teachers should spend instructional time teaching students to blend, segment, and manipulate individual phonemes in words; this is the phonemic awareness level. For students who have difficulty at the phoneme awareness level, teachers should emphasize blending, segmenting, and manipulating activities that focus on individual phoneme sounds in the initial, final, and medial positions. Some students may require onset-rime blending and segmenting activities to prepare them for individual phoneme instruction.

Difficulties with Phonological Awareness

It is not uncommon for young students to have trouble with phonological awareness tasks. A number of beginning readers have difficulty with the following tasks

TABLE 10.2 Types of Phonological Awareness

Type of Phonological Awareness	Description
Phoneme: Individual sounds	• Blending individual phonemes to form words (blend sounds /s/, /u/, /n/ to say *sun*) • Segmenting individual phonemes of words (segment sounds in *sun* as /s/, /u/, /n/) • Manipulating (deleting, substituting) individual phonemes to say new words (substitute the /n/ in *man* with /t/ to say *mat*)
Phoneme: Initial, final, medial	• Matching (*run, rat*) and isolating initial sounds (/d/ begins *dog*) • Matching (*fun, sun*) and isolating (/t/ is last sound in *hat*) final sounds • Matching (*twig, big*) and isolating (middle sound in *set* is /e/) medial sounds
Onset-rime	• Blending the onset (initial consonant or consonant cluster) from the rime (vowel and consonant sounds following the onset) (blend sounds /s/ /ick/ to say *sick*) • Segmenting the onset (initial consonant or consonant cluster) from the rime (vowel and consonant sounds following the onset) (segment sounds in *sick* as /s/, /ick/)
Syllable	• Blending syllables to say words (blend *fun*-ny to say *funny*) • Segmenting words into syllable parts (segment *base/ball*) • Deleting part of a syllable (*baseball* without the *base/ball*)
Rhyme/alliteration	• Identifying if words have matching ending sounds • Producing words with matching ending sounds (*rat, cat*) • Identifying similarities and differences in beginning sounds of words (alliteration)
Word	• Segmenting sentences into individual spoken words

Source: Adapted from *Teaching Reading Sourcebook for Kindergarten Through Eighth Grade,* by B. Honig, L. Diamond, & L. Gutlohn, 2000, Novato, CA: Arena Press.

● This student is listening to a book on tape while also reading the same text in print. What reading skills is the student practicing? What other activities may help to reinforce these skills?

(Bryant et al., 2004; Bryant, Wiederholt, & Bryant, 2004; Chard & Dickson, 1999a; Torgesen & Mathes, 2000):

- Recognizing or producing words that rhyme
- Blending or segmenting syllables
- Blending or segmenting onset-rimes
- Recognizing that two words begin or end with the same sound or different sounds
- Recognizing that two words contain the same or different medial sounds
- Segmenting or blending a word's individual sounds
- Manipulating sounds to identify a new word when a sound is deleted or substituted in a word

Teaching Phonological Awareness

Effective phonological awareness instruction can be accomplished by adhering to the following guidelines (Bos & Vaughn, 2002; Chard & Dickson, 1999a; Torgesen & Mathes, 2000).

- **Assessment:** Consider students' developmental level when planning instruction. Referring to Table 10.2, note that instruction may need to be focused on syllables or onset-rimes if students are not ready for individual phoneme activities. Through assessment, the type of phonological awareness most appropriate for instruction can be determined.
- **Instructional content:** Take into consideration phonological features when selecting words for instruction. First, words with fewer sounds (e.g., *cat, it*) are easier to blend, segment, and manipulate than words with more sounds (e.g., *thread, splash, flat*). Second, the location of the phoneme (initial, medial, or

what WORKS 10.1

Elkonin Procedures to Connect Phonemic Awareness and the Alphabetic Principle

- Type of PA: Phoneme: Initial, Final, Medial

Letter–sound correspondence:

1. Give students a mat with blank boxes.
2. Give students letters that represent sounds in words to be practiced.
3. Present sounds in words following a sequence of initial, final, and medial sounds. Then, mix up the presentation of sound location.
4. Have students place letters in boxes that represent the location of the sounds.

Consider the following example:

- Students are given the letters *m, n, r, s,* and *t* (consonants) in one color and the letters *a, i,* and *u* (vowels) in a second color (red, for example).
- Students are given the mat and asked to put a letter that represents the sound and location in the correct box.

Put the letter that represents the /mmm/ sound in the word *man* in the correct box.
What sound? (/mmm/) What letter? (m) What location? (beginning)

Put the letter that represents the /nnnn/ sound in the word *run* in the correct box.
What sound? (/nnnn/) What letter? (n) What location? (end)

Put the letter that represents the /a/ sound in the word *rat in* the correct box.
What sound? (/a/) What letter? (a) What location? (middle)

Source: Adapted from *Road to the Code: A Phonological Awareness Program for Young Children,* by B. A. Blachman, E. W. Ball, R. Black, & D. M. Tangel, 2000, Baltimore: Brookes.

final) influences the level of difficulty. It is easier to change *man* to *ran* than it is to change *man* to *men* or to *map*. Third, the properties of sounds should be considered when words are selected for instruction. Continuous sounds, /sssss/, are easier to blend than stop sounds, /p/.

- **Instructional materials:** Include concrete objects as part of teaching. Objects such as blank tiles, blocks, and chips offer students opportunities to manipulate physical representations of individual sounds. Students can even use their fingers to show each sound as they segment and blend sounds in words.

- **Connections to letters:** Add letters to phonological awareness activities. Once students are familiar with blending, segmenting, and manipulating onsets and rimes and individual phonemes, include letter–sound correspondence. Connecting PA with letters helps students develop an understanding of the alphabetic principle. For example, teachers can replace blank tiles with letter tiles to have students blend and segment words. More information on phonological awareness is presented in What Works 10.1 on page 399. Read about the Elkonin (1973) procedure that can be used to teach blending and segmenting skills. These procedures can also be used to help students connect oral responses with letter correspondences to promote an understanding of the alphabetic principle.

What Is Word Identification and How Do I Teach It?

The ability to read words quickly and effortlessly means that students can recognize words on sight. However, for those words that are not known automatically, good readers possess effective decoding strategies to decipher unknown words (Chard & Osborn, 1999b; Ehri, 1998; LaBerge & Samuels, 1974). Word identification instruction consists of teaching sight word recognition and decoding skills.

Sight word recognition means that students are able to read a word automatically when encountering it in text or in an isolated list of words. Sight words include

- High-frequency words (*the, you, little, friend*), which are the most commonly occurring words in text
- Irregular words (*some, what*), in which some or all of the letters do not make their common sounds
- Important vocabulary words in content-area textbooks (Vaughn, Bos, & Schumm, 2007)

Two factors contribute to the difficulty of an irregular word: (1) how the word is sounded out and pronounced and (2) how familiar the word is to students (Carnine, Silbert, & Kameenui, 1997). For those students who have not mastered a high-frequency sight word list (see Table 10.3 for an example), instruction on these words is crucial. Fluent reading depends on the student's ability to recognize automatically those words that appear most often in text (Chard & Osborn, 1999a, b).

Difficulties with Sight Word Recognition

Teaching students to recognize sight words is an important part of word identification instruction. Oftentimes, struggling readers at the elementary and secondary

TABLE 10.3 Dolch Basic Word List Organized by Grade Level

Preprimer	Primer	Grade 1	Grade 2	Grade 3
1. the	45. when	89. many	133. know	177. don't
2. of	46. who	90. before	134. while	178. does
3. and	47. will	91. must	135. last	179. got
4. to	48. more	92. through	136. might	180. united
5. a	49. no	93. back	137. us	181. left
6. in	50. if	94. years	138. great	182. number
7. that	51. out	95. where	139. old	183. course
8. is	52. so	96. much	140. year	184. war
9. was	53. said	97. your	141. off	185. until
10. he	54. what	98. may	142. come	186. always
11. for	55. up	99. well	143. since	187. away
12. it	56. its	100. down	144. against	188. something
13. with	57. about	101. should	145. go	189. fact
14. as	58. into	102. because	146. came	190. through
15. his	59. than	103. each	147. right	191. water
16. on	60. them	104. just	148. used	192. less
17. be	61. can	105. those	149. take	193. public
18. at	62. only	106. people	150. three	194. put
19. by	63. other	107. Mr.	151. states	195. thing
20. I	64. new	108. how	152. himself	196. almost
21. this	65. some	109. too	153. few	197. hand
22. had	66. could	110. little	154. house	198. enough
23. not	67. time	111. state	155. use	199. far
24. are	68. these	112. good	156. during	200. took
25. but	69. two	113. very	157. without	201. head
26. from	70. may	114. make	158. again	202. yet
27. or	71. then	115. would	159. place	203. government
28. have	72. do	116. still	160. American	204. system
29. an	73. first	117. own	161. around	205. better
30. they	74. any	118. see	162. however	206. set
31. which	75. my	119. men	163. home	207. told
32. one	76. now	120. work	164. small	208. nothing
33. you	77. such	121. long	165. found	209. night
34. were	78. like	122. get	166. Mrs.	210. end
35. her	79. our	123. here	167. thought	211. why
36. all	80. over	124. between	168. went	212. called
37. she	81. man	125. both	169. say	213. didn't
38. there	82. me	126. life	170. part	214. eyes
39. would	83. even	127. being	171. once	215. find
40. their	84. most	128. under	172. general	216. going
41. we	85. made	129. never	173. high	217. look
42. him	86. after	130. day	174. upon	218. asked
43. been	87. also	131. same	175. school	219. later
44. has	88. did	132. another	176. every	220. knew

Source: From Dolch Word List Reexamined, by D. D. Johnson, 1971, *The Reading Teacher, 24,* pp. 455–456.
Copyright 1971 by the International Reading Association. Reprinted with permission. All rights reserved.

level possess a limited sight word vocabulary and have difficulty recalling words automatically, even after instruction has occurred. For these students, constant practice and review of sight words, along with reading the words in text, is a critical component of daily instruction. The guidelines for sight word instruction in the next section offer ways to provide the extra practice needed by struggling readers.

Teaching Sight Word Recognition

The following guidelines for sight word instruction provide helpful tips for providing effective teaching in an area that typically requires practice and review for mastery and retention. The following guidelines should help teachers plan their instruction and should be implemented regularly (Honig et al., 2000).

- **Assessment:** Use a sight word list (see Table 10.3 for an example) to determine which words should be targeted for intervention.
- **Instructional content:** Teach targeted words that most commonly occur in informational text, literature, and basal readers that students encounter during reading. Teach the words before students read text containing these words.
- **Instructional content:** Teach irregular words with common parts and similar sound patterns as word families, such as *would, could,* and *should* and *other, mother,* and *brother.*
- **Instructional content:** Teach words that have visually similar patterns separately. Words such as *though, thought,* and *through; was* and *saw;* and *were* and *where* should not be taught together.
- **Instructional content:** Teach a limited number of new words in each lesson.
- **Instructional materials:** Use flashcards for instruction and review. Color-code parts of words that require more attention (e.g., color the *w* in *was* and the *s* in *saw* green to focus student attention on the initial sound of the word).
- **Instructional delivery:** Focus student attention on all of the letters and sounds of irregular words, including letters or letter combinations that do not follow common English sounds or spellings.

● This teacher uses a variety of instructional materials in her reading classroom. What are some other examples of instructional materials that may help your students with reading skills?

- **Review/maintenance:** Include a cumulative review of key high-frequency words (2 to 3 minutes daily).
- **Fluency:** Build fluency once words have been learned. Have students read groups of sight words on flash cards. Show the flashcard and ask, "What word?" Students should respond correctly within 3 seconds. Put unknown words in a separate pile for further instruction.
- **Progress monitoring:** Daily, at the conclusion of the lesson, review the words taught to determine which words were learned. Review previously taught words on a weekly basis. Put words not remembered back into the instructional content pool of words.

Refer to ADAPT Framework 10.1 for an example of using the ADAPT framework when students exhibit difficulties with sight word recognition.

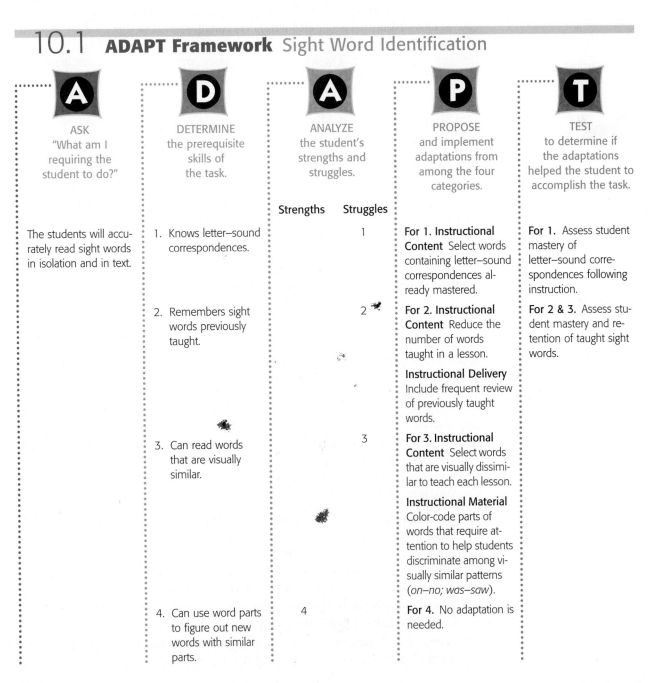

10.1 ADAPT Framework Sight Word Identification

A	D	A	P	T
ASK "What am I requiring the student to do?"	DETERMINE the prerequisite skills of the task.	ANALYZE the student's strengths and struggles.	PROPOSE and implement adaptations from among the four categories.	TEST to determine if the adaptations helped the student to accomplish the task.

		Strengths	Struggles		
The students will accurately read sight words in isolation and in text.	1. Knows letter–sound correspondences.		1	**For 1. Instructional Content** Select words containing letter–sound correspondences already mastered.	**For 1.** Assess student mastery of letter–sound correspondences following instruction.
	2. Remembers sight words previously taught.		2	**For 2. Instructional Content** Reduce the number of words taught in a lesson. **Instructional Delivery** Include frequent review of previously taught words.	**For 2 & 3.** Assess student mastery and retention of taught sight words.
	3. Can read words that are visually similar.		3	**For 3. Instructional Content** Select words that are visually dissimilar to teach each lesson. **Instructional Material** Color-code parts of words that require attention to help students discriminate among visually similar patterns (on–no; was–saw).	
	4. Can use word parts to figure out new words with similar parts.	4		**For 4.** No adaptation is needed.	

Decoding is the process of identifying unknown words by using knowledge of letter–sound correspondences. The ability to decode is important, because students will encounter many unknown words in a variety of texts that necessitate the use of strategies to read them (Pressley, 1998). Decoding includes phonic analysis, structural analysis, and multisyllabic word recognition.

Phonic analysis, or phonics, refers to making connections between units of print and units of sound (Stanovich, 1992). Sometimes called *grapheme–phoneme correspondence*, *sound–symbol relationships*, or *letter–sound correspondence*, phonic analysis uses common elements to form print–sound relationships. Letter–sound correspondence is the association of a common sound with specific letters or letter combinations in a word. Letter combinations are two or more consecutive letters that represent a single sound (/sh/) or multiple sounds (/bl/) in words.

The alphabetic principle is an important component of phonics. The alphabetic principle is the understanding that speech can be converted into print, print can be changed into speech, and letters represent sounds in our language. A part of learning how to read involves applying the most common letter–sound correspondences to a word. The letters that are associated with sounds are learned as single letters or letter combinations.

Difficulties with Phonic Analysis

Phonic analysis difficulties vary among students with reading problems. Many students are able to identify letter–sound correspondences and know how to say letter combinations in isolation. For these students, the problem often lies in blending letter sounds together to read words. This is especially apparent as they try to decode pseudowords (nonwords such as *zim*) that are used to assess phonic analysis skills. Conversely, good readers have developed automaticity in reading words. They easily and immediately apply their phonic analysis skills so that it is impossible to tell whether words are in their sight vocabularies or they are applying their phonics skills rapidly and effortlessly.

Teaching Phonic Analysis

Teaching phonic analysis is an important part of early reading instruction. Students must establish a strong understanding of letter–sound correspondence and combinations. They must also be able to identify word parts such as phonograms, or rimes, which are parts of a word to which consonants or blends are added to make a word (e.g., *an, ip, un*). The following practices can help struggling readers learn to decode using phonic analysis skills (Bear, Invernizzi, Templeton, & Johnston, 2000; Bear & Templeton, 1998; Chard & Osborn, 1999a; Chard & Osborn, 1999b; Chard, Simmons, & Kame'enui, 1998; Cunningham, 2000; Templeton & Morris, 2000).

- **Instructional content:** Teach letter–sound correspondence in a logical order. Most useful initially are the consonants *b, c, d, f, g, h, k, l, m, n, p, r, s,* and *t,* and the vowels. Present continuous letter sounds (e.g., *s* and /sss/, *m* and /mmm/, *n* and /nnn/) before stop letter sounds (*p* and /p/, *k* and /k/). Select letters that represent sounds found in decodable text that students will read.
- **Instructional content:** Introduce the most common sounds of the letters first. Lowercase letters should be taught before uppercase ones.
- **Instructional content:** Teach the letter combinations that most frequently occur in text.

- **Instructional content:** Avoid teaching letter–sound correspondence and letter combinations that sound similar and may confuse students. For instance, /m/ and /n/ and /sh/ and /ch/ should not be taught together. Letter combinations with the same sound, such as /ir/ and /ur/ and /ee/ and /ea/ can be taught at the same time.

- **Instructional content:** Teach phonograms containing letter–sound correspondences that have been introduced. Phonograms or rimes such as *ap, at, ip, it, un,* and *et* paired with initial consonants or onsets provide opportunities to segment and blend sounds to make words. These words should be featured in the decodable text that students will read.

- **Instructional delivery:** Teach students to blend the letter sounds together in a seamless fashion. For instance, students should be taught to say *mmmaaannn* rather than separating the sounds /m/ /a/ /n/.

- **Instructional materials:** Have students read decodable texts—texts that contain words with the sounds and patterns you have previously taught and students have mastered.

- **Connections to spelling:** Have students spell the words so their phonics instruction can be reinforced. Spelling and reading are closely related skills. Here are some examples of ways to make connections to spelling:

  - Introduce letter–sound correspondences for spelling as they are being introduced and taught in reading.

  - Have students sort words into spelling patterns.

  - Have students identify words from their text with patterns that match what they are learning in phonics.

The following are guidelines for English language learners:

- Discuss letters that may have pronunciations in English that differ from those in the student's first language (e.g., the letter *h* in Spanish is silent). Correct differences of speech sounds carefully.

- Add pictures of words (e.g., pictures on the back of word cards) where appropriate to help students associate words and meanings and to learn vocabulary.

- Use charts and word banks to categorize words according to patterns.

- Teach rules for decoding words that contain letters that do not make their most common sound (e.g., silent-*e* words, double-vowel words).

ADAPT in Action • Alexandra—Phonics Analysis

Mrs. Evans considers Alexandra, who seems to struggle in nearly all academic areas, but who is very social and popular with her classmates. Alexandra was assessed to be in the "highly at risk" area for reading difficulties. Alexandra's spoken vocabulary is limited, and she has a reading sight vocabulary of only about 50 words. She has considerable difficulty making letter–sound correspondences and has trouble comprehending even the easiest reading materials. English is her first language and is the only language spoken in the home. Her vision and hearing skills are excellent. She uses a power wheelchair to move about and has no difficulty navigating throughout her school and classroom. Consider the ADAPT framework as you read the following phonics analysis activity in Instructional Activity 10.1.

Using the ADAPT framework to consider the task and prerequisite skills needed to complete the activity, think about how Alexandra's strengths and struggles fit within the framework. What adaptations in content, delivery, and materials might you propose for Mrs. Evans to try? Do they match the following adaptations?

- **Instructional content:** Focus on one beginning- and middle-letter sound or one ending-letter sound.
- **Instructional materials:** Use magnetic letters and a metal letter board.
- **Instructional delivery:** Have the student work one-on-one with an older peer tutor or the teacher.

Structural analysis involves using knowledge of word structure to decode unknown words. Spache and Spache (1986) stated that the purpose of teaching structural analysis is "the development of the habit of recognition by larger, more meaningful units within words" (p. 492). Structural analysis components include prefixes, suffixes, inflectional endings, compound words, and contractions.

Instructional activity 10.1

Phonics Analogies

INSTRUCTIONAL OBJECTIVE: The students will learn to decode VC and CVC words.

INSTRUCTIONAL CONTENT: Letter–sound correspondence, VC and CVC words

INSTRUCTIONAL MATERIALS: Card with squares, letter tiles, list of VC or CVC words

INSTRUCTIONAL DELIVERY
Grouping: Small group of students who require instruction in phonics analysis

TEACHING PROCEDURE

1. Place the letter tiles in the boxes *m, a,* and *n.*
2. Say the first letter sound, /mmm/, while pointing to the letter *m*. The second letter sound, /aaa/, is spoken as the second letter tile is pointed to. The process continues for the final letter sound, /nnn/.
3. Slide your finger below the tiles in a left-to-right sequence as you say the word in elongated fashion (*mmmaaannn*), then quickly (*man*).
4. Say, "If this is *man,* and I change the *m* to *r* (replaces the *m* tile with an *r* tile), now I have *rrraaannn . . . ran.*"

5. Model the process for other words.

Guided Practice

6. Repeat the process with the students. The process continues with a change of the ending letter tile (e.g., *ran* becomes *rat,* then *rag*). Middle letters can also be replaced. The process continues with a variety of VC and CVC words.

Error Correction

7. If students make an error, say, "Stop. I will model the process. Listen, my turn." Model another word. Have students repeat. Then continue with guided practice.

Independent Practice

8. Give each student a couple of words to do alone. Tell the other students to sound out each letter, blending them and then saying the word quickly.

PROGRESS MONITORING: After the lesson, give the student 10 words to decode; check for mastery.

Difficulties with Structural Analysis

Students who exhibit difficulties using knowledge of word structure for decoding purposes struggle with reading multisyllabic words. These students may have difficulty identifying base or root words and recognizing word parts, such as affixes (suffixes and prefixes) and inflectional endings. Also, students may have decoding problems when free morphemes (the smallest units of language that conveys meaning) are combined, which is what happens with compound words and contractions.

Good readers recognize affixes and inflectional endings in words immediately and know how to use these structural cues to decode words. They recognize contractions at sight because there are only a few of them and they encounter them often in text. These students recognize that compound words are composed of two words and that multisyllabic words are composed of letter combinations, word parts, affixes, and inflectional endings. Good readers tend to know the meanings of most affixes, and they apply the meanings of affixes to understand what they read.

Teaching Structural Analysis

Struggling readers require extra instruction to learn to use word parts to decode words. Careful selection of words helps students acquire structural analysis decoding skills by focusing on parts of words, such as prefixes and suffixes. Words should be taken from text students read so that they can learn how to decode harder words. Words should contain parts that students will encounter in their reading. For instance, in social studies, words with *trans* and *ex* prefixes should be included in structural analysis instruction. The following guidelines can help struggling readers with structural analysis skills.

- **Instructional content:** Begin instruction with easier words and then proceed to more difficult words. Start with compound words containing short vowels, followed by words with vowel/consonant combinations. Shorter, single-syllable words such as *fast, run,* and *base* (faster, running, baseball) should be introduced before longer words with multiple syllables, such as *contract, remember,* and *candle* (contractor, remembering, candlelight).
- **Instructional content:** Teach affixes beginning with easier inflectional endings (*-s, -ing*), prefixes (*re-, un-*), and suffixes (*-ly, -est, -er*). For content-area material, teach prefixes that are commonly found in a particular content area (e.g., social studies, *trans*; science, *bio*).
- **Word selection/instructional content:** Use authentic text—nonfiction and fictional literature—and content-area textbooks as a source for words to illustrate different word structures.
- **Instructional activities:** Provide a number of different activities during instruction (such as word sorts and locating affixes, compounds, prefixes, and contractions in content-area books).
- **Connections to spelling:** Integrate spelling into word identification instruction. Have students write down words with affixes, contractions, and compounds to reinforce structural analysis instruction. What Works 10.2 provides prompts to help students decode unknown words.

what WORKS 10.2

Decoding Unknown Words

Students can be instructed to decode unknown words by using the following questions and prompts.

● **Self-Questioning**

1. Is there any part of the word that I can pronounce? If no, then go to step 4.

2. Say the word part that I know. Then try to sound out the rest of the word. If I cannot say the rest of the word, then go to step 4.

3. Say the word. Is this a word that I know? Does it make sense in the sentence? If no, then go to step 4.

4. Does this word have a spelling pattern like another word that I know? If no, then go to step 6.

5. Say the word. Is this a word that I know? Does it make sense in the sentence? If no, then go to step 6.

6. Say "blank" for the unknown word. Finish the sentence. Then ask what word makes sense in the blank.

● **Teacher Prompting**

Strategy	Usage	Prompt
Word parts	Unknown word contains a part the student can pronounce: *un* in *unkind* *mak* in *making.*	Can you say a part of the word? What part?
Analogy	Unknown word contains a spelling pattern that is similar to a known word: unknown word *shameless* is like known word *blameless.*	Is the word like another word that you know? What word?
Sound by sound	Unknown word is sounded out sound by sound: /t/, /r/, /ai/, /n/–ing/–*training.*	Say the first sound, the next sound, and the next sound. What word?
Context	The text provides sufficient clues to help the student verify pronunciation. The student is unable to use structural analysis skills alone for identification purposes.	What word makes sense? Finish the sentence and then tell what word makes sense. What word?

Source: Adapted from *Building Words,* by T. G. Gunning, 2001, Boston: Allyn and Bacon.

ADAPT in Action ● Phillip—Structural Analysis

Mr. Williams has determined that Phillip has problems identifying multisyllabic words. Phillip does not use word structure to decode unknown words in the text. He does not use word parts such as prefixes and suffixes to break the word into manageable units for decoding purposes. He often looks at a "hard" word and says he doesn't know what it says or he mumbles over the word when reading. He is able to read single-syllable words with CCVCC (e.g., *blend, stand*), CVCe (e.g., *bike, make*), and vowel-team patterns (e.g., *ea, ee, oa*). Phillip tends to spend time talking with friends or fidgeting in his desk when it is time to read with a partner. His content-area teachers report that his difficulties decoding subject-area words are interfering with his ability to comprehend the subject material.

Mr. Williams notes that of his 20 students with identified reading problems, one-third had difficulties decoding multisyllabic words. He decides to teach the HINTS strategy to these students for one week across class periods. He plans on reinforcing student application of the strategy by posting the strategy on the wall

Instructional activity 10.2

HINTS

INSTRUCTIONAL OBJECTIVE: The students will identify multisyllabic words using letter–sound correspondence, letter combinations, and structural analysis.

INSTRUCTIONAL CONTENT: Multisyllabic words containing affixes

INSTRUCTIONAL MATERIALS: HINTS poster, blank transparency, overhead projector, marker, highlighter, word list from reading material

INSTRUCTIONAL DELIVERY

Grouping: Small group of students who require instruction in structural analysis

TEACHING PROCEDURE

1. Identify multisyllabic words containing targeted affixes.
2. Tell students they are going to learn a procedure called HINTS for identifying unknown multisyllabic words.
3. Use the HINTS poster to teach the procedure:
   - Tell students what each letter in HINTS stands for and have them echo.
   - Point to and name each letter in HINTS and have students chorally read the descriptor.
   - Cover the poster and review HINTS, having students name the letters and the descriptors from memory.

- Review this procedure daily until students can say the letters and descriptors with 100 percent accuracy from memory.

4. Refer to the poster and model how to divide a word following the HINTS procedures:

Write a word (*unacceptable*) on the overhead projector. Say and do:

   H—**H**ighlight the prefix (*un*) and the suffix (*able*).

   I—**I**dentify the consonant and vowel sounds in the base word (*ac* says /ak/, *cept* says /sept/).

   N—**N**ame the base word (*accept*).

   T—**T**ie the parts together fast (/un/ /accept/ /able/).

   S—**S**ay the word (unacceptable).

5. Model the process for other words.
6. Repeat the process with the students.
7. Give each student a list of words to divide. Meet with each student to check his or her work and hear the words read quickly.

PROGRESS MONITORING: First, have students individually tell you HINTS (letters and descriptors). Next have them divide words using HINTS. Then have them read the words quickly.

Source: Adapted from *Effective Instruction for Secondary Struggling Readers: Research-based Practices,* 2003, Austin: University of Texas, Vaughn Gross Center for Reading and Language Arts.

and reminding students to use HINTS. He will share the strategy and poster with his sixth-grade colleagues. Instructional Activity 10.2 describes the HINTS activity. An example of how Mr. Williams collaborates with the other sixth-grade teachers is shown in the Working Together feature on page 412.

Following the HINTS activity, Mr. Williams notes that Phillip and two other students are not successful during progress monitoring. He decides to use the ADAPT framework to make decisions about next steps.

Ask, "What am I requiring the student to do?" Mr. Williams thinks about the task: "I want students to memorize the HINTS strategy and to apply it to decode unknown words from their reading."

Determine the prerequisite skills of the task. "Students must know what a prefix and suffix are and how to decode letter combinations in the base word."

Analyze the student's strengths and struggles. The data indicate that the students can memorize the letters of HINT, but remembering what each letter stands for is not at 100 percent accuracy. Mr. Williams also notes that knowledge of letter combinations is good, but knowledge of prefixes and suffixes is lacking.

Propose and implement adaptations from among the four categories. He decides to teach the prefixes and suffixes (*instructional content and instructional activity*) separately, including the meaning of the word parts. He will teach only those affixes that are in words from the book. He will also provide more practice (*instructional delivery*) on the HINTS descriptors.

Test to determine if the adaptations helped the student accomplish the task. Mr. Williams will continue to monitor progress as specified in the HINTS lesson.

Multisyllable word recognition involves identifying words that have two or more syllables. A *syllable* is a unit of pronunciation that contains a single vowel sound. *Syllabication* involves analyzing combinations of vowels and consonants in a word to determine where the word should break into syllables. This process helps students to decode manageable units or chunks—that is, *syllable types*—which can be blended together to make a multisyllabic word (Honig et al., 2000). To decode multisyllabic words, students should be able to

- Understand the concept of syllable
- Recognize phonic "chunks" in single-syllable words (i.e., phonograms)
- Identify vowels and consonants
- Recognize syllable types and patterns

Syllable Types and Patterns

Syllable types include the phonic elements taught in decoding that help students to read single and multisyllable words. Syllable patterns tell students where to divide a multisyllabic word and how to pronounce it (Honig et al., 2000). Table 10.4 displays the six syllable types and associated patterns (VCCV) that students can use to identify long words containing more than one syllable. The six syllable patterns are (1) closed syllables, (2) open syllables, (3) vowel–consonant–e syllables, (4) vowel–r syllables, (5) vowel team syllables, and (6) consonant–le syllables. Struggling readers need to learn syllable types and patterns.

Difficulties with Multisyllabic Word Recognition

Beginning readers often struggle with long words. Because beginning readers sometimes struggle with decoding, they also struggle with identifying each syllable. Also, beginning readers often struggle with blending, so combining syllables to form longer words can be problematic. Because they may have limited spoken-language vocabularies, even if they are able to decode the syllable parts and blend them together successfully, no connection is made between print vocabulary and spoken vocabulary, so they may think they mispronounced the word and continue to decode the word differently until they come up with a match between written word and spoken word. After a while, they simply give up.

TABLE 10.4 Syllable Types and Patterns

Syllable Type	Examples and Pattern	
Closed. The closed syllable type follows the CVC, CCVC, or VC pattern. It ends with a consonant and the vowel sound usually is short.	man	on-set
	stop	kit-chen
	at	hap-py
Open. The open syllable type follows the CV, CCV, or the V pattern. The vowel usually makes its long sound.	no	ga-ble
	be	o-pen
	so	cho-sen
Vowel–consonant–e. The vowel-consonant-e type follows the CVC–e, CCVC–e, or VC–e pattern. The vowel usually makes its long sound and the e is usually silent.	shape	like-ness
	bike	ig-nite
	ate	in-cite
Vowel–r. The vowel-r type follows the CV+r, CCV+r, or V+r pattern. The vowel makes an unexpected or unusual sound that is neither short nor long.	carp	sur-name
	stir	car-pet
	fort	ur-gent
Vowel team. The vowel team type has two vowels next to each other and follows the CVVC or VVC pattern. If the team is a vowel digraph, the first sound usually is long and the second vowel is usually silent. If the team is a diphthong, the vowels form a unique sound.	mail	heat-er
	hoop	ea-ger
	shout	soy-bean
	soot	seed
Consonant–le. The consonant-le type appears at the end of a syllable and follows the CCV+le, CV+le, or V+le pattern. The e is silent and the consonant is unaccented.	muz-zle	bri-dle
	ca-ble	rus-tle

Sources: M. Adams, 1990; S. Carreker, 1999; D. J. Chard & J. Osborn, 1999; B. Honig, L. Diamond, & L. Gutlohn, 2000; Moats, 1995.

In contrast, good readers find long words to be less challenging and have little trouble recognizing multisyllabic words. They know syllable types and can use patterns to divide words into syllable parts. Their blending skills are well developed, as are their spoken-language vocabularies, so the process quickly results in a written word–spoken word match. Thus, reading multisyllabic words is efficient and leads to the same level of automaticity with longer words as with shorter words.

Teaching Multisyllabic Word Recognition

Students who encounter multisyllabic words in content-area textbooks must have strategies for decoding them. Teaching syllable patterns and types and implementing the following guidelines can help struggling readers learn how to decode difficult words (Honig et al., 2000).

- **Instructional content:** Use letters and combinations that the students have already mastered. These may be prefixes and suffixes, or they may be familiar letter–sound correspondences and letter combinations. For instance, the prefix *re* (open syllable) with *tool* (vowel team) for *retool* can be used as an example. Or, for a closed syllable, *sun* (closed syllable) can be used with *shine* (vowel–consonant *e*) to form *sunshine* (compound word).

WORKING together

Strategy Instruction Across Classes

Mr. Williams decides to teach the HINTS strategy to his students who require support decoding multisyllabic words. He teaches the strategy to the students and has them apply it to words from texts used in his class. Other sixth-grade teachers have expressed a concern to Mr. Williams that some of his students cannot identify words in their content-area textbooks, much less figure out the meaning of the unknown words. He knows that the HINTS strategy can be used in all classes. He decides to provide an explanation to the other sixth-grade teachers on the strategy, including how students can use their knowledge of prefixes to understand the meaning of the words.

Mr. Williams can use the following suggestions to improve the collaborative process:

- The sixth-grade teachers can create a poster of the strategy to place on their classroom walls as a reminder for all students who need help decoding words.
- The sixth-grade teachers can praise students for using the strategy to help them be independent learners.
- Mr. Williams should ensure that his students have mastered the HINTS strategy and can apply it successfully to identify multisyllabic words.
- Mr. Williams should meet with the sixth-grade teachers periodically to determine how the strategy is working in the content-area classes.
- Mr. Williams should check with his students to determine their perspective on the effectiveness of the strategy in other classes and for doing homework.

- **Instructional content:** Integrate longer words into instruction to challenge the students. All of the syllables in these longer words (such as *incubation*) should be examples of previously learned syllable types and should introduce readers to content-area words.
- **Instructional delivery:** Teach students how to label letters as consonants or vowels and to identify the pattern for dividing the word (e.g., VCCV).
- **Instructional delivery:** Introduce each syllable type after reviewing and reinforcing any previously learned types. Demonstrating the differences between the types helps students compare and contrast similarities and differences.
- **Instructional delivery:** Provide practice opportunities using both expository and narrative texts. This allows students to use context to help them confirm their pronunciations in text. For instance, consider the sentence "The incubation period for the common cold is usually between 2 and 5 days." If students use their knowledge of syllable types to sound out *incubation* and continue to read the sentence, they can determine that they pronounced (identified) the word correctly based on the context of the sentence.
- **Progress monitoring:** Test your students' ability to name the syllable types and patterns. Provide examples of words containing each type and pattern; have students explain how to divide the word into syllables, say the parts, and blend the parts together to read the word. A sorting activity in which students sort words according to type and pattern is another way to monitor their progress with this skill.

In concluding the word identification section, examples of word identification activities can be found in What Works 10.3 on page 414. Elementary and secondary teachers can use this information to help students struggling with word identification skills.

What Is Reading Fluency and How Do I Teach It?

Adams (1990) observed, "The most salient characteristic of skillful readers is the speed and effortlessness with which they seem able to breeze through text" (p. 409). The ability to read with "speed and effortlessness" is what fluency is all about. Duffy and Roehler (1986) described fluency in greater detail: "Fluent reading reflects the reader's clear understanding of the words used, the topic, the author's purpose, and the text structure and is evidenced by correct intonation and an absence of interruptions" (p. 472). After reviewing the reading disability literature, Lyon (1995) stated that fluent word recognition is the most frequently cited factor in reading disorders.

There are two types of reading fluency: oral reading fluency and silent reading fluency. Oral reading fluency is the combination of rate (i.e., how fast one reads) and accuracy (i.e., correct word identification). For oral reading, fluency may also involve expression or *prosody*, which means altering pitch, tone, and so forth. Silent reading fluency is a combination of rate and comprehension.

Despite its importance, most teachers do not spend a lot of instructional time building students' fluency. Some teachers spend *no* time on this important reading element. However, time spent on fluency building is time well spent.

Reading fluency is an important skill for older readers who have to read large quantities of material for school assignments. We suspect that you, as a student and teacher, understand the importance of fluency and how it affects how much time you allocate to completing your reading. Repeated reading, the process of developing fluency through multiple readings of the same passage, increases reading accuracy, reading rate, and comprehension. Researchers have found repeated reading to be very effective in developing the reading fluency and reading comprehension abilities of students with reading difficulties (Adams, 1990).

Fluency is influenced by numerous factors (e.g., purpose for reading, content), and the fluency expectations for oral and silent reading differ. Findings from a study that examined oral reading fluency rates for first grade (beginning in winter) through eighth grade are presented in Table 10.5 (Hasbrouck & Tindall, 2005).

TABLE 10.5 Reading Rates for Oral Reading (in words per minute)

Grade	Fall	Winter	Spring
1	X	23–81	53–111
2	51–106	72–125	89–142
3	71–128	92–146	107–162
4	94–145	112–166	123–180
5	110–166	127–182	139–194
6	127–177	140–195	150–204
7	128–180	136–192	150–202
8	133–185	146–199	151–199

Source: From *Oral Reading Fluency: 90 Years of Assessment* (BRT Technical Report No. 33), by J. Hasbrouck & G. Tindall, 2005, Eugene, OR: Author. Reprinted with permission.

what WORKS 10.3

Word Identification Activities

● Read, Spell, and Write

OBJECTIVE: The students will learn to identify partially decodable words.

INSTRUCTIONAL MATERIALS: Eight irregular-word cards, pencil, and sheet of paper

TEACHING PROCEDURE

1. Show and pronounce the word *should.*

2. Ask the student to read the word *should.*

3. Ask the student to spell the word aloud (*s-h-o-u-l-d*).

4. Say, "What does *s-h-o-u-l-d* spell?"

5. Have the student write and read the word.

6. Repeat the procedure for each word. After each word is written and read, the student reads aloud each word on the list.

PROGRESS MONITORING: After the lesson, give the student 10 irregular words to read; check for mastery. Once a month or so, provide a list of practiced words for the student to read. Unknown words (not read correctly within 3 seconds) are put back in the pool of words for instruction.

● Sorting Words

OBJECTIVE: The student will sort words according to a skill being taught.

INSTRUCTIONAL MATERIALS: Word cards with words containing a skill or pattern being taught. Examples: onset-rimes, syllable types, number of syllables, vowel teams, root words with affixes, compound words, irregular high-frequency words that are partially decodable.

TEACHING PROCEDURE

1. Identify words that contain examples of spelling patterns being taught (guided practice) and previously taught (review).

2. Model for students how to

   - Read the word looking for the pattern being taught and reviewed

   - Find other words in the list that contain a similar spelling pattern

   - Sort the words according to the spelling pattern, explaining why the words are sorted in a particular way

3. Have students work in pairs, small groups, or learning centers to sort words. Be sure students can explain their reason for sorting words into specific piles.

PROGRESS MONITORING: Give students a list of words containing various spelling patterns. Have them sort and explain their sorting rationale.

Source: Adapted from *Words Their Way: Word Study for Phonics, Vocabulary, and Spelling Instruction,* 2nd ed., by D. R. Bear, M. Invernizzi, S. Templeton, & F. Johnston, 2000, Upper Saddle River, NJ: Merrill–Prentice Hall.

● Building Words

OBJECTIVE: The student will create words correctly using root words, prefixes, and suffixes and make a sentence using the word correctly.

INSTRUCTIONAL MATERIALS

- Word cards containing root words, prefixes, and suffixes

- Blank word cards

- Three envelopes per group and teacher

- Poster of selected prefixes and suffixes and their meanings

- Transparency of Word Building handout

- Word Building handout—one per student

TEACHING PROCEDURE

1. Identify several root words, prefixes, and suffixes to target.

2. Tell the students that they are going to work in small groups to build words. This activity involves building multisyllable words, using root words, prefixes, and suffixes, and then developing sentences for the new words.

3. Briefly review the list of targeted prefixes and suffixes on the affix poster.

4. Demonstrate the procedure as follows:

   Place the Word Building transparency on the overhead projector.

   - Show the students the three envelopes. Explain that envelope 1 contains cards with root words, envelope 2 contains cards with prefixes, and envelope 3 contains cards with suffixes.

   - Choose a root word card (e.g., *reason*) from envelope 1 and write the word on the transparency under the word *root.*

- Choose a prefix from envelope 2 and write the prefix (e.g., *un*) on the line before the root word *if it makes sense*. If it doesn't make sense, place it back in the envelope.
- Choose a suffix from envelope 3 and write the suffix (e.g., *able*) on the line after the root word *if it makes sense*. If it doesn't make sense, place it back in the envelope.
- Say and write the new word (e.g., *unreasonable*) under "New Word" on the handout and think aloud what the word means (e.g., *un* means "not," *able* means "capable of," if I put those with *reason*, it would mean that it's not a good cause for doing something.
- Think of and write a sentence on the next line using the new word.

5. Give each group three envelopes and each student a handout.
6. Have the students review the procedure as provided on the top of the handout.
7. Instruct the groups to begin making words, one at a time, referring to the affix poster as needed. When there are no more root words in envelope 1, the group is finished.
8. Post the words next to the poster chart and review them with the class. Select students to read their sentences for some of the words.

PROGRESS MONITORING: Have students create words using roots and affixes and use them in sentences. The sentences should make sense.

Word Building Handout

	PREFIX	ROOT	SUFFIX	NEW WORD
1.	_____	_____	_____	_____

Sentence:

_____

_____

_____

	PREFIX	ROOT	SUFFIX	NEW WORD
2.	_____	_____	_____	_____

Sentence:

_____

_____

_____

● SPLIT

OBJECTIVE: The students will use their knowledge of syllable types to identify multisyllabic words.

MATERIALS: SPLIT poster, blank transparency, overhead projector, marker, highlighter, word list from reading material

TEACHING PROCEDURE

1. Teach or review the six syllable types and patterns (see Table 10.4).
2. Show the students the SPLIT poster and go over each step of the mnemonic SPLIT:

    S—**S**ee the syllable types.

    P—**P**lace a line between the syllables.

    L—**L**ook at each syllable.

    I—**I**dentify the syllable sounds.

    T—**T**ry to say the word.

3. Use the SPLIT poster to teach the procedure:
    - Tell students what each letter in SPLIT stands for and have them echo.
    - Point to and name each letter in SPLIT and have students chorally read the descriptor.
    - Cover the poster and review SPLIT, having students name the letters and the descriptors from memory.
    - Review this procedure daily until students can say the letters and descriptors with 100 percent accuracy from memory.
4. Refer to the poster and model on how to divide a word following the SPLIT procedure.
5. Model the process for other words.
6. Repeat the process with the students.
7. Give each student a list of words to SPLIT. Meet with each student to check his or her work and hear the words read quickly.

PROGRESS MONITORING: First, have students individually tell you SPLIT (letters and descriptors). Next have them divide words using SPLIT. Then have them read the words quickly.

Sources: Adapted from *Effective Instruction for Secondary Struggling Readers: Research-based Practices,* 2003, Austin: University of Texas, Vaughn Gross Center for Reading and Language Arts; *Teaching Reading Sourcebook for Kindergarten Through Eighth Grade,* by B. Honig, L. Diamond, & L. Gutlohn, 2000, Novato, CA: Arena Press.

Difficulties with Fluency

Beginning readers read more slowly than mature readers, make more oral reading errors than mature readers, read with very little prosody, and struggle with silent-reading comprehension (Allington, 1984; Bryant & Rivera, 1997; Moats, 1999; Schreiber, 1980; VGCRLA, 2003). More specifically, beginning readers

- Exhibit problems with accuracy and speed
- Present basic word reading difficulties
- Have a small sight vocabulary
- Read word by word
- Rarely self-correct their errors during their reading
- Struggle reading aloud in ways that reflect understanding of the text and are unable to engage listeners

Conversely, good readers

- Exhibit automatic word identification skills
- Self-correct most errors while reading
- Change their reading rate based on the purposes for reading
- Read at a rate that helps facilitate comprehension
- Read independent-level materials that are challenging yet manageable
- Read and comprehend diverse texts
- Have a rich vocabulary
- Read orally in ways that reflect understanding of the text and engage their listeners

Assessing Fluency

As you prepare to assess a student's reading fluency, you need to plan how you will note errors, whether you will be assessing oral or silent reading, and how current and subsequent performances will be charted.

ERRORS   For purpose of evaluating fluency, a slash marking system can be used to identify deviations from print, which refers to words that are not identified correctly in oral reading (Wiederholt & Bryant, 2003). When using the slash marking system, slash only those words that are examples of mispronunciations, substitutions, hesitations, and omissions. Only these types of deviations from print are recorded in fluency assessment. It takes a while to develop sufficient skills to separate errors from the other deviations from print, but it becomes easier with practice.

PROCEDURES FOR ASSESSING ORAL READING FLUENCY   Have all the materials on hand (i.e., copies of the reading passage for you and the reader; a stopwatch; a tape recorder, if needed; and a pencil). Begin with a passage written at the student's grade level, and have increasingly difficult and easier passages available. Thus, if the student is in the third grade, start with a third-grade passage and have easier and more difficult passages on hand. However, for older students who are struggling with reading select an easier passage (several years below grade level) as a starting point. Selecting a sixth-grade reading passage for a sixth-grade student who has reading difficulties will not create a good assessment situation for the student. Be prepared with easier and more difficult passages until the right reading level can be determined.

Start timing when the student reads the first word. On your copy of the passage, place a slash over every reading error. After 1 minute, stop the student from reading. Count the total number of words read, and subtract the number of errors; the resulting number represents words correct per minute (wcpm), a measure of reading fluency. The wcpm has to be accompanied by the reading level of the passage, so one might report, "Tom reads third-grade-level passages at 73 words correct per minute." Reading levels include the following.

- **Independent reading level:** The level at which the student demonstrates word recognition of 95 percent or above and comprehension of 95 percent or above.
- **Instructional reading level:** The level at which the reader demonstrates word recognition of 90 to 94 percent and comprehension of 90 to 100 percent, *or* word recognition of 95 percent or above and comprehension of 90 to 94 percent.
- **Frustration reading level:** The level at which the student demonstrates word recognition of less than 90 percent and comprehension less than 90 percent.

When conducting fluency assessments with passages that do not have accompanying comprehension questions, you may delete comprehension from consideration. Thus,

- **Independent reading level:** Word recognition of 95 percent or greater
- **Instructional reading level:** Word recognition of 90 to 94 percent
- **Frustration reading level:** Word recognition of less than 90 percent

Continue evaluating for fluency until the student reaches the frustration level (reads less than 90 percent of the words accurately).

PROCEDURES FOR ASSESSING SILENT READING FLUENCY   Assessing silent reading fluency adds a twist to fluency assessment. First, it is impossible to check for errors, so the resulting value for rate is words per minute (wpm), not words correct per minute, because wpm does not take into account deviations from print. Also, the directions are a little different. Begin timing when you say "begin," and the student points to the word he or she is reading when you say "stop." The total number of words read from *begin* to *stop* is the silent reading rate.

Second, oral reading fluency is a combination of rate and accuracy. For silent reading, fluency is a combination of rate and comprehension. Rate without comprehension is a relatively useless statistic in silent reading, because a student can so quickly read a passage that comprehension is reduced. Silent reading rate must be accompanied by a measure of comprehension. Silent reading fluency refers to the number of words read at a certain comprehension level at a certain reading level. For example, Margarita is a ninth grader who has been given a seventh-grade reading passage to read silently. She read 158 words in 1 minute. Ten comprehension questions were asked, of which she answered nine correctly. So her silent fluency is 158 words per minute with 90 percent comprehension at the seventh-grade reading level. Testing continues until the student's frustration level is attained. For silent reading, only comprehension is considered when determining the student's independent level, instructional level, and frustration level.

- **Independent reading level:** Comprehension of 95 percent or greater
- **Instructional reading level:** Comprehension of 90 to 94 percent
- **Frustration reading level:** Comprehension less than 90 percent

CHARTING FLUENCY At the start of fluency instruction, the student's current fluency level becomes the baseline (the starting point) for monitoring progress. Fluency progress should be charted one reading level at a time. For example, consider Tom, a seventh grader who has an oral reading fluency level for independent-reading-level materials at 79 words correct per minute for third-grade passages. A fluency goal of between 92 and 146 words per minute (winter goal) for third-grade passages is established. Fluency progress using third-grade passages is charted until the student meets or exceeds that goal. If the student continues building fluency at another grade level, say, fourth-grade-level passages (provided the student is now reading independently at that level), gather baseline data at that level and begin charting progress on a new chart. The reason for beginning with this new chart is quite simple. Tom's fluency for fourth-grade-level materials is likely to be lower than his goal for third-grade materials.

Teaching Fluency

The ability to read fluently is important so that students can focus on reading comprehension (LaBerge & Samuels, 1974; Rasinski, 2000). Students should have opportunities to practice reading words in isolation (e.g., sight words) and text at their independent level to build fluency. The following practices can be used to help students develop fluency.

- **Instructional content:** Select appropriate text. Fluency instruction is best accomplished using materials at the student's independent reading level. When students read independent-level materials, they recognize many of the words at sight and have no trouble identifying unknown words quickly. Students should concentrate on reading with an increased rate and not worry about decoding unknown words. Instructional-level materials can be used, but avoid frustration-level texts. Beginning readers can practice building their fluency by reading decodable texts. In addition, texts used during fluency building should be of interest to the students.
- **Instructional delivery:** Model fluent reading. Teachers should model fluent reading or have a fluent reader do so with students who require fluency-building instruction.
- **Instructional delivery:** Teach students word identification skills to automaticity. Students should have proficient word identification skills and a core sight word vocabulary to help build fluency. Help students build fluency with isolated words, phrase reading (i.e., reading three or four word phrases, such as "in the tree" and "on the large ball"), and connected text.
- **Progress monitoring:** Assess students' oral reading ability at least biweekly. Graph the number of words per minute that are correct. Compare progress to the benchmark fluency rates in Table 10.5 (see page 413). Students must make steady progress on each assessment so that they will reach the winter and spring benchmarks.

ADAPT in Action ● Mark—Oral Reading Fluency

Mark is a 12-year-old sixth grader who is reading on a third-grade level. He attends Mr. Williams's reading class. Mark has a sight vocabulary of several hundred words and has good letter–sound correspondence skills. He needs instruction with vowel teams (*ee, oa, ai*), especially consonant digraphs (*sh, th, wh*) and diphthongs (*ou, ow*). He needs help with structural analysis and multisyllabic word recognition skills to decode harder words. He reads in a word-by-word manner and lacks expression as he reads aloud. He is eager to please and is a hard worker. Mr. Williams plans on implementing a whole-class (peer-mediated) reading fluency program, because many of his students can benefit from fluency building. Instructional Activity 10.3 presents paired reading, which is modeled after class-wide peer tutoring and uses repeated reading.

While circulating during graphing time, Mr. Williams notices that Mark and several other students' graphs are not showing an upward trend in the number of words read during "best read." Mr. Williams decides to use the ADAPT framework.

A sk, "What am I requiring the student to do?" Mr. Williams wants Mark and other students who need help to become more fluent readers. He knows this is critical so that Mark can read his textbooks more easily and focus on comprehension.

D etermine the prerequisite skills of the task. Mr. Williams knows that to read fluently, one must be able to recognize words quickly (on sight) and to quickly decode any difficult words. In paired reading (*task*), students must be able to practice with a partner, to read the passage, and to read quickly.

A nalyze the student's strengths and struggles. Mr. Williams notices that Mark has difficulty keeping up with his partner and reading the passage when it is his turn.

P ropose and implement adaptations from among the four categories. Mr. Williams decides that he will provide Mark with a shorter selection of text (*instructional content*), use easier material (*instructional material*), and serve as Mark's partner (*instructional delivery*).

T est to determine if the adaptations helped the student accomplish the task. Mr. Williams will continue to monitor progress as specified in the paired reading lesson.

What Is Reading Vocabulary and How Do I Teach It?

Reading vocabulary refers to an understanding of words, or word comprehension. When readers understand individual words, they are better able to understand phrases and sentences. This, in turn, can help readers understand words with the help of context clues, or surrounding text, particularly when a word has more than one meaning. Once sentences are comprehended, paragraphs can be better understood, finally leading to passage comprehension, the ultimate goal of reading.

Instructional activity 10.3

Paired Reading

INSTRUCTIONAL OBJECTIVE: Students will read passages aloud with increased rate and accuracy.

INSTRUCTIONAL CONTENT: Fluency; reading instructional-level passages

INSTRUCTIONAL MATERIALS: Copies of reading materials for students, timer, chart paper

INSTRUCTIONAL DELIVERY

Paired Reading (Partner 1 is a slightly better reader than partner 2.)

Paired reading is an effective method for developing the oral reading fluency skills of students who read at about the first-grade level (e.g., know some sight words, can blend CVC words). This method works well with students who read haltingly and make careless errors.

Teaching Procedure

1. Divide students into pairs.
2. Select reading passages that the lower-level reading partner can read at no less than the instructional level.
3. Set the timer for 2 minutes for partner 1 to read the passage out loud while partner 2 follows along.
4. Repeat step 3, but have partner 2 read out loud and partner 1 follow along, helping with unknown words.
5. Repeat step 3 for 1 minute. Partner 1 charts the number of words read in 1 minute (best read).
6. Repeat step 4 for 1 minute. Partner 2 charts the number of words read in 1 minute (best read).
7. Present a new reading passage each Monday for the weekly practice sessions.

PROGRESS MONITORING: Review graphs on a daily basis to determine the trend of the data. An upward trend shows that progress is being made with daily practice. A flat or downward trend shows that the passage may be too hard, that not enough practice time has been allotted, or that students are no longer motivated with the reading passage.

McGee and Richgels (1990) provide a listing of vocabulary skills that proficient readers can accomplish:

- Describe pictures.
- Classify objects.
- Identify and understand concrete nouns (*dog, cat, man, horse*).
- Identify and understand pronouns (*it, she, he, they, us, we*).
- Identify synonyms, antonyms, and homonyms.
- Identify descriptive words.
- Identify and understand abstract words (*democracy, honesty*).

Types of Vocabularies

Cheek and Collins (1985) note that there are several kinds of vocabularies. A person's general vocabulary is composed of words that are used on a regular basis during conversation. A specialized vocabulary is made up of words that have multiple meanings depending on the context. For instance, the word *range* may be in a person's general vocabulary when it refers to a series of mountains, but it moves into specialized vocabulary when used in statistics to describe all items from the lowest number to the highest number, inclusive, in a data set. A technical vocabulary consists of those words that are used in a particular content area (i.e., *decoding* when used to describe a reading act).

As readers mature, their vocabularies increase as they continue to read. High school and college students encounter words in their readings that, through the use of context and glossaries, will expand their meaning vocabularies.

Understanding words is more than simply having words in one's meaning vocabulary. It also involves using many of the skills associated with decoding, described earlier. For instance, knowing the meaning of prefixes, suffixes, and inflectional endings helps a person comprehend a combination of free and bound morphemes (e.g., *mis-manage-ment*). The ability to use context clues to derive meaning is also important. For example, the meaning of the word *magnanimous* in the sentence "The philanthropist's donation to the Boy Scouts of America was a *magnanimous* gesture" may not be fully understood, yet it is likely that the reader can use the context of the sentence to know that it's probably a good thing to be magnanimous.

FUNCTION WORDS   Reading vocabularies are composed of function words. Function words, such as *on, in,* and *from,* are relatively easy for most students to learn because they help sentences make sense and because they compose about half of the words seen in text.

DENOTATIVE AND CONNOTATIVE MEANINGS   Words can have denotative meanings and connotative meanings. A denotative meaning is the literal dictionary meaning of a word. A connotative meaning can be considered a "read between the lines" meaning. Connotative meaning has to do with the implications, undertones, and feelings a person may add to the denotative meaning.

Consider the word *parachute,* for example. A dictionary may define the word *parachute* as an "umbrella-shaped device designed to slow the descent of someone jumping from an airplane." This denotative meaning, of course, is accurate, but *connotative meanings* of *parachute* would include a person's associations and personal meanings ("escape," "being let down gently," or the like).

LEVELS OF UNDERSTANDING   It is important to understand that students' knowledge of word meaning develops along three levels (Stahl, 1986). The first level is called the association-processing level. At this level, words are thought of in terms of synonyms, definitions, or contexts. Let's consider an earlier example: "The philanthropist's donation to the Boy Scouts of America was a *magnanimous* gesture." At the association level the word seems familiar. A person might think, "I know what that word is, sort of. I've heard it used to describe people who are charitable, so it probably has something to do with being generous. In this context generous would fit, so maybe *magnanimous* and *generous* are synonyms." At the association level, a person has to think about the meaning of the word in relation to something he or she knows, but it is not deeply rooted.

The next stage is known as the comprehension-processing level. Here, students' knowledge of word associations can be used to place words in categories, to create sentences, and to generate multiple word meanings. This level builds upon the first and represents a deeper understanding.

Finally, the generation-processing level expands vocabulary for discussion purposes or in activities. For example, students can create new sentences using vocabulary words, make connections between existing and prior knowledge, and apply vocabulary words across different contexts.

Making a Difference

Specialized Reading Instruction in Collaboration with Classroom Teaching Brings Success

Vivian M. LaColla

Special Education Teacher, Grade 2
Noxon Road Elementary School
Poughkeepsie, New York

One of my second-grade students was a 7-year-old boy named Robert who had been classified as Speech and Language Impaired with delays in auditory processing. He had significant deficits in reading, had difficulty writing the letters of the alphabet, and could not identify the names and sounds of most letters. He could not consistently write his name correctly. Robert had trouble reading words with short vowels or high-frequency sight words. In the beginning of his second-grade year, Robert's reading skills were equivalent to those of a kindergartener. Despite—or perhaps because of—the daily struggles his reading problems caused him, Robert was a motivated learner, and I felt strongly that he had the potential to improve his reading abilities significantly. He was also a very quiet child who showed little or no facial expression and did not have much interaction with his peers or involvement in school activities.

Robert's classroom teacher, Mrs. Taryn, and I met at a scheduled time once a week for 30 minutes, as stipulated on Robert's IEP. Mrs. Taryn had had students with disabilities in her classroom before, but never a student with Robert's level of reading difficulty. During this meeting time, we discussed the upcoming week's plans and activities. I explained the verbal and visual cues I use in teaching reading as part of my reading program, gave Mrs. Taryn suggestions for breaking down her oral instruction for Robert into smaller steps, and modified her reading assignments and handouts to Robert's reading level. Through this collaboration, I was able to support Mrs. Taryn's instruction by previewing or re-teaching a classroom lesson to Robert during my time with him.

Robert's individualized education program (IEP) required me also to provide him with direct instruction for reading and writing outside of his regular classroom for an hour a day. When Mrs. Taryn began her reading groups and the other students were settled working on their independent assignments, I would give Robert a secret signal, such as a nod, and we would go to my reading room. Robert never hesitated to leave; the reading

Difficulties with Vocabulary

Considerable research has been conducted to determine the vocabulary differences between beginning and good readers. Good readers have a deep understanding of words. They use background knowledge to understand the meaning of unknown words, and they can select from multiple meanings the correct definition of a word in context. Good readers have an understanding of word origins and know that many words are based on Greek and Latin words. They know word parts (i.e., base words, prefixes, and suffixes), and they understand both denotative and connotative definitions of words. Good readers are able to apply context clues, and if they still do not know the definition of a word, they can use reference materials such as a dictionary or a thesaurus. Finally, they are confident in their ability to identify word meanings using a variety of strategies.

Basically, beginning readers are deficient in all of the skills just mentioned. They lack confidence to apply context clues, or they don't know the clues to begin with. They struggle with using dictionaries and often lack the reading ability to use guide words to access unknown words in the dictionary. As we have seen in word identification, beginning readers struggle with identifying prefixes and suffixes, so it stands to reason that they would have difficulty understanding word

room was his safe haven. He felt confident there to read without the pressures of making a mistake in front of his peers. I tried to make sure Robert always felt a sense of success during reading. He never needed redirection or refocusing during our sessions, and he often completed his assignments. There were times when I had to reschedule our reading sessions because of an assembly or because the class was working on whole-group projects that I did not want to take Robert away from. Because of his lack of peer interaction, I knew it was very important for Robert to feel a part of the classroom and school community, and I was confident that rescheduling a reading session would not interfere with his progress.

I used the practices and strategies from the Orton-Gillingham Reading Method and the Alphabetic Phonics Program. These methods teach spelling simultaneously with reading. I used basic word families for his weekly spelling list (we started with words ending with -at, etc.). I used controlled readers that had simple word patterns that reflected the lessons we were learning. Robert read a short story many times until he was able to read it fluently, and I charted the time it took him to read the story the first time and the last. Robert enjoyed seeing his graph get higher.

Robert began to make significant progress toward the end of the school year. In the spring, as part of his annual review, I gave Robert the same informal assessments I had used in the fall. I had been certain I would see some growth, but not to this extent. His instructional reading level had improved to the beginning second-grade level. It jumped up two grade levels! When Robert finished reading the second-grade passage I was using as an assessment, I told Robert I wanted everyone in the school to hear how wonderfully he had just read. I asked him if he would read for Mrs. Taryn so that she would know how well he had done. Robert agreed. As Robert read for Mrs. Taryn, tears welled up in my eyes. Mrs. Taryn began calling on Robert to read in class. We then decided to have Robert integrated into Mrs. Taryn's lower-level reading group. Another wonderful milestone was when Robert was able to take his Friday morning spelling test with his classroom peers! He had been doing so well with the modified spelling list that we decided he should try taking the test with the rest of the class. Robert was so excited to be a part of the class. The first day he was called to read before his reading group, Robert stood tall and proud. As he looked at me with pride, he fought back a huge grin. So I grinned for him! ●

parts. Knowledge of word origins is virtually nonexistent. Finally, beginning readers may be able to apply denotative meanings to words, but connotative meanings are rarely understood. All in all, beginning readers not only have difficulty identifying words but also struggle with word meanings.

Teaching Vocabulary

Vocabulary instruction that produces in-depth word knowledge and increases reading comprehension is important for all students (Simmons & Kameenui, 1990). Instructional practices must focus on enhancing retention of new vocabulary to help students comprehend text. Students must learn strategies for independently developing a deeper understanding of the meanings of words that often constitute vocabulary found in content-area text. The following practices can help focus more attention on vocabulary learning.

- **Instructional content:** Teach students to use context clues to figure out meaning in conjunction with other vocabulary instructional approaches. Like the dictionary approach, context clues alone are not sufficient for struggling readers.

For example, the meaning of the word *magnanimous* in the sentence "The philanthropist's donation to the Boy Scouts of America was a *magnanimous* gesture," may not be fully understood, yet the reader can use the context of the sentence to know that it's probably a good thing to be *magnanimous*. Table 10.6 provides an overview of four types of context clues. As you look at the types of clues and their descriptions and examples, think about how you might use the clues in this textbook and others that you have.

- **Instructional delivery:** Integrate vocabulary instruction within the context of a reading lesson. Have students use graphic organizers to map meanings of words. Teach students to use word parts, such as prefixes and suffixes, to understand word meanings. Identify a few words to preteach before the lesson, especially if the words are technical words. When possible, combine the definition and contextual approaches for identifying word meanings. Review word meanings after reading by playing games (such as *Jeopardy* and *Concentration*) with words and definitions, and by creating or elaborating on semantic maps.

- **Instructional delivery:** Provide students with multiple opportunities to practice using words they know. Researchers have noted that it takes multiple exposures to words (about 10 times) to understand them well enough to incorporate them into one's vocabulary (Ruben, 1995).

- **Instructional activity:** Use the dictionary approach in conjunction with other approaches. By itself, the dictionary approach is not effective to teach vocabulary to struggling readers. Because of the possible number of definitions for words, students should have a good conceptual and contextual understanding of the words for which they are locating definitions.

TABLE 10.6 Types of Context Clues

Type	Example	Signal Words
Definition: The meaning of the target word is identified elsewhere in the sentence.	The *fibula* is the outer (and usually the smaller) of the two bones that are located between the ankle and the knee.	is, means
Restatement: The target word is explained through a different way of saying the same thing.	Huck thought about the *vastness,* that is, greatness, of the Mississippi River.	or, that is, in other words
Contrast: The target word is compared with another word, most often of opposite meaning.	The desert sun was *sizzling;* on the other hand, the oasis pool was cool enough to provide temporary relief.	different, in contrast, on the other hand
Comparison: The target word is compared to another word or phrase to demonstrate a likeness or correspondence.	Tom was alone on the *desolate* island, which was like wandering through an uninhabited village.	like, just as, similar

Source: Adapted from *Teaching reading,* by B. Honig, L. Diamond, & L. Gutlohn, 2000, Novato, CA: Arena Press.

Otherwise, this approach may not be effective in promoting vocabulary development (Carlisle, 1993).

- **Instructional material:** Teach students to use reference materials. Make them one, but not the *only,* strategy for finding word meanings. Show students how to identify which meaning to apply in a particular context. Have students make connections between their background knowledge and word meaning. The Making a Difference feature on page 422 describes more about how collaborative efforts can affect reading instruction in the classroom.

ADAPT in Action • Martello—Vocabulary

Consider the case of Martello. He grew up in Cuba and came to the United States at 9 years of age. He lives with his uncle and aunt and attends public schools as an 11-year-old sixth grader. Spanish is his first language, but he is fairly proficient in English. He has a good spoken vocabulary in Spanish, but his English vocabulary lags. His reading instruction has been solely in English, and he is reading two grade levels below his current grade placement. He seems to do well with word identification skills but struggles with vocabulary and comprehension of content-area text. He is outgoing and very popular. He has no behavior problems and gets along well with his teachers. Mr. Williams helps Martello and other students with vocabulary difficulties to use context clues to figure out unknown word meanings. Instructional Activity 10.4 on page 427 presents the lesson.

Unfortunately, Martello and two other students did not benefit from the lesson on contextual searching. Mr. Williams considers what went wrong by using the ADAPT framework.

Ask, "What am I requiring the student to do?" Mr. Williams considers the task: "The students need to learn the context clues and apply this knowledge to unknown words in sentences. They need to be able to read and understand dictionary definitions as well. The students in question scored poorly on progress monitoring when asked about the meanings of words."

Determine the prerequisite skills of the task. "Students need to be able to read the sentences, understand the clues, and read and understand the dictionary meanings."

Analyze the student's strengths and struggles. Mr. Williams thought about the students' response to the lesson. It seemed that there were too many parts of the lesson for them to handle. The clues were too abstract, and the dictionary was hard for them to understand. They could decode most of the words, but the meanings were lacking for the vocabulary words.

Propose and implement adaptations from among the four categories. Mr. Williams decides to try a different instructional activity as an adaptation. He will use a word map, which limits the amount of content and focuses on processing the meaning at different levels to aid understanding. Figure 10.4 shows an example of a word map.

Test to determine if the adaptations helped the student accomplish the task. Mr. Williams will continue to test the students on the meanings of words once instruction has concluded.

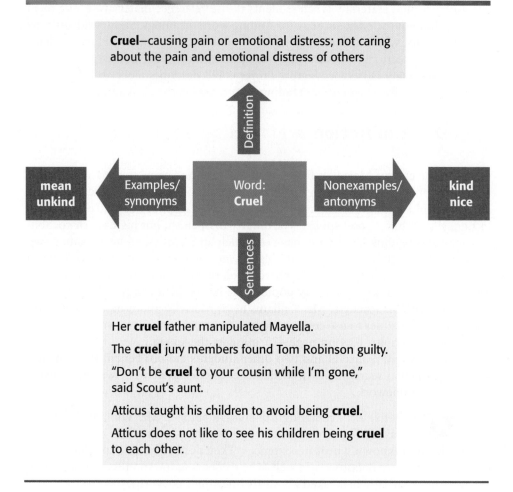

FIGURE 10.4 Sample Completed Word Map

Cruel—causing pain or emotional distress; not caring about the pain and emotional distress of others

Definition

mean unkind ← Examples/synonyms — Word: **Cruel** — Nonexamples/antonyms → kind nice

Sentences

Her **cruel** father manipulated Mayella.

The **cruel** jury members found Tom Robinson guilty.

"Don't be **cruel** to your cousin while I'm gone," said Scout's aunt.

Atticus taught his children to avoid being **cruel**.

Atticus does not like to see his children being **cruel** to each other.

What Is Reading Comprehension and How Do I Teach It?

Reading comprehension involves the following skills: recalling word meanings; using context to make word-meaning inferences; finding answers to questions either explicitly or in paraphrase of the content; weaving together ideas from the content; recognizing a writer's purpose, attitude, tone, and mood; identifying a writer's technique; and following the structure of a passage (Davis, 1968, cited in Barr & Johnson, 1991).

Types of Comprehension

Literal comprehension deals specifically with the material on the printed page; inferential comprehension focuses on what is "behind the scenes" (i.e., that which is not directly stated). An example of literal comprehension would be reading a passage on Mount Vesuvius and being able to recall factual information obtained

Instructional activity 10.4

Contextual Searching

INSTRUCTIONAL OBJECTIVE: Students will learn the meaning of unknown words by applying their knowledge of context clues.

INSTRUCTIONAL CONTENT: Using context clues to identify meanings of words in expository text

INSTRUCTIONAL MATERIALS: Narrative or expository texts, sentence strips, dictionary

INSTRUCTIONAL DELIVERY

Grouping: Small group of students who require vocabulary instruction

Teaching Procedure

1. Select 5 to 10 vocabulary words. These words should be key vocabulary for understanding the topic or important concepts that appear in the text being read.

2. Develop a context for each word by selecting a type of context clue (see Table 10.6, page 424). For instance, the contrast type of context clue could be used for one of the vocabulary words and a sentence considered that typifies that type of clue.

3. Make context clue sentence strips, whereby a sentence is written with a vocabulary word containing one context clue type. For example, for contrast the teacher could write, "The elephant was lethargic, yet the leopard was very energetic." An explanation and example are written on the sentence strip for each context clue type.

4. Present the vocabulary words in isolation and ask the students for a definition of each word; the students' definitions are written on the chalkboard. Students are then asked to provide an explanation for how each definition was derived (e.g., a student might use word parts to understand the meaning of a word).

5. Model how to use the type of context clue to figure out the meaning of each unknown word. Display the sentence strips for student reference.

6. Have students work in pairs to analyze the context (using the sentence strips as a reference) to figure out the meaning of each vocabulary word. The students record their definitions for each word and note the type of context clue that was used to identify its meaning. The dictionary is then used to determine whether each definition derived from the context matches that provided in the dictionary. Group discussion follows, and a member of each student pair explains how they used context clues to figure out each word's meaning. The students also explain how the dictionary definition fits with their definition from context clues.

7. Have students compare their definitions from context to their definitions in isolation.

PROGRESS MONITORING: After the lesson, have the student read an independent-level passage. Target certain words to check the student's knowledge of word meanings.

Source: Adapted from *Effective Instruction for Struggling Secondary Readers: Research-based Practices,* 2003, Austin: University of Texas, Vaughn Gross Center for Reading and Language Arts.

in the passage (e.g., Vesuvius destroyed the city of Pompeii; there were no known survivors). Inferential comprehension requires the reader to go beyond the facts stated in the passage and project his or her own ideas to imagine the writer's thoughts and feelings or those of the people who were affected by the volcano.

Types of Text

Text is either narrative or expository, and each type contains specific features. Narrative text includes myths, folktales, legends, autobiographies, biographies, fantasies, historical fiction, mysteries, science fiction, and plays. Narrative text

● Teaching students to use effective strategies to foster reading comprehension is important. What strategies might these students use to increase their reading comprehension?

entertains readers; it may be fictional or tell of actual real-life experiences. Narrative text uses a story structure. This structure organizes events in a way that helps the reader understand character development and relationships among events.

Expository text includes content found in textbooks, magazines, newspapers, and brochures. This type of text is also known as *informational text*. The information is conveyed in a variety of ways through the use of text structures such as cause–effect, problem–solution, and compare–contrast. These structures differ across types of content and sometimes within a single paragraph. The text may be organized by headings and subheadings and may contain graphics, such as tables and charts. The understanding of expository text is important for students' successful learning in upper elementary and secondary school (Bryant & Lehr, 2001; Dickson, Simmons & Kame'enui, 1998).

Types of Comprehension Questions

When checking reading comprehension, it is important to use a variety of questioning strategies. Comprehension questions that require students to remember facts about what was read often begin with the word *define, identify, label, list, match, name, recall, recognize,* or *repeat*. Students are prompted to understand or construct meanings from what was written when questions begin with such words as *describe, discuss, classify,* and so forth.

Sometimes comprehension questions ask students to apply what they have learned. Key words in application questions include *implement, predict, relate,* and *show*. Students sometimes are asked to analyze, or separate and explain, the content in paragraphs. When this happens, key words such as *distinguish, cause and effect, compare and contrast, draw conclusions, infer,* and *point out* are often used.

When students have to evaluate text, they are asked to make judgments or decisions by responding to questions having words such as *conclude, critique, judge,* or *rate*. Finally, some comprehension questions require students to synthesize what has been written—that is, to put the elements together and make connections. These *create* types of questions may contain words such as *generate, rearrange, produce,* or *imagine*.

Difficulties with Reading Comprehension

Much has been written about the struggles that students face as they try to comprehend what they are reading. Beginning readers do not understand the multiple purposes for reading; either they have little background knowledge about the topic or they don't know how to activate the knowledge they have. When their understanding breaks down, they continue to read without monitoring their reading. They have great difficulty creating mental images of what is going on in the passage and struggle to identify the main ideas and how those ideas are supported by specific details. When asked to summarize what they read, they either produce a blank stare or repeat the story verbatim as best they can. They have difficulty summarizing important information and may be able to answer literal questions, at best.

Conversely, good readers are strategic readers. They demonstrate the ability to use effective strategies before, during, and after reading to enhance comprehension. They possess strategies to access and understand text, and they can generalize their strategies to all kinds of reading materials.

For those students who struggle with word identification skills or reading print because of a sensory impairment, assistive technology can be used to help them compensate for these difficulties so that they can focus on comprehending text and vocabulary. The Tech Notes feature on page 430 shows an example of how technology can promote access to text.

Reading Comprehension Strategy Instruction

Reading comprehension strategy instruction plays an important role in helping students become strategic readers. This type of instruction focuses on teaching students to construct meaning *before, during,* and *after* reading by integrating text information with the reader's background knowledge (Snider, 1989). Background knowledge, or prior knowledge, helps a reader to understand what has been written. Thus, students who can activate and apply whatever background knowledge they have regarding a topic are more likely to understand a passage than those who cannot (Bryant & Lehr, 2001; Carr & Ogle, 1987; Pressley et al., 1995). The ability to strategically monitor comprehension by asking questions, identifying main ideas and supporting details, paraphrasing, and summarizing is crucial to comprehension. Thus, it is important to teach students to use effective strategies to foster reading comprehension (Pressley, 1998).

Comprehension strategy instruction has proved especially helpful for promoting the learning opportunities of students with reading disabilities (Pressley et al., 1995). Consider one type of comprehension strategy instruction, collaborative strategic reading (CSR). Research has validated the effectiveness of CSR in a variety of studies across elementary and middle school classes (Bryant, Vaughn et al., 2000; Klingner, Vaughn, & Schumm, 1998).

tech
NOTES

Using Audio Devices to Access Print

Mark, Dan, and Maureen have used recorded books for years to help them access print materials that would have been inaccessible otherwise. Dan has a learning disability in reading, Mark is visually impaired, and Maureen is blind. As Mark states, "Audiobooks have been a godsend to my education. I would definitely recommend audiobooks for all those people that print is not an option for. Audiobooks provide an invaluable resource which brings the printed word to the visually impaired world."

Tape recorders or compact disc players can be used as playback units or for listening to books on audiotape or CD. Such devices may help students with reading difficulties bypass their disability by listening to prerecorded text (e.g., books, journals, newspapers). Prerecorded texts (audiobooks) are available from a number of sources, including Recordings for the Blind and Dyslexic, The Library of Congress, and several private companies.

Audiobooks can help level the playing field for students with print disabilities. As Dan mentions, "There is no reason that a student with a print disability should be at a disadvantage to anyone. They just have to find the way that they learn and work in their own way."

Maureen, discussing how audiobooks can help with pleasure reading, adds, "Books are usually a good companion when there is no one around to talk to. I like to go into the world of characters I'm reading about, getting involved with their problems, because sometimes it's easier to solve their problems than my own." To that we agree wholeheartedly.

Source: Some of this material was used with permission from M. Raskind and B. R. Bryant, 2002, *Functional evaluation for assistive technology,* Psycho-educational Services.

● Using audio books can help level the playing field for students with print disabilities.

CSR consists of four reading strategies (preview, click and clunk, get the gist, and wrap up). These strategies are combined with cooperative learning to teach students how to comprehend what they are reading. Before they read, students activate their prior knowledge by *previewing* the text. Students brainstorm what they know about the topic and then predict what they will read about based on the text's features (e.g., illustrations and headings). Making predictions is an important activity for strategic readers because it gets them involved and gives them a reason for reading ahead. Will their prediction turn out to be right or wrong? Compare this to a person who is simply reading to be able to turn the page and get closer to the end of an assignment.

Next, students read short segments of the text (a paragraph or two) during what is called *click and clunk*. Students read along (click) until they come to a word they do not know. Students are taught to use fix-up strategies, which are written on clunk cards, and vocabulary strategies, such as context clues, to determine the meaning of unknown words, concepts, or phrases, which are called *clunks*. For each paragraph, *get the gist* (or find the main idea) requires students to tell *who* or *what* they read about and the most important information about the "who" or "what" in 10 or fewer words. Finally, students *wrap-up* by summarizing key concepts and by asking questions (e.g., Who? What? Why? How?) to reflect on important information in the reading passage. Students record their predictions, clunks, gists, and wrap-up questions on a graphic organizer called a *learning log*. They complete the four strategies in cooperative groups to learn from each other and to resolve questions about vocabulary and concepts.

CSR should be taught in two stages (Klingner, Vaughn, Domino, Schumm, & Bryant, 2001). In stage 1, the teacher uses think-aloud and modeling to introduce the four strategies, followed by students practicing the strategies for several days. During stage 2, students learn cooperative learning roles and then are divided into small groups to implement CSR with minimal adult assistance. The graphic organizers in What Works 10.4 can be used to support CSR instruction.

what WORKS 10.4

Graphic Organizers to Support CSR

The following graphic organizers can be used as part of the preview, get the gist, and wrap-up parts of collaborative strategic reading. Students should have their own copy of each graphic organizer to complete before, during, or after reading. Teachers can use the completed forms during class discussion and as a way to assess understanding.

● **Preview Log—Before Reading**

Topic: _____

  - ● How does this topic relate to something I have learned?
  - ● What are the key vocabulary?
  - ● What are the proper nouns?
  - ● What are my two predictions? How did I make my predictions?

I think that I am going to learn about _____

How do I know this? _____

I think that I am going to learn about _____

How do I know this? _____

● **Gist Log—During Reading**

  - ● *Who* or *what* was this paragraph about?

  - ● What was the most important information about the *who* or *what*? (Use this information to develop the gist statement.)

  - ● Write a gist statement/main idea (use 10 or fewer words):

● **Summarization Log—After Reading**

  - ● Identify three or four important ideas from the entire passage (use your gist statements):

    1. _____

    2. _____

    3. _____

    4. _____

  - ● Write a summary statement for the entire passage (10 or fewer words):

  - ● Generate three questions about the important ideas (use who, what, when, where, why, and how):

    1. _____

    2. _____

    3. _____

  - ● Create one question about the passage that might be on a test:

Source: Adapted from *Collaborative Strategic Reading: Clunk to Click,* by J. K. Klingner, S. Vaughn, J. Domino, J. S. Schumm, & D. P. Bryant, 2001, Longmont, CO: Sopris West.

Teaching Reading Comprehension

- **Instructional delivery:** Use think-alouds to model what students should be thinking as they interact with text. Employ a variety of strategies while conducting before-, during-, and after-reading activities (Burns Griffin, & Snow, 1999; Cunningham & Allington, 1999; Dickinson, Cote, & Smith, 1993; Moats, 1999; Vaughn & Klingner, 2000; VGCRLA, 2002).

- **Instructional delivery:** In before-reading activities, activate students' background knowledge, teach key vocabulary terms, give students a purpose for reading ("Read this section to find out . . ."), and have students preview what they will be reading. As they preview, have students make predictions about what they expect to read.

- **Instructional delivery:** With during-reading activities, use a variety of questioning techniques. Have them recall information, apply the information in various ways, and evaluate text. Graphic organizers should be used to help students visually depict what they are reading. Learning logs and story maps are excellent resources. Show students how to self-monitor as they read. By using think-alouds, you can model how to read and reread sections of text to ensure comprehension. Have students use fix-up strategies to clarify the meaning of unknown words, concepts, or phrases.

Considering *Diversity*

Anchoring Reading to Culture

Some students experience a disconnect between the instructional materials assigned at school and their personal backgrounds. (Grantham & Ford, 2003). When students cannot relate new learning to what they have experienced or what they know, learning challenges increase. Also, when some students see relationships between curriculum content and others can't make such associations, some students feel affirmed, whereas others sense that they are not valued (Ford et al., 2000). The result is often negative feelings about school, as well as disengagement.

Culturally responsive classrooms include culturally relevant teaching and materials that children with different interests and backgrounds can relate to. Teachers can enhance content by using books that include an array of characters from different backgrounds for students to select for book reviews. They can also provide multiple perspectives about historical events in their lectures and examples. For example, books about both Thomas Jefferson's and Sally Hemings's lives can stimulate interesting discussions about the lives of people of different races and different cultures living in America before the Civil War. Activities that represent many diverse cultures broaden everyone's knowledge and understanding of each other.

1. How might teachers provide more culturally responsive instruction to their students?
2. What instructional materials or instructional content might you add to a unit about American history?

- **Instructional delivery:** In after-reading activities, use various types of questions to determine the depth of student understanding. Vocabulary terms that were presented in previous activities should be reviewed and their importance in the text discussed. Students should be able to summarize what has been read. Graphic organizers can be completed and discussed.
- **Connections to diversity:** Information about culturally responsive instruction is presented in the Considering Diversity feature.

The following are guidelines for teaching reading comprehension to English language learners (Echevarria, 1995; Gersten & Jimenez, 1994; Goldenberg, 1992; Snow et al., 1998; VGCRLA, 2000).

- Review any unfamiliar vocabulary. English language learners may be able to decode words but may not know their meaning.
- Stop at various intervals throughout a reading passage, and review what has happened up to that point to reinforce comprehension.
- Use story mapping. Stop at various intervals to review story elements. Add new information to story maps as it appears in the story.
- Discuss the content of the book and students' background experiences with the topic.
- Correct differences of speech sounds carefully. Speech sounds in English may be different from those of the students' first language and do not need to be corrected continuously.
- Enhance language development and vocabulary by engaging in instructional conversations with students (e.g., "Tell me more about . . ." and "What do you mean by . . ."). Instructional conversations also include restating what the student has said (e.g., "In other words . . .").
- Use cognates to help students make connections between English and their native language.

ADAPT in Action • Max—Reading Comprehension

Max is a student in Mr. Williams's class. In addition to having a learning disability, he also exhibits behavior problems. The behavior problems are an inability to get along well with classmates (and teachers) and a lack of task completion. However, when involved with something that interests him, Max can be quiet, attentive, and productive. He is usually able to read words written at a fourth-grade level. His reading is fairly fluent. He is able to understand most spoken instructions. He has some difficulty understanding abstract concepts, and his vocabulary of specialized and technical meanings is limited. His family travels a great deal in the summer and during school vacations, so Max has a variety of experiences that he likes to talk about. As you read Instructional Activity 10.5, think about the challenges that Mr. Williams and Max face to meet the instructional objectives. Consider the task that is associated with the activity. What must the student be able to do (requisite skills) to complete the task and meet the objective? Which of the skills fall within Max's strengths, and with which skill(s) does Max struggle? Then look at the sample adaptations provided. Instructional Activity 10.5 describes the story mapping, and Figure 10.5 is an example of a story map.

After the lesson, Mr. Williams evaluated Max's understanding of the story elements. He was not satisfied, based on the progress-monitoring data, that Max understood the elements or could locate the correct information in the text. He decided to make the following adaptations after considering the ADAPT framework.

- **Instructional content:** Reduce the number of pages to be read. Limit the number of map categories.
- **Instructional materials:** Use computer-based visual mapping programs. Provide a controlled vocabulary or audiobook version of the text.
- **Instructional delivery:** Pair the student with a stronger reader or student volunteer. If computer-based visual mapping programs are used, model effective use.

Instructional activity 10.5

Story Mapping for Narrative Text

INSTRUCTIONAL OBJECTIVE: Students will comprehend reading material by participating in before-reading activities.

INSTRUCTIONAL CONTENT: Reading comprehension, making predictions to review text

INSTRUCTIONAL MATERIALS: Copies of a narrative text (e.g., *To Kill a Mockingbird*), story maps for each student, story map transparency

INSTRUCTIONAL DELIVERY
Grouping: Small group of students who require structural analysis instruction

Teaching Procedure
There are six story elements:

1. *Setting.* Introduction of main characters, time, and place
2. *Beginning.* Event that triggers the story (problem)
3. *Reaction.* Response of main characters, what they do
4. *Attempt.* What effort do the characters make to attain the goal? (action)
5. *Outcome.* Results or attempts to reach the goal
6. *Ending.* Consequences of the main characters' actions and final response

Several procedures have been suggested to assist students in mapping a story. Students can arrange a jumbled short story in the correct order of the various elements, as just described. Or students can sort the sentences for each of the elements into separate piles.

An example of a story map is shown in Figure 10.5. Use three phases to teach students how to use the story map to assist in comprehending the story. In the first phase, model how to (a) read a story, (b) stop at points in the story where information for each component of the map was presented, and (c) fill in the story map. Have students complete their maps with the same information during the modeling phase. In the second phase, ask students to read a story independently and complete their story maps with teacher assistance, as necessary; this is the lead phase. Finally, in the third phase, the test phase, have students complete a story and map and then answer teacher questions about the story.

PROGRESS MONITORING: After the lesson, check the students' story maps for accuracy.

Source: Adapted from *Journal of Learning Disabilities,* by L. Idol, 1987, *20,* 196–205.

FIGURE 10.5 Group Story Mapping

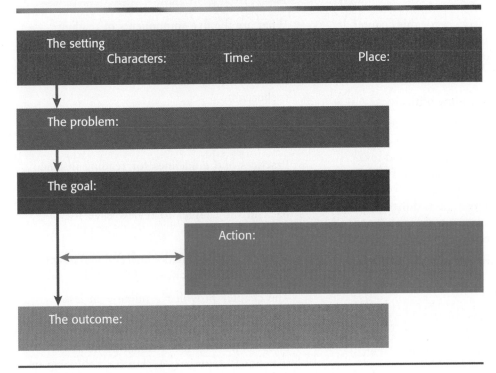

● s u m m a r y

A successful reading program must consider the phonological awareness, word identification, reading fluency, reading vocabulary, and reading comprehension abilities of individual students and the development of instruction tailored to individual needs. A comprehensive and effective reading program must include a balanced approach to instruction. Students demonstrate a variety of reading characteristics in the five components of reading as they develop reading skills. Effective reading in-struction includes features that encompass delivery of instruction and what should be included, such as strategy training and opportunities for students to read good literature. Guidelines for teaching each component of reading were provided and should be used when planning and delivering instruction. Finally, instructional adaptations make it possible to teach these reading components to all struggling readers, including those who have reading or other disabilities.

• self-test QUESTIONS

Let's review the learning objectives for this chapter. If you are uncertain and cannot "talk through" the answers provided for any of these questions, reread those sections of the text.

- **Who are students with reading difficulties?**

  Students may exhibit difficulties with phonological awareness, word identification, reading fluency, and understanding vocabulary and text. Researchers have attributed reading difficulties to a variety of factors, such as genetics, poor teaching, phonological awareness difficulties, and low intelligence, but no single cause exists, and those that have been proposed are debated.

  Dyslexia may be manifested in some of the following areas:

  - Learning to speak
  - Decoding unknown words
  - Word recognition
  - Learning letter–sound associations
  - Memorizing facts
  - Comprehension
  - Spelling
  - Writing
  - Discriminating sounds
  - Learning a foreign language

- **What are the five components of reading?**

  The five components of reading are phonological awareness, word identification, reading fluency, reading vocabulary, and reading comprehension.

- **How can teachers provide effective reading instruction for the components of reading?**

  Practices and guidelines for reading instruction have been provided for each of the five components. Take a few minutes to look back in the chapter to review each list of recommendations.

- **How can teachers make instructional adaptations for the components of reading?**

  The chapter provided a number of lessons for teaching skills in each area. Each lesson includes an instructional activity, an instructional objective, instructional content, instructional materials, a plan for delivering instruction, and methods to monitor progress. Review the lesson presented in each area, focusing on the individual case studies and the adaptations provided to meet individual learning needs.

• Revisit the OPENING challenge

Check your answers to the Reflection Questions from the Opening Challenge and revise them on the basis of what you have learned.

1. What specific difficulties might students in Mrs. Evans's and Mr. Williams's classes exhibit in phonological awareness, word identification, reading fluency, reading vocabulary, and reading comprehension?

2. How can Mrs. Evans and Mr. Williams use practices for effective reading to structure their reading activities?

3. How can these teachers provide adapted lessons to students who require additional instruction, while meeting the needs of the rest of the class?

4. How can teachers monitor their students' progress or response to intervention?

Professional Standards and Licensure

CEC Knowledge and Skill Core Standard and Associated Subcategories

CEC Content Standard 2: Development and Characteristics of Learners

Special educators understand the similarities and differences in human development and the characteristics between and among individuals with and without disabilities. Moreover, special educators understand how exceptional conditions can interact with the domains of human development and they use this knowledge to respond to the varying abilities and behaviors of individuals with ELN.

CEC Content Standard 4: Instructional Strategies

Special educators select, adapt, and use instructional strategies to promote challenging learning results in general and special curricula and to appropriately modify learning environments for individuals with disabilities. They enhance the learning of critical thinking, problem solving, and performance skills of individuals with disabilities, and increase their self-awareness, self-management, self-control, self-reliance, and self-esteem.

CEC Content Standard 7: Instructional Planning

Individualized decision making and instruction is at the center of special education practice. Special educators develop long-range individualized instructional plans anchored in both general and special curricula. Individualized instructional plans emphasize explicit modeling and efficient guided practice to assure acquisition and fluency through maintenance and generalization. Understanding of these factors, as well as the implications of an individual's exceptional condition, guides the special educator's selection, adaptation, and creation of materials, and the use of powerful instructional variables. Instructional plans are modified based on ongoing analysis of the individual's learning progress.

CEC Content Standard 8: Assessment

Special educators conduct formal and informal assessments of behavior, learning, achievement, and environments to design learning experiences that support the growth and development of individuals with disabilities.

INTASC Core Principle and Associated Special Education Subcategories

1. Subject Matter

1.01 All teachers have a solid base of understanding of the major concepts, assumptions, issues, and processes of inquiry in the subject-matter content areas that they teach.

2. Student Learning

2.04 All teachers are knowledgeable about multiple theories of learning and research-based practices that support learning and use this information to inform instruction.

4. Instructional Strategies

4.03 All teachers use research-based practices to support learning and generalization of concepts and skills.

4.04 All teachers understand that it is particularly important to provide multiple ways for students with disabilities to participate in learning activities. They modify tasks and accommodate individual needs of students with disabilities.

7. Instructional Planning

7.02 All teachers plan ways to modify instruction to facilitate positive learning results within the general education curriculum for students with disabilities.

Praxis II: Education of Exceptional Students: Core Content Knowledge

I. Understanding Exceptionalities

Characteristics of students with disabilities, including the influence of

- Cognitive factors
- Genetic, medical, motor, sensory, and chronological age factors

III. Delivery of Services to Students

Curriculum and instruction and their implementation across the continuum of educational placements, including

- Instructional development for implementation
- Teaching strategies and methods
- Instructional format and components

Assessment, including

- How to select, construct, conduct, and modify informal assessments

Structuring and managing the learning environment.

Professional roles, including

- Specific roles and responsibilities of teachers

Video—"Blending Individual Sounds (Phonemic Awareness)"

Students learn to blend individual stretched sounds into words. In this video, the teacher uses direct instruction to teach phonological awareness to struggling readers.

Log onto **www.mylabschool.com**. Under the **Courses** tab, in **Special Education,** go to the **video lab**. Access the "**Reading**" videos and watch the "**Blending Individual Sounds (Phonemic Awareness)**" video.

 OR

Use the **www.mylabschool.com Assignment Finder** to go directly to these videos. Just enter Assignment ID **SPV13**.

1. What strategy does the teacher in this video use to teach phonological awareness?

2. Describe the developmental sequence that occurs when children learn phonological awareness.

3. Describe three activities (other than the one demonstrated in the video) that could be used to teach phonological awareness.

Video—"Post-Alphabetic Multisyllable Regular Words"

In this video, students use decoding strategies to read new regular multisyllable words from a word list.

Log onto **www.mylabschool.com**. Under the **Courses** tab, in **Special Education,** go to the **video lab**. Access the **"Reading"** videos and watch the **"Post-Alphabetic Multisyllable Regular Words"** video.

 OR

Use the **www.mylabschool.com Assignment Finder** to go directly to these videos. Just enter Assignment ID **SPV13**.

1. What decoding skills must students have mastered prior to this practice?

2. What does the teacher do to correct errors during this activity?

3. What recommendations are provided in Chapter 10 for teaching students to decode multisyllable words?

4. Which of these recommendations are demonstrated in the video?

Companion Website

To access chapter objectives, practice tests, weblinks, and flashcards, go to the companion website at **www.ablongman.com/bryantsmith1e.**

chapter

Teaching Writing

After studying this chapter, you will have the knowledge to answer the following questions:

- Who are students with writing difficulties?
- What are the stages of the writing process?
- How can teachers provide effective writing instruction for the stages of writing?
- How can teachers make instructional adaptations for the stages of writing?

● OPENING challenge

Ensuring Appropriate Writing Instruction

Elementary Grades ● Mr. Nu is in his ninth year of teaching in an urban school district. The demographics of the district reflect a rich cultural diversity, and many students are eligible for free or reduced-cost meals. Mr. Nu taught kindergarten for 4 years and is now in his fifth year of teaching fourth grade. He is reviewing results from the screening assessment that was administered to identify students with writing problems. The district's policy requires teachers in second through fifth grades to assess all of their students in the fall, winter, and spring to identify students who are at risk for writing difficulties and to monitor their writing progress as they are taught throughout the school year. In his class of 21 students, 5 are at risk for writing difficulties. In examining the results, he reflects, *"The students exhibited problems across the board. In the mechanics portion of the test, they spelled poorly and failed to follow capitalization and punctuation rules. In their writing passage, the word counts were very low, they tended to write using simple sentences, and there were numerous agreement errors. I had a difficult time reading their passages because of poor handwriting. We have no assess-*

Secondary Grades ● Mrs. Sago is in her third year of teaching 11th-grade English, literature, and reading in a small, rural high school. In her school district, all students are required to take at least two years of English composition. Across her five classes, the number of students ranges from the smallest class size of 11 to the largest class of 21. During the summer, Mrs. Sago attended several workshops on the writing process. In applying what she learned, she noticed that most of her students were adept at brainstorming and topic selection and could produce a first draft. For the most part, students were able to adjust their writing to the purpose of the passage and to the hypothetical audience who would be reading their works. Some students, however, had considerable difficulty in this regard. Nearly all students had some level of difficulty in organization, but a few of her students continued to write disjointed paragraphs even after guidance from her. Spelling, capitalization, and punctuation were not problematic for most of her students, but a small group of students produced errors across the board and were ill equipped to edit their work for errors. She reflects on her efforts, *"I have to admit that it was a*

column continues on next page

column continues on next page

ment data that deal with the stages of the writing process per se, but we teach the writing process at our school. I can see by the results of the assessments that some of my students are really going to struggle with some or all of the stages of the writing process." ●

frustrating experience at first. I divided each class into groups of five students, who were to brainstorm about a topic of their choosing. One group decided to write letters to admissions directors at their favorite colleges to inquire about scholarships and academic opportunities. They went online to the Web site of their school of choice and to the guidance counselor's office to get some brochures. Each created a rough draft of his or her letter. When I met individually with them in a writing conference to discuss the revision, editing, and publishing stages, two students were completely lost. They didn't understand why their letter couldn't just go out "as is." For the two reluctant students, each stage presented its own challenge. Their revised letters looked almost identical to their originals, with the same disorganization, simple sentence construction, and immature vocabulary as their first draft. Editing proved extremely difficult. They simply could not spell and struggled correcting their errors. Capitalization and punctuation were not problem areas, because every sentence began with a capital letter and ended with a period or a question mark. There were no other punctuation marks or capital letters because of the simplicity of their sentences. I really struggle with how to help them." ●

Although teaching at opposite ends of the education spectrum, Mr. Nu and Ms. Sago both have students who "get it" and students who don't. Although Mr. Nu is teaching early writing skills and Ms. Sago is having her students apply skills they supposedly learned many years earlier, they both were faced with the challenge of helping their students put words on paper in a meaningful way.

● Reflection Questions

In your journal, write down your answers to the following questions. After completing the chapter, check your answers and revise them on the basis of what you have learned.

1. What specific difficulties might students in both teachers' classes exhibit in the writing stages?

2. How can the teachers effectively work with their students during each stage of the writing process?

3. How can these teachers provide lessons adapted to students who require additional instruction?

4. How can writing assessments (see Chapter 7) be used to identify struggling students and to monitor their response to intervention?

Writing is a very important skill for all students, regardless of their grade level. Very often, students' academic achievement is related directly to their ability to express themselves through writing. For example, students might be asked to take weekly spelling tests, write letters, and write stories, all of which require efficient writing abilities. Thus, students need to possess a range of writing abilities (such as generating content, using correct punctuation and capitalization, and using appropriate penmanship). Furthermore, writing is an important life skill for personal communication, postsecondary education, and adult adjustment.

Over the past years, writing instruction has assumed a prominent position in all classroom settings. Spurred by national interest in improving academic skills, research findings in cognitive psychology, and the renewed emphasis on writing in postsecondary settings and adult life, writing instruction requires a teacher's attention across all academic subjects (Graham & Harris, 1988a, 1988b; Scardamalia & Bereiter, 1986; Shapiro, 2004). As a result, more instructional time has been allotted to writing, and increased writing competency testing has been implemented nationwide (Finn, Petrilli, & Julian, 2006).

In special education, a body of research on writing instruction and students with learning difficulties identified specific learning characteristics, highlighted instructional strengths and weaknesses, and probed the efficacy of writing intervention programs. Newcomer, Barenbaum, and Nodine (1988) raised five important issues related to this body of research. First, the research has focused on the writing process (discussed below), and less attention has been devoted to developing "convention skills" (correct spelling, punctuation, capitalization). Paying less attention to convention skills is problematic because of the difficulties exhibited by students with learning disabilities in these areas. The issue is how best to address instruction in writing conventions and yet retain an emphasis on developing the writing process.

The second issue involves peer conferencing, which is often mentioned as an effective feedback and editing activity in the writing process. Effective peer conferencing requires that peers have abilities in reading and critiquing stories—skills that students with special needs lack. Thus, teachers must be aware of their students' abilities in understanding and critiquing text structures, using convention skills, editing, and providing socially acceptable, constructive feedback.

The third issue raised by Newcomer and her colleagues centers on the efficacy of instructional methods. They found problems with methods, such as journal writing and expressive writing, where students select their own topics and style of writing. Adopted in the hope of increasing creativity and fluency, these methods do not, however, address writing conventions and story structure.

The fourth issue revolves around assessment. It is important for teachers to determine how they will conduct assessments and apply criteria to judge improvements in writing. Teachers must monitor students carefully to ensure that those with special needs are indeed benefiting from instruction. Using assessment findings to identify student needs and instructional adaptations is important.

Finally, the fifth issue focuses on the need for continued research into the writing abilities of students with special needs and the best writing instruction for them. Newcomer and her colleagues caution that research findings about interventions in writing for typically achieving students must be validated with students who have learning problems before teachers can generalize those findings to students who have difficulty in writing.

Writing is a complex act that is difficult to master. To help students learn how to write, teachers are increasingly having their students produce written works by using a "recursive" writing process that involves five stages of writing (Graves, 1983; Scott & Vitale, 2003). Recursive means that writers move back and forth between stages as they write and polish their work. The prewriting stage involves activities such as planning and organizing that the writer engages in prior to writing. The drafting stage is the author's attempt to put words on paper using the planning and organization of information developed during prewriting. The revising stage involves making changes to the sequencing and structure of the written work to refine the content. In the editing stage, writers focus on the mechanical aspects of writing, such as spelling, capitalization, and punctuation. Finally, in the publishing stage, the author's work is complete and is publicly shared in some format.

In this chapter, we examine each stage by describing the stage, showing how students struggle with the tasks it entails, providing instructional guidelines for one particular skill at that stage, and showing how a representative lesson within the stage can be adapted to accommodate struggling students' needs.

How do we, as teachers, teach writing to students who struggle with the demands of writing? That is the primary question to be answered in this chapter. We will focus on teaching writing by addressing three key areas. First, we will examine writing difficulties experienced by students who struggle with writing. Second, we will present a series of writing strategies that have been used with students throughout the grades across the five stages of writing. Finally, we will provide sample adaptations to show how struggling students can progress through the writing stages.

Who Are Students with Writing Difficulties?

Students who find the task of writing to be challenging exhibit a variety of difficulties. Some students manifest characteristics that are identified as dysgraphia.

Writing Difficulties

Research results show that elementary and secondary students with learning problems are unable to express themselves successfully in written communication. For example, compared to their typical same-age peers, students with learning problems write fewer, shorter, less cohesive narrative story compositions (Cavey, 1993; Hammill & Bryant, 1998; Montague, Maddux, & Dereshiwsky, 1988; Newcomer et al., 1988) and include fewer story elements (Graves, Montague, & Wong, 1990; Laughton & Morris, 1989). Students with learning problems typically lack effective writing strategies (Englert et al., 1989; Graham, Schwartz, & MacArthur, 1993), spell poorly because they do not associate letters with sounds (Moats, 2005/2006), detect and edit fewer errors (Espin & Sindelar, 1988), revise ineffectively (Graham, Harris, & Larson, 2001), and write using fewer different words and fewer sentences (Graham et al., 2001; Houck & Billingsley, 1989). When studying self-efficacy as a variable for promoting successful writers, Graham and colleagues (1993) found that students with learning problems tend to rely on others for assistance in solving writing problems, rather than relying on their knowledge of the writing process. Such students lack confidence and ability with the writing process and seek assistance from their teachers more often than their peers who possess developmentally adequate writing skills. Clearly, writing instruction is necessary for elementary and secondary students with learning difficulties to improve their skill in written communication.

Dysgraphia

Dysgraphia is a disorder in writing that involves problems with handwriting, spelling, and composition. Don Hammill and Brian Bryant (1998) surveyed the research and intervention literature to identify writing behaviors that students with dysgraphia exhibit. Their review of the literature found that students with writing disabilities are reluctant to write at all. When they do write, they do so awkwardly and slowly and with limited output (that is, their essays are too short, and they write relatively few words and sentences). With regard to spelling, they spell poorly, omit letters, confuse vowels, sometimes spell words with the correct letters but in the wrong sequence (for example, *htnig* for *thing*), repeat letters, add unnecessary letters, and often either do not attempt to spell phonetically or misspell words by attempting to spell phonetically. Some students misspell words so badly that one has no idea what they are (e.g., *camelu, huete*). Some writers struggle by reversing letters (such as *b* for *d*), using unconventional pencil grips, writing in mirror fashion, and forming letters correctly but tending to slant the line upward across the page.

From a syntactic and semantic perspective, students with dysgraphia use too many short words, omit words in sentences, omit endings in words, write the wrong words (for instance, write *hotel* for *house*), produce sentence fragments, and avoid writing complex sentences. Qualitatively, some with writing disabilities write wordy but content-empty passages and sequence ideas improperly when

● Students with dysgraphia may struggle with handwriting, spelling, and composition. For these students, help with the stages of writing is critically important.

writing a paragraph. Not all students with writing disabilities or difficulties exhibit all of these characteristics. But if you have had the chance to observe writers, you probably have observed several of these behaviors. In fact, you could form a checklist of these behaviors and use it to screen for students who either may be developing poor writing habits or may already have dysgraphia. For these students, help with the stages of writing is critically important. Let's take a look at the prewriting stage and at some ideas for teaching it.

What Is the Prewriting Stage and How Do I Teach It?

We have often compared writing to a competition between the mind and the blank piece of paper (or computer screen) that sits before the writer. Many times, the writer has plenty of ideas but struggles to get those ideas onto the page. Soon, the blankness of the page begins to win out; what was in the mind begins to disappear, and the mind itself becomes the blank page! The prewriting stage can serve to help the writer win the competition by allowing the student to do some constructive planning before he or she puts pen to paper (or fingers to keyboard) to write a first draft. During the prewriting stage, the student has to select a topic, gather research or information about the topic, determine who the audience will be (that is, who will read the paper), and so on (Gunning, 2003). Many consider the prewriting stage (or planning stage, as it is sometimes called) the most important stage in the writing process. Proper research, planning, and organizing set the stage for what is to come and save a lot of time and energy "down the writing road."

Difficulties with Prewriting

Hammill and Bryant's (1998) research has significant relevance to the prewriting stage, as can be seen by the behaviors exhibited by students with learning disabilities. As you read each characteristic, think about how it would affect students as they brainstorm, select a topic, conduct research, organize their paper, and so forth—all key features of the prewriting stage. When they tackle the prewriting stage of a writing task, struggling students

- Do not move from one idea to another.
- Approach complex problems in a concrete way.
- Provide abbreviated, unelaborated solutions to problems.
- Veer off from the subject at hand to pursue some minor detail.
- Are inconsistent in thinking and make illogical arguments.
- Have difficulty learning abstract concepts (such as *freedom, pronoun,* and *nation*).
- Have difficulty organizing, grouping, and forming concepts.
- Do not see cause/effect relationships.
- Organize time poorly.
- Are easily distracted from tasks or projects.

what WORKS 11.1

Prewriting Stage

● Brainstorming[1]

Objective: The students will brainstorm three types of words for use in their writing: action words, descriptive words, and adverbs.

Instructional Materials: Sheet of paper divided into thirds, one for each word type.

Teaching Procedure

1. Provide explicit instruction in how to brainstorm.

2. Have students brainstorm three types of words: action words, descriptive words, and adverbs.

3. Have students use their words to generate ideas before writing and to demonstrate current knowledge about a topic.

4. Have students categorize their information for further writing development.

Progress Monitoring: During the lesson, check the words and provide corrective feedback. After the revising process, have the students check the worksheet to make sure that the words they selected were put to good use.

● Planning Form[2]

Objective: The students will (a) identify a topic, (b) list brainstormed ideas, (c) determine the writing structure and components, (d) identify the audience, and (e) establish a purpose for writing.

Instructional Materials: Planning Form, a sheet of paper divided into five sections.

Teaching Procedure

1. Review brainstorming procedures.

2. Provide a Planning Form containing boxes for information about each component associated with their writing. For example, boxes could be designated for (a) the topic, (b) a list of brainstorm ideas, (c) the writing structure and components, (d) the audience, and (e) the purpose for writing.

3. Have students brainstorm information to place in each of the five boxes.

4. Use this framework for expository and narrative writing.

Progress Monitoring: During the lesson, check the boxes and provide corrective feedback. After the revising process, have the students check the worksheet to make sure that their draft builds on their brainstorming session.

● Organizational Form[2]

Objective: The students will brainstorm ideas for narrative or expository writing.

Instructional Materials: Sheet of paper divided into sections.

Teaching Procedure

1. Review brainstorming procedures.

2. Review the differences between narrative and expository writing. Provide examples of narrative and expository text.

3. Model for students how they can use information they generated during brainstorming and planning to complete the Organizational Form.

4. Have the students create an Organizational Form that contains space designated for each component of writing. For instance, in narrative writing, a form would contain the story grammar elements. In compare-and-contrast expository writing, the form might contain boxes for the introduction, categories in which comparing and contrasting will occur, comparisons, contrasts, and an ending.

Progress Monitoring: During the lesson, check the form and provide corrective feedback. After the revising process, have the students check the Organizational Form to make sure that their draft builds on their brainstorming session.

Sources: [1]K. R. Harris and S. Graham, 1985, Improving learning disabled students' composition skills: Self-control strategy. *Learning Disability Quarterly, 8,* 27–36.

[2]C. S. Englert et al., 1989, Exposition: Reading, writing, and the metacognitive knowledge of learning disabled students. *Learning Disabilities Research, 5,* 5–24.

- Are rigid and resistant to changes in thought.
- Lack "stick-to-it-iveness," or persistence.
- Reason illogically.
- Are unable to generate worthwhile ideas.
- Cannot organize ideas into a cohesive plan of action.
- Jump to premature conclusions.
- Show poor judgment.

All students may show one or more of these characteristics to some extent. But pervasive problems, such as those exhibited by students with serious learning problems, can cause difficulties during the prewriting stage of the recursive writing process.

Teaching Prewriting

Here are a few implementation tips to use during the prewriting stage. Other ideas for the prewriting stage are presented in What Works 11.1 on page 447.

- **Instructional content:** Review the purposes for writing and how to select from the various purposes.
- **Instructional content:** Discuss audience sense, the process for determining the probable reader.
- **Instructional content:** Review how form and tone will be influenced by the purpose and audience.
- **Instructional delivery:** Teach students to consider questions and topics that they think about at one time or another.
- **Instructional delivery:** Show students how to brainstorm (Allen & Mascolini, 1996). Model how to think of several ideas related to a topic, write notes while you think, and use the notes to generate more ideas.
- **Instructional delivery:** Teach students how to use software programs to "map" their ideas and create an outline. Programs such as Inspiration and Kidspiration help students enhance their brainstorming by using graphics to expand their ideas.

Next, you will read how Mrs. Sago addresses Arthur's writing difficulties.

ADAPT in Action • Arthur—Prewriting

Arthur is a student in Mrs. Sago's 11th-grade class. In addition to his diagnosis of having a writing learning disability, he is poorly motivated. He knows he has difficulty writing and doesn't understand why he needs to spend time on something he does not do well. But Arthur typically is a hard worker and likes to please his teachers, even though he struggles with reading and writing tasks. Specifically with regard to writing, he has difficulty generating ideas on what to write about, is disorganized, writes using simple sentences and immature vocabulary, and lacks writing convention skills. He tends to write simple sentences and run-ons and is reluctant to engage in any kind of revision activities. As you read the lesson below, think about the challenges that Mrs. Sago and Arthur face in meeting the instructional objectives. Consider the task that is associated with the lesson. What must Arthur be able to do (prerequisite skills) to perform the task and meet the objective? Which of the skills fall within Arthur's strengths, and which of the skills might he struggle with? Examine the sample adaptations we provide, and then think of others that may be uniquely suited to Arthur and other students with similar characteristics. Instructional Activity 11.1 on page 450 describes the activity, and the Tech Notes feature on page 451 offers examples of writing programs that can be used during the writing process.

Following the lesson, Mrs. Sago reviewed the progress-monitoring data for each student and decided to use the ADAPT framework to make decisions about the next steps in Arthur's instruction.

Ask, "What am I requiring the student to do?" Mrs. Sago thinks about the task she had the students complete. "They have to understand the role that purpose, audience sense, and other important variables play in the prewriting process, and they have to demonstrate the ability to plan their writing accordingly."

Determine the prerequisite skills of the task. Mrs. Sago comments, "The students need to be able to understand the different parts of the graphic organizer, complete each section, and create their own version of Planet Wright."

Analyze the student's strengths and struggles. All of the students have the requisite skills except Arthur. "He does well working in small groups, and he should be able to understand the components of the graphic organizer as we discuss them. But he will struggle with completing his own graphic organizer and will perhaps have difficulty recognizing the purpose and the intended audience."

Propose and implement adaptations from among the four categories. Mrs. Sago decides to work with Arthur alone before the small-group work to help him learn the components of Planet Wright (instructional delivery). She will focus on the audience sense and purpose (instructional content). And she will let him tape-record notes about his prior knowledge (what he already knows about the topic) and help him transcribe them later (instructional material).

Test to determine if the adaptations helped the student accomplish the task. Mrs. Sago will collect progress-monitoring data to determine if the adaptations helped Arthur complete his own graphic organizer.

After the lesson, Mrs. Sago evaluated Arthur's understanding of the lesson. She was not satisfied, based on the progress-monitoring data, that Arthur understood the notions of audience and how to adjust the style to the reader. She decided to make the following adaptations after considering the ADAPT framework.

- **Instructional content:** Reduce the prewriting elements to audience sense and purpose.
- **Instructional materials:** Arthur could use a tape recorder to record his knowledge of the topic and to transcribe his ideas later on.
- **Instructional delivery:** Mrs. Sago would work one-to-one with Arthur to help him learn the components of the graphic organizer before meeting in a small group to go over the lesson. She would also alter the delivery so that it deals with the limited instructional content.

Now let's consider the drafting stage and how to teach it.

Instructional activity 11.1

Planet Wright (Plan-it Right)

INSTRUCTIONAL OBJECTIVE: The students will learn to write with a purpose, to write for a specific audience, and to generate ideas related to a topic.

INSTRUCTIONAL CONTENT: Prewriting: Idea generation

INSTRUCTIONAL MATERIALS: Planet Wright (Plan-it Right) Graphic Organizer (Figure A); tape recorder

INSTRUCTIONAL DELIVERY

Grouping: Small group of students who require prewriting strategies.

INSTRUCTIONAL PROCEDURE

1. Point out to the students the importance of answering *who, why, what,* and *how* questions when identifying the reader, selecting the purpose, activating prior knowledge, and organizing thoughts, respectively.

2. Introduce the graphic organizer (Figure A) by stating that there is a new planet that has just been discovered and named Planet (Plan-it) Wright (Right) in honor of its discoverer, a famous astronomer known for his scholarly textbooks on the solar system. State that the planet seems to have three distinct land masses, which he has called Who, Why, and What, and four orbiting moons he named How I, How II, How III, and How IV.

3. Continue introducing the following sections of the graphic organizer.

Figure A

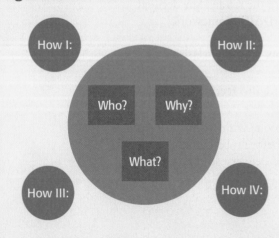

Who (the audience): Who am I writing this for? Who will be the reader? How will that affect how I write? Identify the reader, and write the person's name or position here.

Why (the purpose): Why am I writing this? What is the specific reason you have for writing? You may want to write an e-mail to friends about a weekend get-together. Or you may be writing a letter to the school or community newspaper editor. State your purpose in clear terms, and keep it under ten words long.

What (activating prior knowledge): What do I know? What have I already read or seen or learned about this topic? Brainstorm with two or three other students to identify facts that you know about the topic you have chosen. (*Note:* This is a good time to remind students about K-W-L charts that they have used in the past or to introduce K-W-L charts to students.)

How (organization): How can I group my ideas? Look at the "What" you generated in the previous step. Are there ideas that fit together in conceptual categories? What will be the sequence I use to inform the reader? How can I present my ideas in a logical manner?

4. Model how to complete the graphic organizer. Use think-alouds as you provide examples and nonexamples.

5. Using guided practice, work with the students to complete a graphic organizer on a topic you have been studying. Check for understanding as they complete their work.

6. Have the students create their own graphic organizer, in teams of two or three.

PROGRESS MONITORING: As you check for understanding during the lesson, provide error correction or praise. As you participate in the writer's conference with the students as they are writing the papers, have them refer to the graphic organizer to check whether they have used in their paper what they wrote on Planet Wright.

Source: Adapted from *Differentiating Instruction in Inclusive Classrooms* (p. 249), by D. Haager and J. E. Klingner, 2005, Boston: Allyn and Bacon.

tech NOTES

Writing Programs

In their textbook on assistive technology, Bryant and Bryant (2003) discuss programs that are intended to teach and reinforce the writing process, although further research is needed to demonstrate their effectiveness for this purpose. These programs often target primary-grade students who are in the beginning stages of learning the writing process, but they may also be used with older students who require remediation.

- *Write:OutLoud* (Don Johnston, Inc.) is a talking word processor with a talking spell checker so students can hear what they typed. Equipped with a text-to-speech function, Write:Outloud can speak words and sentences and even read whole passages. The program also highlights word-by-word as students write. Because Write:OutLoud speaks while students write, the students can hear what they have written and perhaps detect inaccuracies.
- *IntelliTalk II* (IntelliTools, Inc.) is a talking word processor combining speech, graphics, and text. IntelliTalk II includes functions such as a speech synthesizer, a talking spell checker, and built-in scanning. Text-to-speech features allow students to listen to letters, words, sentences, and entire entries as they write. Picture menus provide prompts for students who have difficulty reading the typical text-based menu in a word processor.
- *Writing with Symbols 2000* (Mayer-Johnson, Inc.) is a symbol-supported reading and writing program that contains over 8,000 pictures. Students can write with picture stories, read and follow picture directions, and communicate with pictures and speech. Features include a built-in talking word processor that highlights the words as students write, and a spell checker that uses pictures.

● **Stanley's Sticker Stories is a software program that helps struggling writers create stories through animated pictures.**

- *ULTimate KidBooks* (CAST) is a multimedia publishing program with which teachers can create electronic books that use images and text. It is a template into which content can be entered. It focuses on accessibility by providing a variety of functions, including highlighting, text enlargement, speech synthesis, and built-in switch access.
- *Stanley's Sticker Stories* (Edmark, Inc.) is a writing program that includes a word processing function with animated characters. The program provides students with a way to create stories and make their own animated storybooks. Students can create stories by choosing sticker characters, dialog for characters, backgrounds, and music. A Sticker Spelling Book is provided for spelling, and stories can be read for students with limited reading skills.

What Is the Drafting Stage and How Do I Teach It?

After students select a topic, they begin writing their first draft. They do so by writing sentences and paragraphs that express the ideas that they brainstormed, mapped, or otherwise generated in the prewriting stage. As students explain, support, and illustrate those ideas fully, they should not be concerned with writing mechanics (such as spelling, capitalization, and punctuation), nor should they be too concerned about their grammar or the words they select as they write. Instead, students should simply put their ideas on paper as best they can.

It is important that during drafting, students follow the organization they outlined during prewriting and planning. Remind students that their draft is not a finished product. Their draft will be improved on and developed further during the revision and editing stages. To help prepare for later editing, have students write their draft by skipping every other line of lined paper or double-spacing as they type. This procedure will leave them space to revise during the next stage.

Students should understand that during the drafting stage, the process is primarily about *them*—what they want to write about, how they want to write it, and what they have to say. However, students should also spend time considering who is going to read their papers (that is, who their audience will be). Even though the primary focus is on the writer, giving some thought to the reader will help students reduce the amount of revising that is needed later on.

Difficulties with Drafting

When preparing students to make initial drafts of their work, remember that there are differences between struggling writers and their same-age peers during drafting (Hammill & Bryant, 1998; Graham et al., 2001; VGCRLA, 2003). Struggling writers typically

- Write without considering the purpose for their work, who will read what they write, or the form their writing should take
- Focus too little attention on meaning, concentrating instead on mechanics and writing "rules"
- Have little knowledge about the elements of text structure, such as word order and vocabulary
- Avoid taking risks

In contrast, stronger writers typically

- Write their draft with a plan in mind, based on their prewriting efforts
- Check periodically to ensure that the draft and plan effectively fulfill their purpose for writing
- Consider questions the reader might ask and answer some of those questions as they construct their draft
- Use a variety of drafting strategies

Take a moment to think about a particular aspect of drafting that seems to be especially troublesome. What is it? How do you approach the problem? How might your students approach it?

Teaching Drafting

A variety of strategies can be used during the drafting stage to help writers generate effective sentences. See the Considering Diversity feature for examples of how to provide writing assistance for bilingual students.

- **Instructional content:** Begin by having the students write simple sentences; then move to compound, complex, and compound-complex sentences.

- **Instructional delivery:** Use examples and "nonexamples" to demonstrate effective text structure—and the lack of it.
- **Instructional delivery:** Provide students with multiple opportunities to practice writing effective sentences.
- **Instructional delivery:** Model how to write a variety of sentences in a paragraph. Check for student understanding, and provide corrective feedback (Adapted from Schumaker & Sheldon, 1985, as presented in Wood, Woloshyn, & Willoughby, 1995).

You will read about Marian and how Mr. Nu addresses her struggles with writing in ADAPT in Action on page 454.

Considering *Diversity*

Writing Assistance for Culturally and Linguistically Diverse Students with Special Needs

Culturally and linguistically diverse students who have special learning needs, such as writing difficulties, can benefit from the following suggestions.

1. Designate adequate time for writing. Thirty minutes each day should be allotted to writing instruction and opportunities for students to practice under the teacher's guidance and with feedback.

2. Provide a variety of writing topics that include topics with which students are most familiar. Students who are learning to write in a second language and have writing difficulties should be allowed to select topics that are related to their background knowledge and experiences. Allowing student to choose their own topics at first can enhance success, because students will probably select topics with which they are most comfortable.

3. Establish a "writing environment." Teachers can create positive associations with writing by engaging students in different types of writing (informational, making lists, writing directions, keeping journals) throughout the school day. Students should view writing as a natural means of expression, with links to academic areas such as reading, mathematics, and social studies. Conferencing with students regularly reinforces their writing efforts by providing enthusiastic feedback about written work, as well as suggestions for improvement.

4. Incorporate culturally diverse materials. Surround students with books and materials that depict various cultural heritages. Teachers can use these materials (pictures in the books, for example) as story starters. For older students, global and national current events can serve as topics for students to write about.

5. Include technology. Students should learn keyboarding skills and have access to computers with word processing programs, spellcheck tools, and specialized assistive technology (text-to-speech, voice recognition) to facilitate the writing process.

6. Provide explicit instruction during the writing process. Model and "think aloud" the steps involved in each stage of the writing process. Provide many opportunities for students to hone their writing skills. Carefully assess their progress, and use the results to inform further instruction.

7. Facilitate vocabulary development. For students who are learning new vocabulary, provide word walls and instruction on vocabulary building. Teachers can use the vocabulary strategies discussed in the chapter on reading to help students develop their written vocabulary.

Sources: Adapted from *Teaching strategies for students with mild to moderate disabilities* (6th ed.), by C. S. Bos and S. Vaughn, 2006, Boston: Allyn and Bacon; "Instructional recommendations for teaching writing to exceptional students," by S. Graham and K. R. Harris, 1988, *Exceptional Children, 54*(6), 506–512.

ADAPT in Action ● Marian—Drafting

Marian is a student in Mr. Nu's fourth-grade class. In academics she struggles when writing. She is one of the few students Mr. Nu has taught who is a prolific reader and has excellent spoken-language skills yet who has great difficulty writing. Marian is a hard worker who wants desperately to write because she has so many ideas and hopes to be a writer of children's stories when she grows up. Mr. Nu is determined to help her apply the skills she has in reading to develop those she needs to be an effective writer.

Prior to the lesson, Mr. Nu decided to use the ADAPT framework to make decisions about any adaptations that might be needed for Marian's instruction.

Ask, "What am I requiring the student to do?" Mr. Nu thinks about the task he will ask the students to complete. "I want the students to learn how to write concise paragraphs that have appropriate topic sentences, supportive details, and concluding sentences. This will mean they will have one less thing to worry about when they revise and edit their papers. I will teach them how to use a mnemonic (WIPES UP, see Instructional Activity 11.2 on page 456) and a supported report graphic organizer to write concise paragraphs that contain an appropriate topic sentence, supportive details, and concluding sentences."

Determine the prerequisite skills of the task. "The students will need to pay attention to the mnemonic and memorize it. They will have to learn each of the steps the mnemonic represents. From there, they will have to write their own sentences. I won't worry about mechanical errors—that will come in the next lesson."

Analyze the student's strengths and struggles. According to Mr. Nu, "Marian should have little trouble paying attention to the mnemonic and memorizing it. She should be able to learn each of the steps the mnemonic represents. Writing her own sentences will be a problem, even though I won't worry about mechanical errors. She struggles putting her thoughts on paper."

Propose and implement adaptations from among the four categories. Mr. Nu decides that the best adaptation for Marian would be to teach her to use voice-to-text technology (instructional material) to write her sentences in the supported report graphic organizer. This will allow her to take advantage of her excellent spoken-language skills. She will then transcribe what appears on the computer screen onto paper, which will be turned in.

Test to determine if the adaptations helped the student accomplish the task. Mr. Nu will have Marian print out what appears on her computer monitor and will check it for accuracy. He will then examine her written paper to determine if there were transcription errors when she copied from the screen.

After the lesson, Mr. Nu examined Marian's sentences. Through this progress monitoring, he determined that she needed additional practice transcribing her sentences from the screen onto paper.

- **Instructional content:** Reduce the number of paragraphs she has to copy. Transcribing is tiring for Marian, so this will decrease the physical workload. She will still need to create multiple sentences, however, using the voice-to-text technology.
- **Instructional materials:** The voice-to-text system seems appropriate, so Mr. Nu will have Marian use this device.

> • **Instructional delivery:** Because Marian is the only student who requires the assistive technology device, she will work alone and go over her work with the teacher individually. Mr. Nu will have to adapt the instructional delivery in order to train Marian on the new technology.

See the Making a Difference feature for an account of one teacher's discovery of the importance of modeling in assigning a writing task, whether or not students will be "publishing" their work. Next, we examine the revising stage and techniques for teaching it.

What Is the Revising Stage and How Do I Teach It?

After students have identified a topic during the prewriting stage and have organized those ideas into a first draft, they progress to the revising stage. Students need to revise their drafts to clarify the meaning of what they have written. They

Making a Difference

Modeling Both Process and Product Helps *All* Students Become Better Writers

Karin Sandmel
*Former Special Education Teacher
Grades 6, 7, and 8
Vanderbilt University
Nashville, Tennessee*

Over the course of 4 years, I was a writing teacher at two different schools for the deaf. Despite the specialized nature of these schools, which might suggest a rather homogeneous student body, my classrooms were nonetheless *very* inclusive environments! Even though all of my students were deaf, some students had additional disabilities, such as learning disabilities, emotional or behavioral disorders, and cerebral palsy. Therefore, I had to respond to a diverse range of learning needs in order to help these children succeed.

My students had writing class with me four times a week: three 50-minute sessions and one 90-minute session. I learned the importance of *modeling* when I assigned my students to write a newsletter. At first, I had explained to them what should be included in the newsletter but had not provided a model. At the end of the class, my students handed in large, sloppy newsletters written with magic markers on colored construction paper. This was *not* how I had envisioned the assign-

ment! From that moment on, I modeled every sentence, every paragraph, every composition, and every project. I stood in front of the class with the overhead projector and explained how to complete each assignment, showed an example of what the final product of the assignment should look like, and clarified all expectations for each assignment. It may help some students to suggest that they imagine their final product will be published.

Writing is an important skill for all students to possess. I've found that the ability to write is natural for some students but quite a struggle for others. My teaching experiences with children who were deaf taught me that all students can learn to write when the teacher models the writing process, gives them time to practice their writing, and succinctly defines her or his expectations for their writing assignments. ●

Instructional activity 11.2

Web-Based Supported Writing

INSTRUCTIONAL OBJECTIVE: The students will learn to create the first draft of a paper about a pet.

INSTRUCTIONAL CONTENT: Drafting: Paragraph writing with topic sentences

INSTRUCTIONAL MATERIALS: Supported report graphic organizer (Figure A); WIPES UP poster (Figure B)

FIGURE A: Supported Report Graphic Organizer

Title: _____

Introduction to Paper: _____
_____

Topic Sentence 1: _____
Paragraph 1: _____
_____
_____
_____

Concluding Sentence: _____

Source: Adapted from Englert et al., 2005, Scaffolding the writing of students with disabilities through procedural facilitation: Using an Internet-based technology to improve performance, *Learning Disability Quarterly, 30*(1), 18.

FIGURE B

WIPES UP Poster

Write a title that describes the paper (no more than five words).

Introduce the paper.

Provide the topic sentence for your paragraph. It should contain no more than ten words.

Expand on your topic sentence using supportive details. Write from two to five sentences that relate specifically to the topic sentence.

Select a concluding sentence that sums up the paragraph.

Use PES steps to write more paragraphs.

Proofread your paper for errors and revise as needed.

can also spend time thinking about, and perhaps reorganizing, what they drafted. Having students revise their papers is easier said than done. Here is a great comment about revising that illustrates this point:

> Tell any group of teachers in a workshop that revision is the key to good writing and you'll generally see hearty nods of agreement. The trouble is, so much energy has been spent on pre-writing and drafting before we ever get there. Revision is like the last stop on a long, long vacation. Everybody is tired and really wants to get on home, even if it means missing a few things. (Spandel & Stiggins, 1990, p. 106)

Those of us who have labored through the prewriting and drafting stages understand this statement completely. Writing is difficult, and revising what we have written is a laborious process. The first step in the revising stage is examining sec-

INSTRUCTIONAL DELIVERY

Grouping: Small group of students who require drafting strategies

Teaching Procedure

1. Tell students they will write a paper about a pet for someone who does not know anything about that pet.
2. Discuss the importance of generating concise paragraphs that have appropriate topic sentences.
3. Show the students a sample supported report graphic organizer.
4. Introduce the WIPES UP mnemonic (you can show the poster and then place it on the wall for support) that can be used to work through the supported report graphic organizer.
   - **W**rite a title that describes the paper (no more than five words).
   - **I**ntroduce the paper.
   - **P**rovide the topic sentence for your paragraph. It should contain no more than ten words.
   - **E**xpand on your topic sentence using supportive details. Write from two to five sentences that relate specifically to the topic sentence.
   - **S**elect a concluding sentence that sums up the paragraph.
   - **U**se PES steps to write more paragraphs.
   - **P**roofread your paper for errors and revise as needed.

5. Work through the sections of the supported report graphic organizer. As you discuss the components, model the procedure as you provide the following prompts to generate content for each box on the supported report graphic organizer.
   - Give a title.
   - Tell what the pet is.
   - Describe what the pet looks like.
   - State what the pet eats.
   - Discuss what the pet does that is funny or strange.
   - Explain how to take care of the pet.
   - State why it is a good pet.
6. Using guided practice, work with the students to complete the supported report graphic organizer for a real or "made-up" pet (perhaps a unicorn or some other imaginary animal that the students can brainstorm about). Check for understanding as they complete their work.
7. Discuss with students the importance of proofreading and editing/revising their work.

PROGRESS MONITORING: As you check for understanding during guided practice, provide error correction or praise. As you participate in the writer's conference with the students as they are writing their papers, have them refer to the supported report graphic organizer to check whether they have used in their paper what they wrote on their supported report graphic organizer.

Source: Adapted from Englert et al., 2005.

tions of the draft and finding problems in the text. Do not ask students to tackle their writing as a whole to make improvements. Instead, have them keep it simple by thinking about and revising one paragraph at a time, perhaps even sentence by sentence.

During the revising stage, the focus shifts from the writer to the reader. How do students revise what they have written so that it will be easy for the reader to understand and will fully demonstrate the writers' knowledge of the topic using the most appropriate form and tone?

Difficulties with Revising

Struggling writers have difficulty revising their work because they lack revising skills. Their approach to the revision process is quite different from the approach used by their same-age typical peers (Bryant & Hammill, 1998; Espin & Sindelar, 1988; Graham et al., 1993; VGCRLA, 2003). Struggling writers

- Have little knowledge about how to improve their writing
- Have trouble recognizing errors in word order and vocabulary use that might affect meaning
- Lack strategies and skills for correcting errors that are found in their paper
- Make revisions that do not address the errors they made in their draft (thus the overall quality of the paper remains the same)

On the other hand, proficient writers

- Evaluate all sections of their text to ensure that each contributes to the overall effectiveness of the written product
- Make meaningful revisions that improve the overall quality of the text
- Check their word order and vocabulary selection
- Focus on the overall organization of the text

Teaching Revising

As students look at each section of their paper during the revising stage, have them participate in peer revision conferences. Prior to these conferences, writers can examine their own work for possible improvements.

- **Instructional content:** Have students ask themselves the following questions (adapted from Rubin, 1995, p. 292):
  - Does what I have written express what I want to say?
  - Should I add anything?
  - Should I delete some material?
  - Did I organize the material? Can it be better organized?
  - Is there any new information that I should incorporate into my writing?
  - Am I pleased with what I have written?
- **Instructional content:** As students answer these questions, they should highlight parts of their text that deal with each question they asked.
- **Instructional delivery:** Model how to ask the questions and how to revise a paper on the basis of the answers to the questions.

Next, you will read about Miguel's difficulties with reading and writing and how Mrs. Sago uses the ADAPT framework to address his problems.

ADAPT in Action • Miguel—Revising

Miguel is a student in Mrs. Sago's class. He has learning disabilities in reading, writing, and thinking/reasoning. He has difficulty problem solving, is easily distracted, makes illogical arguments, has trouble with abstract concepts, and exhibits several other problems associated with reasoning learning disabilities. He struggles with reading text beyond the primary level and has limited comprehension, although his listening comprehension is excellent. In writing, he writes short, choppy sentences and goes off on tangents from sentence to sentence. His mechanical skills are poor to nonexistent.

What must Miguel be able to do (prerequisite skills) to complete the task and meet the objective? Which of the skills fall within his strengths, and with which skill(s) might he struggle? How might the sample adaptations we provide work for Miguel, and what others might be suited for Miguel and other students with similar characteristics? Instructional Activity 11.3 describes an approach known as peer revision. Will it be suitable for Miguel?

After teaching a peer revision lesson, Mrs. Sago checked her notes and decided to use ADAPT Framework 11.1 (page 461) to help Miguel meet the objective.

Ask, "What am I requiring the student to do?" Mrs. Sago thought about the task she had the students complete. "The students need to learn to work in pairs to help one another revise their papers."

Determine the prerequisite skills of the task. After looking at her lesson, Mrs. Sago noted, "In order to accomplish the task, the students have to be able to work in pairs, communicate effectively, read their partner's passage, ask questions, provide comments, and make suggestions. They also have to be able to respond to the critique to improve their draft."

Analyze the student's strengths and struggles. Mrs. Sago considered what might be strengths and struggles for Miguel. Responding candidly, Mrs. Sago noted that Miguel is socially able to work in pairs and communicate effectively. But he would be unable to read his partner's passage, ask appropriate questions, provide critical commentary, or make constructive suggestions. He would also struggle when asked to respond to his partner's critique to better his draft.

Propose and implement adaptations from among the four categories. Mrs. Sago decides to work one-to-one with Miguel (instructional delivery). She will focus on one section of his paper and have Miguel provide comments only on the purpose of the paper, rather than on audience, content, and form as well (instructional content). She will also have Miguel use text-to-speech technology to read her paper prior to making comments.

Test to determine if the adaptations helped the student accomplish the task. Mrs. Sago will examine how Miguel responds to the adaptations she has made. If he has done well, she will repeat the process and expand the instructional content to audience, content, and form.

After the lesson, Mrs. Sago evaluated Miguel's understanding of the revision process. She was pleased with the comments regarding the purpose of "her" paper. But when they reversed roles, Miguel was unable to use Mrs. Sago's input to revise his paper effectively. She decided to make the following adaptations after considering the ADAPT framework.

- **Instructional content:** Focus on a single paragraph at a time.
- **Instructional materials:** Provide sentence strips with multiple options to replace a poor sentence, and have Miguel select the best sentences.
- **Instructional delivery:** Continue to work one-to-one with Miguel. Adjust the instructional delivery to include the sentence strips.

Instructional activity 11.3

Peer Revision

INSTRUCTIONAL OBJECTIVE: The students will revise their documents.

INSTRUCTIONAL CONTENT: Revising of whole passage

INSTRUCTIONAL MATERIALS: None

INSTRUCTIONAL DELIVERY
Grouping: Students in pairs

Teaching Procedure

1. Have the students divide into pairs.

2. Model how to consider questions before giving the paper to a peer reviewer (adapted from Gunning, 2003).

   - Does the paper fulfill its intended purpose?
   - Will the audience understand what you have written?
   - Does the form of the paper fit the purpose and intended audience?
   - Is the paper interesting?
   - Is there anything that can be done to make the paper more interesting?
   - Are there enough details or examples in the content of the paper?
   - Does it "read right"?

3. Teach the students explicitly how to make revision symbols during peer revisions. Provide examples and nonexamples, and provide multiple opportunities to practice (adapted from Haager & Klingler, 2005).

4. Have peer reviewers also answer the questions in procedure 2 above. Model appropriate interactions between peer reviewers and writers, such as providing constructive criticism and avoiding caustic remarks. Give examples and nonexamples of appropriate comments.

5. Give exactly the same passage to all student pairs. Direct each pair to role-play and practice peer revision. Check for student understanding, and provide praise or corrective feedback as warranted.

6. Have students revise their own drafts and then exchange papers with a peer for a peer review. Periodically check for understanding, and provide praise and corrective feedback. Ensure that students are staying on task and taking this revision process seriously. If need be, stop the process and model once again how to provide constructive criticism.

PROGRESS MONITORING: As you check for understanding during guided practice, provide error correction or praise. Meet with the students in a conference after they have revised their papers following peer revision. As you participate in this conference, examine the actual edits and see how the students have revised their papers on the basis of the revision suggestions. After the final paper has been turned in, be sure to grade in terms of what was taught during the revision process. It does little good to teach revising skills if students are not to be held accountable for errors that "slip through."

To add words, insert ^ between the words and write the added word above the ^.	Tom had a ^big dog.
To take words out, draw a line through the word to be omitted.	Marcy didn't ~~not~~ think she could help.
To change the order of two consecutive words, draw a ⌒ around the words.	Pedro and ⌢sister his⌣ went shopping for new school clothes.
As a reminder to add ideas, use this mark: ↙	↙ tell which dog The dog is furry and friendly.
To insert a space between run-on words, use a / and the # sign.	Marcus enjoyed/playing football with his teammates.
When a lowercase letter needs to be uppercase, use a triple underline: ≡.	Tom likes m̲ary a lot.

11.1 ADAPT Framework Peer Reviews

ASK "What am I requiring the student to do?"	DETERMINE the prerequisite skills of the task.	ANALYZE the student's strengths and struggles.		PROPOSE and implement adaptations from among the four categories.	TEST to determine if the adaptations helped the student to accomplish the task.
		Strengths	**Struggles**		
I want Joseph to work with a student to revise each other's papers for spelling errors.	1. Reads the passage.		1	**For 1. Instructional Materials** Scanner and text-to-speech technology	**For 1.** Check for accuracy of scanned document.
	2. Checks for spelling errors.		2	**For 2. Instructional Materials** Spellcheck of electronic copy of the peer's paper. Text-to-speech technology for alternative spellings.	**For 2.** Monitor spellings, especially for incorrect words spelled correctly (e.g., student wrote *form* instead of *from; form* spelled correctly).
	3. Works cooperatively with a partner.	3		**For 3.** No adaptations needed.	
	4. Is able to stay on task for 15 minutes.	4		**For 4.** No adaptations needed.	

What Is the Editing Stage and How Do I Teach It?

After students revise their drafts, they move to the editing stage, where they focus on ensuring that the written piece is grammatically and mechanically correct. They want to produce a paper that contains as few errors as possible. Some writing experts differentiate between editing and proofreading, but we see them as similar and interrelated.

During the editing stage, students clean up mechanical errors after they have fully developed the meaning of what they have written. Students edit their work to keep the reader from being distracted while reading for meaning. Students look for inconsistencies in writing mechanics and grammar choices, such as subject–verb agreement, pronoun–antecedent agreement, and sentence fragments or run-ons.

Editing requires a variety of strategies that must be explicitly taught to help writers become competent at finding and correcting their mistakes. As writers become better editors, they can often correct grammar and mechanical errors during the revising stage. In fact, common errors occur less frequently during drafts.

During the editing stage, students can first edit their own papers and then share their papers with at least one other person. This opportunity to practice makes the readers/editors better at finding mistakes in their *own* writing, thus helping them to create drafts with fewer errors.

● Editing requires a variety of strategies that must be explicitly taught to help writers become competent at finding and correcting their mistakes.

Difficulties with Editing

We discussed many of these difficulties when we considered the characteristics of students with writing disabilities earlier in this chapter. Many of these characteristics are particularly relevant during the editing stage. To review, struggling students

- Spell poorly
- Use too many short words
- Omit words in sentences
- Omit endings in words
- Write the wrong words
- Write sentence fragments
- Avoid writing complex sentences
- Sequence ideas improperly when writing a paragraph

In addition, McGhee, Bryant, Bryant, and Larsen (1992) found that students with writing problems make considerably more errors in capitalization and punctuation than do their more effective peers. Thus it is easy to see why struggling students would have difficulty with the editing process. They are unable to find their mistakes and therefore cannot correct them.

Teaching Editing

Here are some helpful tips that your students can use as they continue the editing process.

- **Instructional materials:** Have the writers use checklists while they act as the first editor of their own work. Have students ask themselves the following questions:
  - Did I express myself clearly? Will the reader understand what I wrote?
  - Did I write any sentence fragments?
  - Did I capitalize the first word in each sentence?
  - Did I capitalize proper nouns?
  - Did I end each sentence with the correct punctuation mark?
  - Did I spell all of the words correctly?
  - Did I use semicolons in the right places?
  - Did I use proper verb tenses?
  - Did I use apostrophes correctly?
  - Did I vary the length of my sentences?
  - Did I capitalize "I" whenever I used it?
  - Did I use commas when I listed lots of things?

  (Adapted from Gunning, 2003; Rubin, 1995)

- **Instructional delivery:** Model editing strategies and teach students to check their work against the checklist they use.
- **Instructional delivery:** Teach explicitly one editing skill at a time.
- **Instructional delivery:** Teach students explicitly how to proofread others' work, and provide corrective, supportive feedback.
- **Instructional delivery:** Teach students how to use specific editing marks that show the different types of errors.

You will now read about Simon's editing skills and how Mr. Nu made adaptations for Simon using the ADAPT framework.

ADAPT in Action ● Simon—Editing

Simon is a student in Mr. Nu's class. He has been retained once and yet still struggles with nearly all of his academic subjects. He has improved his reading skills somewhat and is able to grasp sound–symbol correspondences, which should help him improve his spelling. So far that has not been the case. Regarding his editing skills, he struggles with almost all aspects of grammar, but he knows his capitalization and punctuation rules.

During the CHECK lesson (see Instructional Activity 11.4 on page 465), Mr. Nu observed Simon and noted that he benefited from instruction but was overwhelmed with all the different syllable patterns and all the spelling rules. Therefore, he applied the ADAPT framework to make appropriate adaptations.

Ask, "What am I requiring the student to do?" Mr. Nu understands that his students were asked to learn and apply a spelling strategy, apply a previously learned SPLIT strategy (see What Works 10.3 on page 415) and recall the syllable patterns, and apply spelling rules in their editing.

Determine the prerequisite skills of the task. "I realize that I asked a lot of my students. They had to learn a new strategy, apply a previously learned strategy to a new skill, and learn a variety of spelling rules. They also had to review the SPLIT strategy and syllable patterns. And they had to look at their drafts and apply their newly learned skills to their editing responsibilities."

Analyze the student's strengths and struggles. Simon had learned strategies in the past by memorizing them through listening, so he should have been able to add a new strategy. He memorized the SPLIT strategy and syllable patterns, and he has shown the ability to apply those to his reading skills to some extent. However, he is unsure of some of the syllable patterns and struggles with them. Therefore, he would be expected to have difficulty applying the previously learned SPLIT strategy to the CHECK strategy, which he did. He also was overwhelmed with all of the spelling rules. Therefore, he has trouble looking at his draft and applying the newly learned skills to his editing.

Propose and implement adaptations from among the four categories. Mr. Nu decided to reduce the number of spelling rules. He also limited the number of syllable patterns that Simon had to remember and apply to his editing. Both of these are instructional content adaptations. He will assign a mentor (older student) to work with Simon (instructional delivery) as he edits.

Test to determine if the adaptations helped the student accomplish the task. Mr. Nu will examine Simon's work and check for errors on words that fit the spelling patterns and rules that are the subject of study. He will make additional adaptations as needed or have Simon work on new patterns and rules if he has been successful.

After the lesson, Mr. Nu evaluated Simon's understanding of what was taught in the lesson and his ability to apply the CHECK strategy as he edited his draft. He found that Simon was still overwhelmed by the number of spelling rules and was unsure of all the syllable patterns, so he made the following adaptations.

- **Instructional content:** Select a single spelling rule and syllable pattern to be studied and applied.
- **Instructional materials:** Place a miniature version of the CHECK poster on Simon's desk. Write the syllable pattern and examples on Post-it notes that Simon can stick to his desk during editing.
- **Instructional delivery:** Pair Simon with a proficient writer (mentor). Make sure that the instructional delivery includes prompts to use the materials on his desk.

What Works 11.2 on page 467 describes the POWER strategy that students can use in all stages of writing.

What Is the Publishing Stage and How Do I Teach It?

We have already discussed the prewriting, drafting, revising, and editing stages of the recursive writing process. At the end of the writing process, we arrive at the publishing stage, where we determine that the paper is finished. Of course, it is possible that minor changes may still remain, because in writing there will always be some revisions and edits that *can* be made. Eventually the earlier stages of writing must be put to rest, and the students can publish their papers.

Instructional activity 11.4

CHECK

INSTRUCTIONAL OBJECTIVE: The students will be able to CHECK their passages for spelling errors.

INSTRUCTIONAL CONTENT: Editing, specifically spelling

INSTRUCTIONAL MATERIALS: CHECK poster handout on spelling rules, SPLIT (see What Works 10.3), handout on syllable patterns (see Table 10.6)

INSTRUCTIONAL DELIVERY
Grouping: Small group of students who require instruction in structural analysis

Teaching Procedure

1. Introduce the lesson by showing the importance of spell checking during the editing phase.

2. Create a handout with the following spelling rules (adapted from Rubin, 1995, pp. 318–329):
   - To form the plural, *s* is added to nouns (such as *tree, airplane,* and *truck*).
   - To form the plural, *es* is usually added to nouns that end in *s, ss, sh, ch,* or *x* (such as *bus/buses, class/classes, brush/brushes, bench/benches,* and *box/boxes*).
   - For nouns that end in *y* with a consonant before the *y,* change the *y* to *i* and add *es* (such as *baby/babies* and *story/stories*).
   - For most nouns that end in *o* with a consonant before the *o,* add *es* (such as *hero/heroes, tomato/tomatoes*). But some nouns that end in *o* are made plural by adding *s* (such as *piano/ pianos, solo/solos*).
   - Most nouns that end in *f* or *fe* are made plural by changing the *f* or *fe* to *ves* (such as *shelf/shelves, knife/knives*). But some nouns that end with *f* are made plural by adding *s* (such as *chief/chiefs* and *roof/roofs*).
   - Some nouns are exceptions. They are made plural by changing the letters within the word or adding letters so that the spelling is changed (such as *foot/feet, mouse/mice*); other noun exceptions include those that are the same in both the singular and the plural (such as *bison* and *sheep*).
   - The letter *q* is always followed by *u* in common words (such as *queen* and *quite*).
   - Words ending in silent *e* usually drop the *e* before adding a suffix beginning with a vowel (such as *use/using*) and retain the *e* if the suffix begins with a consonant (such as *blame/ blameless*).
   - When the sound is long *e,* it is *i* before *e* except after *c* (such as *belief* and *brief*), but when the sound is long *a,* it is *ei* (such as *neighbor* and *weight?*) But there are some exceptions (such as *weird* and *leisure*).
   - Words that retain the hard *c* sound when adding endings beginning with *i, e,* or *y* add a *k* before the ending (such as *picnicking* and *panicky*).
   - The prefixes *dis* and *mis* are spelled with one *s* (such as *disappear* and *mistrust*). But when the root word begins with *s,* there will be two *s*'s, one for the prefix and one for the root word (such as *dissatisfied* and *misspell*).
   - When a word ends in a short vowel followed by a consonant, double the consonant before adding a suffix that starts with a vowel (such as *grip/gripping*).
   - The suffix *ful* is spelled with a single *l* (such as *help/helpful*).

3. Reintroduce the SPLIT strategy, and tell the students that instead of using the strategy to decode unfamiliar words, they will use the strategy to help them spell words. If the strategy has not yet been introduced, make sure to do so in an earlier reading lesson.

4. When ready, continue by reviewing the syllable patterns using the syllable pattern handout. If the syllable patterns have yet to have been discussed, introduce the patterns as part of an earlier SPLIT lesson in reading.

5. Continue by introducing the CHECK strategy by showing the CHECK poster (Figure A). Teach each section of the mnemonic, and have the students memorize it.

(continues)

Instructional activity 11.4

CHECK (Continued)

FIGURE A

> # CHECK Poster
>
> **C**orrectly pronounce the word.
>
> **H**ave each syllable "in your head."
>
> **E**nter your SPLIT and Spelling Rules "memory rooms."
>
> **C**onsider how each syllable sound should be represented by a letter or letters; write the letter(s) down.
>
> **K**eep separate what you wrote for each syllable, and then blend the syllables together. Is it the word you pronounced in first C above?

- **C**orrectly pronounce the word. (If you are not sure how to pronounce the word, use another word that fits.)
- **H**ave each syllable "in your head." Break down the word into syllables, and remember each one.
- **E**nter your SPLIT and Spelling Rules "memory rooms." (Remember what you have learned before: the SPLIT strategy and the syllable patterns and the spelling rules.)

- **C**onsider how each syllable sound should be represented by a letter or letters; write the letter(s) down. (Think about the spelling pattern and the letters that represent the sounds of the patterns.)
- **K**eep separate what you wrote for each syllable, and then blend the syllables together. Is it the word you pronounced in the first C above? (Write each syllable part separately—such as *mis un der stand*—and then blend the parts together.)

6. Teach the spelling rules. Pass out the handouts, and have the students keep them on their desks as a ready reference.

7. Give the students a list of spelling words, some of which have been spelled correctly, some of which have not. Spelling words should all be phonetically regular and should fit the spelling rules. Use modeling and guided practice to demonstrate the procedure.

8. Give the students a paragraph that contains some words that have been spelled correctly and some that have not. Spelling words should all be phonetically regular and should fit the spelling rules. Use modeling and guided practice to demonstrate the procedure.

9. Model for the students how to apply these rules to their written products during the drafting and revising stages. Provide multiple practice opportunities.

PROGRESS MONITORING: During the lesson, check student understanding of the mnemonic, CHECK, and spelling rules. Monitor whether they can apply the mnemonic and spelling rules to the lesson. Have the students add the CHECK strategy, SPLIT strategy, and spelling rules to their writing journal. During the editing portion of the writing conference, meet with the students and check their application of the material taught in the lesson. Have the students discuss how they used the strategies to check for spelling errors.

Before they can do so, students have to make sure that the paper is neatly written and is ready to be read. Looking at an unreadable paper is exasperating, and the reader has little idea how to decipher what has been written. At the publishing stage, students must ensure that the paper is easy to read (that is, handwritten neatly).

what WORKS 11.2

POWER Strategy

Instructional Objective: The students will use the POWER strategy to assist them in all the stages of writing.

Instructional Materials: POWER Poster (large wall poster with the mnemonic listed)

Teaching Procedure

1. Tell the students that they will be learning a strategy that will help them in every stage of the writing process. Specific tasks and self-talk occur at each step of this strategy. In the planning step, students identify their audience, purpose for writing, and supportive background information. The organizing step involves structuring the information obtained in the planning step by categories in preparation for the writing step. Editing involves monitoring the content so that changes can readily be made in the revising step. (*Note:* Some teachers teach students to edit their work after they have revised their paper. POWER has the students revise their work after they have made their edits.)

2. Show the POWER poster: **P** lan, **O** rganize, **W** rite, **E** dit, and **R** evise.

3. Say, "P stands for Plan. Plan means that I identify the audience, purpose for writing, and supportive background information."

4. Say, "O stands for Organize. Organize means that I arrange my ideas in a reasonable fashion." Graphic organizers can assist students as they organize their thoughts.

5. Say, "W stands for Write. I write my first draft based on the ideas I have organized in the previous step."

6. Say, "E stands for Edit. I check my work for any mistakes."

7. Say, "R stands for Revise. I make any changes that I need to before I turn in my final paper."

8. Teach each stage explicitly, and have students practice each step. Have the students memorize the information on the POWER poster so that they can use the strategy as they write.

Progress Monitoring: During the lesson, have students repeat each step of the mnemonic. As the paper is being written, check that each student is following the steps appropriately.

Source: From Making strategies and self-talk visible: Writing instruction in regular and special education classrooms by C. S. Englert et al., 1991, *American Education Research Journal, 28*(2), 337–372.

Publications That Publish Student Writing, Poetry, and Art

Once the paper is publishable, you may want to make the student aware of a number of potential sources wherein a particularly outstanding paper can be widely shared. Here are a few such sources.

STONE SOUP This magazine by young writers and artists is unique among children's magazines. It's the only magazine made up entirely of the creative work of children. Young people from all over the world contribute their stories, poems, book reviews, and artwork to *Stone Soup*. You and your students will be inspired and moved by these young published authors and artists.

MERLYN'S PEN This is perhaps the oldest of all publishers devoted exclusively to teens in Grades 6 through 12. Merlyn's Pen, Inc., is in the process of reorganizing

● Publishing is a way for students to share their writing with an audience both at school and at home.

as a nonprofit foundation, the Merlyn's Pen Foundation. Its mission is to build a vast and friendly library of great works by teens from the last 20 years. The library, which is open all day and night and free to teachers, librarians, kids, and anyone interested in the lives of teens, will never close. It is online, which means it's on every teacher's desk and on every young writer's laptop. Works in its library are often beautifully illustrated, appearing exactly as they did when first printed in *Merlyn's Pen* magazine. Even the design and typography of the poems have been reworked for viewing online and printing out at home. Best of all, any teacher anywhere can use the powerful search index to find exactly the right piece for his or her purposes: Teachers in New York can locate, in mere seconds, 50 poems by top New York student writers. A seventh-grade teacher attempting to teach the difficult art of character development in fiction can locate 25 stories noted for their exquisite character development—and all written by seventh graders just like her own!

SKIPPING STONES   This nonprofit children's magazine encourages cooperation, creativity, and celebration of cultural and environmental richness. *Skipping Stones,* an award-winning resource in multicultural education, is published bimonthly during the school year, and it accepts art and original writings in every language and from all ages. Its staff invites you to participate in this exciting project with your submissions, subscriptions, suggestions, and support. Non-English writings are accompanied by English translations to encourage the learning of other languages. Each issue also contains international pen pals, book reviews, news, and a guide for parents and teachers, which offers creative activities and resources for making the best use of *Skipping Stones* in your home or classroom. This is truly an essential reader for teachers looking outward and wanting to open their students to the world and its many cultures. The student samples on the site are first rate.

POTLUCK CHILDREN'S LITERARY MAGAZINE This "magazine for the serious young writer" is intended for writers between 8 and 16 years of age, who fill each issue with their poems, short stories, fables, and book reviews.

POTATO HILL POETRY This bimonthly magazine (except July and August) is for teachers and students K through 12. The magazine publishes poems written by students, along with writing exercises, interviews with poets, book reviews, contests, and other poetry-related material. Its staff is also interested in submissions of cartoons, writing exercises, artwork (black ink on plain white paper), essays on the writing process, and black-and-white photographs.

TEEN VOICES This magazine is written by, for, and about teenage and young adult women, ages 13 to 19. Regular features include Family, Health, Arts and Culture (music, the Web, and book reviews), an advice column, and creative writing. This magazine honors young women's potential as leaders.

TEENINK This national magazine, book, and Web site feature teen writing, art, photos, poetry, information on issues of interest to teens; and more. All articles are written by teenage authors.

THE CLAREMONT REVIEW This international magazine showcases young adult writers. The editors seek to publish exemplary fiction and poetry by young authors between 13 and 19 years of age. They publish slice-of-life stories that also focus on language and character, not simply plot-driven stories. In poetry, their preference is free verse without rhyme.

THE CONCORD REVIEW This is a quarterly journal of exemplary history essays by high school students. Editors ask that students submit essays approximately 5,000 words in length.

THE WRITER'S SLATE This magazine comes out three times a year and publishes original poetry, exposition, and narration from students enrolled in kindergarten through grade 12.

WRITES OF PASSAGE This literary journal for teenagers is published twice a year. It offers poems and short stories by teens nationwide, as well as special features by established authors offering insight into writing.

BLUE JEAN MAGAZINE This alternative to the glamor and beauty magazines targeting teen girls is the only magazine written and edited by young women around the world between the ages of 13 and 19. It publishes teen fiction, poetry, art, commentary, and nonfiction works. Its mission is to publish what young women are thinking, saying, and doing.

NEW MOON: THE MAGAZINE FOR GIRLS AND THEIR DREAMS *New Moon* is a magazine created by girls, for all girls who want their voices heard and their dreams taken seriously. It's edited entirely by a Girls Editorial Board (16 girls ages 8 to 14).

Difficulties with Publishing

Publishing involves creating a written product that is easy for the reader to read. When students use word processing programs, legibility is rarely an issue

WORKING together

Taking on Technology

Many teachers are uncomfortable working with technology, especially sophisticated technology such as speech-to-text or text-to-speech technology. We encourage you to get to know and collaborate with your assistive technology (AT) specialist. Not every school has an expert in assistive technology in the building. Many school districts or regional service centers hire itinerant professionals, who move from school to school and provide consultant services with classroom teachers and special educators. If you need help with assistive technology devices or services, contact the AT specialist and arrange for a meeting to discuss your students who have special needs. Raskind and Bryant (2002) discuss information that teachers should provide the specialist.

Skills. Teachers should be able to rate the student (weak, average, or strong) in the following skills:

- Applies capitalization rules.
- Spells correctly.
- Writes neatly with little difficulty.
- Uses appropriate grammar.
- Edits/proofs well.
- Writes well conceptually.
- Applies a sense of audience effectively.
- Demonstrates overall writing skills.

Setting demands. The teacher should also share the extent to which the following tasks are accomplished in the classroom:

- Writes test answers.
- Writes papers (reports, term papers).
- Writes stories/essays/poems.
- Copies from the chalkboard/text (words and numbers).
- Takes notes.
- Spells words (in isolation and in continuous text).

Having this information available will give the AT specialist some of the information he or she requires to help you work with your students who have special needs. You will probably be asked many more questions. Also, be sure to ask questions that *you* have regarding how AT devices and services can help you meet the needs of your struggling students. Together, you can examine the student ratings and the writing requirements of the classroom setting. The writing programs in the Tech Notes feature can be evaluated to determine which ones should be applied to help the student meet the writing demands of the setting. The use of any AT device should be evaluated by the classroom teacher and AT specialist to confirm that this support is helping the student improve in writing abilities.

---

if printer quality is good. The Working Together feature discusses collaboration with an assistive technology specialist to determine whether AT devices will be helpful in teaching writing to your students with special needs. For handwritten products, penmanship is important, and penmanship can be a struggle for some students. Cecil Mercer and Paige Pullen (2004) described a variety of handwriting difficulties:

- Slowness
- Incorrect direction of letters and numbers
- Too much or too little slant
- Spacing
- General messiness
- Inability to stay on a horizontal line
- Too much or too little pencil/pen pressure
- Mirror writing
- Closing letters

- Closed top loops in letters (forming *e* like *i*)
- Looped strokes that should not be looped (forming *i* like *e*)
- Omission of parts of letters

Teaching Publishing

Graham and Miller (1980) outlined several ingredients of an effective handwriting program to enhance the appearance of published works.

- **Instructional content:** Establish desirable habits such as short daily learning periods.
- **Instructional content:** Do not accept poorly written work.
- **Instructional delivery:** Have students over-learn (continue to practice beyond mastery) skills such as letter formation and alignment in isolation and then apply them in meaningful contexts and assignments.
- **Instructional delivery:** Have students evaluate their own handwriting.
- **Instructional delivery:** Teach handwriting skills explicitly.

summary

Successful writers engage in a multistep process that includes five stages: prewriting, drafting, revising, editing, and publishing. In the prewriting stage, students generate a topic, develop ideas about the topic, determine the purpose for their writing, select an audience who will be the reader, organize their thoughts and the paper, and determine the form and tone for what will be written.

During the drafting stage, students write down the ideas they generated in the preceding section. Little attention is paid to mechanical and grammatical errors. This is a free-flowing stage wherein the writer is relatively unencumbered by the rules of writing.

The revising stage allows the writers to return to their first drafts and improve what they have written. Care is taken to consider the reader, whose understanding of what is written will be enhanced by the author's choice of words, grammar, and paragraph structure. Corrections of spelling and other mistakes of mechanics and grammar can be made during the revising stage, but they are more likely to be made during the editing stage. In this writing stage, the writer serves as his or her own editor, but he or she also might enlist the aid of a peer.

In the final stage, the publishing stage, the writer prepares a final draft that will be read by the intended audience. The paper should be free of errors and neatly written.

Throughout each stage, struggling writers confront a variety of challenges that can greatly reduce the quality of their written product. Specifically, struggling writers display numerous problems (e.g., organizing their thoughts, generating sentences and paragraphs, making semantic and syntactic adjustments associated with the reader, correcting mechanical errors, and writing a legible document) that, if not dealt with, result in short, hollow writings that are full of errors of all types. However, teachers can use the ADAPT framework to identify the tasks associated with each writing stage, determine the requisite skills that are needed to complete the tasks, examine the student's strengths and struggles with regard to each requisite ability, and propose and monitor adaptations to help the student create and write a decipherable document.

self-test **QUESTIONS**

Let's review the learning objectives for this chapter. If you are uncertain and cannot "talk through" the answers provided for any of these questions, reread those sections of the text.

- **Who are students with writing difficulties?**

  Struggling writers exhibit a variety of characteristics, depending on the writer. These characteristics include writing awkwardly, slowly, and with limited output; spelling poorly; omitting letters; confusing vowels; spelling words with the correct letters but in the wrong sequence; repeating letters; adding unnecessary letters; misspelling words by attempting to spell phonetically; misspelling words so badly that readers have no idea what they are; reversing letters; using unconventional pencil grips; writing in mirror fashion; forming letters correctly but tending to slant the line upward across the page; using too many short words; omitting words from sentences; omitting endings from words; writing the wrong words; writing sentence fragments; avoiding writing complex sentences; writing wordy but content-empty passages; and/or sequencing ideas improperly when writing a paragraph.

- **What are the stages of the writing process?**

  Prewriting, drafting, revising, editing, and publishing.

- **How can teachers provide effective writing instruction for the stages of writing?**

  Here are a few suggestions for teaching each writing stage: *Prewriting:* Review the purposes for writing and how to select from the various purposes; discuss audience sense, the process for determining the probable reader; and review how form and tone will be influenced by the purpose and audience. *Drafting:* Present a sentence pattern (beginning with simple sentences and moving to compound sentences, complex sen-

tences, and then compound-complex sentences); use examples and "non-examples" to illustrate the critical features of a particular sentence pattern; and provid students with many opportunities to practice identifying parts of sentences and the associated sentence patterns. At this point, students should begin to memorize the basic patterns. *Revising:* Students should determine whether their writing tells the reader the answer to the question "What is this writing about?" and determine whether the purpose is clear. If not, how can the content of the writing be made clearer? Also, determine whether there is any part of the writing that does not help achieve the purpose. *Editing:* Have the writer serve as the first editor of his or her own work, using checklists and other strategies. Model editing strategies and teach the students to make appropriate comments, and then have the students use peers as editors. Have students put a well-edited piece in an editing basket for a final editing conference with the teacher. Teachers can briefly edit the student's writing and then confer with the student about one or two editing skills. *Publishing:* Teach handwriting skills explicitly, establish desirable habits in short daily learning periods, and have students over-learn skills in isolation and then apply them in meaningful contexts and assignments.

- **How can teachers make instructional adaptations for the stages of writing?**

  This chapter provides several lessons for teaching writing skills in each writing stage. Each lesson provided an instructional activity, instructional objective, instructional content, instructional materials, ways to deliver instruction, and methods to monitor progress. Examine each lesson presented in each writing stage, and focus on the specific case studies and the adaptations that were suggested to meet the learning needs of each of the students.

Revisit the
OPENING challenge

Check your answers to the Reflection Questions from the Opening Challenge, and revise them on the basis of what you have learned.

1. What specific difficulties might students in both teachers' classes exhibit in the writing stages?

2. How can the teachers effectively work with their students during each stage of the writing process?

3. How can these teachers provide the adapted lessons to students who require additional instruction?

4. How can writing assessments (see Chapter 7) be used to identify struggling students and to monitor their response to intervention?

Professional Standards and Licensure

CEC Knowledge and Skill Core Standard and Associated Subcategories

CEC Content Standard 2: Development and Characteristics of Learners

Special educators know and demonstrate respect for their students first as unique human beings. Special educators understand the similarities and differences in human development and the characteristics between and among individuals with and without ELN. Moreover, special educators understand how exceptional conditions can interact with the domains of human development, and they use this knowledge to respond to the varying abilities and behaviors of individuals with ELN.

CEC Content Standard 4: Instructional Strategies

Special educators select, adapt, and use instructional strategies to promote challenging learning results in general and special curricula and to appropriately modify learning environments for individuals with disabilities. They enhance the learning of critical thinking, problem solving, and performance skills of individuals with disabilities, and increase their self-awareness, self-management, self-control, self-reliance, and self-esteem.

CEC Content Standard 6: Language

Special educators understand typical and atypical language development and the ways in which exceptional conditions can interact with an individual's experience with and use of language. Special educators are familiar with augmentative, alternative, and assistive technologies; match their communication methods to individuals' language proficiency and cultural and linguistic differences; provide effective language models; and use communication strategies and resources to facilitate understanding of subject matter for individuals with ELN whose primary language is not English.

CEC Content Standard 7: Instructional Planning

Individualized decision-making and instruction is at the center of special education practice. Special educators develop long-range individualized instructional plans anchored in both general and special curricula. Individualized instructional plans emphasize explicit modeling and efficient guided practice to assure acquisition and fluency through maintenance and generalization. Understanding of these factors, as well as the implications of an individual's exceptional condition, guides the special educator's selection, adaptation, and creation of materials, and the use of powerful instructional variables. Instructional plans are modified based on ongoing analysis of the individual's learning progress.

INTASC Core Principle and Associated Special Education Subcategories

1. Subject Matter

1.01 All teachers have a solid base of understanding of the major concepts, assumptions, issues, and processes of inquiry in the subject matter content areas that they teach.

1.03 All teachers understand that students with disabilities may need accommodations, modifications, and/or adaptations to the general curriculum.

2. Student Learning

2.04 All teachers are knowledgeable about multiple theories of learning and research-based practices that support learning and use this information to inform instruction.

4. Instructional Strategies

4.03 All teachers use research-based practices to support learning and generalization of concepts and skills.

4.04 All teachers understand that it is particularly important to provide multiple ways for students with disabilities to participate in learning activities. They modify tasks and accommodate individual needs of students with disabilities.

4.08 All teachers expect and support the use of assistive and instructional technologies to promote learning and independence of students with disabilities.

5. Learning Environment

5.04 All teachers recognize factors and situations that are likely to promote intrinsic motivation, and create learning environments that encourage engagement and self-motivation.

6. Communication

6.01 All teachers have knowledge of the general types of communication strategies and assistive technologies that can be incorporated as a regular part of instruction. They understand that students with disabilities may have communication and language needs that impact their ability to access the general education curriculum.

7. Instructional Planning

7.02 All teachers plan ways to modify instruction to facilitate positive learning results within the general education curriculum for students with disabilities.

Praxis II: Education of Exceptional Students: Core Content Knowledge   PRAXIS

I. Understanding Exceptionalities

Human development and behavior as related to students with disabilities, including

- Language development and behavior.
- Cognition.
- Physical development, including motor and sensory.

Characteristics of students with disabilities, including the influence of

- Cognitive factors.
- Affective and social-adaptive factors, including cultural, linguistic, gender, and socioeconomic factors.
- Genetic, medical, motor, sensory, and chronological age factors.

III. Delivery of Services to Students

Background knowledge, including

- Integrating best practices from multidisciplinary research and professional literature into the educational setting.

Curriculum and instruction and their implementation across the continuum of educational placements, including

- Instructional development and implementation.
- Teaching strategies and methods.
- Instructional format and components.
- Technology for teaching and learning in special education settings.

Video—"The Writing Process: Prewriting"

The teacher in this video uses prewriting activities to prepare students to write the first paragraph of a personal narrative.

Log onto **www.mylabschool.com**. Under the **Courses** tab, in **Language Arts,** go to the **video lab**. Access the "**Reading and Writing**" videos and watch the "**The Writing Process: Prewriting**" video.

 OR

Use the **www.mylabschool.com** **Assignment Finder** to go directly to these videos. Just enter Assignment ID **LA5.**

1. What prewriting activities does the teacher use in this video? How will each activity assist students in writing their personal narratives?

2. The chapter describes several problems that students with special needs may encounter during the prewriting stage of the writing process. What additional strategies could the teacher in this video use for students with special needs?

3. List three adaptations the teacher could make to the prewriting map in the video in order to use it effectively for students with dysgraphia.

Video—"The Writing Process: Editing"

In this video, a third-grade teacher confers with a student on a writing project. She explains how the students work on multiple skills with these projects.

Log onto **www.mylabschool.com**. Under the **Courses** tab, in **Language Arts,** go to the **video lab**. Access the "**Reading and Writing**" videos and watch the "**The Writing Process: Editing**" video.

 OR

Use the **www.mylabschool.com Assignment Finder** to go directly to these videos. Just enter Assignment ID **LA5**.

1. What is the goal of the editing stage and what types of problems might students with writing difficulties encounter during this stage?

2. In what ways do the methods used by the teacher in the video match the recommendations for editing provided in the chapter?

3. What additional techniques could a teacher use to teach editing skills to students?

Companion Website

To access chapter objectives, practice tests, weblinks, and flashcards, go to the companion website at www.ablongman.com/bryantsmith1e.

chapter 12

Teaching Mathematics

After studying this chapter, you will have the knowledge to answer the following questions:

- Who are students with mathematics difficulties?
- Who are mathematically gifted and talented students?
- How can teachers provide effective mathematics instruction?
- How can teachers make instructional adaptations for mathematics instruction?

● OPENING challenge

Helping Struggling Students Access the Mathematics Curriculum

Elementary Grades ● Ms. Hart is a third-grade teacher who teaches in a large urban school district. Her class of 23 students is ethnically and linguistically diverse and includes several students who have reading and mathematics problems. She has three English language learners who speak Spanish fluently at home with their families and qualify for English as a second language (ESL) support in school. After administering the school district's curriculum based assessment in mathematics, Ms. Hart learns that one-third of her students do not perform at the competent level on end-of-second-grade skills and concepts. Of those students, several are performing closer to first-grade level in basic skills. She is quite concerned about these results because she knows that third grade is the year that her students take the state's assessment in reading and mathematics. She realizes she must focus extra attention on the number and operations standards that are part of the school district's curriculum and that present the greatest challenges for her students. She starts thinking about her plan to help her students learn basic skills. *"I have to begin teaching the third-grade mathematics curriculum to all of my students. But I will provide extra instruction on basic*

column continues on next page

Secondary Grades ● Mrs. Reid is sitting at her desk after school reviewing her seventh-grade students' papers from the quiz on problem solving that she gave that day. She is using a problem-based approach to teaching the curriculum standards that are required by her school district. Her approach involves having students work in small groups to generate solutions to problems that require the use of measurement, geometry, and pre-algebra skills and concepts. She starts lessons with a quick vocabulary lesson, a review of what was taught the previous day, and introduction of materials for the day's lesson. She reflects on the quiz results. *"Of my 120 students that I teach each day, most of them got the majority of the problems correct. They used different strategies to solve the problems, which suggests that their group work helps them identify ways to solve problems correctly. But I have this stack of 32 papers where most of the answers are incorrect. A quick look at the students' work tells me that many of their mistakes are due to inaccurate calculations and faulty strategies. There are few pictorial representations to show how the data should be organized. In some cases, no work is shown, so*

column continues on next page

skills and concepts to my struggling students to give them the support that they will need to learn more advanced mathematics. I'll use word problems to reinforce student use of the basic number and operation skills so that they can apply what they learn to a problem situation. I know what I need to do, but how am I going to find time for the extra instruction in mathematics and reading? How can I use peer-mediated strategies to support my teaching? What should I do about monitoring the students' progress in mathematics? I am afraid that the language of mathematics might be an issue for some of my students, particularly my English language learners. I need more hours in the day!" ●

I don't know what they were thinking as they tried to solve the problems. Some problems weren't even attempted. Maybe they ran out of time. I've spent weeks on problems that focus on specific skills, yet some of my students aren't getting it. I am stumped about what to do next."

Ms. Hart and Mrs. Reid share a similar concern—they have a significant number of students in their classes who lack prerequisite skills to perform grade-level mathematics. These teachers must decide how to provide extra intervention for their students, what interventions to implement, and how to monitor student progress to determine whether the interventions are working. ●

● Reflection Questions

In your journal, write down your answers to the following questions. After completing the chapter, check your answers and revise them on the basis of what you have learned.

1. What mathematical learning characteristics might be contributing to the students' learning difficulties?

2. How can Ms. Hart and Mrs. Reid use the features of effective mathematics instruction to structure their lessons?

3. What instructional adaptations can be implemented to help students access the mathematics curriculum?

4. What suggestions do you have on ways in which these teachers can monitor student progress?

Mathematical literacy is the ability to use skills and concepts to reason, solve problems, and communicate about mathematical problems in the classroom and in everyday life (National Council of Teachers of Mathematics [NCTM], 1989). According to NCTM (2000) in that body's *Principles and Standards for School Mathematics*, "the need to understand and be able to use mathematics in everyday life and in the workplace has never been greater and will continue to increase" (p. 4). Moreover, NCTM noted in the *Standards* that "those who understand and can do mathematics will have significantly enhanced opportunities and options for shaping their futures. A lack of mathematical competence keeps those doors closed" (p. 5). Thus, the development and application of mathematical competence are important educational goals for *all* students. The NCTM *Standards* guide the states and districts in their development of mathematics curricula, instruction, and assessment. States, school districts, researchers, higher education teacher preparation faculty, and textbook publishers have embraced the *Standards* nationally. Most important, the *Standards* are reflected in states' accountability assessments, which are raising the stakes for student performance and high school graduation. Table 12.1 presents information about NCTM's (2000) *Principles and Standards for School Mathematics*.

TABLE 12.1 NCTM Content and Process Standards for Grades Pre-K–12

Content Standards

Number and Operations Standard

- Understand numbers, ways of representing numbers, relationships among numbers, and number systems.
- Understand meanings of operations and how they relate to one another.
- Compute fluently and make reasonable estimates.

Algebra Standard

- Understand patterns, relations, and functions.
- Represent and analyze mathematical situations and structures using algebraic symbols.
- Use mathematical models to represent and understand quantitative relationships.
- Analyze change in various contexts.

Geometry Standard

- Analyze characteristics and properties of two- and three-dimensional geometric shapes and develop mathematical arguments about geometric relationships.
- Specify locations and describe spatial relationships using coordinate geometry and other representational systems.
- Apply transformations and use symmetry to analyze mathematical situations.
- Use visualization, spatial reasoning, and geometric modeling to solve problems.

Measurement Standard

- Understand measurable attributes of objects and the units, systems, and processes of measurement.
- Apply appropriate techniques, tools, and formulas to determine measurements.

Data Analysis and Probability Standard

- Formulate questions that can be addressed with data and collect, organize, and display relevant data to answer them.
- Select and use appropriate statistical methods to analyze data.
- Develop and evaluate inferences and predictions that are based on data.
- Understand and apply basic concepts of probability.

Process Standards

Problem Solving Standard

- Build new mathematical knowledge through problem solving.
- Solve problems that arise in mathematics and in other contexts.
- Apply and adapt a variety of appropriate strategies to solve problems.
- Monitor and reflect on the process of mathematical problem solving.

Reasoning and Proof Standard

- Recognize reasoning and proof as fundamental aspects of mathematics.
- Make and investigate mathematical conjectures.
- Develop and evaluate mathematical arguments and proofs.
- Select and use various types of reasoning and methods of proof.

Communication Standard

- Organize and consolidate their mathematical thinking through communication.
- Communicate their mathematical thinking coherently and clearly to peers, teachers, and others.
- Analyze and evaluate the mathematical thinking and strategies of others.
- Use the language of mathematics to express mathematical ideas precisely.

Connections Standard

- Recognize and use connections among mathematical ideas.
- Understand how mathematical ideas interconnect and build on one another to produce a coherent whole.
- Recognize and apply mathematics in contexts outside of mathematics.

Representation Standard

- Create and use representations to organize, record, and communicate mathematical ideas.
- Select, apply, and translate among mathematical representations to solve problems.
- Use representations to model and interpret physical, social, and mathematical phenomena.

Source: National Council of Teachers of Mathematics, 2000, *Principles and standards for school mathematics.*
Available online at www.nctm.org/standards/. Reprinted with permission. All rights reserved.

WORKING together

Instructional Adaptations for Inquiry-Based Instruction

For each instructional adaptation category, initial instruction is described, and then examples of adaptations follow.

How can we adapt the instructional delivery?

- **Initial instructional delivery—Student-directed**
  Students figure out how to solve problems using their own solution strategies in a small-group setting.
- **Adapted instructional delivery—Teacher-directed**
  - Teachers demonstrate how to solve a problem by going through the steps of the process.
  - Teachers use "thinking aloud" to demonstrate the thinking processes for seeking problem solutions.

A "thinking aloud" character can be created and posted for the teacher to remind students that she is using the "thinking aloud" process to demonstrate how to use a cognitive strategy to solve certain problems or how to get started with an activity. "Thinking aloud" involves the teacher saying the steps she is using to start an activity and to solve a problem.

1. Teachers list specific steps for students to use, coupled with questions for solving a word problem. Key questions can include the following. (a) When reading the problem: "Are there words I don't know?" "Are there number words?" (b) When restating the problem: "What information is important?" "What is the question asking?" "What are the facts?" (c) When developing a plan: "How can I organize the facts?" "What operation will I use?" (d) When computing the answer: "What steps do I use?" "What is the answer?" "Did I get the same answer using the calculator?" (e) When determining the reasonableness of the answer: "Does this answer make sense with the information I used?"

2. Teachers distribute "Key Questions" sheets to help students solve a problem. For example, here are some key questions to use in dividing whole numbers: What does the problem say? What are the steps? What step did you just do? What step comes next?

- **Initial grouping:** Students are grouped in small, mixed-ability groups.
- **Adapted grouping**
  - Students are paired with higher-performing students to complete activities (peer-mediated strategy).
  - Students are paired into foursomes to share their ideas. They then turn to a new foursome and each group again shares its solutions.
  - Teachers use flexible grouping arrangements to allow for more instructional input for those stu-

In response to the *Standards*, mathematics instruction in many of today's classrooms focuses on an inquiry-based approach to solving mathematical problems (Baxter, Woodward, & Olson, 2001). Even though teachers teach computational skills, more time and effort are devoted to students interacting with their teachers and peers to develop multiple solution strategies for problems. Students share their mathematical reasoning and solutions with their teacher and peers during small-group or whole-class instruction (Baxter et al., 2001). Mathematics instruction focuses on activities that allow students to demonstrate their understanding of mathematical concepts (NCTM, 2000). With this inquiry-based approach to instruction, the general education teacher collaborates with the special education teacher to help struggling students access the mathematics lessons. The Working Together feature provides examples of instruction and how instructional adaptations for the four categories (delivery, materials, content, and activity) can be made during co-teaching when students need additional instructional support.

We know that mathematics instruction should involve approaches, activities, and interventions to teach mathematical skills and concepts that promote mathematics literacy for *all* students. It is important for teachers to challenge their students to achieve mathematical competence. It is equally important for teachers to

dents who require additional teacher assistance. For instance, some groups may include students who need extra help, whereas other groups are able to work independently.

- **Initial discourse**
  - Teachers ask students to think about different ways to solve problems.
  - Students discuss problems together.
  - Students share solution strategies with the whole class.
- **Adapted discourse**
  - Teachers provide specific questions for students to answer: "What if . . . ?" "How do you know . . . ?" "How can you show . . . ?" "What is another way to explain . . . ?" "What steps did you use to . . . ?"
  - Teachers have students write their responses in a journal. This ensures that every student has a chance to respond. The journal is a good alternative for students who prefer not to respond orally in class in front of their peers.

How can we adapt the instructional materials?

- **Initial materials—Abstract level:** Numbers, formulas
- **Adapted materials—**Concrete and pictorial levels

  - Calculators
  - Connecting cubes, base-10 blocks
  - Geoboards, protractors, three-dimensional shapes

- Fraction strips, fraction/decimal/percent equivalency charts
- Basic facts charts
- Number lines
- Place-value charts
- Graphic organizers
- Tallies

How can we adapt the instructional content?

- **Initial instructional content:** Teachers provide lessons to teach specific instructional objectives related to the *Standards.*
- **Adapted instructional content**
  - Teachers break tasks down into smaller steps and teach the steps.
  - Teachers teach the vocabulary of upcoming lessons.
- **Initial instructional content:** This is the lesson teachers provide to all students.
- **Adapted instructional content**

  Teachers provide "mini-lessons" on smaller steps of the original lesson.
  Teachers provide "mini-lessons" on requisite abilities.

Source: From Standards-based mathematics instruction and teaching middle school students with mathematical disabilities by D. P. Bryant, Sun A. Kim, P. Hartman, & B. R. Bryant, in M. Montague & A. Jitendra (Eds.), *Teaching Mathematics to Middle School Students with Learning Difficulties,* 2006, (pp. 7–28). New York: Guilford. Reprinted with permission.

provide appropriate instructional adaptations for those students who are most in need of academic assistance. For students with mathematical disabilities, adaptations are important to help them participate in classroom discussions and learn mathematical skills and concepts emphasized in the NCTM *Standards.*

In recent years, discussions about "number sense" have emerged as a way to emphasize the importance of conceptual reasoning using one's understanding of mathematical skills and concepts. Number sense means "a good intuition about numbers and their relationships. It develops gradually as a result of exploring numbers, visualizing them in a variety of contexts, and relating them in ways that are not limited by traditional algorithms" (Howden, 1989, p. 11). Number sense, then, includes the ability to understand the magnitude of numbers, facility with using mental computation, and the ability to employ appropriate representations (Gersten, Jordan, & Flojo, 2005; Okamoto & Case, 1996). As you read this chapter, keep in mind the idea of number sense and how it is developed and taught to students who have trouble learning mathematics. Some of their difficulties stem from number sense not having been developed. Through multiple opportunities to use representations to show and talk about numbers, students can develop this important number sense to help them reason mathematically.

In this chapter, you will learn about students with mathematics difficulties and students who are mathematically gifted and talented. You will learn about ways to provide effective mathematics instruction and ways to teach mathematics to struggling students using the ADAPT framework. Instructional activities and adaptations based on the ADAPT framework are provided to help you teach students who need extra instructional support.

Who Are Students with Mathematics Difficulties?

Research findings have shown that 5 to 8 percent of school-age children are identified as having a mathematics disability (Geary, 2004) and that some of these students have difficulties in both reading and mathematics instruction. In one survey, teachers reported that 26 percent of their students with learning disabilities (LD) received services primarily for mathematics difficulties encountered in the general education curriculum (McLeod & Armstrong, 1982).

Research on understanding what constitutes a mathematics disability and how it affects learning has lagged behind similar work in the area of reading disabilities. For example, compared to the research base in early reading difficulties, less attention has been paid to early difficulties in mathematics and to the identification of mathematics disability. Fortunately, this pattern is changing at the national and state levels. Increased research attention has focused on students who demonstrate challenges learning and applying mathematics skills and concepts. Research findings show that students struggle learning basic mathematics skills, mastering more advance mathematics (e.g., algebra), and solving math problems.

● Research findings have shown that 5 to 8 percent of school-age children are identified as having a mathematics disability.

Mathematics Difficulties

Mathematics difficulties appear to be persistent and evident across elementary and secondary levels and into adulthood (Garnett, 1987). For example, Gersten, Jordan, and Flojo (2005) examined the results from a series of studies that compared the abilities of young students in kindergarten through grade 2 who exhibited mathematics difficulties to the abilities of their typically achieving peers. Learning problems were noted in arithmetic combinations (i.e., basic facts), counting strategies (e.g., counting all, counting on), and number sense (e.g., basic counting techniques, understanding of size of number, number relationships). Gersten and colleagues found that over a period of time, limited mastery of arithmetic combinations (basic facts) was a "hallmark of mathematics difficulties" (Gersten et al., 2005). They suggested that difficulties learning arithmetic combinations seem to be a characteristic of a developmental difference that involves memory or cognitive problems (Geary, 2004).

In another study on mathematics difficulties, Bryant, Bryant, and Hammill (2000) asked a group of teachers who taught students with learning disabilities and mathematics difficulties to rate the frequency at which specific mathematical skills were problematic for their students. Rank-ordering their responses showed that certain mathematics problems were troublesome for students with mathematics weaknesses across ages. Not surprisingly, word problems were ranked as most problematic for students with learning disabilities and math weaknesses. Table 12.2 shows the ranking of mathematics difficulties of second- through eighth-grade students with learning disabilities and mathematics weaknesses.

TABLE 12.2 Rank-Ordering of Mathematics Difficulties Exhibited by Students with Learning Disabilities and Math Weaknesses

- Has difficulty with word problems
- Has difficulty with multistep problems
- Has difficulty with the language of math
- Fails to verify answers and settles for first answer
- Cannot recall number facts automatically
- Takes a long time to complete calculations
- Makes "borrowing" (i.e., regrouping, renaming) errors
- Counts on fingers
- Reaches "unreasonable" answers
- Calculates poorly when the order in which digits are presented is altered
- Orders and spaces numbers inaccurately in multiplication and division
- Misaligns vertical numbers in columns
- Disregards decimals
- Fails to carry (i.e., regroup) numbers when appropriate
- Fails to read the value of multidigit numbers accurately because of their order and spacing

- Misplaces digits in multidigit numbers
- Misaligns horizontal numbers in large numbers
- Skips rows or columns when calculating (i.e., loses his or her place)
- Makes errors when reading Arabic numbers aloud
- Experiences difficulties in the spatial arrangement of numbers
- Reverses numbers in problems
- Does not remember number words or digits
- Writes numbers illegibly
- Starts the calculation from the wrong place
- Cannot copy numbers accurately
- Exhibits left–right disorientation of numbers
- Omits digits on the left or right side of a number
- Does not recognize operator signs (e.g., +, −)

Source: Adapted from D. P. Bryant, B. Bryant, & D. Hammill, 2000, Characteristic behaviors of students with LD who have teacher-identified math weaknesses, *Journal of Learning Disabilities, 33*(2), 168–177. Adapted by permission.

Finally, we know that the mathematics performance of struggling students can plateau at the fifth- to sixth-grade level. Such stunted achievement can affect the ability to learn curriculum presented at the secondary level and the ability to master mathematics competence that are critical for living in today's society (Cawley, Baker-Kroczynski, & Urban, 1992; Cawley & Miller, 1989).

Factors Contributing to Mathematics Difficulties

Several factors have been identified that contribute to mathematics difficulties. First, language difficulties can interfere with reading and understanding the vocabulary of the curriculum. For instance, students must understand the meaning of terms and symbols related to mathematics instruction. Years ago, Wiig and Semel (1984) referred to mathematics as "conceptually dense," which means that students must understand the meaning of each mathematical symbol and word because context clues, such as appear in reading, are limited or nonexistent. Abstract symbols (e.g., Σ, σ, π, $\geq$) have precise meanings, and all must be understood in order to solve problems. Take $4 < 9$, for example, the student must understand each symbol to decide whether this number statement is true or false. You can spend time

Considering *Diversity*

Focusing on the Language of Mathematics for English Language Learners

English language learners (ELLs) from diverse backgrounds who have learning problems also may find the language of mathematics problematic. Scott and Raborn (1996) identified the linguistic and symbolic features of mathematics as "tricky spots" because words may be used in unfamiliar ways (e.g., *odd* and *even*), structural relationships between words and syntax must be discerned (e.g., relationship of adjectives and nouns in sentence structure), and algorithmic formats (e.g., reading from left to right or from top to bottom) may be contrary to cultural procedures. Therefore, teachers must be sure that *all* students have the necessary semantic, linguistic, and symbolic understanding of the mathematics concepts and skills presented for instruction. Scott and Raborn offer the following pointers to help English language learners acquire the vocabulary of mathematics.

- Provide math instruction in the primary language if the student is stronger in math than in English.

- Identify the terms most frequently used in math instruction. Help the student learn these words in English or in the student's primary language. Refer to information about vocabulary instruction elsewhere in this book for strategies to teach word meanings.
- Use different ways (e.g., gesturing, pictures, rewording) to communicate.
- Create story problems that are relevant to the student's personal cultural identity.
- Share examples of the math heritage of various cultural groups.
- Have students develop picture files of new vocabulary.
- Provide games (e.g., Concentration, Go Fish, Jeopardy) to teach and review abstract symbols (e.g., $\leq$, Σ, π, $\%$, $=$, $>$, $<$, $\neq$).

Source: Adapted from P. Scott & D. Raborn, 1996, Realizing the gifts of diversity among students with learning disabilities. *LD Forum*, 21(2), 7–29.

during mathematics lessons teaching and reviewing this symbolic language. Posting the symbols with a brief explanation is a good reference tool for students.

Language difficulties are also noted in the inability to read and comprehend word problems, including understanding what the problem is asking, understanding the sentence structure, and identifying extraneous information (Rivera, 1997). The language of word problems is another area that requires instructional time. Sometimes the syntax (grammar) is misunderstood or the word meanings are unknown. Consequently, difficulties with syntax and word meaning can affect students' ability to solve problems successfully.

The language and symbolism of mathematics must be taught directly as part of a mathematics lesson (Capps & Cox, 1991). This is especially true for secondary-level students, who are often faced with abstract mathematical concepts, such as algebra and geometry, that require a solid foundation of mathematical skills (e.g., computation, mathematical properties) and language. Teaching ideas include (a) determine prerequisite symbols, syntactic language, and word meanings for the lesson; (b) determine current student understanding of this language; (c) provide explicit instruction to teach the language; and (d) include sufficient practice and review.

We also know that for many English language learners, the language of mathematics may be an obstacle to learning mathematical skills and concepts. Think back to Ms. Hart's concerns about her English language learners in the Opening Challenge. She needs ideas for helping her students learn the language of mathematics. Refer to the Considering Diversity feature to learn about ways to enhance vocabulary development for English language learners. Also, Table 12.3 provides examples of the language or vocabulary associated with mathematics curricula. For struggling students and English language learners, the preview and review of

TABLE 12.3 Examples of Vocabulary Terms for Mathematics Instruction

Addend	Equivalent	Linear	Place value	Second
Area	Estimate	Logarithmic	Polynomial	Sort
Circle	Exponent	Least common denominator	Positive	Square
Circumference	Expression	Magnitude	Product	Square root
Coefficient	Fraction	Matrix	Proper fraction	Sum
Commutative	Function	Minus	Proportion	Symmetry
Coordinate	Greater than	Minute	Pyramid	Theorem
Decimal	Greatest common factor	Month	Ratio	Tomorrow
Denominator		Negative	Rational	Triangle
Diagonal	Improper fraction	Notation	Rectangle	Variable
Diameter	Integer	Numerator	Regrouping	Vectors
Dividend	Inverse	Pattern	Relationship	Volume
Divisor	Isosceles	Percent	Remainder	Yesterday
Equal	Length	Perimeter	Right angle	Zero
Equation	Less than		Round	

new terms are critical. Consider using the instruction ideas for teaching vocabulary found in Chapters 10 and 13 for teaching the language of mathematics.

Second, problems with memory and executive functioning contribute to mathematics difficulties (Hallahan, Lloyd, Kauffman, Weiss, & Martinez, 2005). Working memory entails processing and storing information simultaneously. Long-term memory is the permanent storage of information, which may be by the way information is stored. Executive functioning is the ability to self-monitor by using working memory, inner speech, attention, and rehearsal (Swanson, Cooney, & O'Shaughnessy, 1998). Students who have memory problems (Garnett & Fleischner, 1983) and who process information slowly (Geary, 1993) lack the automatic ability to remember arithmetic combinations (i.e., facts). Memory difficulties can also influence the child's ability to recall the steps that are needed to solve more difficult word problems in the upper grades (Bryant et al., 2000), to recall the steps in solving algebraic equations, or to remember what specific symbols mean. It is common to hear a teacher say, "He knew the math facts yesterday, but he just can't seem to remember them today." Memory difficulties play an important role in how successfully students can perform mathematical operations.

Third, cognitive developmental problems contribute to mathematics difficulties. Cognitive development involves understanding and using declarative knowledge (understanding of factual information), procedural knowledge (knowledge of rules and procedures), and conceptual knowledge (understanding of relationships). Difficulties with cognitive development are seen in problems with understanding number systems, noting relationships among numbers (e.g., fractions and decimals), solving word problems, and using calculation strategies (e.g., counting on, near doubles) (Geary, 1990).

The concrete-semiconcrete-abstract (CSA) teaching sequence is an example of how instruction can be delivered to help students understand the abstract nature of mathematics and to develop conceptual understanding. The CSA teaching sequence was examined as a way to teach place value (Peterson, Mercer, & O'Shea, 1988) and arithmetic combinations (Miller & Mercer, 1993; Miller, Mercer, & Dillon, 1992). Research results indicated that students learned the skills to the criterion level, which suggests that the CSA teaching procedure is highly effective for some students with learning disabilities and mathematics difficulties. The CSA technique can also be applied to the teaching of rational numbers such as fractions (Butler, Miller, Crehan, Babbitt, & Pierce, 2003). An example of this research-based teaching procedure is presented in What Works 12.1.

Finally, visuospatial problems may interfere with a student's ability to solve mathematics problems correctly. Examples of visuospatial difficulties include misaligning numerals in columns for calculation, having trouble with place value, and having difficulty interpreting maps and understanding geometry (Geary, 2004).

Dyscalculia

Dyscalculia refers to problems in learning mathematics skills and concepts. The term means "a severe or complete inability to calculate" (Hallahan et al., 2005, p. 457). However, the terms *learning disabilities in mathematics* and *mathematics disability* are more widely used today. According to the Individuals with Disabilities Education Act of 2004, a learning disability can be identified in mathematics calculation and/or mathematics problem solving. Students with math

what WORKS 12.1

Concrete-Semiconcrete-Abstract

The concrete-semiconcrete-abstract teaching procedure involves several steps.

STEP 1. *Concrete:* Use manipulatives to physically represent a number concept or skill being taught, such as whole-number computation of addition with regrouping. Refer to Figure 12.1 for examples of manipulatives and materials for mathematics instruction.

STEP 2. *Semiconcrete:* After several lessons where students achieve 90 percent accuracy on problems using manipulatives, change the representation to semiconcrete. Use pictorial representations such as tally marks or pictures of base-10 materials for several lessons.

STEP 3. *Abstract:* After several lessons where students achieve 90 percent accuracy on problems using pictorial representations, change the representation to abstract. Have students solve problems that employ only numbers but are otherwise similar to those presented in step 1 and step 2. Again, expect 90 percent accuracy for the problems presented.

The following instructional procedures are used to guide students through the CSA process.

The CSA teaching procedures begin with the teacher providing an advance organizer about the purpose of the lesson. Next, the teacher models how to solve the problem, while verbalizing the steps ("thinking aloud"). The teacher asks questions, such as "What is the first thing that I do?" Then guided practice is implemented. Students work on several problems, and the teacher provides prompts and cues. A prompt might go something like this: "You have the correct number of blocks for the first number. Now which number do you look at?" Corrective feedback and assistance are provided immediately. Finally, students work independently to complete ten problems. To solve problems during guided practice, students use manipulatives in the concrete phase, tallies are used in the semiconcrete phase, and in the abstract phase, students are instructed to solve the problem using only numerals.

calculation difficulties may demonstrate problems with some or most of the following skills:

- Identifying the meaning of signs (e.g., $+$, $-$, $\times$, $<$, $=$, $>$, %, Σ)
- Remembering answers to basic arithmetic combinations (e.g., $8 + 9 = ?$, $7 \times 7 = ?$)
- Using effective counting strategies to calculate answers to arithmetic problems
- Understanding the commutative property (e.g., $5 + 3 = 8$ and $3 + 5 = 8$)
- Solving multidigit calculations that require regrouping
- Misaligning numbers
- Ignoring decimal points

Difficulty solving word problems can be observed in any of the following skills:

- Reading the problem
- Understanding the meaning of the sentences

FIGURE 12.1
Examples of Manipulatives and Materials for Mathematics Instruction

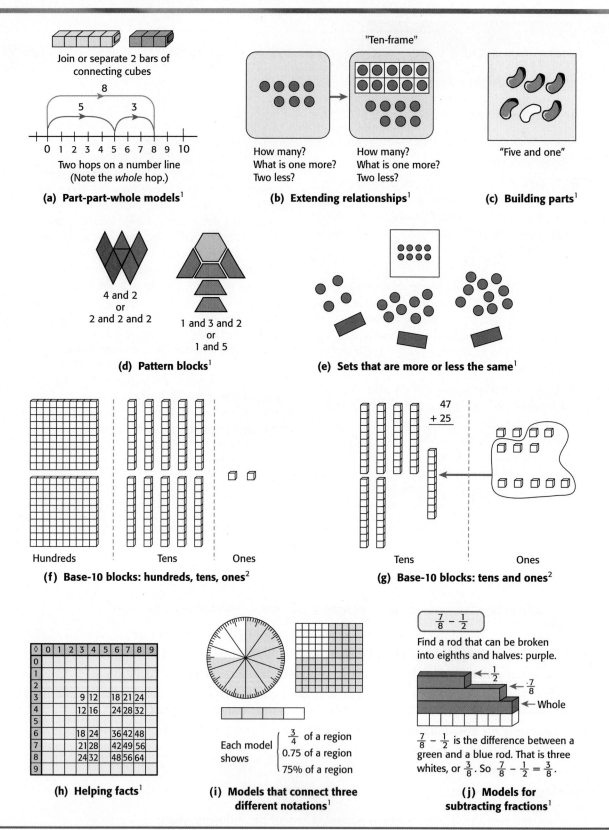

Join or separate 2 bars of connecting cubes

Two hops on a number line
(Note the *whole* hop.)

(a) Part-part-whole models[1]

"Ten-frame"

How many?
What is one more?
Two less?

How many?
What is one more?
Two less?

(b) Extending relationships[1]

"Five and one"

(c) Building parts[1]

4 and 2
or
2 and 2 and 2

1 and 3 and 2
or
1 and 5

(d) Pattern blocks[1]

(e) Sets that are more or less the same[1]

Hundreds Tens Ones

(f) Base-10 blocks: hundreds, tens, ones[2]

47
+ 25

Tens Ones

(g) Base-10 blocks: tens and ones[2]

(h) Helping facts[1]

Each model shows
$\frac{3}{4}$ of a region
0.75 of a region
75% of a region

(i) Models that connect three different notations[1]

$\frac{7}{8} - \frac{1}{2}$

Find a rod that can be broken into eighths and halves: purple.

$\frac{1}{2}$
$\frac{7}{8}$
Whole

$\frac{7}{8} - \frac{1}{2}$ is the difference between a green and a blue rod. That is three whites, or $\frac{3}{8}$. So $\frac{7}{8} - \frac{1}{2} = \frac{3}{8}$.

(j) Models for subtracting fractions[1]

Sources: [1]Adapted from J. A. Van de Walle, 2007, *Elementary and Middle School Mathematics: Teaching Developmentally* (6th ed.) (pp. 116, 124, 125, 129, 139, 171, 267, 289). Boston: Allyn and Bacon. [2]From P. Hudson and S. P. Miller, 2006, *Designing and Implementing Mathematics Instruction for Students with Diverse Learning Needs* (pp. 222, 237). Boston: Allyn and Bacon.

- Understanding what the problem is asking
- Identifying extraneous information that is not required for solving the problem
- Developing and implementing a plan for solving the problem
- Solving multiple steps in advanced word problems
- Using the correct calculations to solve problems

Let's turn our attention next to students who are mathematically gifted and talented.

Who Are Mathematically Gifted and Talented Students?

It is not only students who have difficulty with mathematics, but also students with unusual math aptitude, who need teachers' special attention to achieve their full potential.

Learning Characteristics

Students who are mathematically gifted and talented exhibit a variety of characteristics that can challenge teachers to respond appropriately to their students' academic capabilities during typical mathematics instruction. For example, some teachers may be surprised that mathematically gifted and talented students have uneven mathematical development and conceptual understanding (Rotigel & Fello, 2004). This means that some students may do very well with abstract reasoning in solving problems but lack proficiency with basic computational skills (Rotigel, 2000). In this case, it is important to balance computational instruction with mathematics instruction that offers advanced problem solving opportunities, such as algebraic reasoning. Although you may spend less time teaching computational skills to the point of mastery than on algebraic problem solving, you still need to ensure that students can compute proficiently.

On the other hand, teachers are probably not surprised to know that students who are mathematically gifted and talented are quite adept at inferential thinking skills (reasoning skills), deductive reasoning (reasoning from the general to the specific), and problem solving (Rotigel & Fello, 2004). These students also possess intuitive abilities that enable them to reach solutions with speed and accuracy. This suggests that they don't need all of the steps of formal mathematics instruction that most students, particularly at-risk students and students with mathematics disabilities, require (Greenes, 1981; Heid, 1983).

Teachers can offer their brightest students, who may be identified as mathematically gifted and talented, challenging activities that tap their intellectual ability. We know that mathematically gifted and talented students benefit from differentiated instruction that focuses on enrichment programs and resources to help them reach their potential (NCTM, 2000; VanTassel-Baska, 1998).

Differentiating Instruction

Students who are mathematically gifted and talented begin formal schooling in kindergarten with already developed mathematical "number sense." Consequently, the early mathematics curriculum (with its emphasis on counting principles, simple geometry, number recognition, and patterns) contains skills and

what WORKS 12.2

Differentiate Instruction

- Assessment

- Pre-assess students before teaching to avoid making students repeat material they already know. Instead, provide them with activities that enrich current objectives.

- Conduct a variety of assessments that give students opportunities to demonstrate understanding in creative ways. Students should be required to explain their thinking in a variety of ways, including written and orally.

- To avoid boredom, conduct ongoing assessments so that enrichment is provided once students demonstrate mastery.

- Curriculum and Resources

- Select textbooks that include enrichment activities to extend stimulate the reasoning and thinking of those students who benefit from a challenging curriculum. Consider textbooks that emphasize an inquiry-based approach to instruction for your gifted and talented students.

- Include speakers, Web-based activities, connections with math and science organizations, and professional organizations that focus on the academic and emotional needs of gifted and talented students.

- Work on basic skills along with more complex, higher-order thinking skills, because elementary students must learn the basics as well.

- Ensure that the school curriculum includes advanced placement courses in calculus, statistics, and computer science.

- Establish partnerships with local colleges so that gifted students can take classes that will count toward their higher-education degree.

- Enroll students in contests such as Mathematical Olympiads for the Elementary School (grades 4–6), Math Counts (grades 7–8), and the American Junior High School Mathematics Exam (grades 7–8) or the American High School Mathematics Exam (grades 9–12).

- Establish a mentoring program linking students with community experts who represent diverse linguistic and cultural groups.

- Instructional Practices

- Consider variations in pacing for different needs of students. Some students may be ready to move on to other activities such as enrichment or extension lessons, whereas others may require additional support.

- Focus on inquiry-based learning experiences that include open-ended problems that allow for multiple solution strategies. Challenge students by allowing them to discover ways to solve complex problems.

- Use lots of higher-level questions in justification of problems. Ask "why" and "what if" questions.

- Provide instructional activities that include challenging games and puzzles.

- Differentiate activities. Merely providing more of the same types of problems does not challenge gifted and talented students. Provide choices in activities at different ability levels.

- Provide concrete experiences. Students who are gifted and talented benefit from the use of manipulatives and "hands-on" activities.

- Ensure that students use calculators as an exploration tool to solve complex problems. The graphing calculator or scientific calculator can facilitate advanced data analysis.

- Create opportunities for students to use databases, spreadsheets, and other types of electronic software that are employed in research, including statistics and data analyses.

- Grouping

- Provide activities that can be done independently and shared within groups for feedback.

- Provide homogeneous grouping by ability with some activities to allow gifted and talented students the opportunity to work together on challenging problems. This grouping practice will promote interaction with other gifted students.

Source: Adapted from D. T. Johnson, 2000, Teaching mathematics to gifted students in a mixed-ability classroom, *ERIC Digest E94* (ERIC Document Reproduction Service No. ED441302).

concepts that these students already understand. As students progress through the grades, they can benefit from more depth and breadth of topics and from open-ended experiences where multiple approaches can be identified for solving complex problems (Sheffield, 1994). Activities that challenge students to think about and discuss the "how," "why," and "what if" of mathematical situations offer more appropriate instruction to meet their academic capabilities (Sheffield, 1994).

By becoming knowledgeable about these students' characteristics and working with a specialist who knows how to plan for these students, you can successfully address their mathematical potential. Differentiating instruction for students who are mathematically gifted and talented involves additional resources, small-group interaction, and modification of lessons (Tomlinson, 1995). Experts who focus on this field recommend the following areas in which to differentiate instruction for this group of students: (a) assessment, (b) curriculum and resources, (c) instructional practices, and (d) grouping (Johnson, 2000). What Works 12.2 provides examples of ways in which instruction can be differentiated to meet the unique learning abilities of this group of students. Next, we will look at early number development.

What Is Early Number Development and How Do I Teach It?

Early number development involves a variety of skills and concepts that typically emerge and are taught in preschool, kindergarten, and first grade. The ability to count is a crucial skill that many young children develop well before they enter formal schooling in kindergarten. Through informal experiences at home, on the playground, and in the grocery store, young children are frequently exposed to counting principles. Along with basic knowledge about counting, young children acquire the vocabulary that describes mathematical relationships. They use "more" to ask for another cookie and "all gone" when the cookies are finished. They may hear an adult ask, "Do you want another cookie?" or "Do you want one more cookie?" Their experiences with objects teach the early language of mathematics via physical representations that children understand. Finally, young children often know how to read and write some numerals, such as 1, 2, and 3.

Numbers may be paired with objects in sets so that children are counting objects, saying how many, and selecting the numeral that represents the count. Children may be asked by a preschool teacher or parent to make the number 1. Although markings may be rudimentary at the early stage, children are hearing, representing, seeing, and writing numbers. It is through these types of informal experiences with their environment, the media, other children, and adults that young children develop the early understanding about mathematical concepts from which more formal instruction evolves.

● Experience with objects, such as the manipulatives used by these students, teach the early language of mathematics using physical representations that children understand.

Difficulties with Early Number Development

Students who demonstrate difficulty with early number development exhibit problems with many of the following skills: counting in order, knowing that the last number named is the number of objects in a set, knowing that the result is the same no matter how sets are counted, and demonstrating one-to-one correspondence. Counting up and back two or three numbers from a given number and understanding "bigger than" and "less than" in number magnitude are other important skills that may be problematic. Number reversals may persist long after instruction in writing numbers has occurred. Initial place-value activities may be difficult. For example, problems may arise when using the ten-frame (see Figure 12.1 on page 488 for an example) to show the concept of 10 to find that 2 more are needed with 8 to make 10. Finally, reading, writing, and representing the teen numbers are consistently problematic for struggling students (Bley & Thornton, 2001).

Teaching Early Number Development

We will begin with some general notes on teaching early number development and then look more closely at several specific skills.

- **Diagnosis:** Conduct an informal assessment asking students to read and write numerals, count objects, count from memory, and tell how many are in a group. Use the results to help you determine early number skills and focus beginning instruction in early number development.

- **Instructional content—Comparing and grouping objects:** Provide many opportunities for students to show set equivalency, to make groups based on problems, and to decompose (take apart) larger numbers into smaller sets. Use story problems for students to form and manipulate sets. Pair number symbols with groupings to reinforce the connection between concrete representations and abstract symbols.

- **Instructional content—Reading and writing numerals:** Pair instruction of reading numerals with writing numerals. Writing proficiency may take longer to master as young children learn how to hold the pencil correctly and make correct stroke formations. Provide models of correctly written numerals, including directional arrows for stroke formation. Do not allow messy work, because if you do, it will persist throughout the school years.

- **Instructional materials—Place value and the ten-frame:** Use the ten-frame frequently to help students make and see the concept of ten. Use two ten-frames to build the teen numbers. Use a five-frame initially for students who struggle with the ten-frame.

- **Instructional materials:** Use counting cubes, number lines, ten-frames, and objects for counting, comparing, grouping, and decomposing activities, number magnitude, number sequencing, and number recognition. Refer to Figure 12.1 for examples of manipulatives and materials.

- **Language:** Provide multiple opportunities for students to use the language of mathematics. See Table 12.3 on page 485 for examples of the language to emphasize. Model the use of these terms, such as *same, equal, more,* and *less,* in early number development activities.

- **Fluency and progress monitoring:** Build fluent responding for number recognition and number writing. Use flashcards for "fact numbers," where students see the number and respond within 3 seconds ("look and say"). Focus instruction on numbers that are not named rapidly. Use "quick write," where students write numbers in sequence, beginning with 0, for 1 minute. Count the number of correctly formed numerals. Then focus instruction on those numerals that are not in order or are not written correctly.

COUNTING   Develop basic counting skills. Conduct warm-ups by giving students a number and having them count up "two more" or count back "two less." Have students tap the count or show fingers so that they get the count right. This builds counting skills and reinforces the concepts of more and less. Give students two groups of objects. Have them count the first group and place it in a cup. Then, beginning with the last number named "in the cup," have them count on the second group of objects. This develops the "counting on" strategy. Have students count groups of objects, and then say, "How many?" This builds the counting principles of one-to-one correspondence and cardinality.

TEEN NUMBERS   Tell students that they will learn the names of the teen numbers and how to write them. Teach 14, 16, 17, 18, and 19 first by emphasizing that you say the second number first such as four-teen. Try "fast numbers" with these five numbers; that is, the student looks and says the number quickly (within 3 seconds). Once students know these numbers, move to 13 and 15. Tell students how to read thir-teen and fif-teen. Once students know these two numbers, mix them up with the other five numbers. Next, teach 11 and 12. They are not teen numbers but fall in the 10–20 number range. Tell students that they just have to learn these numbers by sight. Once students know these two numbers, mix them up with the other teen numbers. Pair the reading and writing of the teen numbers with making the numbers in the ten-frame during instruction. Have students name the numbers out of order and write them when dictated. Conduct magnitude comparison activities (see below) with these numbers.

MAGNITUDE COMPARISON   Give students two numbers and have them tell which number is bigger, smaller, more, or less than the other number. At first provide numbers that are further apart, such as 3 and 8, 22 and 36, or 105 and 116. Then provide numbers that are closer together, such as 9 and 11, 28 and 30, or 111 and 115. Focus on the teen numbers and on numbers with 0, such as 50, 106, and 207. For smaller numbers, have students use cubes to make trains or use the number line to show magnitude. For larger numbers, have students use the 100's chart to explain number magnitude. Connect magnitude comparison with place-value activities (see below).

NUMERAL RECOGNITION: FAST NUMBERS   Show students the number cards 0 through 5. Model "Look and Say" quickly. Implement error correction if needed. If the incorrect response is given, provide the correct response right away. Put correctly named number cards in one pile and incorrectly named number cards in another pile. Spend more time on the incorrect pile. Have students say numbers quickly for 30 seconds to see how many they can get right. Increase the range of numbers gradually. Keep numbers done correctly in a special pile that is presented once a week to be sure students can still name those numbers quickly.

NUMERAL WRITING: QUICK WRITE   Have students write numbers, beginning with zero, for 1 minute . After the timing, have students count the number of numerals written. Numerals that are written backwards, are very messy, or are not in sequence are considered errors. Provide error correction for those numerals that are counted as errors by providing a number line for students to see how numerals are written correctly. Have students graph the number of numerals they can write correctly in 1 minute. This is a good warm-up activity and can be done several times a week.

REVERSALS   Reversals may occur with single-digit numerals, such as 6 for 9, and with multidigit numbers, such as 24 for 42. Give students many opportunities to practice writing numerals correctly using a variety of materials. Use stencils for tracing, models of correctly formed numerals, and models with directional cues showing where to start making the numeral and in what direction to go. Have students correct reversals.

PART-PART-WHOLE RELATIONSHIPS   Having students identify ways to compose and decompose numbers is a foundation skill that helps students think about the concept of numbers. The part-part-whole and missing-parts relationships are the building blocks for learning arithmetic combinations and solving word problems. It is important for students to develop an understanding of these relationships; however, some students may have difficulty doing so. The ADAPT framework can be employed for these students. An example is provided in ADAPT Framework 12.1.

12.1 **ADAPT Framework** Part-Part-Whole

A ASK "What am I requiring the student to do?"	**D** DETERMINE the prerequisite skills of the task.	**A** ANALYZE the student's strengths and struggles.		**P** PROPOSE and implement adaptations from among the four categories.	**T** TEST to determine if the adaptations helped the student to accomplish the task.
		Strengths	Struggles		
The students will build the number 8 using the ten-frame and two different-colored cubes. I have two students who may demonstrate problems with this task.	1. Understands that the ten-frame represents ten ones.	1		**For 1. No adaptation needed** The students can say the name of the material: ten-frame.	
	2. Counts 8 cubes.		2	**For 2. Content** Focus on the number 5. Counting 8 cubes was too difficult. **Material** Use just cubes.	**For 2.** Give a number and have students count out cubes. Ask students, "What number?" They should tell the last number named.
	3. Represents the number 8 in different groupings or parts using the cubes and the ten-frame.		3	**For 3. Instruction/Material** Provide more prompts "Show me another way" to make 5. Model the commutative property, showing 4 + 1 = 1 + 4 by using the colored cubes and the five-frame. Make 5 with 4 + 1; then turn the frame around so that students see 1 + 4 also equals 5. **Instructional Content** Provide multiple opportunities to practice using numbers up to 5; then gradually increase to 6, 7, and 8.	**For 3.** Give students a number and have them make the number using cubes and the five-frame. Record the number of ways they can represent a number; all possibilities should be shown by students.

Arithmetic combinations are often difficult for students. In the next section we will examine ways to teach them.

What Are Arithmetic Combinations and How Do I Teach Them?

Instruction in arithmetic combinations (sometimes called basic facts) consists of developing knowledge and understanding. Students need to develop declarative and procedural knowledge and conceptual understanding. Arithmetic combinations include 100 addition, subtraction, and multiplication facts and 90 division facts (Hudson & Miller, 2006). In the elementary grades, students are taught strategies for learning these arithmetic combinations, so most students remember the answers automatically. These students demonstrate computational fluency with arithmetic combinations. Computational fluency consists of knowing and using efficient methods for accurate computing (NCTM, 2000). However, for students who find mathematics challenging, computational fluency with arithmetic combinations remains a persistent problem (Geary, 2004; Jordan, Hanich, & Kaplan, 2003).

Difficulties with Arithmetic Combinations

Difficulty with learning and remembering arithmetic combinations is a typical problem among students who struggle with mathematics and students who are identified as having mathematics disabilities. Problems in retrieval of arithmetic combinations seem to inhibit the ability to grasp the more complex algebraic concepts that are taught in later years (Geary, 2004; Jordan et al., 2003). Lack of efficient and effective counting strategies (e.g., counting on and counting back) is another problem commonly associated with arithmetic combinations and students who struggle with mathematics (Gersten, Jordan, & Flojo, 2005). These students require instruction to develop both conceptual understanding of arithmetic combinations and procedural knowledge to figure out the answers. We know that instruction for struggling students is most enhanced through the use of physical, visual, and abstract representations of arithmetic combinations.

Teaching Arithmetic Combinations

Let's begin with some general notes and then look more closely at some specific skills.

- **Diagnosis:** Assess to determine which arithmetic combinations are known as "fast facts" and which are not. Use observation and clinical interviews to determine what strategies (for example, counting on fingers) the students use to solve facts when a quick response is not provided. The clinical interview is a procedure to examine a student's knowledge of and thinking about how to solve problems (Ginsberg & Pappas, 2004).
- **Instructional content—Sequence:** Teach arithmetic combinations systematically. Although there is no "best" sequence, you should generally teach easier

FIGURE 12.2　Card Reader Notched Card Example

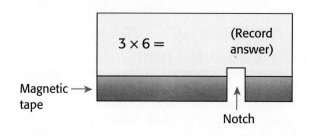

Source: From D. Rivera and B. R. Bryant, 1992, Mathematics instruction for students. *Intervention in School Clinic,* *28*(2), p. 82. Reprinted with permission.

strategies first (count on $+0, +1, +2, +3$; count back or down $-0, -1, -2, -3$; doubles $-4+4$). Then teach turnaround combinations (for example: $1+4 = 4 + 1$, also known as the commutative property) for addition. Teach fact families $(5 + 3, 3 + 5, 8 - 3, 8 - 5)$ once some addition facts are mastered.

- **Instructional content—Decomposition:** Present multiple opportunities for students to practice decomposition of numbers to solve arithmetic problems. For example, students can use the "doubles $+ 1$" strategy to arrive at the answer for $7 + 8$: What double is in $7 + 8$? $7 + 7$. What is double $+ 1$? $7 + 7 + 1 = 15$, so $7 + 8 = 15$.

- **Acquisition:** For students who are learning facts, practice is an important component of instruction. For teachers, such as Ms. Hart in the Opening Challenge, who are looking for ways to give students more practice, students can use the card reader machine to engage in much-needed extra practice. As seen in Figure 12.2, a fact is written (and recorded) on a card with a notch. When inserted into the machine, the card stops at the notch, giving the student time to answer the problem. Then the card can be pushed through the machine to reveal the prerecorded answer.

- **Fluency:** Conduct 1-minute timings ("fast facts") on arithmetic combinations to build fluency. Show flash cards with combinations and give students up to 3 seconds to say the answer (no fingers). Facts that are not answered quickly remain in the practice pile.

- **Generalization:** Promote generalization by having students answer problems with mixed signs and whole-number computational problems.

In Adapt in Action, Ms. Hart uses the ADAPT framework to help students who have difficulty with some addition combinations.

Ms. Hart—
ADAPT in Action • Arithmetic Combinations

Ms. Hart is concerned about three students who have not learned addition combinations to 18. Through informal diagnostic teaching, Ms. Hart notes that the three students can recognize and write numerals quickly. They can also solve simple addition combinations, including sums to 10 and "doubles." However, more difficult combinations involving sums to 11 through 18 are challenging for the students. Ms. Hart uses a clinical interview procedure wherein she asks each student to "think aloud" how they would solve problems such as 7 + 4, 8 + 6, and 9 + 7. Consistently, the three students read the first number and use their fingers to count on to arrive at the solution. Ms. Hart recalls from her teacher preparation program that "counting on" is a good strategy when students are first learning some facts, particularly when one addend is 1, 2, or 3. But it is not an efficient procedural strategy to solve harder combinations. She decides to teach the three students the Make Ten Plus More strategy. Keep in mind that Ms. Hart has other students who have trouble with more difficult addition combinations, so they too may benefit from the adaptations. Also, Ms. Hart can use this lesson for any of her students who are still not proficient with addition combinations. Instructional Activity 12.1 shows the Make Ten Plus More strategy.

Following the lesson, Ms. Hart reviews the progress-monitoring data for each student. She learns that an important concept of "Ten Plus More" is missing for the students. She decides to use the ADAPT framework to make decisions about the next steps for instruction.

Ask, "What am I requiring the student to do?" Ms. Hart wants the students to add combinations with sums 11 to 18. She wants them to show the addition strategy using concrete representations (ten-frames and counters). The students can make ten but cannot say automatically what "Ten Plus More" equals. This is an important step in solving harder addition combinations.

Determine the prerequisite skills of the task. "I know students need to decompose one number to make 10 and know how much to add to get to 10. Students also need to be able to say the answer to "Ten plus ? equals."

Analyze the student's strengths and struggles. The students did a good job of listening and using the ten-frames to make ten. However, quickly saying the answer to "Ten plus a number equals what number?" was problematic. For example, quickly saying 10 + 3 = 13 or 10 + 6 = 16 was difficult for the students.

Propose and implement adaptations from among the four categories. Ms. Hart decides to adapt the Make Ten Plus More lesson by teaching a lesson just on "Ten Plus More" (instructional content). She will have students use the ten-frames and counters to show 10 + more and to tell what number. She will then put these combinations on flash cards and have students say the answers quickly.

Test to determine if the adaptations helped the student accomplish the task. Ms. Hart will continue to collect progress-monitoring data to determine whether the reduced instructional content helps the students learn the Ten Plus More strategy. Then she will return to Make Ten Plus More and add a "fast facts" component to progress monitoring.

PROCEDURAL STRATEGIES   Teach strategies that are most efficient to use with specific types of arithmetic combinations. Table 12.4 presents a list of strategies and gives examples of arithmetic combinations for each strategy. Examine What Works 12.3 on page 501 for examples of teaching procedures, progress monitoring, and prerequisite abilities and adaptations for procedural strategies.

Instructional activity 12.1

Make Ten Plus More

INSTRUCTIONAL OBJECTIVE: The students will compute addition combinations with 7, 8, or 9 as one of the addends.

INSTRUCTIONAL CONTENT: NCTM Standards—Number & Operations: Whole Number Computation—Arithmetic Combinations (Building Conceptual & Procedural Knowledge)

INSTRUCTIONAL MATERIALS: Ten-frames; red counters and blue counters, mat

INSTRUCTIONAL DELIVERY

Grouping: Small group of students

Vocabulary: Turnaround combination
Before teaching the lesson, review the concept of turnaround combination. Give students examples, have students provide examples, and have students explain why the answer remains the same regardless of the sequence in which the elements of the addition fact is presented (e.g., 9 + 4 = 4 + 9).

Teaching Procedure

1. Tell students they are going to learn a strategy to add big numbers up to 18. These facts have big numbers. Show fact cards: 9 + 8, 9 + 7, 8 + 7, 8 + 6, 7 + 9, 7 + 8. Explain that the strategy is called Make Ten Plus More. This strategy can be used when the problem has 7, 8, or 9 as one addend.
   - **Instructional sequence:** 9 + 4 =, 9 + 5 =, 9 + 6 =, 9 + 7 =, 9 + 8 =; Show turnaround facts; 8 + 4 =, 8 + 5 =, 8 + 6=, 8 + 7 =; Show turnaround facts; 7 + 4 =, 7 + 5 =, 7 + 6 =; Show turnaround facts (*Note:* 9 + 8, 8 + 7, and 7 + 6 can also be taught as "near doubles" facts.)
2. Place the fact card 9 + 4 next to the two ten-frames on the mat.

3. Say, "Nine is the first number in the fact problem. I count out 9 counters (blue) and place them in a ten-frame. Now, I count out 4 counters (red) in the second ten-frame." Make these numbers in the two ten-frames.

4. Say, " I will make 10 and then add more. It is easy to take 1 counter from 4 to add to 9 to make 10. I will take 1 counter from the group of 4 and place it with the 9 to make 10. Now, I have 10 plus 3 more. We know that 10 + 3 is 13; 9 + 4 is also 13." (Point to frames above.) "9 + 4 is the same as 10 + 3 = 13."

 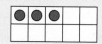

5. Say, "I also know that 3 + 10 = 13, and 4 + 9 = 13."
6. Repeat the steps with the students and the remaining facts from the instructional sequence.

PROGRESS MONITORING (Independent Practice):
After the lesson, give each student a different Make Ten fact card from the instructional sequence, as well as counters and ten-frames. Students should make 10, say the problem with the answer, and explain how the strategy worked.

Source: Adapted from J. A. Van de Walle, 2007, *Elementary and Middle School Mathematics* (6th ed.), Boston: Allyn and Bacon.

BENCHMARK Use the "benchmark" procedure to build fluency. For instance, given a worksheet of facts and working from left to right, a fact (benchmark) is designated as the target to reach by the end of the 1-minute timing. The designated fact can be starred, circled, or identified in any manner by students.

(text continues on page 500)

TABLE 12.4 Arithmetic Strategies and Combinations

Addition Strategies	Addition Combinations
Facts with zero Zero rule: "Any number + 0 is the same number."	(0, 1, 2, 3, 4, 5, 6, 7, 8, 9) + 0 and the turnaround facts
Count on: + 1 One more than	(0, 1, 2, 3, 4, 5, 6, 7, 8, 9) + 1 and the turnaround facts
Count on: + 2 Two more than	(0, 1, 2, 3, 4, 5, 6, 7, 8, 9) + 2 and the turnaround facts
Count on: + 3 Three more than	(0, 1, 2, 3, 4, 5, 6, 7, 8, 9) + 3 and the turnaround facts
Doubles Count by 2's	(3 + 3, 4 + 4, 5 + 5, 6 + 6, 7 + 7, 8 + 8, 9 + 9)
Near doubles Doubles + 1 Doubles − 1	(4 + 5, 5 + 6, 6 + 7, 7 + 8, 8 + 9) and the turnaround facts
9, 8, 7: Make ten plus more	(9 + 4, 9 + 5, 9 + 6, 9 + 7, 8 + 4, 8 + 5, 8 + 6, 7 + 4, 7 + 5, 7 + 8) and the turnaround facts

Subtraction Strategies	Subtraction Combinations
Facts with zero Zero rule: "Any number take away zero is the same number."	(0, 1, 2, 3, 4, 5, 6, 7, 8, 9) − 0
Facts with the same number: "Any number minus the same number is zero."	$n - n = 0$
Count back: − 1 One less than	(10, 9, 8, 7, 6, 5, 4, 3, 2) − 1
Count back: − 2 Two less than	(11, 10, 9, 8, 7, 6, 5, 4, 3) − 2
Count back: − 3 Three less than	(12, 11, 10, 9, 8, 7, 6, 5, 4) − 3
Count up +1, +2, +3 Start with the smaller number and count up to the bigger number (e.g., 9 − 7, start with 7 and count up to 9, the answer is 2).	(12, 11) − 9 (11, 9) − 8 (9, 8) − 7 (9, 8, 7) − 6 (8, 7, 6) − 5 (7, 6, 5) − 4
Double, then "fact family" (4 + 4 = 8; 8 − 4 = 4)	(8 − 4, 10 − 5, 12 − 6, 14 − 7, 16 − 8, 18 − 9)
9, 8, 7: Up to 10, then add	(17 − 9, 17 − 8, 16 − 9, 15 − 9, 15 − 8, 15 − 7, 14 − 9, 14 − 8, 13 − 9, 13 − 8, 13 − 7, 12 − 9, 12 − 8, 12 − 7, 11 − 9, 11 − 8, 11 − 7)
Down to 10, then add	(16 − 7, 16 − 9, 15 − 7, 15 − 6, 14 − 9, 14 − 6, 14 − 5, 13 − 7, 13 − 6, 13 − 5, 13 − 4, 12 − 7, 12 − 5, 12 − 4, 11 − 7, 11 − 6, 11 − 5, 11 − 4)

(continues)

TABLE 12.4   Continued

Multiplication Strategies	Multiplication Combinations
Skip counting: 2's, 5's	(2, 3, 4, 5, 6, 7, 8, 9) × 2; (2, 3, 4, 5, 6, 7, 8, 9) × 5; and the turnaround facts
Nifty 9's: Multiply, then check	$9 \times 2 = 18 (1 + 8 = 9)$, $9 \times 3 = 27 (2 + 7 = 9)$, $9 \times 4 = 36 (3 + 6 = 9)$, $9 \times 5 = 45 (4 + 5 = 9)$, $9 \times 6 = 54 (5 + 4 = 9)$, $9 \times 7 = 63 (6 + 3 = 9)$, $9 \times 8 = 72 (7 + 2 = 9)$, $9 \times 9 = 81 (8 + 1 = 9)$ and the turnaround facts
Zero rule: Any $n \times 0 = 0$	(0, 1, 2, 3, 4, 5, 6, 7, 8, 9) × 0
Identity rule: Any $n \times 1 = n$	(1, 2, 3, 4, 5, 6, 7, 8, 9) × 1
Same n: Count by itself	$3 \times 3, 4 \times 4, 6 \times 6, 7 \times 7, 8 \times 8$ Example: $3 \times 3 = 3, 6, 9$
Harder facts: Distribute, then add	$8 \times 7 = 8 \times 2 = 16 + 8 \times 5 = 40 = 56$ $8 \times 6 = 8 \times 1 = 8 + 8 \times 5 = 40 = 48$ $8 \times 4 = 8 \times 2 = 16 + 8 \times 2 = 16 = 32$

Division Strategies	Division Combinations
Zero rule: Any $n \div 0 = 0$	(9, 8, 7, 6, 5, 4, 3, 2, 1) ÷ 0
Any $n \div n = 1$	$9 \div 9, 8 \div 8, 7 \div 7, 6 \div 6, 5 \div 5, 4 \div 4, 3 \div 3, 2 \div 2, 1 \div 1$
Any $n \div 1 = n$	(9, 8, 7, 6, 5, 4, 3, 2, 1) ÷ 1
Related facts in division	Example: $72 \div 8 = 9$ and $72 \div 9 = 8$
Fact families Divide/multiply	Example: $72 \div 8 = 9$, $72 \div 9 = 8$, $9 \times 8 = 72$, $8 \times 9 = 72$

Sources: Adapted from N. Bley and C. Thornton, 2001, *Effective Primary Mathematics Instruction for Struggling Students.* Austin: TX: PRO-ED; M. Stein, D. Kinder, J. Silbert, and D. Carnine, 2006, *Designing Effective Mathematics Instruction.* Upper Saddle River, NJ: Prentice Hall; J. A. Van de Walle, 2007, *Elementary and Middle School Mathematics: Teaching Developmentally* (6th ed.). Boston: Allyn and Bacon.

Rewards can be distributed to students who reach their benchmark. The benchmark fact can be determined by (a) identifying the number of correct problems previously answered in a 1-minute timing, (b) multiplying that number by 25 percent, and (c) adding the 25 percent figure to the original figure. This new number becomes the benchmark for the next 1-minute marathon. The benchmark strategy is very motivating because it promotes self-competition ("beat yesterday's score").

TIMED DRILLS   Periodic timed drills, distributed practice (over several days or across weeks), and data analysis of student performance can be used to monitor automaticity abilities on lower-level, cognitive skills. Developing automaticity of such cognitive skills is particularly important at the elementary level because students are learning mathematical skills. At the secondary level, automaticity development must continue in life skills areas (e.g., money, time). However, such development in basic facts may be questionable (if, say, a strong proficiency program existed at the elementary level but was unsuccessful) and should be discussed in light of the student's educational goals, transitional needs, and curricular program. For some students with more severe learning problems, automaticity in basic facts might be limited. In these cases, calculator instruction is the obvious choice. For many students, place values is a challenging concept. In the next section we discuss how to teach it.

What Is Place Value and How Do I Teach It?

Place value, which is crucial to understanding our base-10 number system, is a mathematics concept that students must fully grasp (Van de Walle, 2007). Understanding place value helps students understand numerical relationships and the "how" and "why" of procedures used to solve problems. Yet instruction in place value is frequently limited. It often develops conceptual understanding using concrete representations too briefly and moves on to pictorial representations (pictures, tallies) sooner than appropriate for some students.

what WORKS 12.3

Strategies to Teach Arithmetic Combinations

● Addition: Count On (+ 1, + 2, + 3)[1, 3]

Procedure

1. Tell students to "start big" by selecting the larger of the two addends and then to count on by the amount of the second number.

2. Emphasize + 1, + 2, or + 3, depending on the number. For example, 9 + 3 = is computed by saying, "Start big"—9 plus three more, 10, 11, 12 to arrive at 12 as the answer.

3. Have students verbalize the process to ensure accuracy in using the "count on" procedure,

Progress Monitoring: Monitor progress by conducting "fast facts" containing facts with + 1, + 2, and + 3 where students have to say or write the response quickly (within 3 seconds).

Adaptations: Instructional materials, instructional delivery, instructional content

Representations: Concrete and pictorial

Prerequisite Skills	Adaptations
1. Ability to identify larger number to "start big." 2. Ability to "count on" a designated amount (e.g., 2, 3) from a designated number (7, 9). 2. Ability to write the last number spoken.	1. Provide two numbers, one of which is 1, 2, or 3. Have students state which number is larger. Use the number line or concrete objects to represent each number if necessary. Have students tap + 1, + 2, or +3 or show a finger for each number counted on. 2. Conduct warm-up of rote counting from designated number (e.g., 7) and counting on by 1, 2, or 3. Use number line as pictorial representation if necessary.

(continues)

Continued

3. Provide number line or number strip with numbers as a referent.

● Addition: Doubles[1]

Procedure

1. Teach doubles as one of the first strategies.

2. Pair doubles with counting by 2's.

3. Have students count by 2 the number of times represented by the first numeral to arrive at the answer. For example, 4 + 4: 4 is the first number, so count by 2's four times –2, 4, 6, 8; 4 + 4 = 8.

4. Fade the count by 2's as students recall the answers to doubles quickly.

5. Provide a worksheet with different addition arithmetic combinations, and have students circle the doubles and say the answer.

Progress Monitoring: Monitor progress by conducting "fast facts" containing facts with doubles where students have to say or write the response quickly (within 3 seconds).

Adaptations: Instructional materials, instructional delivery, instructional content

Representations: Concrete and pictorial

Prerequisite Skills	Adaptations
1. Ability to count by 2's. 2. Ability to count by 2's a designated number of times. 3. Ability to recall the answers.	1. Conduct warm-up of counting by 2's using a number line as a pictorial representation. 2. Have students tap, hold up a finger, or move a marker for each 2 counted, up to the designated number of times. For example, adding 5 + 5, hold up a total of five fingers while counting by 2's to arrive at the answer of 10. 3. Use a concrete or pictorial cue to associate doubles with a known object. For example, 6 + 6 can be the "egg carton" double; 5 + 5 can be the "hands" double.

● Addition: Near Doubles (Double + 1, Double – 1)[3]

Procedure

1. Have students learn doubles before teaching near doubles. Near doubles are addition fact problems with one numeral being close (+1 or –1) to a double.

2. Show students a "near double" fact—for example, 6 + 7. Ask, "What fact is this close to?" Students should read the problem, identify the related double (6 + 6; 7 + 7), and solve the double problem.

3. Ask whether the original problem is one more or one less than the double (6 + 6 + 1; 7 + 7 – 1).

Students should solve the original problem by adding 1 or subtracting 1 to arrive at the answer.

4. Show students a "near double" fact. Ask what double it is close to and whether it is a + 1 or a – 1 double.

5. Play matching games where students match the near double with the double + 1 and the double – 1.

Progress Monitoring: Monitor progress by conducting "fast facts" containing facts with near doubles where students have to say or write the response quickly (within 3 seconds).

Adaptations: Instructional materials, instructional delivery, instructional content

Representations: Pictorial

Prerequisite Skills	Adaptations
1. Knowledge of doubles. 2. Ability to add 1 to, or subtract 1 from, designated numbers.	1. Review doubles using "fast facts" procedures. 2. Give students a number between 1 and 9 and ask for + 1, What number? – 1 What number? Provide a number line as a pictorial cue if necessary. 3. Teach "one more than, one less than" vocabulary.

Subtraction: Count Back or Down (− 1, − 2, − 3)[1]

Procedure

1. Tell students to "start big" by selecting the larger of the two numerals.
2. Have students count back by the amount of the second number, − 1, − 2, or − 3, and then write the answer.
3. Have students verbalize the process to ensure accuracy in using the "count back" procedure.

Progress Monitoring: Monitor progress by conducting "fast facts" containing facts with − 1, − 2, and − 3 where students have to say or write the response quickly (within 3 seconds).

Adaptations: Instructional materials, instructional delivery, instructional content

Representations: Concrete and pictorial

Prerequisite Skills	Adaptations
1. Ability to identify the larger number to "start big." 2. Ability to write the last number spoken.	1. Conduct a warm-up where students start at 12, 11, or 10 and count back. Have them use a number line if necessary. 2. Give students two numbers between 2 and 12 and ask them to say which number is bigger. 3. Give students a number between 1 and 9 and have them tell the number that is one less than, two less than, or three less than. Have students show a finger for each number counted back. 4. Have students practice writing numbers presented orally.

Subtraction: Up to Ten Then Add (Minuend: 9, 8)[3]

Procedure

1. Tell students to start with the smaller number (9, 8, 7) and add up to 10. Ask, "How much did you need to make 10?"
2. Tell students to use 10 and make the top number. Ask, "How much did you need to make the top number?"
3. Have students add the two numbers from steps 1 and 2.
4. Have students say the problem with the answer.

Example: 13 − 8 = ?

1. I start with 8 and make 10 by adding 2.
2. I add 3 to 10 to make 13.
3. I say, 2 + 3 = 5.
3. I say, 13 − 8 equals 5.

Progress Monitoring: Monitor progress by conducting "fast facts" where students have to say or write the response quickly (within 3 seconds).

Adaptations: Instructional materials, instructional delivery, instructional content

Representations: Concrete and pictorial

Prerequisite Skills	Adaptations
1. Ability to identify the smaller number. 2. Ability to make 10. 3. Ability to build from 10 to the subtrahend number. 4. Ability to add two numbers.	1. Give students two numbers between 7 and 17 and ask them to say which number is smaller. 2. Give students a ten-frame with dots equaling 7, 8, or 9. Have students tell how many dots are needed to make the ten-frame. 3. Conduct "fast facts" with 7, 8, or 9 and an addend that builds to 10. 4. Conduct 10 + ? equals 11, 12, 13, 14, 15, 16, 17. Use two ten-frames or base-10 blocks to show the 10 + concept. 5. Conduct "fast facts" with easier facts to 10 (showing facts and allowing for a 3-second response).

(continues)

what WORKS 12.3

Continued

● Multiplication: Count By

Procedure

1. Tell students to identify a number in the problem they know how to count by.
2. Make tallies or hold up the number of fingers for the other number in the problem.
3. Count by the number from 1 until all of the tallies or fingers are accounted for; the last number named is the answer.

Example: $4 \times 8 = ?$

1. I know how to count by 4's.
2. I will hold up 8 fingers.
3. I count by 4's 8 times: 4, 8, 12, 16, 20, 24, 28, 32.
4. 32 is the answer.

Progress Monitoring: Monitor progress by conducting "fast facts" where students have to say or write the response quickly (within 3 seconds) to a group of facts (e.g., the 3's, 4's, 5's, 6's, 7's, 8's, 9's). Then mix up the facts.

Adaptations: Instructional materials, instructional delivery, instructional content

Representations: Concrete and pictorial

Prerequisite Skills	Adaptations
1. Ability to count by 2, 3, 4, 5, 6, 7, 8, 9. 2. Ability to keep track of how many counting by.	1. Conduct count-by warm-ups. Use a chart to show the count-by number patterns. 2. Have students hold up a finger for each number to be counted.

● Multiplication: "Clock" Strategy (Count by 5's)[2]

Procedure

1. Tell students they will learn a strategy to count by 5's for multiplication by using the clock.
2. Start at 12:00. Count the number of minutes (5) to 1. Explain that you can count by 5's to make it easier. Count: 12:**05**, 12:**10**, 12:**15**, and so forth. Point to each number on the face clock.

3. Ask: If we have two 5's, how many? 10, for 12:10; If we have four 5's, how many? 20, for 12:20.

Progress Monitoring: Monitor progress by pointing to a time on the clock and having students count by 5's to say the time. Written responses can be used also to reinforce writing time.

Adaptations: Instructional materials, instructional delivery, instructional content

Representations: Concrete and pictorial

Prerequisite Skills	Adaptations
1. Ability to count by 5's. 2. Ability to keep track of how many counting by.	1. Conduct count-by warm-ups. 2. Have students hold up a finger for number counted by 5. For example, if it's 4×5, then 5 fingers end up being displayed. 3. Display a count-by-5's chart as a pictorial cue.

● **Division: How Many Groups?[2]**

Procedure

1. Tell students to read the division problem "How many groups of 9 are in 81?"

$$9\overline{)81}$$

2. Have students count by 9's until they reach 81.

3. Tell them that the number of times they count by 9 represents the number of groups of 9 in 81.

Progress Monitoring: Monitor progress by having students say answers for "fast facts."

Adaptations: Instructional materials, instructional delivery, instructional content

Representations: Concrete and pictorial

Prerequisite Skills	Adaptations
1. Ability to count by a number. 2. Ability to keep track of how many counting by.	1. Show students pictorial groups of the number being counted by. 2. Focus initially on easier count-by facts, such as count by 2's and count by 5's. 2. Have students hold up a finger for the number counted by.

● **Division: What's My Family?[2]**

Procedure

1. Show students cards with the commutative problems for a fact family. For example, on the card show $6 \times 7 = 42$ and $7 \times 6 = 42$.

2. Have students use the numbers to create the division facts for the "family."

3. Shuffle the cards and have students match those cards that come from the same "family."

Progress Monitoring: Monitor progress by having students sort cards into families, by saying the family "members" based on one problem, and by doing "fast facts." The first two techniques check for accuracy, and the last technique promotes fluency.

Adaptations: Instructional materials, instructional delivery, instructional content

Representations: Concrete and pictorial

Prerequisite Skills	Adaptations
1. Ability to understand the commutative property. 2. Ability to understand the "family" of facts. 2. Ability to become accurate and fluent.	1. Use manipulatives to reteach the concept of the commutative property. 2. Use manipulatives to demonstrate the connection among the fact family "members." 3. Reduce the amount of fact families until mastery is reached on a smaller number. 4. Have students graph the number of facts they can say correctly in a minute each day.

Sources: [1]Adapted from N. Bley and C. Thorton, 2001, *Teaching Mathematics to Students with Learning Disabilities* (4th ed.). Austin, TX: PRO-ED. [2]Adapted from D. P. Rivera and D. D. Smith, 1997, *Teaching Students with Learning and Behavior Problems* (3rd ed.). Boston: Allyn and Bacon. [3]Adapted from J. A. Van de Walle, 2007, *Elementary and Middle School Mathematics* (6th ed.). Boston: Allyn and Bacon.

Difficulties with Place Value

Students may demonstrate a variety of problems related to their conceptual understanding of place value. Insufficient time spent with concrete representations results in poor understanding of the notion of place and value. According to Ross (1989), as cited in Van de Walle, there are five levels of place-value understanding.

1. **Single numeral:** Individual digits in numerals such as 52 are not understood as representing specific values in the number. Rather, 52 is regarded as a single numeral.

2. **Position names:** The student can name the position of the digits (in 52, 5 is in the tens place and 2 is in the ones place), but value is not associated with the position.

3. **Face value:** Each digit is taken at face value. In 52, the student selects 5 blocks to go with 5 and selects 2 blocks to go with 2. The value of the position is not understood.

4. **Transition to place value:** In 52, 2 blocks are selected for the ones place, and the remaining 50 blocks are selected for the 5; no grouping of tens is demonstrated.

5. **Full understanding:** In 52, five groups of 10 are selected for the 5, and 2 remaining blocks are chosen for the 2.

Young children, of course, do not fully understand place value, and it should not be surprising that older students who struggle learning mathematics have not achieved full understanding of the base-10 system. Diagnostic teaching—giving problems and asking students questions—can help teachers understand what level of development students have reached in learning about place value.

Teaching Place Value

The following techniques can be applied to teaching place-value concepts.

- **Diagnosis:** Using the clinical interview procedure and manipulatives, determine the level of place-value understanding demonstrated by students. Include having students write numbers to represent place values.

- **Instructional materials:** A variety of manipulatives can be used to teach place value and the concept of whole-number computation with and without regrouping. Teachers can use rods, cubes, base-10 blocks, and bean sticks to teach whole-number computation at the concrete level. Base-10 mats and place-value charts can also be used as instructional materials. Figure 12.1 shows examples of manipulatives and materials that can be used during place-value instruction.

- **Vocabulary:** Teach and use regularly the vocabulary of place value. Students should use base-10 language, 5 tens and 3 ones, and standard language, 52, to describe groupings. Other vocabulary should include regrouping to describe how 10 ones are "bundled" to add to the tens place or how a 10 is "unbundled" to add to the ones place during whole-number addition. Similarly, the vocabulary related to hundreds and thousands should be used for larger place-value groupings. Refer to Table 12.3 on page 485 for examples of terms to teach.

- **Instructional content:** The idea of zero as a placeholder is one of the most challenging concepts for many students, including struggling students.

Provide multiple opportunities for students to use manipulatives to represent numbers containing zero as a placeholder in order to carry out whole-number operations.

- **Concrete, pictorial, and abstract representations:** Pair the use of manipulatives to concretely represent the place and value of numbers with the use of written numerals in order to demonstrate how to write the numbers (abstract representation). For example, base-10 blocks are used on the place-value mat to represent numbers; students then write the numbers to show how many in each place. Then move to pictorial representations paired with concrete along with abstract. For example, pictures of blocks depicting numbers can be used, where students build the number using base-10 blocks to check their pictures; the numbers then can be written as the final step.

- **Progress monitoring:** Assess student understanding of place value by giving them numbers to represent with base-10 blocks, having them tell the numbers in two ways (base-10 number and standard number), and writing the number. Include numbers with zero as a placeholder on a regular basis, because numbers with zero are the most problematic for students to understand.

TEEN NUMBERS   Have students spend time on teen numbers. These numbers are most problematic for struggling students to learn. Use two ten-frames to represent quantity for the teen numbers. Provide a number. Have students build the number in the frames, read the number, and write the number. Ask questions such as: How many more is 14 than 11? How many do I need to add to 12 to get 15? How many is 2 less than 17? How much is 10 plus 8? Teen numbers should also be taught within the context of hundreds. Repeat the activities above by using hundreds and teen numbers such as 215, 317, and 411.

NEED TO TRADE?   Need to Trade? is a prerequisite activity to renaming in addition. This intervention can be introduced once students have had practice with addition with no renaming. Students are presented with a variety of addition problems with and without renaming. They are to identify those problems in which renaming is required, or they need to trade 10 ones for 1 ten (Bley & Thornton, 2001). Have students use base-10 blocks to represent numbers initially and then move to visual representation such as tally marks.

ARE THERE ENOUGH?   Are There Enough? is used for subtraction problems with and without renaming. Students are given different subtraction problems and must decide whether the top number in the ones place is large enough from which to subtract the bottom number. Numbers with various places up to thousands can be used, as well as numbers with zeros as placeholders. This activity focuses students' attention on the ones place, number discrimination, and on place value (Bley & Thornton, 2001). The application of place value to whole-number computation is discussed next.

What Is Whole-Number Computation and How Do I Teach It?

Solving problems that contain whole numbers requires an understanding of the relationship between numbers and place value, as well as skill in estimating, determining the reasonableness of answers, using a calculator, and using appropriate algorithms. Instruction in place value and whole numbers should occur throughout the curriculum. It is not necessary for students to master addition before being introduced to subtraction or to be proficient in basic arithmetic combinations before being introduced to whole-number problems.

Whole-number operations include addition, subtraction, multiplication, and division without and with regrouping. According to the NCTM *Standards* (2000), students should understand the meanings of the operations and how they are related to one another. Students should also be able to compute fluently. Place-value abilities are a fundamental skill for whole-number computations. Estimation and rounding strategies are important companion skills, particularly with advanced multiplication and division computation (Cathcart, Pothier, Vance, & Bezuk, 2000; Hudson & Miller, 2006). Whole-number computation should involve the development of conceptual understanding, instruction in procedural strategies, and the application of computation in story problems (Hudson & Miller, 2006).

Difficulties with Whole-Number Computation

Bley and Thornton (2001) identify the process of solving whole-number computation as complex because it involves symbols, multiple steps, and a level of abstraction that may be problematic for struggling students. Difficulty with arithmetic combinations can interfere with students' ability to attempt whole-number computations. Students may view the task as too difficult because they lack fluency with basic facts. The multistep process of computing whole-number problems can be overwhelming to students who have difficulty remembering multiple steps and sequences for solving problems. Difficulties with understanding number relationships and place value can affect the ability to apply important fundamental skills, such as estimating, rounding, recognizing reasonableness of answers, and doing mental computation when solving whole-number computations. Finally, using algorithmic procedures to compute whole-number problems may cause difficulties for students well beyond the elementary school years.

Teaching Whole-Number Computation

The general steps involved in teaching whole-number computation follow. Note that calculators and other technology have an important role to play.

- **Diagnosis:** Provide three problems each of addition, subtraction, multiplication, and division computation, including problems with and without regrouping and division with remainders. Include problems with zero as a value in the ones, tens, and hundreds place. Provide reasonable time for students to complete the problems. Correct the work, noting what types of errors are made. Refer to What Works 12.4 for examples of error patterns identified in whole-number computation and remedial strategies to address these error patterns (Ashlock, 2006).
- **Instructional materials:** Use materials from place-value instruction to support conceptual understanding of whole-number operations. Students who struggle with remembering answers quickly for arithmetic combinations can use a basic facts table. Figure 12.1 on page 488 shows examples of manipulatives and materials that can be used during instruction in whole-number operations.
- **Calculators:** Provide students with calculators to check their answers for whole-number computations.

Error Patterns and Remedial Techniques

Operations	Type of Errors	Remedial Techniques
1. 76 $+\ 49$ $\overline{1115}$	No regrouping of the ones in the ones place.	• Use base-10 blocks to model regrouping. • Use grid paper so only one digit can be recorded in each box, "forcing" the need to regroup. Include highlighted grid boxes above the problem to cue the need to write a numeral from regrouping tens or hundreds.
2. 34 729 $+\ 694$ $\overline{1117}$	Work begins on left rather than right. Regrouping done backwards.	• Insert ⇓ above the ones place as the place to start. • Explain that in math, we start opposite from where we start with reading.
3. $4\ \ 14$ $\cancel{574}$ $-\ 268$ $\overline{206}$	Work begins on left with "borrowing" 1 from 5 to "regroup" to the tens and to the ones in order to be able to subtract.	• Insert ⇓ above the ones place as the place to start. • Use base-10 blocks and base-10 mat to model the conceptual understanding of regrouping.
4. $4\ \ 10$ $\cancel{500}$ $-\ 286$ $\overline{214}$	Regrouping for the ones place is partially conducted. No regrouping for the tens place.	• Use base-10 blocks to model the conceptual understanding of regrouping. • Use D + PM to teach the procedural steps. • Give examples of subtraction problems with the zero in the minuend and with it in the subtrahend. Have students circle only those problems that can be computed without regrouping.
5. 532 $\times\ 24$ $\overline{1068}$	Each column is treated as separate multiplication. The left multiplier continues to be used when the multiplicand has more digits than the multiplier.	• Teach the use of the distributive property as an alternative algorithm. $532 \times 24 =$ $(20 \times 532) + (4 \times 532)$ • Create a cover so that only one digit of the multiplier is revealed at a time. • Have students check their work using a calculator. • Give students grid paper to help with placement issues.
6. 95 $4)\overline{3620}$ 36 $\overline{20}$ $\ 20$	The zero in the tens place is missing from the quotient. When the student "brings down" and division is not possible, the next digit is "brought down" with no zero used as a place holder.	• Have students use the pyramid technique: $\dfrac{905}{5}$ $\overline{900}$ $4)\overline{3620}$ $\overline{3600}$ $\overline{20}$ 20

(continues)

what WORKS 12.4

Continued

Operations	Type of Errors	Remedial Techniques
7. $\dfrac{1}{4} = \dfrac{1}{12}$ $+\dfrac{1}{3} = \dfrac{1}{12}$ $\dfrac{2}{12}$	The student can identify the lowest common multiplier but merely copies the original numerator.	• Explain the purpose of the equals sign—that it means the same fractional part. • Have students use manipulatives to demonstrate that fractional parts on either side of the equals sign are equivalent.
8. $6\dfrac{1}{3}$ $-2\dfrac{2}{3}$ $4\dfrac{1}{3}$	The whole numbers are subtracted. There is no regrouping when the subtrahend is larger than the minuend.	• Have students use fractional parts to work through the problem. Use a cue to signal the need to start working with the fractions before the whole numbers. Have students regroup the whole-number unit for an equal set of fractional parts so the subtraction can be performed. • Have students use markings to signal regrouping of a whole into fractional parts. • Provide examples of mixed fractions that require regrouping for subtraction purposes.
9. 6.8 $+5.5$ 11.13	The decimal point is in the wrong place in the sum. The tenths are not regrouped as units.	• Have students use rods to show a unit for comparison. Have students use rods to show each addend as tenths as compared to the unit. Have students combine the tenths rods and trade for a unit. • Have students use grid paper with the instruction that only one digit can be placed in each box.

Source: Adapted from R. B. Ashlock, 2006, *Error Patterns in Computation,* Columbus, OH: Merrill.

- **Vocabulary:** Use visuals to demonstrate concepts such as regrouping and remainder. Refer to Table 12.3 on page 485 for examples of terms to teach.
- **Instructional materials:** Provide a facts table to support students who need help recalling arithmetic combinations. Pair arithmetic combinations instruction with whole-number computations.
- **Instructional content—task analysis:** Provide similar types of problems when initially teaching whole-number computation at the abstract representation level. Similar types of problems include 2 digit + 2 digit with no regrouping, 3 digit – 3 digit with 0 in the tens place, and 2 digits × 1 digit with regroup-

ing. Then provide mixed-problem worksheets with the same operation, such as 2 digits + 1 digit with regrouping, 2 digits + 2 digits with regrouping, and 3 digits + 3 digits with regrouping. Finally, provide mixed-problem worksheets with mixed operations.

- **Strategies:** Teach students procedural strategies (examples are described below) to solve whole-number computations. Use "invented strategies" for those students who can benefit from representing whole-number computations in nontraditional ways. Refer to What Works 12.5 for examples of "invented algorithms." Choose judiciously which strategies to teach; too many strategies can confuse students. Work with students to determine the strategy that makes sense to them and that they can use independently, efficiently, and effectively.

- **Generalization:** Promote generalization by having students answer problems with mixed signs and in whole-number computational problems.

- **Technology:** Software programs can be used to support the extra instruction that students may require to learn whole-number computation. Some programs offer excellent visualizations of the process using manipulatives, which is often the type of instruction that teachers do not have sufficient time to provide. In the Tech Notes feature, the Unifix cubes software program is shown, illustrating how the cubes are partitioned for a simple division problem with a remainder.

tech NOTES

Using Software to Show Pictorial Representations of Math Concepts

Unifix Software (Didax Educational Resources) is a program that shows pictorial representations of abstract math concepts. Unifix Software is modeled after the materials, called Unifix, which are interlocking cubes. Employing the software, students can use the cubes to display patterning, counting, and operations. Unifix Software provides many pictorial representations of number concepts, showing sets of objects and numbers associated with the cubes. Unifix Software supports switch access.

The following procedures can be used with the Unifix cubes software to pictorially represent and solve the equation $5\overline{)17}$.

Teaching Procedure

1. Identify higher- and lower-performing students who can work together at the computer station.

2. Review the previous lesson involving division and the base-10 blocks.

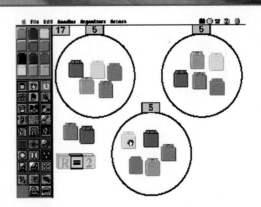

● Pictorial Experiences with Math Concepts in Unifix Software. Unifix ® software is a registered trademark of Philograph Publications, Ltd.

3. Have students work in pairs at the computer with the Unifix software.

Progress Monitoring: Have students complete four division problems independently, using paper and pencil.

Invented Algorithms

Add Tens, Add Ones, Then Combine

46 + 38

40 and 30 is 70.
6 and 8 is 14.
70 and 14 is 84.

$$\begin{array}{r} 46 \\ +38 \\ \hline 70 \\ 14 \\ \hline 84 \end{array}$$

Add on Tens, Then Add Ones

46 + 38

46 and 30 more is 76.
Then I added on the other 8.
76 and 4 is 80, and 4 more is 84.

46 + 38
76 + 4 → 80
80 + 4 → 84

Move Some to Make Tens

46 + 38

Take 2 from the 46 and put it with
the 38 to make 40. Now you have
44, and 40 more is 84.

46 + 38
44 + 40
84

Use a Nice Number and Compensate

46 + 38

46 and 40 is 86.
That's 2 extra, so it's 84.

46 + 38
46 + 40 →
86 − 2 → 84

(a) Invented strategies for addition with two-digit numbers

Add Tens to Get Close, Then Ones

73 − 46

46 and 20 is 66.
   (30 more is too much.)
Then 4 more is 70 and 3 is 73.
That's 20 and 7, or 27.

46 → 20
66 → 4
70 → 3
73 —
27

Add Tens to Overshoot, Then Come Back

73 − 46

46 and 30 is 76.
That's 3 too much,
so it's 27.

73 − 46 →
46 + 30 → 76 − 3 → 73
30 − 3 = 27

Add Ones to Make a Ten, Then Tens and Ones

73 − 46

46 and 4 is 50.
50 and 20 is 70, and 3 more
is 73. The 4 and 3 is 7, and
20 more is 27.

$$\begin{array}{r} 73 - 46 \\ 46 + 4 \to 50 \\ + 20 \to 70 \\ + 3 \to 73 \\ \hline 27 \end{array}$$

Similarly,

46 and 4 is 50.
50 and 23 is 73.
23 and 4 is 27.

46 + 4 → 50
50 + 23 → 73
23 + 4 = 27

(b) Invented strategies for subtraction by counting up

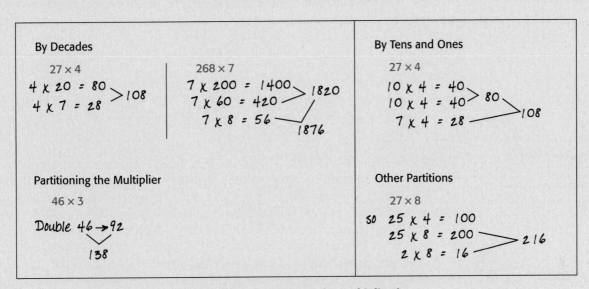

By Decades

27 × 4

4 × 20 = 80
4 × 7 = 28 〉108

268 × 7

7 × 200 = 1400
7 × 60 = 420 〉1820
7 × 8 = 56
1876

Partitioning the Multiplier

46 × 3

Double 46 → 92
138

By Tens and Ones

27 × 4

10 × 4 = 40
10 × 4 = 40 〉80
7 × 4 = 28 〉108

Other Partitions

27 × 8

so 25 × 4 = 100
25 × 8 = 200 〉216
2 × 8 = 16

(c) Partitioning strategies for multiplication

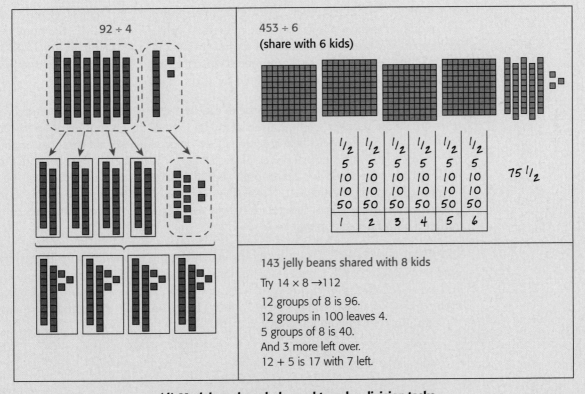

143 jelly beans shared with 8 kids

Try 14 × 8 →112

12 groups of 8 is 96.
12 groups in 100 leaves 4.
5 groups of 8 is 40.
And 3 more left over.
12 + 5 is 17 with 7 left.

(d) Models and symbols used to solve division tasks

Source: Adapted from J. A. Van de Walle, 2007, *Elementary and Middle School Mathematics: Teaching Developmentally* (6th ed.). Boston: Allyn and Bacon.

- **Progress monitoring:** Give students ten problems to work independently. Check for accuracy to determine whether reteaching is needed or you can move on to the next computational skill.

Now let's look at some specific strategies to teach during instruction in whole-number computation.

ROUNDING   Rounding numbers up or down to the nearest 10 or the nearest 100 is a prerequisite skill for whole-number computation, column addition, mental computation, estimation, and determining the reasonableness of an answer. For example, in the division problem 286 divided by 72, it is easy to discover that 4 is a reasonable estimate of how many times 286 can be divided by 72 because $70 \times 4 = 280$.

ESTIMATION: THE FRONT-END STRATEGY   The front-end strategy is useful for computing column addition (Reys, 1986). Provide students with a list of numbers to be added, such as 376 + 87 + 432 + 11 =. Show the students that first the numbers in the "front" (that is, the hundreds column: 300 + 400 = 700) are added. Then the numbers in the tens and ones columns are adjusted to form 100 (i.e., 87 + 11 is about 100, and 76 + 32 is about 100, which makes 200). Third, add the "front" number (700) plus the adjusted number (200). Finally, estimate the answer (900 in this case). This strategy can be applied to adding money as well.

ESTIMATION: THE CLUSTERING STRATEGY   The clustering strategy is useful when all the numbers have about the same numerical value. For instance, the numbers of people who attended a football game during one month might be 15,833, 17,021, and 16,682. All of the numbers cluster around 16,000, so a reasonable estimate is $16,000 \times 3 = 48,000$ people for three games.

BEAN STICK COMPUTATION   Bean sticks can be used to teach addition and subtraction whole-number computation with and without regrouping (Rivera & Smith, 1997). Sticks of 10 beans demonstrate place value for the tens place, and remaining beans represent the ones place. Demonstrations of using the beans to trade 10 ones for a ten for regrouping should be conducted with students. The Demonstration Plus Permanent Model (D + PM, see below) technique can be used for instructional purposes. Figure 12.3 shows an example of using bean sticks for addition with no regrouping.

ALTERNATIVE ALGORITHMS   An algorithm is a routine, step-by-step procedure used in computation. Examples of alternative algorithms include partial products and expanded notation. Partial products can be used to teach division (McCoy & Prehm, 1987). Partial products help students focus on place value and the quantity that is actually being partitioned:

```
428 ÷ 2 = ?
400 ÷ 2 = 200          200
 20 ÷ 2 =  10          +10
  8 ÷ 2 =   4            4
                      _____
                       214
```

Expanded notation can be used for whole-number subtraction and division. The expanded-notation algorithm helps students to show place-value representa-

FIGURE 12.3   Using Bean Sticks to Solve Computational Problems

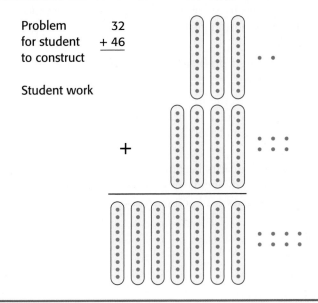

Problem for student to construct

32
+ 46

Student work

Source: From D. Rivera and B. R. Bryant, 1992, Mathematics instruction for students with special needs, *Intervention in School and Clinic, 28*(2), p. 79. Copyright 1992 by PRO-ED. Reprinted with permission.

tions of numerals and to calculate answers (Cawley & Parmar, 1992), as illustrated in the following array.

Subtraction		Division
457	400 + 50 + 7	428 ÷ 2 = ?
−35	− 30 + 5	(400 + 20 + 8) ÷ 2 =
	400 + 20 + 2 = 422	(200 + 10 + 4) = 214

For both types of alternative algorithms, teachers model and "think aloud" how they solve a division problem. Students imitate and verbalize the steps in applying these algorithms, use manipulatives to represent the process, or work with a partner to solve problems.

DEMONSTRATION PLUS PERMANENT MODEL   The Demonstration Plus Permanent Model (D + PM) intervention has proved successful in teaching students explicitly how to solve problems that include addition, subtraction, and multiplication whole-number computation. This intervention takes only a short time to implement, is best applied individually or in small groups, and can greatly facilitate mastery of computation. Teachers using this intervention often report that students catch on very quickly and learn the steps efficiently. The D + PM intervention is at the level of abstract representation but can easily be adapted with visual representations (problems shown using base-10 pictures) and physical representations (problems completed using base-10 manipulatives or bean sticks). Thus, an instructional materials adaptation can be used to help students who require additional conceptual development to understand place value, as well as computing with and without regrouping. The following steps make up the Demonstration (D) + Permanent Model (PM) intervention:

- Demonstrate (D) how to solve a problem by "thinking aloud" the steps in whole-number computation. Stress place-value and regrouping language if regrouping is involved.
- Leave the demonstrated problem as a referent (PM) on the student's worksheet or the chalkboard.
- Have students compute the next problem, saying the steps out loud. If the problem is worked correctly, then have students complete the remaining problems (Rivera & Smith, 1987; 1988).

KEY QUESTIONS   Some students become confused when doing multistep whole-number computation (e.g., division, multiplication). The following key questions can be asked to help students get back on track:

- What is the problem?
- What are the steps?
- What did you just do?
- What do you do next?

Mercer and Mercer (2005) recommend teaching students the following cue or "family strategy" to remember the steps required to solve division problems: **D**addy (divide), **M**other (multiply), **S**ister (subtract), and **B**rother (bring down). Students can be taught to use the "family strategy" or to ask themselves the "key questions" by referring to a chart or cue card, an approach that promotes more self-regulated learning. These techniques can be paired with the D + PM intervention to teach students how to solve division problems (Rivera & Smith, 1997).

SEQUENCE OF INSTRUCTION   Traditionally, teachers present information to students in a task-analyzed, sequenced format. Students are taught the easiest skill in the sequence first. Once that skill is mastered, the next one is presented, and so on. Investigations have revealed that students do not have to be taught whole-number computational skills in an easy-to-difficult sequence in order for learning to occur. Rather, the most difficult skill within a group can be taught; in general, students tend to generalize the algorithmic process to the easier problems. Concrete representations such as bean sticks and base-10 models can be used to promote understanding of place value and renaming.

The following guidelines are suggested:

1. Develop a task analysis of whole-number computation (e.g., two digits + one digit, two digits + two digits, three digits + two digits, three digits + three digits—all with no regrouping; two digits + one digit, two digits + two digits, three digits + two digits, three digits + three digits—all with renaming)
2. Test students to determine which skills within the sequence are mastered and which skills require instruction.
3. Group skills by "no renaming" and "renaming."

4. Select the most difficult skill within a group as the instructional target (e.g., three digits + three digits with no renaming; three digits + three digits with renaming)

5. Teach this most difficult skill using the Demonstration Plus Permanent Model intervention.

6. Present problems representing all of the skills within a group for practice (e.g., two digits + one digit, two digits + two digits, three digits + two digits, three digits + three digits—all with renaming)

7. Collect student performance data on all of the skills on the practice sheet. (Rivera & Smith, 1987; Rivera & Smith, 1988)

We now talk about areas that can be challenging as students progress through the grades.

What Are Fractions, Decimals, and Percents and How Do I Teach Them?

Instruction in fractions, decimals, and percents involves helping students to understand, represent, estimate, and compute across the three numeration systems (NCTM, 2000). Students work flexibly with fractions, decimals, and percents, applying the use of these rational numbers in solving real-life problems that involve money, cooking, shopping, and measurement (NCTM, 2000). According to Van de Walle (2007), developing students' understanding of fraction concepts is critical to their success in learning and understanding computing with fractions. Students should be taught to view fraction and decimal systems as representing the same concepts. Once students understand the relationship between fractions and decimals, they should be introduced to percents. Students should also be taught the interrelatedness of decimals, fractions, and percents (Hudson & Miller, 2006).

Difficulties with Fractions, Decimals, and Percents

Students encounter a variety of challenges as they engage in work with fractions, decimals, and percents. According to Bley and Thornton

● Students encounter a variety of challenges as they engage in work with fractions, decimals, and percents.

(2001), students who demonstrate problems with abstract reasoning have difficulties with rational numbers even with the use of concrete representations. Extra instruction using concrete objects will be necessary to help these students grasp concepts related to each numeration system and the relationships among them. The vocabulary associated with these three systems may be problematic and thus require explicit instruction in the definitions and use of the terms. Number sense regarding the relative sizes of parts, such as thirds, tenths, .60, and 25 percent, and their relationship to a whole unit may be difficult for some students. Problems of this nature will interfere with the ability to judge the reasonableness of answers to questions such as "Is 3/4 or 1/3 closer to a whole?" Relating fractions, decimals, and percents requires a sense of number size and relationship, and without a good sense of number, even numeral relationships become challenging. Difficulty remembering the meaning of symbols can interfere with interpreting how to solve problems. Finally, understanding and recalling the procedural steps necessary in computations is yet another difficult area for students who are struggling.

Teaching Fractions, Decimals, and Percents

Our overview of teaching these skills reflects the fact that many students, with and without special needs, need lots of help learning to work with fractions, decimals, and percents.

- **Diagnosis:** Refer to What Works 12.4 on page 510 for examples of error patterns identified in whole-number computation and remedial strategies to address the error patterns (Ashlock, 2006).
- **Vocabulary:** It is important to teach terms related to fractions, decimals, and percents explicitly. Use *part, whole, percent,* and *fraction* interchangeably (Van de Walle, 2007). Examples of key vocabulary terms are found in Table 12.3 on page 485.
- **Instructional materials:** Use rods, fraction tiles, grid paper, Geoboards, number lines, and pattern blocks to provide activities with quantities in different forms and shapes. Provide multiple exercises for students to represent similar values across the three numeration systems using various materials. For example, use a paper strip to show 1/4 of a region, a Geoboard to show .25 of a region, and grid paper to show 25 percent of a region. Figure 12.1 on page 488 shows examples of manipulatives and materials that can be used for instruction in fractions, decimals, and percent.
- **Instructional content:** Focus on percents that connect to familiar fractions such as halves, thirds, fourths, and eighths (Van de Walle, 2007).
- **Instructional content:** Teach the "big idea" of partitioning and equivalence explicitly, demonstrating its relationship to fractions, decimals, and percents (Carnine, Jones, & Dixon, 1994; Coyne, Kameenui, & Carnine, 2007).
- **Strategies:** Use the CSA or D + PM procedure for teaching addition, subtraction, multiplication, and division algorithms. Refer to ADAPT Framework 12.2 for an example of making adaptations for adding unlike fractions.
- **Technology:** Encourage students to check their work using calculators.

12.2 **ADAPT Framework** Adding Unlike Fractions

ASK "What am I requiring the student to do?"	**DETERMINE** the prerequisite skills of the task.	**ANALYZE** the student's strengths and struggles.	**PROPOSE** and implement adaptations from among the four categories.	**TEST** to determine if the adaptations helped the student to accomplish the task.

		Strengths Struggles		
The students will add unlike fractions.	1. Understands that the denominators need to be the same when we use the least common multiple (LCM) in order to add.	1.	**For 1. No adaptation needed** The students can say that with unlike fractions, the first step is to find the LCM.	
	2. Is able to find the LCM.	2.	**For 2. Content** Provide pairs of numbers for students to identify the LCM. Have students conduct count-bys to help them find answers. **Material** Provide a multiplication facts table.	**For 2.** Record the LCMs for the pairs of numbers as right or wrong. Record count-bys for 2's, 3's, 4's, 5's as right or wrong.
	3. Converts the numerator to represent the change in value in the denominator to the least common denominator.	3.	**For 3. Material** Provide a multiplication facts table. **Content** Drill multiplication facts that represent the most challenges when finding the LCM.	**For 3.** Record answers to multiplication facts. Provide extra drill on those facts not mastered.
	4. Solves the problem.	4.	**For 4.** Provide answer key for students to check their work.	**For 4.** Give ten problems for three days to determine mastery. Record the percent correct of problems computed. Students should achieve 90% accuracy.

- **Making connections to money:** Talk about and show how decimals such as .25, .10, and .05 are related to money.
- **Making connections to telling time:** Connect simple fractions (1/2, 1/4) to telling time: half-past the hour, quarter after an hour, or quarter to an hour.

- **Progress monitoring:** On a weekly basis, conduct assessments on concepts and skills taught to determine whether students are benefiting from instruction. Error analysis can pinpoint misunderstandings that can be targeted for further instruction and review.

SORTING FRACTIONS AND DECIMALS   Given a variety of fractions (or decimals) and the three choices Close to Zero, Close to 1/2, and Close to 1, have students sort the fractions (or decimals) according to their relationship to the choices. To do this accurately, students must understand the relative sizes of the fractions (or decimals). Have students use manipulatives to "prove" the accuracy of their choices (Bley & Thornton, 2001). The Making a Difference feature describes how one community found a way to enhance the social and academic experience of all of its students, as well as their understanding of fractions, via a special summer camp.

Choices

Close to Zero	Close to 1/2	Close to 1

Fractions and Decimals to Sort

2/3	7/8	1/9	4/5	1/20	5/8	6/7	2/4	1/3
	.53	.91	.01	.47	.87	.05	.39	

Making a Difference

Summer Camp Yields Academic and Social Benefits Throughout the Year

Yvette Netzhammer
Special Education Teacher, Grade 4
Green Park Elementary School
Metairie, Louisiana

The idea for the Green Park Friendship League came to my daughter, Noel, in a dream! After witnessing students make fun of a classmate with autism, she dreamed of starting a "Friendship Club" to promote friendship and understanding at our inclusive school. "From the mouths of babes," I thought to myself. By working with Doriana Vicedomini, an inspiring parent of a child with special needs, I learned of state grant money available for tutoring. Combining academic tutoring with social skills instruction seemed ideal. She and I got together and created a proposal to submit to the Special Education Department of our district. It was approved, so our free, 3-week summer camp, Green Park Friendship League, was born.

Students are chosen for the camp on the basis of special needs, standardized test scores, and teacher recommendations. Twenty-five children are chosen, and the camp takes place on our school campus from 8 a.m. to 12 noon, Monday through Friday. We staff the camp with special and general educators and paraeducators from our school. The camp is a true collaboration of general and special education teachers, paraeducators, parents, siblings, general and special education students, adminis-

trators, and community members. Although teachers and paraeducators are paid, many others volunteer their time. Teenage alumni from our school work well with the campers, while receiving credit for community service hours that are sometimes required of them by their middle and high schools. Older siblings of the campers with special needs provide daily help and insight as well. Parents and family members are always invited to share their special skills and interests with the kids. One of our grandfathers performs a magic show each year! Local firefighters, police officers, and professionals also contribute.

We combine interactive academic instruction with social skills instruction to foster friendship, understanding, and acceptance. We engage the campers in reading circles, writing activities, phonics instruction, drills on math facts, partner activities, reader's theater, computer centers, and hands-on activities that reinforce instruction on money, time, and number sense. All of these activities are permeated with instruction on social skills. Taking turns,

FRACTIONS AS EQUAL TO OR GREATER THAN 1   Teach students a range of fractional representations when first introducing the concept of a fraction to help develop number sense about relative size. Rather than limiting instruction to 1/2, 1/4, and 1/3, include fractions such as 5/5, 3/1, and 12/4, using fraction strips and shapes such as squares, rectangles, and circles to illustrate physical representations of the fractional concepts. Students learn from the beginning of fraction instruction that fractions represent relationships, not specific amounts (Kelly, Gersten, & Carnine, 1990).

COMPARISONS   Comparisons help students see comparative sizes of fractions and the relationship between the sizes (Baroody & Hume, 1991). For example, younger children might state that 1/3 is greater than 1/2 because 3 is greater than 2; however, comparisons using manipulatives such as fraction strips or connecting cubes can help students develop an understanding of relative sizes. Note that students must know the identity of the whole (e.g., a cake, a slice of pizza) to discern that 1/2 is indeed greater than 1/3.

ARITHMETIC COMBINATIONS AND FRACTIONS   Combine instruction on arithmetic combinations with simple fraction problems. Build fluency in responding to problems involving arithmetic combinations, and then present fractions containing

using manners, maintaining eye contact, greeting people, complimenting others, and accepting compliments from others are some of the social skills we stress.

This past year, camp teacher Susan Doell noticed that our older campers were struggling with fractions. Through wonderful collaboration, the school cafeteria and playground were transformed into a "Fraction Fair." Booths were set up to reinforce Mrs. Doell's lessons. At one booth the students used measuring skills to prepare trail mix. At another station, the campers balled up wads of paper and tossed them into a trash can. Tallying their attempts and the baskets they made was a fun way to help them understand what fractions represent. Many other exciting activities were employed to show the role math plays in daily life. For instance, campers played "miniature golf" and then showed their "holes in one" in fraction form. Bowling activities were used to show campers what fractions of pins were knocked down with each roll. Hershey bars were divided and shared. Mrs. Doell found the camp curricula very beneficial for her instruction in the following school year. Some of the campers were in her class for the regular school year, and she was able to refer to these activities and let the campers serve as the "experts" on the classroom game or activity.

During the school year we see positive effects from the camp. Natalie Ortiz, a special educator and camp counselor, found that spending the summer with one of her students with autism gave her a real jumpstart on working effectively with her. The student became familiar with Ms. Ortiz's classroom management and expectations. Carla Harrison, a regular educator and camp counselor, thinks the camp gives the students more of a feeling of belonging to the school. She is impressed when she sees campers participate more in school activities, such as the talent show, school plays, and extracurricular activities. Paraeducator Janel Cimo noticed more independence in one of her students and more willingness to volunteer in class. Paraeducator Sam Granger was thrilled to see a camper's name on the school Honor Roll! Of course, there are still challenges to be met each day in the classroom, but the relationships formed at the camp can sometimes help make them less daunting.

The most rewarding aspect of the camp is feedback from the families. Besides the academic benefits, campers learn to help others in their communities. They learn from each other. They learn acceptance and tolerance. The friendships formed at the camp spill over into the regular school year and provide support and encouragement to all students. So you see, dreams *can* come true! ●

the combinations students have been practicing. If the targeted multiplication facts are ×8, then fraction problems might include the following example:

$$\frac{8}{9} \times \frac{6}{8} = \frac{48}{72} = \frac{2}{3}$$

This technique helps students make the connection between learning multiplication combinations and computing problems with fractions.

MONEY, DECIMALS, AND PERCENTS   Teach money and decimals skills together. Use number combinations that have been taught and mastered during study of whole-number computation. Money and decimals have a natural connection, are a life skill, and may have more relevance for students if taught together. Give students problems, such as 35 pennies and 40 dimes, and have them write both the fraction and the decimal for the problems. Use the newspaper to teach and reinforce money, decimals, percents, and computational skills. Computing the prices of items, spending a designated amount of money by "shopping the sales," and comparison shopping are all activities that require students to use money, decimals, percents, and computational skills. Algebra is an important area that requires careful attention. We will take a look at it in the next section.

What Is Algebra and How Do I Teach It?

Algebra is identified in the NCTM (2000) *Standards* as an area that is important to teach beginning in the elementary grades as students prepare for more formalized study in middle and high school mathematics courses. Algebraic reasoning and the development of algebraic concepts involve using models and algebraic symbols to represent problems and quantitative relationships and strategies to construct and solve simple to complex equations. Algebraic reasoning involves patterns; variables, equality, and equations; symbolism; and relations, functions, and representations (Allsopp, Kyger, & Lovin, 2007; Van de Walle, 2007). It is important for students to pass algebra because of the connection between higher-level mathematics and postsecondary education. For students who are at risk and students with mathematics disabilities who find mathematics difficult, adaptations to help them succeed with algebraic thinking are critical for developing their potential to enter higher education.

Difficulties with Algebra

Difficulties with algebra stem from a variety of problems, including difficulties mastering arithmetic combinations and understanding the vocabulary used in algebraic reasoning. As noted in the problem-solving section of this chapter, students who demonstrate mathematical difficulties typically exhibit poor performance in the processes involved in solving word problems, which are an important component of algebraic study. Finally, difficulties with patterns and functions challenge teachers in providing instruction to help students understand algebraic concepts and reasoning.

Teaching Algebraic Reasoning

Students who are well on their way to mastering the concepts and skills addressed earlier in this chapter are ready for the exciting challenge of algebraic reasoning.

- **Diagnosis:** Use the clinical interview procedure with specific problems to determine the level of student reasoning.
- **Language:** Check student understanding of the key vocabulary of algebraic instruction. Refer to Table 12.3 on page 485 for examples of terms to teach.
- **Instructional content:** Make connections in activities among patterns, functions, and variables. For example, students can identify and extend a pattern, represent the relationship in a table, identify the functional relationship as a formula for the step number, and predict the next response in a table by using the formula.
- **Instructional content:** Teach the arithmetic properties that are presented in Table 12.5. These properties are part of algebraic reasoning and are important concepts for students to understand. Even if remembering the name of the property is an issue, students must develop conceptual understanding of how numbers are related and how values are influenced by the properties in this table.

TABLE 12.5 **Mathematical Properties**

Identity Property of Addition: Any number plus zero equals the number; the value does not change.

$$n + 0 = n$$

Commutative Property of Addition: The order in which numbers are added does not change the answer.

$$a + b = b + a$$

Associative Property of Addition: When adding, the grouping does not change the answer.

$$a + (b + c) = (a + b) + c$$

Identity Property of Multiplication: Any number times one equals the number; the value does not change.

$$n \times 1 = n$$

Commutative Property of Multiplication: The order in which numbers are multiplied does not change the answer.

$$a \times b = b \times a$$

Associative Property of Multiplication: When multiplying, the grouping does not change the answer.

$$a \times (b \times c) = (a \times b) \times c$$

Distributive Property of Multiplication: The product can be written as the sum of two products.

$$a \times (b + c) = (a \times b) + (a \times c)$$

- **Strategies:** Provide specific strategies and teach them using the "think aloud" procedure so that students learn how to solve equations and word problems. Strategies in What Works 12.6 on page 527 can be used to guide understanding when setting up and solving equations.
- **Technology:** Teach students how to use graphing calculators to plot points and draw curves when graphing patterns (Van de Walle, 2007). Refer to the applets on the *e-Standards* published by the NCTM. The applets feature the connection between word problems as real-life situations and tables, graphs, and equations. For instance, students can manipulate a situation involving runners and their speed, distance, and time from a starting point. The relationship among these variables is graphed as the variables are manipulated.
- **Instructional materials:** Use a mathematics balance to help students visualize equalities. Use objects (keys, buttons, blocks, or geometric shapes) that students can categorize according to color, size, and shape.

FACT FAMILIES   By illustrating with manipulatives, explain to students that fact families are three numbers that are related just as the people in a family are related. For example, the numbers 2, 5, and 7 can be used to make two addition problems ($2 + 5 = 7$ and $5 + 2 = 7$) and two subtraction problems ($7 - 5 = 2$ and $7 - 2 = 5$). Demonstrate with the manipulatives the commutative property and that subtraction is the inverse of addition. Provide students with many opportunities to create their own "families." Have students write equations for their problems. Figure 12.4 can be used to convey the notion of family and to give students a place to write the number sentences for their fact families.

SOLVING ALGEBRAIC EQUATIONS   Teach students a strategy for solving algebraic equations. The following strategy requires students to ask themselves questions to guide their thinking through the steps (Allsopp et al., 2007).

Solve: $5x = 25$

1. Is there a letter?

   "There is a letter that represents a variable. I need to figure out the value of the variable."

FIGURE 12.4   **Family of Facts**

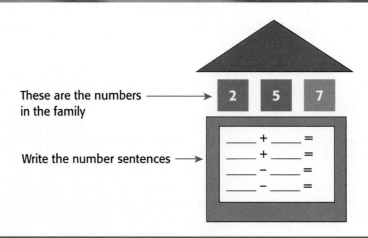

These are the numbers in the family

Write the number sentences

2. What is on each side of the equals sign?

    "There is $5x$ and 25, and $5x$ means 5 times x."

3. What is the value for x?

    "I know that 5 times 5 equals 25, so the value of x is 5."

ORDER OF OPERATIONS   Teach students the order in which operations are used to solve equations. The correct order is

- Perform all operations within "fences" (parentheses and brackets).
- Evaluate each power (exponent).
- Do all multiplications and divisions, from left to right.
- Do all additions and subtractions, from left to right.

Provide examples of equations where students have to explain how to solve the problem using the order of operations rules. Create a poster and bookmark with the order information as a cue for those students who may need help remembering the order of operations.

GRAPHIC ORGANIZERS   Use graphic organizers as a way to help students visualize mathematical relationships, vocabulary, and concepts. Venn diagrams can be used to demonstrate similarities and differences between two concepts; hierarchical diagrams can be used to show subordinate relationships to a superordinate concept; and mapping diagrams (see Figure 12.5) can be used to visually depict how information about concepts can be organized (Maccini & Gagnon, 2005). Figure 12.5 shows the four operations and terms that convey each operation. Students must understand what operation each term represents as they encounter them in algebraic equations. Problem solving is one of the most important areas in mathematics. In the next section, we discuss a variety of ways to teach this area.

FIGURE 12.5 **Graphic Organizer**

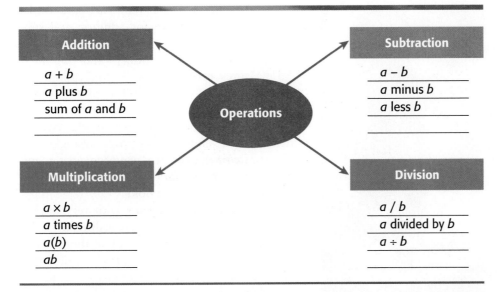

Source: Adapted from P. Maccini and J. C. Gagnon, 2005, *Math Graphic Organizers for Students with Disabilities.* Washington, DC: The Access Center: Improving Outcomes for all Students K–8. Reprinted with permission. Available at www.k8accescenter.org/training_resources/documents/MathGraphicOrg.pdf

What Is Problem Solving and How Do I Teach It?

Problem solving is an essential component of a total mathematics program because it is a major life skill and an area where other skills (such as computation, estimation, and reasoning) can be taught and reinforced (Cawley & Parmar, 1992; NCTM, 2000). Solving real-world word problems is a basic life skill and is recommended as a major component of the mathematics curriculum (NCTM, 2000). Word problems can be developed through contextualized problems by turning classroom situations into word problems and using daily situations that link to problem solving. Conceptual and skill development should be connected to problem solving so that whole-number computations, fractions, decimals, percentages, and algebraic equations are integrated into word problems that students solve reflecting real-life situations.

Mayer (1992) identified five types of knowledge that are necessary to solve word problems: linguistic (i.e., English language and syntax), semantic (i.e., understanding of the meaning of words), schematic (i.e., word problem types, relevant and irrelevant information), strategic (i.e., planning and monitoring solution strategies), and procedural (i.e., performing a sequence of operations). As noted by Montague (2006), good problem solvers use a variety of cognitive and metacognitive strategies (e.g., rereading, drawing pictures, identifying important information, and disregarding extraneous information) to solve word problems.

● Solving real-world word problems is a basic life skill and is recommended as a major component of the mathematics curriculum.

Types of Word Problems

The word problems typically found in elementary curricula involve (1) join, part-part-whole, separate, and compare for addition and subtraction, and (2) equal-groups, multiplicative comparisons, combinations, and product-of-measures problems for multiplication and division (Van de Walle, 2007). Mayer (1992) indicated that interest, area, mixture, river current, probability, number, work, navigation, progressions, exponentials, triangle, distance/rate/time, averages, scale conversion, and ratio problem categories are typically included in secondary-level textbooks.

In some cases, students with very limited reading abilities may have great difficulty solving story problems simply because they are unable to read the words in the problem. Adapting instruction might be the answer to this type of problem. For instance, story problems could be presented on audiotape as well as on paper; in this way, difficult words are read aloud to the

what WORKS 12.6

Problem Solving Strategies

One of the most useful applications of algebraic reasoning is in using equations to solve word problems. The following are four multistep strategies that have been suggested for analyzing and solving problems.

- ● Six-Step Problem Solving Strategy[1]

1. State the question.
2. Identify the operation.
3. Eliminate extraneous information.
4. State how many steps are involved.
5. Solve the problem.
6. Check your work.

- ● Cognitive and Metacognitive Problem Solving Strategy[2]

1. Read the problem.
2. Paraphrase the information.
3. Visualize the information.
4. Identify the problem.
5. Develop a hypothesis.
6. Estimate the answer.
7. Compute the problem.
8. Check your work.

- ● FAST DRAW[3]

1. **F** ind what you're solving for.
2. **A** sk yourself, "What are the parts of the problem?"
3. **S** et up the numbers.
4. **T** ie down the sign.

1. **D** Discover the sign.
2. **R** Read the problem.
3. **A** Answer, or draw and check.
4. **W** Write the answer.

- ● Questions and Actions[4]

Step	Questions	Actions
a. Read the problem.	Are there words I don't know?	Underline words.
	Do I know what each word means?	Find out definitions.
	Do I need to reread the problem?	Reread.
	Are there number words?	Underline.
b. Restate the problem.	What information is important?	Underline.
	What information isn't needed?	Cross out.
	What is the question asking?	Put in own words.
c. Develop a plan.	What are the facts?	Make a list.
	How can they be organized?	Develop a chart.
	How many steps are there?	Use manipulatives.
	What operations will I use?	Use smaller numbers.
		Select an operation.
d. Compute the problem.	Did I get the correct answer?	Estimate.
		Check with partner.
		Verify with a calculator.
e. Examine the results.	Have I answered the question?	Reread the question.
	Does my answer seem reasonable?	Check the question and answer.
	Can I restate the question and answer?	Write a number sentence.

Sources: [1]Adapted from E. Marzola, 1985, *An arithmetic problem solving model based on a plan for sets to solution, mastery learning, and calculator use in a resource room setting for learning disabled students.* New York: Teachers College Press. [2]Adapted from M. Montague and C. S. Bos, 1986, The effect of cognitive strategy training on verbal math problem solving performance of learning disabled adolescents. *Journal of Learning Disabilities, 19,* 26–33. [3]Adapted from C. D. Mercer and S. P. Miller, 1992, Teaching students with learning problems in math to acquire, understand, and apply basic math facts. *Remedial and Special Education, 13*(3), 19–35, 61. [4]Adapted from D. P. Rivera, 1994, April, *Teaching mathematics using direct instruction and cooperative learning.* Paper presented at the International Conference of the Council for Learning Disabilities. San Diego, CA.

students. Another way to address the issue of reading level is to have students work in cooperative learning or peer tutoring arrangements. A student with a more advanced reading level could be the designated "reader" for the other student or students. A third possibility is to have students work individually or in small groups with the teacher, a family member volunteer, or the paraprofessional. This individualized attention could easily address the reading-level problem and provide additional support in solving story problems. A fourth option could include controlling the reading level of the word problems to more closely match the reading level of the students. By carefully selecting words, teachers can address the reading level more adequately in some cases.

Difficulties with Problem Solving

In the area of solving word problems, students have trouble understanding and setting up problems and solving different types of word problems. Parmar (1992) noted that students ages 8 to 14 who were identified as having learning disabilities or behavior disorders had difficulties with reading the problem, identifying the operation, setting up problems, self-correcting, and excluding extraneous information. Rivera (1997) summarized the difficulties commonly observed in student attempts to solve word problems as difficulties with vocabulary, sentence structure complexity, extraneous information, reading problems, computational skills, multistep problem representation, and word problem types.

Teaching Problem Solving

The general steps involved in teaching problem solving follow.

- **Diagnosis:** Use clinical interview procedures to assess the reasons for difficulty solving problems. (These might include language, numbers too big, reading problems, extraneous information, or linguistic structure.) Rewrite problems accordingly. In some cases, problems may have to be read to students who have serious reading problems.
- **Strategy instruction:** Teach explicit strategies. Refer to What Works 12.6 on page 527 for examples of strategies that can be used to teach problem solving.
- **Instructional delivery:** Include problems with too little or too much information; ask students to tell what is needed or what is extra.
- **Instructional delivery:** Have students write story problems for peers to solve.
- **Instructional delivery:** Have students substitute smaller numbers for larger numbers that may be troublesome. Students can (a) use manipulatives to depict problems, (b) use charts and tables to organize information, (c) solve problems containing more than one "right" answer, (d) devise their own story problems, (e) solve "real" problems (e.g., situations in the classroom or current events), and (f) focus on the "language" of the story problem by explaining, in their own words, problems with varying linguistic, symbolic, and extraneous information.
- **Calculations:** Have students use calculators to check their work.
- **Progress monitoring:** Monitor student performance regularly. Provide several problems for students to solve independently. Ask them to show their work, including both the ways they "make a plan" and their calculations.

ADAPT in Action • Mrs. Reid—Problem Solving Instruction

Mrs. Reid is very concerned that solving word problems in small groups is difficult for many of her students. She has students with identified mathematics disabilities who are having trouble, but she notes that other students are struggling as well. She decides to provide a problem solving lesson that incorporates skills from the different areas of the curriculum. She likes to contextualize problems, so her "real-life" problem will involve the use of geometry, measurement, and algebra to solve a problem. She wants students to develop their strategies for solving the problems and to present their solution strategies to the whole class as a learning experience. Mrs. Reid will conduct observation during group work. She will look for students' ability to read the problem, paraphrase what the problem is asking, identify relevant information, identify and use a strategy with visuals, and calculate the answer. She will also observe involvement of students by sitting with each group for 10 minutes and recording the quantity and quality of student comments to determine who is participating, how frequently, and what is being discussed. Instructional Activity 12.2 outlines the resulting lesson.

Following the lesson, Mrs. Reid reviews her progress-monitoring data about how students performed on the assignment. She learns that at least one student in each group makes no or infrequent contributions to the discussion on how to solve the problem. Some of the contributions are quite good, where students identify strategies for problem solution and visuals to depict the problem. But her struggling students who did not perform well on the progress-monitoring problems need adapted instruction. She decides to use the ADAPT framework to figure out her next steps.

Ask, "What am I requiring the student to do?" Mrs. Reid wants the students to solve problems using strategies, including visual representations. She also wants them to compute the calculations correctly.

Determine the prerequisite skills of the task. "I know students need to read the problem, figure out what it is asking (including identifying whether there is extraneous information and whether it is a multistep problem), set up a plan using visuals, and calculate the answer."

Analyze the student's strengths and struggles. At least five students in each class period had difficulty identifying a plan to solve the problem, did not show the work for each step of a multistep problem, and made calculation errors.

Propose and implement adaptations from among the four categories. Mrs. Reid decides to use the "Questions and Actions" strategy shown in What Works 12.6 on page 527 to help students work through each step of the problem solving process. This strategy taps both the cognitive (steps) and metacognitive (self-questioning) aspects of problem solving.

Test to determine if the adaptations helped the student accomplish the task. Ms. Hart will continue to collect progress-monitoring data and group observation information to determine whether students use the steps of the "Questions and Actions" strategy in their small-group work and whether their independent performance improves.

Instructional activity 12.2

Geometry, Measurement, Problem Solving: Buying Sod for the Backyard

INSTRUCTIONAL OBJECTIVE: The student will use a strategy to solve a multistep problem.

INSTRUCTIONAL CONTENT: NCTM Standards— Problem solving, number and operation, geometry, measurement, algebra (conceptual understanding)

INSTRUCTIONAL MATERIALS: Graph paper, recording sheet

INSTRUCTIONAL DELIVERY

Grouping: Small group of students

Vocabulary: area, square, foot
Before teaching the lesson, review the vocabulary terms. Have students define the terms in their own words. Use visuals for English language learners.

Teaching Procedure

1. Provide directions to the whole class for the activity.

   In small groups, you are going to work together to generate a solution to the following problem. You are going to lay sod in your backyard. Sod is sold in squares measuring 12 inches by 12 inches. The backyard is 50 feet by 72 feet. Draw, on graph paper, a diagram of the backyard area you wish to sod. Sod goes for $.85 a square. How much will enough sod to complete the project cost? Solve the problem and record your group's answer and reasoning.

2. Tell students that each one of them should write, on his or her recording sheet, what the problem is asking, strategies for solving the problem, and the calculations.

3. Circulate among groups, asking questions to promote discussion and problem solving.

4. Have a speaker from each small group explain to the whole class how the group solved the problem.

PROGRESS MONITORING (Independent Practice): After the lesson, give each student four problems to solve independently. Ask students to draw a diagram to represent each problem and to show all calculations.

Source: Adapted from D. P. Bryant, Sun A. Kim, P. Hartman, and B. R. Bryant, 2006, Standards-based mathematics instruction and teaching middle school students with mathematical disabilities. In M. Montague and A. Jitendra (Eds.), *Teaching Mathematics to Middle School Students with Learning Difficulties.* New York: Guilford.

summary

We know that mathematics instruction should involve approaches, activities, and interventions to teach mathematical skills and concepts that promote mathematics literacy for *all* students. It is important for teachers to challenge their students to achieve mathematical competence. It is equally important for teachers to provide appropriate instructional adaptations for those students who are most in need of academic assistance. For students with mathematics disabilities, adaptations are important to help them participate in classroom discussions and learn mathematical skills and concepts emphasized in the NCTM *Standards.*

Several factors contribute to mathematical difficulties for students who struggle with learning mathematics. Language processing and vocabulary are challenging for some students. Memory and executive functioning may interfere with learning mathematical skills and concepts. Cognitive developmental problems may hamper students' understanding of declarative, procedural, and conceptual knowledge. Finally, visuospatial difficulties may cause difficulties with alignment of problems, place value, and geometry.

Instructional adaptations are necessary to help students benefit from instruction in the general education setting. This chapter offers ideas about adaptations for early number development; arithmetic combinations; place value; whole-number computation; fractions, decimals, and percents; algebra; and problem solving. Keep in mind that other areas addressed in the NCTM *Standards* (such as measurement, geometry, and statistics and probability) also require adapted instruction.

self-test QUESTIONS

Let's review the learning objectives for this chapter. If you are uncertain and cannot "talk through" the answers provided for any of these questions, reread those sections of the text.

- **Who are students with mathematics difficulties?**

  Such students demonstrate difficulties with language processing, memory and executive functioning, cognitive development, and visuospatial skills.

- **Who are mathematically gifted and talented students?**

  Students who are mathematically gifted and talented have uneven mathematical development and conceptual understanding. They are quite adept with inferential thinking, deductive reasoning, and problem solving, and they possess intuitive abilities that allow them to reach solutions with speed and accuracy.

- **How can teachers provide effective mathematics instruction?**

  Teachers should apply diagnostic procedures and use strategies that can help students learn to solve problems and become self-regulated learners. Representations at the concrete, pictorial, and abstract levels should be used to help students understand and improve abstract mathematical reasoning. It is important to teach the language of mathematics, and English language learners need extra support. Computational fluency should be promoted with those skills that require fluent responding, such as arithmetic combinations and naming and writing numerals. Progress monitoring ensures that teachers know whether students are responding to instruction or reteaching is necessary.

- **How can teachers make instructional adaptations for mathematics instruction?**

  This chapter provided several Instructional Activities and ADAPT frameworks for mathematics instruction. Reexamine all of these to review how instruction can be conducted in such a way as to meet individual learning needs.

Revisit the OPENING challenge

Check your answers to the Reflection Questions from the Opening Challenge and revise them on the basis of what you have learned.

1. What mathematical learning characteristics might be contributing to the students' learning difficulties?

2. How can Ms. Hart and Mrs. Reid use the features of effective mathematics instruction to structure their lessons?

3. What instructional adaptations can be implemented to help students access the mathematics curriculum?

4. What suggestions do you have on ways in which these teachers can monitor student progress?

CEC Knowledge and Skill Core Standard and Associated Subcategories

CEC Content Standard 2: Development and Characteristics of Learners

Special educators know and demonstrate respect for their students first as unique human beings. Special educators understand the similarities and differences in human development and the characteristics between and among individuals with and without ELN. Moreover, special educators understand how exceptional conditions can interact with the domains of human development and they use this knowledge to respond to the varying abilities and behaviors of individuals with ELN.

CEC Content Standard 4: Instructional Strategies

Special educators select, adapt, and use instructional strategies to promote challenging learning results in general and special curricula and to appropriately modify learning environments for individuals with disabilities. They enhance the learning of critical thinking, problem solving, and performance skills of individuals with disabilities, and increase their self-awareness, self-management, self-control, self-reliance, and self-esteem.

CEC Content Standard 7: Instructional Planning

Individualized decision-making and instruction is at the center of special education practice. Special educators develop long-range individualized instructional plans anchored in both general and special curricula. Individualized instructional plans emphasize explicit modeling and efficient guided practice to assure acquisition and fluency through maintenance and generalization. Understanding of these factors as well as the implications of an individual's exceptional condition, guides the special educator's selection, adaptation, and creation of materials, and the use of powerful instructional variables. Instructional plans are modified based on ongoing analysis of the individual's learning progress.

CEC Content Standard 8: Assessment

Special educators conduct formal and informal assessments of behavior, learning, achievement, and environments to design learning experiences that support the growth and development of individuals with disabilities.

INTASC Core Principle and Associated Special Education Subcategories

1. Subject Matter

1.01 All teachers have a solid base of understanding of the major concepts, assumptions, issues, and processes of inquiry in the subject matter content areas that they teach.

1.03 All teachers understand that students with disabilities may need accommodations, modifications, and/or adaptations to the general curriculum.

2. Student Learning

2.02 All teachers examine their assumptions about the learning and development of students with disabilities and use this information to create challenging and supportive learning opportunities.

2.04 All teachers are knowledgeable about multiple theories of learning and research-based practices that support learning and use this information to inform instruction.

4. Instructional Strategies

4.03 All teachers use research-based practices to support learning and generalization of concepts and skills.

4.04 All teachers understand that it is particularly important to provide multiple ways for students with disabilities to participate in learning activities. They modify tasks and accommodate individual needs of students with disabilities.

7. Instructional Planning

7.02 All teachers plan ways to modify instruction to facilitate positive learning results within the general education curriculum for students with disabilities.

8. Assessment

8.02 All teachers use a variety of assessment procedures to document student's learning, behavior, and growth within multiple environments appropriate to the student's age, interests, and learning.

Praxis II: Education of Exceptional Students: Core Content Knowledge PRAXIS

I. Understanding Exceptionalities

Human development and behavior as related to students with disabilities, including

- Cognition

Characteristics of students with disabilities, including the influence of

- Cognitive factors
- Affective and social-adaptive factors, including cultural, linguistic, gender, and socioeconomic factors

III. Delivery of Services to Students

Background knowledge, including

- Integrating best practices from multidisciplinary research and professional literature into the educational setting

Curriculum and instruction and their implementation across the continuum of educational placements, including

- Instructional development and implementation
- Teaching strategies and methods
- Instructional format and components

Assessment, including

- How to select, construct, conduct, and modify informal assessments

Video—"Using Manipulatives as Models"

Using manipulatives as models, provide opportunities for students to see and experience mathematical relationships. In this video, pinto beans are used to represent the variables in the story, allowing students to learn by doing and to discover outcomes on their own.

> Log onto **www.mylabschool.com**. Under the **Courses** tab, in **Math Methods,** go to the **video lab**. Access the **"Math Foundations"** videos and watch the **"Using Manipulatives as Models"** video.

 OR

> Use the **www.mylabschool.com Assignment Finder** to go directly to these videos. Just enter Assignment ID **MMV1**.

1. What do the students gain from using manipulatives while the teacher reads the story in this video?
2. In what ways might this lesson in particular, and manipulatives in general, be especially effective for students who struggle in math?
3. If you used this activity in your classroom, list any modification you might make for (a) a student with ADHD, (b) a student with fine motor coordination problems, and (c) a student with behavioral or emotional problems.

Case Study—"Algebra (Part 1): Applying Learning Strategies to Beginning Algebra"

This case study unit outlines some of the common problems students face when beginning to learn more advanced math subjects, such as algebra. It also provides strategies for teaching algebra using math vocabulary, the Concrete-Representational-Abstract method, graphic organizers, and mnemonic devices.

> Log onto **www.mylabschool.com**. Under the **Resources** tab, navigate to the **Case Archive**, and read **"Algebra (Part 1): Applying Learning Strategies to Beginning Algebra"**

 OR

> Use the **www.mylabschool.com Assignment Finder** to go directly to the case study. Just enter Assignment ID **MMCS**.

To answer the following questions, read one of the case studies provided in this case study unit.

1. Read the STAR (Strategies and Resources) sheets recommended for the case you selected. Briefly summarize each strategy and describe the ways in which it could assist you in meeting the needs of the student outlined in the case study.
2. Describe three other strategies outlined in the chapter that you could use to support the student in the case study.

To access chapter objectives, practice tests, weblinks, and flashcards, go to the companion website at **www.ablongman.com/bryantsmith1e**.

chapter *13*

Facilitating Content-Area Instruction and Study Skills

chapter **OBJECTIVES**

After studying this chapter, you will have the knowledge to answer the following questions:

- What difficulties do students demonstrate with content-area instruction?
- How can teachers facilitate content-area instruction?
- What difficulties do students demonstrate with study skills?
- How can teachers facilitate study skills?

● OPENING challenge

Facilitating Content-Area Instruction and Study Skills

Elementary Grades ● Mr. Davis is in his 13th year of teaching fifth grade in a suburban school district. The demographics of the neighborhood reflect a rich cultural diversity in a middle-class setting. Less than 30 percent of enrolled students are eligible for free or reduced-cost meals. He has several students with learning disabilities in his class, and two are being referred for possible ADHD. Mr. Davis gave his students a survey to complete so that he could examine the reading and study skills of his students. Reviewing results from the survey, he found that a majority of his 27 students had few strategies to help them understand content-area expository texts and lacked time management skills. He reflects, *"Most of my students have good decoding skills and can read fairly fluently. However, when I gave my survey, only a few students could identify strategies to help them read and understand the textbook. I have to help my students read their content textbooks successfully. Time management skills showed similar poor results on the survey. Results suggest that few students spend uninterrupted time studying. They did not identify a plan for taking notes or studying for tests."*

Secondary Grades ● Mrs. Marks is in her 9th year of teaching tenth-, eleventh-, and twelfth-grade history. In her urban school district, she is the only history teacher with over 2 years of experience. She teaches honors history and general history classes. Her students have a range of academic abilities. She has several students with reading disabilities, one student with a mild developmental disability, and several students who are English language learners. Most of her students are eligible for free or reduced-cost lunch. Her students have diverse ethnic and linguistic backgrounds. Across her classes, the number of students ranges from the smallest class size of 15 to the largest class of 37.

Mrs. Marks recognizes that students need strategies to learn content and concepts taught in their history textbooks. She reflects, *"I have been frustrated over the years with my students' inability to understand the information that is provided in their textbooks. I use the textbooks as a starting point for my teaching. I build upon the information in the texts through lectures and hands-on activities. History has to come alive for my students, not just be a recounting of the past. But my*

column continues on next page

column continues on next page

"I am especially excited about working with my students who have learning disabilities. They are extremely capable, but they need help to benefit from content-area instruction and to implement effective study skills. I know that some of my English language learners also need help with vocabulary and comprehension strategies for textbook reading. I am concerned that if they do not develop these skills by the end of the year, they will be at a serious disadvantage when they go into middle school next year." ●

students have to be able to get the concepts and vocabulary from the text to understand what I am teaching."

Also, through informal conversations with her students, she learns that study skills are not adequate, especially for students in her general history class. Many of her students cannot describe what good note-taking and test preparation practices look like or how to budget their time. Mrs. Marks wants her students to go on to college. She knows that something needs to be done to prepare them to handle the studying demands of postsecondary education. ●

Mr. Davis and Mrs. Marks recognize that they have to help their students benefit from content-area instruction and use study skills so that they can be efficient, independent learners. The teachers realize that many students continue to need help across the grades using effective strategies to tackle content-area textbooks and applying study skills to ensure that work is done accurately and in a timely manner.

● Reflection Questions

In your journal, write down your answers to the following questions. After completing the chapter, check your answers and revise them on the basis of what you have learned.

1. What difficulties might students in both teachers' classes exhibit with regard to content-area instruction and study skills?

2. How can the teachers effectively work with their students to help them become efficient learners in content-area instruction and study skills?

3. How can these teachers provide adapted lessons to students who require intensive intervention, while keeping the rest of the class busy with relevant work?

4. How can study skills assessment be used to identify how students, including struggling students, become more efficient learners?

As students progress from the upper elementary grades to middle school and high school, a new pattern evolves, wherein teachers teach their content-area material and students employ study skills such as taking notes and learning subject matter. As part of content-area instruction at the secondary level, students are required to read textbooks at their grade level or above, write reports and papers, and participate in discussions and activities (Lenz & Schumaker, 1999; Raskind & Bryant, 2002). Additionally, students must complete homework, take tests, conduct research, and manage their time across multiple subject areas. Secondary teachers, those who teach in middle school and high school, are required to teach content-area knowledge so that students will learn the material and be successful on end-of-semester exams and state assessments. Notably, because of the need for teachers to teach a great deal of instructional content, the pacing of instruction may not match the learning needs of struggling students who require a lot of practice to master material. Thus, students with special learning needs may be challenged to keep up with their classmates.

Content-area instruction focuses on teaching students subject knowledge in areas such as social studies, science, and literature. Secondary teachers use various instructional approaches for teaching content-area material to students. For example, middle and high school content-area instruction is teacher-directed; that is, teachers present lectures on textbook content, and students read their textbooks to identify important facts and concepts in preparation for weekly tests (Armbruster & Anderson, 1988; Bean, Zigmond, & Hartman, 1994; Kinder & Bursuck, 1991). Content-area instruction may also include **student-centered activities,** which actively engage students in the learning process to solve problems, discuss issues, and create products. Abdullah (2001) notes that self-directed learners are "responsible owners and managers of their own learning process" (p. 1). Teachers focus more of their time on facilitating student learning through hands-on activities, questioning, and discussions. Thus, in content-area classes, students must be able to read and understand textbooks and engage in activities such as class discussions and questioning.

To learn from textbooks, teachers' lectures, and class discussions, students must use effective study skills. Study skills are techniques students use to obtain, write, remember, and apply content (Hoover & Patton, 1995). Students must be able to manage their time and to concentrate in class and while they are studying (Rivera & Smith, 1997). They must be able to listen effectively to lectures and discussions so that they can distinguish important from irrelevant information to take notes. Students must know how to memorize information and take tests so that they can learn content and pass their classes. Students must be able to demonstrate their mastery of content by taking objective tests and answering short-answer essays on tests. Unfortunately, study skills are not often directly taught to students (Larkin & Ellis, 1998; Strichart, Mangrum, & Iannuzzi, 2002); rather, students may have to acquire these skills by getting tips from helpful teachers, peers, or parents.

We know that secondary teachers who teach in inclusive settings must help all students access and learn the general education curriculum. Because of the problems many students demonstrate with literacy skills, there is increasing emphasis at the state and national levels on the literacy needs of this group of students and on identifying ways to help them learn content-area material. Teachers want strategies to help their students comprehend material in textbooks, including key concepts and terminology, and to engage in classroom activities that lead to successful learning (Bryant et al., Ugel, 2001). Students must possess effective study skills to understand and learn the content material for which they are responsible across multiple subject areas.

In this chapter, we provide an overview of content-area instruction and study skills. You will learn about the difficulties faced by students who struggle with content-area instruction and study skills. Instructional activities and adaptations based on the ADAPT framework are provided to help you teach students who need extra instructional support.

What Difficulties Do Students Demonstrate with Content-Area Instruction?

Reading and understanding content in textbooks is one of the major challenges of students with reading difficulties. Research reveals that many struggling older students read at the fourth-grade level and have difficulty learning content (Bryant et al., 2001). They lack strategies for learning vocabulary and concepts, monitoring their reading, and tackling content in textbooks. Additionally, activities that demand discussion and small-group participation may be problematic because students have not learned the content enough to contribute.

For students with reading difficulties, content-area instruction is "overwhelmingly difficult" because they lack the strategies and skills that enable their typically achieving peers to benefit fully from textbook-based instruction (Bryant, Ugel, Thompson, & Hamff, 1999). Most students with reading difficulties need assistance in content area instruction to integrate the new information with their prior knowledge and to learn important information from the text (Bryant et al., 2000; Ciborowski, 1992; Lenz & Schumaker, 1999).

In terms of vocabulary and concept knowledge, research shows that not all of your students will learn meanings at the same rate. Students who have reading disabilities will have poorer vocabularies than your better readers, because a great deal of vocabulary learning occurs through reading different types of materials. Thus, the vocabulary gap between your good and poor readers will widen over time (Simmons & Kameenui, 1990). Students who lack strategies for learning vocabulary and concepts typically are not familiar with the multiple meanings of words, word origins, or derivational meanings (word parts). Using a dictionary to look up the meanings of words and using context clues in text may not be helpful strategies. Dictionaries may be too difficult to understand, or the context may not provide helpful clues for figuring out word meanings.

Reading comprehension consists of thinking and constructing meaning before, during, and after reading by integrating information from the author with the reader's background knowledge (Snider, 1989). Readers must employ strategies to activate their prior knowledge about a topic, self-question, identify main ideas and supporting details, paraphrase, and summarize information. Monitoring reading comprehension requires many skills. Good readers monitor their understanding of reading as they read text, and they use strategies to promote comprehension and retention (Honig, Diamond, & Gutlohn, 2000, Ward & Traweek, 1993). We know that students who struggle with monitoring their reading comprehension do not establish a purpose for reading or activate background knowledge. Also, they lack self-questioning abilities to ensure comprehension, and their summarizing strategies are deficient (Deshler, Ellis, & Lenz, 1996). Any one of these problems can seriously interfere with reading text and learning new concepts. Combined, they impose serious reading challenges on struggling students.

Content-area instruction in science, history, and social studies that focuses primarily on the textbook as a source of information implies that students can read and comprehend expository text (text structure that is explanatory/factual), which includes multisyllabic, technical words; various expository text structures (e.g., cause/effect, compare/contrast); and concepts and facts (Lenz & Hughes, 1990). Students with reading difficulties do not understand text structures and thus have difficulty getting meaning from their content-area reading materials. Research has shown a strong relationship between students' understanding of text structure and reading comprehension (Bryant et al., 1999; Deshler et al., 1996). Furthermore, struggling readers do not take advantage of the physical features of the text, such as headings, tables, boldfaced terms, and chapter organizers and summaries.

Finally, in classrooms where teachers include student-centered activities, students with special needs may be challenged by instruction that requires group interactions, discussions, and product development. For example, students may not possess the prerequisite skills (such as basic reading and writing skills) to function well in group work. They may not be able to make connections to or remember previously taught material from an earlier chapter or unit that is now integrated into group activities. Difficulty understanding figurative and literal meanings, and trouble distinguishing connotative meanings (associated meanings that enrich a word's primary meaning) from denotative meanings (dictionary definitions), may hamper students' ability to understand readings and engage in discussions. Let's turn now to ways to teach content-area vocabulary and concepts.

How Can I Teach Content-Area Vocabulary and Concepts?

Students learn about 3,000 new words each year as they read content-area materials and read independently. By the time most of them graduate from high school, your students will have encountered over 88,500 word families (i.e., a base word and its derivatives, such as *success* and *successfully*), and many of these words will have been learned during the course of their independent reading (Beck, McKeown, & Kucan, 2002). Good readers learn vocabulary rapidly during their school years (Honig et al., 2000).

Each discipline has its own technical vocabulary and concepts that your students will have to learn if they are to comprehend specific content-area information. Students must learn the definitions and meanings of these discipline-specific

● What methods is this teacher using to teach vocabulary? What other methods might be helpful?

what WORKS 13.1

Word Meaning Associations

Word associations with synonyms, antonyms, and visuals can facilitate student learning and enhance retention of word meanings.

● **Picture and Associations**

Teaching Procedure

1. Select a vocabulary word and write it in the top left-hand box of the chart (see below).

2. Draw a picture that depicts the word in the picture box.

3. Write a synonym and an antonym, or "nonexample" (tells what the word does *not* mean), in the boxes.

4. Write a definition of the word using meaning from the picture and the synonym or antonym.

5. Write a sentence that uses the word and is personally meaningful.

6. Have students work in small groups to complete the same activity for the next vocabulary word.

7. The students can make posters of their words, share their charts, or create a *Jeopardy*-type game with the words.

Progress Monitoring: Have students define the words in a quiz or group project.

Adaptations

● Instructional content: Provide fewer words for students to define.

● Instructional materials: Eliminate one or two boxes on the chart initially.

● Instructional delivery: Have students make posters of their charts showing variations in pictures, synonyms, and antonyms (nonexamples) for vocabulary words.

● **Keyword Mnemonics**

The keyword mnemonic technique is used to help students learn and remember vocabulary words in subject-area material.

Name _____

Vocabulary word	Picture of word
Associate: Synonym	**Associate: Antonym, or nonexample**
Write the definition in your own words.	

words and concepts to understand content-area text. For example, in history, students must understand the meaning of the word *transcontinental* as they read about westward migration in the United States and railroad expansion. Students also need to understand the conceptual relationship of *transcontinental* to the reasons why people migrated west and to migratory patterns. Thus, to master reading comprehension, your students need to develop an understanding of the

Teaching Procedure

1. Recoding: Change part of an unknown word into a familiar-sounding word (keyword). For example, part of the vocabulary word *grapnel* could be recoded to the keyword *grab*. The keyword is familiar to students and sounds similar to part of the vocabulary word.

2. Relating: Associate the keyword to the definition of the vocabulary word. The relation between the keyword and the definition is illustrated to provide a visual cue of the vocabulary word's definition. In this example, *grapnel* means "a small anchor with several flukes." Thus, a picture of a person grabbing at boxes with a small anchor and flukes could be shown.

3. Retrieving: Activate prior knowledge about the vocabulary words and related keywords with pictures by instructing students to define their vocabulary words by (a) remembering the keywords, (b) visualizing the keyword illustration and the related definition, and then (c) defining their vocabulary words.

4. Displaying: Using a handout with columns, in column 1 provide the vocabulary words, in column 2 provide the keywords, in column 3 write the definitions, and in column 4 show the pictures.

Progress Monitoring: Have students use their keywords to define vocabulary.

Adaptations

- Instructional content: Select words that are easy to picture.
- Instructional delivery: Have students work in small groups to get ideas from each other for keywords.

Source: From M. A. Mastropieri, T. E. Scruggs, & B. J. M. Fulk, 1990. Teaching abstract vocabulary to LD students with the keyword method: Effects on comprehension and recall. *Journal of Learning Disabilities, 23,* 92–107.

● Conceptual Relationships: Semantic Mapping

Semantic maps are procedures that help students to make connections between new vocabulary and prior knowledge and to see the relationships among conceptual ideas. Semantic maps can be done before, during, and after reading as a way to determine what students know prior to instruction and what they learn as they read text or engage in activities. Figure 13.1 on page 547 shows an example of a completed semantic map for a reading selection on seabirds.

Teaching Procedure

1. Identify the main topic and place it at the center of the graphic organizer.

2. Have students brainstorm words that are associated with the main topic.

3. Discuss how to group these words into broad categories, and discuss the meanings and relationships of the words.

4. Ask students to provide labels for the categories.

5. Have students generate words or subcategories for each category.

6. Discuss the vocabulary and the interrelationships of categories and subcategories.

Source: Adapted with permission from Bryant, Ugel, Thompson, & Hamff, 1999.

Progress Monitoring: Give students concepts to create their own semantic maps.

Adaptations

- Instructional content: Limit the amount of mapping "branches" or ideas.
- Instructional material: Have students use Inspiration® software instead of paper and pencil.
- Instructional delivery: Have students work together in small groups to generate ideas, or provide a list of words that students should organize. Give students prompts for organizing.

meaning of concepts and their relationships to the content and the meaning of vocabulary words (Honig et al., 2000). Students needs strategies for understanding the meaning of words and concepts as they read text or handouts or engage in hands-on activities in class. What Works 13.1 provides strategies to help students learn the meanings of words and concepts. Let's take a look at additional strategies for teaching technical vocabulary and concepts.

Teaching Technical Vocabulary and Concepts

Vacca and Vacca (2002) and Bryant et al. (1999) provide suggestions for helping students learn the meanings of new words and concepts that they encounter in content-area texts.

- **Instructional delivery:** Present new vocabulary in semantically related groups, which are groups of words with meaningful relationships (e.g., semantic feature analysis) (Stahl & Nagy, 2006).

- **Instructional delivery:** Teach students the meaning of the prefixes and the Greek and Latin roots used most frequently in specific content areas. For example, in social studies, teach *trans* (over, across, beyond), *geo* (earth), and *port* (carry), and in science teach *bio* (life), *ex* (from, former), and *meter* (measure).

- **Instructional activity:** Have students link new vocabulary with background knowledge by describing what they already know about the topic (Beck, McKeown, & Kucan, 2002).

Considering *Diversity*

Cognates in the Bilingual Classroom

English language learners benefit from formal instruction in using cognates to improve their English reading and vocabulary. *Cognates* are words that are similar in both form and meaning in English and Spanish. Cognates that have similar spelling patterns are easier to recognize. Other cognates are more difficult to identify, because they have variations in their spelling and function. Students need to have knowledge of the word in their native language in order to make the connection between the two words. Post a list of cognates on the wall to remind students to use what they know in Spanish to help them read and comprehend English.

Spanish	English	Spanish	English
animal	animal	lava	lava
imaginación	imagination	mineral	mineral
doctor	doctor	oxígeno	oxygen
océano	ocean	cebra	zebra
vitamina	vitamin	jirafa	giraffe
familia	family	elefante	elephant
telescopio	telescope	hipopótamo	hippopotamus
fruta	fruit	dinosaurio	dinosaur
importante	important	control	control
guitarra	guitar		

Source: Adapted from G. E. Garcia, & W. Nagy, 1993, Latino students' concept of cognates. In D. J. Leu and C. K. Kinzer (Eds.), *Examining central issues in literary research, theory, and practice: Forty-second Yearbook of the National Reading Conference* (pp. 367–373). Chicago, IL.

- **Instructional activity:** Have students make up sentences using new vocabulary (Stahl & Nagy, 2006).
- **Instructional materials:** Have students develop word lists or banks.
- **Instructional materials:** Have students use typographic cues such as footnotes, italics, boldface print, and parenthetical definitions to define words.
- **Instructional materials:** Have students use visual displays, including such graphic organizers as hierarchical charts (charts with broader concepts listed first, connected to supporting narrower concepts); Venn diagrams (intersecting shapes that show how concepts are similar and different); and graphs.
- **Instructional delivery:** Help English language learners by teaching cognates. See the Considering Diversity feature for information about teaching cognates.

You will now read about Samantha and how her struggles with reading and vocabulary are addressed by Mrs. Marks.

Samantha—
ADAPT in Action • Organizing to Learn

Samantha is a student in Mrs. Marks's class. Her diagnosis of having learning disabilities affecting spoken language (with particular deficits in listening) and reasoning/thinking (executive functioning) explains in part why she gets confused with verbal directions and is extremely disorganized. According to a psychological report in her cumulative folder, Samantha was in an automobile accident at 4 years of age and sustained central nervous system damage that caused her learning disabilities.

Mrs. Marks finds Samantha one of her greatest challenges. "She's challenging because she is so bright but seemingly doesn't care a bit about her schoolwork. I know that's not the case, because she often shares with me her frustration at not being able to get straight A's. She likes to read, when she can find her books, but she is constantly misplacing assignment due dates and what is needed for each assignment, and then she loses her completed assignment when she does get something done. Her attention span is short compared to the other students, which affects her ability to listen to directions and her peers. Sustaining attention on reading varies; thus, her comprehension abilities vary. Tackling new vocabulary, which is related to comprehension, is also hampered by her difficulties focusing and keeping her attention on her reading. The referral for an ADHD evaluation may reveal why she has organization and concentration difficulties, which in turn affect her academics."

Read Instructional Activity 13.1 on page 545, which has been assigned to Samantha and her classmates. Consider the ADAPT framework, and then identify adaptations that might be useful.

Following the lesson, Mrs. Marks reviewed the progress-monitoring data for each student and used the ADAPT framework to make decisions about the next steps in instruction for Samantha.

Ask, "What am I requiring the student to do?" Mrs. Davis noted, "They have to create a visual display to connect Civil War battles with related words and ideas in print."

Determine the prerequisite skills of the task. Mrs. Marks comments, "The students need to be able to skim the chapter to find the battles and then read carefully to find out where and when the battles were fought, learn who won the battles, and determine whether General Ulysses S. Grant was a participant. So they have to find key vocabulary terms (the battles) and comprehend what they read in the sections that describe each battle. Also, they need to have their materials (textbook, notebook, and Semantic Feature Analysis Grid) available, take notes, and then decipher what they have written so they can complete their grid. This will take some time, so they must stay on task and keep from being distracted, all the while attending to what they are doing as they work in small groups."

Analyze the student's strengths and struggles. All of the students have the requisite skills except Samantha. "She does well working in small groups, but she has trouble understanding the semantic features as we discuss them before moving into small groups. She has no problem reading the text, adjusting her reading rate, or comprehending text, but she didn't have her book or notebook with her. She stays on task for about 10 minutes at a time. If she is able to stay on task, and if she has her book, she should be able to complete part of the grid."

Propose and implement adaptations from among the four categories. Mrs. Marks decides to pair a student with Samantha before the small-group work to help her understand the semantic features they will be discussing (instructional delivery). She will have Samantha work on only one battle at a time (instructional content). And the day before the lesson, Mrs. Marks will make sure that Samantha records in her "Schoolwork Diary" that she needs to bring her history book to class (instructional material).

Test to determine if the adaptations helped the student accomplish the task. Mrs. Marks will collect progress-monitoring data to determine whether the adaptations helped in completing the grid.

After the lesson, Mrs. Marks evaluated Samantha's understanding of the lesson. She was satisfied, based on the progress-monitoring data, that Samantha understood semantic features and was able to complete a section of the grid successfully. Let's take a look at the adaptations Mrs. Marks chose to help Samantha. She decided to continue with the following adaptations, which she had made earlier while considering the ADAPT framework.

- **Instructional content:** Samantha will work on only one battle at a time.
- **Instructional materials:** The day before the work is to be done, Mrs. Marks will make sure that Samantha records in her "Schoolwork Diary" that she needs to bring her history book to class.
- **Instructional delivery:** Samantha will be paired with another student before the small-group work to help her understand the semantic features they will be discussing.

Now, we will focus on ways in which students can monitor their reading comprehension.

Instructional activity 13.1

Semantic Feature Analysis: Civil War Battles

INSTRUCTIONAL OBJECTIVE: The student will create a graphic display to relate a concept to related words.

INSTRUCTIONAL CONTENT: Vocabulary from lessons

INSTRUCTIONAL MATERIALS: Concept, Semantic Feature Analysis Grid, vocabulary

INSTRUCTIONAL DELIVERY

Grouping: Whole class for initial instruction; small groups for practice and sharing

Teaching Procedure

1. Identify the concept to teach.
2. Model how to complete a Semantic Feature Analysis Grid.
3. List the related vocabulary words down the left-hand column, and write the names of the features across the top row.

4. Review the vocabulary words to see whether they contain any of the features listed under characteristics. If so, have the students put a + in the corresponding box. If not, have students put a – in the box.
5. Have students provide a reason why they chose to put + or – in the box.
6. Have students work in small groups to complete a Semantic Feature Analysis Grid for a concept to be studied and related vocabulary words.
7. Have students explain their grids to the class.

An example of a completed Semantic Feature Analysis Grid for the Civil War is shown in the accompanying table.

PROGRESS MONITORING: Give students key concepts from a lesson, and have them generate related vocabulary.

Concept: Civil War Battles	Characteristics			
	Fought in South	South Victories	1863	Ulysses S. Grant Involved
Vicksburg	–	–	+	+
Gettysburg	–	–	+	–
First Bull Run	+	+	–	–
Chattanooga	+	–	+	+

How Can Students Monitor Their Reading Comprehension?

Good readers monitor their understanding of reading as they proceed through the text and use strategies to comprehend and retain the reading material. Students who are able to monitor their comprehension are aware of whether they are understanding and/or remembering what they are reading. Thus monitoring entails regulating comprehension during reading so students can prevent faulty understanding. Comprehension monitoring involves (a) activating background knowledge, (b) clarifying the purposes for reading, (c) identifying the important information, (d) summarizing information, (e) engaging in self-questioning about the text, (f) using text structure formats to comprehend text, and (g) correcting problems when comprehension is inadequate (Baker & Brown, 1984; Pressley et al., 1995). Students benefit from instruction on when and how to use different strategies to monitor comprehension so that they will be able to "fix" comprehension problems. Let's review ways to facilitate monitoring of reading comprehension.

Facilitating Students' Monitoring of Their Reading Comprehension

Students should engage in multiple activities before, during, and after reading to ensure that comprehension monitoring is an ongoing process. The following ideas can also be used to facilitate comprehension monitoring.

- **Instructional delivery:** Teach students self-monitoring questions (Baker [1991], cited in Vacca & Vacca, 2002, p. 358; Bryant et al., 1999).

  Questions to Ask Before Reading

  1. What is my purpose for reading?
  2. What do I already know about this topic?
  3. What do I think I will learn about this topic (make predictions)?

  Questions to Ask During Reading

  1. Does what I am reading make sense?
  2. Is this what I expected? Should I revise my predictions or suspend judgment until later?
  3. How are the important points related to one another? What parts are similar and/or different?
  4. Should I read on, reread, or stop and use a fix-up strategy? Are there any words I don't understand?

  Questions to Ask After Reading

  1. What were the most important points?
  2. What is my opinion? How do I feel? Do I agree or disagree?
  3. What new information did I learn?

- **Instructional delivery**
  1. Help students link background knowledge with topics to be studied before reading.
     - Students can make predictions about the reading based on such physical features of the text as pictures, graphs, and headings.
     - Students can watch a video that depicts a time era or science concept to be studied.
     - Students can make concept maps (see Figure 13.1) to activate their prior knowledge.

FIGURE 13.1   Semantic Map for Seabirds

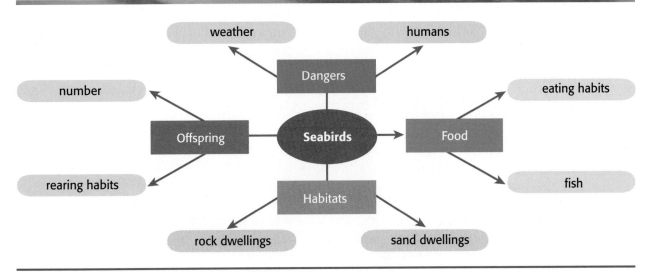

Source: D. P. Bryant, N. Ugel, S. Thompson, & A. Hamff, 1991, Instructional strategies for content-area reading instruction. *Intervention in School & Clinic, 34*(5), 293–302. Reprinted with permission.

- Students can use the technique of asking specific questions designed to help them preview the chapter they are about to read.

2. Help students think about the content during reading.

- Students can use the paraphrasing strategy to help monitor their understanding of content in each paragraph (see What Works 13.2 for more information about this strategy).

- Students can use fix-up strategies to repair faulty comprehension, such as checking their understanding using the questions listed above, rereading difficult sentences, and paraphrasing sentences or paragraphs.

- Students can benefit from seeing visuals such as charts and pictures that can be informative and support important content information. For example, Depression Era photos are powerful sources of information that can stimulate discussions and support text reading (see www.memory.loc .gov for photograph images).

- Students can complete graphic organizers (discussed in the next section) to organize their thoughts about the reading. For instance, Figure 13.2 shows a character map for Stuart Little that was constructed during reading in response to questions about character traits.

3. Help students think about the content after reading.

- Students can summarize text in small chunks, such as chapter sections, and then combine the smaller summaries into a chapter summary.

- Students can write reports to answer questions about the reading.

On page 549, you will meet Andre and read about how Mr. Davis plans accommodations to help him monitor his comprehension of instructional material.

Comprehension-Monitoring Activities

● Questions to Preview a Chapter

Teaching Procedure

1. Provide students with the following questions to serve as an overview before reading their chapter.

   ● What's familiar? Skim to identify content that is familiar and that connects with what you know. Record what is familiar.

   ● What topics are covered? Read the summary, and record the topics that seem to be most important.

   ● What questions do you have? Write the questions that you have about the chapter and topic.

   ● How is it organized? Write the main headings, and take notes under each heading.

   ● What words don't I know? Write on note cards any words you notice that are unfamiliar.

2. Have them monitor their comprehension in small groups by

   ● Skimming portions of a chapter and recording familiar content.

   ● Using pictures and graphics to help identify information.

3. Have students read sections of the chapter to identify information with which to answer these questions:

   ● What topics are covered?

   ● What questions do you have?

4. Have students note technical, unfamiliar vocabulary on note cards and define the terms if possible.

FIGURE 13.2 Stuart Little Character Map

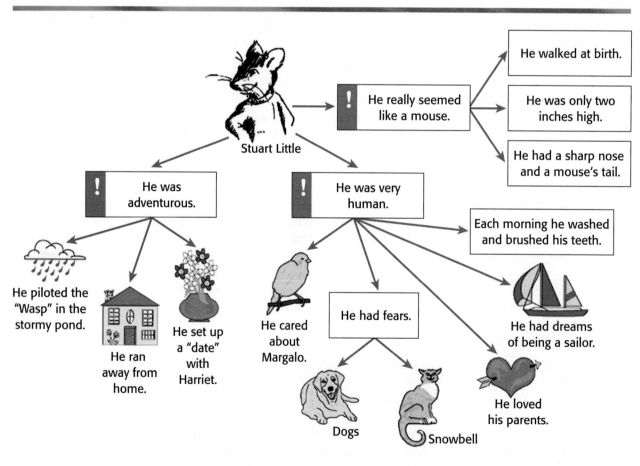

Source: D. P. Bryant & B. R. Bryant, 2003, *Assistive technology for people with disabilities.* Boston: Allyn and Bacon.

This activity can be combined with a vocabulary activity such as keyword mnemonics and a summary activity (see What Works 10.4: Graphic Organizers to Support CSR, Summarization Log) to increase understanding of text, including vocabulary.

Progress Monitoring: Have students answer chapter summary and test questions.

Adaptations

- Instructional content: Have students complete handout for only one or two sections rather than for the entire chapter.
- Instructional delivery: Preteach selected technical vocabulary.

Source: Adapted from D. Buehl, 2001, *Classroom strategies for interactive learning,* Newark, DE: International Reading Association.

● **Paraphrasing Strategy**

Teaching Procedure

1. Model how to use the strategy.
2. Teach to mastery the strategy steps for "RAP":
   - **R**ead a paragraph.

- **A**sk, "What were the main ideas and details in this paragraph?"
- **P**ut the main idea and details into your own words.

3. Provide text that is below the student's reading ability so that the focus falls squarely on using the strategy.
4. Provide multiple practice opportunities with feedback.

Progress Monitoring: Have students state the steps in the strategy and explain the meaning of paragraphs in their own words. Provide comprehension test questions to further determine student understanding of text.

Adaptations

- Instructional content: Provide fewer paragraphs for students to practice initially.
- Instructional delivery: Have students practice the strategy in pairs.
- Instructional materials: Use material at an easier reading level.

To receive a full description of the procedures and materials used for the paraphrasing strategy, and to learn about training in its use, contact The University of Kansas Center for Research on Learning: www.ku-crl.org.

ADAPT in Action ● Andre—Self-Monitoring Comprehension

Andre is a student in Mr. Davis's class. Andre knows a great deal about science and knows how to find the answers to questions. Andre has great spoken-language skills, both listening and speaking, and can make incredible displays for his class presentations and science fairs. He is a hard worker (when it comes to science), but he becomes easily bored with other topics. Andre has a reading disability that makes reading content-area text difficult. He has difficulty with decoding skills and comprehension monitoring. His reading fluency is slow.

As you read Instructional Activity 13.2, think about the challenges that Mr. Davis and Andre face in their efforts to meet the instructional objectives. Consider the task that is associated with the lesson. What must Andre be required to do (requisite skills) in order to do the assigned task and meet the objective? Which of the skills draw on Andre's strengths, and which might be struggles? Examine our sample adaptations, and then think of others that might be ideally suited to Andre and to students with similar characteristics.

Following the lesson, Mr. Davis reviewed the progress-monitoring data for each student and decided to use the ADAPT framework to make decisions about next steps for instruction for Andre.

Ask, "What am I requiring the student to do?" Mr. Davis thinks about the task he had the students complete. "They have to complete each section of the KWLS Chart as they read the section on the years leading up to the American Revolution."

Determine the prerequisite skills of the task. Mr. Davis comments, "Students have to be able to think abut the topic and write down what they know about it. They also need to be able to skim the text and gather clues about the content from headings, key vocabulary terms in boldface print, pictures, and the like so that they can write down what they need to learn. Then students have to read the text and write down information about what they noted they want to learn. Finally, all of the students have to think about what may still be missing from their readings and write that down on the chart. So what does all that involve? Accessing prior knowledge; skimming; getting clues as they skim and scan; reading individual words; understanding what those words mean, especially key vocabulary terms; comprehending passages; writing legibly; and thinking about what they now know and what they still need to find out."

Analyze the student's strengths and struggles. All of the students except Andre have the prerequisite skills. "Andre has a great memory. But when given a textbook to read, he quits before he starts. He lacks important reading skills to do the task."

Propose and implement adaptations from among the four categories. Mr. Davis decided to work with Andre alone to help him complete the KWLS chart (instructional delivery). He will have Andre complete the first section of the chart by himself. Mr. Davis was at a workshop recently where he heard about a Recordings for the Blind and Dyslexic program titled Learning Through Listening. This program makes CD-ROMs available for students who are blind or who have reading disabilities. Because Andre has a reading learning disability, he qualifies for such a program that can provide electronic books (instructional materials; instructional delivery).

Test to determine if the adaptations helped the student accomplish the task. Mr. Davis will collect progress-monitoring data to determine whether the adaptations helped Andre access the chapter and complete the KWLS chart.

Before the lesson, Mr. Davis evaluated the activity and determined that Andre's reading disability presented a major challenge to his accessing print. He decided to make the following adaptations after considering the ADAPT framework.

- **Instructional content:** None. Andre would meet the content demands as assigned.
- **Instructional materials:** Andre would use a CD player to listen to a recorded version of the chapter on a CD-ROM supplied by Recordings for the Blind and Dyslexic. Mr. Davis found that the school district had a subscription with the organization.
- **Instructional delivery:** Mr. Davis would help Andre complete sections of the chart by working with Andre as he first learned to access the chapter via CD-ROM. Mr. Davis's involvement would diminish (fade) throughout the lesson, allowing Andre to work more and more independently.

In the next section, we focus on ways to help students use textbooks effectively.

KWLS

INSTRUCTIONAL OBJECTIVE: Before, during, and after reading, the students will create a KWLS chart to determine what they know about the topic and what they are learning as they read.

INSTRUCTIONAL CONTENT: Reading comprehension: Activating prior knowledge and acquiring new knowledge

INSTRUCTIONAL MATERIALS: KWLS chart, history text

INSTRUCTIONAL DELIVERY
Grouping: Whole class group

Teaching Procedure

1. Determine the core concept.

2. Develop a KWLS chart with the core concept stated in question form.

3. Before they read the material, ask the students what they think they already **know** about the core concept. That information is to be recorded in the K column.

4. Ask the students what they **want** to find out while reading the material. That information is to be recorded in the W column.

5. After reading a portion of the text, return to the KWLS chart and confirm or deny the knowledge in the K (What I know) column.

6. Complete the L (What I learned) column by writing the answers to the questions written in the W (What I want to find out) column and entering other pertinent information that students have **learned** from the reading.

7. Complete the S (What I **still** need to learn) column as they are reading.

8. Repeat steps 5, 6, and 7 until the reading has been completed.

PROGRESS MONITORING: Review students' charts after they finish filling them in to determine the accuracy of the information. Provide a comprehension check to determine how well students are understanding their reading.

A sample of a completed KWLS chart is shown in the following table for the core concept question, "What were the American colonists' attitudes toward England before the American Revolution?"

K What I know	W What I want to find out	L What I learned	S What I still need to learn
American colonists did not like their connection to England.	What issues did the American colonists have with England? What was the English attitude toward the American colonists? Were there American colonists who still were happy with their connection with England? If so, what were their disagreements with those colonists who were unhappy with their connection to England?	There were many disagreements. For example, many American colonists did not like to be taxed and yet have no representation in government. Nor did they like having to house English troops serving in the colonies. England viewed the colonies as part of England, or at least as subjects of the English crown. Thus the colonists had to obey whatever edicts England handed down. Yes; they were called Tories, or Loyalists. Some served in Tory Militias, which took the British side during the Revolutionary War. In some instances, Tories and the other colonists lived together without malice. But in other instances, considerable conflict arose, including armed conflicts. Some Tory colonists who were not unhappy with the colonies' connection to England supported independence nonetheless.	What happened to the Tories after the Revolutionary War? Were there factions in England who understood the issues raised by the American colonists? If so, how did they make their opinions known, or did they keep silent?

Source: From D.M. Ogle, 1986, A teaching model that develops active reading of expository text. *The Reading Teacher, 39,* 564–570.

How Can Students Benefit from Textbook Instruction?

Textbooks are an integral part of content-area instruction. They typically consist largely of expository text, although stories (narrative text) are sometimes included to provide a humanistic perspective. For example, in a social studies text, an account of events surrounding the civil war may be personalized with stories about the effects of the war on individuals and their families.

Expository text conveys information in a variety of ways through the use of text structure:

- Problem solution—the text presents a problem and offers possible solutions, usually identifying one solution as most appropriate.
- Description—the text provides details about a topic, person, event, or idea.
- Cause/effect relationships—the text links events (effects) with their causes.
- Enumeration or categorizing—the text is organized by means of lists or by collecting like items.
- Compare/contrast—the text explains similarities and differences between topics, concepts, or issues.

Examples of material that contain expository text include textbooks, magazines, and newspapers. As students read content-area material, they must know how to monitor their comprehension by adjusting to different text structures. Authors and publishers of textbooks work hard to ensure that chapter content is effectively organized and to incorporate a wide variety of study aids. It is important for students to recognize and understand how to use these tools. Teachers can teach their students to get the most out of them by using the text perusal strategy presented in What Works 13.3. This text perusal strategy, known as PARTS, is a cognitive strategy to help readers identify study aids embedded in the chapters and use them to comprehend the text more successfully. These chapter features include components such as introduction, outline, objectives, headings, printing of important new words in boldface type, graphics, and focus questions that help readers comprehend information. Let's explore some ways to help students benefit from textbook instruction.

Facilitating Student Learning from Textbooks

Students can benefit from explicit instruction that helps them to recognize and use text structures as they encounter them in their textbooks. Because textbooks are the materials used most often by content-area teachers as the basis for their instruction, selecting textbooks is an important consideration for teachers and students. The following guidelines can help teachers select textbooks that consider students' learning needs. Also listed are ideas for helping students benefit from textbook instruction.

- **Instructional materials:** Considerations for Selecting Textbooks
  - Textbooks should be examined for coherence (logical flow of ideas) and appropriateness (match between material to be read and reader's knowl-

what
WORKS 13.3

Text Perusal Strategy

- PARTS Cognitive Strategy

Teaching Procedure

1. Model how to use the strategy.
2. Teach to mastery the strategy steps for PARTS:
   - **P**erform goal setting.
     Why are you analyzing the chapter parts?
   - **A**nalyze little parts (chapter features: title, headings, graphics, and italicized words).
     Explain the information indicated by the part.
     Predict what the section under the part is about.
     Tie the parts together.
   - **R**eview big parts (introduction and summary).
     Search for signal words that indicate main ideas.
     Decide what the author thinks is important.
     Relate new information to what you already know.
     Paraphrase the main messages.
   - **T**hink of questions you hope will be answered.
     Check questions provided by the chapter.
     Formulate your own questions.
   - **S**tate relationships.
     How is the chapter related to the rest of the book?
     How is the chapter related to what you already know?
3. Provide multiple opportunities for students to practice using the strategy.

Progress Monitoring: Have students state the steps in the strategy and use the strategy; keep a checklist of each step successfully performed.

Adaptations

- Instructional content: Have students use portions of the PARTS strategy initially and then use the entire strategy.
- Instructional delivery: Have students work in jigsaw groups to identify a part of their textbook and then share with their group.
- Instructional materials: Use materials that explicitly display the features of the text, including boldface terms and graphics to highlight information.

Source: Adapted from E. S. Ellis, 1996, Reading strategy instruction. In D. Deshler, E. S. Ellis, & B. K. Lenz, *Teaching adolescents with learning disabilities* (2nd ed., pp. 61–126). Denver, CO: Love Publishing.

edge and skills). The relationships between main ideas and details should be clear.

- There should be plenty of signal words (words that serve as cues to text structure, such as *first, second,* and *finally* for sequence and *on the other hand* for comparison and contrast).
- Visuals should be informative and should reinforce important content information.
- Graphic organizers (charts, pictures, flowcharts, and diagrams) help students comprehend the text structure.
- Sufficient practice activities give students opportunities to learn and apply concepts and ideas.
- Prereading activities help students link their prior knowledge with topics to be studied.
- Vocabulary activities help students develop a deeper understanding of concepts.

● Textbooks are the materials used most often by content-area teachers as the basis for their instruction. What other kinds of materials are used in this classroom to help students learn about geography and culture?

- **Instructional delivery:** Teach words that signal text structures. Some examples follow. Sequence—*first, second, next;* Cause/Effect—*causes, effects, as a result of;* Problem/Solution—*the problem is, the question is, difficulty;* Compare/Contrast—*is similar, is different, however, in the same way;* Description—*for example, also, another feature;* Enumerative—*includes the following.*
- **Instructional delivery:** Teach text structures using graphic organizers. Model how to use the graphic organizers. Figure 13.3 shows examples of different graphic organizers. These graphic organizers can be used as study guides and sources of information for test questions.

Promoting students' participation is an important part of teaching. In the next section, we take a look at ways to engage students in the learning process.

FIGURE 13.3 Graphic Organizers and Signal Words for Text Structure Formats

Enumerative Format (list and describe)

Description: Facts of similar importance are presented.

Facts may be presented in the order of general to specific:

Many scientists think the **two main reasons** for global warming are the *excessive amounts of carbon dioxide* and *the reduction in the amount of oxygen resulting from our way of life.*

Facts may be presented in the order of specific to general:

Excessive amounts of carbon dioxide and *the reduction in large quantities of oxygen once produced by rainforests* are **two reasons** for global warming.

Enumerative structures usually consist of key words that signal important general and specific information.

Specific facts are elaborated on in subsequent paragraphs.

Example

What is this whole idea about?

Global Warming

What are the main ideas and details?

Excessive amounts of carbon dioxide		Quantities of oxygen	
detail	detail	detail	detail

What is important to understand about this?

If we don't change our lifestyle and stop burning rainforests,

then the global warming trend will continue and increase temperatures worldwide.

Cause/Effect Format

Description: A change results from the occurrence of another factor.

Three types: general to specific, specific to general, and implied

Example

What is this whole idea about?

The Civil War

Start with . . .   Add this . . .   Now this . . .

Economic differences between North and South +		Different viewpoints on slavery =		Battles between the North and South ?	
detail	detail	detail	detail	detail	detail

If there were major differing viewpoints about economic issues and the way the people were treated,

then the nation became divided and civil war broke out.

(continues)

FIGURE 13.3 Continued

Sequential Order Format

Description: Events unfold in a linear (chronological) or cyclical sequence.

Example: Cyclical sequence

What is the whole idea about? _____

What are the main events that happened? _____

What is the cycle? _____

What is important to understand about this cycle? _____

Compare/Contrast Format

Description: Two (and sometimes more) general topics are compared by giving factual information about their characteristics.

Example: Social activism

What is being compared?

1. Progressive Movement of 1990s: General Topic 1
2. Civil Rights Movement of 1960s: General Topic 2

Main Ideas	Topic 1: How Different	How Similar	Topic 2: How Different
Social problems	Discrimination against minorities, price fixing	Discrimination	Discrimination against minorities, segregation
_____	_____	_____	_____

Source: Adapted from E. Ellis, 1996, Reading strategy instruction. In D. Deshler, E. S. Ellis, & B. K. Lenz, *Teaching adolescents with learning disabilities* (2nd ed., pp. 61–126). Denver, CO: Love Publishing.

How Can I Facilitate Student Participation?

It is important to actively engage students in the learning process through discussions, questioning, and small-group activities. Active engagement can be used along with textbook instruction to help students with learning difficulties understand and interact with material. For example, Okolo and Ferretti (1997) worked with adolescent students with learning disabilities on events leading up to the American Revolution. Students created multimedia design projects to explain their understanding of the events. Preliminary study findings suggested that it is feasible to engage students with learning disabilities in activities involving historical topics using many sources of information. In another study that focused on student participation and engagement, Ferretti, MacArthur, and Okolo (2001) used project-based learning, which involves students investigating relevant problems and discussing their work with other students, to teach about the migration of groups of people. They used a conceptual framework as a strategy to help students understand migratory practices of groups of people in the late nineteenth and early twentieth centuries and make comparisons to contemporary migratory practices. Students also used a compare/contrast strategy to help them understand key ideas. The researchers found that students both with and without disabilities significantly improved their historical knowledge and reasoning. Additional research on the effects of activity-based learning with students with learning difficulties is warranted.

In Chapter 6, we discussed using cooperative learning groups to engage students in learning and offered some ideas for increasing the likelihood that all students have a role to play during group work. In this section, we describe ways to engage students during class discussions. We provide an overview of anchored instruction, using multimedia research projects as an example of actively involving students in learning. You will now read about ways to help engage students in class discussions and to promote participation.

Facilitating Class Discussions to Engage Students

Teachers can include all students in class discussions through various activities and techniques. Using questioning strategies can facilitate discussions by engaging students in activities to ask and answer questions. Also, requiring students to write their responses and to share their ideas within a small group is good preparation for whole-class instruction. Teachers should work among small groups checking for understanding, modeling how to respond to questions, and asking probing questions to stimulate student thinking. The following suggestions can be implemented in all content-area classes.

- **Instructional materials/delivery:** Provide a discussion guide with questions that students should answer before class discussions begin. Students can work with a partner to complete the guide. Discussion guides can also include sections for each small group to complete in preparation for class discussion. For example, a novel can be analyzed according to story elements such as setting, characters, problem, and resolution, where each group is responsible for summarizing content for each element. In social studies or science, students

● Teachers can include all students in class discussions through various activities and techniques. What are some examples of techniques that may be useful in your classroom?

may be assigned a specific part of a chapter to summarize or chapter headings to turn into questions and then answer.

- **Instructional materials/delivery:** Provide a question stem card (these are cards with questions such as "How are ___ alike and different?" "What explanation can you offer about . . . ?" "Why do you think . . . ?" "How would you describe . . . ?") and a topic, character, event, or issue to go with the question stem. Students should prepare an answer to the question before discussion, working with a partner or in a small group.

- **Instructional activity/delivery:** Divide students into small groups and give them one question representing each level of Bloom's taxonomy: knowledge, comprehension, application, analysis, synthesis, and evaluation. Questions can be the same across groups so that groups can share their responses after the activity to determine multiple perspectives about questions that require higher-order thinking such as synthesis and evaluation.

- **Instructional activity:** Have students record their questions about content and put the questions in a box. Draw questions and have students answer the questions.

Using Anchored Instruction to Facilitate Participation

Anchored instruction is an instructional technique that begins with an event or problem situation that may be presented in a video or movie. The video is used to provide background information about the event or problem situation and to create a context that contributes to a shared experience among students to facilitate learning (The Cognition and Technology Group at Vanderbilt, 1990; Rieth, Colburn, Bryant, 2003). Although more research is needed, anchored instruction shows promise for teaching secondary students with academic problems (Glaser, Rieth, Kinzer, Colburn, & Peter, 1999; Rieth, Bryant, et al., 2003; Rieth et al., 2003). Video-based anchors can help students with significant reading disabilities gain access to subject-area content rather than relying solely on textbooks and teacher lectures (Kinzer, Gabella, & Rieth, 1994; Rieth, Colburn, et al., 2003). The anchor can be used as the main focus for class discussion to facilitate student–teacher interactions (Glaser et al., 1999; Rieth, Bryant et al., 2003). For example, anchored instruction has been shown to increase the types of questions and answers (higher-level thinking) generated by teachers and students during class discussions (Glaser et al., 1999; Rieth, Colburn, et al., 2003). In studies, anchored instruction has used *To Kill a Mockingbird* and *Playing for Time* video anchors to teach human relationships, social studies events (e.g., post–World War I, World War II, the Great Depression), and themes such as racism, authority, power, and socioeconomic status. Anchored instruction consists of questioning, discussions, video-based learning, and multimedia projects wherein students engage in research and conduct class presentations.

Rieth, Bryant, and colleagues (2003) identified the following phases and associated activities for anchored instruction. The video *To Kill a Mockingbird* is the anchor used for the description of the phases.

PHASE 1: Setting the Stage. This phase consists of activities to help students develop interviewing and research skills for their final multimedia project. In this phase, students learn how to conduct interviews, ask questions to research a topic, and use their background knowledge to learn more about a topic. Table 13.1 shows the three procedures employed in Phase 1.

TABLE 13.1 Anchored Instruction Procedures for Phase 1

Learning How to Interview

1. Ask students to bring in boxes that contain two to four objects that they feel best represent them. Ask students to brainstorm possible items to include in their boxes.

2. Tell students that today they will work in small groups to learn more about each other by examining the objects each person brought in and by asking questions about the objects. They should ask different types of questions. These might be "why," "how," or "what" questions. Or they might come up with other types of questions.

3. Divide students into groups of three. Assign students the following roles: recorder, question asker, responder. These roles will be changed every time.

4. Students begin questioning another student about his or her object box. Allow approximately 10 minutes per person for questioning. Encourage students to ask questions that explore issues such as "Who is this person?" "What do these objects tell me about him or her?"

5. Once the small groups of three have finished questioning, join each group with another group of three. Ask this group of six:
   - What types of questions gave you the most information about a person? Why?
   - What types of questions didn't seem to give you much information? Why not?

Ask students to share their responses from the small-group sessions, and record their responses on paper.

Learning How to Research a Topic

1. Show students a picture depicting a scene from the 1930s.

2. Ask students, "What's going on in this picture?" "What do you see?" Encourage students to discuss the photograph.
   - Who are the people in this picture?
   - What do you think they are doing? Why?
   - When do you think this took place?
   - Where do you think it took place?
   - How would you describe what is going on in the photograph?

3. Tell the students to think of the photograph as similar to an object box. Different elements of the photograph come together to give us a portrait of a particular time and place, just as different objects come together to give us a portrait of a person. Ask:
   - What did the photographer want to capture when she took this picture? What is she trying to show us?
   - What message do you think she wanted to convey?
   - What elements of the photograph are essential for our understanding of that message?
   - What information is missing? (What are you wondering about that would help your understanding of the photographer's message?)

4. Record students' questions on the board.

Transitioning to the Anchor

1. Following student responses, return to the photograph. Ask students:
   - Do you think this picture is typical of the 1930s? Why or why not?
   - What have you learned about this time in history?
   - What are you learning about the kinds of questions that get you the most information?
   - What did you learn about people in the 1930s?
   - Who had power? Who had money? How did people get along with one another?

Source: Adapted from H. J. Rieth, D. P. Bryant, C. K. Kinzer, L. K. Colburn, S.-J. Hur, P. Hartman, & H.-S. Choi, 2003, An analysis of the impact of anchored instruction on teaching and learning activities in two ninth-grade language arts classes, *Remedial and Special Education, 24*(3), 173–184. PRO-ED. Reprinted with permission.

PHASE 2: Watching the Anchor / Retelling. This phase occurs over several days. Students are introduced to the themes of power, money, and human relationships. They also watch the video (anchor). After watching the video, students retell the events and identify scenes that they think are important to the story. Retelling descriptions are written on sentence strips. Students answer questions about the movie related to the themes, setting, characters, and events. Students then engage in a discussion to confirm conclusions and clarify misconceptions.

PHASE 3: Segmenting. In this phase, students segment the movie into scenes and label them to be able to use these scenes during Phase 5, when they conduct their research. Strategies used for segmenting include looking for logical breaks between scenes based on plot, scene changes, and character appearances. For instance, if the students choose Mayella Ewell's courtroom scene as a segment, it might be labeled "Mayella's Testimony."

PHASE 4: Characterization. In this phase, students conduct character analysis. Students work in small groups, and each group chooses one character to portray. The students create an acrostic for their character. For example, for Scout: S—secretive, c—curious, o—outward, u—unpredictable, and t—tomboy. Students identify scenes from the video that depict that character's personality. Scenes should show how the character displays examples of the themes power, money, and human relationships. Characterization activities are shown in Table 13.2.

PHASE 5: Student Research and Presentations. Students work in small groups to develop a research question on issues that stem from their discussions. Group members conduct research to gather information to answer their question and create a multimedia presentation. Students must use library and Internet

TABLE 13.2 Anchored Instruction Phase 4 Characterization

Character Research Procedure

1. Explain to the students that they will use video segments to develop portraits of important characters in *To Kill a Mockingbird*. Ask the class to identify orally the main characters of the story.
   - What are the most important relationships in *To Kill a Mockingbird*?

2. Model how to create a character web and how to find scenes using film segments. For example:
   - Choose Mayella Ewell. On the board, create a character web around her name. Ask students to identify Mayella's qualities, her relationships with others, her power in Macon, and her financial situation.
   - Choose the scene from the movie that best illustrates Mayella's character in terms of money, power, and human relationships (Mayella's courtroom testimony).

3. Explain that students will choose a character and, working in groups, will find the most important scenes for that character that reveal money, power, and human relationships. Students will then present their findings to the class.

4. Have groups present their findings on characters to the class.

resources. For instance, one question might be "How did the stock market work?" Students would research this question and relate it to the stock market crash that occurred during the Great Depression in the United States, the period of time depicted in *To Kill a Mockingbird*. The teacher helps students with researching their topic and developing their presentation. A group multimedia presentation is the final event.

You will now read about Colleen and how Mrs. Marks uses the ADAPT framework to ensure Colleen's successful participation in group work.

ADAPT in Action • Colleen—Creating a Group Presentation

Colleen is a student in Mrs. Marks's class. Colleen has a mild developmental disability that manifests itself in numerous ways. She reads at the fourth-grade level, struggles with abstractions, has trouble with fine motor activities, and has some social skills challenges. At the same time, Colleen is eager to please and interacts well with her fellow students. She takes notes when she is assigned a task and has a time management calendar that she uses regularly. She is "technology adept" because her mother is a media specialist in a neighboring middle school and has shown Colleen how to operate cameras (both digital and video) and computers. Colleen spends 2 hours a night on the Internet, researching information on a topic for school and chatting with her online friends.

As you read Instructional Activity 13.3 on page 563, think about the challenges that Mrs. Marks and Colleen face to meet the instructional objective. Consider the activity's task and requisite skills. Which of the skills fall within Colleen's strengths, and which of the skills might be problematic? Examine our list of sample adaptations, and then think of others that may help Colleen and other students with similar characteristics.

Following the lesson, Mrs. Marks reviewed the progress-monitoring data for each student and decided to use the ADAPT framework to make decisions about next steps for instruction for Colleen.

Ask, "What am I requiring the student to do?" After considering the question, Mrs. Marks thinks, "The objective of the lesson is for students to use research and technology skills to create a presentation on a topic about *To Kill a Mockingbird*. Students have to learn skills to do their part of the project, complete their part of the project, and share new information with their peers."

Determine the prerequisite skills of the task. Mrs. Marks notes, "They have to be able to work in small groups to obtain information and then share that information when they convene in their original groups. While in their groups learning specific skills related to the task, they have to be able to access the Internet, read the content presented, extract useful information, determine how to use that information when they return to their jigsaw groups (see Instructional Activity 13.3), know what to present to their fellow students, and then use their individual skills to fulfill their roles. I know it's my job not only to facilitate their success but also to provide explicit instruction and give them practice opportunities."

Analyze the student's strengths and struggles. All of the students have the prerequisite skills except Colleen, but even she has skills that she can utilize. "Colleen works well in small groups, and I have made sure that she will be the Webmaster, because she is comfortable with the Internet. She knows PowerPoint, also. But I think she'll struggle with accessing information off the Internet, because Webmaster information may be written at a reading level that exceeds her abilities. She will also need help in her presentation to other members of the jigsaw cooperative learning group."

Propose and implement adaptations from among the four categories. Mrs. Marks decides to work with Colleen alone before her group convenes so that they can access Web sites containing Webmaster information. In that way, Colleen will have prior knowledge that she can use in Webmaster discussions. She will also pair Colleen with another member of the group to jointly prepare their presentation to their original groups. And Mrs. Marks has asked Colleen's mother to edit Colleen's work and suggest modifications to Mrs. Marks for ways to improve the final project. All of these involve adaptations of instructional delivery. Mrs. Marks sees no reason to adapt the instructional content. She will have Colleen verbally record notes into a tape recorder (instructional materials), rather than writing notes in a notebook. She will instruct Colleen to speak softly into the recorder so as not to disturb others as they take their notes.

Test to determine if the adaptations helped the student accomplish the task. Mrs. Marks will collect progress-monitoring data to determine whether the adaptations helped Colleen learn the material and share that material with her classmates.

After the lesson, Mrs. Marks evaluated the extent to which Colleen met the instructional objective. She was satisfied, on the basis of the progress-monitoring data, that Colleen fulfilled her cooperative learning role of Webmaster. In fact, Colleen's group achieved the highest score.

We now turn our attention to study skills, which are critical for successful learning at all grade levels. Students develop study skills in the elementary grades, maintain their use in the middle grades, refine their skills in high school, and generalize the use of study skills to postsecondary education (Hoover & Patton, 1995). Students with learning difficulties exhibit problems with study skills. Thus, teachers must be prepared to facilitate the development and use of effective study skills for all students.

What Difficulties Do Students Demonstrate with Study Skills?

Students with special learning needs lack effective and efficient study skills that would help them work successfully in inclusive settings, especially at the secondary level (Schloss, Schloss, & Schloss, 2007). Research indicates that students with special learning needs must be taught study skills (Deshler et al., 1996) because they have not "learned how to learn" (Ellis & Lenz, 1987).

Managing one's time to study and prepare for exams is critically important for success in secondary and postsecondary classes. Students with special needs may demonstrate problems with time management because they organize their

Instructional activity 13.3

Conducting Research and Creating a Multimedia Presentation

INSTRUCTIONAL OBJECTIVE: The students will use research and technology skills to create a presentation on a topic about *To Kill a Mockingbird*.

INSTRUCTIONAL CONTENT: Conducting research and creating a multimedia presentation

INSTRUCTIONAL MATERIALS: Computer with Internet access, PowerPoint tutorial, interview script

INSTRUCTIONAL DELIVERY

Grouping: Whole class divided into small cooperative learning groups

Teaching Procedure

1. Divide the class into four groups of four students each. Assign one member of each group to identify pictures (in books or on the Internet) depicting their topic and to use his or her interviewing skills to learn more about the topic; one member to be the Webmaster to conduct research on the Internet for additional information about their topic; and two members to put together the multimedia presentation of information about the topic.

2. Have students meet in role groups and use the jigsaw cooperative learning technique (see Chapter 6 for a review of this procedure). For more information, see http://www.jigsaw.org/tips.htm.

3. Assign the interviewers to learn about conducting interviews in multimedia activities by accessing the Web site http://pblmm.k12.ca.us/PBLGuide/Activities/Interviewing.html

4. Assign the Webmasters to conduct research on the Internet.

5. Assign students to learn how to use PowerPoint via a tutorial (http://www.actden.com/pp/) and to develop a multimedia presentation using PowerPoint.

6. Have the students reconvene into their original cooperative learning groups and share their knowledge with their classmates to complete the project.

Source: Adapted from 4-Empowerment.com, 2004, *Conducting research using* To Kill a Mockingbird. Austin, TX: Author.

---

time poorly, are easily distracted from tasks or projects, lack "stick-to-it-ness," or persistence, and are unable to organize their ideas into a cohesive plan of action (Hammill & Bryant, 1998). Difficulty in any one of these areas results in trouble completing a task. When students have multiple difficulties, their time management problems are exacerbated.

Students must listen to take notes during lectures or discussions and to follow directions (Hoover & Patton, 1995). Listening involves understanding spoken language, including sentence structure and vocabulary. Students must also be able to understand the meaning of the message that is being conveyed by organizing the content and ignoring irrelevant information. Students with special learning needs may exhibit the following listening problems (Hammill & Bryant, 1998):

- Misunderstanding simple spoken sentences and questions
- Having difficulty recognizing that sentences that differ in syntax can mean the same thing
- Having difficulty understanding the meaning of long, multisyllabic words
- Misunderstanding sentences that are spoken at a rapid rate

tech NOTES

Technology to Boost Study Skills

Screen magnification. Screen magnification consists of enlarged character display on the monitor. For individuals with low vision, screen magnification is an adaptation that can promote access to print displayed on the monitor. Using a large-screen monitor (17 inches, for example) is one way to create a larger visual display for easier print access. A simple adaptation is to enlarge the print displayed on the screen through the word processing software program. A large type size, such as 18 point, may provide sufficient magnification for some individuals, depending on their acuity.

Speech synthesis / Screen reading. Screen-reading software makes possible electronic spoken language (i.e., a speech synthesizer). Most computers today come with speakers to amplify sound. Speech synthesis is helpful for individuals who are blind or have low vision, who have a mild hearing loss, or who have difficulties with written language, both reading and writing, and can benefit from listening to information for learning purposes. JAWS (Job Access With Speech; Henter-Joyce) is an example of a speech synthesis program for the Windows operating system. JAWS works with e-mail, word processing programs, spreadsheets, and Web browsers.

Personal frequency-modulated transmission device. A frequency-modulated (FM) transmission device helps students with hearing impairments listen to their teacher via a student receiver or hearing aid. FM transmission devices consist of a wireless transmitter with a microphone and a receiver with a headset or earphone. Students with hearing impairments can more readily listen to lectures and other information presented by the teacher.

Tape recorders. The tape recorder is a simple adaptation of the notetaking process. Tape-recording a class lecture or a discussion in a work session helps the student focus on the speaker and content and not on the tasks of listening, identifying the important information, and taking notes. Tape recording is a good adaptation for students with listening and writing difficulties and students with physical disabilities.

Notetakers. Carbonless paper can be used to aid notetaking. A student who can take good notes should be recruited to use the carbonless paper for notetaking. A copy of the notes can then be shared with the student who has difficulties taking notes, listening, writing, and identifying important information.

- Having difficulty with metaphors and other nonliteral language
- Having difficulty remembering multiple commands

As students listen to lectures and discussions, they are expected to take notes to study. Students with special learning needs may have trouble taking notes for several reasons (Boyle, 2001). They may not be able to identify the most important information or write fast enough to keep up with the lecturer. Even when they do record notes, students may have problems making sense of their notes after the lecture, mostly because their notes are illegible or unorganized.

Students with special learning needs demonstrate difficulties with short- and long-term and working memory. Short-term memory is a temporary store of information that is tapped for immediate types of task (e.g., remembering a list of items to buy in the supermarket, remembering two tasks to accomplish in a day). As we discussed in Chapter 12, long-term memory is a permanent store of information that is assisted by how information is stored. Working memory consists of the simultaneous processing and storing of information. Memorizing information for class work and tests involves these types of memory. Struggling students experience a number of difficulties related to memorizing and test taking (Hammill

● Braille 'n Speak is a notetaking device that can be used by individuals with visual impairments.

The Braille 'n Speak (Blazie Engineering) is a notetaking device that can be used by individuals with visual impairments. It operates using refreshable braille cells, which are an alternative format to the embossed paper used with conventional braille. The individual inputs information in braille. The information is stored electronically and can later be transferred to a computer for editing purposes or read back by screen-reading software. Voice output is also included in braille note takers.

Magnification aids. Magnification aids focus on size, spacing, and contrast. Because over 90 percent of people with visual impairments have some degree of usable vision, optical aids can be employed to promote access. Optical aids include magnifying glasses and magnifiers on stands. Magnifiers on stands are particularly helpful if the individual is doing a task that requires the use of both hands. A closed-circuit television (CCTV) device (see page 294) is one of the most common examples of an electronic magnification aid. A CCTV includes a camera, a video display, and a unit that manages how the material is presented (zoom feature, scanning table). Individuals place their reading material on the scanning table; the camera captures the image, and the lens projects the image, which is shown on the video display. The use of color, contrast, and type size allows users with varying acuity to access and read the material.

Source: Adapted from D. P. Bryant and B. R. Bryant, 2003, *Assistive technology for people with disabilities.* Boston: Allyn and Bacon.

& Bryant, 1998). For memorizing, they may lack efficient strategies such as chunking, rehearsing, and creating mnemonics for studying material that will be tested. They may not make associations between new and former material to help them memorize content (Hughes, 1996). Chunking is organizing information by groups or topics. For test taking, students may lack efficient strategies for approaching the task of taking a test, such as managing time or tackling multiple-choice questions methodically. Students may not use memory strategies to retrieve information as they take the test. Finally, they may have difficulties reading and understanding test instructions. Given this list, it is not surprising that students struggle taking exams, even if they know the content being tested.

We return to Mr. Davis, who had his students complete a study skills survey to help him learn about their content-area and study skills. The survey is shown in Table 13.3, which you may want to use with your students. Also, assistive technology can play an important role in helping students develop study skills. Ways in which assistive technology can be used in the classroom to facilitate study skills instruction for students with different types of disabilities are shown in the Tech Notes feature. Next, we talk about ways to help students improve their time management skills.

TABLE 13.3 Study Skills Survey

The purpose of this survey is to find out about your own study habits and attitudes. Read each statement and indicate (by writing 1, 2, 3, or 4) how it applies to you.

1 = Sounds not at all like me   2 = Sounds a little like me

3 = Sounds quite a bit like me   4 = Sounds just like me

1. _____ I spend too much time studying for what I am learning.
2. _____ I usually spend hours studying the night before an exam.
3. _____ When I study enough, I don't have time for a social life.
4. _____ I usually try to study with the radio and TV turned on.
5. _____ I can't sit and study for long periods of time without becoming tired or distracted.
6. _____ I go to class, but I usually doodle, daydream, or fall asleep.
7. _____ My class notes are sometimes difficult to understand later.
8. _____ I usually seem to get the wrong material into my class notes.
9. _____ I don't review my class notes periodically throughout the chapter in preparation for tests.
10. _____ When I get to the end of a chapter, I can't remember what I've just read.
11. _____ I don't know how to pick out what is important in the text.
12. _____ I have strategies to figure out the meaning of new vocabulary words in my textbooks.
13. _____ I lose a lot of points on essay tests even when I know the material well.
14. _____ I study enough for my test, but when I get there my mind goes blank.
15. _____ I often study in a jumbled, disorganized way when I'm getting ready to take a test.
16. _____ I often find myself getting lost in the details of reading and have trouble identifying the main ideas.
17. _____ I usually don't change my reading speed in response to the difficulty level of the selection or to my familiarity with the content.
18. _____ I often wish that I could read faster.
19. _____ I wish I knew better ways to remember what I have read for tests.
20. _____ I easily forget information I read and learned.
21. _____ I use techniques for remembering information in my textbook.

- Time Management—1, 2, and 3
- Concentration—4, 5, and 6
- Listening and Note Taking—7, 8, and 9
- Reading—10, 11, and 12
- Test taking—13, 14, and 15
- Reading—16, 17, and 18
- Thinking, Learning, and Remembering—19, 20, and 21

Source: Adapted from http://www.ucc.vt.edu/stdysk/checklis.html

How Can Students Learn Time Management Skills?

Some students with learning problems have difficulties with organizational skills in general; managing and organizing time is one component of the bigger self-management picture. Time management requires students to (1) identify what they must accomplish, (2) understand how long each task will take to complete, and (3) schedule blocks of time to get the job done efficiently. Time management entails making judgments and estimates about the time requirements of various tasks; your students may struggle with time management if they lack good estimation skills and conceptual understanding of time. For example, the student who does not begin a research paper until 3 days before the due date either has not demonstrated sufficient understanding of the demands of the task or lacks the time management skills to complete the task by the deadline. Let's take a look at ways to promote time management skills with your students.

Promoting Time Management Skills

Hoover (1995) identified eight guidelines for teaching effective time management skills to help guide your instruction in this area:

- Help students budget their time to complete assigned tasks.
- Reward students for effective use of time.
- Create situations periodically in which students are required to budget their own time.
- Verbally encourage on-task behaviors, especially during independent work times.
- Ensure that students know the time allotted to completing each activity.
- Provide sufficient time for students to manage their time as well as to complete assigned tasks.
- Have students keep a notebook in which they record daily assignments and due dates.
- Instruct students to list their daily or weekly activities in order of importance, to list them again in the order in which they are actually completed, and to then compare the two lists (adapted from Hoover, 1995).

Teachers can have students keep a record of how their time was spent for 1 week. Then, an analysis of their time management can be performed. The analysis should reveal issues related to time management so that a plan can be developed to address these issues. What Works 13.4 provides information about the time management evaluation process.

What Are Ways to Facilitate Listening and Notetaking?

Listening is a skill that students use to obtain meaning from spoken language, to promote more efficient study habits, and to foster communication in general. Listening is not synonymous with paying attention, nor is it synonymous with hearing, although both contribute to good listening.

You can facilitate listening skills in your students, yet research studies show that despite the amount of time students spend listening to someone and its importance as a study skill, teachers spend little time on listening instruction (Hoover & Patton, 1995). For example, Rankin's study (as cited in Devine, 1987)

what WORKS 13.4

Time Management Evaluation

● Recording and Analyzing Time

Teaching Procedure

1. Have students keep a daily log of how their time is spent. A chart can be developed containing days of the week and blocks of time for students to complete. They can designate specific activities and the amount of time it takes to complete each activity.

2. Work with students at the end of the week to examine their daily logs, categorize into groups the activities that occur, and record amounts of time taken to complete various tasks.

3. With students, examine the logs for "time leaks"; that is, identify any time used inefficiently, mismanaged, or wasted. For example, it might be determined that too much time was spent talking on the telephone during the designated study time. Or perhaps activities were not well organized and thus demanded extra time to reorganize tasks or search for materials.

Progress Monitoring: Examine trends in students' logs to see if fewer "time leaks" are occurring weekly.

Adaptations

● Instructional content: Focus on daily, rather than weekly, reviews of logs.

● Instructional delivery: Work with individual students who seem to have the most difficulty managing their time.

● Instructional content: Provide fewer categories of activities to consider managing during the day.

● Developing and Implementing a Scheduling Plan

Teaching Procedure

1. Have students develop a "Things to Do Today" list that is realistic and manageable. Listed tasks could be sequenced from difficult to easy, and an estimated amount of time to complete each task could be included.

2. Focus on weekly schedules with designated time slots for accomplishing activities on the "Things to Do Today" list, as well as for completing the "givens" (going to school, taking out the trash, practicing a musical instrument).

3. Work with parents and other teachers to ensure that schedules are followed and that students are reinforced for developing better time management skills.

Progress Monitoring: Monitor completion of tasks that are on the "Things to Do Today" list to determine whether and how they are being accomplished. Look for quality of task completion as well as quantity of tasks finished.

Adaptations

● Instructional content: Focus on one day at a time.

● Instructional delivery: Work individually with students who require extra assistance in getting things done.

● Instructional materials: Work with each student to make a list that has only a few items on it, and add a section for some type of reinforcement (sticker, smiley face, points).

Source: B. J. Bragstad, & S. M. Stumpf, 1987, *A guidebook for teaching study skills and motivation* (2nd ed.). Boston: Allyn and Bacon.

showed that about 45 percent of daily verbal communication was spent listening to someone talk about something. In the school setting, Wilt's research (as cited in Devine, 1987) found that about 60 percent of time was devoted to listening. Putnam, Deshler, and Schumaker (1992) reported that at the secondary level, lecturing was the major form of instructional delivery in English, science, social studies, and mathematics classes. Only a small percentage of time was devoted to peer interactions via independent small-group work. Thus the ability to listen, to receive and understand information, is a crucial skill for students to possess.

According to Hoover (1995), listening requires attending, applying meaning to messages, and filtering out distractions. Devine (1987) suggested that listening skills involve determining a purpose, noting transitional words (e.g., *next, first,* and *finally*), using a study guide, recognizing the speaker's main points, noting the details, predicting possible test questions, and drawing conclusions. Thus, your students must know how to listen effectively to obtain the information for which you will hold them accountable.

Notetaking requires students to be able to listen, recognize important points and supporting details, utilize an organizational framework, know some "shorthand" method for abbreviating information, and write quickly. As they listen to a lecture, students must implement listening skills and use some means for recording pertinent information. Research has demonstrated a relationship between how effectively students take notes and how well they do on exams (Devine, 1987). Therefore, students need to learn how to apply their listening skills to taking notes. Here are some ways to help students with their listening and notetaking skills.

Facilitating Listening and Notetaking

You can help your students develop better listening skills by using the following practices:

- Asking questions and then calling on a student—this keeps the "level of concern" heightened.
- Using a variety of media (e.g., overhead projector, chalkboard, computer and projection panel, manipulatives) to keep lessons interesting and presentations diverse.
- Providing a small amount of information followed by a "check for understanding."

● These students are writing out notes as they listen. How can you help your students to develop better listening and notetaking skills?

Making a Difference

Teaching Study Skills Helps Students Throughout Their Academic Lives and Beyond

Margaret P. Weiss
*Learning Specialist, Student Athlete
Academic Support Services
Blacksburg, Virginia*

"Dear Jack."

That is how everyone began any discussion of Jack with me. I was in my second semester as a learning specialist in student athlete academic support services at a local university. Having been a high school and middle school special educator, I found this position both new and very familiar. The schedule was more flexible, the courses tougher, and NCAA rules more strict, but the students still struggled with time management, organization, and study skills.

I met Jack when everyone else in the program was at their wits' end. Jack had a very difficult time focusing on tasks, organizing his time, breaking down and completing tasks, and advocating for himself. He also was very intelligent, could talk his way out of almost anything, and was a starting player on the baseball team. I learned that college baseball teams play 50 or more games during the spring semester, missing as many as seven class days and spending countless hours on a bus.

When I began meeting with Jack, he was taking a course in business law that he claimed was incomprehensible and overwhelming. We decided to meet for an hour twice a week, but by the third week of our study sessions, we were meeting every day. Business law required learning a tremendous amount of new vocabulary and an equal number of major concepts. For example, Jack had to understand the different types of business organizations—their structures, rights, powers, and taxation—and how they all fit together. He had attempted to memorize the vocabulary involved and the characteristics of each type (there were four main types and three subtypes), only to fail miserably. He had convinced himself that this course was impossible and that it was not worth his time to read the material or attempt to study.

I taught Jack how to use graphic organizers to relate concepts to one another, instead of memorizing terms. After reading over professor notes and individual chapters together, we determined the main concept (e.g.,

business organizations), and then we started to identify the characteristics that were given for each type of organization (e.g., leadership, rights, form of taxation). With this basic structure, Jack was able to identify the different qualities of each type of organization and relate the material to the overall concept, instead of just trying to memorize the terms involved. The visual link made more sense to him.

Jack set the goal of creating an organizer for each major concept that appeared in an assigned reading. With this goal, Jack was able to understand what he had to accomplish before our next meeting—a big improvement over the ambiguous task of simply "studying." He was also able to monitor his understanding of the material as he read. When we met, we would try to integrate the organizers and understand the context of the unit. When he did not do well on his next test, he took the organizers to his professor and asked for help understanding the questions he had missed. Jack developed a rapport with the professor and was able to establish a purpose for meeting with him.

After much practice, Jack was able to create graphic organizers for other classes on his own. For him, the graphic organizers served several purposes: (a) monitoring his understanding of material, (b) setting a purpose for reading, (c) offering a springboard for discussions with his professors, and (d) providing study materials to use in preparation for tests. Jack passed his business law course, even though the final exam was more difficult than he had anticipated. Jack completed our semester together with a better understanding that he needs to process information in order to learn it and that he has to take the initiative to articulate his needs to his instructors. He has also become much more confident in his ability to do well in classes.

- Asking students to summarize, either on paper or with a neighbor, content that was just presented. (That is, have students think about the information, summarize the information, pair with a partner, and share the information.)
- Using transitional words (e.g., "I am going to mention three important points. First, . . .").

- Telling students there will be a quiz following the activity.
- Providing an outline of the information that is presented so students can fill in the blanks.

Bragstad and Stumpf (1987) identified notetaking steps with key words and procedures that students can learn to help them recall lecture and textbook material. Modeling how to perform the steps and then allowing students opportunities to practice with teacher feedback should teach each of the following steps. Teachers can provide examples of poorly written notes and compare them to well-written notes. (Do not use your students' own work as examples of poor notes.) Students can take notes from a lecture or textbook and then work in small groups to discuss what they did for each step. Teachers can use students' notes in the Note Shrink quiz box (see below) to construct quizzes to test student understanding of the lecture or textbook material. The following steps are recommended to improve students' notetaking skills.

STEP 1: *Note take,* which requires taking notes of important facts during the lecture.

STEP 2: *Note shrink,* wherein students survey their notes, identify important points and "thought chunks," and record chunks in a quiz box.

STEP 3: *Note talk,* which involves self-recitation on the content—that is, putting the content into one's own words.

STEP 4: *Note think,* which entails linking the new information to previous knowledge and experiences.

STEP 5: *Note review,* which requires 10 minutes a day for going over the notes.

Teachers can model this technique by (1) distributing a copy of a lecture for students to read, (2) locating the main ideas and details in the lecture notes, and (3) providing a completed outline of the lecture for students to review.

Finally, Susan Vogel (1997), one of the leading researchers in postsecondary learning disabilities, offers the following suggestions to help students learn and remember information. These steps can be placed on a handout and given to students to help them remember how to take notes more effectively.

- Color code, enlarge, underline, and highlight your notes to learn the material.
- Copy your notes over if, for you, the act of writing facilitates memorizing.
- Rehearse, either orally or in writing, material to be mastered.
- Write out concepts in full.
- Read your notes silently or aloud.
- Paraphrase or explain concepts to a friend.

The Making a Difference feature illustrates how effective instruction in study skills can help learners.

What Are Ways to Facilitate Memorization and Test Taking?

Students need memorization skills to facilitate the learning of information. For example, they will be asked to memorize a great deal of information in various subject areas and to produce that information on tests and in class discussions.

Therefore, it is vital for students to possess strategies that help them to learn, store, and retrieve information. Research studies have shown that students with learning problems tend to exhibit difficulties with short-term and working memory that result from ineffective information processing abilities (Swanson, Cochran, & Ewers, 1990). Their problems stem from lack of efficient memory strategies (e.g., chunking, organizing), lack of automaticity with basic knowledge (e.g., computational facts, sight words), and inefficient self-regulation (metamemory) strategies.

You can help students improve their memory skills by (1) teaching students how to create mnemonic devices to assist them in memorizing and recalling content such as lists of information, important people, and steps in a procedure; (2) discussing how some information can be remembered by creating mental images—have students provide specific examples of images they create; (3) teaching students to "chunk" related information for easier memorization and recall—this necessitates discussing the concepts of compare and contrast, where students must attend to specific categorical features in order to be able to state how things are similar and how they are different; and (4) giving students opportunities to recite information through verbal rehearsal—you can do this in student-mediated groups or in a whole-group setting. Clearly, if your students with special needs are to learn, retain, and recall content information, they have to know and apply strategies to facilitate these cognitive, or thinking, processes.

Students take tests (e.g., multiple-choice, true-false, fill-in-the-blanks, and short-answer tests) so that content-area teachers can determine the degree to which the students have mastered instruction. Students must rely on the study skills we have discussed: time management, learning and remembering, listening and note taking, and conducting research. However, possessing knowledge in an organized format is only the first step toward successful test taking. Students must learn efficient and effective ways to retrieve their knowledge, to read and understand test questions, to monitor their test time, and to make educated guesses.

Bassett (1995) offered several guidelines for students to consider when taking tests: Read the entire test first, including the instructions. Complete the easier questions first. Use strategies to tackle multiple-choice questions (for example, avoid answers with absolute words such as *never*, eliminate answers, and look for the detailed answer). Review your responses. And maintain a positive attitude.

Now let's look at some ways to help students recall information and take tests successfully.

Facilitating Memorization and Test Taking

Memorizing information in preparation for tests requires reviewing the material frequently and committing it to memory. Memory strategies that enhance recall, such as listing, categorizing, drawing, visualizing, alphabetizing, devising acronyms, and creating associations, are techniques that students with good study skills use (Rivera & Smith, 1997).

There are several ways in which teachers can help their students become better test takers. Hoover (1995) offers the following suggestions.

- Show students how to take different types of tests.
- Explain different methods of study and types of materials necessary to study for objective and essay tests.
- Review completed tests with students, highlighting test-taking errors.

- Explore test-taking procedures with students, and explain different types of questions.
- Identify and discuss key vocabulary terms found in test instructions, such as *compare, contrast, match,* and *evaluate.*
- Teach students general strategies to use when taking tests: Review the entire test, know the time allotted for test completion, recognize the point values of specific test items, read and reread the directions and test questions, identify key words in questions, and respond to more difficult items after answering the easier items.
- Teach students specific strategies to use when taking multiple-choice tests: Know the number and kind of answers to select, remember the question, narrow down the possible correct answers by eliminating obviously incorrect answers, and record each answer carefully.
- Figure 13.4 offers the PIRATES strategy for helping students learn effective test-taking steps.

The ADAPT framework can be used to help teachers think about ways to alter practice to accommodate specific student needs. In ADAPT Framework 13.1, we provide an example of how a teacher uses ADAPT to consider ways to meet the needs of Pedro, a student who is blind, to be able to take tests like the other students. Additionally, instructional considerations must be addressed to enable a student such as Pedro to access instructional content and materials during

FIGURE 13.4 The PIRATES Test-Taking Strategy

Step 1: Prepare to succeed.

Put "PIRATES" and name on the test.

Allot time and order to sections.

Say something positive.

Start within two minutes.

Step 2: Inspect the instructions.

Read the instructions carefully.

Underline how and where to respond.

Notice special requirements.

Step 3: Read, remember, and reduce.

Read the whole question.

Remember with memory strategies.

Reduce choices.

Step 4: Answer or abandon.

Answer the question.

Abandon the question if you're not sure.

Step 5: Turn back.

Turn back to abandoned questions when you get to the end of the test.

Tell yourself to earn more points.

Step 6: Estimate.

Estimate unknown answers using the "ACE" guessing technique.

Avoid absolutes.

Choose the longest or most detailed choice.

Eliminate identical choices.

Step 7: Survey.

Survey to ensure that all questions are answered.

Switch an answer only if you're sure.

Source: The Test Taking Strategy: PIRATES, by J. Hughes, J. Schumaker, D. D. Deshler, and C. Mercer, 1988, Lawrence: University of Kansas, Institute for Research in Learning Disabilities. Copyright 1987 by Edge Enterprises. Reprinted with permission.

content-area reading and study skills time. Fortunately, there are resources to help classroom teachers prepare for and accommodate individual needs related to visual impairments. For instance, school districts have personnel who are specifically trained to work with students who have visual impairments and to provide support to their classroom teachers. Examples of instructional considerations and resources are given in the Working Together feature.

13.1 **ADAPT Framework** Using Braille for Multiple-Choice Tests

ASK "What am I requiring the student to do?"	DETERMINE the prerequisite skills of the task.	ANALYZE the student's strengths and struggles.		PROPOSE and implement adaptations from among the four categories.	TEST to determine if the adaptations helped the student to accomplish the task.
		Strengths	**Struggles**		
I want Pedro, who is blind and who reads braille, to be a better multiple-choice test taker, especially with the "fill in the bubble" format.	1. Reads the test item.		1	**For 1. Materials** A braille version of the test is prepared; or test items are recorded on tape for playing on a variable-speed tape player.	**For 1.** Check for reading or listening comprehension.
	2. Identifies what is being asked.	2		**For 2. No adaptations needed.**	
	3. Reads the response choices.		3	**For 3. Instructional Materials** Tape player or braille version of textbook.	**For 3.** Check for reading or listening comprehension.
	4. Recalls knowledge about the content of the test question.	4		**For 4. No adaptations needed.**	
	5. Identifies obviously incorrect response choices.	5		**For 5. No adaptations needed.**	
	6. Selects the best choice and fills in the correct bubble.		6	**For 6. Instructional Materials** The student records his or her response on a tape; student records responses using a pen and stylus.	**For 6.** Answers are checked to ensure that they are the students' correct response choices.
	7. Checks the answers to make sure no items were skipped.	7		**For 7. No adaptations needed.**	

Collaborating to Teach the Visually Impaired

Most teachers need assistance when they are working with students who have sensory disabilities. Access to the general education curriculum for students with sensory impairments is of great importance, so consultation about their needs is a critical part of a special educator's and general educator's job. Professionals collaborating in their work with students who are blind or visually impaired should address the following issues. Together, these professionals can make decisions about materials, braille text, and grading.

- When material adaptations are required, especially for braille readers, a 2-week lead time is often necessary. The teacher of the visually impaired or someone else who knows how to use braille materials will need to prioritize the materials required for all the students served.
- Appropriate materials may need to be ordered. This ordering will require more than 2 weeks of lead time. Allow ample lead time.
- Materials for the new school year will need to be ordered no later than February for the following academic year. Start working together early.
- Decisions need to be made regarding how to grade students' work, especially braille papers. Discuss how grading decisions will be made on the basis of mutually agreed-upon criteria.
- Teachers who don't read braille need to understand how braille texts are organized and become familiar with their use of titles and subtitles.
- Print in the classroom needs to be accessible to the braille reader. This includes bulletin boards, posted rules and charts, names on cubbies used for possessions, schedules, job wheels, and other instructional materials.

summary

Content-area instruction is the focus of secondary teaching. Students use textbooks to learn content, listen to teachers lecture on subjects, and engage in activities that help them apply their knowledge. Study skills become increasingly important and are crucial at the secondary level because students must manage their time efficiently to study notes from class and the textbook, must memorize material, and must take tests that enable them to advance to the next grade level and eventually to graduate from high school. Yet we know that students with special needs demonstrate a variety of difficulties in learning and studying content that interfere with their ability to access and master content-area material. For example, reading and understanding textbooks is often a major problem for students with reading problems. Acquiring information through lectures and learning this information well enough to take tests successfully are challenging for many struggling students.

Strategies, adaptations, and technology were presented in this chapter as means of facilitating content instruction and study skills for students with special needs. Examples of the ADAPT framework illustrate how teachers can respond to individual learning needs. For content-area instruction, we discussed instructional techniques to facilitate student learning in the areas of content-area vocabulary and concepts, self-monitoring of reading comprehension, textbook reading, and student participation. For study skills, techniques were identified for time management, listening and notetaking, and memorization and taking tests. Content-area instruction and study skills are important components of a total curriculum for students with special needs to foster academic success in elementary and secondary school instruction, as well as in postsecondary settings.

self-test QUESTIONS

Let's review the learning objectives for this chapter. If you are uncertain and cannot "talk through" the answers provided for any of these questions, reread those sections of the chapter.

- **What difficulties do students demonstrate with content-area instruction?**

  We discussed many but will review a few here. For content-area instruction, some students are slow readers orally and silently, have limited sight vocabularies, have trouble decoding words with inflectional endings and multisyllabic words, and have difficulty constructing mental images of text descriptions and structures. They have particular difficulty when they attempt to summarize text, generate and answer different types and levels of questions, draw inferences, and monitor their comprehension. Also, problems are noted in understanding derivational meanings (word parts), understanding denotative and connotative meanings, and applying word meanings across content areas.

- **How can teachers facilitate content-area instruction?**

  When using textbooks, it is helpful for students to use graphic organizers and comprehension-monitoring strategies. Students should learn how to figure out the meaning of unfamiliar words through mapping, associations, and context clues. Student participation can be facilitated by structuring class discussions using discussion guides and questioning. Students can also participate in learning by conducting research, using anchors to promote understanding, and using technology to create multimedia projects.

- **What difficulties do students demonstrate with study skills?**

  Students who struggle manage time poorly; reason illogically; are unable to generate important ideas; misunderstand simple spoken sentences and questions; have difficulty recognizing that sentences that differ in syntax can mean the same thing; are unable, even when they do record notes, to make sense of their notes after the lecture; misspell words; read slowly; and make illogical arguments.

- **How can teachers facilitate study skills?**

  You can teach your students time management skills such as auditing their time. You can help your students learn content by teaching them how to color-code, enlarge, underline, and highlight notes to strengthen their recall of the material and encouraging them to copy their notes over if the act of writing facilitates memorizing. Finally, you can teach them tips for being more astute test takers.

Revisit the
OPENING challenge

Check your answers to the Reflection Questions from the Opening Challenge and revise them on the basis of what you have learned.

1. What difficulties might students in both teachers' classes exhibit with regard to content-area instruction and study skills?

2. How can the teachers effectively work with their students to help them become efficient learners in content-area instruction and study skills?

3. How can these teachers provide adapted lessons to students who require intensive intervention, while keeping the rest of the class busy with relevant work?

4. How can study skills assessment be used to identify how students, including struggling students, become more efficient learners?

Professional Standards and Licensure

CEC Knowledge and Skill Core Standard and Associated Subcategories

CEC Content Standard 2: Development and Characteristics of Learners

Special educators know and demonstrate respect for their students first as unique human beings. Special educators understand the similarities and differences in human development and characteristics between and among individuals with and without ELN. Moreover, special educators understand how exceptional conditions can interact with the domains of human development, and they use this knowledge to respond to the varying abilities and behaviors of individuals with ELN.

CEC Content Standard 4: Instructional Strategies

Special educators select, adapt, and use instructional strategies to promote challenging learning results in general and special curricula and to appropriately modify learning environments for individuals with disabilities. They enhance the learning of critical thinking, problem solving, and performance skills of individuals with disabilities, and increase their self-awareness, self-management, self-control, self-reliance, and self-esteem.

CEC Content Standard 7: Instructional Planning

Individualized decision making and instruction is at the center of special education practice. Special educators develop long-range individualized instructional plans anchored in both general and special curricula. Individualized instructional plans emphasize explicit modeling and efficient guided practice to assure acquisition and fluency through maintenance and generalization. Understanding of these factors as well as the implications of an individual's exceptional condition, guides the special educator's selection, adaptation, and creation of materials, and the use of powerful instructional variables. Instructional plans are modified based on ongoing analysis of the individual's learning progress.

INTASC Core Principle and Associated Special Education Subcategories

1. Subject Matter

1.01 All teachers have a solid base of understanding of the major concepts, assumptions, issues, and processes of inquiry in the subject matter content areas that they teach.

1.03 All teachers understand that students with disabilities may need accommodations, modifications, and/or adaptations to the general curriculum.

2. Student Learning

2.02 All teachers examine their assumptions about the learning and development of students with disabilities and use this information to create challenging and supportive learning opportunities.

2.04 All teachers are knowledgeable about multiple theories of learning and research-based practices that support learning and use this information to inform instruction.

4. Instructional Strategies

4.03 All teachers use research-based practices to support learning and generalization of concepts and skills.

4.04 All teachers understand that it is particularly important to provide multiple ways for students with disabilities to participate in learning activities. They modify tasks and accommodate individual needs of students with disabilities.

7. Instructional Planning

7.02 All teachers plan ways to modify instruction to facilitate positive learning results within the general education curriculum for students with disabilities.

Praxis II: Education of Exceptional Students: Core Content Knowledge

I. Understanding Exceptionalities

Human development and behavior as related to students with disabilities, including
- Language development and behavior.
- Cognition.
- Physical development.

Characteristics of students with disabilities, including the influence of
- Cognitive factors.
- Affective and social-adaptive factors.

III. Delivery of Services to Students

Background knowledge, including
- Integrating best practices from multidisciplinary research and professional literature into the educational setting.

Curriculum and instruction and their implementation across the continuum of educational placements, including

- Instructional development and implementation.
- Teaching strategies and methods.

- Instructional format and components.
- Technology for teaching and learning in special education settings.

Where the classroom comes to life!

Video—"Vocabulary Strategies"

In this video clip, students use several vocabulary strategies while reading content-area texts.

Log onto www.mylabschool.com. Under the **Courses** tab, in **Content Area Reading,** go to the **video lab**. Access the "**Vocabulary Instruction**" videos and watch the "**Vocabulary Strategies**" video.

OR

Use the www.mylabschool.com **Assignment Finder** to go directly to these videos. Just enter Assignment ID **CRV2**.

1. What is a vocabulary strategy and why is it important in school and in life?
2. List five vocabulary strategies demonstrated in the video or described in Chapter 13.

Video—"Content Area Reading"

In this video clip, educators discuss the purpose of and several strategies for teaching content-area reading. A third-grade teacher demonstrates teaching content-area reading in science.

Log onto **www.mylabschool.com**. Under the **Courses** tab, in **Reading Methods**, go to the **video lab**. Access the "**Content Area Reading**" videos and watch the "**Content Area Reading**" video.

Use the **www.mylabschool.com Assignment Finder** to go directly to these videos. Just enter Assignment ID **RMV6**.

1. What is front loading and how does it help readers prepare to engage in content-area reading?
2. What are some of the techniques for previewing text that are described in the video and in Chapter 13?
3. Once students have completed the previewing phase demonstrated in the video, list several comprehension-monitoring strategies that could be used *during* reading.

To access chapter objectives, practice tests, weblinks, and flashcards, go to the companion website at **www.ablongman.com/bryantsmith1e**.

references

CHAPTER 1   Inclusive Teaching as Responsive Education
20 U.S.C. section 1400 (b & c).

Allen, M., & Ashbaker, B. Y. (2004). Strengthening schools: Involving paraprofessionals in crisis prevention and intervention. *Intervention in School and Clinic, 39,* 139–146.

American Association on Mental Retardation (AAMR). (2002). *Mental retardation: Definition, classification, and systems of support* (10th ed.). Washington, DC: AAMR.

American Psychiatric Association (APA). (2003). *Diagnostic and statistical manual of mental disorders, fourth edition, text revision* (DSM-IV-TR) (4th ed.). Washington, DC: Author.

Americans with Disabilities Act of 1990. PL No. 101-336, 104 STAT.327.

Artiles, A. J. (1998). The dilemma of difference: Enriching the disproportionality discourse with theory and context. *The Journal of Special Education, 32,* 32–36.

Artiles, A. J. (2003). Special education's changing identity: Paradoxes and dilemmas in views of culture and space. *Harvard Educational Review, 73,* 164–202.

Assistive Technology Act of 2004. PL No. 108-364.

Ballard, J., Ramirez, B. A., & Weintraub, F. J. (1982). *Special education in America: Its legal and governmental foundations.* Reston, VA: Council for Exceptional Children.

Branson, J., & Miller, D. (2002). *Damned for their difference: The cultural construction of deaf people as disabled.* Washington, DC: Gallaudet University Press.

Browder, D. M., & Cooper-Duffy, K. (2003). Evidence-based practices for students with severe disabilities and the requirement for accountability in "No Child Left Behind." *The Journal of Special Education, 37,* 157–163.

Brown v. Board of Education, 347 U.S. 483 (1954).

Burlington School Committee v. Department of Education, 471 U.S. 359 (1985).

Carter v. Florence County School District 4, 950 F. 2d 156 (1993).

Cedar Rapids School District v. Garret F., 106 F.3rd 822 (8th Cir. 1997), cert. gr. 118 S. Ct. 1793 (1998), aff'd, 119 S. Ct. 992 (1999).

Children's Defense Fund (CDF). (2001). *The state of America's children: 2001.* Washington, DC: Author.

Children's Defense Fund (CDF). (2004). *The state of America's children: 2004.* Washington, DC: Author.

De Bettencourt, L. U. (2002). Understanding the differences between IDEA and Section 504. *Teaching Exceptional Children, 34,* 16–23.

Deno, S. (2003). Developments in curriculum-based measurement. *The Journal of Special Education, 37,* 184–192.

Deshler, D. (2001). SIM to the rescue? Maybe . . . maybe not! *Stratenotes, 9,* 1–4.

Deshler, D. D. (2003 May/June). A time for modern-day pioneers. *LDA Newsbriefs, 38,* 3–24.

Doe v. Withers, 20 IDELR 422 (1993).

Dymond, S. K., & Orelove, F. P. (2001). What constitutes effective curricula for students with severe disabilities? *Exceptionality, 9,* 109–122.

Education for All Handicapped Children Act (EHA). PL No. 94-142.

Education for All Handicapped Children Act (EHA) (reauthorized). PL No. 99-457.

Elementary and Secondary Education Act. PL No. 107-110.

Erevelles, N. (1996). Disability and the dialects of difference. *Disability & Society, 11,* 519–537.

Finn, Jr., C. E., Rotherham, A. J., & Hokanson, Jr., C. R. (Eds.). (2001). *Rethinking special education for a new century.* Washington, DC: Thomas B. Fordham Foundation and the Progressive Policy Institute.

Fisher, D., Frey, N., & Thousand, J. (2003). What do special educators need to know and be prepared to do for inclusive schooling to work? *Teacher Education and Special Education, 26,* 42–50.

Florian, L. (2007). Reimagining special education. In L. Florian (Ed.), *The Sage handbook of special education* (pp. 7–20). Thousand Oaks, CA: Sage.

Friend, M. (2000). Myths and misunderstandings about professional collaboration. *Remedial and Special Education, 21,* 130–132, 160.

Fuchs, D., Fuchs, L. S., & Compton, D. L. (2004). Identifying reading disabilities by responsiveness-to-instruction: Specifying measures and criteria. *Learning Disabilities Quarterly, 27,* 216–227.

Fuchs, L., Fuchs, D., & Powell, S. (2004). *Using CBM for progress monitoring.* Washington, DC: American Institutes for Research.

Fuchs, L. S., & Fuchs, D. (2001). Principles for the prevention and intervention of mathematics difficulties. *Learning Disability Research & Practice, 16,* 85–95.

Futernick, K. (2006). A possible dream: Retaining California teachers so all students learn. Sacramento: CSU Center for Teacher Quality.

Gaetano, C. (2006, August 31). General ed. teachers face special ed. realities. *Sentinel, Schools,* East Brunswick, New Jersey. Retrieved from ebs.gmnews.com/news/2006/0831/Schools/043.htm/

Garcia, E. E., (2001). *Hispanic education in the United States.* New York: Rowman & Littlefield.

Gartner, A., & Lipsky, D. K. (1987). Beyond special education: Toward a quality system for all students. *Harvard Educational Review, 57,* 367–395.

Gregg, N., & Mather, N. (2002). School is fun at recess: Informal analyses of written language for students with learning disabilities. *Journal of Learning Disabilities,* 7–22.

Gresham, F. (2002). Responsiveness to intervention: An alternative approach to the identification of learning disabilities. In R. Bradley, L. Danielson, and D. P. Hallahan (Eds.), *Identification of learning disabilities: Research to practice.* Mahwah, NJ: Erlbaum.

Grossman, H. (1998). *Ending discrimination in special education.* Springfield, IL: Charles C Thomas.

Harry, B. (2007). The disproportionate placement of ethnic minorities in special education. In L. Florian (Ed.), *The Sage handbook of special education* (pp. 67–84). Thousand Oaks, CA: Sage.

Hitchcock, C., & Stahl, S. (2003). Assistive technology, universal design, universal design for learning: Improved learning opportunities. *Journal of Special Educational Technology, 18,* 45–52.

Honig v. Doe, 484 U.S. 305, 108 S. Ct. 592 (1988).

Hoover, J. J., & Patton, J. R. (2004). Differentiating standards-based education for students with diverse needs. *Remedial and Special Education 25,* 74–78.

Individuals with Disabilities Education Act. PL No. 101-476.

Individuals with Disabilities Education Act. PL No. 105-17, 111 STAT.37.

Individuals with Disabilities Education Improvement Act of 2004. PL No. 108-446.

Irving Independent School District v. Tatro, 468 U.S. 833 (1984).

Katsiyannis, A., & Yell, M. L. (2000). The Supreme Court and school health services: *Cedar Rapids v. Garret F. Exceptional Children, 66,* 317–326.

Kauffman, J. M. (1997). Caricature, science, and exceptionality. *Remedial and Special Education, 18,* 130–132. Newark, NJ: Harwood.

Kauffman, J. M., & Hallahan, D. P. (2005). *Special education: What it is and why we need it.* Boston: Allyn and Bacon.

Knitzer, J. (1982). *Unclaimed children: The failure of public responsibility to children and adolescents in need of mental health services.* Washington, DC: Children's Defense Fund.

Knitzer, J., Steinberg, Z., & Fleisch, B. (1990). *At the schoolhouse door: An examination of programs and policies for children with behavioral and emotional problems.* New York: NY Bank Street College of Education.

Longmore, P. (2002). *San Francisco State University: Institute on disability.* Retrieved June 21, 2002, from http://online.sfsu.edu/~longmore/

Longmore, P. (2003). *Why I burned my book and other essays on disability.* Philadelphia: Temple University Press.

Lynch, E. W., & Hanson, M. J. (2004). *Developing cross-cultural competence: A guide for working with children and their families* (3rd ed.). Baltimore, MD: Brookes.

MacMillan, D. L., & Siperstein, G. N. (2002). Learning disabilities as operationally defined by schools. In R. Bradley, L. Danielson, and D. P. Hallahan (Eds.), *Identification of learning disabilities: Research to practice* (pp. 287–333). Mahwah, NJ: Erlbaum.

McMasters, K., Fuchs, D., Fuchs, L., & Compton, D. (2000). Monitoring the academic progress of children who are unresponsive to generally effective early reading intervention. *Assessment for Effective Intervention, 27,* 23–33.

Mills v. Board of Education of the District of Columbia, 348 F. Supp. 866 (1972).

Moody, S. W., Vaughn, S., Hughes, M. T., & Fischer, M. (2000). Reading instruction in the resource room: Set up for failure. *Exceptional Children, 66,* 305–316.

Müller, E., & Markowitz, J. (2004). *Disability categories: State terminology, definitions & eligibility criteria.* Washington, DC: Project Forum, National Association of State Directors of Special Education (NASDSE).

National Center for Learning Disabilities. (2004). *No Child Left Behind and students with learning disabilities: Ensuring full participation and equal accountability.* Retrieved September 14, 2004, from www.ld.org/advocacy

National Council on Disability (NCD). (2001 June 21). *The accessible future: Transmittal letter.* Washington, DC.

National Institute of Environmental Health Sciences (NIEHS). (2005). *Hot topic packs: Asthma and the environment.* Retrieved December 20, 2006, from www.niehs.nih.gov /outreach-education/Resources/HTasthma.cfm

No Child Left Behind Act of 2001. PL 107-110.

Office of Special Education Programs (OSEP). (2000). High school graduation. *Twenty-second annual report to Congress on the implementation of the Individuals with Disabilities Education Act,* (pp. IV-15–IV-21). Washington, DC: U.S. Department of Education.

Office of Special Education Programs (OSEP). (2006). Students served under IDEA, Part B, by disability category and state: Fall 2005. Retrieved October 24, 2006, from www.ideadata.org

Pennsylvania Association for Retarded Children v. Commonwealth of Pennsylvania, 343 F. Supp. 279 (E.D. Pa. 1972).

Phyler v. Doe, 102 S. Ct. 2382 (1982).

Rehabilitation Act of 1973. Section 504, 19 U.S.C. section 794.

Riddell, S. (2007). A sociology of special education. In L. Florian (Ed.), *The Sage handbook of special education* (pp. 34–45). Thousand Oaks, CA: Sage.

Roos, P. (1970). Trends and issues in special education for the mentally retarded. *Education and Training of the Mentally Retarded, 5,* 51–61.

Rowley v. Hendrick Hudson School District, 458 U.S. 176 (1982).

Sailor, W. (1991). Special education in the restructured school. *Remedial and Special Education, 12,* 8–22.

Schettler, R., Stein, J., Reich, F., Valenti, M., & Wallinga, D. (2000). In harm's way: Toxic threats to child development. Cambridge, MA: Greater Boston Physicians for Social Responsibility. Available at www.igc.org/psr

Smith v. Robinson, 468 U.S. 992 (1984).

Snell, M. E., & Brown, F. (2006). *Instruction of students with severe disabilities* (6th ed.). Upper Saddle River, NJ: Merrill–Prentice-Hall.

Stroul, B., & Friedman, R. (1986). *A system of care for children and youth with severe emotional disturbances.* Tampa, Florida: University of South Florida, Louis de la Parte Florida Mental Health Institute, The Research and Training Center for Children's Mental Health.

Timothy W. v. Rochester, New Hampshire, School District, 875 F. 2d 945 (1989).

Torgeson, J. K. (1996). Thoughts about intervention research in learning disabilities. *Learning Disabilities, 7,* 55–58.

Trautman, M. L. (2004). Preparing and managing paraprofessionals. *Intervention in School and Clinic, 39,* 139–146.

Turnbull, A., Turnbull, H. R., III, & Wehmeyer, M. (2007). *Exceptional lives: Special education in today's schools* (5th ed.). Upper Saddle River, NJ: Prentice-Hall.

U.S. Department of Education. (1995). *Seventeenth annual report to Congress on the implementation of the Individuals with Disabilities Education Act.* Washington, DC: U.S. Government Printing Office.

U.S. Department of Education. (1999). Assistance to states for the Education of Children with Disabilities Program and the Early Intervention Program for Infants and Toddlers with Disabilities; Final Regulations. *Federal Register, 34,* CRF Parts 300 and 303.

U.S. Department of Education. (2006). Assistance to states for the Education of Children with Disabilities Program and the Early Intervention Program for Infants and Toddlers with Disabilities; Final rule. *Federal Register, 34.* CRF Parts 300 and 301.

U.S. Senate (2004, September 13). Health, Education, Labor and Pensions Committee (HELP): *Democrats testimony on No Child Left Behind Act of 2001.*

Utley, C. A., & Obiakor, F. (2001). Multicultural education and special education. In C. A. Utley and F. Obiakor (Eds.), *Special education, multicultural education, and school reform: Components of quality education for learners with mild disabilities* (pp. 1–29). Springfield, IL: Charles C Thomas.

Vaughn, S., Elbaum, B., & Boardman, A. G. (2001). The social function of students with learning disabilities: Implications for inclusion. *Exceptionality, 9,* 47–65.

Villa, R. A., Thousand, J. S., & Nevin, A. I. (2004). *A guide to co-teaching.* Thousand Oaks, CA: Corwin Press.

Wehmeyer, M. L., Lattin, D. L., Lapp-Rincker, G., & Agran, M. (2003). Access to the general education curriculum of middle school students with mental retardation: An observational study. *Remedial and Special Education, 24,* 262–272.

West, J. (1994). *Federal implementation of the Americans with Disabilities Act, 1991–1994.* New York: Milank Memorial Fund.

Winzer, M. A. (2007). Confronting difference: An excursion through the history of special education. In L. Florian (Ed.), *The Sage handbook of special education* (pp. 21–33). Thousand Oaks, CA: Sage.

Ziegler, D. (2002). *Reauthorization of the Elementary and Secondary Education Act: No Child Left Behind Act of 2001.* Arlington, VA: The Council for Exceptional Children, Public Policy Unit.

Zigmond, N. (2003). Where should students with disabilities receive special education services? Is one place better than another? *The Journal of Special Education, 37,* 193–199.

Zobrest v. Catalina Foothills School District, 963 F. 2d 190 (1993).

CHAPTER 2 Understanding Learners with Special Needs: High Incidence Disabilities or Conditions

American Association on Mental Retardation (AAMR). (2002). *Mental retardation: Definition, classification, and systems of support* (10th ed.). Washington, DC: AAMR.

American Psychiatric Association (APA). (2003). *Diagnostic and statistical manual of mental disorders* (DSM-IV-TR). Washington, DC: Author.

American Speech–Language–Hearing Association Ad Hoc Committee on Service Delivery in the Schools. (1993). Definitions of communication disorders and variations, *ASHA, 35,* (Suppl. 10), 40–41.

Arc, The. (2005 May). Causes and prevention of mental retardation. *Frequently Asked Questions.* Retrieved on June 17, 2005, from www.thearc.org

Archwamety, T., & Katsiyannis, A. (2000). Academic remediation, parole violations, and recidivism rates among delinquent youth. *Remedial and Special Education, 21,* 161–170.

Baca, L. M., & Cervantes, H. T. (Eds.). (2004). *The bilingual special education interface* (4th ed.). Columbus, OH: Merrill.

Bakken, J. P., & Whedon, C. K. (2002). Teaching text structure to improve reading comprehension. *Intervention in School and Clinic, 37,* 229–233.

Bender, W. N. (2004). *Learning disabilities: Characteristics, identification, and teaching strategies* (5th ed.) Boston: Allyn and Bacon.

Bernthal, J. E., & Bankson, N. W. (2004). *Articulation and phonological disorders* (5th ed.). Boston: Allyn and Bacon.

Bishop, A. G., & League, M. B. (2006). Identifying a multivariate screening model to predict reading difficulties at the onset of kindergarten: A longitudinal analysis. *Learning Disability Quarterly, 29,* 235–253.

Bradley, R., Danielson, L., & Hallahan, D. P. (Eds.) (2002). *Identification of learning disabilities: Research to practice.* Mahwah, NJ: Erlbaum.

Bryan, T. (1997). Assessing the personal and social status of students with learning disabilities. *Learning Disabilities Research and Practice, 12,* 63–76.

Bryan, T., Burstein, K., & Ergul, C. (2004). The social-emotional side of learning disabilities: A science-based presentation of the state of the art. *Learning Disability Quarterly, 27,* 45–51.

Bryant, D. P., Bryant, B. R., Gerten, R., Scammacca, M., & Chavez, M. (in press). Mathematics interventions for first- and second-grade students with mathematics difficulties: The effects of Tier 2 intervention delivered as booster lesson. *Remedial and Special Education.*

Bryant, D. P., Bryant, B. R., & Hammill, D. D. (2000, March/April). Characteristic behaviors of students with LD who have teacher-identified math weakness. *Journal of Learning Disabilities, 33,* 168–177, 199.

Bullis, M., Walker, H. M., & Sprague, J. R. (2001). A promise unfulfilled: Social skills training with at-risk and antisocial children and youth. *Exceptionality, 9,* 67–90.

Carlson, C. L., Booth, J. E., Shin, M., & Canu, W. H. (2002). Parent, teacher-, and self-rated motivational styles in ADHD subtypes. *Journal of Learning Disabilities, 35,* 103–113.

Centers for Disease Control (CDC). (2004). Fetal alcohol syndrome. *Fast Facts.* Retrieved June 17, 2005, from www.cdc.gov

Chadsey, J., & Beyer, S. (2001). Social relationships in the workplace. *Mental Retardation and Developmental Disabilities Research Reviews, 7,* 128–133.

Children and Adults with Attention-Deficit/Hyperactivity Disorder (CHADD). (2004). *Fact Sheet.* Retrieved August 29, 2004, from www.chadd.org

Conture, E. G. (2001). *Stuttering: Its nature, diagnosis, and treatment.* Boston: Allyn and Bacon.

Davis, S., & Davis, L. A. (2003). Fetal alcohol syndrome. *Frequently Asked Questions.* Retrieved on June 18, 2005, from www.thearc.org

Dimitrovsky, L., Spector, H., & Levy-Schiff, R. (2000). Stimulus gender and emotional difficulty level: Their effect on recognition of facial expressions of affect in children with and without LD. *Journal of Learning Disabilities, 33,* 410–416.

Donahue, M. L. (1997). Beliefs about listening in students with learning disabilities: "Is the speaker always right?" *Topics in Language Disorders, 17,* 41–61.

Fisher, D., Frey, N., & Thousand, J. (2003). What do special educators need to know and be prepared to do for inclusive schooling to work? *Teacher Education and Special Education, 26,* 42–50.

Fletcher, J. M., Lyon, G. R., Barnes, M., Stuebing, K. K., Francis, D. J., Olson, R. K., Shaywitz, S. E., & Shaywitz, B. A. (2002). Classifications of learning disabilities: An evidence-based evaluation. In R. Bradley, L. Danielson, and D. P. Hallahan (Eds.), *Identification of learning disabilities: Research to practice* (pp. 185–250). Mahwah, NJ: Erlbaum.

Forness, S. R., & Kavale, K. A. (2001). Are school professionals missing their best chance to help troubled kids? *Emotional & Behavioral Disorders, 1,* 80–83.

Forness, S. R., & Knitzer, J. (1992). A new proposed definition and terminology to replace "serious emotional disturbance" in IDEA. *School Psychology Review, 21,* 13.

Freeman, S. N., & Kasari, C. (2002). Characteristics and qualities of the play dates of children with Down syndrome: Emerging or true friendships? *American Journal on Mental Retardation, 107,* 16–31.

Frey, K. S., Hirschstein, M. K., & Guzzo, B. A. (2000). Second step: Preventing aggression by promoting social competence. *Journal of Emotional and Behavioral Disorders, 8,* 102–112.

Fuchs, D. (2002, July 17). *Identification of students with LD: From IQ–achievement discrepancy to response-to-treatment.* Paper presented at Kansas University's Center for Research on Learning International SIM Trainers Conference, Lawrence, KS.

Fuchs, D., & Fuchs, L. S. (2006, July). *Curriculum Based Measurement and Response to Intervention (RTI).* Kansas City: Progress Monitoring Center, Summer Institute.

Fuchs, D., Fuchs, L. S., Mathes, P. G., Lipsey, M. W., & Roberts, P. H. (2002). Is "learning disabilities" just a fancy term for low achievement? A meta-analysis of reading differences between low achievers with and without the label. In R. Bradley, L. Danielson, and D. P. Hallahan (Eds.), *Identification of learning disabilities: Research to practice* (pp. 747–762). Mahwah, NJ: Erlbaum.

Fuchs, D., Fuchs, L. S., Thompson, A., Al Otaiba, S., Yen, L., Yang, N. J., Svenson, E., & Braun, M. (2002). Exploring the importance of reading programs for kindergarteners with disabilities in mainstream classrooms. *Exceptional Children, 68,* 295–311.

Fuchs, L. S. (2004). *Curriculum Based Measurement: Perspectives and Resources.* IRIS Module. Available at http://iris.peabody.vanderbilt.edu

Fuchs, L. S., & Fuchs, D. (2001). Principles for the prevention and intervention of mathematics difficulties. *Learning Disabilities Research & Practice, 16,* 85–95.

Fuchs, L. S., & Fuchs, D. (2003). Enhancing the mathematical problem solving of students with mathematics disabilities. In H. L. Swanson, K. R. Harris, and S. E. Graham (Eds.), *Handbook on learning disabilities* (pp. 306–322). New York: Guilford.

Futernick, K. (2006). *A possible dream: Retaining California teachers so all students learn.* Unpublished paper. Sacramento: Center for Teacher Quality at the California State University.

Gargiulo, R. M. (2003). *Special education in a contemporary society: An introduction to exceptionality.* Belmont, CA: Wadsworth–Thomson.

Goldberg, R. J., Higgins, E. L., Raskind, M. H., & Herman, K. L. (2003). Predictors of success in individuals with learning disabilities: A qualitative analysis of a 20-year longitudinal study. *Learning Disabilities Research and Practice, 18,* 222–236.

Gotsch, T. (2002, March 13). Medication issue could emerge in IDEA debate. *Special Education Report, 28,* 1–2.

Graham, S., & Harris, K. R. (2005). *Writing better: Teaching writing process and self-regulation* (2nd ed.). Baltimore, MD: Brookes.

Gregg, N., & Mather, N. (2002, February). School is fun at recess: Informal analyses of written language for students with learning disabilities. *Journal of Learning Disabilities, 35,* 7–22.

Gresham, F. (2002). Responsiveness to intervention: An alternative approach to the identification of learning disabilities. In R. Bradley, L. Danielson, and D. P. Hallahan (Eds.), *Identification of learning disabilities: Research to practice* (pp. 467–519). Mahwah, NJ: Erlbaum.

Gresham, F. M., Lane, K. L., & Lambros, K. M. (2000, Summer). Comorbidity of conduct problems and ADHD: Identification of "fledgling psychopaths." *Journal of Emotional and Behavioral Disorders, 8,* 83–93.

Hall, B. J., Oyer, H. J., & Haas, W. H. (2001). *Speech, language, and hearing disorders: A guide for the teacher.* Boston: Allyn and Bacon.

Hallahan, D. P., & Kauffman, J. M. (2000). *Exceptional children: Introduction to special education* (8th ed.). Boston: Allyn and Bacon.

Hammill, D. (2004). What we know about correlates of reading. *Exceptional Children, 70,* 453–468.

Harris, K. R., & Graham, S. (1999). Programmatic intervention research: Illustrations from the evolution of self-regulated strategy development. *Learning Disability Quarterly, 22,* 251–262.

Hartung, C. M., & Scambler, D. J. (2006). Dealing with bullying and victimization in schools. *Emotional & Behavioral Disorders in Youth, 6,* 73–96.

Hock, M. (1997, June). Student motivation and commitment: A cornerstone of strategy instruction. *Strategram, 9,* 1–2.

Hughes, C., & Carter, E. W. (2006). *Success for all students: Promoting inclusion in secondary schools through peer buddy programs.* Boston: Allyn and Bacon.

Hussar, W. J., & Bailey, T. M. (2006). *Projections of education statistics to 2015* (NCES 2006-084). U.S. Department of Education, National Center for Education Statistics. Washington, DC: U.S. Government Printing Office.

IDEA Practices. (2002). *Youth with disabilities in the juvenile justice system.* Retrieved July 17, 2002, from www.ideapractices.org

The IRIS Center (2006). *The Response to Intervention (RTI) Module Series.* Nashville, TN: Vanderbilt University. Available at www.iris.peabody.vanderbilt.edu

Jenkins, J. R., & O'Connor, R. E. (2002). Early identification and intervention for young children with reading/learning disabilities. In R. Bradley, L. Danielson, and D. P. Hallahan (Eds.), *Identification of learning disabilities: Research to practice* (pp. 99–149). Mahwah, NJ: Erlbaum.

Jensen, P. S. (2000). ADHD: Advances in understanding its causes, and best treatments. *Emotional and Behavioral Disorders in Youth, 1,* 9–10, 19.

Kauffman, J. M. (2005). *Characteristics of behavioral disorders of children and youth* (8th ed.). Columbus, OH: Merrill.

Kavale, K. A., & Forness, S. R. (2000). What definitions of learning disability say and don't say. *Journal of Learning Disabilities, 33,* 239–256.

Kennedy, C. H., & Horn, E. (2004). *Including students with severe disabilities.* Boston: Allyn and Bacon.

Kuhne, M., & Wiener, J. (2000). Stability of social status of children with and without learning disabilities. *Learning Disability Quarterly, 23,* 64–75.

Kukic, S., Tilly, D., & Michelson, L. (2005). *Addressing the needs of students with learning difficulties through the response to intervention (RtI) strategies.* Alexandria, VA: National Association of State Directors of Special Education (NASDSE).

Lane, K. L. (2004). Academic instruction and tutoring interventions for students with emotional/behavioral disorders: 1990 to present (pp. 462–486). In R. B. Rutherford, M. M. Quinn, and S. R. Mathur (Eds.), *Handbook of research in emotional and behavioral disorders.* New York: Guilford.

Lane, K. L., & Wehby, J. (2002). Addressing antisocial behavior in the schools: A call for action. *Academic Exchange Quarterly, 6,* 4–7.

Lerner, J., & Kline, F. (2006). *Learning disabilities and related disorders* (10th ed.). Boston: Houghton Mifflin.

Lipsky, D. K., & Gartner, A. (1991). Restructuring to quality. In J. Lloyd, N. Singh, and A. Repp (Eds.), *The regular education initiative: Alternative perspectives on concepts, issues, and models* (pp. 43–56). Sycamore, IL: Sycamore.

Luckasson, R., Borthwick-Duffy, S., Buntinx, W. H. E., Coulter, D. L., Craig, E. M., Reeve, A., Schalock, R. L., Snell, M. E., Spitalnik, D. M., Spreat, S., & Tassé, M. J. (2002). *Definition of mental retardation.* Washington, DC: American Association on Mental Retardation (AAMR).

Luckasson, R., Coulter, D. L., Polloway, E. A., Reis, S., Schalock, R. L., Snell, M. E., Spitalnik, D. M., & Stark, J. A. (1992). *Mental retardation: Definition, classification, and systems of supports.* Washington, DC: American Association on Mental Retardation (AAMR).

Maag, J. W. (2000). Managing resistance. *Intervention in Schools and Clinics, 35,* 131–140.

Manley, R. S., Rickson, H., & Standeven, B. (2000). Children and adolescents with eating disorders: Strategies for teachers and school counselors. *Intervention in School and Clinic, 35,* 228–231.

Mayes, S. D., Calhoun, S. L., & Crowell, E. W. (2000). Learning disabilities and ADHD: Overlapping spectrum disorders. *Journal of Learning Disabilities, 33,* 417–424.

McLaughlin, M. J. & Nolet, V. (2004). *What every principal needs to know about special education.* Thousand Oaks, CA: Corwin.

Mercer, A. (2004). *Students with learning problems* (7th ed.). Columbus, OH: Merrill–Prentice Hall.

Müller, E., & Markowitz, J. (2004). *Disability categories: State terminology, definitions & eligibility criteria.* Alexandria, VA: National Association of State Directors of Special Education (NASDSE), Project Forum.

National Center for Educational Statistics (NCES). (2005). *Quick tables and figures.* www.nces.ed.gov/quicktables

National Down Syndrome Society. (2006). *Education and schooling.* Retrieved November 16, 2006, from www.ndss.org

National Institutes of Health, National Institute of Neurological Disorders and Stroke. (2006). *"What is learning disabilities?"* NINDS Learning Disabilities Information Page. Retrieved November 6, 2006, from www.ninds.nih.gov

National Institute of Mental Health (2005). *Attention Deficit Hyperactivity Disorder.* Bethesda, MD: National Institutes of Health. Retrieved March 15, 2005, from www.nimh.nih.gov

Newcorn, J. H. (2001). New medication treatment for ADHD. *Emotional and Behavioral Disorders in Youth,* pp. 59–61.

Office of Special Education Programs (OSEP). (2001). Special education in correctional facilities. In U.S. Department of Education, *The twenty-third annual report to Congress on the implementation of IDEA.* Washington, DC: U.S. Government Printing Office.

Office of Special Education Programs (OSEP). (2006). *Students served under IDEA, Part B, by disability category and state: Fall 2005.* Retrieved on October 24, 2006, from www.ideadata.org

Olmeda, R. E., Thomas, A. R., & Davis, C. P. (2003). An analysis of sociocultural factors in social skills training studies with students with attention deficit/hyperactivity disorder. *Multiple Voices, 6,* 58–72.

Pappadopulos, E., & Jensen, P. S. (2001, Spring). What school professionals, counselors, and parents need to know about medication for emotional and behavioral disorders in kids. *Emotional and Behavioral Disorders in Youth,* pp. 35–37.

Parrish, T., & Esra, P. (2006). The special education expenditure project (SEEP): Synthesis of findings and policy implications. In *Forum: Policy Brief Analysis.* Alexandria, VA: Project Forum, The National Association of State Directors of Special Education.

Payne, K. T., & Taylor, O. L. (2006). Multicultural influences on human communication. In N. B. Anderson and G. H. Shames (Eds.), *Human communication disorders: An introduction* (7th ed., pp. 93–125). Boston: Allyn and Bacon.

Pierangelo, R., & Guiliani, G. (2006). *Learning disabilities: A practical approach to foundations, assessment, diagnosis, and teaching.* Boston: Allyn and Bacon.

Pierce, K. (2003). Attention-deficit/hyperactivity disorder and comorbidity. *Primary Psychiatry, 10*(4), 69–70, 75–75.

Polloway, E. A. (1997). Developmental principles of the Luckasson et al. (1992). AAMR definition of mental retardation: A retrospective. *Education and Training in Mental Retardation and Developmental Disabilities, 32,* 174–178.

Prabhala, A. (2007, February 20). Mental retardation is no more—New name is intellectual and developmental disabilities. *Information form AAIDD.* News release to members online.

Ramig, P. R., & Shames, G. H. (2006). Stuttering and other disorders of fluency. In N. B. Anderson and G. H. Shames (Eds.), *Human communication disorders: An introduction* (7th ed, pp. 183–221). Boston: Allyn and Bacon.

Ratner, N. B. (2005). Atypical language development. In J. B. Gleason (Ed.), *The development of language* (6th ed.). Boston: Allyn and Bacon.

Reid, R., & Lienemann, T. O. (2006). Strategy instruction for students with learning disabilities. In K. R. Harris and S. Graham (Series Eds.), *What works for special-needs learners.* New York: Guilford.

Reid, R., Riccio, C. A., Kessler, R. H., DuPaul, G. J., Power, T. J., Anastopoulos, A. D., Rogers-Adkinson, D., & Noll, M. B. (2000). Gender and ethnic differences in ADHD as assessed by behavior ratings. *Journal of Emotional and Behavioral Disorders, 8,* 38–48.

Reschly, D. J. (2002). Minority overrepresentation: The silent contributor to LD prevalence and diagnostic confusion. In R. Bradley, L. Danielson, and D. P. Hallahan (Eds.), *Identification of learning disabilities: Research to practice* (pp. 361–368). Mahwah, NJ: Erlbaum.

Roizen, N. J. (2001). Down syndrome: Progress in research. *Mental Retardation and Developmental Disabilities Research Reviews, 7,* 38–44.

Salend, S. J. (2005). *Creating inclusive classrooms: Effective and reflective practices for all students* (5th ed.). Columbus, OH: Merrill–Prentice Hall.

Sexton, M., Harris, K. R., & Graham, S. (1998). Self-regulated strategy development and the writing process: Effects on essay writing and attributions. *Exceptional Children, 64,* 295–311.

Small, L. H. (2005). *Fundamentals of phonetics: A practical guide for students* (2nd ed.) Boston: Allyn and Bacon.

Smith, D. D. (2007). *Introduction to special education: Making a difference* (6th ed.). Boston: Allyn and Bacon.

Sunderland, L. C. (2004). Speech, language, and audiology services in public schools. *Intervention in School and Clinic, 39,* 209–217.

TASH (2004). *Inclusive quality education.* Retrieved August 18, 2004, from www.tash.org/inclusion/index.htm

Taylor, R. L., Richards, S. B., & Brady, M. P. (2005). *Mental retardation: Historical perspectives, current practices, and future directions.* Boston: Allyn and Bacon.

Torgesen, J. K. (2002). Empirical and theoretical support for direct diagnosis of learning disabilities by assessment of intrinsic processing weaknesses. In R. Bradley, L. Danielson, and D. P. Hallahan (Eds.), *Identification of learning disabilities: Research to practice* (pp. 565–652). Mahwah, NJ: Erlbaum.

Torgesen, J. K., & Wagner, R. K. (1998). Alternative diagnostic approaches for specific developmental reading disabilities. *Learning Disabilities Research & Practice, 13,* 220–232.

U.S. Department of Education. (1999). Assistance to states for the Education of Children with Disabilities Program and the Early Intervention Program for Infants and Toddlers with Disabilities; Final regulations. *Federal Register, 34,* CRF Parts 300 and 303.

U.S. Department of Education. (2001). *Twenty-third annual report to Congress on the implementation of the Individuals with Disabilities Education Act.* Washington, DC: U.S. Government Printing Office.

U.S. Department of Education. (2002). *Twenty-fourth annual report to Congress on the implementation of the Individuals with Disabilities Education Act.* Washington, DC: U.S. Government Printing Office.

U.S. Department of Education. (2006). Assistance to states for the Education of Children with Disabilities Program and the Early Intervention Program for Infants and Toddlers with Disabilities; Final rule. *Federal Register, 34.* CRF Parts 300 and 301.

U.S. Senate Appropriations Committee. (2004 September 15). *Senate Appropriations Committee report on the Labor/HHS/Education bill.* Washington, DC: U.S. Senate.

Vaughn, S. (2005). *Evidence-based Reading Interventions for the 2%.* OSEP 15th Annual Technical Assistance and Dissemination Conference. Washington, DC. June 8, 2005.

Vaughn, S., Bos, C., & Schumm, J. S. (2006). *Teaching exceptional, diverse, and at-risk students in the general education classroom, IDEA update* (3rd ed.). Boston: Allyn and Bacon.

Vaughn, S., Elbaum, B., & Boardman, A. G. (2001). The social function of students with learning disabilities: Implications for inclusion. *Exceptionality, 9,* 47–65.

Vaughn, S., & Fuchs, L. S. (2003). Redefining learning disabilities as inadequate response to instruction: The promise and potential problems. *Learning Disabilities Research and Practice, 18,* 137–146.

Vaughn, S., & Linan-Thompson, S. (2004). *Research-based methods of reading instruction: Grades K–3.* Alexandria, VA: Association for Supervision and Curriculum Development.

Wagner, M., & Blackorby, J. (2004). *Overview of findings from Wave 1 of the Special Education Elementary Longitudinal Study (SEELS).* Menlo Park, CA: SRI International.

Walker, H. M., Nishioka, V., Zeller, R., Bullis, M., & Sprague, J. R. (2001). School-based screening, identification, and service delivery issues. *Emotional and Behavioral Disorders in Youth, 1,* 51–52.

Walker, H. M., Ramsey, E., & Gresham, F. M. (2004). *Antisocial behavior in school: Evidence-based practices* (2nd ed.). Belmont, CA: Wadsworth.

Walker, H. M., & Sprague, J. (1999). The path to school failure, delinquency, and violence: Causal factors and potential solutions. *Intervention in School and Clinic, 35,* 67–73.

Wetherby, A. M. (2002). Communication disorders in infants, toddlers, and preschool children. In G. H. Shames and N. B. Anderson (Eds.), *Human communication disorders: An introduction* (6th ed., pp. 186–217). Boston: Allyn and Bacon.

CHAPTER 3   Understanding Learners with Special Needs: Low Incidence Disabilities or Conditions

American Council on Education, Health Resource Center. (2005). *Students who are deaf or hard of hearing on postsecondary education.* Washington, DC: Author.

American Foundation for the Blind. (2005). *Statistics and sources for professionals.* Retrieved on August 7, 2005, from www.afb.org

American Psychiatric Association (APA). (2003). *Diagnostic and statistical manual of mental disorders* (DSM-IV-TR). Washington, DC: Author.

American Speech–Language–Hearing Association (ASHA). (2002, May 4). *Facts on hearing loss in children.* Retrieved from www.asha.org

American Speech–Language–Hearing Association (ASHA). (2005). *Causes of hearing loss in children.* Retrieved on July 23, 2005, from www.asha.org/public/hearing/disorders/cuases.htm

Arthritis Foundation of America. (2002). *Juvenile rheumatoid arthritis: What is it?* Retrieved July 7, 2002, from http://www.arthritis.org/conditions/DiseaseCenter/jra.asp

Asthma Foundation of America. (2005). *Asthma facts and figures.* Retrieved July 7, 2005, from www.aafa.org/display.cfm

Autism Society of America (2006). *What is autism?* Retrieved November 24, 2006, from www.autism-society.org

Baldwin, V. (1995). *Annual Deaf-Blind Census.* Monmouth, OR: Teaching Research, Western Oregon State College.

Baron-Cohen, S., Wheelwright, S., Skinner, R., Martin, J., & Clubley, E. (2001). The autism spectrum quotient (AQ): Evidence from Asperger syndrome/high functioning autism, males and females, scientists and mathematicians. *Journal of Autism and Developmental Disorders, 31,* 5–17.

Bruno, L. (2006, September 19). GPS helps lead the way for the blind. *USA Today,* p. 8D.

Bryant, D., & Bryant, B. (2003). *Assistive technology for people with disabilities.* Boston: Allyn and Bacon.

Burton, D. (2002, April 18). *The autism epidemic: Is the NIH and CDC response adequate?* Committee on Government Reform, Opening Statement, U.S. Congress.

Centers for Disease Control (CDC). (2005). *Vision impairment.* Atlanta: National Center on Birth Defects and Developmental Disabilities. Retrieved on August 7, 2005, from www.cdc.gov /ncbddd/dd/ddvi.htm

Centers for Disease Control (CDC). (2006). *How common are Autism Spectrum Disorders?* Atlanta: National Center on

Birth Defects and Developmental Disabilities. Retrieved on November 26, 2006, from www.cdc.gov/ncbddd/autism/asd_common.htm

Centers for Disease Control (CDC), National Center on Birth Defects and Developmental Disabilities. (2004). *Developmental disabilities*. Retrieved on November 24, 2006, from www.cdc.gov/cnbdd

Chen, D., Downing, J., & Rodriguez-Gil, G. (2000–2001, Winter). Tactile learning strategies for children who are deaf-blind: Concerns and considerations from Project SALUTE. *Deaf-Blind Perspectives, 8*, 1–6.

Corn, A. (1989). Instruction in the use of vision for children and adults with low vision: A proposed program model. *RE:view, 21,* 26–38.

Corn, A., & Koenig, A. J. (2002). Literacy for students with low vision: A framework for delivering instruction. *Journal of Visual Impairments and Blindness, 96,* 305–321.

Cox, P., & Dykes, M. (2001). Effective classroom adaptations for students with visual impairments. *Teaching Exceptional Children, 33,* 68–74.

Davey, M. (2005, March 21). As town for Deaf takes shape, debate on isolation re-emerges. *New York Times*, National Desk. Retrieved on July 23, 2005.

DB Link, National Technical Assistance Consortium for Children and Youth Who Are Deaf-Blind. (2006). *National deaf-blind census*. Monmouth, OR: Teaching Research, Western Oregon University. Retrieved November 24, 2006, from www.dblink.org

Dote-Kwan, J., Chen, D., & Hughes M. (2001). A national survey of service providers who work with young children with visual impairments. *Journal of Visual Impairment and Blindness, 95,* 325–337.

Ellison, J. (2002). *Miracles happen: One mother, one daughter, one journey*. New York: Hyperion.

Emory University School of Medicine. (2005). *Sickle cell information for teachers, students, and employers*. The Sickle Cell Information Center. Retrieved July 8, 2005, from www.scinfo.org

Epilepsy Foundation of America (EFA). (2005a). *Epilepsy and seizure statistics*. Retrieved July 7, 2005, from www.efa.org/answerplace/statistics.cfm

Epilepsy Foundation of America (EFA). (2005b). *Managing seizures at school*. Retrieved July 7, 2005, from www.efa.org/answerplace/teachers/managing.cfm

Evans, C. J. (2004). Literacy development in deaf students: Case studies in bilingual teaching and learning. *American Annals of the Deaf, 149,* 17–127.

Gallaudet Research Institute. (1994). *Working Papers 89-3*. Washington, DC: Gallaudet University.

Gordon-Langbein, A. L., & Metzinger, M. (2000, January/February). Technology in the classroom to maximize listening and learning. *Volta Voices, 7,* 10–13.

Haller, A. K., & Montgomery, J. K. (2004). Noise-induced hearing loss in children: What educators need to know. *Teaching Exceptional Children, 36,* 22–27.

Hatton, D. (2001, July). Model registry of early childhood visual impairment: First-year results. *Journal of Visual Impairment and Blindness, 95,* 418–433.

Helman, S. W. (2002, May 28). A disabled student's battle could aid others' struggles. *Boston Globe*, pp. B1–2.

Johnson, R. C. (2001–2002, Fall/Winter). High stakes testing and deaf students: Comments from readers. *Research at Gallaudet, 1*.

Johnson, K. C., & Winter, M. E. (2003). Audiologic assessment of infants and toddlers. *The Volta Review, 103,* 221–251.

Keller, H. (1988). *The story of my life*. Mineola, NY: Dover Thrift Editions.

Kochhar-Bryant, C. A., Shaw, S., & Izzo, M. (2007). *What every teacher should know about transition and IDEA 2004*. Boston: Allyn and Bacon.

Lash, M., & DePompei, R. (2002). *Kids' corner*. Available from the Brain Injury Association of America. Retrieved August 31, 2002, from www.biausa.org/children.htm

Laurent Clerc National Deaf Education Center. (2006). *Deaf children with multiple disabilities*. Retrieved November 16, 2006, from www.clerccenter.gallaudet.edu/InfoToGo/141.htm

Marschark, M. (2001). *Language development in children who are deaf: A research synthesis*. Alexandria, VA: Project Forum, National Association of State Directors of Special Education (NASDSE).

McCormick, L., & Wegner, J. (2003). Supporting augmentative communication. In L. McCormick, D. F. Loeb, and R. L. Shiefelbusch (Eds.), *Supporting children with communication difficulties in inclusive settings: School-based language intervention* (pp. 435–460). Boston: Allyn and Bacon.

McDonnell, J. J., Hardman, M. L., & McDonnell, A. P. (2003). *Introduction to persons with moderate and severe disabilities: Educational and social issues* (2nd ed.). Boston: Allyn and Bacon.

Miles, B. (2005). *Overview on deaf-blindness*. Retrieved November 24, 2006, from http://tr.wou.edu/dblink/overview.html

Moores, D. F. (2001). *Educating the deaf: Psychology, principles, and practices* (5th ed.). Boston: Houghton Mifflin.

Müller, E., & Markowitz, J. (2004). *Disability categories: State terminology, definitions & eligibility criteria*. Alexandria, VA: National Association of State Directors of Special Education (NASDSE), Project Forum.

National Federation of the Blind (NFB). (2006). *About vision loss for . . . .* Retrieved November 24, 2006, from www.nfb.org

National Human Genome Research Institute. (2005). *Learning about sickle cell disease*. Retrieved July 6, 2005, from www.genome.gov

National Institute of Allergy and Infectious Diseases. (2004, July 8). *Backgrounder-HIV infections in infants and children*. Retrieved August 9, 2004, from www.niaid.nih.gov/newsroom/simple/background.htm

National Institute on Deafness and Other Hearing Disorders. (2006). *Cochlear implants*. Retrieved November 24, 2006, from www.nidcd.nih.gov/health/hearing/coch.asp

National Institute of Environmental Health Sciences (NIEHS). (2005). *Asthma and the environment*. Hot topics packs. Retrieved July 10, 2005, from www.niehs.nih.gov/outreach/education/Resources/HTasthma.cfm

National Institutes of Health, National Heart, Lung and Blood Institute. (2006). *Sickle cell anemia: Who is at risk for sickle cell anemia?* Diseases and conditions index. Retrieved November 24, 2006, from www.nhlbi.nih.gov/health/dci/Diseases/Sca/SCA_WhoIsAtRisk.html

National Institute of Mental Health (NIMH). (2006). *Addendum to autism spectrum disorders, March 2006*. Retrieved November 24, 2006, from http://www.nimh.nih.gov/publicat/autism.cfm

National Institute of Neurological Disorders and Stroke (NINDS). (2006). *NINDS Traumatic Brain Injury Information Page*. Retrieved on November 24, 2006, from www.ninds.nih.gov/disorders/tib/tbi.htm

National Research Council. (2001). *Educating children with autism*. Washington, DC: National Academy Press.

NICHCY (2004). *Severe and/or multiple disabilities*. Fact Sheet 10. Washington, DC: National Dissemination Center for Children with Disabilities. Retrieved on August 30, 2005, from www.nichcy.org

NICHCY (2006). *Traumatic brain injury*. Fact Sheet 18. Washington, DC: National Dissemination Center for Children with Disabilities. Retrieved on November 24, 2006, from www.nichcy.org

Noonan, M. J., & Siegel, E. B. (2003). Special needs of students with severe disabilities or autism. In L. McCormick, D. F. Loeb, and R. L. Shiefelbusch (Eds.), *Supporting children with communication difficulties in inclusive settings: School-based language intervention* (pp. 409–434). Boston: Allyn and Bacon.

Office of Special Education Programs (OSEP). (2000). High school graduation. *Twenty-second annual report to Congress on the implementation of the Individuals with Disabilities Education Act* (pp. IV–15 to IV–21). Washington, DC: U.S. Department of Education.

Office of Special Education Programs (OSEP). (2006). *Students served under IDEA, Part B, by disability category and state: Fall 2005.* Retrieved on October 24, 2006, from www.ideadata.org

Owens, R. E., Metz, D. E., & Haas, A. (2007). *Introduction to communication disorders: A lifespan perspective.* Boston: Allyn and Bacon.

Powers, M. D. (2000). What is autism? In M. D. Powers (Ed.), *Children with autism: A parent's guide.* Bethesda, MD: Woodbine House.

Reichle, J., Beukelman, D. R., & Light, J. C. (2002). *Exemplary practices for beginning communicators: Implications for ACC.* Baltimore, MD: Brookes.

Safran, S. P. (2001). Asperger syndrome: The emerging challenge to special education. *Exceptional Children, 67,* 151–160.

Simeonsson, R. J., Huntington, G. S., McMillen, J. S., Danaher, J., Aberl-Boone, H., & McMillan, V. J. (2001). *Study of classification of disability in special education: Extending the definition of developmental delay from 6 through 9 years.* (CDC R04/CCR414143-03). Chapel Hill, NC: Frank Porter Graham Child Development Institute.

Simpson, R. L., de Boer-Ott, S. R., Griswold, D. E., Myles, S. B., Bryd, S. E., Ganz, J., B., Cook, K. R., Otten, K. L., Ben-Arieh, J., Kline, S. A., & Adams, L., G. (2005). *Autism spectrum disorders: Interventions and treatments for children and youth.* Thousand Oaks, CA: Corwin.

Snell, M. E., & Brown, F. (2006). *Instruction of students with severe disabilities* (6th ed.). Upper Saddle River, NJ: Merrill–Prentice Hall.

Stremel, K. (1998, August). *Communication interactions: It takes two.* Retrieved August 29, 2002, from DB Link, http://tr.wou.edu/dblink/comm.htm

Strock, M. (2004). *Autism spectrum disorders (pervasive developmental disorders).* NIH Publication No. NIH-04-5511, National Institute of Mental Health (NIMH), National Institutes of Health, U.S. Department of Health and Human Services, Bethesda, MD, 40 pp. Retrieved from www.nimh.nih.gov/publicat/autism.cfm

Switzky, H. N., & Greenspan, S. (2006). *What is mental retardation? Ideas for an evolving disability in the 21st century.* Washington, DC: American Association of Mental Retardation.

Talay-Ongan, A., & Wood, K. (2000). Unusual sensory sensitivities in autism: A possible crossroads. *International Journal of Disability, Development and Education, 47,* 201–212.

TASH. (2000). *TASH resolution on the people for whom TASH advocates.* Baltimore: Author. Definition originally adopted April 1975; revised December 1985 and March 2000. Available at www.tash.org/resolutions/R21PEOPL.html

United Cerebral Palsy Association (UCP). (2001). *Cerebral palsy—Facts and figures.* Retrieved November 24, 2006, from www.ucp.org

U.S. Department of Education. (1996). *Nineteenth annual report to Congress on the implementation of the Individuals with Disabilities Education Act.* Washington, DC: U.S. Government Printing Office.

U.S. Department of Education. (2002). *Twenty-fourth annual report to Congress on the implementation of the Individuals with Disabilities Education Act.* Washington, DC: U.S. Government Printing Office.

U.S. Department of Education. (2006). Assistance to states for the Education of Children with Disabilities Program and the Early Intervention Program for Infants and Toddlers with Disabilities; Final rule. *Federal Register, 34.* CRF Parts 300 and 301.

Van Kuren, L. (2001, March). Traumatic brain injury—The silent epidemic. *CEC Today, 7,* 1, 5, 15.

Yoshinaga-Itano, C., & Sedey, A. (2000). Early speech development in children who are deaf or hard of hearing: Interrelationships with language and hearing. *Volta Review, 100,* 181–211.

Zazove, P., Meador, H. E., Derry, H. A., Gorenflo, D. W., & Saunders, E. W. (2004). Deaf persons and computer use. *American Annals of the Deaf, 148,* 376–384.

CHAPTER 4   Other Students with Special Learning Needs

Aguirre, N. (2003). ESL students in gifted education. In J. A. Castellano (Ed.), *Special populations in gifted education* (pp. 17–27). Boston: Allyn and Bacon.

American Association of University Women. (1992). *How schools short-change girls.* Washington, DC: AAUW Education Foundation.

Arreaga-Mayer, C., & Greenwood, C. R. (1986). Environmental variables affecting the school achievement of culturally and linguistically different learners: An instructional perspective. *Journal of the National Association of Bilingual Education, 10*(2), 113–135.

Artiles, A. J., Rueda, R., Salazar, J., & Higareda, I. (2005). Within-group diversity in minority disproportionate representation: English language learners in urban school districts. *Exceptional Children, 71,* 283–300.

Au, K. (1995). Multicultural perspectives on literacy research. *Journal of Reading Behavior, 27,* 85–100.

August, D., & Shanahan, T. (2006). *Developing literacy in second-language learners: Report of the national literacy panel on language-minority children and youth.* Mahwah, New Jersey: Erlbaum.

Baca, L. M., & Cervantes, H. T. (Eds.). (2004). *The bilingual special education interface* (4th ed.). New Jersey: Merrill–Prentice Hall.

Baca, L., & de Valenzuela, J. S. (1994, Fall). Reconstructing the bilingual special education interface. *NCBE Program Information Guide Series, 20.* Retrieved August 2, 2001, from www.ncela.gwu.edu/ncbepubs/pigs/pig20.htm

Baldwin, A. Y. (1999). Learning disability: The mysterious mask—The USA perspective. In A. Y. Baldwin and W. Vialle (Eds.), *The many faces of giftedness* (pp. 103–134). Belmont, CA: Wadsworth.

Banks, J., (2001). *Cultural diversity and education: Foundations, curriculum, and teaching* (4th ed.). Boston: Allyn and Bacon.

Baum, S., & Owen, S. (1988). Learning disabled students: How are they different? *Gifted Child Quarterly, 32,* 321–326.

Bianco, M. (2005). The effects of disability labels on special education and general education teachers' referrals for gifted programs. *Learning Disability Quarterly, 28*(4), 285–293.

Bos, C. S., Allen, A. A., & Scanlon, D. J. (1989). Vocabulary instruction and reading comprehension with bilingual learning disabled students. In S. McCormick and J. Zutell (Eds.), *Cognitive and social perspectives for literacy research and instruction: Thirty-eighth yearbook of the National Reading Conference* (pp. 173–179). Chicago: National Reading Conference.

Campbell, L., Campbell, D., & Dickinson, D. (1999). *Teaching and learning through the multiple intelligences* (2nd ed.). Boston: Allyn and Bacon.

Castellano, J. A. (2002). Renavigating the waters. The identification and assessment of culturally and linguistically diverse students for gifted and talented education. In J. A. Castellano and E. I. Diaz (Eds.), *Reaching new horizons* (pp. 94–116). Boston: Allyn and Bacon.

Children's Defense Fund. (2004). *The state of America's children: 2004.* Washington, DC: Author.

Clark, B. (2002). *Growing up gifted* (6th ed.). Upper Saddle River, NJ: Prentice-Hall.

Coben, S. S., & Vaughn, S. (1989). Gifted students with learning disabilities: What does the research say? *Journal of Learning Disabilities, 5*(2), 87–94.

Cole, M. (1998). Can cultural psychology help us think about diversity? *Mind, Culture, and Activity, 5*(4), 291–304.

Cox, S., & Galdo, L. (1990). Multicultural literature: Mirrors and windows on a global community. *The Reading Teacher, 43,* 582–589.

D'Anguilli, A., Siegel, L., & Maggi, S. (2004). Literacy instruction, SES, and word-reading achievement in English-language learners and children with English as a first language: A longitudinal study. *Learning Disabilities Research & Practice, 19*(4), 202–213.

Davis, G. A., & Rimm, S. B. (2004). *Education of the gifted and talented* (5th ed.). Boston: Allyn and Bacon.

Donovan, S., & Cross, C. (Eds.). (2002). *Minority students in special and gifted education.* Washington, DC: National Academy Press.

Echevarria, J., & McDonough, R. (1995). An alternative reading approach: Instructional conversations in a bilingual special education setting. *Learning Disabilities Research and Practice, 10*(2), 108–119.

Education Statistics Quarterly (2000). High school dropouts, by race/ethnicity and recency of migration. *Education Statistics Quarterly, 2*(3), 25–27.

Ford, D. Y., Grantham, T. C., & Milner, R. H. (2004). Underachievement among gifted African American students: Cultural, social, and psychological considerations. In D. Boothe and J. C. Stanley (Eds.), *Critical issues for diversity in gifted education* (pp. 15–32). Waco, TX: Prufrock Press.

Fox, L., Engle, J., & Sooler, J. (1999). The math-science mystique. *Understanding Our Gifted, 11*(2), 3–7.

Frasier, M., Hunsaker, S. L., Jongyeun, L., Mitchell, S., Cramond, B., Krisel, S., Garcia, J. H., Martin, D., Frank, E., & Vernon, S. F. (1995). *Core attributes of giftedness: A foundation for recognizing the gifted potential of minority and economically disadvantaged students* (Report No. RM-95210). Storrs, CT: National Research Center on the Gifted and Talented. (ERIC Document Reproduction Service No. ED 402 703)

Friend, M. (2008). *Special education: Contemporary perspectives for school professionals* (2nd ed.). Boston: Allyn and Bacon.

Gallagher, J. J. (2000). Unthinkable thoughts: Education of gifted students. *Gifted Children Quarterly, 44,* 5–12.

Gardner, H. (1983). *Frames of mind.* New York: Basic Books.

Gardner, H. (1993). *Multiple intelligences: The theory in practice.* New York: Basic Books.

Gersten, R., & Baker, S. (2000). What we know about effective instructional practices for English-language learners. *Exceptional Children, 66,* 454–470.

Gollnick, D. M., & Chinn, P. C. (2006). *Multicultural education in a pluralistic society* (7th ed.). Columbus, OH: Merrill.

Gottlieb, J., Alter, M., Gottlieb, B. W., & Wishner, J. (1994). Special education in urban America: It's not justifiable for many. *The Journal of Special Education, 27,* 453–465.

Granada, J. (2003). Casting a wider net: Linking bilingual and gifted education. In J. A. Castellano (Ed.), *Special populations in gifted education* (pp. 1–16). Boston: Allyn and Bacon.

Grantham, T. C. (2004, Winter). Underrepresentation in gifted education: How did we get here and what needs to be changed? *Roeper Review, 24,* 50–51.

Greene, J. (1998). *A meta-analysis of the effectiveness of bilingual education.* Claremont, CA: The Tomás Rivera Policy Institute.

Gutierrez, K., & Rogoff, B. (2003). Cultural ways of learning: Individual traits or repertoires of practice. *Educational Researcher, 32*(5), 19–25.

Harry, B., & Klingner, J. K. (2006). *Why are so many minority students in special education? Understanding race and disability in schools.* New York: Teachers College Press.

Heath, S. B. (1983). *Ways with words: Language, life, and work in communities and classrooms.* New York: Cambridge University Press.

Hébert, T. P., & Olenchak, F. R. (2000). Mentors for gifted underachieving males: Developing potential and realizing promises. *Gifted Child Quarterly, 44,* 196–207.

Henning-Stout, M. (1996). "Que Podemos Hacer?": Roles for school psychologists with Mexican and Latino migrant children and families. *School Psychology Review, 25,* 152–164.

Hoover, J. J., & Collier, C. (1989). Methods and materials for bilingual special education. In L. M. Baca and H. T. Cervantes (Eds.), *The bilingual special education interface* (pp. 231–255). Columbus, OH: Merrill.

Individuals with Disabilities Education Improvement Act of 2004. PL No. 108-446.

Jacob K. Javits Gifted and Talented Students Education Act of 1988. PL 100-297. U.S. Department of Education, 1994. Washington, DC: U.S. Government Printing Office.

Kauffman, J. M. (1999). Commentary: Today's special education and its message for tomorrow. *Journal of Special Education, 32*(4), 244–254.

Kerr, B. (1994). *Smart girls.* Scottsdale: AZ: Gifted Psychology Press.

Kitano M., & Espinosa, R. (1995). Language diversity and giftedness: Working with gifted English language learners. *Journal of the Education for the Gifted, 18*(3), 234–254.

Klingner, J. K., Artiles, A. J., Kozleski, E., Harry, B., Zion, S., Tate, W., Durán, G. Z., & Riley, D. (2005). Addressing the disproportionate representation of culturally and linguistically diverse students in special education through culturally responsive educational systems. *Education Policy Analysis Archives, 13*(38), 1–39. Available at http://epaa.asu.edu/epaa/v13n38/

Klingner, J., & Bianco, M. (2006). What is special about special education for culturally and linguistically diverse students with disabilities? In B. Cook and B. Schirmer (Eds.), *What is special about special education?* (pp. 37–53). Austin, TX: PRO-ED.

Klingner, J. K., & Vaughn, S. (2000). The helping behaviors of fifth-graders while using collaborative strategic reading (CSR) during ESL content classes. *TESOL Quarterly, 34,* 69–98.

Lee, C. D. (2003). Why we need to re-think race and ethnicity in educational research. *Educational Researcher, 32*(5), 3–5.

Lee, V. E., & Burkam, D. T. (2003). Dropping out of high school: The role of school organization and structure. *American Educational Research Journal, 40*(2), 353–393.

Linan-Thompson, S., Vaughn, S., Hickman-Davis, P., & Kouzekanani, K. (2003). Effectiveness of supplemental reading instruction for second-grade English language learners with reading difficulties. *Elementary School Journal, 103,* 221–238.

Lopez-Reyna, N. A. (1996). The importance of meaningful contexts in bilingual special education: Moving to whole language. *Learning Disabilities Research & Practice, 11,* 120–131.

Markowitz, J. (Ed.). (1999). Education of children with disabilities who are homeless. *Proceedings of Project FORUM convened April 5–7, 1999,* 1–24. Alexandria, VA: NASDSE.

Moje, E. B., & Hinchman, K. (2004). Culturally responsive practices for youth literacy learning. In T. L. Jetton and J. A. Dole (Eds.), *Adolescent literacy research and practice* (pp. 321–350). New York: Guilford.

National Center for Education Statistics (2005). *The condition of education 2005.* Washington, DC: National Center for Educational Statistics.

Neu, T. W. (2003). When the gifts are camouflaged by disability. In J. A. Castellano (Ed.), *Special populations in gifted education* (pp. 151–162). Boston: Allyn and Bacon.

Nielsen, M. E. (2002). Gifted students with learning disabilities: Recommendations for identification and programming. *Exceptionality, 10*(2), 93–111.

Nieto, S., & Bode, P. (2008). *Affirming diversity: The sociopolitical context of multicultural education* (5th ed.). Boston: Allyn and Bacon.

No Child Left Behind Act of 2001. PL 107-110.

Ortiz, A. A. (2001). *English language learners with special needs: Effective instructional strategies.* Washington, DC: ERIC Education Reports.

Patton, J. M. (1997). Disproportionate representation in gifted programs: Best practices for meeting this challenge. In A. J. Artiles and G. Zamora-Duran (Eds.), *Reducing disproportionate representation of culturally diverse students in special and gifted education.* Reston, VA: The Council for Exceptional Children.

Patton, J. M. (1998). The disproportionate representation of African-Americans in special education: Looking behind the curtain for understanding and solutions. *Journal of Special Education, 32,* 25–31.

Piirtro, J. (1999). *Talented children and adults.* Upper Saddle River, NJ: Prentice-Hall.

Ramírez, D. (1992). Executive summary: Longitudinal study of structured English immersion strategy, early-exit and late-exit transitional bilingual education programs for language minority children. *Bilingual Research Journal, 16*(1 & 2), 1–62.

Rehabilitation Act of 1973. Section 504, 19 U.S.C. section 794.

Reis, S. M., & McCoach, D. B. (2002). Underachievement in gifted and talented students with special needs. *Exceptionality, 10*(2), 113–25.

Renzulli, J. S. (1978). What makes giftedness? Reexamining a definition. *Phi Delta Kappan, 60*(3), 180–184.

Renzulli, J. S. (2004). The myth: The gifted constitute 3–5% of the population. In J. S. Renzulli (Ed.), *Identification of students for gifted and talented programs.* Thousand Oaks, CA: Corwin Press and the National Association for Gifted Children.

Renzulli, J. S., & Reis, S. M. (1997). The schoolwide enrichment model: New directions for developing high-end learning. In N. Colangelo and G. A. Davis (Eds.), *Handbook of gifted education* (2nd ed., pp. 136–154). Boston: Allyn and Bacon.

Richert, E. S. (1997). Excellence with equity in identification and programming. In N. Colangelo and G. A. Davis (Eds.), *Handbook of gifted education* (2nd ed., pp. 75–88). Boston: Allyn and Bacon.

Robisheaux, J. A. (2002). Addressing the curriculum, instruction, and assessment needs of the bilingual/bicultural students. In J. A. Castellano and E. I. Diaz, (Eds.), *Reaching new horizons* (pp. 154–174). Boston: Allyn and Bacon.

Rogoff, B. (2003). *The cultural nature of human development.* New York: Oxford University Press.

Ruiz, N. T. (1995). The social construction of ability and disability: II. Optimal and at-risk lessons in a bilingual special education classroom. *Journal of Learning Disabilities, 28,* 491–502.

Schuler, P. A. (2002). Perfectionism in gifted children and adolescents. In M. Neihart, S. M. Reis, N. M. Robinson, and S. M. Moon (Eds.), *The social and emotional development of gifted children: What do we know?* (pp. 71–79). Washington, DC: National Association for Gifted Children.

Silverman, L. K. (2003). Gifted children with learning disabilities. In N. Colangelo and G. A. Davis (Eds.), *Handbook of gifted education* (3rd ed., pp. 533–543). Boston: Allyn and Bacon.

Slavin, R. E., & Cheung, A. (2005). A synthesis of research on language of reading instruction for English language learners. *Review of Educational Research, 75,* 247–284.

Smith, D. D. (2007). *Introduction to special education: Making a difference* (6th ed.). Boston: Allyn and Bacon.

Stephens, K., & Karnes, F. (2000). State definitions for the gifted and talented revisited. *Exceptional Children, 66,* 219–238.

Suarez-Orozco, C., & Suarez-Orozco, M. (2001). *Children of immigration.* Cambridge, MA: Harvard Education Publishing Group.

Tannenbaum, A. J. (1997). A triarchic view of giftedness: Theory and practice. In N. Colangelo and G. A. Davis (Eds.), *Handbook of gifted education* (2nd ed., pp. 43–53). Boston: Allyn & Bacon.

Tannenbaum, A. J., & Baldwin, L. J. (1983). Giftedness and learning disability: A paradoxical combination. In L. Fox, L. Brody, and D. Tobin (Eds.), *Learning disabled/gifted children: Identification and programming* (pp. 11–36). Baltimore, MD: University Park Press.

Taylor, B. M., Pearson, P. D., Clark, K., & Walpole, S. (2000). Effective schools and accomplished teachers: Lessons about primary-grade reading instruction in low-income schools. *Elementary School Journal, 101,* 121–165.

Thomas, W., & Collier, V. (2003). *A national study of school effectiveness for language minority students' long term academic achievement.* Santa Cruz, CA: Center for Research on Education, Diversity and Excellence.

Tomlinson, C. A. (2004a). Introduction to differentiation for gifted and talented students. In C. A. Tomlinson (Ed.), *Differentiation for gifted and talented students.* Thousand Oaks, CA: Corwin Press and the National Association for Gifted Children.

Tomlinson, C. A. (Ed.). (2004b). *Differentiation for gifted and talented students.* Thousand Oaks, CA: Corwin Press and the National Association for Gifted Children.

Tornatzky, L. G., Pachon, H. P., & Torres, C. (2003). *Closing achievement gaps: Improving educational outcomes for Hispanic children.* Los Angeles: The Center for Latino Educational Excellence, The Tomás Rivera Policy Institute, University of Southern California.

U.S. Census Bureau. (2000). *Census 2000 redistricting.* PL 94-171. Summary file, Tables PL1 and PL2. Washington, DC: U.S. Department of Commerce.

U.S. Census Bureau (2001, April 2). *U.S. Census Bureau, Population Division.* Retrieved March 26, 2003, from www.census.gov/population/www/cen2000/phc-t1.html

U.S. Department of Education. (1993). *National excellence: A case for developing America's talent.* Washington, DC: Author.

U.S. Department of Education. (1994). *The Improving America's Schools Act of 1994: Summary sheets.* Washington, DC: Author.

U.S. Department of Education. (2003). *Turning around low performing high schools.* National High School Summit. Retrieved April 14, 2007, from www.ed.gov/about/offices/list/ovae/pi/hs/reform.html

U.S. Department of Education (2003, June). *Key indicators of Hispanic student achievement: National goals and benchmarks for the next decade.* Retrieved June 27, 2003, from www.ed.gov/pubs/hispanicindicators/

Van Tassel-Baska, J., & Stambaugh, T. (2006). *Comprehensive curriculum for gifted learners* (3rd ed.). Boston: Allyn and Bacon.

Vaughn, S., Bos, C. S., & Schumm, J. S. (2007). *Teaching exceptional, diverse, and at-risk students in the general education classroom* (4th ed.). Boston: Allyn and Bacon.

Vaughn, S., Cirino, P. T., Linan-Thompson, S., Mathes, P. G., Carlson, C. D., Hagan, E. C., Pollard-Durodola, S. D., Fletcher, J. M., & Francis, D. J. (2006). Effectiveness of a Spanish intervention and an English intervention for English-language learners at risk for reading problems. *American Educational Research Journal, 43,* 449–487.

Vaughn, S., Mathes, P. G., Linan-Thompson, S., & Francis, D. J. (2005). Teaching English language learners at risk for reading disabilities to read: Putting research into practice. *Learning Disabilities Research & Practice, 20,* 58–67.

Wright, P. W. D., & Wright, P. D. (2007). *Wright's law: Special education law* (2nd ed.). Available from www.wrightslaw.com/bks/feta2/feta2.htm

Yates, J. R., & Ortiz, A. A. (2004). Classification issues in special education for English language learners. In A. M. Sorrells, H. J. Rieth, and P. T. Sindelar (Eds.), *Critical issues in special education* (pp. 38–56). Boston: Allyn and Bacon.

Zehler, A., Fleischman, H., Hopstock, P., Stephenson, T., Pendzick, M., & Sapru, S. (2003). *Policy report: Summary of findings related to LEP and SPED-LEP students.* Submitted by Development Associates, Inc., to U.S. Department of Education, Office of English Language Acquisition, Language Enhancement, and Academic Achievement of Limited English Proficient Students.

Zima, B. T., Forness, S. R., Bussing, R., & Benjamin, B. (1998). Homeless children in emergency shelters: Need for prereferral intervention and potential eligibility for special education. *Behavioral Disorders, 23,* 98–10.

Zirkel, P. A. (2005). State laws for gifted education: An overview of the legislation and regulations. *Roeper Review, 27,* 228–232.

CHAPTER 5 Delivery of Special Services Through Individualized Plans

Barnett, D. W., Daly, E. J., Jones, K. M., & Lentz Jr., F. E. (2004). Response to intervention: Empirically based special service decisions from single-case designs of increasing and decreasing intensity. *Journal of Special Education, 38,* 66–79.

Barnhill, G. P. (2005). Functional behavior assessment in schools. *Intervention in School and Clinic, 40,* 131–143.

Bigby, L. M. (2004). Medical and health related services: More than treating boo-boos and ouchies. *Intervention in School and Clinic, 39,* 233–235.

Borthwick-Duffy, S. A., Palmer, D. S., & Lane, K. L. (1996). One size doesn't fit all: Full inclusion and individual differences. *Journal of Behavioral Education, 6,* 311–329.

Bradley, R., Danielson, L., & Hallahan, D. P. (Eds.). (2002). *Identification of learning disabilities: Research to practice.* Mahwah, NJ: Erlbaum.

Brown, M. R., Paulsen, K., & Higgins, K. (2003). Remove environmental barriers to student learning. *Intervention in School and Clinic, 39,* 109–112.

Bryant, D. P., & Bryant, B. R. (2003). *Assistive technology for people with disabilities.* Boston: Allyn and Bacon.

Buehler, V. (2004, July/August). Easy as 1-2-3 IEPs. *Volta Voices, 11,* 20–23.

Cartledge, G., Kea, C. D., & Ida, D. J. (2000). Anticipating differences, celebrating strengths: Providing culturally competent services for students with serious emotional disturbance. *Teaching Exceptional Children, 32,* 30–37.

Chambers, A. C. (1997). *Has technology been considered? A guide for IEP Teams.* Reston, VA: Council of Administrators of Special Education and Media Division of The Council of Exceptional Children.

Cook, B. G. (2001). A comparison of teachers' attitudes toward their included students with mild and severe disabilities. *Journal of Special Education, 34,* 203–213.

Cook, B. G., Tankersley, M., Cook, L., & Landrum, T. J. (2000). Teachers' attitudes toward their included students with disabilities. *Exceptional Children, 67,* 115–135.

Council for Exceptional Children (CEC). (1999). *IEP Team guide.* Reston, VA: Author.

Curran, C. M., & Harris, M. B. (1996). *Uses and purposes of portfolio assessment for general and special educators.* Albuquerque: University of New Mexico.

Dabkowski, D. M. (2004). Encouraging active parent participation in IEP Team meetings. *Teaching Exceptional Children, 36,* 34–39.

Darling-Hammond, L. (2005). *Correlation between teachers and student achievement.* Presentation at The American Education Research Association (AERA). Annual conference. Montreal, April 2005.

Darling-Hammond, L. (2006a). Constructing 21st-Century teacher education. *Journal of Teacher Education, 57,* 300–314.

Darling-Hammond, L. (2006b). *Developing a profession of teaching.* Presentation to 2006 CalTEACH Annual Faculty Professional Conference, San Jose, November 2006.

de Fur, S. H. (2003). IEP transition planning—from compliance to quality. *Exceptionality, 11,* 115–128.

Downing, J. A. (2004). Related services for students with disabilities: Introduction to the special issue. *Intervention in School and Clinic, 39,* 195–208.

Dworetzky, B. (2004). Effective practices for involving families of children with disabilities in schools. *Newsline: The Federation of Children with Special Needs, 24,* 1, 12.

Earles-Vollrath, T. L. (2004). Mitchell Yell: IDEA 1997 and related services. *Intervention in School and Clinic, 39,* 236–239.

Etzel-Wise, D., & Mears, B. (2004). Adapted physical education and therapeutic recreation in schools. *Intervention in School and Clinic, 39,* 223–232.

Fisher, D., Frey, N., & Thousand, J. (2003). What do special educators need to know and be prepared to do for inclusive schooling to work? *Teacher Education and Special Education, 26,* 42–50.

Fuchs, L. S., & Fuchs, D. (2001). Principles for the prevention and intervention of mathematics difficulties. *Learning Disabilities Research & Practice, 16,* 85–95.

Fuchs, L. S., Fuchs, D., Hosp, M., & Jenkins, J. R. (2001). Oral reading fluency as an indicator of reading competence: A theoretical, empirical, and historical analysis. *Scientific Studies of Reading, 5,* 239–256.

Fuchs, L., Fuchs, D., & Powell, S. (2004). *Using CBM for progress monitoring.* Washington, DC: American Institutes for Research.

Futernick, K. (2006). *A possible dream: Retaining California teachers so all students learn.* Sacramento: CSU Center for Teacher Quality.

Haager, D., & Klingner, J. K. (2005). *Differentiating instruction in inclusive classrooms: The special educator's guide.* Boston: Allyn and Bacon.

Hammond, H., & Ingalls, L. (2003). Teachers' attitudes toward inclusion: Survey results from elementary school teachers in three southwestern rural school districts. *Rural Special Education Quarterly, 22,* 22–30.

Hanley, G. P., Iwata, B. A., & McCord, B. E. (2003). Functional analysis of problem behavior: A review. *Journal of Applied Behavior Analysis, 36,* 147–185.

Hébert, T. (2001, June). Man to man: Building channels of communication between fathers and their talented sons. *Parenting for High Potential,* pp. 18–22.

Hoover, J. J., & Patton, J. R. (2004). Differentiating standards-based education for students with diverse needs. *Remedial and Special Education, 25,* 74–78.

Hughes, M. T., Valle-Riestra, D. M., & Arguelles, M. E. (2002). Experiences of Latino families with their child's special education program. *Multicultural Perspectives, 4,* 11–17.

Individuals with Disabilities Education Improvement Act of 2004. PL No. 108-446. 118 STAT. 2647.

Kern, L., Delaney, B., Clarke, S., Dunlap, G., & Childs, K. (2001, Winter). Improving the classroom behavior of students with emotional and behavioral disorders using individualized curricular modifications. *Journal of Emotional and Behavioral Disorders, 9,* 239–247.

Kravetz, J. (2005, January 7). Under new IDEA, districts no longer required to provide, maintain implants. *The Special Educator, 20,* 1, 6.

Layton, C. A., & Lock, R. H. (2007). Use authentic assessment techniques to fulfill the promise of No Child Left Behind. *Interventions, 27,* 169–173.

Lovitt, T. C., & Cushing, S. S. (1994). High school students rate the IEPs: Low opinions and lack of ownership. *Intervention in School and Clinic, 30,* 34–37.

Madaus, J. W., & Shaw, S. F. (2006). The impact of the IDEA 2004 on transition to college for students with learning disabilities. *Learning Disabilities Practice, 21,* 273–281.

Magiera, K., Smith, C., Zigmond, N., & Gebauer, K. (2005). Benefits of co-teaching in secondary mathematics classes. *Teaching Exceptional Children, 37,* 20–24.

McMaster, K. L., Fuchs, D., Fuchs, L. S., & Compton, D. L. (2005). Responding to nonresponders: An experimental field trial of identification and intervention methods. *Exceptional Children, 71,* 445–463.

McNamara, K., & Hollinger, C. (2003). Intervention-based assessment: Evaluation rates and eligibility findings. *Exceptional Children, 69,* 181–193.

National Alliance of Black School Educators (NABSE), & ILIAD Project (2002). *Addressing over-representation of African American students in special education.* Arlington, VA: Council for Exceptional Children, and Washington, DC: National Alliance of Black School Educators.

National Association of School Nurses (NASN). (2004). Impact of *Cedar Rapids community school district* vs. *Garret F.* on school nursing services. *School Health Nursing Services' Role in Health Care: Issue Brief.* Retrieved December 12, 2004, from www.nasn.org

National Center for Educational Statistics (NCES). (2002). *Condition of education: 2002.* Washington, DC: U.S. Department of Education.

National Center for Educational Statistics (NCES). (2006). *Fast facts: Dropout rates of high school students.* Retrieved on December 29, 2006, from www.nces.ed.gov

National Center on Secondary Education and Transition [NCSET]. (2005). Key provisions on transition: IDEA 1997 compared to H.R. 1350 (IDEA 2004). Minneapolis: University of Minnesota. Retrieved December 5, 2005, from www.ncset.org

National Research Council. (2002). *Minority students in special education and gifted education.* Washington, DC: National Academy Press.

Neal, J., Bigby, L. M., & Nicholson, R. (2004). Occupational therapy, physical therapy, and orientation and mobility services in public schools. *Intervention in School and Clinic, 39,* 218–222.

Neubert, D. A. (2003). The role of assessment in the transition to adult life process for students with disabilities. *Exceptionality, 11,* 63–75.

Nichols, P. (2000). Role of cognition and affect in a functional behavioral analysis. *Exceptional Children, 66,* 393–402.

Obiakor, F. W., & Ford, B. A., (2002). Educational reform and accountability: Implications for African Americans with exceptionalities. *Multiple Voices, 5,* 83–93.

Office of Special Education Programs (OSEP). (2006a). *Building the legacy of IDEA 2004.* Topical Brief: Individualized Education Program (IEP), Team Meetings, and Changes to the IEP. Retrieved on December 20, 2006, from http://idea.ed.gov

Office of Special Education Programs (OSEP). (2006b). *Building the legacy of IDEA 2004.* Model Forms: IEP. Available from http://idea.ed.gov

Office of Special Education Programs (OSEP). (2006c). *Students served under IDEA, Part B, by disability category and state: Fall 2005.* Retrieved on December 30, 2006, from www.ideadata.org

Ortiz, A. A. (1997). Learning disabilities occurring concomitantly with linguistic differences. *Journal of Learning Disabilities, 20*(3), 321–332.

Ortiz, A. A. & Yates, J. R. (2002). Considerations in the assessment of English language learners referred to special education. In A. J. Artiles and A. A. Ortiz, *English language learners with special education needs* (pp. 65–86). McHenry, IL: Delta Systems.

Praisner, C. L. (2003). Attitudes of elementary principals toward the inclusion of students with disabilities. *Exceptional Children, 69,* 135–145.

Robertson, P., Kushner, M. I., Starks, J., & Drescher, C. (1994). An update of participation rates of culturally and linguistically diverse students in special education: The need for a research and policy agenda. *Bilingual Special Education Perspective, 14,* 1, 3–9.

Rodríguez, M. A., Gentilucci, J., & Sims, P. G. (2005). *Preparing principals to support special educators: Interactive modules that enhance course content.* Paper presented at the Annual Meeting of the University Council for Educational Administration, Nashville, Tennessee, November 11, 2005.

Ryan, A. L., Halsey, H. N., & Matthews, W. J. (2003). Using functional assessment to promote desirable student behavior in schools. *Teaching Exceptional Children, 35,* 8–15.

Sataline, S. (2005, January 30). A matter of principal. *The Boston Globe Magazine.*

Shippen, M. E., Simpson, R. G., & Crites, S. A. (2003). A practical guide to functional behavioral assessment. *Teaching Exceptional Children, 35,* 36–44.

Shriner, J. G., & Destefano, L. (2003). Participation and accommodation in state assessment: The role of individualized education programs. *Exceptional Children, 69,* 147–161.

Smith, D. D. (2007). *Introduction to special education: Making a difference.* Boston: Allyn and Bacon.

Smith, R., Salend, S., & Ryan, S. (2001). Closing or opening the special education curtain. *Teaching Exceptional Children, 33,* 18–23.

Sopko, K. M. (2003). *The IEP: A synthesis of current literature since 1997.* Washington, DC: National Association of State Directors of Special Education (NASDSE), Project Forum.

Test, D. W., Mason, C., Hughes, C., Konrad, M., Neale, M., & Wood, W. M. (2004). Student involvement in individualized education program meetings. *Exceptional Children, 70,* 391–412.

Thompson, S., Lazarus, S., Clapper, A., & Thurlow, M. (2004). *Essential knowledge and skills needed by teachers to support the achievement of students with disabilities: EPRRI Issue Brief Five.* College Park, MD: The Institute for the Study of Exceptional Children and Youth, Educational Policy Reform Research Institute.

Tomlinson, C. A., Brighton, C., Hertberg, H., Callahan, C. M., Moon, T. R., Brimijoin, K., Conover, L. A, & Reynolds, T. (2003). Differentiating instruction in response to student readiness, interest, and learning profile in academically diverse classrooms: A review of the literature. *Journal for the Education of the Gifted, 27,* 119–145.

Tornatzky, L. G., Pachon, H. P., & Torres, C. (2003). *Closing achievement gaps: Improving educational outcomes for Hispanic children.* Los Angeles: The Center for Latino Educational Excellence, The Tomás Rivera Policy Institute, University of Southern California.

U.S. Department of Education. (2006). Assistance to states for the Education of Children with Disabilities Program and the Early Intervention Program for Infants and Toddlers with Disabilities: Final rule. *Federal Register, 34,* CRF Parts 300 and 301.

Vaughn, S., & Fuchs, L. S. (2003). Redefining learning disabilities as inadequate response to instruction: The promise and potential problems. *Learning Disabilities Research and Practice, 18,* 137–146.

Wagner, M., Newman, L., Cameto, R., Levine, P., & Garza, N. (2006). *An overview of findings from Wave 2 of the National Longitudinal Transition Study-2 (NLTS2).* (NCSER 2006-3004). Menlo Park, CA: SRI International.

Wood, W. M., Karvonen, M., Test, D. W., Browder, D., & Algozzine, B. (2004). Promoting student self-determination skills in IEP planning. *Teaching Exceptional Children, 36,* 8–16.

Yates, J. R., & Ortiz, A. A. (2004). Classification issues in special education for English language learners. In A. M. Sorrells, H. J. Rieth, and P. T. Sindelar, *Critical issues in special education* (pp. 38–56). Boston: Allyn and Bacon.

Ziegler, D. (2002). *Reauthorization of the elementary and secondary education act: No Child Left Behind Act of 2001.* Arlington, VA: The Council for Exceptional Children, Public Policy Unit.

CHAPTER 6 Differentiating Instruction to Promote Access to the Curriculum

Algozzine, B., Ysseldyke, J. E., & Elliott, J. E. (1997). *Strategies and tactics for effective instruction.* Longmont, CO: Sopris West.

Americans with Disabilities Act of 1990. PL No. 101-336, 104 STAT.327.

Anderson-Inman, L., Knox-Quinn, C., & Horney, M. A. (1996). Computer-based study strategies for students with learning disabilities: Individual differences associated with adoption level. *Journal of Learning Disabilities, 29*(5), 461–484.

Assistive Technology Act of 2004. PL No. 108-364.

Ayllon, T., & Azrin, N. H. (1964). Reinforcement and instructions with mental patients. *Journal of the Experimental Analysis of Behavior, 7*(4), 327–331.

Babkie, A., Goldstein, P., & Rivera, D. (1992). Evaluation criteria for the selection of materials and instructional program. *LD Forum, 17*(2), 10–14.

Bloom, B. (1984). The search for methods of group instruction as effective as one-to-one tutoring. *Educational Leadership, 41*(8), 4–18.

Bos, C. S., & Anders, P. L. (1990). Effects of interactive vocabulary instruction on the vocabulary learning and reading comprehension of junior-high learning disabled students. *Learning Disability Quarterly, 13,* 31–42.

Bowser, G., & Reed, P. (1995). Education TECH points for assistive technology planning. *Journal of Special Education Technology, 12*(4), 325–338.

Bryant, D. P., & Bryant, B. R. (1998). Using assistive technology adaptations to include students with learning disabilities in cooperative learning activities. *Journal of Learning Disabilities, 31,* 41–54.

Bryant, D. P., & Bryant, B. R. (2003). *Assistive technology for people with disabilities.* Boston: Allyn and Bacon.

Bryant, D. P., Vaughn, S., Linan-Thompson, S., Ugel, N., Hamff, A., & Hougen, M. (2000). Reading outcomes for students with and without reading disabilities in general education middle-school content area classes. *Learning Disability Quarterly, 23*(4), 238–252.

Carnine, D., Silbert, J., & Kameenui, E. J. (1990). *Direct instruction reading.* Columbus, OH: Merrill.

Cooke, N. L., Heron, T. E., & Heward, W. L. (1983). *Peer tutoring: Implementing classwide programs in the primary grades.* Columbus, OH: Special Press.

Cloud, N. (2002). Culturally and linguistically responsive instructional planning. In A. J. Artiles and A. A. Ortiz (Eds.), *English language learners with special education needs* (pp. 107–133). McHenry, IL: Delta Systems.

Cloud, N., Genesee, F., & Hamayan, E. (2000). *Dual language instruction: A handbook for enriched education.* Boston: Heinle & Heinle.

Cooper, H. (1989). *Homework.* White Plains, NY: Longman.

Cooper, H., & Nye, B. (1994). Homework for students with learning disabilities: The implications of research for policy and practice. *Journal of Learning Disabilities, 27*, 470–479.

Delquadri, J., Greenwood, C. R., Stretton, K., & Hall, R. V. (1983). The peer tutoring game: A classroom procedure for increasing opportunity to respond and spelling performance. *Education and Treatment of Children, 6*, 225–239.

Delquadri, J., Greenwood, C. R., Whorton, D., Carta, J. J., & Hall, R. V. (1986). Classwide peer tutoring. *Exceptional Children, 52*, 535–542.

Deshler, D., Ellis, E. S., & Lenz, B. K. (1996). *Teaching adolescents with learning disabilities.* Denver, CO: Love.

Elbaum, B., Vaughn, S., Hughes, M., & Moody, S. (1999). Grouping practices and reading outcomes for students with disabilities. *Exceptional Children, 65*(3), 399–415.

Ellis, E. (1992). *LINCS: A starter strategy for vocabulary learning.* Lawrence, KS: Edge Enterprises.

Engelmann, S., & Carnine, D. (1991). *Theory of instruction: Principles and applications.* Eugene, OR: ADI Press.

Epstein, M. H., Polloway, E. A., Foley, R. M., & Patton, J. R. (1993). Homework: A comparison of teachers' and parents' perceptions of the problems experienced by students identified as having behavioral disorders, learning disabilities, or no disabilities. *Remedial and Special Education, 14*(5), 40–50.

Fuchs, D., Fuchs, L. S., & Burish, P. (2000). Peer-assisted learning strategies: An evidence-based practice to promote reading achievement. *Learning Disabilities Research and Practice, 15*, 85–91.

Fuchs, L. S., Fuchs, D., & Kazdan, S. (1999). Effects of peer-assisted learning strategies on high-school students with serious reading problems. *Remedial and Special Education, 20*, 309–318.

Gelzheriser, L. M., & Meyers, J. (1991). Reading instruction by classroom, remedial, and resource room teachers. *Journal of Special Education, 24*, 512–527.

Gersten, R., Carnine, D., & Woodward, J. (1987). Direct instruction research: The third decade. *Remedial and Special Education, 8*(6), 48–56.

Golden, D. (1998). *Assistive technology in special education: Policy and practice.* Arlington, VA: Council for Exceptional Children.

Harper, G. F., Maheady, L., Mallette, B., & Karnes, M. (1999). Peer tutoring and the minority child with disabilities. *Preventing School Failure, 43*(2), 45–51.

Hasselbring, T. S., Goin, L., & Bransford, J. D. (1987). Effective mathematics instruction: Developing automaticity. *Teaching Exceptional Children, 19*(3), 30–33.

Hopkins, B. I. (1968). Effects of candy and social reinforcement, instructions, and reinforcement schedule learning on the modification and maintenance of smiling. *Journal of Applied Behavior Analysis, 1*, 121–129.

Individuals with Disabilities Education Act of 2004 (IDEA). PL No. 108-446.

International Business Machines. (1991). *Technology and persons with disabilities.* Atlanta: IBM Corporate Support Programs.

Johnson, D. W., Johnson, R. T., & Holubec, E. J. (1994). *Cooperative learning in the classroom* (6th ed.). Alexandria, VA: Association for Supervision & Curriculum Development.

Kagan, S. (1990). *Cooperative learning resources for teachers.* San Juan Capistrano, CA: Resources for Teachers.

King-Sears, M. E. (1997). Best academic practices for inclusive classrooms. *Focus on Exceptional Children, 29*, 1–22.

King-Sears, M. E., Mercer, C. D., & Sindelar, P. T. (1992). Toward independence with keyword mnemonics: A strategy for science vocabulary instruction. *Remedial and Special Education, 13*, 22–33.

Lemons, C. J. (2000). *Comparison of parent and teacher knowledge and opinions related to augmentative and alternative communication.* Unpublished master's thesis, The University of Texas at Austin.

Lenz, B. K., Alley, G. R., & Schumaker, J. B. (1987). Activating the inactive learner: Advance organizers in the secondary content classroom. *Learning Disability Quarterly, 10*, 53–62.

Mastropieri, M. A., & Scruggs, T. E. (2002). *Effective instruction for special education* (3rd ed.). Austin: PRO-ED.

Mastropieri, M. A., & Scruggs, T. E. (2007). *The inclusive classroom* (2nd ed.). Upper Saddle River, NJ: Pearson.

Mercer, C. D., & Mercer, A. R. (2001). *Teaching students with learning problems* (6th ed.). Columbus, OH: Merrill–Prentice Hall.

Miller, S. P. (2002). *Validated practices for teaching students with diverse needs and abilities.* Boston: Allyn and Bacon.

Miller, A. D., Barbetta, P. M., Drevno, G. E., Martz, S. A., & Heron, T. E. (1996). Math peer tutoring for students with specific learning disabilities. *LD Forum, 21*(3), 21–28.

No Child Left Behind Act of 2001 (NCLB). PL No. 107-110.

O'Connor, R., & Jenkins, J. (1994). *Cooperative learning as an inclusion strategy: A closer look.* Unpublished manuscript. University of Washington.

Orkwis, R., & McLane, K. (1998, Fall). A curriculum every student can use: Design principles for student access. *ERIC OSEP Topical Brief,* 1–20.

Ortiz, A. A., & Yates, J. R. (2001). A framework for serving English language learners with disabilities. *Journal of Special Education Leadership, 14*(2), 72–80.

Polloway, E. A., Epstein, M. H., Bursuck, W. D., Jayanthi, M., & Cumblad, C. (1994). Homework practices of general education teachers. *Journal of Learning Disabilities, 27*(8), 500–509.

Pressley, M., Scruggs, T. E., & Mastropieri, M. A. (1989). Memory strategy instruction for learning disabilities: Present and future directions. *Learning Disabilities Research, 4*, 68–77.

Price, K. M., & Nelson, K. L. (2003). *Daily planning for today's classroom* (2nd ed.). Belmont, CA: Wadsworth–Thomson.

Raskind, M., & Bryant, B. R. (2002). *Functional evaluation for assistive technology.* Austin, TX: Psycho-Educational Services.

Rich, Y. (1993). *Education and instruction in the heterogeneous class.* Springfield, IL: Charles C Thomas.

Rieth, H. J., Colburn, L. K., & Bryant, D. P. (2004). Trends and issues in instructional and assistive technology. In A. M. Sorrells, H. J. Rieth, and P. T. Sindelar (Eds.), *Critical issues in special education* (pp. 205–225). Boston: Allyn and Bacon.

Rivera, D. (1996). Using cooperative learning to teach mathematics to students with learning disabilities. *LD Forum, 21*(3), 29–33.

Rivera, D. P., & Smith, D. D. (1997) *Teaching students with learning and behavior problems* (3rd ed.). Boston: Allyn and Bacon.

Roderique, T. W., Polloway, E. A., Cumblad, C., Epstein, M. H., & Bursuck, W. H. (1994). Homework: A survey of policies in the United States. *Journal of Learning Disabilities, 27*, 481–487.

Schumm, J. S., Moody, S. M., & Vaughn, S. (2000). Grouping for reading instruction: Does one size fit all? *Journal of Learning Disabilities, 33*(5), 477–488.

Scruggs, T. E., & Mastropieri, M. A. (1992). Classroom applications of mnemonic instruction: Acquisition, maintenance, and generalization. *Exceptional Children, 58*, 219–229.

Scruggs, T. E., & Mastropieri, M. A. (2000). The effectiveness of mnemonic instruction for students with learning and behavior problems: An update and research synthesis. *Journal of Behavioral Education, 10*, 163–173.

Simmons, D. C., Fuchs, D., Fuchs, L. S., Pate Hodge, J. P., & Mathes, P. G. (1994). Importance of instructional complexity and role reciprocity to classwide peer tutoring. *Learning Disabilities Research and Practice, 9*, 203–212.

Slavin, R. E. (1991). Synthesis of research on cooperative learning. *Educational Leadership, 48*(5), 71–82.

Smith, D. D., & Lovitt, T. C. (1976). The differential effects of reinforcement contingencies on arithmetic performance. *Journal of Learning Disabilities, 9,* 11–29.

Stokes, T. F., & Baer, D. M. (1977). An implicit technology of generalization. *Journal of Applied Behavior Analysis, 10,* 349–367.

Stowitschek, J. J., Stowitschek, C. E., Hendrickson, J. M., & Day, R. M. (1984). *Direct teaching tactics for exceptional children.* Rockville, MD: Aspen Publications.

Swanson, H. L. (2001). Research on intervention for adolescents with learning disabilities: A meta-analysis of outcomes related to high-order processing. *The Elementary School Journal, 101,* 331–348.

Swanson, H. L., Cooney, J. B., & O'Shaughnessy, T. E. (1998). Learning disabilities and memory. In B. Wong (Ed.), *Learning about learning disabilities* (2nd ed., pp. 107–162). San Diego, CA: Academic Press.

Swanson, H. L., Hoskyn, M., & Lee, C. (1999). *Interventions for students with learning disabilities: A metaanalysis of treatment outcomes.* New York: Guilford.

Technology and Media (n.d.). *The AT quick wheel.* Arlington, VA: Council for Exceptional Children.

Todis, B. (1996). Tools for the task? Perspectives on assistive technology in educational settings. *Journal of Special Education Technology, 13*(2), pp. 49–61.

Utley, C. A., Mortweet, S. L., & Greenwood, C. R. (1997). Peer-mediated instruction and intervention. *Focus on Exceptional Children, 29*(1), 1–23.

Vaughn, S., Hughes, M. T., Moody, S. W., & Elbaum, B. (2001). Instructional grouping for reading for students with learning disabilities: Implications for practice. *Intervention in School and Clinic, 35,* 131–137.

Wong, B. Y. (1993). Pursuing an elusive goal: Molding strategic teachers and learners. *Journal of Learning Disabilities, 26*(6), 354–357.

Zehler, A. M. (1994). *Working with English language learners: Strategies for elementary and middle school teachers* (Program Information Guide, No. 19). Washington, DC: National Clearinghouse for Bilingual Education. Retrieved May 20, 2002, from http://www.ncbe.gwu.edu/ncbepubs/pigs/pig19.htm

CHAPTER 7 Assessing Students with Special Needs

Anastasi, A., & Urbina, S. (1997). *Psychological testing* (7th ed.). New York: Macmillan.

Brown, L. L., & Hammill, D. D. (1990). *Behavior Rating Profile–Second Edition.* Austin, TX: PRO-ED.

Bryant, B. R., Bryant, D. P., Hammill, D. D., & Sorrells, A. M. (2004). Characteristic reading behaviors of poor readers who have learning disabilities. *Assessment for Effective Intervention, 19,* 39–46.

Bryant, B. R., & Rivera, D. P. (1997). Educational assessment of mathematics skills and abilities. Special Series, *Journal of Learning Disabilities, 30*(1), 57–68.

Bryant, B. R., Seay, P. C., & Bryant, D. P. (1999). Assistive technology and adaptive behavior. In R. Schalock (Ed.), *Adaptive behavior and its measurement* (pp. 81–98). Washington, DC: AAMR.

Bryant, B. R., Wiederholt, J. L., & Bryant, D. P. (2004). *Gray Diagnostic Reading Test–Second Edition.* Austin, TX: PRO-ED.

Bryant, D. P., Patton, J. R., & Vaughn, S. (2000). *Step-by-step guide for including students with disabilities in state and districtwide assessments.* Austin, TX: PRO-ED.

Conners, C. K. (1997). *Conners Teacher Rating Scale–Revised.* N. Tonawanda, NY: Multi-Health Systems.

Deno, S. L., & Merkin, P. K. (1977). *Data-based program modification.* Reston, VA: Council for Exceptional Children.

Dolan, R. P., & Hall, T. E. (2001). Universal design for learning: Implications for large-scale assessment. *IDA Perspectives 27*(4): 22–25.

Elliott, S. N., Kratochwill, T. R., & Gilbertson, A. (1998). The assessment accommodation checklist: Who, what, where, when, why, and how? *Teaching Exceptional Children 31*(2), 10–14.

Frase-Blunt, M. (2000, September). High stakes testing a mixed blessing for special students. *CEC Today, 7,* 1, 5, 7, 15.

Fuchs, L. S. (2003) Assessing intervention responsiveness: Conceptual and technical issues. *Learning Disabilities Research and Practice, 18*(3), 172–186.

Ginsberg, H. (1987). Assessing arithmetic. In D. D. Hammill (Ed.), *Assessing the abilities and instructional needs of students* (pp. 412–503). Austin, TX: PRO-ED.

Hammill, D. D. (1987). An overview of assessment practices. In D. D. Hammill (Ed.), *Assessing the abilities and instructional needs of students* (pp. 5–48). Austin, TX: PRO-ED.

Hammill, D., Brown, L., & Bryant, B. R. (1992). *A consumer's guide to tests in print* (2nd ed.). Austin, TX: PRO-ED.

Hammill, D. D., & Bryant, B. R. (1991). Standardized assessment and academic intervention. In H. L. Swanson (Ed.), *Handbook on the assessment of learning disabilities: Theory, research, and practice* (pp. 373–406). Austin, TX: PRO-ED.

Hammill, D. D., & Bryant, B. R. (1998). *Learning Disability Diagnostic Inventory.* Austin, TX: PRO-ED.

Heubert, J. P., & Hauser, R. M. (1999). *High stakes: Testing for tracking, promotion, and graduation.* Washington DC: National Academy Press.

Kubiszyn, T., & Borich, G. (2003). *Educational testing and measurement.* New York: Wiley.

Linn, R. L., & Gronlund, N. E. (2000). *Measurement and assessment in teaching* (8th ed.). Upper Saddle River, NJ: Prentice-Hall.

McLoughlin, J. A., & Lewis, R. B. (2005). *Assessing students with special needs.* Upper Saddle River, NJ: Pearson.

Ochoa, S. H., Robles-Pina, R., Garcia, S. B., & Breuning, N. (1999). School psychologists' perspectives on referrals of language minority students. *Multiple Voices, 3,* 1–14.

Overton, T. (2000). *Assessment in special education.* Upper Saddle River, NJ: Pearson.

Raskind, M., & Bryant, B. R. (2002). *Functional evaluation for assistive technology.* Austin, TX: Psycho-Educational Services.

Reynolds, C. R., Livingston, R. B., & Willson, V. (2006). *Measurement and assessment in education.* Boston: Allyn and Bacon.

Rivera, D. M., & Bryant, B. R. (1992). Mathematics instruction for students with special needs. *Intervention in School and Clinic, 28*(2), 71–86.

Rivera, D. P., & Smith, D. D. (1997). *Teaching students with learning and behavior problems* (3rd ed.). Boston: Allyn and Bacon.

Salvia, J., & Ysseldyke, J. (2001) *Assessment in special and remedial education* (8th ed.). Boston: Houghton Mifflin.

Sattler, J. (2001). *Assessment of children* (4th ed.). La Mesa, CA: Author.

Smith, D. D. (2004). *Introduction to special education* (5th ed.). Boston: Allyn & Bacon.

Smith, F. (1982). *Writing and the writer.* New York: Holt, Rinehart, & Winston.

Spinelli, C. G. (2002). *Classroom assessment for students with special needs in inclusive settings.* Upper Saddle River, NJ: Pearson.

Swicegood, P. (1994). Portfolio-based assessment practices. *Intervention in School and Clinic, 30*(1), 6–15.

Taylor, R. L. (2003). *Assessment of exceptional students.* (6th ed.). Boston: Allyn and Bacon.

Thompson, S. J., Johnstone, C. J., & Thurlow, M. L. (2002). *Universal design applied to large scale assessments.* Minneapolis, MN: National Center on Educational Outcomes.

Thurlow, M., & Liu, K. (2001). *State and district assessments as an avenue to equity and excellence for English language learners with disabilities.* Minneapolis, MN: National Center on Educational Outcomes.

Torgesen, J. K., Alexander, A., Wagner, R., Rashotte, C., Voeller, K., & Conway, T. (2001). Intensive remedial instruction for children with severe reading disabilities: Immediate and long-term outcomes from two instructional approaches. *Journal of Learning Disabilities, 34,* 33–58.

Torgesen, J., & Bryant, B. R. (2005). *Test of Phonological Awareness* (2nd ed.; TOPA-2+). Austin, TX: PRO-ED.

Torgesen, J. K., Wager, R., & Rashotte, C. (1999). *Test of Word Reading Efficiency.* Austin, TX: PRO-ED.

Turner, M. D., Baldwin, L., Kleinert, H. L., & Kearns, J. F. (2000). The relation of statewide alternate assessment for students with severe disabilities to other measures of instructional effectiveness. *Journal of Special Education, 34,* 69–76.

Vaughn Gross Center for Reading and Language Arts. (2003). *Secondary institute: Effective instruction for secondary struggling readers: Research-based practices.* Austin, TX: University of Texas System/Texas Education Agency.

Vellutino, F. R., Scanlon, D. M., Sipay, E., Small, S., Pratt, A., Chen, R., & Denckla, M. (1996). Cognitive profiles of difficult to remediate and readily remediated poor readers: Toward distinguishing between constitutionally and experientially based causes of reading disability. *Journal of Educational Psychology, 88,* 601–638.

Venn, J. J. (2004). *Assessing students with special needs.* Upper Saddle River, NJ: Pearson.

Wager, R., Torgesen, J. K., & Rashotte, C. (1999). *Comprehensive Test of Phonological Awareness.* Austin, TX: PRO-ED.

White, E. M. (1994). *Teaching and assessing writing* (2nd ed.). San Francisco: Jossey-Bass.

Woodcock, R., & Mather, N. (1989, 1990). *Woodcock-Johnson-Revised.* Itasca, IL: Riverside Publishing.

Zigmond, N., Vallecorsa, A., & Silverman, R. (1983). *Assessment for instructional planning in special education.* Englewood Cliffs, NJ: Prentice Hall.

CHAPTER 8   Developing Collaborative Partnerships

Baca, L. M. (2002). Educating English language learners with special education needs: Trends and future directions. In A. J. Artiles and A. A. Ortiz (Eds.), *English language learners with special education needs* (pp. 191–202). Washington, DC: Center for Applied Linguistics; and McHenry, IL: Delta Systems.

Balshaw, M., & Farrell, P. (2002). *Teacher assistants: Practical strategies for effective classroom support.* London: David Folton.

Bernal, C., & Aragon, L. (2004). Critical factors affecting the success of paraprofessionals in the first two years of career ladder projects in Colorado. *Remedial and Special Education, 25*(4), 205–213.

Blalock, G. (1990). *Paraprofessional training program activity, 1989–1990.* Unpublished report, University of New Mexico, Albuquerque.

Blalock, G. (1991). Paraprofessionals: Critical team members in our special education programs. *Intervention in School and Clinic, 26*(4), 200–214.

Brown, L., Farrington, K., Ziegler, M., Knight, T., & Ross, C. (1999). Fewer paraprofessionals and more teachers and therapists in educational programs for students with significant disabilities. *The Journal of the Association for Persons with Severe Handicaps, 24,* 249–252.

Bryant, D. P., & Bryant, B. R. (2003). *Assistive technology for people with disabilities.* Boston: Allyn and Bacon.

Chalfant, J. C., & Van Dusen Pysh, M. (1989). Teacher assistance teams: Five descriptive studies on 96 teams. *Remedial and Special Education, 10*(6), 49–58.

Chopra, R. V., Sandoval-Lucero, E., Aragon, L., Bernal, C., De Balderas, H. B., & Carroll, D. (2004). The paraprofessional role of connector. *Remedial and Special Education, 25*(4), 219–231.

Cloud, N. (2002). Culturally and linguistically responsive instructional planning. In A. J. Artiles and A. A. Ortiz (Eds.), *English language learners with special education needs* (pp. 107–133). Washington, DC: Center for Applied Linguistics; and McHenry, IL: Delta Systems.

Cook, L., & Friend, M. (1993). Educational leadership for teacher collaboration. In B. Billingsley (Ed.), *Program leadership for serving students with disabilities* (pp. 421–444). Richmond, VA: Virginia Department of Education.

Downing, J., Ryndak, D., & Clark, D. (2000). Paraeducators in inclusive classrooms. *Remedial and Special Education, 21,* 171–181.

Figueroa, R. (2002). Toward a new model of assessment. In A. J. Artiles and A. A. Ortiz (Eds.), *English language learners with special education needs* (pp. 51–63). Washington, DC: Center for Applied Linguistics and McHenry, IL: Delta Systems.

Foly, R. M., & Mundschenk, N. A. (1997). Collaboration activities and competencies of secondary school special educators: A national survey. *Teacher Education and Special Education, 20*(1), 47–60.

French, N. K. (2004). Connecting schools and communities: The vital role of paraeducators. *Remedial and Special Education, 25*(4), 203–204.

French, N. K., & Chopra, R. V. (1999). Parent perspectives on the roles of paraprofessionals. *JASH, 24*(4), 259–272.

Friend, M. (2006). *Special education: Contemporary perspectives for school professionals.* Boston: Allyn and Bacon.

Friend, M., & Bursuck, W. (2006). *Including students with special needs: A practical guide for classroom teachers* (4th ed.). Boston: Allyn and Bacon.

Friend, M., & Cook, L. (2000). *Interactions: Collaboration skills for school professionals* (3rd ed.). White Plains, NY: Longman.

Garcia, S. (2002). Parent-professional collaboration in culturally sensitive assessment. In A. J. Artiles and A. A. Ortiz (Eds.), *English language learners with special education needs* (pp. 87–103). Washington, DC: Center for Applied Linguistics; and McHenry, IL: Delta Systems.

Giengreco, M. F., & Doyle, M. B. (2007). Teacher assistants in inclusive schools. In L. Florian (Ed.) *The Sage handbook of special education* (pp. 429–439). London: Sage.

Giangreco, M. F., Edelman, S. W., Broer, S. M., & Doyle, M. B. (2001). Paraprofessional support of students with disabilities: Literature from the past decade. *Exceptional Children, 68*(1), 45–63.

Gordon, T. (1980). *Leadership effectiveness training.* New York: Wyden.

Halvorsen, A. T., & Neary, T. (2001). *Building inclusive schools: Tools & strategies for success.* Boston: Allyn and Bacon.

Harris, K. C. (1991). An expanded view on consultation competencies for educators serving culturally and linguistically diverse exceptional students. *Teacher Education and Special Education, 14*(1), 25–29.

Heron, T. E., & Harris, K. C. (1993). *The educational consultant* (3rd ed.). Austin, TX: PRO-ED.

Individuals with Disabilities Education Improvement Act of 2004. PL No. 108-446.

Idol, L. (2001). *Creating collaborative and inclusive schools* (2nd ed.). Austin, TX: PRO-ED.

Idol, L., Nevin, A., & Paolucci-Whitcomb, P. (1994). *Collaborative consultation* (2nd ed.). Austin, TX: PRO-ED.

Kozleski, E., Mainzer, R., & Deshler, D. (2000). Bright futures for exceptional learners: An action agenda to achieve quality conditions for teaching and learning. *Teaching Exceptional Children, 32*(6), 56–69.

Minondo, S., Meyer, L., & Xin, J. (2001). The roles and responsibilities of teaching assistants in inclusive education: What's appropriate? *Journal of the Association for Persons with Severe Handicaps, 24*(4), 253–256.

Mostert, M. P. (1998). *Interprofessional collaboration in schools.* Boston: Allyn and Bacon.

Murawski, W. W., & Swanson, H. L. (2001). A meta-analysis of co-teaching research: Where are the data? *Remedial and Special Education, 22*(5), 258–267.

No Child Left Behind Act of 2001. PL No. 107-110.

Ortiz, A. (2002). Prevention of school failure and early intervention for English language learners. In A. J. Artiles and A. A. Ortiz

(Eds.), *English language learners with special education needs* (pp. 31–50). Washington, DC: Center for Applied Linguistics; and McHenry, IL: Delta Systems.

Ortiz, A. A., & Yates, J. R. (2001). A framework for serving English language learners with disabilities. *Journal of Special Education Leadership, 14*(2), 72–80.

Pickett, A. L. (1999). *Strengthening and supporting teacher/provider-paraeducator teams: Guidelines for paraeducator roles, supervision, and preparation.* New York: National Resource Center for Paraprofessionals in Education and Related Services, Graduate Center, City University of New York. (ERIC Document Reproduction Service No. ED 440 506).

Pickett, A. L., & Gerlach, K. (2003). *Supervising paraeducators in school settings* (2nd ed.). Austin, TX: PRO-ED.

Pugach, M. C., & Johnson, L. J. (1995). *Collaborative practitioners, collaborative schools.* Denver, CO: Love.

Riggs, C. G. (2005). To teachers: What paraeducators want you to know. *Teaching Exceptional Children, 36*(5), 8–12.

Riggs, C. G., & Mueller, P. H. (2001). Employment and utilization of paraeducators in inclusive settings. *Journal of Special Education, 35*, 54–62.

Rivera, D. P., & Smith, D. D. (1997). *Teaching students with learning and behavior problems* (3rd ed.). Boston: Allyn and Bacon.

Salend, S. J., Gordon, J., & Lopez-Vona, K. (2002). Evaluating cooperative teaching teams. *Teaching Exceptional Children, 37*(4), 195–200.

Smith, D. D. (2007). *Introduction to special education: Making a difference* (6th ed.). Boston: Allyn and Bacon.

Smith, D. D., & Rivera, D. (1993). *Effective discipline* (2nd ed.). Austin, TX: PRO-ED.

Trent, S. C. (1998). False starts and other dilemmas of a secondary general education collaborative teacher: A case study. *Journal of Learning Disabilities, 31*(5), 503–513.

Turnbull, A. P., Turnbull, H. R., Rewin, E. J., & Turnbull, E. (2005). *Families, professionals, and exceptionality: Positive outcomes through partnership and trust* (5th ed.) Upper Saddle River, NJ: Pearson Education.

Vasa, S. F., Steckelberg, A. L., & Hoffman, P. (1986). *Resource guide for the development of policies and practices in the use of paraprofessionals in special education.* Lincoln: Department of Special Education and Communication Disorders, University of Nebraska-Lincoln.

Vaughn, S., Bos, C. S., & Schumm, J. S. (2007). *Teaching exceptional, diverse. and at-risk students in the general education classroom* (4th ed.). Boston: Allyn and Bacon.

Vaughn, S., Schumm, J. S., & Arguelles, M. E. (1997). The ABCDEs of co-teaching. *Teaching Exceptional Children, 30*(2), 4–10.

Walther-Thomas, C. (1997). Co-teaching experiences: The benefits and problems that teachers report. *Journal of Learning Disabilities, 30*(4), 395–407.

Walther-Thomas, C., Korinek, L., McLaughlin, V. L., & Williams, B. T. (2000). *Collaboration for inclusive education: Developing successful programs.* Boston: Allyn and Bacon.

Weiss, M. P., & Lloyd, J. W. (2002). Congruence between roles and actions of secondary special educators in co-taught and special education settings. *The Journal of Special Education, 36*(2), 58–68.

Werts, M. G., Harris, S., Tillery, C. Y., & Roark, R. (2004). What parents tell us about paraeducators. *Remedial and Special Education, 25*(4), 232–239.

West, J. F., & Idol, L. (1990). Collaborative consultation in the education of mildly handicapped and at-risk students. *Remedial and Special Education, 11*(1), 22–31.

West, J. F., Idol, L., & Cannon, G. (1993). *Collaboration in the schools.* Austin, TX: PRO-ED.

White, R. (2004). The recruitment of paraeducators into the special education profession: A review of progress, select evaluation outcomes, and new initiatives. *Remedial and Special Education, 25*(4), 214–218.

Yates, J. R., & Ortiz, A. A. (2004). Classification issues in special education for English language learners. In A. M. Sorrells, H. J. Rieth, and P. T. Sindelar (Eds.), *Critical issues in special education* (pp. 38–56). Boston: Allyn and Bacon.

CHAPTER 9   Promoting Positive Behavior and Facilitating Social Skills

Alberto, P. A., & Troutman, A. C. (2005). *Applied behavior analysis for teachers* (7th ed.). Englewood Cliffs, NJ: Merrill.

Allen, K. E., Hart, B. M., Buell, J. S., Harris, F. R., & Wolf, M. M. (1964). Effects of social reinforcement on isolate behavior of a nursery school child. *Child Development, 35*, 511–518.

Asher, S. R., & Gazelle, H. (1999). Loneliness, peer relationships, and language disorder in childhood. *Topics in Language Disorders, 19*, 16–33.

Axelrod, S., & Hall, R. V. (1999). *Behavior modification: Basic principles.* Austin, TX: PRO-ED.

Babyak, A. E., Luze, G. J., & Kamps, D. M. (2000). The good student game: Behavior management for diverse classrooms. *Intervention in School and Clinic, 35*, 216–223.

Bacon, E. H. (1990). Using negative consequences effectively. *Academic Therapy, 25*, 599–611.

Barrish, H. H., Saunders, M., & Wolf, M. M. (1969). Good behavior game: Effects of individual contingencies for group consequences on disruptive behavior in a classroom. *Journal of Applied Behavior Analysis, 2*, 119–124.

Bender, W. N., & Wall, M. E. (1994). Social-emotional development of students with learning disabilities. *Learning Disability Quarterly, 17*, 323–341.

Bryan, T. H., & Bryan, J. H. (1978). Social interaction of learning disabled children. *Learning Disability Quarterly, 1*, 33–38.

Burke, J. C. (1992). *Decreasing classroom behavior problems.* San Diego, CA: Singular Publishing Co.

Canter, L., & Canter, M. (2001). *Assertive discipline: Positive behavior management for today's classroom* (3rd ed.). Santa Monica, CA: Lee Canter & Associates.

Carr, E. G., Horner, R. H., Turnbull, A. P., McLaughlin, D. M., McAtee, M. L., Smith, C. E., Ryan, K. A., Ruef, M. D., & Doolabh, A. (1999). *Positive behavior support for people with developmental disabilities: A research synthesis.* Washington, DC: American Association on Mental Retardation.

Center, D. B., Deitz, S. M., & Kaufman, N. E. (1982). Student ability, task difficulty, and inappropriate classroom behavior: A study of children with behavioral disorders. *Behavior Modification, 6*, 355–374.

Cloud, N. (2002). Culturally and linguistically responsive instructional planning. In A. J. Artiles and A. A. Ortiz (Eds.), *English language learners with special education needs: Identification, assessment, and instruction* (pp. 107–132). Washington, DC: Center for Applied Linguistics and McHenry, IL: Delta Systems.

Cloud, N., Genesee, F., & Hamayan, E. (2000). *Dual language instruction: A handbook for enriched education.* Boston: Heinle & Heinle.

Colvin, G., Kame'enui, E. J., and Sugai, G. (1993). School-wide and classroom management: Re-conceptualizing the integration and management of students with behavior problems in general education. *Education and Treatment of Children, 16*, 361–381.

Costa, A. L., & Garmston, R. J. (2002). *Cognitive coaching* (2nd ed.). Norwood, MA: Christopher-Gordon.

Craig, W., & Peplar, D. (1996). Understanding bullying at school: What can we do about it? In S. Miller, J. Brodine, and T. Miller (Eds.), *Safe by design* (pp. 247–260). Seattle, WA: Committee for Children.

Demchak, M., & Bossert, K. W. (1996). *Assessing problem behaviors. Innovations* (no. 4). Washington, DC: American Association on Mental Retardation.

Dreikurs, R. (1968). *Psychology in the classroom: A manual for teachers* (2nd ed.). New York: Harper & Row.

Dreikurs, R., & Cassel, P. (1972). *Discipline without tears.* New York: Hawthorn Books.

Emmer, E. T., Evertson, C. M., & Worsham, M. E. (2003). *Classroom management for secondary teachers* (6th ed.). Boston: Allyn and Bacon.

Evertson, C. M., Emmer, E. T., & Worsham, M. E. (2003). *Classroom management for elementary teachers* (6th ed.). Boston: Allyn and Bacon.

Fad, K. M., Patton, J. R., & Polloway, E. A. (2000). *Behavioral intervention planning*. Austin, TX: PRO-ED.

Freeman, S. F. N., & Alkin, M. C. (2000). Academic and social attainments of children with mental retardation in general education and special education settings. *Remedial and Special Education, 21*, 3–18.

Gagnon, J. C., & Leone, P. E. (2002). Alternative strategies for school violence prevention. In R. J. Skiba and G. G. Noam (Eds.), *Zero tolerance: Can suspension and expulsion keep schools safe?* (pp. 101–125). San Francisco: Jossey-Bass.

Gast, D. L., & Nelson, C. M. (1977). Legal and ethical considerations for the use of timeout in special education settings. *The Journal of Special Education, 11*, 457–467.

Glasser, W. (1992). *The quality school: Managing students without coercion* (2nd ed.). New York: Harper Perennial.

Gordon, T. (1988). *Teaching children self-discipline: At home and at school*. NY: Times Books.

Gresham, F. M., Sugai, G., & Horner, R. H. (2001). Interpreting outcomes of social skills training for students with high-incidence disabilities. *Exceptional Children, 67*, 331–344.

Haager, D., & Vaughn, S. (1995). Parent, teacher, peer, and self-reports of the social competence of students with learning disabilities. *Journal of Learning Disabilities, 28*, 205–231.

Hazel, J. S., Schumaker, J. B., Sherman, J. A., & Sheldon-Wilgen, J. (1981). *ASSET: A social skill program for adolescents*. Champaign, IL: Research Press.

Hernandez, H. (2001). *Multicultural education: A teacher's guide to linking context, process, and content*. Upper Saddle River, NJ: Prentice-Hall.

Horner, R. H. (1999). Positive behavior supports. In M. Wehmeyer and J. Patton, (Eds.), *Mental retardation in the 21st century* (pp. 181–196). Austin, TX: PRO-ED.

Horner, R. H., & Carr, E. G. (1997). Behavioral support for students with severe disabilities: Functional assessment and comprehensive intervention. *The Journal of Special Education, 31*, 84–104.

Hughes, C. A., & Boyle, J. R. (1991). Effects of self-monitoring for on-task behavior and task productivity on elementary students with moderate mental retardation. *Education and Treatment of Children, 14*, 96–111.

Huitt, W. (2001). *Motivation to learn: An overview*. Educational Psychology Interactive. Valdosta, GA: Valdosta State University. Retrieved December 11, 2004, from http://chiron.valdosta.edu/whuitt/col/motivation/motivate.html

Jones, F. (2004). *Positive classroom discipline*. Retrieved May 14, 2007, from www.fredjones.com

Kennedy, C. H., Long, T., Jolivettel, K., Cox, J., Tang, J., & Thompson, T. (2001). Facilitating general education participation for students with behavior problems by linking positive behavior supports and person-centered planning. *Journal of Emotional and Behavioral Disorders, 9*(3), 161–171.

Kounin, J. S. (1970). *Discipline and group management in classrooms*. New York: Holt, Rinehart, & Winston.

LaGreca, A. M. & Stone, W. L. (1990). LD status and achievement: Confounding variables in the study of children's social status, self-esteem, and behavioral functioning. *Journal of Learning Disabilities, 23*, 483–490.

Lane, H. (1976). *The wild boy of Aveyron*. Cambridge MA: Harvard University Press.

Lane, K. L., Gresham, F. M., & O'Shaughnessy, T. (2002). Identifying, assessing and intervening with children with or at-risk for behavior disorders: A look to the future. In K. L. Lane, F. M. Gresham, and T. E. O'Shaughnessy (Eds.), *Interventions for children with or at risk for emotional and behavioral disorders* (pp. 317–326). Boston: Allyn and Bacon.

Larrivee, B. (1992). *Strategies for effective classroom management: Creating a collaborative guide*. Boston: Allyn and Bacon.

Lewandowski, J. A. (1989). Using peer forums to motivate students. *Teaching Exceptional Children*, pp. 14–15.

Lovitt, T. (2000). *Preventing school failure: Tactics for teaching adolescents* (2nd ed.). Austin, TX: PRO-ED.

Marquis, J. G., Horner, R. H., Carr, E. G., Turnbull, A. P., Thompson, M., Behrens, G. A., Magito-McLaughlin, D., McAtee, M., L., Smith, C. E., Anderson Ryan, K., & Doolabh, A. (2000). In R. M. Gersten, E. P. Schiller, and S. Vaughn (Eds.), *Contemporary special education research: A syntheses of the knowledge base on critical instructional issues* (pp. 137–178). Mahway, NJ: Erlbaum.

Martin, J. E., & Marshall, L. H. (1995). ChoiceMaker: A comprehensive self-determination transition program. *Intervention in School and Clinic, 30*(3), 147–156.

Maurer, R. (1988). *Special education discipline handbook*. West Nyack, NY: Center for Applied Research in Education.

McCart, A., & Turnbull, A. (2003). *Behavioral concerns within inclusive classrooms*. Retrieved December 14, 2003, from The Issues Article Archive www.pbis.org

McLane, K. (1997). School-wide behavioral management systems. *Research Connections in Special Education, 1*, 1–5.

Morgan, D. P., & Jensen, W. R. (1988). *Teaching behaviorally disordered students: Preferred practices*. Columbus, OH: Merrill.

Nansel et al. (2001). *Journal of the American Medical Association*. Retrieved from www.nichd.nih.gov/new/releases/bullying.cfm

Neal, L. V. I., McCray, A. D., Webb-Johnson, G., & Bridgest, S. T. (2003). The effects of African American movement styles on teachers' perceptions and reactions. *The Journal of Special Education, 37*, 49–57.

Obiakor, F. E. (1999). Teacher expectations of minority exceptional learners: Impact on "accuracy" of self-concepts. *Exceptional Children, 66*, 39–53.

Pepler, D. J., & Craig, W. (1997). *Bullying: Research and interventions. Youth update*. Publication of the Institute for the Study of Antisocial Youth.

Polsgrove, L., & Ochoa, T. (2004). Trends and issues in behavioral interventions. In A. M. Sorrells, H. J. Rieth, and P. T. Sindelar (Eds.), *Critical issues in special education: Access, diversity, and accountability* (pp. 154–180). Boston: Allyn and Bacon.

Premack, D. (1959). Toward empirical behavior laws: Positive reinforcement. *Psychological Review, 66*, 219–233.

Repp, A. C. & Horner, R. H. (Eds.) (1999). *Functional analysis of problem behavior: From effective assessment to effective support*. Pacific Grove: CA: Brooks/Cole.

Rivera, D. P., & Smith, D. D. (1997). *Teaching students with learning and behavior problems* (3rd ed.). Boston: Allyn and Bacon.

Rosenberg, M. S., Wilson, R., Maheady, L., & Sindelar, P. T. (1997). *Educating students with behavioral disorders* (2nd ed.). Boston: Allyn and Bacon.

Rosenblum, P. L. (1998). Best friendships of adolescents with visual impairments: A descriptive study. *Journal of Visual Impairments & Blindness, 92*, 593–608.

Sleeter, C. E. (1995). An analysis of critiques of multicultural education. In J. A. Banks and C. A. McGee Banks (Eds.), *Handbook on research on multicultural education* (pp. 81–94). New York: Simon & Schuster Macmilan.

Smith, D. D. (2007). *Introduction to special education: Making a difference* (6th ed.). Boston: Allyn and Bacon.

Smith, D. D., & Rivera, D. (1993). *Effective discipline* (2nd ed.). Austin, TX: PRO-ED.

Smith, D. D., & Rivera, D. P. (1995). Discipline in special education and general education settings. *Focus on Exceptional Children, 27*(5), 1–4.

Swanson, H. L. (2001). Reading intervention research outcomes and students with learning disabilities: What are the major instructional ingredients for successful outcomes? *Perspectives, 27*(2), 18–20.

Taylor-Greene, S., Brown, D., Nelson, L., Longton, J., Gassman, T., Cohen, J., Swartz, J., Horner, R. H., Sugai, G., & Hall, S. (1997). School-wide behavioral support: Starting the year off right. *Journal of Behavioral Education, 7*, 99–112.

U.S. Census Bureau. (1999). *Statistical abstract of the United States*. Washington, DC: Author.

U.S. Department of Education (2002). *Twenty-fourth annual report to Congress on the implementation of the Individuals with Disabilities Education Act.* Washington, DC: U.S. Government Printing Office.

Vaughn, W. (2004). Prospective teachers' attitudes and awareness towards culturally responsive teaching and learning. *Teacher Education and Practice, 17*(1), 45–55.

Vaughn, S., & Lancelotta, G. X. (1990). Teaching interpersonal social skills to low accepted students: Peer-pairing versus no peer-pairing. *Journal of School Psychology, 28,* 181–188.

Walker, H. M., & Gresham, F. M. (1997). Making schools safer and violence free. *Intervention in School and Clinic, 32,* 199–204.

Walker, H. M., McConnell, S., Holmes, D., Todis, B., Walker, J., & Golden, N. (1983). *The Walker social skills curriculum—The ACCEPTS program.* Austin, TX: PRO-ED.

Walker, H. M., & Sprague, J. R. (2000, Winter). Intervention strategies for diverting at-risk children and youth from destructive outcomes. *Emotional and Behavioral Disorders in Youth, 1,* 5–8.

Walker, H. M., Todis, B., Holmes, D., & Horton, G. (1983). *The Walker social skills curriculum: ACCESS.* Austin, TX: PRO-ED.

Wehmeyer, M. L. (1995). Policy supporting self-determination in the environments of children with disabilities. *Education and Training in Mental Retardation and Developmental Disabilities* (March), 3–14.

White, M. A., (1975). Natural rates of teacher approval and disapproval in the classroom. *Journal of Applied Behavior Analysis, 8,* 367–372.

White, G. D., Nielsen, G., & Johnson, S. M. (1972). Time-out duration and the suppression of deviant behavior in children. *Journal of Applied Behavior Analysis, 5,* 111–120.

Wolfgang, C. H. (1995). *Solving discipline problems* (3rd ed.). Boston: Allyn and Bacon.

CHAPTER 10   Teaching Reading

Adams, M. J. (1990). *Beginning to read: Thinking and learning about print.* Cambridge, MA: The MIT Press.

Al Otaiba, S., & Fuchs, D. (2002). Characteristics of children who are unresponsive to early literacy intervention. *Remedial and Special Education, 23*(5), 300–316.

Allington, R. L. (1984). Oral reading. In P. D. Pearson (Ed.), *Handbook of reading research* (pp. 829–864). New York: Longman.

Barr, R., & Johnson, B. (1991). *Teaching reading in elementary classrooms: Developing independent readers.* Reading, MA: Addison-Wessley.

Bear, D. R., Invernizzi, M., Templeton, S., & Johnston, F. (2000). *Words their way: Word study for phonics, vocabulary, and spelling instruction* (2nd ed.). Upper Saddle River, NJ: Merrill–Prentice Hall.

Bear, D. R., & Templeton, S. (1998). Explorations in developmental spelling: Foundations for learning and teaching phonics, spelling, and vocabulary. *The Reading Teacher, 52,* 222–242.

Blachman, B. A., Ball, E. W., Black, R., & Tangel, D. M. (2000). *Read to the code: A phonological awareness program for young children.* Baltimore, MD: Brookes.

Bos, C. S., & Vaughn, S. (2002). *Strategies for teaching students with learning and behavior problems* (5th ed.). Boston: Allyn and Bacon.

Bryant, D. P., & Lehr, F. (2001). *Research-based content area instruction.* Austin: Texas Education Agency.

Bryant, B. R., Bryant, D. P., Hammill, D. D., & Sorrells, A. M. (2004). Characteristic reading behaviors of poor readers who have learning disabilities. *Assessment for Effective Intervention, 19,* 39–46.

Bryant, B. R., & Rivera, D. P. (1997). Reading. In D. P. Rivera & D. D. Smith (Eds.), *Teaching students with learning and behavior problems* (3rd ed., pp. 268–309). Boston: Allyn and Bacon.

Bryant, B. R., Wiederholt, J. L., & Bryant, D. P. (2004). *Gray Diagnostic Reading Test* (2nd ed.). Austin: PRO-ED.

Bryant, D. P., Ugel, N., Thompson, S., & Hamff, A. (1999). Strategies to promote content area reading instruction. *Intervention in School and Clinic, 34*(5), 293–302.

Bryant, D. P., Linan-Thompson, S., Ugel, N., Hamff, A., & Hougen, M. (2001). The effects of professional development for middle school general and special education teachers on implementation of reading strategies in inclusive content area classes. *Learning Disability Quarterly, 24*(4), 251–264.

Bryant, D. P., Vaughn, S., Linan-Thompson, S., Ugel, N., Hamff, A., & Hougen, M. (2000). Reading outcomes for students with and without reading disabilities in general education middle-school content area classes. *Learning Disability Quarterly, 23,* 238–252.

Burns, M. S., Griffin, P., & Snow, C. E. (Eds.). (1999). *Starting out right: A guide to promoting children's reading success.* Washington, DC: National Academy Press.

Carlisle, J. F. (1993). Selecting approaches to vocabulary instruction for the reading disabled. *Learning Disabilities Research & Practice, 8*(2), 97–105.

Carnine, D. W., Silbert, J., & Kameenui, E. J. (1997). *Direct instruction reading* (3rd ed.). Upper Saddle River, NJ: Merrill.

Carreker, S. (1999). Teaching reading: Accurate decoding and fluency. In J. R. Birsh (Ed.), *Multisensory teaching of basic language skills* (pp. 141–182). Baltimore, MD: Brookes.

Carr, E., & Ogle, D. (1987). K-W-L Plus: A strategy for comprehension and summarization. *Journal of Reading, 30*(7), 626–631.

Caswell-Tuley, A. (1998). *Never too late to read: Language skills for the adolescent dyslexic.* Timonium, MD: York Press.

Chall, J. S. (1996). *Stages of reading development* (2nd ed.). New York: McGraw-Hill.

Chard, D. J., & Dickson, S. V. (1999). Phonological awareness: Instructional and assessment guidelines. *Intervention in School & Clinic, 34,* 261–270.

Chard, D. J., & Osborn, J. (1999a). Phonics and word recognition instruction in early reading programs: Guidelines for accessibility. *Learning Disabilities Research & Practice, 14,* 107–117.

Chard, D. J., & Osborn, J. (1999b). Word recognition instruction: Paving the road to successful reading. *Intervention in School & Clinic, 34,* 271–277.

Chard, D. J., Simmons, D. C., & Kame'enui, E. J. (1998). Word recognition: Instructional and curricular basics and implications. In D. C. Simmons and E. J. Kame'enui (Eds.), *What reading research tells us about children with diverse learning needs: Bases and basics* (pp. 169–181). Mahwah, NJ: Erlbaum.

Cheek, E. H., & Collins, M. D. (1985). *Strategies for reading success.* Columbus, OH: Merrill.

Cunningham, P. M. (2000). *Phonics they use: Words for reading and writing* (3rd ed.). New York: Addison-Wesley–Longman.

Cunningham, P. M., & Allington, R. L. (1999). *Classrooms that work: They can all read and write.* New York: Longman.

Dickinson, D. K., Cote, L., & Smith, M. W. (1993). Learning vocabulary in preschool: Social and discourse contexts affecting vocabulary growth. In C. Daiute (Ed.), *New directions for child development (No. 61). The development of literacy through social interactions* (pp. 67–78). San Francisco: Jossey-Bass.

Dickson, S. V., Simmons, D. C., & Kame'enui, E. J. (1998). Text organization: Research bases. In D. C. Simmons and E. J. Kame'enui (Eds.), *What reading research tells us about children with diverse learning needs: Bases and basics* (pp. 239–277). Mahwah, NJ: Erlbaum.

Duffy, G., & Roehler, L. (1986). Constraints on teacher change. *Journal of Teacher Education, 35,* 55–58.

Echevarria, J. (1995). Sheltered instruction for students with learning disabilities who have limited English proficiency. *Intervention in School and Clinic, 30*(5), 302–305.

Ehri, L. C. (1998). Grapheme-phoneme knowledge is essential for learning to read words in English. In J. L. Metsala and L. C. Ehri (Eds.), *Word recognition in beginning literacy* (pp. 3–40). Mahwah, NJ: Erlbaum.

Elkonin, D. B. (1973). U.S.S.R. In J. Downing (Ed.), *Comparative reading* (pp. 551–579). New York: Macmillan.

Gersten, R. M., & Jiménez, R. T. (1994). A delicate balance: Enhancing literacy instruction for students of English as a second language. *The Reading Teacher 47*(6), 438–449.

Goldenberg, E. P. (1992). The difference between graphing software and *educational* graphing software. In F. Demana, and B. Waits (Eds.), *Proceedings of the Second Annual Conference on Technology in Collegiate Mathematics.* Reading, MA: Addison-Wesley, 1991. Co-published in W. Zimmerman & S. Cunningham (Eds.), *Visualization in teaching and learning mathematics,* Mathematical Association of America.

Grantham, T. C., & Ford, D. Y. (2003). Beyond self-concept and self-esteem for African American students: Improving racial identity improves achievement. *The High School Journal, 87,* 18–29.

Gunning, T. G. (2001). *Building words: A resource manual for teaching word analysis and spelling strategies.* Boston: Allyn and Bacon.

Guzak, F. (1985). *Diagnostic reading instruction in the elementary grades.* New York: Harper & Row.

Hammill, D. D., & Bartel, N. R. (2004). *Teaching students with learning and behavior problems.* Austin, TX: PRO-ED.

Hammill, D. D., & Bryant, B. R. (1998). *Learning Disabilities Diagnostic Inventory.* Austin, TX: PRO-ED.

Hasbrouck, J., & Tindall, G. (2005). Oral reading fluency: 90 years of measurement. Available at http://brt.uoregon.edu/techreports/TR_33_NCORF_DescStats.pdf

Honig, B., Diamond, L., & Gutlohn, L. (2000). *Teaching reading sourcebook.* Novato, CA: Arena Press.

Idol, L. (1987). Group story mapping: A comprehension strategy for both skilled and unskilled readers. *Journal of Learning Disabilities, 20,* 196–205.

Johnson, D. D. (1971). The Dolch list reexamined. *The Reading Teacher, 24,* 455–456.

Klingner, J., Vaughn, S., Domino, J., Schumm, J. S., & Bryant, D. P. (2001). *Collaborative strategic reading.* Longmont, CO: Sopris West.

Klingner, J. K., Vaughn, S., & Schumm, J. S. (1998). Collaborative strategic reading during social studies in heterogeneous fourth-grade classrooms. *Elementary School Journal, 99*(1): 3–21.

LaBerge, D., & Samuels, S. I. (1974). Toward a theory of automatic information processing in reading. In H. Singer and R. D. Riddell (Eds.), *Theories, models, and processes of readiness* (2nd ed., pp. 549–579). Newark, DE: International Reading Association.

Lundberg, I. (1991). Phonemic awareness can be developed without reading instruction. In S. Brady and D. Shankweiler (Eds.), *Phonological processes in literacy.* Hillsdale. NJ: Erlbaum.

Lyon, G. R. (1995). Learning disabilities. In E. Marsh and R. Barkley (Eds.), *Childhood psychopathology* (pp. 390–434). New York: Guilford.

McGee, L. M., & Richgels, D. J. (1990). *Literacy's beginnings: Supporting young readers and writers.* Boston: Allyn and Bacon.

Moats, L. C. (1999). Reading, spelling, and writing disabilities in the middle grades. In B. Wong (Ed.), *Learning about learning disabilities* (2nd ed., pp. 367–389). San Diego: Academic Press.

Morais, J. (1991). Constraints on the development of phonological awareness. In S. Brady and D. Shankweiler (Eds.), *Phonological processes in literacy.* Hillsdale, NJ: Erlbaum.

National Assessment of Educational Progress. (2000). *The nation's report card.* Washington, DC: National Center for Educational Statistics.

National Reading Panel. (2000). *Teaching children to read: An evidence-based assessment of the scientific research literature on reading and its implications for reading instruction.* Bethesda, MD: National Institutes of Health, National Institute of Child Health and Human Development.

Ogle, D. M. (1986). A teaching model that develops active reading of expository text. *The Reading Teacher, 39, 564–570.*

Orton Dyslexia Society. (1993). *Basic facts about dyslexia.* Baltimore, MD: The Orton Dyslexia Society.

Pressley, M. (1998). *Reading instruction that works. The case for balanced teaching.* New York: Guilford.

Pressley, M., Brown, R., El-Dinary, P. B., & Afflerbach, P. (1995). The comprehension instruction that students need: Instruction fostering constructively responsive reading. *Learning Disabilities Research and Practice, 10,* 215–224.

Rasinski, T. V. (2000). Speed does matter in reading. *The Reading Teacher, 54*(2), 146–151.

Raskind, M., & Bryant, B. R. (2002). *Functional Evaluation for Assistive Technology.* Austin, TX: Psycho-Educational Services.

Rubin, D. (1995). *Teaching elementary language arts* (5th ed.). Boston: Allyn and Bacon.

Scarborough, H. S. (1998). Predicting the future achievement of second graders with reading disabilities: Contributions of phonemic awareness, verbal memory, rapid serial naming, and IQ. *Annals of Dyslexia, 48,* 115–136.

Schreiber, P. A. (1980). On the acquisition of reading fluency. *Journal of Reading Behavior, 12,* 177–186.

Simmons, D. C., & Kame'enui, E. J. (1990). The effect of task alternatives on vocabulary knowledge: A comparison of students with and without learning disabilities. *Journal of Learning Disabilities, 23,* 291–297, 316.

Snow, C. E., Burns, M. S., & Griffin, P. (1998). *Preventing reading difficulties in young children.* Washington, DC: National Academy Press.

Spache, G. D., & Spache, E. B. (1986). *Reading in the elementary school* (5th ed.). Boston: Allyn and Bacon.

Stahl, S. A. (1986). Three principles of effective vocabulary instruction. *Journal of Reading, 29*(7), 662–668.

Stanovich, K. E. (1992). Developmental reading disorder. In S. R. Hooper, G. W. Hynd, and R. E. Madison (Eds.), *Developmental disorders: Diagnostic criteria and clinical assessment* (pp. 173–208). Hillsdale, NJ: Erlbaum.

Templeton, S., & Morris, D. (2000). Spelling. In M. L. Kamil, P. B. Mosenthal, P. D. Pearson, and R. Barr (Eds.), *Handbook of reading research: Vol. 3* (pp. 525–543). Mahwah, NJ: Erlbaum.

Torgesen, J. K., & Bryant, B. R. (2004). *Test of Phonological Awareness—Second edition (TOPA 2+).* Austin, TX: PRO-ED.

Torgesen, J. K., & Mathes, P. G. (2000). *A basic guide to understanding, assessing, and teaching phonological awareness.* Austin, TX: PRO-ED.

U.S. Department of Education. (2002). *Guidance for the Reading First program.* Washington, DC: Author. Retrieved September 5, 2004, from www.ed.gov/programs/readingfirst/guidance.doc.

Vaughn, S., Bos, C. S., & Schumm, J. S. (2007). *Teaching exceptional, diverse. and at-risk students in the general education classroom* (4th ed.). Boston: Allyn and Bacon.

Vaughn, S., & Klingner, J. K. (1999). Teaching reading comprehension through collaborative strategic reading. *Intervention in School & Clinic, 34*(5), 284–292.

Vaughn Gross Center for Reading and Language Arts (2000). *Coordinating for reading instruction: General education and special education working together.* Austin, TX: University of Texas System/Texas Education Agency.

Vaughn Gross Center for Reading and Language Arts (2003). *Effective instruction for secondary struggling readers: Research-based practices.* Austin, TX: University of Texas System/Texas Education Agency.

Wiederholt, J. L., & Bryant, B. R. (1987). *Assessing the reading abilities and instructional needs of students.* Austin, TX: PRO-ED.

Wiederholt, J. L., & Bryant, B. R. (2003). *Gray Oral Reading Tests* (4th ed.). Austin, TX: PRO-ED.

CHAPTER 11   Teaching Writing

Allen, R., & Mascolini, M. (1996). *The process of writing: Composing through critical thinking.* Upper Saddle River, NJ: Prentice-Hall.

Bos, C. S., & Vaughn, S. (2006). *Teaching strategies for students with mild to moderate disabilities* (6th ed.). Boston: Allyn and Bacon.

Bryant, D. P., & Bryant, B. R. (2003). *Assistive technology for people with disabilities.* Boston: Allyn and Bacon.

Cavey, D. W. (1993). *Dysgraphia.* Austin, TX: PRO-ED.

Englert, C. S., Raphael, T. E., & Anderson, L. M. (1989). *Socially-mediated instruction: Improving students' knowledge and talk about writing.* Unpublished manuscript, Michigan State University: Institute for Research on Teaching, East Lansing.

Englert, C. S., Raphael, T. E., Anderson, L. M., Anthony, H. M., & Stevens, D. D. (1991). Making strategies and self-talk visible: Writing instruction in regular and special education classrooms. *American Educational Research Journal, 28*(2), 337–372.

Englert, C. S., Raphael, T. E., Anderson, L. M., Gregg, S. L., & Anthony, H. M. (1989). Exposition: Reading, writing, and the metacognitive knowledge of learning disabled students. *Learning Disabilities Research, 5,* 5–24.

Englert, C. S., Zhao, Y., Dunsmore, K., Collings, N. Y., & Wolbers, K. (2005). Scaffolding the writing of students with disabilities through procedural facilitation: Using an Internet-based technology to improve performance. *Learning Disability Quarterly, 30*(1), 9–29.

Espin, C., & Sindelar, P. (1988). Auditory feedback and writing: Learning disabled and nondisabled students. *Exceptional Children, 55,* 45–51.

Finn, C. E., Petrilli, M. J., & Julian, L. (2006). *The state of state standards 2006.* Washington, DC: Fordham Foundation.

Graham, S., & Harris, K. R. (1988a). Instructional recommendations for teaching writing to exceptional students. *Exceptional Children, 54,* 506–512.

Graham, S., & Harris, K. R. (1988b). Research and instruction in written language: Introduction to the special issue. *Exceptional Children, 54,* 495–496.

Graham, S., Harris, K. R., & Larsen, L. (2001). Prevention and intervention of writing difficulties with students with learning disabilities. *Learning Disabilities Research & Practice, 16,* 74–84.

Graham, S., & Miller, L. (1980). Handwriting research and practice: A unified approach. *Focus on Exceptional Children, 13*(2), 1–16.

Graham, S., Schwartz, S. S., & MacArthur, C. A. (1993). Knowledge of writing and the composing process, attitude toward writing, and self-efficacy for students with and without learning disabilities. *Journal of Learning Disabilities, 26*(4), 237–249.

Graves, D. (1983). *Writing: Teachers and children at work.* Exeter, NH: Heinemann.

Graves, A., Montague, M., & Wong, Y. (1990). The effects of procedural facilitation on the story composition of learning disabled students. *Learning Disabilities Research, 5,* 88–93.

Gunning, T. G. (2003). *Creating literacy instruction for all children.* Boston: Allyn and Bacon.

Haager, D. & Klingner, J. K. (2005). *Differentiating instruction in inclusive classrooms.* Boston: Allyn and Bacon.

Hammill, D. D., & Bryant, B. R. (1998). *Learning Disabilities Diagnostic Inventory.* Austin, TX: PRO-ED.

Harris, K. R., & Graham, S. (1985). Improving learning disabled students' composition skills: Self-control strategy. *Learning Disability Quarterly, 8,* 27–36.

Houck, C. K., & Billingsley, B. S. (1989). Written expression of students with and without learning disabilities: Differences across the grades. *Journal of Learning Disabilities, 22*(9), 561–567, 572.

Laughton, J., & Morris, N. (1989). Story grammar knowledge of learning disabled students. *Learning Disabilities Research, 4,* 87–95.

McGhee, R., Bryant, B. R., Bryant, D., & Larsen, S. C. (1992). *Test of written expression.* Austin, TX: PRO-ED.

Mercer, C. D., & Pullen, P. C. (2004). *Students with learning disabilities* (7th ed.). Upper Saddle River, NJ: Prentice-Hall.

Moats, L. C. (2005/2006, Winter). How spelling supports reading. *American Educator,* 12–43.

Montague, M., Maddux, C., & Dereshiwsky, M. (1988). Story grammar and comprehension and production of narrative prose by students with learning disabilities. *Journal of Learning Disabilities, 23,* 190–197.

Newcomer, P. L., Barenbaum, E. M., & Nodine, B. F. (1988). Comparison of the story production of LD, normal-achieving, and low-achieving children under two modes of production. *Learning Disability Quarterly, 11,* 82–96.

Rubin, D. (1995). *Teaching elementary language arts* (5th ed.). Boston: Allyn and Bacon.

Scardamalia, M., & Bereiter, C. (1986). Written composition. In M. Wittrock (Ed.), *Handbook of research on teaching* (3rd ed., pp. 778–803). New York: Macmillan.

Schumaker, J. B., & Sheldon, J. (1985). *The sentence writing strategy.* Lawrence: University of Kansas Press.

Scott, B. J., & Vitale, M. R. (2003). Teaching the writing process to students with LD. *Intervention in School and Clinic, 38*(4), 220–224.

Shapiro, E. S. (2004). *Academic skills problems.* San Diego: Sattler.

Spandel, B., & Stiggins, R. V. (1990). *Creative writers: Linking assessment and writing instruction.* New York: Longman.

Wood, E., Woloshyn, V. E., & Willoughby, T. (1995). *Cognitive strategy instruction for middle and high schools.* Cambridge, MA: Brookline.

Vaughn Gross Center for Reading and Language Arts (VGCRLA). (2003). *Professional development guide: Enhancing writing instruction for secondary students.* Austin, TX: The University of Texas System/Texas Education Agency.

CHAPTER 12 Teaching Mathematics

Allsopp, D. H., Kyger, M. H., & Lovin, L. H. (2007). *Teaching mathematics meaningfully: Solutions for reaching struggling learners.* Baltimore, MD: Brookes.

Ashlock, R. B. (2006). *Error patterns in computation.* Columbus, OH: Merrill.

Baroody, A. J., & Hume, J. (1991) Meaningful mathematics instruction: The case of fractions. *Remedial and Special Education, 12*(3), 54–68.

Baxter, J., Woodward, J., & Olson, D. (2001). Effects of reform-based mathematics instruction in five third-grade classrooms. *Elementary School Journal, 101*(5), 529–548.

Baxter, J., Woodward, J., Wong, J., & Voorhies, J. (2002). We talk about it, but do they get it? *Learning Disabilities Research & Practice, 17*(3), 173–185.

Bley, N. & Thornton, C. (2001). *Teaching mathematics to students with learning disabilities* (4th ed.). Austin, TX: PRO-ED.

Bryant, D. P., Bryant, B., & Hammill, D. D. (2000). Characteristic behaviors of students with LD who have teacher-identified math weaknesses. *Journal of Learning Disabilities, 33*(2), 168–177.

Bryant, D. P., Kim, Sun A., Hartman, P., & Bryant, B. R. (2006). Standards-based mathematics instruction and teaching middle school students with mathematical disabilities. In M. Montague and A. Jitendra (Eds.), *Teaching mathematics to middle school students with learning difficulties* (pp. 7–28). New York: Guilford.

Butler, F. M., Miller, S. P., Crehan, K., Babbitt, B., & Pierce, T. (2003). Fraction instruction for students with mathematics disabilities: Comparing two teaching sequences. *Learning Disabilities Research & Practice, 18,* 99–111.

Capps, L. R., & Cox, L. S. (1991). Improving the learning of mathematics in our schools. *Focus on Exceptional Children, 23*(9), 1–8.

Carnine, D., Jones, E. D., & Dixon, R. (1994). Mathematics: Educational tools for diverse learners. *School Psychology Review, 23*(3), 406–427.

Cathheart, W. G., Pothier, Y. M., Vance, J. H., & Bezuk, N. S. (2000). *Learning mathematics in elementary and middle schools.* Upper Saddle River, NJ: Merrill–Prentice Hall.

Cawley, J. F., Baker-Kroczynski, S., & Urban, A. (1992). Seeking excellence in mathematics education for students with mild disabilities. *Teaching Exceptional Children, 24,* 40–43.

Cawley, J. F., & Miller, J. H. (1989). Cross-sectional comparisons of the mathematical performance of children with learning disabilities: Are we on the right track toward comprehensive programming? *Journal of Learning Disabilities, 23,* 250–254, 259.

Cawley, J. F., & Parmar, R. S. (1992). Arithmetic programming for students with disabilities: An alternative. *Remedial and Special Education, 13*(3), 6–8.

Coyne, M. D., Kameenui, E. J., & Carnine, D. W. (2007). *Effective teaching strategies that accommodate diverse learners.* Upper Saddle River, NJ: Pearson.

Garnett, K. (1987). Math learning disabilities: Teaching and learners. *Reading, Writing, and Learning Disabilities, 3,* 1–8.

Garnett, K., & Fleischner, J. E. (1983). Automatization and basic fact performance of normal and learning disabled children. *Learning Disability Quarterly, 6,* 223–231.

Geary, D. C. (1990). A componential analysis of an early learning deficit in mathematics. *Journal of Experimental Child Psychology, 49,* 363–383.

Geary, D. C. (1993). Mathematical disabilities: Cognitive, neuropsychological, and genetic components. *Psychological Bulletin, 114,* 345–362.

Geary, D. C. (2004). Mathematics and learning disabilities. *Journal of Learning Disabilities, 37,* 4–15.

Gersten, R., Jordan, N. C., & Flojo, J. R. (2005). Early identification and intervention for students with mathematics difficulties. *Journal of Learning Disabilities, 38*(4), 293–304.

Ginsberg, H. P., & Pappas, S. (2004). SES, ethnic, and gender differences in young children's informal addition and subtraction: A clinical interview investigation. *Applied Developmental Psychology, 25,* 171–192.

Greenes, C. (1981, February). Identifying the gifted student in mathematics. *Arithmetic Teacher,* 14–17.

Hallahan, D. P., Lloyd, J. W., Kauffman, J. M., Weiss, M. P., & Martinez, E. W. (2005). *Learning disabilities: Foundations, characteristics, and effective teaching* (3rd ed.). Boston: Allyn and Bacon.

Heid, M. K. (1983). Characteristics and special needs of the gifted student in mathematics. *Mathematics Teacher, 76,* 221–226.

Howden, H. (1989). Teaching number sense. *Arithmetic Teacher, 36,* 6–11.

Hudson, P., & Miller, S. P. (2006). *Designing and implementing mathematics instruction for students with diverse learning needs.* Boston: Allyn and Bacon.

Johnson, D. T. (2000). Teaching mathematics to gifted students in a mixed-ability classroom. *ERIC Digest E94* (ERIC Document Reproduction Service No. ED441302). Office of Educational Research and Improvement (OERI), U.S. Department of Education (ED) under Contract No. ED-99-CO-0026.

Jordan, N. C., Hanich, L. B., & Kaplan, D. (2003). Arithmetic fact mastery in young children: A longitudinal investigation. *Journal of Experimental Child Psychology, 85,* 103–119.

Kelly, B., Gersten, R., & Carnine, D. (1990). Student error patterns as a function of curriculum design: Teaching fractions to remedial high school students and high school students with learning disabilities. *Journal of Learning Disabilities, 23*(1), 23–29.

Maccini, P., & Gagnon, J. C. (2005). Math graphic organizers for students with disabilities. Washington, DC: The Access Center: Improving Outcomes for All Students K–8. Used with permission. Available at www.k8accesscenter.org/training_resources/documents/MathGraphicOrg.pdf

Marzola, E. (1985). *An arithmetic problem-solving model based on a plan for sets to solution, mastery learning, and calculator use in a resource room setting for learning disabled students.* New York: Teachers College Press.

Mayer, R. E. (1992). *Thinking, problem solving, and cognition* (2nd ed.). New York: W. H. Freeman.

McCoy, E. M., & Prehm, H. J. (1987). *Teaching mainstreamed students. Methods and techniques.* Denver, CO: Love.

McLeod, T. M., & Armstrong, S. W. (1982). Learning disabilities in mathematics: Skill deficits and remedial approaches at the intermediate and secondary level. *Learning Disability Quarterly, 5*(3), 305–311.

Mercer, C. D., & Mercer, A. R. (2005) *Teaching students with learning problems* (7th ed.). New York: Macmillan.

Mercer, C. D., & Miller, S. P. (1992). Teaching students with learning problems in math to acquire, understand, and apply basic math facts. *Remedial and Special Education, 13*(3), 19–35, 61.

Miller, S. P., & Mercer, C. D. (1993). Mnemonics: Enhancing the math performance of students with learning difficulties. *Intervention in School & Clinic, 29,* 78–82.

Miller, S. P., Mercer, C. D., & Dillon, A. (1992). CSA: Acquiring and retaining math skills. *Intervention in School & Clinic, 28,* 105–110.

Montague, M. (1997). Cognitive strategy instruction in mathematics for students with learning disabilities. *Journal of Learning Disabilities, 30,* 164–177.

Montague, M. (2006). Self-regulation strategies for better math performance in middle school. In M. Montague and A. K. Jitendra (Eds.), *Teaching mathematics to middle school students with learning difficulties* (pp. 89–107). New York: Guilford.

Montague, M., & Applegate, B. (1993). Middle school students' mathematical problem solving: An analysis of think-aloud protocols. *Learning Disability Quarterly, 16,* 19–30.

Montague, M., & Bos, C. S. (1986). The effect of cognitive strategy training on verbal math problem solving performance of learning disabled adolescents. *Journal of Learning Disabilities, 19,* 26–33.

National Council of Teachers of Mathematics. (1989). *Curriculum and evaluation standards for school mathematics.* Reston, VA: Author.

National Council of Teachers of Mathematics (2000). *Principles and standards for school mathematics.* Reston, VA: Author.

Okamoto, Y., & Case, R. (1996). Exploring the microstructure of children's central conceptual structures in the domain of number. *Monographs of the Society for Research in Child Development, 61*(1–2), 27–58.

Parmar, R. S. (1992). Protocol analysis of strategies used by students with mild disabilities when solving arithmetic word problems. *Diagnostique, 17*(4), 227–243.

Peterson, S. K., Mercer, C. D., & O'Shea, L. (1988). Teaching learning disabled students place value using the concrete to abstract sequence. *Learning Disabilities Research, 4*(1), 52–56.

Reys, B. J. (1986). Teaching computational estimation: Concepts and strategies. In H. L. Schoen & M. J. Zweng (Eds.), *Estimation and mental computation: 1986 yearbook* (pp. 31–44). Reston, VA: National Council of Teachers of Mathematics.

Rivera, D. P. (1994, April). *Teaching mathematics using direct instruction and cooperative learning.* Paper presented at the International Conference of the Council for Learning Disabilities. San Diego, CA.

Rivera, D. (1997). Mathematics education and students with learning disabilities: Introduction to the special series. *Journal of Learning Disabilities, 30*(1), 2–19.

Rivera, D., & Smith, D. D. (1987). Influence of modeling on acquisition and generalization of computational skills: A summary of research finding from three sites. *Learning Disability Quarterly, 10,* 69–80.

Rivera, D., & Smith, D. D. (1988). Using a demonstration strategy to teach midschool students with learning disabilities how to compute long division. *Journal of Learning Disabilities, 21,* 77–81.

Rivera D. P., & Smith, D. D. (1997) *Teaching students with learning and behavior problems* (3rd ed.). Boston: Allyn and Bacon.

Rotigel, J. V. (2000) *Exceptional mathematical talent: Comparing achievement in concepts and computation.* Unpublished doctoral dissertation, Indiana University of Pennsylvania.

Rotigel, J. V., & Fello, S. (2004). Mathematically gifted students: How can we meet their needs? *Gifted Child Today, 27*(4), 46–51, 65.

Schoen, H. L., & Zweng, M. J. (Eds.), *Estimation and mental computation* (pp. 31–44). Reston, VA: National Council of Teachers of Mathematics.

Scott, P. B., & Raborn, D. T. (1996). Realizing the gifts of diversity among students with learning disabilities. *LD Forum, 21*(2), 7–29.

Sheffield, L. J. (1994). *The development of gifted and talented mathematics students and the National Council of Teachers of Mathematics Standards* (Report No. RBDM 9404). Storrs: National Research Center on the Gifted and Talented, University of Connecticut. ERIC Document Reproduction Service No. ED388011.

Stein, M., Kinder, D., Silbert, J., & Carnine, D. W. (2006). *Designing effective mathematics instruction.* Upper Saddle River, NJ: Prentice-Hall.

Swanson, H. L., Cooney, J., & O'Shaughnessy, T. (1998). Memory. In B. Wong (Ed.), *Understanding learning disabilities* (pp. 107–162). San Diego: Academic Press.

Tomlinson, C. A. (1995). Deciding to differentiate instruction in middle school: One school's journey. *Gifted Child Quarterly, 39,* 77–87.

Van de Walle, J. A. (2007). *Elementary and middle school mathematics: Teaching developmentally* (6th ed.). Boston: Allyn and Bacon.

VanTassel-Baska, J. (1998). *Excellence in educating gifted and talented learners* (3rd ed.). Denver: Love.

Wiig, E. H., & Semel, E. M. (1984). *Language assessment and intervention for the learning disabled* (2nd ed.). New York: Macmillan.

CHAPTER 13 Facilitating Content-Area Instruction and Study Skills

Abdullah, M. H. (2001). *Self-directed learning* [ERIC digest No. 169]. Bloomington, IN: ERIC Clearinghouse on Reading, English, and Communication. ERIC Document Reproduction Service No. ED459458.

Armbruster, B. B., & Anderson, T. H. (1988). On selecting "considerate content area textbooks." *Remedial and Special Education, 9*(1), 47–52.

Baker, L. (1991). Metacognition, reading, and science education. In C. M. Santa and D. E. Alvermann (Eds.), *Science learning: Processes and applications* (pp. 12–13). Newark, DE: International Reading Association.

Baker, L., & Brown, A. L. (1984). Metacognitive skills and reading. In P. D. Pearson, R. Barr, M. L. Kamil, and P. Mosenthal (Eds.), *Handbook of reading research, Vol. I* (pp. 353–394). White Plains, NY: Longman.

Bassett, D. S. (1995). A guide to the study units in this workbook. In D. D. Smith, *Study guide for introduction to special education* (2nd ed.) (pp. 1–10). Boston: Allyn and Bacon.

Bean, R. M., Zigmond, N., & Hartman, P. K. (1994). Adapted use of social studies textbooks in elementary classrooms: Views of classroom teachers. *Remedial and Special Education, 15*(4), 216–226.

Beck, I. L., McKeown, M. G., & Kucan, L. (2002). *Bringing words to life: Robust vocabulary instruction.* New York: Guilford.

Boyle, J. R. (2001). Enhancing the note-taking skills of students with mild disabilities, *Intervention in School & Clinic, 36,* 221–224.

Bragstad, B. J., & Stumpf, S. M. (1987). *A guidebook for teaching study skills and motivation* (2nd ed.). Boston: Allyn and Bacon.

Bryant, D. P., & Bryant, B. R. (2003). *Assistive technology for people with disabilities.* Boston: Allyn and Bacon.

Bryant, D. P., Ugel, N., Thompson, S., & Hamff, A. (1999). Strategies to promote content area reading instruction. *Intervention in School & Clinic, 34*(5), 293–302.

Bryant, D. P., Linan-Thompson, S., Ugel, N., Hamff, A., & Hougen, M. (2001). The effects of professional development for middle school general and special education teachers on implementation of reading strategies in inclusive content area classes. *Learning Disability Quarterly, 24*(4), 251–264.

Bryant, D. P., Vaughn, S., Linan-Thompson, S., Ugel, N., Hamff, A., & Hougen, M. (2000). Reading outcomes for students with and without reading disabilities in general education middle-school content area classes. *Learning Disability Quarterly, 23,* 238–252.

Buehl, D. (2001). *Classroom strategies for interactive learning.* Newark, DE: International Reading Association.

Ciborowski, J. (1992). *Textbooks and the students who can't read them: A guide to teaching content.* Boston: Brookline Books.

Cognition and Technology Group at Vanderbilt. (1990). Anchored instruction and its relationship to situated cognition. *Educational Researcher, 19*(6), 2–10.

Deshler, D. D., Ellis, E. S., & Lenz, B. K. (1996). *Teaching adolescents with learning disabilities* (2nd ed.). Denver, CO: Love.

Devine, T. G. (1987). *Teaching study skills* (2nd ed.). Boston: Allyn and Bacon.

Ellis, E. S. (1996). Reading strategy instruction. In D. Deshler, E. S. Ellis, and B. K. Lenz (Eds.), *Teaching adolescents with learning disabilities* (2nd ed., pp. 61–126). Denver, CO: Love.

Ellis, E., & Lenz, B. K. (1987). Accompanying analysis of effective learning strategies for LD students. *LD Focus, 2,* 94–107).

Ferretti, R. P., MacArthur, C. A., & Okolo, C. M. (2001). Teaching for historical understanding in inclusive classrooms. *Learning Disability Quarterly, 24,* 59–71.

4-Empowerment.com. (2004). *Conducting research using* To Kill a Mockingbird. Austin, TX: Author.

Garcia, G. E., & Nagy, W. (1993). Latino students' concept of cognates. In D. J. Leu and C. K. Kinzer (Eds.), *Examining central issues in literary research, theory, and practice: Forty-second Yearbook of the National Reading Conference* (pp. 367–373). Chicago, IL.

Glaser, C. W., Rieth, H. J., Kinzer, C. K., Colburn, L. K., & Peter, J. (1999). A description of the impact of multimedia anchored instruction on classroom interactions. *Journal of Special Education Technology, 14,* 27–43.

Hammill, D. D., & Bryant, B. R. (1998). *Learning Disabilities Diagnostic Inventory.* Austin, TX: PRO-ED.

Honig, B., Diamond, L., & Gutlohn, L. (2000). *Teaching reading.* Novato, CA: Arena Press.

Hoover, J. J. (1995). Teaching study skills to students. In D. D. Hammill and N. Bartel (Eds.), *Teaching students with learning and behavior problems* (6th ed., pp. 347–380). Austin, TX: PRO-ED.

Hoover, J. J., & Patton, J. R. (1995). *Teaching students with learning problems to use study skills.* Austin, TX: PRO-ED.

Hughes, C. A. (1996). Memory and test-taking strategies. In D. Deshler, E. S. Ellis, and B. K. Lenz (Eds.), *Teaching adolescents with learning disabilities* (2nd ed., pp. 209–266). Denver, CO: Love.

Hughes, C. A., Schumaker, J. B., Deshler, D. D., & Mercer, C. D. (1988). *The test taking strategy: PIRATES,* Lawrence: University of Kansas, Institute for Research in Learning Disabilities, Edge Enterprises.

Kinder, D., & Bursuck, W. (1991). The search for a unified social studies curriculum: Does history really repeat itself? *Journal of Learning Disabilities, 24*(5), 270–275.

Kinzer, C. K., Gabella, M. S., & Rieth, H. J. (1994). An argument for using multimedia and anchored instruction to facilitate mildly disabled students' learning of literacy and social studies. *Technology and Disability Quarterly, 3*(2), 117–128.

Larkin, M. J., & Ellis, E. S. (1998). Adolescents with learning disabilities. In B. Y. L. Wong (Ed.), *Learning about learning disabilities* (2nd ed., pp. 557–584). San Diego: Academic Press.

Lenz, B. K., & Hughes, C. A. (1990). A word identification strategy for adolescents with learning disabilities. *Journal of Learning Disabilities, 23*(3), 149–163.

Lenz, K., & Schumaker, J. B. (1999). *Adapting language arts, social studies, and science materials for the inclusive classroom* (Vol. 3). Reston, VA: Council for Exceptional Children.

Mastropieri, M. A., Scruggs, T. E., & Fulk, B. J. M. (1990). Teaching abstract vocabulary to LD students with the keyword method: Effects on comprehension and recall. *Journal of Learning Disabilities, 23,* 92–107.

Okolo, C. M., & Ferretti, R. P. (1997). Knowledge acquisition and technology-supported projects in the social studies for students with learning disabilities. *Journal of Special Education Technology, 13,* 91–103.

Pressley, M., Brown, R., El-Dinary, P. B., & Afflerbach, P. (1995). The comprehension instruction that students need: Instruction fostering constructively responsive reading. *Learning Disabilities Research & Practice, 10,* 215–224.

Putnam, M. L., Deshler, D. D., & Schumaker, J. B. (1992). The investigation of setting demands: A missing link in learning strategy instruction. In L. Meltzer (Ed.), *Strategy assessment and instruction for students with learning disabilities: From theory to practice* (pp. 325–353). Austin, TX: PRO-ED.

Raskind, M., & Bryant, B. R. (2002). *Functional Evaluation for Assistive Technology.* Austin, TX: Psycho-Educational Services.

Rieth, H. J., Bryant, D. P., Kinzer, C. K., Colburn, L. K., Hur, S.-J., Hartman, P., & Choi, H.-S. (2003). An analysis of the impact of anchored instruction on teaching and learning activities in two ninth grade language arts classes. *Remedial and Special Education, 24*(3), 173–184.

Rieth, H. J., Colburn, L. K., & Bryant, D. P. (2003). Trends and issues in instructional and assistive technology. In A. McCray, H. J. Rieth, and P. Sindelar (Eds.), *Trends and issues in special education* (pp. 205–225). Boston: Allyn and Bacon.

Rivera, D. P., & Smith, D. D. (1997). *Teaching students with learning and behavior problems* (3rd ed.). Boston: Allyn and Bacon.

Schloss, P. J., Schloss, M. A., & Schloss, C. N. (2007). *Instructional methods for secondary students with learning and behavior problems* (4th ed.). Boston: Allyn and Bacon.

Simmons, D. C., & Kameenui, E. J. (1990). The effect of task alternatives on vocabulary knowledge: A comparison of students with learning disabilities and students of normal achievement. *Journal of Learning Disabilities, 23*(5), 291–297.

Snider, V. E. (1989). Reading comprehension performance of adolescents with learning disabilities. *Learning Disability Quarterly, 12,* 87–96.

Stahl, S. A., & Nagy, W. E. (2006). *Teaching word meanings Series: Literacy teaching series.* Florence, KY: Erlbaum.

Swanson, H. L., Cochran, K. F., & Ewers, C. A. (1990). Can learning disabilities be determined from working memory performance? *Journal of Learning Disabilities, 23,* 59–68.

Strichart, S. S., Mangrum, C. T., & Iannuzzi, P. (2002). *Teaching study skills and strategies to students with learning disabilities, attention deficit disorders, or special needs.* Boston: Allyn and Bacon.

Vacca, R. T., & Vacca, J. L. (2002). *Content area reading: Literacy and learning across the curriculum* (7th ed.). Boston: Allyn and Bacon.

Vogel, S. (1997). *Ways that students can help themselves.* Retrieved from http://www.ldonline.org/article/6145

Ward, L., & Traweek, D. (1993). Application of a metacognitive strategy to assessment, intervention, and consultation: A think-aloud technique. *Journal of School Psychology, 31,* 469–485.

glossary

ability grouping A form of acceleration wherein students of comparable abilities work together in courses or activities in which they excel

academic qualifications In high stakes assessment, determination as to whether a student is eligible, on the basis of his or her curriculum, to be assessed

acceleration An approach that allows gifted and talented students to move through the curriculum at faster rates than their peers who learn in more typical ways

access to the general education curriculum A requirement of IDEA '04; gives students with disabilities the right to receive evidence-based instruction in the general education curriculum, to the greatest extent possible

accommodations Supports to compensate for disabilities; adjustments to assignments or tests

acquired immunodeficiency syndrome (AIDS) A usually fatal medical syndrome caused by infection with the human immunodeficiency virus (HIV)

acquisition stage of learning Stage of learning in which learners may not know how to perform a skill, and the aim is for the individual to learn how to perform it

acronym A memory aid that consists of a word made from the first letters of the words that convey the information to be learned

acrostic A memory aid that consists of a sentence wherein the first letters of the words stand for both the items to be recalled and their proper order

active listening A method of listening that involves ways to listen and respond to communication partners more effectively

active process assessment Flexible interviewing where the student discusses aloud what is being thought during computation

ADAPT framework Steps used to differentiate instruction; provides questions to assist teachers in making instructional and evaluation decisions for individual students

adaptive behavior Performance of everyday life skills expected of adults

adequate yearly progress The progress of students toward their end-of-year goals, as tracked by the use of assessment data

advance organizer Activities to prepare students for the lesson's content

advanced placement courses Classes that provide more in-depth course content and college credit

adventitious blindness Blindness originating after the age of 2 years

affixes Prefixes and suffixes

age equivalents Derived developmental scores reported in years and months

age of onset The time of life when a disability originates

alphabetic principle An understanding that speech can be converted into print, print can be changed into speech, and letters represent sounds in our language

alternate (or alternative) assessment Individualized methods of evaluating the progress of students who do not participate in the general education curriculum

alternative portfolios Schoolwork that becomes part of the documentation about some students' progress at school; usually replaces high stakes tests for students with disabilities

American Sign Language (ASL) The language of Deaf Americans that uses manual communication; a signal of Deaf culture

Americans with Disabilities Act (ADA) Antidiscrimi-nation legislation guaranteeing basic civil rights to people with disabilities

analytical evaluation scale Scoring that is broken down to consider specific elements; contrast with use of a holistic evaluation scale, wherein student work is considered as a whole

anchored instruction An instructional technique that begins with an event or problem situation (a video or movie can be the anchor). The video is used to provide background information about the event or problem situation and to create a context that contributes to a shared experience among students to facilitate learning

anorexia Intense fear of gaining weight, disturbed body image, and chronic absence or refusal of appetite for food, causing severe weight loss (25 percent of body weight)

anxiety disorders Conditions causing painful uneasiness, emotional tension, or emotional confusion

application stage of learning Stage of learning in which the aim is for students to use learning and extend it to new situations

array of services Constellation of special education services, personnel, and educational placements

articulation problems Abnormal production of speech sounds

Asperger syndrome One of the autism spectrum disorders (ASD) wherein cognition is usually in the average or above-average range

assessment Method by which teachers and other professionals gain information about students

assistive technologist A related services provider who assists with the selection, acquisition, or use of assistive technology

assistive technology (AT) Equipment (devices) or services that help compensate for an individual's disabilities

Assistive Technology Act of 2004 (ATA) Law that facilitates increased accessibility through technology

assistive technology device A unit such as an item, piece of equipment, or product system that helps compensate for an individual's disabilities

association–processing level The vocabulary acquisition level wherein words are thought of in terms of synonyms, definitions, or contexts

asthma The most common chronic health condition among children, resulting in difficulty breathing

at risk Students who have experiences, living conditions, or characteristics that have been shown to contribute to school failure

attention deficit hyperactivity disorder (ADHD) A condition characterized by hyperactivity, impulsivity, and inattention; included in the "other health impairments" category in *DSM-IV-TR*

audience In writing, the person(s) who will read the paper

audience sense In writing, the process for determining the probable reader

audiogram A grid or graph used to display a person's hearing abilities

audiologist A related services provider who diagnoses hearing losses and auditory problems

auditory discrimination Ability to identify speech and other sounds, such as environmental sounds

augmentative and alternative communication devices (au com) Methods for communicating, such as communication boards, communication books, sign language, and computerized voices; assistive technology that helps individuals communicate, including devices that actually produce speech

aura Warning of an imminent seizure in the form of heightened sensory awareness; also known as the preictal stage of a seizure

authentic assessments Performance measures that use work generated by the student

authentic text Nonfiction and fictional literature

autism One of the autism spectrum disorders (ASD); ranges from low functioning to high functioning

autism spectrum disorders (ASD) A group of disorders with similar characteristics, including mannerisms and difficulties with communication and social interaction

autistic savant An individual who displays many behaviors associated with autism but also possesses discrete abilities and unusual talents

automaticity Practicing skills until they require less cognitive processing

basal textbook The textbook that is used by the classroom teacher to teach subject-area content

basals Textbooks adopted by school districts to serve as a primary source for subject-area content

base word *See* root word

behavior intervention plan Includes a functional assessment and procedures to prevent behavioral infractions and to intervene if they occur

benchmark In assessment, a predetermined standard for success or failure

bilingual education Instruction that is provided in two languages

bilingual-bicultural approach A method of instruction for students who are deaf that combines practices of ESL and bilingual education. ASL is the native language, and reading and writing in English are taught as a second language

blindness Degree of visual loss wherein the individual uses touch and hearing to learn and does not have functional use of sight

braille A system of reading and writing that uses dot codes embossed on paper; tactile reading. In 1824, Louis Braille created a precursor to the method used today

brainstorm To think of several ideas related to a topic, write notes as one thinks, and use the notes to generate further ideas

bulimia Chronically causing oneself to vomit or otherwise remove food to limit weight gain

bullying Behavior that is deliberate with the intent of harming the victim

categorical approach The organization of special education in terms of different disabilities

cerebral palsy (CP) A neuromotor impairment; a nonprogressive disease resulting in motor difficulties that is associated with communication problems and mobility problems

checking for understanding During a lesson, periodically determining whether students are learning the content

child find A requirement of IDEA '04 that educators help refer and identify children and youth with disabilities

childhood disintegrative disorder (CDD) One of the autism spectrum disorders (ASD) wherein the individual has typical development until about the

age of 5 or 6 years

chromosomal abnormality A gene disorder

chronic illnesses Long-lasting and serious health conditions

chunking Organizing information by groups or topics

classroom management Purposeful planning, delivery, and evaluation of techniques and procedures that ensure a classroom environment conducive to teaching and learning

clinical interview A procedure to examine a student's knowledge of and thinking about how to solve problems

clinical teaching cycle Sequenced instruction, reteaching if necessary, and informal assessment procedures, including assessment of academic and conversational language proficiency

closed-circuit television (CCTV) An assistive visual input technology that uses a television to increase the size of objects or print

clustering Categorizing information in a meaningful way as part of learning

coaching A procedure that focuses on encouraging appropriate behaviors through modeling and feedback

cochlear implant A microprocessor, surgically placed in the hearing mechanism, that replaces the cochlea so that people with sensorineural hearing loss can perceive sounds

coexisting disability The situation of having more than one disability; co-morbidity

cognitive development Understanding and using declarative, procedural, and conceptual knowledge

cognitive disabilities or mental retardation A disability characterized by impaired intellectual functioning, limited adaptive behavior, need for supports, and initial occurrence before age 18; intellectual disabilities

collaboration Professionals working in partnerships to provide educational services

collaborative consultation A partnership between the general education and special education teachers, tapping the expertise of both to provide appropriate services to students with disabilities

communication boards Low-tech assistive technology devices that display pictures or words that the individual can point to in order to communicate

community-based instruction (CBI) Teaching functional skills in real-life situations or in environments where they occur

comprehension-processing level The vocabulary acquisition level wherein knowledge of word associations can be used to place words in categories, cre-

ate sentences, and generate multiple word meanings

computational fluency Knowing and using efficient methods for accurate computing

concepts Categories of knowledge

conceptual knowledge Understanding ideas and relationships

conductive hearing loss Hearing impairment that is due to damage or obstruction to the outer or middle ear and that interferes with transfer of sound to the inner ear

conflict A disagreement of interests or ideas

congenital Present at birth or originating during early infancy

congenital blindness Blindness present at birth or originating during early infancy

connotative meaning An associated meaning added to the primary meaning

construct validity A form of technical adequacy in assessment that reflects whether tests provide results that are associated with the construct being measured

content-area instruction Teaching students subject knowledge in areas such as social studies, science, and literature

content validity A form of technical adequacy in assessment that reflects whether tests contain items that come from a legitimate source and meet basic statistical criteria

contingent observation A behavior management approach in which a disruptive student is removed from an activity but is still able to observe the activity

continuum of services Pattern in which each level of special education services is more restrictive than the one before, and services come in a lock-step sequence

contracting A procedure that involves setting up a written agreement between two parties about a targeted behavior that needs improvement

convention skills In writing, the skills associated with spelling, punctuation, and capitalization; mechanics

convergent, lower-order-questions Questions that usually have one answer and start with *who, what, where,* or *when*

cooperative learning A grouping practice in which small, mixed-ability groups work collaboratively to complete activities

core curriculum Content that is taught to all students in the general education classroom

co-teaching Team teaching by general education and special education teachers

criterion-referenced interpretations Interpretations of assessment measures for purposes of comparing performance to standards that signal mastery of the content being tested

criterion-related validity   A form of technical adequacy in assessment that has to do with whether tests produce results similar to established tests, either presently (concurrent criterion-related validity) or in the future (predictive criterion-related validity)

criterion-specific rewards   A reward system in which students earn privileges only when they reach desirable levels of the target behavior

critical thinking   Reasoning to learn new concepts, ideas, or problem solutions

cues   Visual or verbal prompts provided to increase the likelihood of correct student responses

cultural characteristics   Beliefs, norms, and customs that differ within and between groups

culture   Way of perceiving the world and of interacting within it

cumulative folder   Collective records or files that contain academic and behavioral history data

curriculum based measurement (CBM)   A direct measurement system used to monitor students' progress mastering basic academic skills

deaf   Having profound hearing loss

Deaf   The capital "D" in Deaf signifies membership in the Deaf community, adherence to Deaf culture, and use of American Sign Language (ASL) as the primary means of communication

deafblindness   A dual disability involving problems with both vision and hearing

decibel (dB)   Unit in which the intensity of sound is measured

declarative knowledge   Understanding of factual information

decodable text   Text that contains words made up of the sounds and patterns that students have mastered

decoding   Identifying unknown words by using knowledge of letter–sound correspondences

deductive reasoning   Reasoning from the general to the specific and problem solving

denotative meaning   Literal, dictionary meaning

depression   A state of despair and dejected mood

derivational meanings   The meanings of the parts of words

derived scores   Normative scores (such as age equivalents, grade equivalents, ratio IQs, percentiles, and standard scores) into which raw scores are converted

developmental delay   A noncategorical special education label allowed by IDEA '04 to make children ages 3

through 9 years eligible for special education services

developmental disabilities   Severe disabilities that often combine intellectual and physical problems; often used interchangeably with *multiple-severe disabilities*

deviations from print   In oral reading, words that are not identified correctly

diagnostic teaching   Giving problems and asking students questions to determine their thinking

differentiated curriculum   For gifted and talented students, different learning experiences beyond those provided to typical learners through the general education curriculum

differentiated instruction   Provision of an individualized array of instructional interventions

differentiating instruction   Instruction that is responsive to the diverse needs of all students with a focus on curriculum, instructional adaptations, services, and instruction intensity

direct instruction   Teacher-directed instruction that focuses on using explicit, systematic procedures such as modeling, practice opportunities, pacing, error correction, and progress monitoring

disabilities   Results of impairments or medical conditions

discrepancy formulas   Calculations used to determine the gap between a student's achievement and her or his potential; used to identify students with learning disabilities

discrimination   The ability to distinguish one item (such as a letter, number, letter sound, math sign, state, or piece of lab equipment) from another

distributive practice   Practice opportunities presented over time on skills that have been taught

divergent, higher-order questions   Questions that require students to make inferences, to analyze or synthesize information, and to evaluate content

Down syndrome   A chromosomal disorder associated with identifiable physical characteristics and resulting in delays in physical and intellectual development

drafting   In writing, the stage in which the author attempts to put words on paper using the planning and organization information developed during prewriting

due process hearing   Noncourt proceeding before an impartial hearing officer, used when parents and school personnel disagree on a special education issue

duration recording   An observational system to measure how long a discrete target behavior occurs

dyscalculia   A disorder in learning mathematics skills and concepts

dysgraphia   A disorder in writing that involves problems with handwriting, spelling, and composition

dyslexia   A language-based reading disability

early intervening   Providing explicit and intensive instruction to all young, struggling students to prevent the compounding of learning problems

earned time   *See* free time.

e-books   Electronic versions of textbooks allowing for the application of universal design for learning

echolalia   Repeating words, sounds, or sound patterns with no communicative intent, meaning, or understanding; this repetition may occur immediately or even days later

ecological assessment   An assessment approach that explores the student's relationship to his or her environment, rather than simply focusing on student strengths and deficits

editing   In writing, the stage in which writers focus on the mechanical aspects of spelling, capitalization, and punctuation

Education for All Handicapped Children Act   *See* Public Law (PL) 94-142

educational/diagnostic meeting   A meeting held to determine what students know, and what they do not know, about a topic to be studied

efficacy   The power to produce an effect

elaboration   Adding more details to facts to aid in memorization, retention, and recall

emotional or behavioral disorders (EBD)   A disability characterized by behavioral or emotional responses that are very different from those of all norms and referent groups and that have adverse effects on educational performance

engaged time   The amount of time that students are involved in learning

English language learners (ELLs) or English learners (ELs)   Students who are learning English as their second (or third) language

enrichment   Addition, to the traditional curriculum, of further topics and skills for the instruction of gifted and talented students

epilepsy or seizure disorders   A tendency to experience recurrent seizures resulting in convulsions; caused by abnormal discharges of neurons in the brain

error correction   The teacher's provision of immediate feedback to correct error responses

event recording   An observational system to measure each occurrence of a discrete behavior (that is, a behavior with an observable beginning and end, such as hand raising)

evidence-based practices   Instruction proved effective through rigorous research; also known as validated practices

executive functioning   Ability to self-monitor by using working memory, inner speech, attention, and rehearsal

exempt   In high stakes testing, a student who it has been determined does not have to participate in testing

expanded notation   Shows place value representations of numerals

expository text   Text structure that is explanatory or factual

externalizing behaviors   Behaviors directed toward others (such as aggressive behaviors)

factual knowledge   Information that is based on facts and is memorized, retained, and recalled as part of learning

family systems approach   An approach in which families' needs and support are defined according to resources, interactions, functions, and the life cycle

fetal alcohol effects (FAE)   Congenital conditions caused by the mother's drinking alcohol during pregnancy and resulting in reduced intellectual functioning, behavior problems, and sometimes physical differences; not as severe as fetal alcohol syndrome (FAS)

fetal alcohol syndrome (FAS)   Congenital conditions caused by the mother's drinking alcohol during pregnancy and resulting in reduced intellectual functioning, behavior problems, and sometimes physical differences

flexible grouping practices   Same-ability groups and mixed-ability groups for instructional purposes

form   In writing, the type of written product (such as a letter, story, essay, shopping list, or poem)

fragile X syndrome   The most common inherited reason for mental retardation

free appropriate public education (FAPE)   Ensures that students with disabilities receive necessary education and services without cost to the family

free time   Designated time during the school day that is provided for students who have completed their work; also known as earned time

frustration reading level   The level at which the student has less than 90 percent word recognition and less than 90 percent comprehension

full inclusion or pull-in programming   Special education or related services delivered exclusively in the general education classroom

function words   Words such as *on, in,* and *from* that are relatively easy for most students to learn because their presence helps students make sense of sentences and because they account for about half of the words seen in text

functional behavioral assessment (FBA)   Behavioral evaluations, interviews, observations, and environmental manipulations conducted to determine the exact nature of problem behaviors

functional capability   Student strengths related to specific tasks

functional dissonance   Conflict between what a student is being asked to do and what the student can do

functional skills   Skills used to manage a home, cook, shop, commute, and organize personal living environments with the goal of independent living; also known as life skills

general vocabulary   Words that are used on a regular basis during conversation

generalization   Transfer of learning from particular instances to other environments, people, times, or events

generalization stage of learning   Stage of learning in which the aim is for mastered skills to be employed across all appropriate situations

generation-processing level   Vocabulary acquisition level wherein words can be used for discussion purposes or in activities

gifted and talented   Students who are identified at the preschool, elementary, or secondary level as possessing demonstrated or potential abilities that give evidence of high performance capability

grade equivalent   Derived developmental score reported in years and tenths of years

grade skipping   Process in which students advance to a grade ahead of their classmates of the same age

grading   Assigning a numeric or letter index based on a student's performance during a specified academic calendar period, usually a semester

graphic organizers   Visual aids to help students organize, understand, see relationships, and remember important information

group homes   Community based living arrangements in which a small number of adults with disabilities live together and receive supports they need for independence

guide dog   Assistance animals trained to serve the individual needs of people with disabilities

guided practice   A teacher's providing students with multiple opportunities to respond and practice

hand over hand   Sign language for individuals with deafblindness wherein signs are conveyed through touch

handicap   A challenge or barrier imposed by others, or by society, because of a condition or disability

hard of hearing   Having hearing losses that impair understanding of sounds and communication

hertz (Hz)   Unit in which the frequency of sound is measured

heterogeneity   A great variety, such as a wide range of strengths and abilities in a group

hierarchical charts   Charts on which broader concepts are listed first and then connected to smaller, supporting concepts

high frequency words   The most commonly occurring words in text

high incidence disabilities   Special education categories with the most students

high stakes testing   State- and district-wide assessments to ensure that all students are making satisfactory progress

holistic evaluation scale   Evaluation scale in which a single, overall rating is assigned to achievement in learning the curriculum; contrast with the use of an analytical evaluation scale

home bound instruction   Special education services delivered to the student's home, usually as a consequence of the student's fragile health

honors sections   An example of ability grouping

Hoover cane   A mobility device used by people with severe visual loss to aid them in moving through the environment independently; also known as a long cane

human immunodeficiency virus (HIV)   A microorganism that infects the immune system, impairing the body's ability to fight infections

hyperactivity   Impaired ability to sit or concentrate for long periods of time

I-messages   A communication technique that involves stating the behavior of concern, the effect of the behavior on the person sending the I-message, and the feelings that the person sending the I-message has as a result

impulsivity   Impaired ability to control one's own behavior

inattention   Inability to pay attention or focus

inclusive education   Educational setting in which students with disabilities have access to the general education curriculum, participate in school activities alongside students without disabilities, and attend their neighborhood school

independent practice   Practice that does not require direct teacher supervision or guidance; may occur in the classroom or as homework

independent reading level   The reading level at which the student has at least 95 percent word recognition and at least 95 percent comprehension

independent study   Study of curriculum topics in greater depth or exploration of a topic that is not part of the general education curriculum

individualized education program (IEP)
Management tool to identify needed services and to specify and organize them in detail; developed through collaboration among general and special educators, administrators, medical professionals, related services providers, the student's family, and (if appropriate) the student who will receive special education services

Individualized Family Service Plan (IFSP)
Management tool to identify and organize services and resources for infants and toddlers (birth to age 3) and their families

Individuals with Disabilities Education Act (IDEA)   The special education law that protects the rights of students with disabilities to a free appropriate public education; originated with PL 94-142 in 1975

inferential comprehension   A type of reading comprehension that focuses on what is not directly stated in text

inferential thinking skills   Reasoning skills

informal instruction   The use of assessment data to guide instructional efforts

informal reading inventories (IRI)   Unique reading tests that consist of graded word lists and graded passages and for which test scores are reported in terms of grade equivalents

information processing   The flow of information that leads to understanding, knowledge, and the ability to act on information

input adaptations   How students access test stimuli and questions

inquiry-based approach   An approach to teaching mathematics wherein students interact with their teachers and peers to develop multiple solution strategies for problems

in-school supervision   Removing a student from one or more classes and requiring him or her to spend the time in a designated school area

instructional activity   A lesson that teaches and reinforces skills and concepts; one of four instructional adaptations included in the ADAPT framework described in this book

instructional content   The skills and concepts that are taught; one of four instructional adaptations included in the ADAPT framework described in this book

instructional delivery   How an activity is taught, including grouping, instructional steps, presentation, and practice; one of four instructional adaptations included in the ADAPT framework described in this book

instructional materials   Instructional aids such as textbooks, kits, hardware, software, and manipulatives; one of four instructional adaptations included in the ADAPT framework described in this book

instructional reading level   The reading level at which the reader has either 90–94 percent word recognition and 90–100 percent comprehension *or 95* percent word recognition and 90–94 percent comprehension

intellectual and developmental disabilities   A disability characterized by impaired intellectual functioning, limited adaptive behavior, need for supports, and initial occurrence before age 18; also known as cognitive disabilities or mental retardation

intelligence quotient (IQ)   Score on a standardized test that is supposed to reflect learning ability

intensity of supports   The level of assistance needed for individuals to function as independently as possible; often described as intermittent, limited, extensive, or pervasive

interactional behaviors   Ways in which people interact with one another across cultures

interdependent group contingency   Arrangement in which individuals earn reinforcement when they achieve a goal established for the group

interest inventories   An activity wherein teachers ask specific questions to determine student interests, likes, and dislikes

interim alternative educational setting (IAES)   A special education placement to ensure progress toward IEP goals, assigned when a serious behavioral infraction necessitates removal from current placement

internalizing behaviors   Behaviors directed inward (e.g., withdrawn, anxious, depressed)

internships   A form of enrichment instruction

interval recording   A system designed to measure the number of intervals of time in which continuous, highly frequent behavior occurs during the observation period

intraindividual differences   In assessment, the strengths and weaknesses a person exhibits across test scores

irregular words   Words in which some or all of the letters do not make their common sounds

itinerants   Professionals who work in different locations

juvenile arthritis   A chronic and painful muscular condition seen in children

keyguard   An overlap placed on top of a computer keyboard to minimize the accidental striking of keys during typing

keyword method   A mnemonic device that involves linking information, such as a word, with response information, such as the word's definition. The

information is reconstructed either pictorially or verbally

language delays   Slowed development of language skills; may or may not result in language impairments

language different   Students who are just beginning to learn a second language or are using nonstandard English

language impairment   Difficulty in mastering, or inability to master, the various systems of rules in language, which then interferes with communication

learning disabilities (LD)   A condition that causes significant learning problems, most often related to reading and writing; a disability of unexpected underachievement that is typically resistant to treatment

least restrictive environment (LRE)   Educational placement of students with disabilities that provides as much inclusion in the core curriculum, and as much integration with typical learners, as possible and appropriate

legally blind   A category of blindness used to qualify the individual for federal and state benefits

legibility   The extent to which what is written can be deciphered or understood

letter combinations   Two or more consecutive letters that represent a single sound (/sh/) or multiple sounds (/bl/) in words

letter–sound correspondence   Association of a common sound with specific letters or letter combinations in a word

level of concern   Amount of student interest in the instruction

life skills   See *functional skills.*

limb deficiencies   Missing or nonfunctioning arms or legs resulting in mobility problems

literal comprehension   A type of reading comprehension that deals specifically with recalling the material expressly stated on the printed page

location adaptations   In assessment, changes in the setting in which a test is administered or in the conditions of the test setting

long cane   See Hoover cane

long-term memory   The permanent storage of information

loudness   An aspect of voice, consisting of the intensity of the sound produced while speaking

low incidence disabilities   Special education categories with relatively few students

low vision   Degree of visual loss wherein the individual uses sight to learn and to execute tasks, but visual disabilities interfere with daily functioning

macro culture   The overarching cultural factors exhibited by the society at large

mainstreaming A term formerly used to signify including students with disabilities in school activities alongside students who do not have disabilities

maintenance stage of learning The stage of learning in which the aim is for the mastered skills to remain at the same level of performance as during the proficiency stage

manifestation determination Determination of whether a student's disciplinary problems are due to her or his disability

massed practice Extra practice of a skill to ensure mastery

mathematics learning disabilities Condition wherein a student's learning disability is most significant in areas related to mathematics

medically fragile A term used to describe the status of individuals with health disabilities

mental retardation *See* intellectual and developmental disabilities

mentorships Arrangement in which students with special interests pair with adults who have expertise in those areas

micro culture A group, within the larger society, whose members share similar language, belief systems, and values

mixed-ability grouping structure Arrangement of students into groups whose members are performing at various levels on the skills targeted for instruction

mnemonic devices Techniques for aiding memory by forming meaningful associations and linkages across information that appears to be unrelated

mobility The ability to travel safely and efficiently from one place to another; a topic of instruction for students who are blind

modeling A demonstration of how to perform the steps involved in solving a problem

modifications Adjustments to assignments or tests that reduce the requirements

morpheme The smallest unit of language that conveys meaning

multicultural education Instruction that provides students with ways to see themselves reflected in the curriculum, as well as to learn about others

multidisciplinary teams Groups of professionals with different areas of expertise, assembled to meet the special needs of individual students

multiple means of engagement Involving students in activities by using a variety of modes of representation and expression to address their interests

multiple means of expression Encouraging students to respond in different ways, in accordance with their strengths

multiple means of representation Presenting information in various formats to reduce or avoid sensory and cognitive barriers to learning

multiple-severe disabilities Exceptionally challenging disabilities where more than one condition influences learning, independence, and the range of intensive and pervasive supports the individual and the family require; also known as developmental disabilities

multisyllable word recognition Recognition of words that have two or more syllables

muscular/skeletal conditions Conditions affecting muscles or bones and resulting in limited functioning

National Instructional Materials Standard (NIMAS) A standard in the IDEA '04 regulations requiring states to provide instructional materials in accessible formats to students with disabilities (e.g., electronic versions of textbooks)

neuromotor impairments Conditions involving the nerves, muscles, and motor functioning

No Child Left Behind Act (NCLB) Reauthorization of the Elementary and Secondary Education Act mandating higher standards for both students and teachers, including an accountability system

noncategorical approach Special education services delivered in terms of students' needs, not in terms of an identified disability; cross-categorical special education

non-referenced interpretations Interpretations of assessment measures for purposes of examining performance

normal curve Theoretical construct of the typical distribution of human traits such as intelligence; also known as a bell-shaped curve

normative sample The people who are given a test and whose scores provide a basis with which later test takers' scores are compared

norm-referenced interpretations Interpretations of assessment measures for purposes of comparing performance to those in a normative sample

number sense Good intuition about numbers and the relationships among them

observation In assessment, watching students do something, thinking about what they are doing, determining why they are doing it, and identifying what the behavior means to the students and those around them

occupational therapist (OT) A related services provider who directs activities that improve muscular control and develop self-help skills

on-task behavior Behavior focused on the task at hand

open-ended meeting A meeting in which students discuss how they would deal with problems and take a "What would you do if . . . ?" approach to problem solving

orientation The mental map that people use to move through environments; a topic of instruction for students who are blind

orientation and mobility specialist A related services provider who teaches individuals who are blind or have low vision techniques to move safely and independently at school and in the community

orthopedic impairments The term used in IDEA '04 for physical disabilities or physical impairments

other health impairments In *DSM-IV-TR*, a category that consists of health conditions that create special needs and disabilities but are not described specifically in any other category; also known as special heath care needs

outcome assessments Measurements that allow teachers and others to check the results of instruction

output adaptations Accommodations that enable a test taker with a disability to record responses to test questions

over-learn To continue to practice beyond the point of mastery

overrepresentation The assignment, to a special education category, of more students from a diverse group than would be expected on the basis of the proportion of that diverse group in the overall population of students

pacing Providing instruction at an appropriate rate to keep students engaged in learning and to promote understanding

paraeducators See *paraprofessionals*.

paraprofessionals Teacher assistants who work in a supportive role under the supervision of licensed professionals

partial products Partitioning quantities to help students focus on place value

peer conferencing Students discussing each other's written products; considered an effective feedback and editing activity in the writing process

peer or expert consultation Teachers observing their peers providing interventions to learners, such as English language learners, who need supplemental instruction

peer tutoring A grouping practice wherein pairs of students work on their skills, usually for extra practice

percentiles Scores reported on norm-referenced tests that indicate the percentage of scores (determined from a normative sample) that fall below a person's raw score; percentile rank

performance deficits Lack of consistent performance of a skill or behavior even though it is in the student's repertoire

perinatal During birth

peripheral vision The outer area of a person's visual field

personal readers People who read for others

pervasive developmental disorder–not otherwise specified (PDD-NOS) One of the autism spectrum disorders (ASD); the category used when not all three ASD characteristics (problems with communication, social interaction, and repetitive or manneristic behaviors) are present or when they are mild

phenylketonuria (PKU) Inherited condition that results in mental retardation from toxins that build up because the affected individuals are unable to metabolize amino acids from certain foods (such as milk)

phonemes The smallest units of sound that influence the meaning in words

phonemic awareness Ability to segment, blend, and manipulate individual phonemes

phonic analysis (phonics) Making connections between units of print and units of sound

phonograms Parts of a word to which consonants or blends are added to make a word (examples include *an, ip,* and *un*); also known as rimes

phonological awareness (PA) One's sensitivity to, or explicit awareness of, the phonological structure of words in one's language

physical disabilities Conditions related to a physical deformity or disability of the skeletal system and associated motor function; also known as physical impairments and orthopedic impairments

physical features of the text Headings, tables, bold-faced terms, chapter organizers and summaries, and the like

physical therapist (PT) A related services provider who treats physical disabilities through many nonmedical means and works to improve motor skills

pitch An aspect of voice; its perceived high or low sound quality

planned ignoring Deliberate, systematic withdrawal of attention by the individual from whom attention is sought

portfolio assessment A form of authentic assessment wherein students select their work for evaluation

positive behavioral support (PBS) A behavioral approach designed to link scientifically validated practice applications across settings, such as home, school, work, and community

postlingually deaf Having lost the ability to hear after developing language; having acquired, or adventitious, deafness

postnatal After birth

preictal stage Warning of an imminent seizure in the form of heightened sensory awareness; also known as an aura

prelingually deaf Having lost the ability to hear before developing language

prenatal Before birth

pre-referral process Steps taken before the actual referral of a child to special education

prevalence Total number of cases at a given time

prewriting The writing stage that involves activities, such as planning and organizing, that are conducted by the writer prior to writing

prior knowledge What a student already knows about a topic

problem-solving meeting A meeting that focuses on a problem exhibited in class. Students explain the problems they see, and then the effects of those problems, as well as possible solutions, are discussed. The meeting concludes with an agreed-upon plan

procedural knowledge Understanding of rules and procedures

process assessment Procedures used to determine the manner in which students derive a particular answer when solving a problem

proficiency stage of learning The stage of learning in which the aim is for the learner to perform the skill accurately and quickly

progress monitoring The systematic and frequent assessment of students' improvement in the skills being taught

project-based learning A learning approach wherein students investigate relevant problems and discuss their work with other students

prompts *See* cues.

prosocial behaviors Behaviors that are positive and build relationships

Public Law (PL) 94-142 Originally passed in 1975 to guarantee a free appropriate public education to all students with disabilities; also known as the Education for All Handicapped Children Act (EHA)

publishing In writing, the stage in which the author's work is complete and is publicly shared in some format

pull-out programs Part-time special services provided outside of the general education classroom, such as in a resource room

purpose In writing, the reason for writing (e.g., to convey a message, to make a request, or to express feelings)

question stem card Cards with questions such as "How are _____ alike and different?" "What explanation can you offer about . . . ?" "What do you think . . . ?" "How would you

describe . . . ?" to prompt student discussions

raw scores The total number of points that a person is awarded in a test

reading comprehension The ability to understand what is read

reading fluency The ability to read text accurately, quickly, and (if reading aloud) with expression

reading vocabulary Word comprehension

reading/learning disabilities Condition wherein a student's learning disability is most significant in reading

recreational therapist A related services provider who assesses leisure function, and provides therapeutic recreation and leisure education

recursive In writing, the act of moving back and forth between stages as one writes and polishes one's work

redirection Informing the student that an error was made and asking what the appropriate behavior would be

reinforcement The application of an event that increases the likelihood that the behavior it follows will occur again. Thus reinforcement is functionally related to an increase in frequency of that behavior

related services Special education services from a wide range of disciplines and professions

reliability In assessment, the consistency of measurement results

repeated reading Process of developing fluency through multiple practice opportunities with the same passage; increases reading accuracy, reading rate, and comprehension

reprimand A negative response to problem behavior that does not provide the opportunity to practice and to receive reinforcement contingent on correct behavior

residual vision The amount and degree of vision a person has functional use of despite a visual disability

resistant to treatment A defining characteristic of learning disabilities. Validated methods typically applied in general education settings are not adequate to bring about sufficient learning; the student requires more intensive and sustained explicit instruction

response to intervention (RTI) A multi-tiered pre-referral method of applying increasingly intensive interventions; can be used to identify students with learning disabilities and provide intensive instruction to struggling students

restitution The principle that when the environment is destroyed or altered, the student must restore it to an improved state

Rett syndrome One of the autism spectrum disorders (ASD) that has a known genetic cause and occurs only in girls

revising In writing, the stage in which authors make changes to the sequencing and structure of the written work to refine the content

rewards Representations of targeted improvement, including tangible items, earning privileges, free time, or honors

rimes *See* phonograms.

robotics The use of high-tech devices to perform motor skills

role playing An activity wherein students practice desired behaviors under the guidance of a teacher or counselor

root word The primary lexical unit of a word; also known as the base word

rules Procedures that must be followed

same-ability grouping structure Groups in which all students are performing at a similar level

schizophrenia A disorder, rare in children, that includes bizarre delusions and dissociation from reality

school counselor A related services provider who provides psychological and guidance services

school nurse A related services provider who assists with medical services at school, delivers health services, and designs accommodations for students with special health care needs

screening The use of assessment data to identify quickly and efficiently who is struggling in a particular area

seclusion timeout For severe, out-of-control behavior, the student is placed in an isolated room; removing the student from a situation that is encouraging and maintaining the problem behavior

Section 504 of the Rehabilitation Act of 1973 First law to outline the basic civil rights of people with disabilities

seizure disorder *See* epilepsy

self-advocacy Capacity to understand, ask for, and explain one's need for accommodations; expressing one's rights and needs

self-determination Ability to identify and achieve goals for oneself

self-management The implementation of specific interventions by the targeted student to manage his or her own behavior

self-regulation Individuals monitoring their own behavior by avoiding situations that contribute to inappropriate behavior and stopping inappropriate behavior if it is initiated

semantically related groups Groups of words with meaningful relationships

sensorineural hearing loss Hearing impairment due to damage to the inner ear or the auditory nerve

service animals Animals (dogs, monkeys, guide dogs) trained to serve the individual needs of people with disabilities; also known as assistance animals

service manager A case coordinator who oversees the implementation and evaluation of IFSPs

short-term memory The temporary store of information that is tapped for immediate use

sickle cell anemia A hereditary blood disorder that inhibits blood flow; African Americans are most at risk for this health impairment

sight word recognition The ability to read a word automatically when encountering it in text or in a list of words

signal words Words that indicate the use of a text structure (for example, *first, second,* and *third* for sequence and *on the other hand* for contrast)

signals Visual, auditory, and verbal cues that teachers use to gain student attention

signed English Translation of English into a form of manual communication

silent reading fluency The number of words read at a certain comprehension level at a certain reading level

skill deficits Specific skills that students have not mastered

socially competent Able to perceive when and how to use social skills depending upon the situation and social context

sociogram A depiction of peer relationships in graphic form

sociometric survey A set of questions that students answer regarding their perspectives on their peers; helps teachers learn about students who may be popular, rejected, or isolated within the classroom or peer group

special education categories System used in IDEA '04 to classify disabilities among students

special health care needs *See* other health impairments

special education Individualized education and services for students with disabilities and sometimes for students who are gifted and talented

specialized vocabulary Words that have multiple meanings depending on the context

specific praise Complimenting or verbally rewarding others for their accomplishments

speech impairment A disability characterized by abnormal speech that is unintelligible, is unpleasant, or interferes with communication

speech synthesizers Assistive technology devices that create "voice"

speech/language pathologist (SLP) A related services provider who diagnoses and treats speech or language impairments

sponge Activities that students can complete independently and are intended to "soak up" time

standard scores Derived scores that include an average, or mean, score and a set statistical standard deviation

statement of transition services A component of IEPs for students age 16 or older to help them move to adulthood

stay put provision Prohibits students with disabilities from being expelled because of behavior associated with their disabilities

strategy instruction The use of cognitive strategies to facilitate the learning process

strengths What a student is able to accomplish

structural analysis Using knowledge of word structure to decode unknown words

student-centered activities Activities in which students actively engage in the learning process to solve problems, discuss content issues, and create products

student-centered learning Learning in which students are actively engaged in hands-on tasks, discussions, and decision making

study skills Techniques students use to obtain, write, remember, and use content effectively

stuttering The lack of fluency in an individual's speech pattern, often characterized by hesitations or repetitions of sounds or words; dysfluency; a speech impairment

survey batteries A compilation of tests that assess different areas and provide an overview of achievement

survey tests Tests that survey, or assess, numerous areas

systems of supports Networks of supports that everyone develops to function optimally in life

target behavior A specific behavior, either positive or inappropriate, that the teacher focuses on to increase or decrease that behavior

teacher assistance team process A collaborative approach in which the team discusses a student's problem, identifies possible interventions, and assists the teacher as needed in implementing strategies

teacher presence The use of assertive behaviors, teacher proximity, and nonverbal communication to manage student behavior and promote a positive classroom environment in which effective instruction can occur

teacher proximity The teacher positioning himself or herself close to a student to prevent or eliminate problem behavior

teacher-directed instruction At the secondary level, teachers providing lectures on textbook content and students reading their textbooks to identify important facts and concepts in preparation for weekly tests

technical vocabulary   Words that are used in a particular content area

think aloud   The teacher saying out loud the steps he or she is taking while solving a problem

think-aloud interviews   Asking students to think out loud as they perform a task

time sampling   Recording the number of intervals in which a target behavior occurs during the period of observation

timeout   An intervention that removes the student from a situation that is reinforcing the inappropriate behavior

timeout-seclusion   For severe, out-of-control behavior, placement of the pupil in an isolated room

tone   In writing, the "voice" of a written product, which can be light hearted, serious, optimistic, pessimistic, and so forth

traffic patterns   Paths that students frequently follow as they move about the classroom

transition   The interval of time occurring prior to, during, or after instruction within the classroom and between locations within the school

traumatic brain injury (TBI)   A head injury causing reduced cognitive functioning, limited attention, and impulsivity

typical learners   Students and individuals without disabilities

unexpected underachievement   A defining characteristic of learning disabilities; poor school performance cannot be explained by other disabilities or limited potential

universal design   Barrier-free architectural and building designs that meet the needs of everyone, including people with physical challenges; materials and instructions designed in a way that allows access for all students, including those with sensory, motor, and cognitive disabilities

universal design for learning (UDL)   Design that increases access to the curriculum and instruction for all students, typically by using technology

universal screening   Testing of everyone, particularly newborns, to determine the existence or risk of disability

validated practices   Thoroughly researched or evidence-based practices; scientifically validated instruction

validity   The extent to which an assessment device measures what it is supposed to measure

Venn diagrams   Intersecting shapes that show how concepts are similar and how they are different

visual acuity   Sharpness of response to visual stimuli

visual disabilities   Impairments in vision that, even with correction, affect educational performance, access to the community, and independence

vocabulary   The meaning of words

vocational rehabilitation counselor   A professional who provides training, career counseling, and job placement services

wait time   The amount of time (about 3–4 seconds) between when the student is asked a question and when the teacher provides the response if the student does not answer

weaknesses   What a student is unable to accomplish; limitations

with-it-ness   A teacher's awareness of what is going on in his or her classroom at all times

word family   A base word and its derivatives

words correct per minute   A measure of reading fluency, the number of words a student reads accurately in one minute

work sample analysis   A procedure that helps teachers assess students' academic skills by looking at their permanent products

working memory   The simultaneous processing and storing of information

writing process   A recursive process involving five stages: prewriting, drafting, revising, editing, and publishing

name index

subject index

Page references followed by *f* and *t* refer to figures and tables respectively.